The Societal Foundations of National Competitiveness

MICHAEL J. MAZARR

Prepared for the Office of Net Assessment,
Office of the Secretary of Defense

NATIONAL DEFENSE RESEARCH INSTITUTE

For more information on this publication, visit **www.rand.org/t/RRA499-1**.

About RAND

The RAND Corporation is a research organization that develops solutions to public policy challenges to help make communities throughout the world safer and more secure, healthier and more prosperous. RAND is nonprofit, nonpartisan, and committed to the public interest. To learn more about RAND, visit www.rand.org.

Research Integrity

Our mission to help improve policy and decisionmaking through research and analysis is enabled through our core values of quality and objectivity and our unwavering commitment to the highest level of integrity and ethical behavior. To help ensure our research and analysis are rigorous, objective, and nonpartisan, we subject our research publications to a robust and exacting quality-assurance process; avoid both the appearance and reality of financial and other conflicts of interest through staff training, project screening, and a policy of mandatory disclosure; and pursue transparency in our research engagements through our commitment to the open publication of our research findings and recommendations, disclosure of the source of funding of published research, and policies to ensure intellectual independence. For more information, visit www.rand.org/about/principles.

RAND's publications do not necessarily reflect the opinions of its research clients and sponsors.

Limited Print and Electronic Distribution Rights

About This Report

This report offers the results of a yearlong study conducted by the RAND Corporation, funded by the U.S. Department of Defense, to examine the characteristics of highly competitive societies and apply those criteria to the United States. The report explores the relationship between a nation's social condition and its global standing. Does the character of a society bear on its competitive position? Do its essential societal characteristics decisively influence its ability to generate a potent engine of national power, compete for the respect and allegiance of other countries, sustain technological supremacy, and attract the most-skilled immigrants and global capital? Can we identify which societal characteristics contribute most to competitive success? The study sought to throw light on these questions without offering definitive answers. The eventual goal of this line of work is to perform a societal net assessment of the United States and China and derive a sense of how well equipped the United States is for a long-term competition.

The research reported here was completed in January 2022 and underwent security review with the sponsor and the Defense Office of Prepublication and Security Review before public release.

National Defense Research Division

This research was sponsored by the Office of Net Assessment in the U.S. Department of Defense and conducted within the International Security and Defense Policy Center of the RAND National Security Research Division (NSRD), which operates the National Defense Research Institute (NDRI), a federally funded research and development center sponsored by the Office of the Secretary of Defense, the Joint Staff, the Unified Combatant Commands, the Navy, the Marine Corps, the defense agencies, and the defense intelligence enterprise.

For more information on the RAND International Security and Defense Policy Center, see www.rand.org/nsrd/isdp or contact the director (contact information is provided on the webpage).

Acknowledgments

I would like to acknowledge the sponsor for support and helpful comments through many interim project reviews, especially the thoughts of James Baker, David Epstein, and Caroline Pestel. I am grateful to RAND management, notably Michael McNerney and Michael Spirtas, for help and guidance during the project. I extend the warmest thanks to Libby May for her editorial assistance and Emily Ellinger for her research support.

In addition, the following RAND staff researched and wrote at least one historical country study, which contributed significantly to this analysis: Emily Ellinger, Caitlin McCulloch, Bryan Rooney, Michael Shurkin, Andrew Stravers, and Jordan Willcox. Their work, and participation in associated research team discussions and email threads, offered great insight into key countries and highlighted important themes and sources that contributed greatly to the development of this analysis.

RAND commissioned several noted scholars to produce essays assessing specific countries that considered the project's framework for national competitive advantage. I am extremely grateful for their contributions, which added greatly to my understanding of these cases. These scholars were John Deak, William Anthony Hay, Robert Hellyer, Pieter Judson, Gabriel Paquette, Kenneth Pomeranz, and Nicolas Tackett.

I would also like to acknowledge two peer reviewers, James Goldgeier of American University and Anthony Vassalo at RAND, for their perceptive comments.

I am also grateful to four scholars who read portions of the manuscript and provided more-informal feedback: Kenneth Bartlett, John Deak, William Anthony Hay, and Robert Hellyer.

Of course, none of these scholars should be associated with specific analysis or claims in this final report. I am solely responsible for this content.

Summary

Issue

Nations rise and fall, succeed or fail in rivalries, and enjoy stability or descend into chaos because of a complex web of factors. One critical component of any such recipe is the package of essential social characteristics of a nation. One prominent recent example is the Cold War. The ultimate story of the Cold War is that the United States was simply a more competitive society than the Soviet Union: more energetic, more vibrant, more innovative, more productive, more legitimate. This study explored how the characteristics of a society determine its competitive standing in the context of today's emerging rivalries. The study was designed as an initial, exploratory investigation of this issue. The report does not aspire to offer definitive answers to these questions but rather to provide analytically grounded insights into the factors that underpin national competitive advantage—and in doing so provoke further discussion and debate.

Approach

The research team first sought to define the core terms of the analysis—*societal characteristics* and *national competitive advantage* or *competitive success*. We employed existing literatures and related concepts to offer an understanding of the terms.

This project defined *societal characteristics* as "the essential and persistent social qualities of a nation, including norms, values, institutions, and practices, that shape measurable outputs of national competitive advantage and influence its patterns of behavior." A factor must meet four conditions to count as a societal characteristic in this sense: It must be related to inherent qualities of the society, it must be a sociopolitical or socioeconomic factor rather than a physical one, it must be an enduring trait, and it must reflect multiple individual factors and not be reducible to a single proxy variable. To identify an initial list of societal characteristics, assess their impact on national dynamism and competitive standing, and eventually settle on a final list of characteristics associated with competitive success, we used five main research approaches and sources of data:

1. the insights of global comparative histories
2. specific historical case studies
3. general disciplinary assessments seeking explanatory variables for historical trends, such as studies of the sources of economic development
4. issue-specific empirical research
5. assessment of disconfirming cases or alternate causes.

Key Findings

Our research had five leading findings. First, we identified seven leading societal characteristics associated with national competitive success:

1. national ambition and will
2. unified national identity
3. shared opportunity
4. an active state
5. effective institutions
6. a learning and adapting society
7. competitive diversity and pluralism.

Second, the study highlighted the importance of a *prudent balance* within each of these characteristics. Factors such as national ambition or pluralism can become competitive handicaps when pushed to an extreme, and no nation gains competitive advantage by pushing any characteristic to its limit. Third, the study identified specific *factors other than societal characteristics*, such as membership in networks of trade and exchange of ideas, that help determine national competitive standing.

Fourth, our analysis found that lasting competitive advantage derives from *positive-feedback synergies* among the seven nominated societal characteristics. It is these blended, interactive effects, creating competitive wholes greater than the sum of their parts, that distinguish the strongest and most-competitive nations of each era. Fifth, the study further identified one recipe for national competitive advantage that was most consistently associated with success: Competitive societies tend to be open, tolerant, full of intellectual energy and commitment to learning; they have a powerful sense of their own role in the world and a sense of mission or will; they almost always benefit from strong public and private institutions, as well as a state apparatus that actively promotes advantage; and they embody a pluralistic clash of ideas and an ability of people from many backgrounds to offer their talents and succeed. We term this specific mix of characteristics *the Renaissance spirit*.

We applied the seven characteristics to the United States in an initial effort to create a snapshot of where the country stands on these scales. That application provided some reason for optimism. The United States continues to reflect many of these characteristics, and the overall synergistic engine, more than any other large country in the world. But the analysis also offers reason for grave concern: Multiple trends are working to weaken traditional U.S. advantages. Several, such as the corruption of the national information space, pose acute risks to the long-term dynamism and competitiveness of the nation. These and related trends raise a worrying prospect—that the United States has begun to display classic patterns of a major power on the far side of its dynamic and vital curve.

Contents

Figures and Tables

Figures

Tables

CHAPTER ONE

The Sources of National Competitive Advantage

One of the most gripping scenes in Thucydides's *History of the Peloponnesian War* takes place in 432 BCE. Greece stands on the verge of a generational conflict, and a peace conference has been called in Sparta to head off the looming war. The delegation from Corinth, a Spartan ally, is mightily displeased, accusing the Spartans of letting Athenian power grow and doing nothing about it. As Thucydides presents the scene, the Corinthian argument centers on the inherent character of the rivals.[1] "The Athenians are addicted to innovation," the Corinthian delegation argues,

> and their designs are characterized by swiftness alike in conception and execution; you have a genius for keeping what you have got, accompanied by a total want of invention, and when forced to act, you never go far enough. Again, they are adventurous beyond their power, and daring beyond their judgment, and in danger they are sanguine; your wont is to attempt less than is justified by your power, to mistrust even what is sanctioned by your judgment, and to fancy that from danger there is no release. Further, there is promptitude on their side against procrastination on yours; they are never at home, you are most disinclined to leave it, for they hope by their absence to extend their acquisitions, you fear by your advance to endanger what you have left behind. They are swift to follow up a success, and slow to recoil from a reverse. Their bodies they spend ungrudgingly in their country's cause, their intellect they jealously husband to be employed in her service. . . . To describe their character in one word, one might truly say that they were born into the world to take no rest themselves and to give none to others.[2]

Sparta should fear Athens not because of what it possesses, or where it lies, or the number of its people, the delegation from Corinth was suggesting. Sparta should fear this audacious city-

---

[1] Gregory Crane, "The Fear and Pursuit of Risk: Corinth on Athens, Sparta and the Peloponnesians," *Transactions of the American Philological Association*, Vol. 122, 1992. As always with Thucydides, he is recreating scenes from the memory of participants, some written sources, and most likely a degree of imagination.

[2] Thucydides, *The Landmark Thucydides: A Comprehensive Guide to the Peloponnesian War*, Robert B. Strassler, ed., New York: Free Press, 1998, p. 40.

state because of *the kind of society that it is*. Athens stood to supplant Spartan power because it was more dynamic, vibrant, forward looking, and ambitious. The Corinthians made the case, the classicist Josiah Ober explains, "that a new Athenian approach to state power and its uses was quickly rendering the Spartan approach to power obsolete." The Athenian formula held that "quickness, innovation, and an experimental approach to policy drove the continuous growth of wealth and power."[3]

Although it occurred 2,500 years ago, this episode highlights a fact about the eternal competition among nations, societies, and civilizations that remains relevant to this day. History suggests that the outcome of enduring rivalries is seldom determined by narrow, singular factors. Nations do not prevail in such rivalries because they own one transformative technology (such as the longbow or even the steam engine) or reflect a single decisive structural factor (such as a geographic advantage). Almost always, nations rise and fall or succeed or fail in rivalries because of a complex mixture of factors that provide competitive advantage. And at the core of this mix stand the sort of qualities that the Corinthians were begging Sparta to understand—the essential social characteristics of a nation.

A remarkably similar story would unfold two millennia after the drama in Greece. The ultimate outcome of the Cold War was determined in part because the United States and its democratic partners and allies were simply more-competitive societies than the Soviet Union and its satellites—more energetic, more innovative, more productive, more legitimate. Some commentators cast the United States as the Athens of that drama to the Soviet Union's lethargic, conservative Sparta. The essential message was the same: The qualities of a society, more than any specific actions or investments or capabilities, play the essential role in advancing or degrading its competitive position.

American presidents, national security officials, scholars, and pundits have for decades given lip service to the idea that a dynamic and resilient home front is the foundation for success abroad. But in terms of the public conception of the requirements for national strength (the emphasis of most national security policy) and the level of investment in key capabilities, this focus on the home front slips into the background. Public debate on rivalries usually defaults to measuring competitive position in the size of defense budgets or armies or the relative capabilities of some defense systems. Despite the general agreement on the importance of domestic vibrancy to global position, few studies have tried to determine what a strong home front truly means, in terms of the qualities of a nation that underpin competitive success.

The problem is newly relevant in the context of today's emerging rivalries. Is the United States still a more competitive society than its main rival, China? What *are* the main ingredients in a web of societal advantage, and where does the United States stand in that regard? That was the research agenda of this study: to identify specific societal characteristics that have been historically associated with national dynamism and competitive position and to make an initial, tentative assessment of the U.S. standing in those areas.

---

[3] Josiah Ober, *The Rise and Fall of Classical Greece*, Princeton, N.J.: Princeton University Press, 2015.

Yet even from the case of Athens and Sparta, the complexity of this task starts becoming apparent. In many ways, according to the characteristics that we (the research team) will nominate, Athens was destined to win the Peloponnesian War. It was more energetic and creative. It had a stronger societal commitment to learning, more ambition, and a stronger financial base. It drew on the talents of a wider proportion of its population. And yet Sparta won the Peloponnesian War, at least in military terms.

As with many wars, this outcome was the product of several decisive but idiosyncratic reasons that had little to do with Spartan societal character. A plague struck Athens in 430 BCE and might have killed as much as a third of the city's population (including Pericles, the architect of the Athenian strategy) and weakened Athens physically, spiritually, and strategically. Another factor was Athens's disastrous decision to invade Sicily in 415 BCE, squandering huge numbers of soldiers and massive amounts of resources and leaving Athens much less well equipped for the remainder of the war. Persia leaned on the scales in favor of Sparta, which made the contest an unequal one in key respects.[4]

But then, too, in more lasting historical terms, it is reasonable to ask how much Sparta really won and Athens lost. Of these two city-states, Athens has unquestionably been the more influential, powerful, and lasting in its influence. It remained a significant economic, naval, and geopolitical player a century later in the time of Alexander,[5] and its social and cultural influences echo down to the present day.[6] Athens *was* the more dynamic and competitive society. This did not keep it from losing a war, but it did underwrite timeless social, cultural, political, and scientific influence.[7]

***

The United States has now embarked on a new—and in many ways unprecedented—phase of its role in the world. It is undertaking an extended, challenging, and at times crisis-prone competition with at least two major rivals, Russia and China—one that became even more urgent and intense with Russia's invasion of Ukraine in February 2022. The dominant narra-

---

[4] The defining overall history that describes many of these factors is Donald Kagan, *The Peloponnesian War*, New York: Penguin, 2004.

[5] Fordyce Mitchel, "Athens in the Age of Alexander," *Greece and Rome*, Vol. 12, No. 2, 1965.

[6] As Ober concludes, "The perpetuation of efflorescence in the Hellenistic era, long past the moment of political fall, made possible the 'immortality' of Greek culture" (Ober, 2015, p. 19). See also Tony Spawforth, *The Story of Greece and Rome*, New Haven, Conn.: Yale University Press, 2018, p. 147.

[7] Sparta's victory was in this sense a misleading signal. The Corinthians, Ober argues, were making a more long-term argument—that Sparta was destined to stagnate, while "much of the rest of the Greek world, led by dynamic and aggressive risk-taking Athens, would continue to grow." He continues, "At some time, the tipping point would be reached and Sparta's military specialization would no longer be enough to maintain its superpolis status. And at that time, there would be a cascade of defection from the Peloponnesian League, out of fear or desire, to follow the Athenian path of dynamic growth" (Ober, 2015, p. 210). This same pattern would emerge 2,500 years later, with the end of the Cold War, when a cascading set of defections from the Soviet bloc collapsed its status as a superpower.

tive about the brewing U.S. rivalry with China in particular (certainly the narrative favored by Beijing) is that it pits a tired, declining hegemon (the United States) against a vigorous, rising power (China). Many Chinese officials and scholars see the trajectory in these terms, firmly believing that the 21st century is destined to be shaped by an increasingly Sino-centric global order.[8]

It is no surprise, then, that observers in the United States and abroad have been urgently nominating potential investments, policies, and capabilities that the United States will need to face this challenge. Many draw seemingly obvious implications: The United States must enhance its military capabilities, strengthen its global defense posture, and invest in key areas of technological competition. It should be prepared for a series of tests of will, from proxy wars to major deterrent trials. Success in the overall rivalries with China and Russia, this advice assumes, depends on an accumulating set of victories in these individual contests for supremacy.

Yet if the history surveyed in this report provides an accurate guide to the future, the fate of the United States in these competitions will not be determined solely, or even in significant degree, by the numbers of its weapons or amounts of defense spending or how many proxy wars it wins but by the basic characteristics of its society. Some level of military capability is an important component of national strength and a necessary precondition for avoiding defeat. But the factors that ultimately govern success are societal ones, qualities that reflect the kind of country that a nation is rather than the things it builds or does. A great power can make many mistakes—lose wars, invest in the wrong military capabilities, fail at a significant percentage of its strategic initiatives—and yet still prevail in a long-term contest if its essential societal advantages are robust enough.

If so, then it becomes critical for the United States to identify and nurture the range of characteristics that underpin strategic competitiveness. This report addresses the first part of that challenge, nominating seven leading qualities that distinguish dynamic and competitively successful nations.

Looking for Societal Sources of Competitive Advantage

The idea that a society's inherent qualities make for competitive success goes back a long way—to Thucydides's description of the Peloponnesian War, as we have seen; to Edward Gibbon's claim that an emergent form of decadence helps explain Rome's decline;[9] and to dozens of other histories and theories that tie national character to national fate. Arguably, the Cold

---

[8] William Callahan, "Chinese Visions of a World Order: Post-Hegemonic or New Hegemony?" *International Studies Review*, Vol. 10, No. 4, 2008; Jude Blanchette, "Xi's Confidence Game," *Foreign Affairs*, November 23, 2021.

[9] Edward Gibbon and Hans-Friedrich Mueller, *The Decline and Fall of the Roman Empire*, Vols. 1–3, New York: Modern Library, 2005.

War is the paradigmatic modern case of a rivalry in which societal characteristics played a decisive role. It was the rigidity, inefficient institutions, bureaucratic sclerosis, central planning errors, and quashing of diverse ideas and initiatives that most fundamentally caused the collapse of the Soviet system, as the gap between the claims of state ideology and its material results continually widened.

The societal characteristics of the two rivals arguably played a much more decisive role in determining the Cold War's outcome than any specific strategic choice or defense investment. The Soviet Union possessed unbelievable intelligence assets, world-class military technology, and the ability to focus the investment of a planned economy in areas that were thought capable of ensuring competitive advantage. But pure material capacity applied to key areas did not make the difference. Nor did individual confrontations or even wars: The United States allowed repeated Soviet incursions into Eastern Europe, fought to an unsatisfying draw in Korea, lost in Vietnam—and ultimately prevailed. The United States did so, it now seems clear, in large part because of the essential qualities of its society.

George Kennan certainly thought so. The architect of America's strategy based his approach on the firm expectation that America was more dynamic in essential ways than its competitor, and that this inherent societal advantage would prove decisive in the long run, if the West could keep the Soviet Union from winning in the short run through blunt force. Kennan famously argues in his "Long Telegram" of 1946 that

> much depends on health and vigor of our own society. World communism is like a malignant parasite which feeds only on diseased tissue. . . . [C]ourageous and incisive measure to solve internal problems of our own society, to improve self-confidence, discipline, morale and community spirit of our own people, is a diplomatic victory over Moscow worth a thousand diplomatic notes and joint communiqués. If we cannot abandon fatalism and indifference in face of deficiencies of our own society, Moscow will profit— Moscow cannot help profiting by them in its foreign policies.[10]

These and a dozen other major cases throughout history, from the rise to prominence of the tiny Netherlands, to the decline from hegemony of Spain, to the systemic weaknesses of the Austro-Hungarian and Ottoman Empires, point to a clear connection between the elements of national character and success in the struggle of international politics.

Yet any effort to assess this question turns out to be a minefield of methodological risks. It is easy to fall into sweeping assertions about the superiority of one culture or civilization over another. Even the example with which we opened this report reflects such perils: Many scholars find the supposed claims of the Corinthians about Athens and Sparta to be simpli-

---

[10] George Kennan, "George Kennan's 'Long Telegram,'" History and Public Policy Program Digital Archive, National Archives and Records Administration, Department of State Records, Record Group 59, February 22, 1946.

fied and exaggerated.[11] Others argue that the caution and restraint attributed to Sparta ought to be seen (and probably was seen, in the conservative society of ancient Greece) as a competitive advantage rather than a burden. And Athens's burgeoning energy and ambition hardly served it well when these qualities prompted a condescending mistreatment of its allies or rash adventures, such as the disastrous Sicilian expedition.

Still: Some societies, at some times, *do* have characteristics that make them more dynamic, influential, and ultimately competitive than their contemporaneous rivals.[12] This study sought to take a step forward in examining this question.

Are We Talking About "Culture"?

Many efforts to come to grips with the societal advantages of nations have relied on a freighted concept to do much of the heavy lifting: *culture*. Scholars have argued for centuries that some cultures or civilizations inculcate values and promote behaviors that foster economic development and growth and the effective expression of national power. Other cultural factors constrain the power and competitiveness of their societies with values hostile to progress and governance. Most definitions of culture refer to some combination of persistent values, beliefs, habits, and practices that guide behavior in a society and are transmitted between generations—a definition that would seem to have much in common with our notion of societal characteristics. There is a distinction, though, between classic culturalist theories and the approach we have taken.

Some culturalist theories have aspired to comprehensive, holistic explanations for national competitive advantage: the meta-narrative theorists Oswald Spengler, Herbert Spencer, Talcott Parsons, and Carroll Quigley and such concepts as Max Weber's notion of a Protestant ethic.[13] These are sometimes described as *essentialist* in the sense that they aim to identify unchanging—or at least very deeply ingrained—essences of a civilization or people.

---

[11] The historian Donald Kagan dismissed the comparison, arguing that "a people so sluggish and unimaginative as the Spartans depicted by the Corinthian speech could hardly have won mastery over the Peloponnese, leadership of the Greeks in the successful resistance to Persia, and victory in the first Peloponnesian war" (Donald Kagan, *A New History of the Peloponnesian War*, Ithaca, N.Y.: Cornell University Press, 1969, pp. 290–291).

[12] The famed economist Walt W. Rostow was intrigued with the argument of a scholar who had assessed "the relative weakness in modern France of the propensities to apply science to the economy, to accept innovations, and to seek material advance. He finds French behavior rooted, in these respects, in certain economic, social, and political patterns and scales of value, carried over from preindustrial revolution times." Rostow asks whether such a societal assessment might not provide a better picture of a country's competitive trajectory over time than simpler and more straightforward catalogues of material power (Walt W. Rostow, *The Process of Economic Growth*, New York: W. W. Norton, 1962, p. 50).

[13] Lawrence Harrison and Samuel P. Huntington, eds., *Culture Matters: How Values Shape Human Progress*, New York: Basic Books, 2000. Another example is the simple "individualist versus communitarian" dichotomy proposed by some analysts in the 1980s who were anxious to account for East Asian economic

For obvious reasons, arguments that rely on such enduring factors to explain national outcomes have difficulty accounting for the sometimes wildly varying trajectories of these supposedly unchanging cultures. Europeans disparaged the role of Confucianism in China as a barrier to development—until the Asian economic miracles caused scholars to suddenly discover the virtues of Confucian culture for progress and growth.[14] Nations and societies have displayed many of the same essential cultural characteristics during times of rapid growth and recession, victory and defeat in war, and success or failure in international rivalries. The historian and archaeologist Ian Morris notes that a superior "Western culture" cannot explain both the West's relative advance over China between the 18th and 20th centuries *and* China's equivalent or even superior position before and after that time.[15] The business strategist Michael Porter adds that some qualities named as cultural values have highly contingent effects: They can be a benefit in some periods and a handicap in others. "Frugality," he writes as an example, "served Japan well until its recent prolonged recession; now it is an obstacle to

---

progress (for example, see George C. Lodge and Ezra F. Vogel, eds., *Ideology and National Competitiveness: An Analysis of Nine Countries*, Cambridge, Mass.: Harvard Business School Press, 1987). Some of the "disadvantaged" individualistic societies have since done better, on the scales used in Lodge and Vogel's book, than the communitarian ones. Our research suggests that *certain aspects* of individualism and communitarianism can provide competitive advantage—but in balance with other factors. That book also demonstrates the risks of relying on a single historical period: The 1960s through the early 1980s, the authors' focus of analysis, were the most intense period of postwar industrialization in East Asia for a host of reasons beyond the ideology of societies. Studying Japan pre- and post-1985, for example, gives starkly different indications of the relationship between unchanging cultural values and economic results.

[14] Similarly, as the historian Kenneth Pyle notes, Japan was told that its "culture" was a major barrier to industrialization and that it had to adopt Western norms and institutions—until "Japanese cultural values," such as thrift and hard work, were viewed as responsible for its postwar economic miracle (Kenneth B. Pyle, "The Future of Japanese Nationality: An Essay in Contemporary History," *Journal of Japanese Studies*, Vol. 8, No. 2, 1982, p. 231).

[15] Ian Morris, *Why the West Rules—for Now: The Patterns of History, and What They Reveal About the Future*, New York: Farrar, Straus and Giroux, 2010, pp. 558, 568–571. Jürgen Osterhammel argues, "That such theories can explain success and failure alike appears rather suspicious" (Jürgen Osterhammel, *The Transformation of the World: A Global History of the Nineteenth Century*, Patrick Camiller, trans., Princeton, N.J.: Princeton University Press, 2014, p. 664). Daron Acemoglu and James Robinson similarly suggest that cultural theories are too crude a variable to explain differences in economic performance. Culture and institutions are related in complex ways, and some seemingly cultural norms—a lack of trust, for example—can also be viewed as symptoms rather than causes, as the outputs of bad institutions. Some cultural categories, such as religious belief, are weakly associated with economic performance: A "Protestant ethic" cannot explain the rapid rise of East Asia. The lagging performance of many Middle Eastern countries is as much a product of the institutional legacy of colonialism as it is anything about the implications of Islam (Daron Acemoglu and James A. Robinson, *Why Nations Fail: The Origins of Power, Prosperity, and Poverty*, New York: Currency, 2012, pp. 56–63; see also Armand Clesse, Takashi Inoguchi, E. B. Keehn, and J. A. A. Stockwin, eds., *The Vitality of Japan: Sources of National Strength and Weakness*, Basingstoke, UK: Macmillan Press, 1997, p. 325).

recovery."[16] For all his interest in broad civilizational trends, the historian Arnold Toynbee disparaged Spengler's essentialist vision of the "character" of a society as "arbitrary fantasy."[17]

Trying to pin down a simple list of cultural values associated with national success is further complicated by the fact that competitively dynamic societies do not reflect a single, universal set of cultural qualities. As the historian Joyce Appleby explains, both the United States and Germany gained tremendous industrial and national momentum through the 19th century and into the 20th, surpassing Britain. But the two relied on strikingly different cultural models to achieve that success. "Americans loved novelty; Germans feared it. The Americans practiced religious toleration; Germans had fought bitter wars over differences within the Christian faith. Germans accepted authoritarian politics," whereas Americans insisted on individual liberties.[18] Identifying universal values associated with dynamism becomes more difficult when dynamic competitors betray such differences.[19]

A particular version of the culturalist approach focuses on aspects of sociocultural "weakness" or decline, often depicted as a failure of moral values, as an explanation for national fates. Gibbon's argument may be the most famous example, attributing Rome's ebbing prospects in part to a decline of aggressive martial values in favor of softer Christian values.[20] Another famous example is the British historian Correlli Barnett's argument that Britain's fall from global hegemony was not a technological or material but a moral and psychological process. This process involved the replacement of tough men "hard of mind and hard of will" who accepted the reality of ruthless international competition and applied tough strategic judgment, and a strong commercial ethic, to achieve advantage, with a moralistic and romantic liberal internationalism that had gone soft. He blames "a mutation in the values—indeed the very character—of the British governing classes which began in the early nineteenth century" for the country's decline.[21] He contends that British schools and churches became the propagandists of a kind and generous softness toward the world rather than the powerful assertion of might that characterized Britain's rise to greatness.

---

[16] Michael E. Porter, "Attitudes, Values, Beliefs, and the Microeconomics of Prosperity," in Lawrence E. Harrison and Samuel P. Huntington, eds., *Culture Matters: How Values Shape Human Progress*, New York: Basic Books, 2000, p. 15. Japan has been seen as having frugal and conservative values when considering its high savings rates and bold and dynamic competitive habits in its industries (Clesse et al., 1997, p. 319).

[17] Arnold J. Toynbee, *A Study of History: Abridgement of Volumes I–VI by DC Somervell*, New York: Oxford University Press, 1947, p. 242.

[18] Joyce Appleby, *The Relentless Revolution: A History of Capitalism*, Kindle ed., New York: W. W. Norton, 2010, loc. 3369.

[19] In a more recent example, seeming cultural similarities between the nations of the "Anglosphere"—such as the United States, Britain, Australia, and New Zealand—managed to generate vast differences in these countries' responses to the COVID-19 pandemic. Janan Ganesh, "How the Pandemic Exposed the Myth of the Anglosphere," *Financial Times*, January 18, 2022.

[20] Gibbon and Mueller, 2005.

[21] Correlli Barnett, *The Collapse of British Power*, New York: William Morrow & Company, 1972.

These sorts of "moral degeneration" arguments about culture have been rightly criticized for being analytically mushy and empirically suspect. There were, for example, plenty of factors at work in both Rome and Britain other than the moral fiber of their leaders and elites. For Rome, an arguably much more decisive threat was the arrival in Europe of massive Hun incursions, which then displaced Germanic tribes that put pressure on Roman imperial territory. In the British case, another factor was the relative growth of the much larger U.S. and German economies, an objective demographic and material reality for which no amount of moral fiber would have compensated. Then, too, the concept of moral strength and weakness in a nation is notoriously ill-defined, making it extremely difficult to measure at any given time.[22]

We can, though, downgrade the role of culture—as abstract and difficult to define as it can be—too much. The rich literature on culture and economic development has identified many habits, beliefs, or behaviors that tend to be associated with competitive advantage in more-limited and issue-specific ways.[23] Classical economists and social scientists, from Adam Smith to John Stuart Mill, Max Weber, and Karl Polanyi, all theorized causal links between cultural factors and economic outcomes.[24] An explosion of more-empirical efforts has gathered persuasive data on culture's effect:[25] Values associated with economic success include cooperation, reciprocity, high levels of interpersonal trust beyond the family or tribe, initiative, a strong orientation toward the future rather than the present, a belief in the value of thrift and savings, a commitment to education, and a belief in the moral and instrumental value of discipline, hard work, and self-control.[26] The extensive literature on social capital or

---

[22] Barry Supple, review of *The Verdict of Peace: Britain Between Her Yesterday and the Future*, by Correlli Barnett, *English Historical Review*, Vol. 117, No. 472, June 2002.

[23] Paul DiMaggio, "Culture and Economy," in Neil Smelser and Richard Swedberg, eds., *The Handbook of Economic Sociology*, Princeton, N.J.: Princeton University Press, 1994; Stephen Knack and Philip Keefer, "Does Social Capital Have an Economic Payoff? A Cross-Country Investigation," *Quarterly Journal of Economics*, Vol. 112, No. 4, 1996; Stephen Knack and Paul Zak, "Trust and Growth," *Economic Journal*, Vol. 111, No. 470, 2001.

[24] These scholars define *culture* as "those customary beliefs and values that ethnic, religious, and social groups transmit fairly unchanged from generation to generation," and they found, for example, that people with certain cultural values (such as adherence to a religious faith) tended to teach thriftiness to their children at higher rates, and so countries with more adherents to those religions tended to save more, controlling for other factors (Luigi Guiso, Paola Sapienza, and Luigi Zingales, "Does Culture Affect Economic Outcomes?" *Journal of Economic Perspectives*, Vol. 20, No. 2, Spring 2006, p. 23).

[25] This literature includes such research as Edward Banfield's studies of the lack of trust (and resulting pattern of "amoral familism") he witnessed in southern Italian villages and, later, the work of Robert Putnam, Lawrence Harrison, William Easterly, and Francis Fukuyama. See Edward C. Banfield, *Moral Basis of a Backward Society*, New York: Free Press, 1958.

[26] Joel Mokyr, *A Culture of Growth: The Origins of the Modern Economy*, Princeton, N.J.: Princeton University Press, 2017, pp. 13–14. Typical causal mechanisms suggest that certain cultural values can reduce transaction costs, promote collective work ethic, encourage ambition and initiative, and encourage learning and education. Just a few examples from this immense literature are Alberto Alesina and Paola Giuliano, "Culture and Institutions," Cambridge, Mass.: National Bureau of Economic Research, Working Paper

civic culture, and the data tying these social patterns to productive outcomes, cannot help but support the argument that aspects of culture, however we define it, are shaping the global standing of nations.[27]

***

Many scholars writing large-scale comparative histories over the past several decades have emphasized the critical role of such softer, cultural qualities in determining national outcomes. The historian David Landes argues that what made the difference in Europe's rise relative to other regions and civilizations was not natural resources or large wealth to begin with, nor "mistreatment by outsiders. It was what lay inside—culture, values, initiative."[28] The economist Dierdre McCloskey's magisterial three-volume study of the sources of Western economic and social progress relies, in the end, on social values to explain those trends.[29] For McCloskey, a strong "bourgeois ethic"—combining an ambition for economic and commercial success with the relevant essential norms, values, and institutions that will allow that ambition to be realized efficiently—is the key competitive advantage. This is surely a cultural trait, however defined.

The historian Margaret Jacob similarly argues for "taking culture seriously," as opposed to more strictly material factors, in determining national fates. She has in mind a particular component of what can be described as culture: "education and the inculcation of knowledge," or what she labels as "the culture of applied science." But those qualities, as central

---

No. 19750, December 2013; Richard H. Franke, Geert Hofstede, and Michael H. Bond, "Cultural Roots of Economic Performance: A Research Note," *Strategic Management Journal*, Vol. 12, No. S1, 1991; Yooshik Gong and Wonho Jang, "Culture and Development: Reassessing Cultural Explanations on Asian Economic Development," *Development and Society*, Vol. 27, No. 1, 1998; Jim Granato, Ronald Inglehart, and David Leblang, "The Effect of Cultural Values on Economic Development: Theory, Hypotheses, and Some Empirical Tests," *American Journal of Political Science*, Vol. 40, No. 3, 1996; Guiso, Sapienza, and Zingales, 2006; Luigi Guiso, Paola Sapienza, and Luigi Zingales, "Social Capital as Good Culture," *Journal of the European Economic Association*, Vol. 6, Nos. 2–3, April–May 2008; Harrison and Huntington, 2000; Geert Hofstede, *Culture's Consequences: Comparing Values, Behaviors, Institutions, and Organizations Across Nations*, Thousand Oaks: Sage, 2001; W. Fred Scharf and Seamus Mac Mathuna, "Cultural Values and Irish Economic Performance," in Susanne Niemeier, Charles P. Campbell, and René Dirven, eds., *The Cultural Context in Business Communication*, Amsterdam: John Benjamins, 1998; Rene M. Stulz and Rohan Williamson, "Culture, Openness, and Finance," *Journal of Financial Economics*, Vol. 70, No. 3, 2003.

[27] "We define social capital as 'good' culture—in other words, a set of beliefs and values that facilitate cooperation among the members of a community," three scholars explain, concluding that such social patterns create deeply embedded effects that last for centuries in a society, in part because these beliefs and values become intergenerationally transferred (Guiso, Sapienza, and Zingales, 2008, p. 296).

[28] David S. Landes, *The Wealth and Poverty of Nations: Why Some Are So Rich and Some So Poor*, New York: W. W. Norton and Co., 1998, p. 252.

[29] Dierdre N. McCloskey, *The Bourgeois Virtues: Ethics for an Age of Commerce*, Chicago: University of Chicago Press, 2010; Dierdre N. McCloskey, *Bourgeois Dignity: Why Economics Can't Explain the Modern World*, Kindle ed., Chicago: University of Chicago Press, 2011; Dierdre N. McCloskey, *Bourgeois Equality: How Ideas, Not Capital or Institutions, Enriched the World*, Chicago: University of Chicago Press, 2016.

as they are to national success, cannot do the job alone, because knowledge and learning do not have the same effects in all contexts—that such a "mechanistic perspective assumes that knowledge is socially disembodied and universally transferable."[30] Supportive cultural values are essential to allow learning to have its full dynamic effect.

Such values, however, can theoretically exist in any nation, any society. Qualities such as a strong work ethic, habits of cooperation and reciprocity, a future orientation, and the celebration of learning have existed in many nations—and some of them have been spurred and nurtured in places where they were initially weak. These factors are *cultural* only in the broadest and most secular meaning of that term and potentially accessible to any civilization. Emphasizing the importance of the cultural values and habits of a society is not the same thing as arguing for the inherent superiority of one nation or civilization over another. It is an argument about the characteristics that can in theory benefit *any* nation, society, or culture that reflects them instead of their opposite.[31] To return to the argument about differences between Athens and Sparta, Ober suggests, the distinction is not about the superiority of "a peculiarly Athenian character," but rather a more generalizable model "that other communities might successfully emulate."[32]

In sum, the extensive literature on elements of what can be called culture, and its relationship to such outcomes as economic development and innovation, hints at the ways in which national character determines national fate. The best examples of that literature do not support crude, simplistic assertions, and they do not go as far, usually, in carving out discrete factors that can be independently assessed as causal variables. But they do offer a useful starting point for this analytical journey by beginning to outline the ways in which societal characteristics shape national competitive success.

---

[30] Margaret C. Jacob, *The First Knowledge Economy: Human Capital and the European Economy, 1750–1850*, New York: Cambridge University Press, 2014, pp. 4–5, 9, 17.

[31] The historian Marc David Baer, for example, takes issue with those who stereotype the Ottoman world of the 17th and 18th centuries as backward and closed and uninterested in commerce—as inherently inferior, from a societal standpoint, to Europe (Marc David Baer, *The Ottomans: Khans, Caesars, and Caliphs*, New York: Basic Books, 2021). Our argument does not require such comparisons. It simply highlights the fact that nations that embody these characteristics gain dynamism and competitive advantage. Some, such as European nations after 1500 and then including the United States and much of the democratic world—Western and non-Western—have come to reflect many of these characteristics very broadly. One can still argue that some specific societies at specific moments (including the Ottoman Empire) demonstrated shortcomings in some of these characteristics that contributed to their competitive decline.

[32] Ober, 2015, p. 210. In Chapter Eleven, we extend this idea to an argument about one enduring dynamic in world politics—the rise of nations whose social habits and structures reflect the dominant competitive paradigm of the period and the urgent effort by others to superimpose that model onto their own society.

Defining Our Terms

A critical first step in any analysis like this is to define its terms as precisely as possible. Appendix B offers an extended discussion of our effort to come to grips with the definitions of the two concepts at the heart of this study—societal characteristics and success in strategic rivalries. We briefly summarize our understanding of each here.

The initial research question for the study aimed at an even broader and more abstract quality of a society—its *dynamism* or *vitality*. Several classic treatments of world politics and national fates embrace the idea that some nations or civilizations are livelier, and have a more potent èlan vital, than others. The historian Paul Kennedy has distinguished between "less active societies" and more dynamic ones by way of several criteria—pluralistic governing structures, lack of orthodoxy, "a concern for the practical rather than the abstract"—and he argues that "although it is impossible to prove it, one suspects that these various general features relate to one another, by some inner logic as it were."[33] The modern historian Peter Turchin uses an Arabic term—*asabiya*—to capture a similar idea, the essential energy or vitality, grounded in collective identity, of a society.[34] The scholar and former diplomat Armand Clesse became fascinated with this issue and convened a series of conferences in the 1980s on national vitality.[35]

But terms such as *dynamism* and *vitality* could mean many things. Absent more-precise conceptualization, they cannot carry much weight as analytical categories.[36] Some scholars have tried to flesh out these basic notions. The famed historian Robert Legvold, for example, participating in one of Clesse's conferences, defined *vitality* in this way:

> First, from my point of view the issue of vitality has to do with the creativity of a society, it has to do with the extent to which it is conceptually innovative in dealing with its environment. Secondly, it has to do with how well it adapts to its environment, whether it understands the world that it lives in, whether it's able to keep pace with that world, even

---

[33] Paul Kennedy, *The Rise and Fall of the Great Powers: Economic Change and Military Conflict from 1500 to 2000*, New York: Random House, 1987, p. 30.

[34] Peter Turchin and Sergey A. Nefedov, *Secular Cycles*, Princeton, N.J.: Princeton University Press, 2009.

[35] See, for example, Clesse et al., 1997; Armand Clesse and Sergei Lounev, eds., *The Vitality of Russia*, Luxembourg: Luxembourg Institute for European and International Studies, 2004.

[36] Dictionary definitions of these terms tended not to be of much help, being largely tautological or circular in nature. Merriam-Webster, for example, defines *vitality* as "lively and animated character," "capacity to live and develop," or "physical and mental vigor" (see *Merriam-Webster.com Dictionary*, "Vitality," Merriam-Webster, undated-b). The *Oxford English Dictionary* places similar emphasis on qualities attached to living things, defining the term in the broadest sense as "active force or power" and noting that it comes from the Latin *vitalitat*, meaning vital force, or life (see *Oxford English Dictionary*, "Vitality," undated-b). Merriam-Webster defines *dynamism* as "a dynamic or expansionist quality," offering such synonyms as *drive, energy, esprit, vigor,* and *vitality*; the *Oxford English Dictionary* relates *dynamism* to *force, energy,* or *dynamic action* (see *Merriam-Webster.com Dictionary*, "Dynamism," Merriam-Webster, undated-a; *Oxford English Dictionary*, "Dynamism," undated-a).

whether it's able to anticipate it in some fashion. Third, vitality has to do with its capacity for mobilizing its people, for engaging its people in order to address its problems. Fourth, it has to do . . . with the self-confidence of its leaders, the self-confidence of its *elites* and the self-confidence of its people, and that has something to do with values. So the opposite of vitality, are things like alienation or, if you will, betrayal of values or cynicism within a society at the elite level and at the public level. In a word, *anomie*, which is what you are now suffering—the absence of values or the uncertainty of values.[37]

That is intriguing and suggestive and in fact hints at many of the factors we ultimately identified as more-discrete societal characteristics associated with competitive success. But we worried that these terms were simply too vast and undifferentiated to support any meaningful analysis. There is a justified sense that some societies have more energy, dynamism, or vitality than others at any given time, but that is a different thing from being able to measure it or to define the more-specific and in some cases measurable component elements that add up to those abstract qualities. As a result, we determined that the best approach was to disaggregate the far-reaching notion of social dynamism into constituent parts—still admittedly expansive and sometimes abstract concepts but at least giving a more detailed sense of the actual characteristics that societies must possess to *be* dynamic or vital.

***

The focus of the study thus shifted to identifying the components of an encompassing quality of national dynamism, the more-specific societal characteristics or qualities that generate such advantage.[38] This involved first defining what we meant by a *societal characteristic*, and then deciding on a way to discover these characteristics.

In broad terms, we had in mind with this concept qualities that reside in the space between abstract cultural values (e.g., trust or hard work) and issue-specific policies, choices, or outcomes (e.g., rates of research and development investment or the size of a country's military).[39] The qualities had to be essential enough to serve as the sources of beneficial

---

[37] Robert Legvold quoted in Clesse and Lounev, 2004, pp. 262–263.

[38] Others have relatively recently outlined principles or factors that produce national success. The investor Ray Dalio, for example, published a thoughtful 2021 book that looks at 18 measures of national strength. Many of these mirror aspects of the qualities we are discussing, but most of them are downstream from true societal characteristics. They are measurable indicators of national power that are produced by those characteristics—e.g., levels of innovation, economic output, share of world trade, and financial strength (Ray Dalio, *Principles for Dealing with the Changing World Order: Why Nations Succeed and Fail*, New York: Avid Reader Press, 2021, p. 41). The economic analyst Ruchir Sharma seeks to identify the "rules of successful nations," several of which, especially those dealing with finance and investment and shared opportunity, overlap with our characteristics (Ruchir Sharma, *The Rise and Fall of Nations: Forces of Change in the Post-Crisis World*, New York: W. W. Norton, 2016; Ruchir Sharma, *The 10 Rules of Successful Nations*, New York: W. W. Norton, 2020).

[39] Building strong alliances may provide competitive advantage, for example, but that strategy is not a societal characteristic and is therefore beyond the scope of this analysis. The issue is complicated, however,

national outcomes, such as growth rates or innovation, but still precise and discrete enough as factors that we could accurately assess their presence or absence. With these thoughts in mind, we settled on the following definition of *societal characteristic*: "the essential and persistent social qualities of a nation, including norms, values, institutions, and practices, that shape measurable outputs of national competitive advantage and influence its patterns of behavior." More specifically, our research suggests four main criteria for a factor to count as a societal characteristic. Such a factor must be

1. *related to inherent qualities of the society*, representing ideas, ideologies, cultural values, or other features of social life, aspects that go beyond individual policy decisions and that are widely internalized as taken-for-granted values or behaviors
2. *sociopolitical or sociocultural rather than physical*, reflecting the competitive advantages of a society rather than a location or some resource endowment
3. *lasting and persistent over time*, although not necessarily permanent (even habitual characteristics undergo change and evolution and can be subject to some intentional revision through intentional policy measures)
4. *representative of multiple individual measures or variables and not reducible to a single proxy variable*, reflecting the fact that societal characteristics are necessarily somewhat abstract and holistic factors.

Physical or structural variables that affect national competitive standing—for instance, geography, demography, or position in global trade networks—therefore do not count as societal characteristics. Some factors that affect national fates came close but were not ultimately included as societal characteristics because we saw them as intervening variables rather than underlying causes. A nation's patterns of investment, for example, have a critical effect on competitive standing, but they are the product of more-foundational societal characteristics.

The resulting factors—characteristics such as shared opportunity and unified national identity—are still expansive. None can be reduced to a single number.[40] But each characteristic has two important aspects: It defines a clear and bounded issue, and it can be understood in terms of at least several measurable subcomponents.

An important issue is what we mean by *lasting and persistent* characteristics. The qualities governing national dynamism need not be, and seldom will be, eternal. That is one of the critiques of essentialist theories of cultural advantage: The behavior patterns in Britain or China or Japan in regard to commerce or education or other sources of advantage will shift over time. On the other hand, if a habit or behavior pattern is fleeting—associated, for

---

by the fact that countries may have national characteristics that make them more capable of advantage-producing international behavior, such as alliances and coalitions. This example illustrates again the difficulty of drawing causal lines from *dynamism* to *competitive advantage*: There can be many intervening variables or factors.

[40] We considered the idea of generating an index value for each, but that would have incorporated so many incommensurable factors as to produce overall ratings that had no real significance.

example, with a specific leader's reign or a single regime—it does not count as an underlying societal characteristic. No single time frame defines a lasting characteristic; broadly speaking, though, we were searching for qualities that survive at least several generations.

We do not claim that the resulting characteristics alone determine national fates: As Chapter Two makes clear, factors other than societal characteristics play a critical role. There may also be societal characteristics beyond those we nominate that convey competitive advantage. Our claim is thus limited and qualified: We believe that there is substantial historical and research-based empirical evidence for the importance of a specific set of societal characteristics—and, critically, the way they work together in a synergistic mix—in providing national competitive advantage. They are

1. national ambition and will
2. unified national identity
3. shared opportunity
4. an active state
5. effective institutions
6. a learning and adapting society
7. competitive diversity and pluralism.

We lay out each of these characteristics in a separate chapter and later describe the default recipe for national success that brings them together into a mutually supporting whole.

***

Having clarified our notion of societal characteristics, we then turned to a second definitional challenge: to understand what we meant by *competitive advantage* or *competitive position*. To make the argument that societal characteristics shape national competitive outcomes, we had to decide how to conceive of those outcomes. Appendix B explains our analysis of this issue in depth; here we offer a summary.

Winning and losing competitions or rivalries, or a country's relative standing in world politics, can be surprisingly difficult to pin down. Who, for example, "won" the long-term contest between France and Germany? It depends on what time frame we are looking at and what criteria we employ to measure success. Both have emerged as highly productive, high-income, territorially secure nations influential in both regional and global terms—and so both have succeeded, as measured in many critical ways.[41]

---

[41] British history since about 1950, to take an example, "cannot really bear the weight of unmitigated gloom heaped on it in" the more polemical narratives of national decline, as Barry Supple concludes. He continues, "The ship did not founder, competitors have not steamed endlessly away, the comparative material achievements have been impressive, the social and democratic experience has not been destructive." Britain's success or failure cannot be judged in simple relative terms next to the United States: "Britain could undoubtedly have done better. But it 'failed'" in the terms sometimes used by the declinists—failed as in

Competitive standing cannot be reduced to winning or losing wars. Many nations have triumphed in specific battles or even wars and gone on to lose a larger competition. Sparta is a good example: At the end of the Peloponnesian War, Athens had been defeated and occupied. Yet through the long lens of history, between these two city-states, apart from some inflated reverence for Spartan values (Sparta was a brutal totalitarian state that routinely terrorized its slave classes and won a smaller percentage of its battles than is commonly supposed), Athens clearly won the historical competition for power and influence. Britain lost an embarrassing counterrevolutionary war in North America and ascended to its peak of imperial power a century later. Germany and Japan lost one or more major conflicts but recurrently displayed societies of significant dynamism and today enjoy high standards of living and regional influence. The United States lost in Vietnam and prevailed 15 years later in the Cold War.

Nor is a measure of material national power an effective proxy for competitive success. Many assessments of the sources of national competitive advantage rely on some index of power—however defined—as their essential output. Yet power indexes frequently weight mass (large population and industrial output) very heavily, which disadvantages smaller but competitively dynamic nations that generate high standards of living and security for their citizens. Russia has a higher strategic power position than Denmark today—but few would argue that Russia's societal characteristics are more effective or dynamic. These analyses also often have difficulty capturing the nonmaterial foundations of dynamism: Nations with impressive material power but very weak societal qualities do not tend to maintain an enduring competitive position.

To deal with these challenges, we reviewed multiple approaches to competitiveness broadly defined (listed in Appendix B). We studied historical accounts of national rise and fall, highlighting periods of peak influence for great powers.[42] We also examined studies that touch on one of the most profound discrepancies in competitive position among great powers ever witnessed—the Great Divergence, the period after 1500 and through the Industrial Revolution, when European nations dramatically outpaced global competitors in measures of

---

losing its dominant position to the United States and others—"because success was impossible" (Supple, 2002, pp. 672–673).

[42] This lens, therefore, has much in common with the ongoing debate about national rise and decline, the ways of understanding national fates over time. The scholar Marshall Goldman reminded an audience in 1995, for example, that, in the 19th century, Russia "was the largest producer of pig iron . . . the biggest producer of grain, bigger even than the United States"; in the first years of the 20th century, Russia led the world in petroleum production; and even under the Soviet system, in 1970, it was "the world's largest producer of all kinds of important products: oil, gas, steel, machine tools." And yet it would keep falling back from those advances and eventually lag badly in many industrial sectors (Marshall Goldman quoted in Clesse and Lounev, 2004, p. 230). Its relative power declined, measurably and significantly, on the global stage. Britain in the 19th century showed the opposite trajectory, powered by its lead in the Industrial Revolution. "For the next 150 years," after roughly 1800, "no other European country could rival Britain's dynamism" (Stephen Broadberry, Bruce M. S. Campbell, Alexander Klein, Mark Overton, and Bas van Leeuwen, *British Economic Growth, 1270–1870*, New York: Cambridge University Press, 2014, p. 426). These are classic statements of relative national trajectories—ones we sought to understand using societal characteristics.

wealth and power. And we reviewed a dozen in-depth historical case studies for hints about the nature of competitive success on the geopolitical stage.

Using these sources as guidance, we eventually conceptualized competitive advantage in three broad ways. These encompassed both absolute and relative measures of success. First, from the historical literature, our case studies, and modern indexes of competitiveness, we identified nine defining indicators of national competitive success—signposts of dynamism and advantage inherent to the society itself. (These nine indicators are listed in Table 1.1.) These are the outputs—both absolute and relative, ranging from relative military power to domestic measures of wealth—that we would expect to see from highly competitive nations. Starting with this yardstick of success, we evaluate how effective a society is in meeting its own domestic needs and goals, which helps us take seriously, for example, the fact that the Netherlands is a hugely successful and competitive society today even though it is no longer a world-spanning great power in classic historical terms. This approach also allows us to assess that vague but suggestive idea of national dynamism in more-precise ways: A dynamic and vital society will be one that shows up well in these nine indicators.

To assess longer-term geopolitical standing, indicators that a nation is succeeding in comparison with others over time, we turned to a second lens: We defined the competitive peak or apex of global power of our case study countries and looked for the factors that drove that success. Assessments of the cycles of great power hegemony tend to identify three major peaks of modern global influence—the Dutch, British, and American. In the case of Britain, we highlighted the period from the mid-19th century through World War I as its moment of peak competitive standing. The Ottoman state rose to prominence in roughly the 15th through the 17th centuries, remaining powerful for an extended period after that but beginning a gradual relative decline—which prompted a series of reform efforts to catch up with European powers—in the 18th century. For Rome's peak of power and influence, we chose the period from the late republic through the early empire. In this sense, although the chapters refer broadly to lessons from national experiences, in each case we had a more specific time frame in mind with our research.

A nation's trajectory of power can be challenging to assess. Some nations remained at a relative peak for a long time—in the case of Rome, for centuries. It is impossible to associate simple, time-specific measures of societal characteristics with such enduring patterns. In some cases, moreover, a nation on the far side of its competitive peak can remain among the world's most potent states for a century or more. This is certainly true of the Ottoman and Austro-Hungarian Empires. It is even true of a former European power sometimes derided as a competitive laggard: Habsburg Spain. It rose to global preeminence in the 15th and 16th centuries and by 1520 controlled huge swaths of Europe. In the face of multiple wars and the gradual erosion of stability in its colonies, Spain began to suffer reverses but also witnessed partial recoveries and remained one of Europe's leading powers into the mid-17th century.

In a more recent case, the Soviet Union had real industrial accomplishments by the 1960s and bursts of creativity and a sort of self-confidence within the society. Between 1956 and 1968, Vladislav Zubok concludes, "the Soviet Union still possessed considerable internal

TABLE 1.1

Outcome Indicators—Factors to Measure Competitive Success

Indicator of Competitive Success and Advantage	Historical and Current Examples and Metrics
Longevity in terms of long-term socioeconomic and geopolitical resilience that maintains national identity over an extended period and promotes extended cultural and social influence	• Trends in measures of national power • Collapse or surrender by rival • Long-term, indirect, and diffuse social, cultural, or political influence
Sovereign ability to protect the safety and prosperity of citizens against capabilities or threats of other states, nonstate actors, and systemic risks	• Power to prevent large-scale territorial aggression against homeland • Ability to prevent harassment or disruption of society short of war
Geopolitical freedom of action in terms of the ability to make free and unconstrained sovereign decisions and to take actions in the international system to greatest degree that relative power will allow	• Absence of coercive control by regional or global hegemon • Self-sufficiency in materials and factors necessary for freedom of action
Military advantage or dominance, locally or globally, and the ability to project power	• Global military dominance, either generally (e.g., Rome, post–Cold War United States) or in specific domains (e.g., British maritime dominance) • Ability to project power from a distance
Leadership of or membership in predominant alignments of military and geopolitical power	• Modern treaty-based alliances, multilateral or bilateral • Less formal security relationships
Predominant economic strength—globally, within a region, or within one or more industries	• Total or per capita gross domestic product (GDP) • Share of global trade, investment, or research in critical industries
Strong to predominant position in global trade, investment, and capital markets (relative to size of GDP and other factors)	• Role in regional or global trade networks (Egypt, Rome, Britain, United States) • Dominance of national currency • Predominant power in economic institutions
Strong to predominant position in ideological and paradigmatic categories and global narratives and norms, attractive power, and international institutions and standards	• Cultural influence • Alignment with leading global norms and values • Leadership of international organizations and norm-setting processes
Strong or leading position in frontier technology; leading or dominant role in key emerging industrial sectors	• Domestic capabilities and industries in leading industries of the era • Measures of relative technological standing • Proportion of research and development (R&D) spending in key industries

energy and even . . . was capable of bouts of ideological vigor and optimistic idealism."[43] Within a decade, though, the Soviet Union was clearly stagnating, and soon after that began a terminal decline, yet it remained one of the world's two dominant powers for more than a decade. Even when such a clear decline is evident—as it surely was in the Spanish case by the

---

[43] Vladislav M. Zubok, *A Failed Empire: The Soviet Union in the Cold War from Stalin to Gorbachev,* Chapel Hill: University of North Carolina Press, 2007, p. 191.

mid-17th century—the trends can take such an immense time to unfold that it becomes very difficult to draw causal connections to the sources of these trends.

Then, too, national power trajectories will almost always seem clearer in retrospect than they were at the time. David Cannadine's magisterial history of 19th-century Britain makes clear that even this most dynamic period of British economic and technological advance, culminating in the peak of British power, was hardly smooth sailing, involving a series of economic crises, social uprisings, and threats of instability. The five years after the Battle of Waterloo (1815), for example, saw nationwide recession, riots, and strikes, which one contemporary government report emotionally claimed sought "a total overthrow of all existing establishments."[44] The government used strong-arm tactics to repress such unruliness, which led to the infamous Peterloo Massacre. The year 1825 brought a severe banking crisis; the 1830s "began and ended with . . . periods of intense and acute depression," while in the 1840s across Britain, "distress and despair, anxiety and anger, were the mood and the modes of the times."[45] By midcentury, the process of industrialization was not remotely complete: The largest portion of the working population remained in agriculture, and more people worked with horses than steam engines. The economic progress that did occur brought with it urban misery, belching smokestacks, dangerous working environments, and often terrible living conditions.

One way to recognize a country, a civilization, or an empire in such a position of competitive dominance is to look at how others see it. When a state or empire is viewed as the clear world leader, or one of a very few dominant powers—and beyond that, when others see the society as dynamic and worthy of emulation—that is a strong indication of position. Beyond public commentary, evidence for such perceptions can arise in the form of a social, political, and military phenomenon known as *competitive isomorphism*: when organizations (or countries) become more similar over time because they are trying to match the competitive advantage of one or a few leading societies.[46] This pattern emerged multiple times in the historical cases: many other peoples copying Roman social patterns in a desire to ape Rome's success; Britain, jealous of the Dutch advantages in finance and trade in the 16th century, trying to learn lessons and overtake its rival; and Meiji Japan sending half its senior ministers on a nearly two-year tour of leading world powers—notably Britain and the United States—to gather best practices that would inform its drive for power. In other cases (Habsburg Spain and Austria-Hungary, the Ottoman Empire, and the Soviet Union), even when a state ranks among the top set of world powers in some objective sense, we do not see the same degree of effort to xerox its social model.

---

[44] Quoted in David Cannadine, *Victorious Century: The United Kingdom, 1800–1906*, New York: Penguin Books, 2017, pp. 130–131.

[45] Cannadine, 2017, pp. 177, 202.

[46] Paul J. DiMaggio and Walter W. Powell, "The Iron Cage Revisited: Institutional Isomorphism and Collective Rationality in Organizational Fields," *American Sociological Review*, Vol. 48, No. 2, April 1983.

For a third and final lens on competitive advantage, we turned to global histories tracking large-scale shifts in power and influence in world politics beyond the fates of individual nations, especially analyses that sought to identify causal factors explaining such shifts. The literature on the Great Divergence was especially useful, since it speaks directly to the factors responsible for Europe attaining a peak of competitive standing.

One of the most helpful concepts we encountered for understanding what societal success looks like is Jack Goldstone's idea of national *efflorescences*. He defines such a development as "a sharp and fairly sudden burst of economic expansion and creative innovation," or more specifically as

> a relatively sharp, often unexpected upturn in significant demographic and economic indices, usually accompanied by political expansion and institution building and cultural synthesis and consolidation. Such efflorescences . . . are often seen by contemporaries or successors as "golden ages" of creativity and accomplishments. Moreover, they often set new patterns for thought, political organization, and economic life that last for many generations.[47]

These golden ages are characterized by interrelated progress in multiple areas of social development: political institutions, economic growth and development, technological innovation, rising productivity, and improving objective measures of national well-being and development. Historically, they also tend to produce military advantage and geopolitical influence.[48] For the purpose of this analysis, our focus was on identifying the societal characteristics associated with periods of national efflorescence.

In sum, then, as we sought to assess competitive success, we assessed relative geopolitical position—the dominance of a Rome or Britain at their heights, for example, or the decline into vulnerability and eventual fragmentation of the Ottoman Empire starting as early as the 18th century, as measured by both narrow geopolitical assessments of relative power and wider global histories of the long-term fates of nations. We also considered evidence of the degree to which a nation succeeded on its own terms, independent of its global position. The result was a complex, qualitative, and qualified judgment about many countries. The analysis did not (and could not) produce anything like mathematical precision; no "index of national competitive success" could hope to accurately measure and include all the necessary factors. But the research did allow us to make provisional conclusions about the association between certain qualities of societies and their dynamism and competitive standing. It produced, in

---

[47] Jack Goldstone, "Efflorescences and Economic Growth in World History: Rethinking the 'Rise of the West' and the Industrial Revolution," *Journal of World History*, Vol. 13, No. 2, Fall 2002, p. 333.

[48] Ober, to take just one example, classifies the rise of ancient Greek city-states as such an efflorescence, involving "increased economic growth accompanied by a sharp uptick in cultural achievement." He contends that this "ancient Greek efflorescence was distinctive for its duration, its intensity, and its long-term impact on world culture" (Ober, 2015, pp. 2–3).

fact, a set of seven societal characteristics very consistently associated with both absolute and relative competitive standing.

Methodology for a Complex Issue: Demonstrated Causal Associations

After defining the two core concepts in our study—societal characteristics and competitive advantage—we had to develop a methodology for testing the causal relationship between them. In the process, we sought to draw relationships between broad and sometimes abstract qualities rather than precise variables, in contexts in which the outcomes are governed by multiple intersecting factors and a relative paucity of information about the precise way in which they affect one another.[49] Appendix A describes our approach to this methodological challenge in more detail.[50]

Any effort to connect societal characteristics to competitive outcomes also confronts the challenge of changing historical context. The factors that provided a competitive advantage in 1300 would not necessarily do so in 1700; societal characteristics essential to success in the 18th century might be irrelevant now. To take one example, classical Egypt, one of the ancient world's most dominant powers, was a profoundly conservative and, in some ways, stagnant society. There was precious little room for social mobility. Patterns of life changed hardly at all. The same essential conservatism created a powerful xenophobia, a sense that foreigners not only had little to offer but also posed risks to the community. And yet this society produced a system that allowed pharaonic rule to persist for 3,000 years—with social habits and beliefs that would make a state terribly uncompetitive in the modern world.[51]

---

[49] Ober in his study of classical Greece, for example, agrees that "it is impossible to employ a perfectly clear identification strategy—that is, to strictly distinguish independent (explanatory) variables from dependent variables and to rigorously test hypotheses through natural, lab, or survey experiments." Partly this is true because highly complex social systems have a substantial degree of endogeneity—"that is, feedback between causes and effects." But he still believes that "quantitative and qualitative methods can be conjoined in ways that are rigorous enough to pass muster as causal explanation," and our approach asserts the same (Ober, 2015, p. xviii). Ober's analysis is one of the most direct efforts to make causal relationships between societal characteristics and competitive outcomes. He claims a resulting causal relationship, as "Athens' quick ascent to the status of superpolis was correlated with the end of tyranny and the institution of more egalitarian democratic rules." To make this case, though, he writes—"to draw a causal arrow from democratic reforms to superior performance"—the analysis must "explain just how the relevant changes made Athens more capable and ultimately wealthier as a polis" (Ober, 2015, p. 170). This neatly describes the challenge we faced as well, to describe the mechanisms by which characteristics deliver competitive advantage. We discuss this challenge in more detail in Appendix A.

[50] We also operated with the constraint of a specified research period: We had just over a year to complete all the basic research in the project.

[51] David Wootton's fascinating account of the origins of the Scientific Revolution draws an important distinction between mindsets even in 17th-century Europe and those after the full force of scientific advances in the following two centuries: a shift in the appreciation for the reality of change and the concept of prog-

The changing basis of national success applies to more modern cases as well. The political scientist William Wohlforth, considering the "vitality" of Russia in historical perspective, suggests that most historians would agree that Russia's best historical advantages were "its territorial expanse and its ability to extract military power from its population." Looking to the future, though,

> it doesn't seem to me that the traditional sources of Russia's relative advantage will be of much use in today's international system. Territory, raw military power, large population, ability to extract resources through authoritarian methods from society—none of these things strikes me as being particularly useful in what I understand to be today's international system.[52]

When considering the causal effects of societal characteristics, therefore, we sought to distinguish between more-timeless ones and those that might have been a product of specific eras and whose relative weight may thus change over time. For example, the former Central Intelligence Agency analyst Kenneth Pollack's study of the societal and cultural basis for Arab military underperformance stresses the importance of a productive match between a nation's societal characteristics and the dominant military paradigm of the day.[53] This same idea can apply to national fates more broadly: The 21st century represents a specific competition paradigm that is very different from those of premodern, early modern, or even 20th-century contexts. Any assessment of societal characteristics essential for success in the future must take this into account while remaining mindful of factors that appear relatively timeless.

Efforts to identify the persistent value of any one societal characteristic also encounter the potential issue of diminishing returns. Do some of these characteristics have a threshold beyond which "more" does not really have any effect? Is it possible that most modern nations have crossed a critical threshold and have "enough" of these characteristics (such as shared opportunity or effective institutions) and that competitive success will be determined by other things?

An added complication is that different countries have assembled these characteristics into packages of success (or failure) in different ways. Some gain competitive advantage through relentless success in a small number of these characteristics. Others—such as the United States—achieve lasting competitive advantage through a robust combination of many societal characteristics. Every nation has its own recipe. But one clear takeaway from our analysis is that national competitive advantage appears to rely on *some* combination of the

---

ress. The lack of qualities associated with an embrace of change and adaptation would not have been as much of a competitive disadvantage in ancient times, but they would be disastrous today. David Wootton, *The Invention of Science: A New History of the Scientific Revolution*, New York: Harper, 2015.

[52] William Wohlforth quoted in Clesse and Lounev, 2004, p. 311.

[53] Kenneth M. Pollack, *Armies of Sand: The Past, Present, and Future of Arab Military Effectiveness*, New York: Oxford University Press, 2019.

seven characteristics we have identified. We have not been able to identify a national or civilizational success story that did not reflect some version of nearly all of them.[54]

***

When we are dealing with multiple, overlapping, and often abstract factors, definitive causal relationships can be difficult to establish. We cannot precisely quantify the degree of unified national identity of Britain in 1850, for example, or the level of national ambition in the United States in 1910. At its worst, such argumentation can become hand-waving assertions about ill-defined terms.[55]

For this and other reasons, anecdotal evidence from historical cases can only prove so much. And yet such evidence can clearly be helpful in trying to identify patterns in history. We have used the historical research not to generate a comprehensive database of historical events or to directly correlate the rise or fall of a given characteristic with the trajectory of national power but rather to find clear patterns of association. In each of the seven characteristics, we can say that multiple anecdotal examples, repeated evidence from many different cases, and issue-specific empirical research suggest a causal relationship between the characteristic and specific measures of dynamism and success.

More specifically, in considering the historical evidence, we disciplined our search in several ways. First, *we undertook more in-depth research, and laid special stress, on the more modern cases*. There are wonderfully suggestive indications from ancient Greece and Rome, Song China, Renaissance Italy, and other premodern cases of these characteristics, and we catalog many of those. But we sought the most in-depth evidence on the modern British, U.S., Soviet–Cold War, and Japanese cases, as those are the ones most likely to offer lessons still relevant today. Second, *we looked particularly for tangible evidence, even if not quantifiable, of connection to competitive outcomes*, examples where a societal characteristic generated some form of national strength or advantage. Third, we sought out *consistent patterns across theories and cases*, evidence of the ways a societal characteristic offered competitive advantage that cropped up in multiple countries and periods. Fourth and finally, we then *backed up the historical indications with issue-specific research* to determine whether the causal relations implied by historical research stood up to empirical analysis. We asked, for example, whether

---

[54] Some analyses look specifically at characteristics associated with societal or civilizational failure or, as Jared Diamond puts it, "collapse." He defines that as "a drastic decrease in human population size and/ or political/economic/social complexity, over a considerable area, for an extended time" (Jared Diamond, *Collapse: How Societies Choose to Fail or Succeed*, New York: Viking, 2005, p. 3). This is somewhat distinct from our focus here: A state could not check any of those boxes yet be doing very poorly in a competition. Nonetheless, Diamond's analysis aims to uncover the sources of social weakness and decay, which can be part of the story of competition.

[55] Peter Turchin recognizes the difficulties of doing objective social science with concepts as abstract as solidarity—and especially of developing causal relationships involving such variables. This work can all too easily fall into the realm of "mystical explanations" (Peter Turchin, *Historical Dynamics: Why States Rise and Fall*, Princeton, N.J.: Princeton University Press, 2003, p. 37).

there is evidence that shared opportunity is associated with positive economic and social outcomes, whether unified national identity has identifiable economic value, or whether competitive diversity and pluralism are indeed a strength of human organizations.

As we undertook this analysis, because of the complexities mentioned above, we did not seek to rigidly fit measures of societal characteristics to peak relative power—to demonstrate, for example, that social opportunity in Britain, or its habit of societal learning and intellectual energy, rose in tandem with its power in the 19th century. These causal relations will generally be too indirect and qualitative to see such alignments in measured trends. In most cases, too, we simply do not have the data to create such quantitative assessments.

Instead, we sought evidence of what we came to term *demonstrated causal associations* across the areas of evidence summarized above. Does the nation generally reflect these societal qualities during its competitive rise? Are there anecdotal examples of the societal characteristic producing specific advantage, especially related to a nation's peak power? Are there research data proving an important component of an overall causal relationship?

We are not able to express the resulting findings in the form of invariant, lawlike causal connections.[56] Yet not all causal relationships are subject to that demanding level of proof. Much social scientific analysis of causal relations is designed to be explanatory and exploratory rather than designed to generate precise, universal relationships.[57] This kind of analysis can build a case for a causal relationship at some broader level even if the precise effect a variable will have in any individual case is unknown. Medical researchers can say with confidence, for example, that exercise *in general* improves long-term health and resistance against various illnesses. Its precise effect on any one individual can vary widely, but that does not deny the truth of the general causal relationship.

It is in this spirit of exploratory modeling and analysis that we approached the methodology of this study. Rather than a replicable, lawlike causal relationship between two precisely defined variables, we looked for a demonstrated causal association between somewhat more general factors. This approach has much in common with an alternative strategy for assessing causation that has been termed *middle-range theory* or sometimes *mechanisms* or *middle-range law mechanisms*.[58] Two scholars have defined *middle-range theory* as

---

[56] Margaret Jacob, for example, highlights the role of scientific culture, but takes pains to note that she is not suggesting that it is "the key, the sufficient cause" (Jacob, 2014, p. 18). There is no single "sufficient" cause, she suggests—only factors that are especially important but depend upon their interaction with others to achieve their real effects.

[57] Ben Connable, Michael J. McNerney, William Marcellino, Aaron B. Frank, Henry Hargrove, Marek N. Posard, S. Rebecca Zimmerman, Natasha Lander, Jasen J. Castillo, and James Sladden, *Will to Fight: Analyzing, Modeling, and Simulating the Will to Fight of Military Units*, Santa Monica, Calif.: RAND Corporation, RR-2341-A, 2018, pp. 34–36.

[58] Nancy Cartwright, "Middle-Range Theory," *Theoria: An International Journal for Theory, History and Foundations of Science*, Vol. 35, No. 3, 2020.

a clear, precise, and simple type of theory which can be used for partially explaining a range of different phenomena, but which makes no pretense of being able to explain all social phenomena. . . . It is a vision of sociological theory as a toolbox of semigeneral theories each of which is adequate for explaining a limited range or type of phenomena.[59]

Nancy Cartwright offers the example of democratic peace theory as a classic modern case of such middle-range theorizing.[60] The claim that democracies tend not to go to war with one another is not an invariant lawlike proposition: It admits exceptions and will be true for different reasons in different cases. Nonetheless, it states a causal relationship, between the characteristics of democracies and choices for war, that is recurrently true across time and geography.[61]

To bring methodological rigor to making the case for such qualified causal associations, we established several conditions for any causal claims we would make. Table 1.2 lays these out, along with examples of each criterion in practice drawn from one of our seven societal characteristics—in this case, the third, which deals with shared societal opportunity. This framework requires the analyst to ask five questions—and to do so while specifying the pathways for causal outcomes, exactly *how* a factor will achieve its effects.[62]

The chapters on the characteristics are organized according to this broad approach. Each chapter first seeks to define the societal characteristic being proposed, both as a general idea and in terms of concrete real-world expressions. Each then outlines the theoretical case for the association between that characteristic and competitive success and surveys the case studies and global histories for anecdotal evidence to support the association. In the process, we looked for clearly disconfirming cases or alternative causes that could cancel out the effect

---

[59] Peter Hedström and Peter Bearman, "Analytical Sociology and Theories of the Middle Range," in Peter Hedström and Peter Bearman, eds., *The Oxford Handbook of Analytical Sociology*, Oxford, UK: Oxford University Press, 2011, p. 31.

[60] "The claim 'democracies do not go to war with democracies' is an example of a middle-range theory par excellence. It is in the middle with respect to the abstractness of the concepts employed and the breadth of the claim's applicability, i.e. between high social theory and more specific social science claims that use more detailed concepts about more specifically identified issues" (Cartwright, 2020, p. 277). In employing such rigorous but less lawlike causal arguments, Nancy Cartwright argues that precision in defining terms is important—democratic peace theorists spend exhaustive effort defining *democracy*. And yet not all of them do so in the same way, and she ends up concluding that useful middle-range theories can get away with "employing loosely characterized concepts."

[61] Jon Elster argues for a similar approach, the use of explanatory mechanisms in social science that make important claims of causal relationships short of lawlike causalities. He defines such mechanisms as "frequently occurring and easily recognizable causal patterns that are triggered under generally unknown conditions or with indeterminate consequences" (Jon Elster, "A Plea for Mechanisms," in Peter Hedström and Richard Swedberg, eds., *Social Mechanisms: An Analytical Approach to Social Theory*, Cambridge, UK: Cambridge University Press, 1998, p. 45). See also Jon Elster, *Explaining Social Behavior: More Nuts and Bolts for the Social Sciences*, Cambridge, UK: Cambridge University Press, 2015.

[62] On the importance of reasons why a factor causes an outcome as opposed to "black box" explanations, see Elster, 1998, pp. 47–48.

TABLE 1.2

Elements of Demonstrated Causal Associations—Shared Opportunity

Question and Criterion	Example
Can we *define the factor we are trying to assess* with sufficient detail, rigor, and precision to test its effect in real settings?	Shared opportunity can be understood as the ability of all or a large part of a population—both in absolute terms and relative to its competitors—to express its talents in economic, political, and social contexts; partial elements include such measurable indicators as social mobility, numbers of entrepreneurs from middle and lower classes, availability of capital, and quality and reach of mass education.
Is there a strong *theoretical reason* to believe in this causal association that specifies the pathways by which the factor will achieve outcomes?	In theory it ought to be the case that a superior ability to tap into a nation's human resources ought to enhance national power and thus competitiveness.
Do historical cases or surveys provide *multiple concrete examples of various types of this association* that confirm some causal relationship and show how the factor generates outcomes?	Such causal ties show up in multiple case studies. The British case, for example, indicates how opening opportunity to a wide range of the population to become inventors and entrepreneurs can provide national access to critical new technologies.
Is there *issue-specific empirical evidence* validating the causal effect of one or more subsets of the association?	Economic research has shown a relationship between greater opportunity, including such proxy factors as social mobility, and aspects of national dynamism, including economic performance; other empirical evidence shows that the denial of opportunity has effects that degrade national stability and coherence.
Are there any cases or alternative causalities that *decisively contract the causal relationship*?	We found no major cases of nations that achieved sustained dynamism or competitive advantage while displaying significantly less shared opportunity than their direct rivals or competitors.

of our nominated factor. And each chapter offers empirical evidence that demonstrates the competitive effects of subcomponents of the characteristic.

To gather this evidence, as briefly mentioned above, we employed five distinct sources of evidence to inform our assessment of causal ties between societal characteristics and competitive outcomes:

1. *The insights of global histories.* Dozens of authors—including classic historical theories by such writers as Gibbon and Toynbee, as well as modern work by such authors as Daron Acemoglu and James Robinson, Jared Diamond, Niall Ferguson, Jack Goldstone, Margaret Jacob, Paul Kennedy, David Landes, Deirdre McCloskey, Joel Mokyr, Kenneth Proneness, and Peter Turchin—have reviewed long-term historical trajectories of nations and offered specific variables that were decisive in shaping these histories.

2. *Case studies.* We undertook a dozen more-detailed case studies of specific major powers and their competitive trajectories to develop additional insights into the role

of societal qualities on national outcomes. We conducted an internal RAND case study of each power; in many of the cases, we also commissioned a supporting evaluation from a leading historian on the country in question. Table 1.3 lists the cases.

3. *General disciplinary assessments seeking explanatory variables for historical trends.* Besides the global histories in the first lens, we also considered analyses from specific scholarly disciplines—mainly economics—that have tried to tie societal qualities to competitive outcomes. These include work by such scholars as Eric Beinhocker, Samuel Huntington, Edmund Phelps, Michael Porter, Walt Rostow, and Dietrich Vollrath.

4. *Issue-specific empirical research.* Wherever possible, once we had identified candidate societal characteristics, we sought to determine whether there was independent empirical confirmation for some version of the causal relationship. For example, when the cases suggested that some degree of diversity and pluralism could be beneficial, we assessed the literature on the effect of diversity on competitive advantage among corporations.

5. *Assessment of disconfirming cases and potential alternative causalities.* Finally, as we assessed the historical record, we looked for cases or discrete alternative causes that would disprove causal connections suggested by the other lenses.

TABLE 1.3
Historical Cases Assessed for the Study

Case	Analyses Conducted
Rome	RAND analysis
China (premodern and modern)	RAND and external analyses
Spain	RAND and external analyses
Austria-Hungary	RAND and external analyses
Ottoman Empire	RAND and external analyses
Renaissance Italy	RAND analysis
Britain	RAND and external analyses
Sweden	RAND analysis
France	RAND analysis
Japan	RAND and external analyses
Soviet Union	RAND analysis
United States	RAND analysis

NOTE: In addition to these more-formal case analyses, project staff conducted significant research into two other historical cases, though less comprehensively than the above cases: ancient Greece, primarily Athens, and the Netherlands during its peak of global trade, economic, and political power.

To settle on our final list, we first used the survey literatures and other broad assessments of national rise and fall to generate candidate societal characteristics. We then compared the evidence of those sources and applied the analysis of the individual case histories to refine the list to search for causal relationships to the competitive outcomes we had highlighted as defining success. As certain characteristics rose to the top, we searched for empirical evidence confirming some of their core elements. During the entire process, we remained on the alert for disconfirming cases or alternate causes that would cancel out the value of a specific characteristic. Ultimately, the process tested each characteristic according to the five criteria listed above. Figure 1.1 summarizes this analytical process. The result is a work of synthesis that relies on the research of hundreds of scholars who have assessed the broad sweep of historical trends, the rise and fall of societies, and the fates of individual countries and the sources of those fates.

In our use of historical cases to buttress the analysis, we do not contend that each case proves or disproves the relationship between a given characteristic and national competitive success. Rather, our research aimed to extract specific examples that show such a causal connection—identifiable times when a characteristic produced competitive advantage. The chapters on the characteristics can only briefly summarize much of the research on the cases; sometimes, a single paragraph must summarize a whole national experience relative to a given characteristic. Such brief references obviously leap over vast complexities in national

FIGURE 1.1
Summary of the Methodology

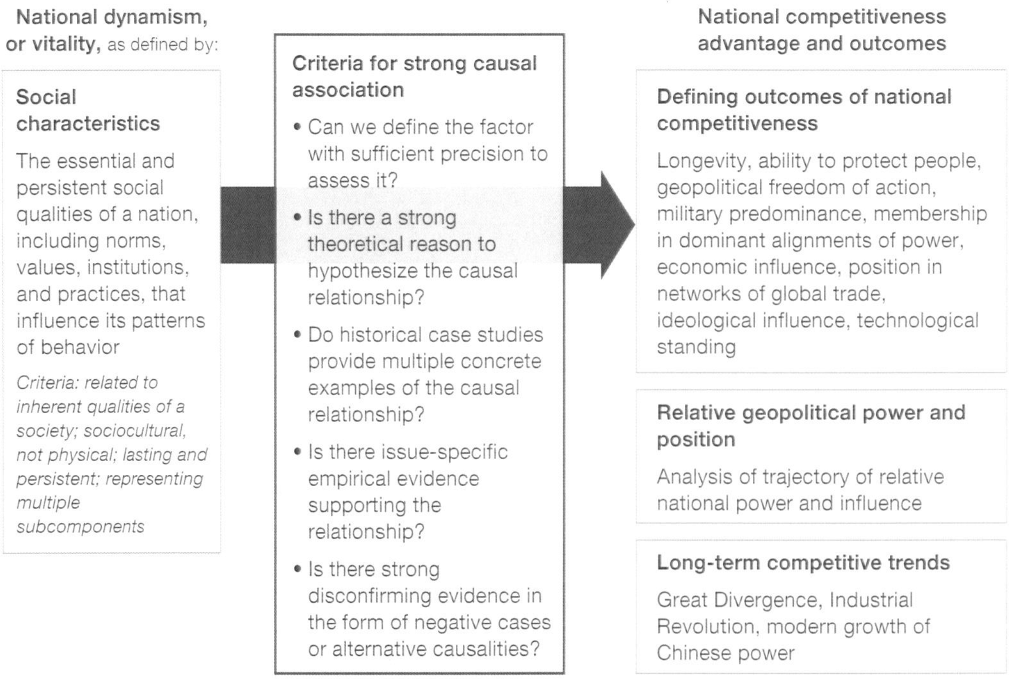

National dynamism, or vitality, as defined by:

Social characteristics

The essential and persistent social qualities of a nation, including norms, values, institutions, and practices, that influence its patterns of behavior

Criteria: related to inherent qualities of a society; sociocultural, not physical; lasting and persistent; representing multiple subcomponents

Criteria for strong causal association

- Can we define the factor with sufficient precision to assess it?
- Is there a strong theoretical reason to hypothesize the causal relationship?
- Do historical case studies provide multiple concrete examples of the causal relationship?
- Is there issue-specific empirical evidence supporting the relationship?
- Is there strong disconfirming evidence in the form of negative cases or alternative causalities?

National competitiveness advantage and outcomes

Defining outcomes of national competitiveness

Longevity, ability to protect people, geopolitical freedom of action, military predominance, membership in dominant alignments of power, economic influence, position in networks of global trade, ideological influence, technological standing

Relative geopolitical power and position

Analysis of trajectory of relative national power and influence

Long-term competitive trends

Great Divergence, Industrial Revolution, modern growth of Chinese power

experience. But those references reflect deeper research, and the case studies are not our sole source of insight—they are only one piece of the analytical approach.

This approach is best understood as a gradual process of discovery, informed by multiple literatures and sources of data. We developed a set of candidate factors and continually refined it, adding and subtracting characteristics and combining and splitting factors as the research suggested better definitional boundaries. The result was a deeply research-informed journey of discovery guided by several clear criteria.

Primary Findings

Our analysis produced five major findings. The first is that *an identifiable set of societal characteristics do appear to be related to competitive success.* Table 1.4 summarizes the verdicts of the cases on our hypothesized characteristics. Our research found significant support for *some* causal relationship (whether positive or negative) between those seven characteristics

TABLE 1.4

Case Study Results: The Role of Hypothesized Societal Characteristics in Determining Competitive Position

	National Ambition and Will	Unified National Identity	Shared Opportunity	An Active State	Effective Institutions	A Learning and Adapting Society	Competitive Diversity and Pluralism
Rome	●	●	◗	●	◗	◗	◗
China	●	●	●	●	●	◗	◗
Spain	●	◗	●	◗	◗	●	
Austria-Hungary	◗	●	◗		◗		●
Ottoman Empire	●	●	●	◗	◗	●	●
Renaissance Italy	●	●	●	●	●	●	◗
Britain	●	●	●	●	●	●	●
Sweden	◗	◗	◗	●	◗		
France	●	●	●	●	●	◗	◗
Japan	●	●	●	●	●	●	
Soviet Union	●	●	◗	●	●	◗	
United States	●	●	●	●	●	●	●

NOTES: ● indicates clear historical evidence to support association—not that the association is necessarily positive, only that the case offers a strong causal link, whether positive or negative. ◗ indicates weaker evidence. Blank cells indicate that the case did not offer clear evidence for the causal effect of that characteristic.

and competitive outcomes in most cases. Taken in total, that research suggests that highly competitive societies

1. possess a strong and widely shared sense of national ambition and will, both externally (to express the power of the nation in the international sphere) and internally (to push the frontiers of scientific knowledge and technological achievement while mastering the natural world)
2. have a unified, coherent national identity that encourages effort, loyalty, sacrifice, and commitment to the common good
3. offer significant and widely accessible degrees of opportunity to express talents and ideas to the largest feasible part of their populations
4. benefit from the targeted, context-appropriate policies and actions of an active and effective state apparatus
5. possess broadly effective institutions—economic, social, political, and military
6. reflect an intellectually curious mindset that emphasizes learning and experimentation and is open to change and adaptation to enhance national power
7. embody significant degrees of diversity (as measured in many different ways) and a competitive pluralism in which various actors or levels of governance can take distinct initiative.

These characteristics offer specific avenues to competitive advantage. Societies that have them become more economically vibrant and scientifically and technologically advanced. They become more innovative. They become more motivated and unified in the pursuit of their objectives. They become more able to govern themselves and display better rule of law and more-effective application of societal resources. They also tend to have stronger national resilience, dealing with threats, crises, and disasters better than nations that reflect weaker societal characteristics.[63] They have greater reservoirs of national willpower, better sources of economic vitality to carry them through difficult times, more innovative and flexible sources of ideas, and better decisionmaking processes. In these and other ways, our research suggests, the nominated characteristics work their competitive magic.

The second finding highlights *the importance of a prudent balance in seeking sources of national advantage.* No nation gains competitive advantage by pushing any one characteristic to its limit. In every case, the chief advantage comes from cultivating a productive balance within each characteristic—a strong national identity that still allows for pluralistic diversity or an active state that does not harden into a stultifying bureaucracy. Some of the characteristics harbor greater risk than others in this regard: Excessive national ambition and will is more dangerous than excessive shared opportunity. But all of them carry some danger when thrown out of balance.

---

[63] We are grateful to William Anthony Hay for suggesting that we emphasize this finding.

Our third finding is that *a set of distinct factors other than societal characteristics is associated with national competitive standing.* Chapter Two outlines these variables. Some are a product of national decisions or strategies; others are systemic factors or momentary events or trends that shape the context for national success. Nations concerned with their competitive position must attend to these issues at the same time as they are working to bolster their societal foundation for competitiveness. Indeed, it is often the interaction of these nonsocietal factors with the qualities of a nation—the ways in which its character matches or falls out of alignment with the demands of the moment—that determines national fates.

The fourth finding constitutes in many ways the core message of the study: *competitive advantage derives from positive-feedback synergies among multiple societal characteristics, which in turn interact with other factors.* Individual characteristics are important. But it is these blended, interactive effects, creating competitive wholes greater than the sum of their parts, that distinguish the strongest and most-competitive nations of each era.[64] Competitive societies are those that benefit from such a whirlpool effect of many factors working together.

Similarly, nations whose competitive standing deteriorates tend to manifest weakness in many factors that compound: Competitive failure typically results from a negative-feedback loop of some kind, in the same way that success derives from a positive-feedback loop. A nation can have thousands of highly talented scientists and welcome people from diverse backgrounds to contribute to its scientific and technological endeavors. But if its markets are too disorganized to turn the outputs of its scientific community into practical innovations, and if the nation has weak financial institutions that prevent entrepreneurs from developing their inventions, then the advantages the state gains from learning and opportunity will be squandered. Building and preserving the efficiency of a nation's competitive ecosystem, its recipe for dynamism, is thus a priority for any great power, irrespective of the quality of any one factor.

Closely related to the idea of synergies of competitive advantage is the fact that dynamic nations that achieve competitive success are always plugged into energetic and productive networks of exchange (commercial, intellectual, or otherwise). These networks (described in Chapter Two) are not a societal characteristic per se. Rather, we might think of them as a natural by-product of certain characteristics, the sort of behavior that arises in societies with shared opportunity, diversity and pluralism, a learning and adapting mindset, an active state

---

[64] Michael Mann, in his assessment of the "sources of social power" that governed national fates, concludes similarly that the "sources of social power and the organizations embodying them are promiscuous—they weave in and out of each other in a complex interplay between institutionalized and emergent, interstitial forces" (Michael Mann, *The Sources of Social Power*: Vol. 3, *Global Empires and Revolution, 1890–1945*, Cambridge, UK: Cambridge University Press, 2012, p. 16). Jack Goldstone points to the essential role of a similar combination of factors in spurring the Industrial Revolution (Jack Goldstone, *Why Europe? The Rise of the West in World History, 1500–1850*, New York: McGraw-Hill, 2009, pp. 129–130, 133–134). Another scholar argues that industrialization in Britain "did not have just one single cause; it depended on the felicitous chemistry of many disposing elements, some only obliquely connected with social features." He mentions the presence of coal, copper, and tin, emerging export markets for British goods, and others (Roy Porter, *English Society in the Eighteenth Century*, rev. ed., London: Penguin, 1990, p. 312).

shaping networks for competitive advantage, and so on. But the same pattern turns out to be critical beyond a nation's borders: Competitively successful nations *always* serve as important hubs in the leading global networks of trade, finance, culture, and intellectual dialogue.

***

Not all recipes for success are equally compelling. Our fifth finding is perhaps the most important: *Our research highlights one default mosaic of success, one recipe that is representative of all the most dynamic, most sustainably competitive societies.* That recipe tends to be built around a national ethos that is open, tolerant, full of intellectual energy and commitment to learning. It is usually characterized by strong and effective public and private institutions, a pluralistic clash of ideas, and the ability of people from many backgrounds to offer their talents and succeed. It reflects a competitive spirit grounded in a clear conception of the community's collective identity and a deeply felt societal reverence for experimentation and new ideas. Beyond these basic societal aspects, nations that embody this recipe for success reside at the hub of international networks—of ideas, norms, and trade—and build their success on some version of a commercial market that provides a spur to and support system for learning, innovation, and productive expression.

We have adopted a shorthand term to describe this recipe: We call it a *Renaissance spirit*. The phrase is not meant to suggest that every competitively vibrant society will mirror the precise aspects of the historical period known as the Renaissance. The comparison is broader and more thematic. The Renaissance was a period of expanded individual empowerment and expression. It was an era in which scientific, artistic, and cultural creativity were valued. It saw the rise of increasingly vibrant commercial markets and the institutions to manage them. The comparison is not exact, but the basic essence of such societies—open-minded, ambitious, competitive, embracing a degree of diversity and pluralism, humanistic in some essential sense, driven to the institutionalized pursuit of knowledge and greatness—closely matches the essential qualities of the most-dynamic and most-competitive nations throughout history.[65]

Although classical Greece is not one of our core cases, Josiah Ober's wonderful survey of the factors that propelled the rise of the leading Greek city-states offers intriguing support for this proposed default mix of variables. He refers to a package including strong civic institutions, robust investment in human capital, "high levels of economic specialization and exchange, continuous technical and institutional innovation, high mobility of people and ideas, low transaction costs, and ready transfer of both goods and ideas." Again, it is the mix-

---

[65] There were other aspects of the Italian Renaissance that reflected limits on its synergy of competitive strength—for example, the somewhat mixed embrace of modern scientific methods and the persistent limits on shared opportunity. Again, our use of this term is meant to highlight the general spirit of intellectual energy and competitive zeal that characterized the time and to refer to the more general definition of a *renaissance* in the life of a nation.

ture or synergy that is the key: It was the "aggregate of those prosocial choices," he argues, that "tipped classical Greece toward sustained economic growth."[66]

The scholar of Japan Carol Gluck describes many elements of the Meiji era in very similar ways: a rising emphasis on education, literacy, and learning; enhanced national institutions in many fields; a "legal leveling of the classes," mass education, and other mechanisms with the effect of broadening opportunity; an "aggressively entrepreneurial private sector"; and the role of a potent, development-oriented active state involved in such fields as infrastructure improvement, trade policy, and industrialization.[67] The investor Ray Dalio highlights a similar list: "Throughout time, the formula for success has been a system in which well-educated people, operating civilly with each other, come up with innovations, receiving funding through capital markets, and own the means by which their innovations are turned into the production and allocation of resources, allowing them to be rewarded by profit-making."[68]

As noted above, the precise way a nation expresses that recipe must be aligned with the demands of the historical era. Ancient societies could build and maintain substantial empires with three or four primary competitive factors working in tandem—large reserves of manpower, some sense of collective identity, and a decisive and catalytic state, for example. Today, that set of factors alone would not get a great power very far.

Yet there is a timeless value to many key factors, and there is reason to believe that our preferred recipe for success remains closely aligned to the demands of 21st-century national competition. One recipe for dynamism and competitive advantage—especially in the modern era—stands head and shoulders above the rest. That leading recipe is all about intellectual energy, openness to change, and new ways of doing things. It is about a society empowered from the grassroots upward to express creativity. It is about a forward-looking, optimistic sensibility that aims to master and change the world. It is a Renaissance spirit.

---

[66] Ober, 2015, pp. xviii–xix. He distinguishes this from appeals to "a mystical Hellenic spirit" or "spurious assumptions about inherent differences between the peoples of the East and West"—in other words, essentialist arguments about culture.

[67] Carol Gluck, *Japan's Modern Myths: Ideology in the Late Meiji Period*, Princeton, N.J.: Princeton University Press, 1985, p. 17.

[68] Dalio, 2021, p. 32. The naval historian Andrew Lambert argues that true "seapower states"—countries that have embraced the sea not merely for strategic reasons but as a cultural choice—reflect a very similar list of characteristics, ones that provided competitive advantage. He highlights such things as "inclusive politics, the central place of commerce in civic life," an openness to change and new ideas, "endless curiosity," and "progressive political ideologies" (Andrew Lambert, *Seapower States: Maritime Culture, Continental Empires and the Conflict That Made the Modern World*, New Haven, Conn.: Yale University Press, 2018, pp. 38, 47–48).

The Basis for a National Competitive Renaissance

Speaking at a conference on Russian vitality in the 1990s, the scholar William Wohlforth regretted the lack of a rigorous analytical approach to the problem of national competitive advantage: "The set of theories that we have to understand international politics doesn't include any strong body of theory about why some states rise in relation to other states and why some states decline." He spoke of the need for more research:

> One way is to look at what seem to be the requirements of vitality in the international con-text, and ask whether Russia, in this case, has the attributes that are necessary for success in international society. . . . One has to ask, what are the requirements of success in the international system and does it look as if Russia now has those qualities. . . . One way to take a first cut at it . . . is to ask what have been the sources of Russia's relative advantage in the past, and whether those sources are likely to lead to success today, and in the future.[69]

The study we undertook was designed to offer just such an assessment. It has produced evidence that at least seven societal characteristics are strongly associated with long-term competitive advantage. There could be more; our claim is not that this initial list is compre-hensive, only that it is a starting point. In some cases, the characteristics feed on one another in ways that produce a tremendous engine of social dynamism and powerful competitive advantage.

This engine of national dynamism has deep roots, as it turns out. National dynamism relies on institutions that take centuries to develop. It is based on a specific view of the bal-ance between the traditional and the new, the established and the innovative, that has been alien to many societies. It requires degrees of national unity and ambition that cannot be easily copied and pasted from one society to another. The result has often been highly imper-fect efforts to do such xeroxing, and there is a constant tension within societies making the attempt.

Capturing this competitive synergy is what generations of reformers in "Westernizing" countries were trying to do. It was not modernization or Westernization per se that they needed; it was national dynamism to let them compete. But mastering all or enough of these seven characteristics, and to light off the explosive interaction of a positive feedback among them in ways analogous to what was going on in the most-dynamic countries, proved to be a herculean task.[70] It involved forcing these societies to become more like the industrializ-ing West, for good and ill, a process that almost always upset tradition, produced social and political upheaval, and generated often bitter resistance. But ultimately it was about a search for national dynamism more than the importation of any foreign social model.

---

[69] William Wohlforth quoted in Clesse and Lounev, 2004, pp. 310–311.

[70] M. Şükrü Hanioğlu, *A Brief History of the Late Ottoman Empire*, Princeton, N.J.: Princeton University Press, 2008, p. 6.

Some of these countries could never resolve the contradictions of trying to shoehorn societies imperfectly adapted to this recipe for national dynamism into this model. In the Ottoman, Austro-Hungarian, and Russian cases, among others, there remained for a long time a societal dual nature—an effort to build the superstructure of modernized industrialization on premodern, dynastic, quasi-feudal, or other unsupportive foundations. Many countries are still grappling with these tensions to this day. As one scholar writes of a self-claimed modernizing political movement in the late Ottoman Empire:

> by promoting the new while preserving the old, [members of the movement] fostered an ambiguous dualism. They kept the sultan, but introduced the Committee; maintained the Islamic identity of the regime, yet endorsed secularism; espoused Turkism, yet professed Ottomanism; advocated democracy, but practiced repression; attacked imperialism, but courted empires; and proclaimed ètatism while promoting liberal economics.[71]

Such straddling of dilemmas will pose intense challenges for any effort to wrench a society into the recipe for success that we have laid out when a nation's social patterns simply do not align with the demands of that recipe.

Chapter Ten offers a snapshot of where the United States stands today in relation to our seven characteristics. This assessment is bracing. There are reasons for hope and confidence, aspects of American society that reflect potent degrees of the seven characteristics: continuing social mobility, strong diversity and political pluralism, a baseline level of unified national identity. But there can be no doubt that there are also reasons for profound concern. Across almost all the seven characteristics but several in particular, abundant evidence suggests that the United States risks losing much of what made it the world's dominant power for a century.

There is, in fact, a worrying historical pattern of nations ascending to the heights of global influence at a moment when their competitive engines have already begun to run down. By the time of a country's measured peak power, it is probably already relatively declining—it just might not be apparent yet. By some measures, for example, Britain's peak power was the first decade of the 20th century—but by then it had been losing ground in industrial dominance, to such countries as Germany and the United States, for decades.[72] The United States may be in the midst of a similar transition. We therefore offer this analysis with the hope of sparking further research and debate on the critical issue of national competitiveness and the qualities that underpin it. From a national security perspective, there is an extensive discussion today about the capabilities that America requires to deal with the China challenge—yet, if history is any guide, much more important will be the strength of the social qualities that underwrite competitive strength.

---

[71] Hanioğlu, 2008, p. 202.

[72] Walter M. Hudson, "Analogy and Strategy: U.S.-China Competition Through an Edwardian Lens," *American Affairs*, Vol. 5, No. 3, Fall 2021. See also Correlli Barnett, *The Pride and Fall: The Dream and Illusion of Britain as a Great Nation*, New York: Free Press, 1986.

We turn first to a brief review of the factors other than societal characteristics that our analysis highlighted and then begin a detailed assessment of each of the seven characteristics we uncovered. We then turn to the United States to assess its current competitive prospects before offering general conclusions.

CHAPTER TWO

Factors Other Than Societal Qualities That Determine Competitive Position

When Napoleon was rampaging across Europe in the first decade and a half of the 19th century, it was not yet clear whether France's neighbors could deal with the juggernaut of the postrevolutionary French armies. To be sure, Napoleon was hardly an unrestrained adventurist. He waged his campaigns partly in response to the exertions by conservative monarchies to quash this revolutionary regime. Yet in part through domestic reforms (some designed to enhance the societal characteristics on our list, such as investments in learning and institutions of governance), Napoleon's France became a feared military power that loomed over European politics. France certainly seemed to possess the raw materials for hegemony: an immense and productive land mass of more than 200,000 square miles; a population of almost 30 million, three times that of Britain; and a potent economy with a GDP of more than $35 billion in 1820, $10 billion more than Germany and nearly equal to that of world-leading Britain.[1] By many of the criteria we outline in this report, France had wide-ranging competitive advantages and the potential to nurture societal characteristics that would make it a regional and world hegemon.

Within roughly a decade, however, Napoleonic France had suffered decisive losses and had to retreat from its position of overwhelming power. Napoleon himself was removed from power and exiled. Postrevolutionary France then fell behind Britain and others in the race to industrialize. France remained a substantial European power but would never again threaten to become the regional hegemon.

As we will catalog in coming chapters, some of the reasons for this uneven performance are grounded in societal characteristics. But other factors played a significant role in dictating France's fate. Napoleonic France, though it brilliantly played various European powers against one another and recruited many formidable allies of its own, ultimately ended up on the wrong side of a lopsided strategic power balance: Arrayed against it at various times were Britain, Prussia, Russia, Austria, and Sweden. Napoleon also made strategic and interpersonal blunders that counteracted his frequent operational military success. His invasion of

---

[1] Angus Maddison, *Contours of the World Economy, 1–2030 AD: Essays in Macro-Economic History*, Oxford, UK: Oxford University Press, 2007.

Russia must top this list, but there are other mistakes—the ruinously expensive Peninsular War in Spain, to take one example.

In other words, France's competitive position in these years was determined by many factors *other than* societal characteristics. Our research pointed to a collection of specific additional variables that work alongside societal characteristics to influence national standing, and it is critical to understand them to comprehend the more sweeping competitive landscape in which societal characteristics play out.[2] Like the societal characteristics themselves, these other factors could have important implications for the United States today. This chapter groups these other factors influencing competitive standing into three major categories:

1. *structural factors*, including geography and demography
2. *exogenous events and factors*, such as disease, climate change, and strength of enemies or proximity to threats and instability
3. *national strategic posture, positioning, and decisionmaking quality*, such as participating in productive networks, being part of a dominant coalition, making productive use of capital, and building a sustainable financial basis for power, as well as the role of specific leaders.

The following sections briefly survey each of these categories.

Structural Factors

The first set of factors other than societal characteristics that bears on national competitive advantage is a nation's structural or physical realities—its scale and size, geography, demography, and proximity to threats and instability.

Scale and Size

In international rivalries, size matters. Countries with bigger land masses, populations, and economies have an inescapable advantage. If the qualities of social characteristics help shape a country's *potential* competitive standing (at least in relative terms), they must be multiplied by the country's scale to produce its actual competitive position.

The economist Dietrich Vollrath provides an excellent example of this law of geopolitical physics in his assessment of the factors that determine economic muscle. New Zealand ranks very high in competitiveness and ease-of-doing-business scales. Yet, Vollrath notes, "there

---

[2] Marc David Baer offers a similarly wide-ranging list of factors that contribute to "explaining Ottoman success" in the rising centuries of its competitive position (the 14th through 16th centuries). There was luck—some surrounding powers fell into periods of weakness just as the Ottomans arrived. Early leaders had strong strategic vision. Geography placed the early empire in a strong position astride burgeoning trade routes, near enough to fertile lands to expand its power, yet far enough from parts of Europe to help insulate it from warfare and plague. Its initial core of nomadic peoples proved expert raiders (Baer, 2021, pp. 34–36).

is not a continual stream of executives flying to Christchurch every day to try to negotiate any kind of deal to get into the New Zealand market." The reason is simple: scale. New Zealand has a population of fewer than 5 million. Its advantages in governance and regulatory environment are important but can only go so far to promote investment when the domestic market is so tiny. This shows up in state investment patterns within the United States: States such as California and New York rank lower on freedom-of-doing-business indexes than some others. But as Vollrath explains, "firms are desperate to get into those markets. Why? Because they are already huge economies in their own right, and scale matters."[3]

To take another international example, in its competition with the Netherlands, Britain was simply bigger and had the ability to generate a critical mass of economic activity, technological development, and military power that the Dutch could not match.[4] Later, the United States shot past Britain as a global economic hegemon: Both became industrial leaders, but eventually the pure size and weight of the U.S. economy proved decisive.[5]

Geography

One classical argument for the relative strength and success of societies is geography—the natural resources offered by a country's territory and its geographic position in its region.[6] The geographer and historian Jared Diamond's original theory about the rise of nations had to do with the numbers and types of plant and animal species that filled their respective territories. This was dependent on geography and in turn shaped levels of agricultural productivity—and, critically, technological advance—and thus early civilizational growth.[7] Ian Morris's first works maintain that "the West rules because of geography" and go on to describe the long-term developmental implications of the "Lucky Latitudes."[8] Europe's geography, split by mountain ranges and rivers, was a major reason Europe ended up fragmented,

---

[3] Dietrich Vollrath, *Fully Grown: Why a Stagnant Economy Is a Sign of Success*, Chicago: University of Chicago Press, 2020, pp. 181–182.

[4] Broadberry et al., 2014, p. 396. The "decline" of the Netherlands from its 17th-century peak may simply be a factor of the "inability of such a small country (population of less than 2 million) to compete in an increasingly consumer-oriented Western economy" because its market simply did not have enough critical mass (Margaret C. Jacob, *The Cultural Meaning of the Scientific Revolution*, Philadelphia: Temple University Press, 1988, p. 192).

[5] In 1890, Britain had a population of 37.4 million; the United States was already bigger, at 62.6 million. Twenty-five years later, the United States had almost triple Britain's population: "Studies have shown that scale, in terms of domestic resource abundance, population, and industrial production, was the key reason why both the United States and Germany surpassed Britain in the late nineteenth and early twentieth centuries. Germany, and especially the United States, were simply bigger countries—with more land, resources, and people" (Hudson, 2021, pp. 118, 120–121).

[6] Morris, 2010, pp. 29–35; A. Wess Mitchell, *The Grand Strategy of the Habsburg Empire*, Princeton, N.J.: Princeton University Press, 2018, p. 26; Harrison, 2000, pp. xxvii–xxviii.

[7] Diamond, 2005.

[8] Morris, 2010, pp. 557–565.

Morris argues, a structural reality that contributed to its dynamism by promoting competition among a multitude of political units.[9] Other scholars have pointed to a "geographic sweet spot" for development and have also suggested that being "landlocked with bad neighbors" can keep a country from developing.[10]

Historians have cataloged ways in which geographic advantages or disadvantages influence the fates of specific nations, empires, and civilizations. Rome, some scholars explain, benefited from the role of several protective bodies of water, including the Bosphorus, the Sea of Marmara, and the Dardanelles, which provided a defensive barrier between it and Europe's and Asia's massive empires. The "evidence is very strong," one scholar concludes, that

> a thin band of water, reinforced by sea power and supported by peace on other fronts, was the eastern empire's greatest defence. Whereas, without this advantage, a series of invasions at the start of the fifth century plunged the West into a vicious spiral of devastation, loss of revenue, and bitter internecine strife—from which it never recovered.[11]

Renaissance Italy benefited from its location at the center of the trade networks in the Mediterranean and astride trade routes from the east toward Europe.[12] The Ottomans too "were fortunate in their geography," being not only at the center of networks of trade but also shoulder to shoulder with powers under pressure from others and thus, for a time, less likely to pose a direct threat.[13]

The United States has certainly benefited from a favorable geographic position. It has been protected from European and Asian wars by vast oceans and bordered—at least in the modern era—by friendly and largely stable neighboring countries. This geography may also, to a degree not often recognized, have served to protect the United States from the conse-

---

[9] We will examine the social and political aspects of this argument—the advantages of pluralism—in Chapter Nine.

[10] Sharma, 2016, pp. 181–211; Paul Collier, *The Bottom Billion: Why the Poorest Countries Are Failing and What Can Be Done About It*, New York: Oxford University Press, 2007. David Landes, while focusing primarily on culture, insists that geographic factors are important: Rich countries cluster in "the temperate zones" and poor ones "in the tropics and semitropics." He argues that there are many direct and indirect links to the level of human development, ranging from heat to disease (Landes, 1998, pp. 5–15). In particular, Landes makes a persuasive case that geographic demands—such as the need to control water in arid regions—were the parents of social structures, which need to respond to the demands of the geography. One example was the manpower-intensive water control techniques of China, which set the stage for later social patterns (Landes, 1998, pp. 27–28). Landes's argument is that geography sets the stage, in a sense, for development or the lack of it, but it is then left up to human institutions, norms, values and actions to take charge.

[11] Bryan Ward-Perkins, *The Fall of Rome: And the End of Civilization*, New York: Oxford University Press, 2006, pp. 59–60.

[12] Kenneth Bartlett, "Italian Renaissance," Great Courses, course no. 3970, 2005, lecture 3.

[13] Caroline Finkel, *Osman's Dream: The History of the Ottoman Empire*, New York: Basic Books, 2005, pp. 7–8.

quences of its foreign policy excesses. Their implications have largely played out far from home, with the U.S. homeland geographically insulated from conflicts in Vietnam, Iraq, or elsewhere.[14]

Yet geography *alone* is not a reliable predictor of national competitive success—at least not after the experiences of ancient civilizations, and not after a nation's boundaries are set. Daron Acemoglu and James Robinson identify both successful and laggard countries in northern or southern, hot or cold, and land-locked or coastal locations. "There is no simple or enduring connection between climate or geography and economic success," they conclude. Vast differences in national competitiveness sometimes exist in the local areas that straddle borders—for example, the United States and Mexico, Haiti and the Dominican Republic— where the geography is basically the same. Nor can geographic factors explain regions that advanced rapidly for a time and then slowed; their geography did not change even though their fortunes did.[15]

A less dramatic claim might be that geography matters—but mostly through its inter-action with other variables, such as the effectiveness of institutions.[16] Favorable geography might have been a precondition or critical factor for a nation's rise to prominence, but it could not guarantee that rise in the absence of other key societal characteristics. Dani Rodrik, Arvind Subramanian, and Francesco Trebbi conducted economic analysis suggesting that institutions rather than geography are the key factors in development; at a minimum, even geographically gifted nations need to take advantage of their position with good governance.[17] Other scholars argue that Europe's geographic advantages emerged only when combined with another factor stressed in this chapter—participation in networks of trade and in intel-lectual exchange, which were made possible, but not inevitable, by geographic proximity.[18]

---

[14] We are grateful to Jim Goldgeier for this insight.

[15] Acemoglu and Robinson, 2012, pp. 48–56. Arnold Toynbee's argument about the value of challenges, including environmental ones, contradicts the argument about geography as well: Civilizations do not emerge "when environments offer unusually easy conditions of life," he suggested, but the opposite (Toynbee, 1947, p. 80). Other scholars have pointed to wild swings in economic development and innovation rates among countries in latitudes identified as geographically productive (McCloskey, 2011, loc. 2450–2593). Josiah Ober argues that geography is not enough to explain efflorescence in ancient Greece (Ober, 2015, pp. 105–108).

[16] Walter Scheidel, *The Failure of Empire and the Road to Prosperity*, Princeton, N.J.: Princeton University Press, 2019, pp. 263–264; Mark Koyama, "Counterfactuals, Empires, and Institutions: Reflections on Walter Scheidel's Escape from Rome," *Journal of Economic Literature*, Vol. 59, No. 2, 2021, p. 640.

[17] Dani Rodrik, Arvind Subramanian, and Francesco Trebbi, "Institutions Rule: The Primacy of Institu-tions over Geography and Integration in Economic Development," Cambridge, Mass.: National Bureau of Economic Research, Working Paper 9305, October 2002.

[18] Roman Studer, *The Great Divergence Reconsidered: Europe, India, and the Rise to Global Economic Power*, Cambridge, UK: Cambridge University Press, 2015. Diamond's (2005) thesis of geography and plant and animal domestication helps explain the origins of civilization but "cannot explain why modern economic growth started in western Europe rather than in China" (Enrico Spolaore, "Commanding Nature by Obey-

Geography may have newfound relevance in the 21st century. Some countries, due solely to their location, will be harder hit by the effects of climate change than others. Some—such as Canada and Russia—stand to gain significant amounts of arable land and other economic value from a gradual warming.[19] Others could see major components of their territory become uncultivatable (and some even unlivable). Countries with a large part of their economic activity near coastlines may pay an especially large price as sea levels rise, coastal storms worsen, and, potentially, climate-induced tsunamis become a rising phenomenon.

Demography

The size, age distribution, and sophistication of a country's population have long been held up as major indicators of competitive advantage. An important baseline factor contributing to Rome's competitive success was the total population of the empire. Especially once it had integrated the surrounding peoples of central Italy, Rome could call on a potential reservoir of perhaps 700,000 military-aged males. This was a tremendous manpower base, with strong resilient capacities, that furnished an ability to overwhelm many potential adversaries—beginning with Carthage.[20] Some theories connect the pure size of a country's population to innovative capacity: More people generate more ideas, which lead to more innovation.[21]

One of the most common demographic arguments connected to national competitive advantage deals with arguments about human capital: Younger, growing populations have more raw material for economic growth and productivity.[22] Such favorable demographic characteristics have historically been associated with growth.[23] A case in point is the Indus-

---

ing Her: A Review Essay on Joel Mokyr's *A Culture of Growth*," *Journal of Economic Literature*, Vol. 58, No. 3, 2020, p. 784).

[19] See, for example, Gregg Easterbrook, "Global Warming: Who Loses—and Who Wins?" *The Atlantic*, April 2007.

[20] Michael P. Fronda, *Between Rome and Carthage: Southern Italy During the Second Punic War*, New York: Cambridge University Press, 2010, pp. 37–40.

[21] Diego Comin, William Easterly, and Erick Gong, "Was the Wealth of Nations Determined in 1000 B.C.?" Boston, Mass.: Harvard Business School, Working Paper 09-052, 2008, p. 3.

[22] Ruchir Sharma focuses one part of his assessment of national economic fates on a single question: "Is the talent pool growing?" (Sharma, 2016, p. 26). So one question is whether forms of equality are expanding the talent pool even without growth in the population by giving more people an opportunity to express their full abilities (including encouraging older people to reenter the workforce, improving the proportion of women in the workforce). U.S. labor force participation rate declined from 67 percent to 62 percent in 2000–2016 period (p. 42). There will be an associated temptation for "aggressive campaigns to attract or steal labor and talent from other countries" (p. 31). In this, the United States has an advantage in that it is a multiethnic democracy and can attract people from anywhere, very different from China's Thousand Talents model, which recruits experts from abroad.

[23] According to Sharma, half of global economic growth is typically attributed to labor force growth: "A 1 percentage point decline in growth in the labor force will shave about 1 percentage point off economic growth," he explains (Sharma, 2016, p. 23). "To produce strong economic growth in a country with a shrink-

trial Revolution, which some believe to have been fueled in part by a significant, and youthful, population surge.[24]

Apart from population size and quality, other demographic factors have also made a difference in national competitiveness. One is the shift toward later childbearing and smaller families. This allowed "greater investment in human capital" because fewer children meant greater family income available to support each; later childbirth allowed women to participate in the workforce to some degree before having children. These demographic trends encourage the emergence of capital-intensive technologies, because a slowing population growth meant that human capital was more precious.[25] Some countries accelerated into these demographic patterns before others, thus providing a competitive advantage.

Yet, like geographic factors, demographic advantages alone do not explain overall national competitive success. During some periods in history, populous countries have been dominated by ones with far fewer people (as when China was humbled by military missions from comparatively tiny European nations). Demographic advantages have also turned out to be fleeting in most cases. France gained significant competitive advantage in the 18th century from its massive population—22 million in 1750, almost twice Britain's population a full half century later, and roughly eighty 80 of the European population west of Russia.[26] But as its population growth slowed, France's demographic advantage narrowed and then disappeared.

"A large, expanding and youthful population has driven the rise of nations for much of human history," the columnist Gideon Rachman argues. "Great powers needed warm bodies to put on a battlefield and citizens to tax."[27] But, he explains, this is changing: Land battles increasingly rely on technology, not masses of troops, and technological sophistication is the route to national power, not simply a large population base. In the 21st century, when national power will flow in part from mastery of advanced technologies, the unique role of classic demographic power is waning. "Demography will continue to shape world politics, as it always has. But the historic connection between a growing and youthful population and increasing national power is giving way to something more complex," Rachman writes.[28]

---

ing population is close to impossible, or as the European Commission warned in 2005, 'Never in history has there been economic growth without population growth'" (Sharma, 2016, p. 34).

[24] Eric J. Hobsbawm, *The Age of Revolution: 1789–1848*, New York: New American Library, 1962, pp. 169–170.

[25] Broadberry et al., 2014, p. 390.

[26] Gordon Wright, *France in Modern Times*, New York: W. W. Norton, 1995, p. 14; Jeremy Black, *From Louis XIV to Napoleon: The Fate of a Great Power*, London: University College London Press, 1999.

[27] Gideon Rachman, "Lousy Demographics Will Not Stop China's Rise," *Financial Times*, May 4, 2021.

[28] Rachman, 2021.

Proximity to Threats and Instability

A consistent lesson from the historical cases we reviewed is both simple and often forgotten: Nations gain or lose competitive advantage in part as a function of their neighborhoods. Countries surrounded by powerful, hostile neighbors with directly conflicting ambitions or interests will face a competitive disadvantage. Major instability in a nation's immediate area also imposes costs. High-threat, high-instability contexts sap a country's resources, overwhelm its decisionmaking structures, and eat away at its long-term competitiveness.[29] This competitive drawback can be expressed in terms of the costs of war: Nations that are constantly caught up in regional conflagrations will be weakened over time and may face catastrophic pressures.

Nations surrounded by weaker powers and peaceful environments, by contrast, may benefit greatly. Sometimes major powers succeed because they advance into a relative vacuum or take advantage of a period of decline in a neighboring country. Rome benefited from this geographic dynamic for a time, when Greek powers were on the decline but before massive external powers or coalitions—such as the Germanic tribes, the Huns, or the Persian (Achaemenid) Empire—posed major threats to the Mediterranean. Once this changed—that is, when the rising threat of outside power and the regional chaos of a Europe being disrupted by massive pressure from the Huns and others pushing in from the east—Rome came under mortal threat.

The same dynamic has played out with many other major powers. The Ottomans in their rise "certainly profited from the weaknesses and confusion of their enemies"; for example, when the Byzantines faced major disruption, the Ottomans took advantage.[30] Later in Ottoman history, the effect of nearby instability reversed itself: A major handicap of the Ottoman Empire was that it lay "in the middle of a predatory struggle for power on three continents."[31] The Austro-Hungarian Empire suffered because of volatility along its southern borders—and World War I, a product of being surrounded by more revisionist, aggressive, or unstable neighbors, was surely a more decisive blow than any weakness in Austro-Hungarian society.[32] Song China confronted the Jin dynasty, and later Mongol invasions, ultimately falling victim not to internal weakness but to invasion by stronger foreign powers. The United States, meanwhile, has long enjoyed an enviable position in a region without major rivals or, for the most part, large-scale instability threatening the country's borders.

---

[29] Jan Vijg is a scientist, not a historian, but he makes a compelling case that, for the most part, "stable societies always collapsed under the influence of disruptive external forces" (Jan Vijg, *The American Technological Challenge: Stagnation and Decline in the 21st Century*, New York: Algora Publishing, 2011, p. 210).

[30] Donald Quataert, *The Ottoman Empire 1700–1922*, 2nd ed., Cambridge, UK: Cambridge University Press, 2005, p. 25.

[31] Hanioğlu, 2008, p. 209; Halil Inalcik, *The Ottoman Empire: The Classical Age, 1300–1600*, Kindle ed., London: Phoenix Press, 2001, loc. 934–937.

[32] John Deak, *Forging a Multinational State: State Making in Imperial Austria from the Enlightenment to the First World War*, Stanford, Calif.: Stanford University Press, 2015, pp. 264, 271–273.

Sometimes an overly ambitious nation can generate a hostile surrounding environment where one did not exist before. Through belligerence and warmongering, a nation may provoke a decisive coalition of power against it and in doing so seal its own fate. Take Napoleon's France: Although Napoleon sought for a time to conduct savvy diplomacy to keep his European rivals from coalescing against him, eventually he produced just such a dominant coalition. And for all its militarism, Germany's catastrophic loss in World War II was a product of undertaking brutal aggression that generated an allied response of massive power and determination.

Statecraft, however, can also create a more amenable surrounding environment, which can provide a competitive advantage. A shared international order among countries committed to a peaceful status quo—for example, the post-1945 version led by the United States—can shape an underlying structural reality that is unfavorable to aggressors. This order can establish norms, rules, and institutions that generate some degree of automatic balancing against aggression, thus putting the system leader in the stronger competitive position. And it can confront would-be revisionists with exactly the prospect threatened by history—triggering a decisive counterbalancing coalition.

The historian Peter Turchin suggests an alternative argument—that conflict and instability can *produce* competitive advantage by generating a requirement for centralized power in response. Turchin contends that a conflictual interethnic frontier spurs a country to develop an empire, in part by fueling national identity and solidarity (which he terms *asabiya*, meaning group feeling or unity, borrowing from the work of Ibn Khaldun). Eventually, in Turchin's theory of history, growing opposition forms at the boundaries of the expanding empire, instability rises, the system collapses, and the cycle repeats.[33]

Although it is true—and some of our later analysis will agree—that competitive pressures can enhance national dynamism, the degree of competitive opposition can quickly get out of hand. Moreover, Turchin's argument about the power-generating spur of nearby instability has most relevance to earlier periods in history. Today, when the central governance systems of major powers are well established, trouble on the borders tends to generate challenges (such as surges of immigration) that weaken, rather than strengthen, internal solidarity. Nations that rise into a relative vacuum of countervailing power, and into a relatively stable arena, have a major competitive advantage over those that are constantly hounded by enemies and chaos.

Exogenous Factors, Mechanisms, and Events

A second general category of factors other than societal characteristics that shape national competitiveness includes major global developments, trends, or events that set the international context for national competition. These can be sudden or slow developing, a fleeting

---

[33] Turchin, 2003.

hammer blow or a drawn-out process. They can be broad and systemic or discrete and unpredictable. They can hit some nations especially hard in ways that help determine outcomes. As Ross Douthat explains,

> The lesson of 1492 and its consequences isn't that misgovernment and human sacrifice invite conquest and guarantee destruction. It's that any civilizational order, decadent or otherwise, is sustainable only until the right black-swan development arrives, at which point it might be doomed in a way that no simple extrapolation, no sociological analysis, could have possibly predicted.[34]

Here we focus on just such events—exogenous shocks to the system that have undermined nations' competitive standing.

Natural Disasters

Throughout history, natural disasters—earthquakes, floods, volcanic eruptions, and the like—have played a significant role in affecting national rise and fall. When writing about the collapse of Bronze Age civilizations, for example, Eric Cline highlights the role of earthquakes.[35] Major flood disasters in the Netherlands during the 14th and 15th centuries, for example, powerfully affected the national history. The floods became "a metaphor for the ebb and flow of national fortune; they virtually took on the role of a historical actor."[36] Although we might think that natural disasters would not pose a mortal threat to large, complex, resilient modern societies, it is possible that a persistent accumulation of such disasters could disrupt national competitive standing over time.

Climate Change

In his examination of the region-wide demise of multiple societies around the same period in the 12th century BCE, "when the Bronze Age Mediterranean civilizations collapsed one after another," plunging the entire region into centuries of decline and stagnation, Cline is admirably humble about his ability to narrow down on a single causal variable.[37] He does stress, however, that climate change was a significant factor, with accompanying effects on regional

---

[34] Ross Gregory Douthat, *The Decadent Society: How We Became the Victims of Our Own Success*, New York: Avid Reader Press, 2020, p. 190.

[35] Eric Cline, *1177 B.C.: The Year Civilization Collapsed*, Princeton, N.J.: Princeton University Press, 2014, pp. 140–142.

[36] Simon Schama, *The Embarrassment of Riches: An Interpretation of Dutch Culture in the Golden Age*, New York: Vintage Books, 1987, pp. 34–40.

[37] No one cause can be adduced for these events, Cline writes; "it is much more likely that a concatenation of events, both human and natural—including climate change and drought, seismic disasters known as earthquake storms, internal rebellions, and 'systems collapse'—coalesced to create a 'perform storm' that brought this age to an end" (Cline, 2014, p. 11).

societies, notably drought and failed harvests.[38] Other historical analysis has also supported the idea that specific periods of climate shift had profound effects on the fates of nations.[39] Yet even the best assessments of this factor tend to assign it a supporting rather than starring role in ruining national fortunes.

Kyle Harper, in his comprehensive exploration of alternative causes for Rome's rise, fall, and competitive position, argues that environmental factors, specifically climate (including volcanic activity) and disease, were responsible for the gradual decline of empire.[40] Others disagree, suggesting that although environmental crises did hurt the empire over time, "it is probably right to see them as subsidiary, rather than primary, causes of the decline of the ancient economy."[41] Even Harper admits that the Antonine Plague, a major pandemic event that forms part of his narrative, did not produce social chaos, was not a "fatal blow," and did not cause "the fabric of the empire" to "come unwound," noting, in fact, that it "roared back" from a second major plague in the third century CE.[42] Indeed, when considering the specific effects of climate change or associated calamities such as disease, Harper's superb analysis cannot assign relative causal weight to any single factor, and he admits that the real story is how these ecological insults combined with pressure from outside forces (such as the Goths and Huns) to fracture the empire.

Perhaps the greatest investigation of the effects of climate on geopolitical outcomes is Geoffrey Parker's monumental study of global governance crises, instability, starvation, and depopulation in the 17th century CE. As he explains: "The mid-seventeenth century saw more cases of simultaneous state breakdown around the globe than any previous or subsequent age: something historians have called 'The General Crisis.'" Parker locates the cause in climate change—specifically, a significant cooling, starting in the 1640s, that prompted many individual extreme weather events, significant and prolonged drought, and severe effects on agriculture. And this "intense episode of global cooling," Parker writes, "coincided with an

---

[38] Cline, 2014, pp. xv, 142–147.

[39] One major study concludes "By combining data from coastal Cyprus and coastal Syria, this study shows that the LBA [Late Bronze Age] crisis coincided with the onset of a ca. 300-year drought event 3200 years ago. This climate shift caused crop failures, dearth and famine, which precipitated or hastened socio-economic crises and forced regional human migrations at the end of the LBA in the Eastern Mediterranean and southwest Asia" (David Kaniewski, Elise Van Campo, Joël Guiot, Sabine Le Burel, Thierry Otto, and Cecile Baeteman, "Environmental Roots of the Late Bronze Age Crisis," *PloS ONE*, Vol. 8, No. 8, 2013).

[40] Kyle Harper, *The Fate of Rome: Climate, Disease, and the End of an Empire*, Princeton, N.J.: Princeton University Press, 2017, p. 4.

[41] Ward-Perkins, 2006, p. 134. "Acts of God tend to occur in all periods of history," Ward-Perkins continues, "but their effects are generally long-lasting only when an economy is already in trouble. Stable economies can survive intermittent crises, even on a grand scale, because they seldom affect the underlying structures of society. . . . The Roman world could have recovered from acts of God; what it could not survive were the prolonged troubles of the end of the empire, and the definitive dissolution of the Roman state."

[42] Harper, 2017, pp. 116, 161.

unparalleled spate of revolutions and state breakdowns around the world."[43] State failure and social crisis afflicted England, France, Spain, the Ottoman Empire, Sweden, Denmark, and even China.

Yet Parker too admits that climactic events alone are not likely to have such profound effects on political processes. Drought and famine on their own do not always cause rebellion but must be combined with political and social factors to achieve dramatic effects. Parker acknowledges the critical importance of contingency—in effect, accidental developments that spurred political outcomes—but concludes that "no convincing account of the General Crisis can now ignore the impact of the unique climatic conditions that prevailed."[44]

Disease

Another factor with potentially dire implications for national standing is disease.[45] Perhaps the most catastrophic example is the collapse of New World populations by a factor of 70 to 90 percent, in parts of both North and South America, as Native American populations were ravaged by diseases unwittingly imported by European explorers and settlers. These events made it virtually impossible for the American societies and tribes to effectively counter European power. It is one reason why Jared Diamond highlights "germs" as one of the major factors shaping national rise and fall.[46] Disease, as noted above, also played a significant role in affecting the power of Athens and Rome in different periods and in the 17th-century General Crisis.[47]

The work of Harper, Parker, and others points to a sort of parallel synergistic effect here, a threatening and competitiveness-destroying mixture as a counterpoint to the engine of national dynamism discussed in Chapter One. As these scholars suggest, great powers at the apex of their competitive standing have been brought down by powerful combinations of these exogenous factors: climate change married to pandemics combined with natural disasters, for example. Cline's analysis of the Bronze Age collapse points to the role of multiple factors operating together to create a critical mass of destructive effect. He suggests that the best answer for the puzzle of parallel collapses "is to suggest that all these factors together"— climate change, natural disasters (specifically earthquakes and presumably associated ocean waves), external attacks, and internal rebellions—produced the collapse of Bronze Age Mediterranean societies. "We may be seeing the result of a systems collapse that was caused by a

---

[43] Geoffrey Parker, *Global Crisis: War, Climate Change and Catastrophe in the Seventeenth Century*, New Haven, Conn.: Yale University Press, 2013, pp. xix–xx, 1053.

[44] Parker, 2013, pp. 1075–1077; also see pp. xxviii, 190–191, 210.

[45] Interestingly, Cline emphasizes that he did not find unique and dramatic reports of disease as being part of the recipe for the collapse of Bronze Age civilizations (Cline, 2014, p. 179).

[46] Diamond, 2005.

[47] Parker, 2013, pp. 82–87.

series of events linked together via a 'multiplier effect,' in which one factor affected the others, thereby magnifying the effects of each."[48]

Path Dependence and Momentum

A final process that constitutes an independent factor explaining national competitive outcome is path dependence. Economic growth and prominence have a certain self-sustaining trajectory and momentum, which in turn influence national power and ambitions. This is part of the legacy of the Industrial Revolution: It generated a cascade of self-sustaining growth that did not become exhausted after an initial venture.[49] The initial patterns of such a process are of course strongly influenced by societal characteristics. But, once underway, trends can be self-sustaining, and then they become exogenous variables.

Diego Comin, William Easterly, and Erick Gong have mounted a striking argument about path dependence, suggesting that patterns of technological advance in place as early as 1000 CE, and certainly by 1500 CE, constitute strong predictors of modern-day per capita income: "There were important technological differences between the predecessors to today's modern nations as long ago as 1000 BC," they argue, "and these precolonial, preindustrial differences have striking predictive power for the pattern of both per capita incomes and technology adoption across nations that we observe today. Our strongest results are for the detailed technology dataset we assemble for 1500 AD, which is an excellent predictor of per capita income today." They refer to this as a "direct propagation effect" of technology, in part because "a higher initial technology level lowers the cost of adopting new technologies."[50] The effect is quite large: "going from having none to having adopted all the technologies available in 1500 AD is associated with an increase in current per capita GDP by a factor of 17. Even after including a battery of controls, this factor is over 5."[51]

One way in which path dependence can emerge is through institutions. Some institutional forms and patterns become effectively locked into place, substantially increasing the cost of alternative approaches.[52] On the other hand, some societies can instead become locked into ineffectual and corrupt institutional patterns, creating a persistent roadblock to embracing the comprehensive recipe for success described in Chapter One.

---

[48] Cline, 2014, p. 165.

[49] Joel Mokyr, "Entrepreneurship and the Industrial Revolution in Britain," in David S. Landes, Joel Mokyr, and William J. Baumol, eds., *The Invention of Enterprise: Entrepreneurship from Ancient Mesopotamia to Modern Times*, Princeton, N.J.: Princeton University Press, 2012a, p. 186.

[50] Comin, Easterly, and Gong, 2008, pp. 3–4.

[51] Comin, Easterly, and Gong, 2008, p. 28.

[52] This can be seen among other places in the Roman case; Bruce W. Frier and Dennis P. Kehoe, "Law and Economic Institutions," in Walter Scheidel, Ian Morris, and Richard Saller, eds., *The Cambridge History of the Greco-Roman World*, Cambridge, UK: Cambridge University Press, 2007, pp. 138–139.

Other National Qualities

National competitiveness can also be shaped by a third category of factors: the qualities or characteristics of a nation other than strictly societal ones. These can be intervening factors—that is, qualities produced by societal characteristics that then contribute to competitiveness. They can also be inherent to the economic factors of the country or the sum of many policy choices.

Ecological Sustainability

A core theme in Jared Diamond's work is how "past societies have undermined themselves by damaging their environments," whether by deforestation, destruction of soil, overhunting and overfishing, species destruction, or overpopulation. Unsustainable practices, such as overuse of land to generate food because of overpopulation, lead to environmental damage, which then puts pressure on social stability through food shortages and other mechanisms.[53]

The broader and more traditional notion of "carrying capacity" (a territory's ability to generate sufficient resources for its population) is more difficult to identify in a global era. In the past, a specific nation might have exhausted its own carrying capacity; now, all states are exhausting fisheries and the productive capacity of soils.[54] In an era of global warming, issues of environmental sustainability have become critical for the whole international community. But these risks are mostly shared, and the issue no longer drives differential rates of competitive success.[55] Malthusian overshoot theories have largely been discredited; technology has

---

[53] Diamond, 2005, p. 6. Diamond admits that not all societies will hit ecological quicksand and decline. Nor does environmental collapse constitute the only reason for such collapses—"there are always other contributing factors," and in some cases collapse had nothing to do with environmental issues (Diamond, 2005, pp. 10–11, 15). In fact, he builds a wider framework of five crucial factors that parallel several of the variables discussed in this chapter: the basic environmental damage a society causes to its environment, the climate change going on in the background, hostile neighbors, declining support from friendly neighbors, and the quality and effectiveness of "the society's responses to its problems." Those responses in turn "depend on [a society's] political, economic, and social institutions and on its cultural values" (Diamond, 2005, pp. 11–15).

[54] A related notion deals with natural resource endowments as the source of civilizational progress, but these approaches refer to the prehistorical and very primitive rise of civilizations. Diamond's "endowments" thesis, in particular, "cannot be extended to explain modern world inequality" because those endowments no longer govern productivity (Acemoglu and Robinson, 2012, p. 52). See also Thomas F. Homer-Dixon, "On the Threshold: Environmental Changes as Causes of Acute Conflict," *International Security*, Vol. 16, No. 2, 1991; Thomas F. Homer-Dixon, "Environmental Scarcities and Violent Conflict: Evidence from Cases," *International Security*, Vol. 19, No. 1, 1994; Thomas F. Homer-Dixon, "The End of Ingenuity," *New York Times*, November 29, 2006.

[55] The exception is some competitive advantage that may accrue to countries in latitudes that become more productive as temperature bands shift with warning; see, for example, Abrahm Lustgarten, "How Russia Wins the Climate Crisis," *New York Times Magazine*, December 16, 2020. Some projections have suggested as much as a 200 percent increase in per capita GDP for some countries relative to their projected future without warming; see Marshall Burke, Sol Hsiang, and Ted Miguel, "Economic Impact of Climate Change on the World," Stanford University, webpage, undated. But these developments mostly lie well beyond the

vastly increased the efficiency of resource extraction, production, and use, and advanced societies today are not risking local overshoot in the way some of Diamond's historical cases did.[56]

Nonetheless, there may be specific ways in which major powers could overstress their local ecologies and thus undermine their competitive advantage. The series of environmental disasters that have plagued both Russia and China in the last several decades, from nuclear meltdowns to massive, health-destroying waves of pollution, have imposed significant competitive disadvantage. Nations that ruin their domestic agricultural foundations through overuse of chemicals and destructive farming practices could pay an especially large competitive price, as could countries that destroy local maritime habitats through overfishing. Attending to ecological sustainability, while perhaps not as decisive a factor as it might have been in premodern societies, remains a critical competitive strategy.

Energy Production

Some scholars have placed special stress on the role of energy and energy supplies in the rise and fall of civilizations. Ian Morris, for example, has "settled" on four societal traits as being most associated with development: energy capture per person, social organization (roughly proxied by the size of a civilization's largest city), information technology, and war-making capacity.[57] For Morris, energy capture is the wellspring of all the other factors, the essential baseline requirement for social development. "Energy," he concludes, "must be the central plan in any index."[58]

Jack Goldstone has made a similar argument: "Wherever breakthroughs in energy use occurred—in wind or waterpower, in peat or coal or charcoal or coke use—gains generally followed."[59] Energy was the main "bottleneck" to sustained growth in the premodern era,

---

time frame of this study, they are locked into environmental trends and not subject to policy, and they do not reflect societal characteristics as much as exogenous factors. Indeed, it is the characteristics we examine here that will determine whether states adapt to climate change—its dangers as well as, for some, opportunities.

[56] For example, Scott Page notes of Diamond's overshoot thesis that, although as history it is brilliant, "As predictive modern social science, the effort is less successful. It does not miss the mark, it is not wide left as some claim, so much as its main argument oversimplifies and overgeneralizes. The book's historical richness is not balanced by an equally sophisticated connection to the modern world and its capabilities." Scott E. Page, "Are We Collapsing? A Review of Jared Diamond's Collapse: How Societies Choose to Fail or Succeed," *Journal of Economic Literature*, Vol. 43, No. 4, December 2005, p. 1050.

[57] As much as Morris eventually relies on data to make key judgments, his selection of these traits is as intuitive as it is based on any formal model. He does not have an approach that identifies dozens of possible traits and tests them against one another; he looks across history and picks four that stand out and then assembles data to support them. See Ian Morris, *The Measure of Civilization: How Social Development Decides the Fate of Nations*, Princeton, N.J.: Princeton University Press, 2013, pp. 39–42.

[58] Morris, 2013, p. 142.

[59] Goldstone, 2002, p. 361; Goldstone, 2009, p. 164.

he believes, and the initiation of an era of steam engines was the key breakthrough.[60] The practical implications of these revolutions in energy generation were immense. By 1850, an average person in England had deployable energy at their disposal at ten times the rate of the world average; England's 18 million residents were using as much energy as the 300 million people of Qing China. By 1900, English coal was generating a quarter of the world's energy output for 3 percent of the world's population.[61] Kenneth Pomeranz has pointed out that Britain benefited not only from significant coal deposits but also from the fact that—unlike in China—they were propitiously located very near to emerging industrial cities, thus reducing transportation costs.[62]

Yet relative standing in energy production cannot be viewed as a sufficient condition for national development.[63] Ian Morris's quantitative case for the centrality of energy supplies, for example, relies on profoundly subjective judgments about relative weights of different factors contributing to national competitive advantage.[64] Some countries with substantial coal deposits did not develop in the way England did. Coal could have been shipped, and it is not clear that the proximity of coal and industrial production sites was economically essential for Britain's industrial advances. And some countries with great energy production handicaps, such as Japan and South Korea, have nonetheless managed to fashion periods of dramatic economic growth.

Access to cheap and reliable supplies of energy is obviously an advantage, but not an absolutely essential one—or one sufficient, on its own, to guarantee national dynamism. Margaret Jacob argues that the presence of this energy supply is not a sufficient explanation for Britain's eventual lead in the Industrial Revolution. The critical supporting factor, she contends, was knowledge—the engineering skill to mine the coal and, more importantly, the ability to develop, build, and employ the technology of steam power that benefited from coal. The

[60] Goldstone, 2002, p. 362.

[61] Goldstone, 2002, pp. 363–364.

[62] Kenneth Pomeranz, *The Great Divergence: China, Europe, and the Making of the Modern World Economy*, Princeton, N.J.: Princeton University Press, 2009. Eric Beinhocker's thoughtful assessment of evolutionary theories of economics discusses the problem of entropy at some length, noting that social systems demand an introduction of new energy to overcome tendencies to entropy. It is when the energy inputs have lagged, in part, that societies have faced evolutionary problems. Eric D. Beinhocker, *The Origin of Wealth: The Radical Remaking of Economics and What It Means for Business and Society*, Boston, Mass.: Harvard Business Review Press, 2007, pp. 400–423.

[63] McCloskey, 2011, loc. 2516–2564.

[64] At times Morris's need to rely on subjective assessments becomes obvious. One truism among military analysts is that military power is the product of many factors. Yet in his discussion he eventually "suggests" a ratio of Western "war-making capacity" between 1800 and 1900 as 1:10, which he admits is a "guess." He later says if a war-making score in 1500 was 0.13, "a score of 0.12 points seems reasonable to me for the year 1 CE" (Morris, 2013, pp. 184, 190).

British, she says, had "more readily available a body of scientifically and technically informed knowledge that could assist profit seekers in coal."[65]

More generally in terms of natural resources, in a high-tech industrial and information economy, resource benefits may be a curse rather than a blessing and are no longer related to economic performance.[66] Michael Porter argues that the *lack* of natural resources was a common feature of the successful nations he studied.[67] The experience of European colonizers, Niall Ferguson argues, shows that it is not so much the resource endowments that make the difference as the institutions that rise up around those endowments.[68]

Nonetheless, one lesson of the historical record is that nations that build a strategic advantage in the generation of sustainable, effective energy supplies have a competitive advantage, even if this alone is not enough to determine the fate of rivalries. The current context may offer a modified but important version of this connection: As the world struggles to transcend the fossil fuel era, countries that build reliable, efficient, very low-emission energy grids—and develop the energy technologies that will dominate this new era—will gain significant advantages.

In this regard, William R. Thompson and Leila Zakhirova contend that leadership in energy production will be critical to competitive advantage in the 21st century. They argue that international "systemic leadership" demands "an energy transition to make and fuel new technological innovations relatively inexpensively." Emerging information and other technologies that will underwrite future national power, they say, demand "a new, relatively inexpensive energy base,"[69] as well as one that finds ways to generate power without calamitous climactic effects. Thompson and Zakhirova do not suggest that energy is the sole criterion for competitive advantage; indeed, it is precisely in how energy is linked to other factors, such as commerce and technology, that is the key to its importance. There can be little question that gaining world leadership in such inexpensive, climate-friendly energy generation would be a competitive advantage of incalculable benefit.

Nonsocietal Sources of Advantage

Another category of factors that can influence national competitive advantage are related, in a sense, to the strategic posture of nations—the ways in which nations choose to position themselves in global networks, markets, and balances of power. These factors are partly the

---

[65] Jacob, 2014, pp. 2, 5–6, 60; see also pp. 57–75.

[66] Bruce R. Scott and George C. Lodge, *U.S. Competitiveness in the World Economy*, Boston, Mass.: Harvard Business School Press, 1985, p. 67.

[67] Michael E. Porter, *The Competitive Advantage of Nations*, New York: Free Press, 2019, p. 464.

[68] Niall Ferguson, *Civilization: The West and the Rest*, New York: Penguin, 2011, p. 105.

[69] William R. Thompson and Leila Zakhirova, *Racing to the Top: How Energy Fuels System Leadership in World Politics*, New York: Oxford University Press, 2019, pp. 3, 8.

product of national choice, but not entirely. A country's ability to position itself at the core of global networks will be partly a function of its regime type, as well as its history and habits of cooperation or conflict with other states. This category of factors can therefore be strongly influenced by a society's societal characteristics.

Many of these factors are by-products of an essential truth: Economic muscle is the essential building block of national competitive position. As Wess Mitchell has pointed out, "Historically, the main reason that empires decline is that uneven economic growth rates cause them to fall behind their peers in power capabilities."[70] Economic strength is also the basis of military power. Paul Kennedy argues that, although this connection is not always linear, it is fundamental in most cases.[71]

All the societal characteristics we will examine in the next seven chapters bear on economic strength. Each of these factors—e.g., a unified national identity, shared opportunity, an active state, a competitive diversity and pluralism—plays a critical role in generating national economic power. But other factors besides societal characteristics influence economic power as well.

Core Position in Networks of Intellectual, Economic, and Technological Exchange

The most important of these is the degree to which a nation positions itself as a hub, or at least a highly integrated and productive node, in global or regional networks of exchange. Nations that do so tend to gain tremendous competitive advantage.

Trade is a leading example. Ancient Rome benefited from a deep, society-wide involvement in productive networks. Rome oversaw and was the force for creating an extensive semi-global trading system.[72] This was a product of state-led development, in the sense of shipping networks associated with the military and Roman administration, but also a large private component of profit-seeking commercial actors. In the process, Rome served as a "complex

---

[70] Mitchell, 2018, p. 257. Mitchell also points out, "Historically, the success of states in strategic competition has been a by-product of the extent to which they can achieve mastery over the internal resources at their disposal" (2018, p. 59).

[71] Kennedy traces how the "staggering increases in productivity emanating from the Industrial Revolution" dramatically shifted power balances among leading nations. Britain raced from 1.9 percent of global manufacturing output in 1750 to 18.5 percent in 1900—whereas the Habsburg empire stagnated, rising from 2.9 percent to just 4.7 percent. France, too, made little progress (growing from 4 percent to 6.8 percent), whereas the collective German states (and then a unified Germany) represented 13.2 percent of world output by 1900—up from 2.9 percent in 1750. Most dramatic of all was the rocket-like rise of America: from 0.1 percent of world output in the prerevolutionary era of 1750 to owning 23.6 percent of world industrial output by the turn of the 20th century (Kennedy, 1987, pp. 148–149). Equally dramatic was China's collapse, from 32.8 percent of output in the mid-18th century to just 6.2 percent by 1900.

[72] William V. Harris, "The Late Republic," in Walter Scheidel, Ian Morris, and Richard Saller, eds., *The Cambridge History of the Greco-Roman World*, Cambridge, UK: Cambridge University Press, 2007, pp. 533–535.

system of production and distribution."[73] Romans prospered in part because of the food and other goods available via trade.[74]

Similarly, the rising Ottoman Empire benefited from sitting "at the hub of the great trading networks of the time,"[75] while Italian Renaissance city-states benefited from a pan-Mediterranean order that linked the countries of the region into networks of trade, finance, and intellectual exchange.[76] Britain was a hegemon and empire built on a central position in trade networks.[77] And the rise of Holland and England was powered in part by their ability to take advantage of global networks of trade but also networks of exchange around technology, science, and finance. Jack Goldstone agrees that his notion of efflorescence occurs in part when "international trade and sustained contact lead to a mixing of cultures and ideas," creating hubs of international trade that are natural incentives for commercial activity.[78]

Seeking prosperity within a club of associated societies can be a more competitively advantageous strategy than going it alone. This is the story of Europe, whose mutual trade, overlapping and interacting scientific and cultural communities, cross-border educational and research efforts, and other combined activities helped promote growth in member countries beginning in earnest after 1500.[79] There is strong evidence that Europe's early advance in the modern era was powered by trade and market networks among European countries and that the quality of transportation networks was critical to this.[80]

The Soviet Union provides something of the inverse example—a nation excluded from full participation in global networks of trade, technology, culture, and intellectual exchange, to its great detriment. Partly this was a product of U.S. and Western sanctions that restricted technology transfer and trade.[81] But it was also inherent to the nature of an autocratic system, which will always see risk in general social openness to exchange of ideas. Soviet citizens, for example, simply could not travel easily, or at all, to join meetings, conferences, or academic programs. Amid its many other competitive handicaps, the Soviet Union thus suffered from weak integration into key networks.

***

---

[73] Ward-Perkins, 2006, pp. 100–102, 120.

[74] Peter Temin, *The Roman Market Economy*, Princeton, N.J.: Princeton University Press, 2013, p. 3.

[75] Finkel, 2005, p. 71.

[76] Bartlett, 2005, lecture 3.

[77] "By the middle of the 1820s the United Kingdom was more fully connected with more parts of the world, as a trading and investing nation, as a maritime force and imperial power, than any other country on earth, or than any other country had ever been" (Cannadine, 2017, p. 122).

[78] Goldstone, 2002, p. 358.

[79] Osterhammel, 2014, pp. 647–648.

[80] Studer, 2015, pp. 5–6, 153–154, 161–162.

[81] Robert Service, *The End of the Cold War: 1985–1991*, New York: PublicAffairs, 2015, p. 6.

A country's choice about the degree of trade in its overall economic strategy, and its relative dependence on trade, can vary significantly, especially in its developmental phase. Many highly competitive nations have retained significantly closed economies, or at least shaped the character of trade and the level of state support for domestic industries, during their periods of rise or peak power. The United States, to take one example, as late as 1961 had a trade-to-GDP ratio of just 10 percent, which led Edward Alden to describe the U.S. economy of that period (and much before) as autarkic. Its vast domestic market provided the basis for rapid growth without much reliance on trade.[82] Even as the post-1945 United States gradually embraced more integration in trade regimes, it mitigated the effects with various domestic protections and trade limits that have been referred to as a system of "embedded liberalism."[83]

But these qualifications do not challenge the essential finding that nations that have become hubs of economic networks enjoy a competitive advantage. The United States before 1960, for example, did not spurn trade; it embraced it but, as Alden explains, simply did not have an overwhelming need for more at that point in its development. By that time, the United States was already becoming the dominant economic magnet of the democratic world. It drew technology and technique from others and had begun to rely on key foreign sources of materials. The pre-1960 U.S. story is not a victory for isolation but merely an example of a massive economy able to thrive with a smaller proportion of trade dependence than some others.

The advantages of being part of global economic networks is common to all the competitive societies we have considered, from ancient Greece and Rome, to the Italian Renaissance city-states, to modern Britain and the United States. All have served as the nexus of a vibrant regional or global trade network that brought both resources and goods to the society: "No national or regional process of incipient industrialization has ever been entirely homemade and isolated from the larger world."[84]

The opposite dynamic has also emerged in many historical cases: The loss of trade markets has been competitively disastrous for countries. When Britain turned to import substitution in the mid-19th century, for example, it cost India and China key export markets for textiles, which had "catastrophic effects" on some areas of the economy.[85] The Ottoman Empire had suffered similar reversals earlier in the century. Periods of Chinese and Japanese history when they isolated themselves from such networks proved competitively disastrous:

---

[82] Edward Alden, *Failure to Adjust: How Americans Got Left Behind in the Global Economy*, New York: Council on Foreign Relations, 2016, pp. 1–5.

[83] John Gerard Ruggie, "International Regimes, Transactions, and Change: Embedded Liberalism in the Postwar Economic Order," *International Organization*, Vol. 36, No. 2, 1982.

[84] Osterhammel, 2014, p. 640.

[85] Osterhammel, 2014, p. 662.

"As a result" of such policies in the later 17th and 18th centuries, "Japan missed out entirely on the benefits associated with a rapidly rising level of global trade and migration."[86]

***

The productive networks that benefit competitiveness go well beyond commerce. Networks of ideas have historically been just as important—from the exchanges of scientific knowledge and philosophy around the Mediterranean during the ancient period, to the Republic of Letters in Italy and elsewhere in Europe during the Renaissance, to modern scientific networks.[87] When nations participate in these networks and supply their most important gathering places or hubs of activity, they gain a tremendous advantage. The flow of ideas, inventions, and concepts through a country not only has economic advantages but also energizes the learning and adaptive engines of the society.

The classicist Josiah Ober emphasizes the importance of networks of knowledge and ideas to the rise of classical Greece. "Exchanging and aggregating diverse and dispersed forms of knowledge is a key factor to the success of contemporary purposeful organizations," he explains, and this sort of open, voluntary intellectual exchange was a central factor in the Greek efflorescence. This networked useful knowledge ties in closely with other social characteristics: It relies on shared opportunity in the form of the development of human capital, as people "voluntarily choose to deepen their own special knowledge and sharpen their skills"; it demands a degree of collective identity that produces "mutual trust and a sense of shared purpose"; and it requires, perhaps most of all, fair and egalitarian social model to create a context in which shared knowledge produces the right incentives to compete and excel.[88]

Other kinds of webs provide competitive advantages. Networks of military professionals, linked through shared education, training, engagement activities, and more, can boost the capabilities of countries involved in these relationships. Cultural and artistic networks contribute to national prestige and creativity. Global systems of corporate consultation produce the standards that govern many products; international domain-specific expert networks (epistemic communities) generate critical ideas and concepts in such areas as finance and medicine. Across the board, nations that join and lead networks of productive exchange become more dynamic, more creative, and more powerful.

The importance of trade and other networks does not undermine the importance of social characteristics. Countries still need to be able to take advantage of these networks, and their ability to do so varies greatly and in part because of institutions, national identity, shared opportunity, and other of our characteristics. Spain and Portugal had just as much access to

---

[86] Ferguson, 2011, pp. 44–45.

[87] Niall Ferguson describes the intellectual networks that rose up in Europe after the mid-17th century as an "intellectual revolution" that laid the foundations of the modern scientific method (Ferguson, 2011, p. 67).

[88] Ober, 2015, p. 15.

Atlantic shipping routes as Holland and England, for example, but their weaker and more-extractive institutions funneled profits to the ruling classes and did not produce a diverse economy, broad commercial classes, or a strong middle class.

It is possible to become *too* dependent on networks—of trade, of ideas, of raw materials and other resources. Our research uncovered several cases of individual countries or groups of them suffering real competitive decline, and sometimes societal ruin, because their competitive position came to rely on erratic sources of essential goods from abroad. One ancient example is the massive societal collapse of the Late Bronze Age, spurred in part by mutual dependencies fostered by a vibrant Mediterranean web of trade. When natural disasters and disease interrupted some of these links, societies suffered. In the modern era, many countries' dependence on global financial networks has led to vulnerability—to both direct pressure (in the form of financial sanctions) and economic dislocation in financial crises. One important source of national competitive advantage is resilience even amid networked power, seeking again that difficult balance.

Membership in Dominant Alignments of Power

Another factor that is partly subject to choice by major powers but also at risk from influences outside their control is whether a nation manages to align itself with coalitions and alliances reflecting the dominant proportion of world power. If a country is part of a dominant coalition or alliance, its chances of competitive success, geopolitically and economically, as well as militarily, will grow.

Rome benefited from this factor not so much through forming alliances with other states or empires—it was the preeminent hegemon of its time—as much as building a dominant superstate through absorption. It made the strategic decision to incorporate subject peoples into the empire. "One cannot overstress the importance," the historian Michael Fronda contends,

> of the practice of absorbing some conquered territory into the ager Romanus, extending forms of Roman citizenship to various Italian communities, and in all cases obliging subordinate states to contribute troops to the Roman army. This threefold policy allowed for the citizen population of Rome to grow so as to dwarf any single potential peninsular competitor, even the largest.[89]

This strategy provided Rome with important competitive advantages. Rome allied itself with local elites, providing them with benefits from membership in the empire in exchange for managing local affairs and providing taxes, manpower, and other support. Critically, Rome granted citizenship to these incorporated peoples—initially on a very selective basis and then, in the later empire, more comprehensively—which departed from typically more exclusive ancient approaches to national membership. Rome punished disloyal elites but

---

[89] Fronda, 2010, p. 29; see also Harper, 2017, p. 9.

also developed family ties through intermarriage and citizenship and trade ties. These were "inclusive policies that integrated many conquered communities, especially in central Italy, into a sort of Roman 'super-state.'"[90]

The more classic version of this factor applies to the geopolitical balance of power and forms of alignment among independent states, such as coalitions and alliances. This was a major focus of British statecraft in the 19th and 20th centuries: remaining largely aloof from large deployments of military power on the Continent but finding ways to avoid becoming the focus of a predominant alignment of power. Some countries violated this rule at great cost—specifically, Napoleonic France, Wilhelmine Germany, Nazi Germany, and imperial Japan. These states ultimately generated responses from a large degree of the global power balance and lost the major wars or series of wars in which they embroiled in large measure because of this. Each had shortcomings in some of our nominated societal characteristics, but all had tremendous strengths as well and could theoretically have developed a stronger competitive position.[91] But they tilted the playing field decisively against themselves by undertaking disastrously ambitious campaigns and provoking a devastating response.

A nation's place in regional or global alignments of power is a factor distinct from a nation's role in productive networks. The two can overlap, but they need not. A country could find itself in a military alliance with most of the world's leading powers yet still have strong trade protectionism and otherwise insulate itself from productive networks. By contrast, a country could be deeply integrated in such networks yet utterly lack security or geopolitical ties to a dominant global coalition. One of the most favorable aspects of the U.S. strategic position since the 1960s, and especially since 1989, is that it has excelled on *both* these collective factors: It has been the hub of many productive world trade, finance, and information networks, *and* it drew to itself partnerships and alliances with the overwhelming share of world economic and military powers.

Imperial Possessions

Some scholars argue that empire and colonies provide a critical competitive advantage. One of the most important arguments on the sources of national competitive standing is Kenneth Pomeranz's 2009 book, *The Great Divergence*. Pomeranz assesses explanations for Europe's economic advance—and Asia's relative stagnation or even decline—during much of the 19th

---

[90] Fronda, 2010, pp. 30, 303, 305. The Ottomans employed a roughly similar approach, building a multiethnic empire through absorbing local societies and polities, ruling through a set of partly assimilated elites, and drawing financial and military strength from the very large resulting mosaic; see Baer, 2021.

[91] It is interesting to imagine, for example, the sort of power a unified Germany would have become had it not undertaken two world wars and instead focused strictly on the development of the sinews of societal advantage—national identity but also science, technology, industry, education, efficient institutions, and more, contenting itself with dominant military power for defensive purposes only. Germany was already surging past Britain as an industrial power before World War II. Without the interruption of the world wars, that trajectory could have led Germany to the apex of world influence.

century. Why was it, he asks, that Europe was able to take advantage of the Industrial Revolution and China and India were not? Classic explanations focus on such issues as culture and institutions, but Pomeranz argues that China actually had better institutions than Europe—and a well-established commercial economy, equivalent capital stock and agricultural technology and potential, and financial mechanisms—in the middle to late 18th century, leading into the Industrial Revolution.[92] Nor was the quality of the rule of law in China, as assessed for example by the number of arbitrary expropriations suffered by companies, dramatically different. Instead, Pomeranz highlights two advantages that Europe enjoyed: colonies and sources of coal. "Some differences that mattered did exist" in areas of institutions, he explains, but "they could only create the great transformation of the nineteenth century in a context also shaped by Europe's privileged access to overseas resources."[93]

There is no question that *some* states, and notably some European powers, gained temporary but weighty strategic advantage from their colonies at certain times and in certain ways. This was true of Rome, whose vast imperial possessions filled the Roman state treasury and, eventually, the ranks of its legions. It was certainly true of Spain and the degree to which its 17th- and 18th-century power projection was fueled by New World precious metals. And it was true to a degree of Britain, which in the late 19th and early 20th centuries sustained much of its economic heft in the form of imperial possessions.

But imperial ambitions have a difficult time explaining the Great Divergence or national competitiveness as a whole. Recent evidence, for example, suggests that India was far behind Europe in development, including in such areas as effective institutions, through much of the 19th century.[94] Newer research argues that Pomeranz's estimates of China's standing in the early 19th century might be somewhat exaggerated.[95] If Europe was already significantly ahead before the peak of its imperial age, then the colonies could not have been critical in explaining its relative success.

The financial benefit of colonies might also have been less than is often supposed. Partly this is because the drive for colonies itself imposed costs, locking countries into an endless search for foreign wealth, which in some cases ended up overextending them. David Landes argues that

---

[92] Pomeranz, 2009. Pomeranz argues "Labor deployment in Chinese families seems to closely resemble the reorientation of labor, leisure, and consumption toward the market that Jan DeVries has called Europe's 'industrious revolution.' . . . Core regions in China and Japan circa 1750 seem to resemble the most advanced parts of western Europe, combining sophisticated agriculture, commerce, and nonmechanized industry in similar, arguably even more fully realized, ways. Thus we must look outside these cores to explain their subsequent divergence" (p. 17). He later adds, "China seemed to conform to neoclassical ideas of efficient economic institutions at least as well as pre-1800 western Europe" (p. 111). For comments on finance in China, see p. 167.

[93] Pomeranz, 2009, p. 3.

[94] Studer, 2015.

[95] Broadberry et al., 2014, p. 386.

the silver of America did little for Spain, which re-exported most of it to pay for military operations in other parts of Europe and for imports of food and manufactures from "less fortunate" countries. Indeed, one might reasonably argue that the colonial windfall did Spain serious harm by encouraging her to rely on tribute rather than work.[96]

Landes also notes that "to say that colonial possessions contributed to the enrichment and development of certain European countries, however, is one thing; to say that they were a necessary or a sufficient condition of this development, is quite another. The necessity argument implies that if there had been no overseas expansion, there would have been no Industrial Revolution."[97]

The historian Walter Scheidel does not deny that European states gained significantly from imperial possessions and from "exporting violence and conquest across the globe." But he argues that this was a symptom of a deeper factor, rather than a discrete and original cause of its own. It was Europe's pluralism and fragmentation—and the resulting intense geopolitical competition, as well as the small to moderate size of its nations—that fueled exploration and the search for colonies. China did not match Europe's explorations because its focus was inward, on the maintenance of a massive, established land empire.[98]

Making and Fostering Productive Investment

Our research also points to the critical importance of one specific sort of economic behavior—productive investment. Societies with habits, institutions, and qualities that more reliably place national wealth in the service of productive activities have a competitive advantage.

The tie between levels of productive investment and economic outcomes is well established.[99] Ruchir Sharma argues that a key indicator of competitive prospects is whether investment is rising or falling as a share of the economy (the consumption-investment balance). Of the 56 fastest-growing postwar economies, for example—countries that grew at more than 6 percent per year for a decade or more—the average investment amount was 25 percent of GDP. As a general rule, Sharma believes that investment totals of 25–35 percent of GDP spur growth and that levels under 20 percent inhibit it.[100] Skimping on investment leads to stagnation in many ways: "Countries that invest too little leave roads unpaved, schools unbuilt, the police ill-equipped, and factories suspended in the blueprint stage." As of 2016, a range of

---

[96] David S. Landes, *The Unbound Prometheus: Technological Change and Industrial Development in Western Europe from 1750 to the Present*, Cambridge, UK: Cambridge University Press, 2003, p. 36.

[97] Landes, 2003, p. 37.

[98] Walter Scheidel, "The Road from Rome," *Aeon*, April 15, 2021.

[99] Timo J. Hämäläinen, *National Competitiveness and Economic Growth: The Changing Determinants of Economic Performance in the World Economy*, Cheltenham, UK: Edward Elgar, 2003, pp. 53–54; Scott and Lodge, 1985, pp. 30–40.

[100] Sharma, 2016, p. 220. When a country's rate of investment was less than 20 percent of GDP for ten years, his research shows, there was a 60 percent chance the country's growth would be under 3 percent.

slower-growing countries were stuck at 20 percent, or slightly under that amount, of GDP in investment: Mexico, Brazil, Italy—and the United States.[101]

But countries also must "distinguish between good and bad investment binges." Sharma contends that investment in manufacturing is most productive of growth. "Good binges" leave behind productive assets, such as infrastructure and new companies; "bad binges" leave behind "little in productive value." The poster child of a bad investment binge is booms in real estate. The quality of investment also depends on how it is financed: Debt financing can lead to stalled growth and an eventual crash.[102]

As Mariana Mazzucato argues, evidence from post-2008 Europe supports the idea that "lack of investment in productivity-enhancing R&D and human capital development" is a handicap to growth and competitiveness.[103] In Britain, for example, the degree to which capital sought out the most productive and advanced industrial applications after about 1850 might have been somewhat limited by Britain's economic structure and its continuing dependence on family firms. In several industries, such as chemicals, it lost out to foreign competitors (for example, Germany) in part because it did not channel the necessary investment to firms that could have competed.[104]

In the case of the Soviet Union, the early relative success of the Soviet system was in part a lesson in the value of productive investment: Significant state support for key industries helps to explain its initial period of growth.[105] But the tendency of the Soviet system to overinvest in unproductive sectors, as well as the strict dividing line between military and civilian research

---

[101] Sharma, 2016, p. 251.

[102] Sharma, 2016, pp. 220, 240–241.

[103] Mariana Mazzucato, *The Entrepreneurial State: Debunking Public vs. Private Sector Myths*, New York: PublicAffairs, 2015, p. 48. Mazzucato continues, "While low spending on R&D is a problem throughout much of the European 'periphery,' it is also true that if a country has lower than average R&D spending, this is not necessarily a problem if the sectors that the country specializes in are not sectors in which innovation occurs necessarily through R&D. For example, the UK specializes in financial services, construction and creative industries (such as music)—all with relatively low needs for basic R&D" (Mazzucato, 2015, pp. 49–50, citing Yannis Pierrakis, *Venture Capital: Now and After the Dotcom Crash*, London: National Endowment for Science, Technology and the Arts, 2010).

[104] By one possible measure—in this case, the rate of return on capital—British investment seems to have been quite productive indeed during key decades of its rise to hegemony: "The rate of profit rose from a pre-industrial level of 9.2 per cent in 1688 and 9.1 per cent in 1759 to 16.8 per cent in 1798. The rate continued to rise gradually, reaching 17.6 per cent in 1846 and 20.3 per cent in 1867. The rates of return are higher than interest rates on government debt and mortgages but in line with estimates of the return on business investments and with aggregate calculations of the real rate of return" (Robert C. Allen, "Class Structure and Inequality During the Industrial Revolution: Lessons from England's Social Tables, 1688–1867," *Economic History Review*, Vol. 72, No. 1, February 2019, p. 102).

[105] Robert C. Allen, "The Rise and Decline of the Soviet Economy," *Canadian Journal of Economics/Revue Canadienne d'Economique*, Vol. 34, No. 4, 2001.

(limiting many of the country's best scientists and most-impressive breakthroughs), was a significant factor in its decay.[106]

A Sustainable Financial Foundation

A related factor associated with competitively successful nations is the maintenance of a vibrant and sustainable basis of national finances.[107] One major finding from historical research is that "endless streams of money equals victory." When states run out of money, they are forced to end wars or withdraw from competitions. "Because of this, a state's economic infrastructure and capacity to generate wealth often became a rival's primary target."[108] Strong, sustainable finances—in terms of access to financial resources (primarily through taxes), the responsible management of those finances, and competent institutions to manage the whole process—repeatedly emerge as a central competitive advantage.[109]

Large-scale debt is especially problematic for national competitive position.[110] Ruchir Sharma points to debt—and the lack of it—as a major factor distinguishing economically successful countries from failures. "The clearest signal of coming financial trouble comes from the pace of increase in . . . debt," Sharma says, noting that there is a "point of no return" when

---

[106] David Reynolds, "Science, Technology and the Cold War," in Melvyn P. Leffler and Odd Arne Westad, eds., *The Cambridge History of The Cold War*: Vol. 3, *Endings*, Cambridge, UK: Cambridge University Press, 2010; Allen, 2001.

[107] Kennedy, 1987, p. 72; see also pp. 76–86.

[108] James Lacey, "Introduction," in James Lacey, ed., *Great Strategic Rivalries: From the Classical World to the Cold War*, New York: Oxford University Press, 2016, p. 37. A major theme of Paul Kennedy's work—the growing price of militaries—meant that countries that could generate sufficient resources to fund them had a huge advantage. Britain was an early and persistent example. The critical factor is the balance of private investment with military expenditure. But this is more of an overreach argument than one specifically about the sustainability of financing. And it is not clear that the United States is anywhere close to historical levels of overreach in these terms (Kennedy, 1987, p. xvii).

[109] Ferguson, 2011, p. 38. In earlier times, the simple baseline existence of monetized exchange—the existence of a trustworthy and common currency and the ability to trade goods using money—provided a competitive advantage for nations that developed this innovation first or most effectively. But this characteristic is now so thoroughly ingrained in all economies that it is a historical observation rather than a factor that will be influential in the future.

[110] This was true in ancient times as well as modern. Ober argues that financial stability was a critical support system for the rise and efflorescence of Athens (Ober, 2015, p. 250). Recently, the investor Ray Dalio put the question of debt right at the center of his recent examination of the principles that make nations successful. Debt-financed bubbles—a common is not unavoidable phase in the civilizational cycle he proposes—are just about always a precursor to national decline, he contends. High levels of borrowing at an empire or nation's peak power "sustains the country's power beyond its fundamentals by financing both domestic overconsumption and international military conflicts required to maintain the empire." Dalio sees a pattern in which states amass large debts and confront an economic downturn, so "the empire can no longer borrow the money necessary to repay its debts," and the leaders confront the choice of whether to default or print more money. They almost always choose the latter, which "devalues the currency and raises inflation" (Dalio, 2021, pp. 11, 36, 47, 49).

debt grows so quickly in a given period of time "that a financial crisis is very likely." Sharma's analysis highlights the risks not only from public or government debt but also from private debt—credit undertaken by companies and individuals. "Of more than 430 severe financial crises since 1970," he writes, the International Monetary Fund "classifies fewer than 70 (or less than one in six) as primarily government or 'sovereign' debt crises."[111]

Perhaps the single most emblematic case of national competitiveness being ruined by poor finances is the Spanish Empire in the 16th century and afterward. Spain's access to New World precious metals, which provided as much as 20 percent of the crown's total revenues, was an essential explanation for its rise and helped to spur a nation whose societal characteristics might not otherwise have generated such a competitive position. No matter how many fiscal crises Spain suffered, there was always the prospect of more gold and silver.[112]

Spain received massive influxes of resources, mostly from New World expropriation, by the mid-16th century but engaged in multiple wars, which meant that "a seemingly insatiable appetite for war finance grew faster."[113] One scholar has calculated that Spain's overall purchasing power rose to a peak of 6 to 8 million pesos in the later decades of the 16th century. But then, as New World silver supplies became harder to acquire, Spain dropped to having just over 3 million pesos by 1616–1620 and then to 1.2 million by 1650. Spain's war expenses were growing in those same decades, a product in part of the financially ruinous war to preserve its Netherlands possessions. By 1557 the monarchy had to declare the first of many bankruptcies, and by 1560 it poured most of its resources into repaying old debts. As late as 1598, two-thirds of state revenues went to debt repayment. Between 1577 and 1580, Spain's debt stood at roughly six times its state revenues; by the end of the century, the ratio was more like ten to one.[114] The resulting shortfalls crippled its economy and society with the resulting taxes.[115] When nationalistic and independence-oriented feelings grew in the New World, cutting many ties to Spain, the effect on the sustainability of Spain's competitive position was devastating.[116]

---

[111] Sharma, 2016, pp. 323–324, 327–328, 330–331, 343. On the risks of private debt, see also Mortiz Schularick, "Public and Private Debt: The Historical Record (1870–2010)," *German Economic Review*, Vol. 15, No. 1, 2013.

[112] We are grateful to Gabriel Paquette for this insight.

[113] Dennis O. Flynn, "Fiscal Crisis and the Decline of Spain (Castile)," *Journal of Economic History*, Vol. 42, No. 1, March 1982, p. 142.

[114] Flynn, 1982, p. 143; Acemoglu and Robinson, 2012, p. 219.

[115] Geoffrey Parker, "Incest, Blind Faith, and Conquest: The Spanish Habsburgs and Their Enemies," in James Lacey, ed., *Great Strategic Rivalries: From the Classical World to the Cold War*, New York: Oxford University Press, 2016, pp. 262–264, 270, 277.

[116] Jeremy Adelman, "The Age of Imperial Revolutions," *American Historical Review*, Vol. 113, No. 2, 2008. The argument is elaborated in Jeremy Adelman, *Sovereignty and Revolution in the Iberian Atlantic*, Princeton, N.J.: Princeton University Press, 2006. Under these financial pressures, Spain "declined from the most powerful nation in the Western world since the Roman empire to a second-rate power," according to Douglass North. He continues, "[D]epopulation of the countryside, the stagnation of industry, and the collapse of

Another leading European power whose position was devastated by decaying finances was France. Its massive commitments, multiple wars, and global ambitions during the Napoleonic period outstripped the resources the state had to generate, and it did not have the finances to fund a navy to counter British rule of the sea.[117] The financial system of the Continent at the time also worked against the French. In the 17th century, Dutch capital helped the British economy grow and provided some of the foundation for a dominant navy. French economic setbacks and later the loss of revenue-generating colonies cut the resources available and forced France to make hard choices among forms of military power.[118]

Financial weakness was also a huge factor in Austria-Hungary's competitive disadvantage. Wess Mitchell argues that his case proves that "the most dangerous frontier is financial."[119] One Austrian chancellor describes the financial problem as an "internal enemy fully as dangerous to the Crown as the more obvious enemies without." The Habsburg Empire accumulated vast amounts of debt, which constantly ate away at its strategic capacities. As Mitchell puts it, "Large-scale external borrowing created debt overhangs that could constrain strategic options and require military retrenchment."[120]

Some scholars argue that, outside the European context, strong financial foundations and institutions provide one piece of the puzzle in explaining differences in industrialization and national technological advances between China and Japan in the 19th century. China, as Jürgen Osterhammel explains, was "fiscally and administratively weak," whereas Japan had strong national financial systems and moved early to embrace modern banking practices, which helped accelerate the arrival of a comprehensive banking system to underwrite economic progress.[121] Yet Japan itself did tumble into a fiscal quicksand at one point, driven by

---

Seville's trading system with the New World were paralleled in the political realm by the revolt of Catalonia and Portugal. The proximate cause was recurrent war and a fiscal crisis that led Olivares (1621 to 1640) to pursue the desperate measures that only exacerbated the fundamental problems" (Douglass C. North, *Institutions, Institutional Change and Economic Performance*, Kindle ed., Cambridge, UK: Cambridge University Press, 1990, p. 115). Eventually, "When [the] market value" of the New World precious metals, especially silver, "withered to production cost, no economic profits remained for merchant or Crown, and the Spanish empire collapsed upon itself" (Flynn, 1982, p. 141).

[117] Michael V. Leggiere, "Napoleon's Quest: Great Britain Versus France III," in James Lacey, ed., *Great Strategic Rivalries: From the Classical World to the Cold War*, New York: Oxford University Press, 2016, p. 340.

[118] Matt J. Schumann, "A Contest for Trade and Empire: England Versus France II," in James Lacey, ed., *Great Strategic Rivalries: From the Classical World to the Cold War*, New York: Oxford University Press, 2016, pp. 316–317, 322, 325, 329, 335.

[119] Mitchell, 2018, pp. 325–326.

[120] Quoted in Mitchell, 2018, pp. 62–69.

[121] Osterhammel, 2014, p. 665.

its imperial ambitions in the 1930s. The costs of its accelerating imperial empire demanded ever-growing expansion, which had more costs: "It was a vicious circle."[122]

The crucial role of sustainable finances in underwriting national power also is apparent in the history of the Ottoman Empire. It developed a series of reasonably effective state mechanisms of taxation that drew financial and military resources from its vast lands.[123] But over time, as burdens grew and the central state apparatus metastasized, the empire began to outrun the resources of the tax base.[124] The later Ottoman Empire was weakened by fragmented tax collection; Ottoman tax revenues grew only 10 percent in the 18th century, and by 1812 the empire was devoting a quarter of total state revenue to paying domestic debt alone.[125] By the mid-19th century, the empire had no alternative but to begin borrowing money from Europe. Then loans piled upon loans, and the empire became gradually insolvent.

Exploding debt eventually landed the empire, humiliatingly, in the hands of the Ottoman Public Debt Administration, which gave European creditors significant near-sovereign control over parts of the Ottoman economy and tax system. One example of the competitive price that the state paid was the constraints on its education system. Although education expanded in the 19th century, it was unable to keep pace with the modernizing world. But the empire could do little better, in part because "strapped Ottoman finances continued to retard the fuller emergence of the state-run school system."[126]

The Critical Role of Individual Personalities

The quality of a nation's leadership is an obvious enough variable but one that deserves specific mention, as the cases provide numerous examples of either individual leaders or a sustained leadership class over a longer period having measurable effects on competitive success or failure. Good or bad leaders might be a symptom of the societal characteristics we review in Chapters Three through Nine, but they are a distinct variable.

Some of the historical cases offer obvious and historic cases of individual leaders who made a difference in their country's competitive positioning. These range from Pericles and Philip of Macedon, to Caesar Augustus (whose extended reign reaffirmed aspects of Roman identity and power),[127] to Cosimo de Medici in Florence, to Prussia's Bismarck, to Napoleon,

---

[122] William M. Morgan, "Pacific Dominance: The United States Versus Japan," in James Lacey, ed., *Great Strategic Rivalries: From the Classical World to the Cold War*, New York: Oxford University Press, 2016, p. 575.

[123] Quataert, 2005, pp. 28–29.

[124] Finkel, 2005, p. 73.

[125] Hanioğlu, 2008, p. 22.

[126] Quataert, 2005, pp. 71–72, 170.

[127] Ober, 2015, p. 263.

who eventually brought strategic ruin to his country but also undertook significant domestic reforms that strengthened the French state and who, for a time, did take his country to the top of the European power hierarchy. Vladislav Zubok places the role of individual personalities at the center of modern Soviet history. That history cannot be understood without comprehending the role of major figures from Stalin to Gorbachev.[128] More broadly, international relations scholars have in recent years reemphasized the role of specific leaders in shaping global outcomes, including the competitive standing of countries.[129]

Individual personalities, it is clear, can make a critical difference in providing (or destroying) competitive advantage through their roles in leadership positions. This factor is not a societal characteristic per se but can interact with them, either fueling or undermining the national dynamism generated by those characteristics. The importance of this factor is another reason why societal characteristics alone can only be counted upon to achieve partial success.

A Complex Mosaic

Our research therefore uncovered many factors beyond societal characteristics that help explain national competitive advantage. The seven societal variables, the focus of our study, must operate in tandem with these structural, exogenous, and national strategic factors to produce the highest degrees of competitive advantage. Although some of the factors listed in this chapter appear to have been primarily relevant during prehistorical, ancient, or early modern periods of national formation and rise, many remain relevant today and can provide useful guidance to the United States, highlighting areas in which it can achieve competitive advantage (and avoid competitive costs).

Table 2.1 outlines five main factors of competitive advantage highlighted in this chapter. They incorporate all the factors noted above that can be shaped by national policy or choice (leaving out such things as path dependence and geography, which are baked into the system as it exists today).

These categories make clear some obvious investments that would boost competitive standing. We return to these in the concluding chapter. But now we turn to our review of the seven societal characteristics associated with national competitive success. We begin with the essential foundation for national power and competitive success—national ambition and will.

---

[128] Zubok, 2007, pp. 303–304, 335.

[129] Daniel L. Byman and Kenneth M. Pollack, "Let Us Now Praise Great Men: Bringing the Statesman Back In," *International Security*, Vol. 25, No. 4, 2001.

TABLE 2.1

Nonsocietal Sources of National Competitive Advantage

Factor	Components and Examples
Demographic indicators	• Population growth rate • Dependency ratio
Resilience	• Ecological sustainability • Climate resilience • Disease preparedness • Natural disaster response and recovery
National policies and characteristics underwriting economic strength	• National investment as a proportion of GDP • Degree of productive investment • Sustainable fiscal position in both public and private sectors • The availability of high-quality, strategically and politically savvy leaders
Role in international webs and networks	• Formal alliances • Informal coalitions, groupings • International institutions • Networks of economic exchange • Scientific and intellectual networks
Sustainable energy sources	• Resilient, secure, reliable energy network • Competitive advantage in accessibility and sustainability of energy sources

CHAPTER THREE

National Ambition and Will

Our first characteristic constitutes the essential fuel of national dynamism and is the foundation on which all periods of international competitive dominance have been built. Countries that reach and sustain high levels of competitive standing typically demonstrate a broad-based sense of ambition and drive to master the world around them, in terms of both knowledge and political-military influence—an urge expressed both domestically (in scientific, technological, and cultural terms) and internationally (in geopolitical ambitions). Of the seven characteristics associated with national competitive advantage, this one holds the most serious risks of overshoot: Seeking mastery over both nature and other nations has often led to geopolitical overreach, environmental disaster, and fiscal ruin. Yet nations that have reached the pinnacle of world politics and technological achievement have almost universally relied on an abundant supply of national ambition and will—an urge for intellectual achievement and superiority and a sense of national destiny and greatness that fuels their competitive drive.

One of our case studies offers a classic example of this characteristic and its effect on competitive standing. Rome's rise to greatness and its competitive success against the major powers of its day was propelled by a powerful societal custom that valorized control, mastery, and conquest. Contemporaneous visitors and Romans alike consistently remarked on the taken-for-granted sense among Romans that their society was destined to rule others. This translated into a form of manifest destiny that infused the Roman elite's perception of the city-state's role on the world stage, seemingly from early periods of Roman history.

When we read the words, "There was one nation in the world which would fight for the liberties of others at its own cost, with its own labor, and at its own danger. It was even ready to cross the sea to make sure there was no unjust rule anywhere and that everywhere justice, right, and law would prevail," we might think we are reading an assessment of modern-day America.[1] But this is from Livy, writing about Rome, speaking to its inherent sense of superiority, duty, and right to expand its power. As the University of Chicago scholar Shadi Bartsch-Zimmer points out, Rome was influenced by "a matrix of . . . cultural and national

---

[1] Quoted in Shadi Bartsch-Zimmer, "The Romans, Just Wars, and Exceptionalism," *Formations* (Stevanovich Institute on the Formation of Knowledge, University of Chicago), September 28, 2017.

beliefs that brought together religion, pride in the Roman expansion, and a firm sense of the moral character of their ancestors, all of this creating a sense that the Romans were special."[2]

Partly, this urge to expand Rome's power was grounded in fundamental societal values built around glory and honor. As the historian Tom Holland put it, Romans "had a deeper thirst for honor than any other people in the world." Alongside a moralistic sense of a right to rule, Romans displayed drive, commitment, and a willingness to suffer to achieve greatness. "Hardness was a Roman idea," Holland explains. "The steel required to hunt out glory or endure disaster was the defining mark of a citizen. It was instilled in him from the moment of his birth."[3]

This sensibility extended from emperors down to soldiers in the field. It reflected economic and personal ambitions, as well as collective ones: Conquering new lands produced booty, which enriched generals and emperors—and to a lesser degree the common soldier. Rome's sway over global trade routes created opportunities for enrichment. But there was more at play here than just material appetites: The Roman sense of superiority and duty was rooted in a sense of exceptionalism and national mission, one justified (again in Rome's self-conception) by self-serving but nonetheless genuinely held moral and legal principles.

But the Romans' drive to master their surroundings was not limited to military predominance or a lunge for empire. Roman society also reflected a significant degree of the internal or domestic aspects of this characteristic, a craving to master the world to discover and apply many tools of understanding, power, and control. Romans sought to understand the techniques of engineering and basic science needed for dramatic logistical and construction achievements—the roads, bridges, walls, aqueducts, cisterns, and other feats of human social organization that became the symbolic (and lasting) hallmarks of the empire. Many modern assessments do not rank Rome especially highly for technological innovation, and, in its intellectual engagement with the natural world, some have viewed it as far behind the Italian Renaissance or 19th-century Britain.[4] Nonetheless, within the confines of an ancient context, Roman engineers' ability to shape and manipulate their surroundings was unprecedented. Indeed, the latest evidence suggests that Rome did advance the technology of its time in areas such as farming, mining, and milling.[5]

---

[2] Bartsch-Zimmer, 2017.

[3] Tom Holland, *Rubicon: The Last Years of the Roman Republic*, New York: Anchor Books, 2005, pp. 220, 110–111. Tony Spawforth argues that Roman elite males "were raised in a moral code familiar in other societies dominated by a warrior aristocracy. This emphasized reputation, glory and masculine excellence, all made manifest in public service" (Spawforth, 2018, p. 196).

[4] Nor did Rome possess revolutionary military technology. As Bryan Ward-Perkins argues, "even at the best of times, the edge that the Romans enjoyed over their enemies, through their superior equipment and organization, was never remotely comparable, say, to that of Europeans in the nineteenth century using rifles and the Gatling and Maxim guns against peoples armed mainly with spears" (Ward-Perkins, 2006, pp. 37–38).

[5] Temin, 2013, p. 217.

Rome's ambitions also extended to commerce and profit. In economic and commercial terms, Rome's economy from the late republican period through the early empire lacked many elements of a modern capitalist economy—most production was by households and not firms, for example. Some historians contend that it is misleading to think of Roman society as having an inherently commercial drive on par with the leading commercial empires in history, from Venice to Britain to the United States. But it still reflected key elements of a market economy, and many members of its elite classes embodied such a commercial zeal.[6]

In all these ways, the Roman case is emblematic of a lesson we found in many historical examples: A nation's competitive vibrancy is, in part, a product of its national ambition and will. This is true in outward-directed ways—the nation's foreign ambitions and determination to force its way to the apex of world politics. But it is also true in more ephemeral expressions within a society, in the generalized sense of the urge to achieve and progress that exists among its people.

Nations, city-states, and empires with strong competitive positions have almost always had such a clear sense of mission, some sense of exceptionalism, and the conviction that they have the right and obligation to place their stamp on world politics. As the writer Ross Douthat argues, "Across human history, the most dynamic and creative societies have been almost inevitably expansionary, going outward from tribes and cities and nations to put their stamp upon a larger world. Sometimes this has meant settlement and sometimes conquest, sometimes it has meant missionary zeal, sometimes simply exploration."[7] Or as a scholar puts it, it was the "spirit of relentless, driving entrepreneurship" that characterized both Britain and then the United States on their rise to global power.[8] Competitive nations are fueled by this appetite to succeed, to understand, to bring normative order to their own lives and to the world.

This commitment is often, indeed almost always, fueled by some dominant and rousing societal idea. The Italian historian Federico Chabod writes of an "energizing myth" of societies.[9] He used this construct in part to explain why the city-states of the Italian Renaissance had such a remarkable degree of intellectual and geopolitical ambition. His construct refers to some central idea or concept that invigorates and propels the society, a mythology about itself—its origins, destiny, rightness, excellence—that galvanizes both its domestic economic power and its foreign actions. Our case studies suggest that countries with an energizing myth, and all the elements of ambition that go with it, have a competitive advantage over those that do not.

---

[6] Temin, 2013, p. 4; Harris, 2007, p. 529.

[7] Douthat, 2020, p. 3.

[8] Hudson, 2021, p. 120.

[9] This concept is discussed in Kenneth R. Bartlett, *Short History of the Italian Renaissance*, Toronto: University of Toronto Press, 2013.

But national ambition and will, as we will see, is a difficult if not impossible characteristic to accurately measure. There were no polls in ancient Rome, or most of our other case study nations. And even if there were, the views of the population alone do not equate to the degree of ambition and willpower the characteristic implies. In a few cases, we will find proxy indicators for this characteristic—indirect measurable ways that a generalized ambition makes itself known in a society. This is an unavoidably qualitative and elusive variable. And yet it is also one for which our historical cases provide extensive support.

Defining the Characteristic

The concept of national ambition and will, as we use it here, highlights the role of a generalized ambition and competitive sensibility, not merely an aggressive foreign policy. It is often fed by a nation's potent sense of exceptionalism, desire for reputation and honor, and right to rule, but that is a secondary aspect of this characteristic. More fundamentally, it implies a societal commitment to power and mastery of the world around them, natural and social—an urge to achieve, control, expand, and influence.

One challenge in assessing such a variable is that any nation's degree of ambition will rise and fall over time. As a European great power, Sweden once harbored a desire for regional hegemony that would be anachronistic today. Spain manifested a relatively brief period of intense national will based on a vision of the country as the rightful hegemon of Europe—which somewhat quickly (in historical terms) gave way to a more constrained sense of national ambitions. It is also worth noting that discussions of national will easily devolve into a kind of culturalist essentialism that cannot explain national competitive advantage—claims that some "peoples" are inherently more aggressive, or acquisitive, than others.

And yet some societies at any given moment in history reflect more ambition, dynamism, and drive than others. Such a drive has characterized many of the great civilizations in their rise and at their zenith. We can recognize it in countries with a potent sense of national exceptionalism; public statements, doctrines, myths, and then national behavior in service to the idea that the nation is destined to have a leading position in the world; ambitious scientific and technological exploration driven by a powerful urge to understand the natural world; and commercial ambitions to dominate markets. Elements of a habit of ambition can be seen in measurable social habits around fatalism, orientation to time, and similar issues. We can bring more scaffolding to our intuitive sense that a vague and abstract concept, such as ambition or willpower, provides indispensable fuel to national competitive advantage.

Elements of the Characteristic

That concept of national ambition and will can take many different forms—some more geopolitically oriented and some more economic or technological in their focus. In practice, these different components are often linked: Nations with potent geopolitical ambitions tend to generate strong economic and scientific-technological goals as well.

***

The geopolitical component of this characteristic is the most straightforward. It identifies nations with a powerful ambition to shape world politics, either their direct neighborhood or the world system. This need not imply a lust for global hegemony, nor does it require that a nation seek to forcibly subordinate others. But it does imply a determination to gain a leading position among nations. Such an aggressive zeal for geopolitical power can be recognized in the strategic documents, public statements, and private official correspondence of major powers, as well as in their behavior.

In some cases, this drive for power can reflect a nation's urgent desire to control its own destiny, in part by becoming the hegemon in its immediate environment, rather than a desire for extensive external power. Sweden in the 17th century and early 18th sought a degree of regional military predominance and engaged in wars that ultimately overextended its power. It did this not out of some missionary conviction that the country was destined to rule large parts of Europe but rather because of more narrow, practical, and material concerns for security and a desire for regional influence. Other cases reflect more-comprehensive ambitions for global influence: Rome, Britain, and the United States sought and acquired tremendous degrees of global hegemony, in some cases through formal empire. The Ottoman Empire and, at various times in their histories, France, Japan, and Spain all tried to acquire dominant regional power, as well as substantial global influence.

***

A corollary of geopolitical ambition is the appetite for global commercial success.[10] National will also typically implies a desire for wealth, and the industriousness that led some populations to work hard in pursuit of a better standard of living. Almost no major power that has reached the top of global competitive rankings has lacked such a basic ambition.

A foundational commercial drive was central to the self-conception, social habits, and global influence of Rome (in premodern terms), Spain, Britain, the United States, and others. Modern Germany and South Korea, as two examples, have followed the same pattern. Major powers that eschewed such commercial goals—and who have tightly constrained trade, immigration, and exchange and provided little support to key industries or trading houses— have tended to lag. Russia, both before and after the Soviet era, is a leading example: its firms "sold to the national market, exported little or nothing. They were simply not competitive— not then, not later—especially not during the Soviet years."[11]

---

[10] Ferguson, 2011, p. 36.

[11] Landes, 1998, p. 251. Similarly, a broad-based commercial drive was lacking, some scholars believe, across Ottoman society. A implication was the "failure of a vital bourgeois class to emerge in the late Ottoman Empire," despite the state's efforts to generate one (Hanioğlu, 2008, p. 209).

Joel Mokyr has in mind elements of such a commercial drive when he describes the critical role played in Europe's advance by "an entrepreneurial or bourgeois culture," in which "people are willing to work harder, save more, provide for the poor, and take more risks. It involves enhanced respect for labor, production, and technology."[12] A rising consumer demand for improved consumer goods and the fruits of trade produced an "industriousness" to work hard and gain the salary needed to purchase these things.[13] Dierdre McCloskey's three-volume argument about the sources of Europe's dramatic economic advances from the 18th century onward highlights the same package of essential qualities: a focus on commerce, honoring labor and ambition, a context that fuels innovation and entrepreneurialism.[14]

A commercially ambitious mindset expresses itself in part in a risk-acceptant drive for innovation and improvement. This mindset spurs a competitive ambition among firms and is associated with market-changing and industry-dominating innovations. As a result, we will argue below, this characteristic tends to be associated with a critical intervening variable of national competitive success: a leading role in frontier industries and technologies.

A powerful commercial ambition also has sociological implications: Such an ambition was associated with the rise of the commercial classes of the Italian Renaissance city-states, the ambitious entrepreneurs in early industrial-era Britain, and generations of capitalist strivers in the United States. It has also helped spur the rise of the petit bourgeoisie of these countries, the small business owners and craftsmen, thereby expanding the pool of people whose creative imagination is engaged in the national project. Commercial ambition is thus associated, in its truly open and inclusive versions, with shared opportunity.[15] In 18th-century Japan, fishers, craftspeople, and others began to produce specialty goods (e.g., herring and sugar) for export and to sponsor the development of new domestic industries, such as silk. The country was gradually nurturing a "proto-industrial" class working in business, crafts, farming, and so on, with the ambitions and talents that would feed naturally into later economic growth.[16]

Some nations can reflect a mostly economic ambition or will without much of a geopolitical overhang. Japan since the 1960s is a good example: It is a country with a potent, even nationalistic, drive to capture market share in key industries and build a world-class industrial and technological foundation.[17] This expression of will justified an intense national

---

[12] Mokyr, 2017, p. 122.

[13] Broadberry et al., 2014, pp. 391, 401, 407–415.

[14] McCloskey, 2010, 2011, 2016.

[15] In turn, societies with a potential commercial ambition tend to break down feudal or aristocratic social boundaries over time, as they search relentlessly for commercial talent. The result is to tend to expand the range of opportunity (Appleby, 2010, loc. 1487–1490).

[16] We are grateful to Robert Hellyer for this insight. See Edward E. Pratt, *Japan's Protoindustrial Elite: The Economic Foundations of the Gōnō*, Cambridge, Mass.: Harvard University Asia Center, 1999.

[17] For Japan after World War II, concludes the eminent scholar Marius Jensen, "Goals of personal consumption had replaced, seemingly forever, the goals of national power" (Marius B. Jansen, *The Making of Modern Japan*, Kindle ed., Cambridge, Mass.: Harvard University Press, 2000, loc. 11149).

commitment, accompanied by a work ethic that can run to self-destructive extremes, that has shaped national investments and come to embody the nation's identity.

South Korea is another example of a society that, at least for a time, had striking levels of will, ambition, dedication, and drive for expressions other than geopolitical assertiveness. South Korea since the 1950s has been characterized by work ethic, a social ethic of accomplishment and drive, tremendous cultural and artistic achievements (such that Korea's cultural influence far exceeds China's), and the development of world-leading industries in sectors ranging from electronics to shipbuilding. And, yet, recurring efforts to generate a stronger South Korean expression of its regional or global role have fallen flat. The country simply does not have a strong sense of an ambitious role in world politics—although it has such a conception in every other realm of society.

***

National will is not merely about the projection of geopolitical and economic power—it has strong domestic connotations as well. In the most-competitive societies, the passion to achieve, to understand, and to master becomes a generalized societal habit. It becomes characteristic of scientists and inventors whose ambition is expressed by pushing the frontiers of knowledge rather than political power. It fires engineers and technological entrepreneurs who seek to build and invent products that shape the world. It is reflected in a generalized urge to understand, and eventually control and manipulate, the natural world.

The relationship between scientific and technological ambitions and national power emerges in a classic case study of national efflorescence—the rise of European power in the so-called Great Divergence. A major catalyst of this advance was the adoption of what has become known as the scientific method, along with associated practices of intellectual curiosity, engagement, and experimentation, across the Continent. The scientific method and a rising urge to understand, and then manipulate, natural phenomena produced many key technological breakthroughs that empowered European nations. But it also reflected, and bolstered, a more generalized sense of intellectual ambition and willpower that is implied by this characteristic.[18] That core idea, habit, or mindset, a driving belief in the ability of human knowledge to push the frontiers of accomplishment, is a form of national ambition and will present in the most-competitive societies.

This determination to express a society's ambitions and creative potential is not limited to scientific and technological applications. It also finds expression in cultural output and a

---

[18] Margaret Jacob (1988) catalogs how the goal of mastery emerged in the post-Cartesian European scientific community and, having once been suppressed by church-affiliated authorities, became the leading intellectual doctrine of important elements of the ruling elite in Britain, the Netherlands, and then elsewhere in Europe. Jack Goldstone describes the same mindset as being critical to the Industrial Revolution. It was a "culture of innovation" that spurred scientific and technological advances, a culture that implied ambitions to master the natural world and derive applicable technologies from its workings (Goldstone, 2009, pp. 134–135).

desire to demonstrate a society's cultural superiority to the world. It is not surprising, then, that during periods of competitive rise and apex nations tend also to reflect vibrant cultural sectors. In Rome, Britain, or the United States at their peak, or in such powers as the 18th-century Ottoman Empire, Song-dynasty China, or even parts of Austria-Hungary around the turn of the 20th century, artists, writers, philosophers, public intellectuals, musicians, composers, and other cultural entrepreneurs sought breakthroughs in technique, glory, and achievement. Cultural ambitions seem to have paralleled geopolitical and economic ones in highly competitive nations.

This societal sense of ambition and drive ultimately translates all the way down to the individual level, and to norms and habits often associated with what is loosely described as a society's work ethic. It correlates closely with two values often nominated by cultural-ist assessments of national development: ambition (as opposed to fatalism), and a forward-looking orientation to time. Advocates of a cultural lens have amassed a degree of evidence (which we will discuss below) for the economic value of certain shared societal norms.[19] As the economist Eric Beinhocker puts it,

> These include norms that support a strong work ethic, individual accountability, and a belief that you are the protagonist of your own life and not at the whim of gods or Big Men. Fatalism greatly reduces personal incentives. It is also important to believe that there is a payoff to hard work and a moral life in this world, and not just in the next.[20]

McCloskey's explanation for Europe's great economic leap focuses on similar factors. She argues that a key variable in explaining economic growth is "the honoring of work apart from manual drudgery or heroic daring." The premodern "European aristocracy delight[ed] rather in haughty idleness."[21] The valorization of work and the values that came with it—drive, ambition, thrift, future orientation—all contributed to the most dramatic economic leap forward in human history.

***

These individual components are part of a larger reality in the most-competitive societ-ies: The zeal to explore, learn, and master reflects something of a dissatisfaction with the way things are and a desire to do and be more as a people. Competitive societies, while confident and self-assertive, also profoundly *dis*satisfied with the current state of affairs.

David Landes catalogs the ways in which European powers were driven to explore, settle, and in some cases steal the wealth of other regions.[22] He writes of the "Faustian spirit of

---

[19] For example, see Harrison and Huntington, 2000.

[20] Beinhocker, 2007, p. 568.

[21] McCloskey, 2010, p. 74.

[22] Landes, 1998.

mastery" over nature that imbued European societies. This combined with other factors to provide European powers with

> a tremendous advantage in the invention and adoption of new technology. The will to mastery, the rational approach to problems that we call the scientific method, the competition for wealth and power—together these broke down the resistance of inherited ways and made of change a positive good. Nothing—not pride, nor honor, nor authority, nor credulity—could stand in the face of these new values.[23]

These qualities are not unique to great powers. And they do not require an urge to conquer or attain geopolitical hegemony but rather a desire to achieve mastery in areas appropriate to the country. Japan's postwar push for industrial prominence, and its focus on market share in key industries, is an example of this quality at work (as is China's similar push today).

The mindset of ambition and achievement is manifest throughout multiple social groups and organizations, generating competitive dynamics that push the nation ahead. This is most obviously true in the business world, where competition within major industries (and in the context of global markets) spurs investment, increases productivity, and produces innovations.

An essential spirit of *competition*, then—welcoming and nurturing a battle to be the best, the leader, the winner, whether of an economic sector or a field of artistic achievement or a class of social institutions—is part and parcel of national will. Societies that compete effectively *among* the community of nations encourage and actively cultivate manifold kinds of competition *within* their borders as well. They spur advances—economic, technological, scientific, cultural—that make them strong by creating a context in which their people, companies, universities, and other institutions compete vigorously against one another.

Landes explains that cooperation and knowledge-sharing were critical to early European scientific advances—but it was a cooperation "enormously enhanced by fierce rivalry in the race for prestige and honor." Even in academic and scientific pursuits, "fame was the spur, and even in those early days, science was a contest for priority.... And that was why scientists, amateur and professional, were so keen to found journals and get dated articles published."[24] This sort of productive rivalry, playing out between individuals or groups in society determined to outdo one another, is characteristic, in some fashion, of every competitively successful society we have identified. Its absence, and the rise of an indolent, satisfied, narrowly materialistic mindset, is characteristic of most cases of competitive decline.

***

---

[23] Landes, 2003, pp. 32–33.

[24] Landes, 1998, p. 205.

National will manifests itself not only in normal times but also in crisis. Indeed, the degree of national ambition and will helps to determine a critical related quality, one that is itself associated with sustained national competitive position: national resilience and the ability to rise to challenges. The ability to use challenge and difficulty as spurs to new forms of greatness is a common feature of competitively dynamic societies.

Arnold Toynbee's central argument about the fates of civilizations focused on the developmental spur of challenge—that is, on how civilizations advanced most when they faced, and effectively surmounted, major trials. Societies that were not challenged in a meaningful way, or failed in their response, eventually collapsed or faded into irrelevance. "Immunity from the challenge of encounters with civilizations is a very serious handicap," he argues, suggesting that challenge may reflect "some social law which may be expressed in the formula, 'the greater the challenge, the greater the stimulus.'"[25]

Toynbee also describes a broader characteristic of civilizations that successfully progress from challenge, to effective response, to further growth, and to new challenges: They have, he suggests, an élan vital "which carries the challenged party through equilibrium to an over-balance which exposes him to a fresh challenge and thereby inspires him to make a fresh response in the form of a further equilibrium ending in a further overbalance, and so on in a progression which is potentially infinite."[26] Toynbee's notion of élan is closely related to our proposed characteristic of ambition and willpower—with one useful addendum: his argument that difficulties can strengthen ambition and forge national will through a demanding series of challenges. If the nations overcome those challenges, their societies become ever stronger. A society without such a drive would never be required to surmount challenges in this way and would thus never be forced into greater excellence.[27]

Indeed, Toynbee makes the fascinating point that sometimes the apparent lowest ebb in a nation's history is only a prelude to a new expansion. For the city-states of Greece, the costly tragedy of the Peloponnesian War gave way to the expansionist surge of Alexander, bringing Greek ideas and culture to more of the world than ever before. But the expansion itself is not the indicator of civilizational success, because the centuries after Alexander's conquest were

---

[25] Toynbee, 1947, pp. 152, 140. Toynbee raises the question of whether some challenges may be "excessive," simply too much for a society to handle, but then also notes that a challenge that "defeated one respondent is afterward proved by the victorious response of some later competitor to be not insuperable" (Toynbee, 1947, p. 142).

[26] Toynbee, 1947, p. 187.

[27] Toynbee also refers to the general sense of national spirit, norms, values, and principles that is an important component of competitive advantage. A "spiritual rift" in a society, as Toynbee puts it, a "schism in the souls of human beings," can be one of the symptoms of a "disintegrating society" (Toynbee, 1947, p. 429) Toynbee himself very much meant this in religious terms (he warned of the decline of Christian values and the rise of "vulgarity and barbarism," and claimed that a path of social "transfiguration" needed to be guided "by the light of Christianity"), but the basic idea can be extended to the abstract but undeniable notion that a society has a spiritual life and that some form of healthy balance in this realm—whether from religious or secular sources—is essential (p. 530).

a period "during which the Hellenic Civilization was palpably in process of disintegration."[28] Nations seemingly at the peak of their competitive position can be decaying inside. The shell of their power has reached its maximum extent, but their dynamism—their élan vital, as he would put it—has long since dimmed.

The Contrast: Satisfied Powers

Another way to understand this characteristic is to define its conceptual opposite. The inverse of a nation fueled by potent degrees of national ambition and will would be a society shackled by a generalized lethargy, a crippling degree of fatalism, an absence of social norms encouraging drive and dedication, and a focus on near-term satisfaction of individual wants rather than expressions of national power and glory. This satisfaction might stem from a sense that the nation had reached a stable level of international influence proportionate to its size, economic power, and national mythology. Such attitudes are perhaps most likely in nations that have achieved a degree of wealth and economic security that makes them concerned largely with preserving the status quo.

Such a society, in some cases, might be a nation on autopilot, living off its accumulated advantages, using path dependence and inertia rather than new dynamism as its major source of strength. It might be able to muster significant degrees of will from time to time, but typically only in a defensive and urgent response to a major crisis or attack, very seldom as a future-oriented choice fired by ambition. Such a society might be one in which the bureaucratic chains grab tighter every year and in which the wealthy and powerful gradually but inexorably shift from productivity-enhancing experimentation to profit skimming and rent seeking. It would likely be stagnant and increasingly governed by various forms of orthodoxy.

Such a society would begin to mirror elements of one classic vision of a nation or society in decline, focusing on the collapse of moral fiber or willpower. Societies become decadent, satisfied, and entitled, goes a common refrain. They lose the willpower that made them great or could make them great. It is a version of Edward Gibbon's argument about Rome: It grew weak, consumerist, and dissolute, partly because of the influence of Christianity.[29]

Such a trend was arguably, for example, part of the slow decline of the vibrancy and competitive spirit of the Italian Renaissance city-states, at least in the commercial realm. "Over the long term," the scholar Lauro Martines explains, "there was a deceleration in the peninsula's productive capacities, a weakening in trade investment and in the upper-class grasp on business initiative, and a decline, at the same social level, in direct personal commitment to trade." Such trends were evident, he contends, among the nobility and wealthy classes

---

[28] Toynbee, 1947, p. 191. A parallel could perhaps be found in the Soviet Union of the late 1970s and early 1980s—empowered by the U.S. loss in Vietnam (and the crisis of the U.S. system during Watergate), believing that Moscow had a certain momentum in the Cold War contest for the developing world, it then overextended itself precisely at a time when it, too, was "in the process of disintegration."

[29] Gibbon and Mueller, 2005.

of Venice: The potential for profits from mainland Italian areas they had seized "lulled the entrepreneurial initiative of the nobility, gradually rendering it more sedentary. In Pareto's classic formulation, entrepreneurs turned into rentiers."[30] Soon the great seafaring power of Venice could not find enough experienced seamen to command its ships.

The Theoretical Case for the Competitive Advantage of National Ambition and Will

A strong dose of national ambition and will, expressed both domestically and internationally, would seem logically related to national dynamism. But that potential relationship has to be tested with analysis. The first step is to consider the theoretical case for its importance.

In one sense, the relationship between national will and competitive position ought to be almost tautological. Nations that possess little desire to improve their standing presumably do not often end up on top. In theory, a national self-identity that points to the right and duty to a strong global role ought to spur efforts to pursue such a role. The nation is likely to inspire competitive success in several ways. In ideological terms, for example, a strong sense of national exceptionalism can provide a theory of national power that demands competition. In political terms, it can help ensure sufficient domestic popular support for such exertions. In internal or domestic terms, as well, the theoretical tie between this characteristic and national success seems obvious enough. A grassroots degree of ambitious energy in a society—rather, as noted above, than a generalized sense of either fatalism or satisfied idleness—would seem naturally associated with productivity, economic output and growth, innovation, and other determinants of a state's economic dynamism. It would logically seem associated with national strength and competitive standing. A potent societal ethic of competitive ambition ought to fuel entrepreneurialism, scientific and technological achievement, cultural expression, and other outcomes that bolster national power.

As with all the characteristics we assess, national ambition and will alone are insufficient to generate competitive success. The Soviet Union is perhaps the best example of a broken connection between an official energizing mythology and a practical belief in that narrative or the ability to carry it through. If a nation has intense willpower but not the institutions or national coherence to express that will, its competitive position will suffer. National will is only one ingredient in a larger recipe for national dynamism. And more than any of the other societal characteristics we assess, this one carries immense risks of getting the balance wrong. A thoughtless, unbounded expression of national willpower is a sure route to competitive, and national, disaster.

In an even more abstract sense, this characteristic may be related to another source of competitive advantage—specifically, that some degree of *national self-actualization*, both in

---

[30] Lauro Martines, *Power and Imagination: City-States in Renaissance Italy*, New York: ACLS Humanities E-Book Project, 2013, loc. 3660, 3684.

collective and individual terms, lies at the core of such advantage. Nations are more vibrant, dynamic, and ultimately stronger when they serve as engines for self-actualization, of both their individual citizens and the society as a whole.

The economist Edmund Phelps speculates about the importance of such abstract but nonetheless potent social values, arguing that nations characterized by a high degree of pursuit of individual and collective self-actualization gain competitive advantage. "Where there is great dynamism, there is also an abundance of its characteristic fruit: achieving, succeeding, prospering, and flourishing," he argues. "And where it is lacking, there is a joyless society." Phelps offers research evidence suggesting that certain values, as identified in the World Values Survey, associated with self-expression and achievement are also associated with higher economic achievement. These values include a commitment to learning and acceptance of new ideas and widely shared opportunity. Attitudes associated with "traditional" values, on the other hand, turned out to be negatively correlated with productivity and growth.[31] An active, dynamic society that is interested in actualizing itself as a nation and creating a context in which its citizens can pursue their goals to the greatest possible degree is likely to be more competitive.

National Ambition and Will and Competitive Outcomes: Evidence from Cases

In reviewing the historical cases for links between national ambition and will and competitive standing, we looked for qualitative or anecdotal evidence that the cases reflected each of the major components of this characteristic. Table 3.1 summarizes these findings. We found meaningful evidence of a national narrative of power and ambition and associated geopolitical ambitions, commercial ambitions, and signs of a strong and vibrant domestic drive for scientific and technological achievement, as well as some evidence of a societal emphasis on hard work and individual achievement in each of these cases.

The cases offered three broad arguments for a connection between national ambition and competitive position. First, this characteristic ranks highest—the sense of national mission and exceptionalism, and its expression in globe-spanning outputs of power, as well as intense engineering and scientific efforts to master the natural world—among the three most dominant historical powers, Rome, Britain, and the United States. Put another way, the three most potent hegemons arguably had the most intense and wide-ranging forms of national will, both domestic and international.

In Britain, for example, we find clear and obvious evidence of a British sensibility, at least by the late 18th century, that Britain had a rightful place as a leading world empire. After a succession of victories in war and a rising industrial ethos, the "English thus fell in love with

---

[31] Phelps, 2013, pp. 11, 211–213.

TABLE 3.1

Assessing Components of National Ambition and Will in Historical Cases

Case	National Narrative, Energizing Myth of Right to Rule	International Commercial Ambitions	Scientific and Technical Ambitions	Degree of Work Ethic, Individual Drive to Succeed
Rome	●	●	◗	●
China	●	●	●	●
Spain	●	●	◗	
Austria-Hungary	◗	◗	●	◗
Ottoman Empire	●	●	●	◗
Renaissance Italy	●	●	●	●
Britain	●	●	●	●
Sweden	◗	◗	◗	●
France	●	●	●	●
Japan	●	●	●	●
Soviet Union	●	●	●	●
United States	●	●	●	●

NOTES: ● indicates clear historical evidence to support association—not that the association is necessarily positive, only that the case offers a strong association, whether positive or negative. ◗ indicates weaker evidence.

themselves in the eighteenth century."[32] This impulse was the product of a complex set of motives ranging from global power considerations to a desire for commercial gain to a racist ideology of the right to rule others.[33] In its national energizing myth of Pax Britannica, British officials and the public came to believe, as the United States later would, that their form of government was unique and that they had a civilizing mission.[34]

But it was the explosion of commercial ambition in Britain in the 18th century, especially the second half, that set the stage for the Industrial Revolution and was most associated with various aspects of national ambition and will.[35] The Industrial Revolution was shaped by the

---

[32] R. Porter, 1990, p. 11.

[33] There is a massive literature on British imperial ambitions and the ideology that lay behind them. See, for example, Ronald Hyam, *Britain's Imperial Century, 1815–1914: A Study of Empire and Expansion*, 2nd ed., Lanham, Md.: Barnes and Noble Books, 1993; Niall Ferguson, *Empire: How Britain Made the Modern World*, London: Allen Lane, 2003. Specifically on the ideological aspects, see David Armitage, *The Ideological Origins of British Empire*, Cambridge, UK: Cambridge University Press, 2000.

[34] We are grateful to William Anthony Hay for a very helpful description of these factors.

[35] There is some debate about the relative lack of a society-wide commercial ambition in Britain, at least among the elite classes in the 19th century. This is the core of Martin Wiener's argument about British

view that science and technology provided a new way—and something of an obligation—to control and master the natural world.[36] The historian Roy Porter describes the rush of economic striving in these decades and associated technological accomplishment: In the century after 1660, records indicate a total of only 210 patents taken out in Britain; in the three decades after 1760, there were almost 1,000.[37] Ambitious entrepreneurs took out loans via the well-developed financial system and made bets on hundreds of new products, techniques, and business models. This flourishing of the scientific method in Britain, and a whole cascade of scientific and technological ambitions to know and master the natural world that flowed from it, has long been held to be a defining characteristic of British elite society from the early 18th century through the Industrial Revolution.[38]

The second broad causal connection suggested by the case studies is that a dramatic advance in a nation's competitive standing was often associated with a parallel flourishing of its sense of national ambition. This has been true, for example, in Japan, which consciously sought to enhance national will and drive during leading periods of competitive advance. This sensibility has waxed and waned, but at times the society has demonstrated a strong sense of rightful leadership position in its region and the world. Japanese Meiji officials looking to Western countries for models "observed the 'civilized' powers to be obsessed with creating patriotic, hard-working, and self-reliant citizens."[39] During this broad period, Japanese

---

industrial decline—the idea that late Victorian and Edwardian elites simply never developed a "business ethic" in the manner of Americans and indeed continued to view commercial endeavors as somehow unworthy. The result was a culture not especially supportive of entrepreneurialism. See Martin Wiener, *English Culture and the Decline of the Industrial Spirit, 1850–1980*, Cambridge, UK: Cambridge University Press, 1981.

[36] On the Enlightenment-based sense of ability and even responsibility to master the natural world, and the role of an urge for "improvement" as a general political and moral principle, in Britain in the Victorian era, see Jacob, 1988; Mark Casson and Andrew Godley, "Entrepreneurship in Britain, 1830–1900," in David S. Landes, Joel Mokyr, and William J. Baumol, eds., *The Invention of Enterprise: Entrepreneurship from Ancient Mesopotamia to Modern Times*, Princeton, N.J.: Princeton University Press, 2010, pp. 237–238.

[37] R. Porter, 1990, p. 311.

[38] Margaret Jacob stressed the ambition—for fame, social position, and riches—of key British inventors and early industrialists, such as Matthew Boulton and James Watt. Coming from middle-class backgrounds, they "coveted a place in a world that would make room for their interests and success." Such ambition was characteristic of many who drove British industrialization—the valorization, Jacob explains, of an "entrepreneurial life" that joined with other factors (such as effective institutions and a learning and experimental culture) to unleash unheard-of levels of productivity. This ambition merged naturally with contexts of shared opportunity to create the potential for advance. The Watt family, for example, was "fiercely intent upon upward mobility. They were quick to indict any family member who could not or would not work" (Jacob, 2014, pp. 42, 45).

[39] Sheldon Garon, "Transnational History and Japan's 'Comparative Advantage,'" *Journal of Japanese Studies*, Vol. 43, No. 1, Winter 2017, p. 75.

pride, sense of cultural superiority, and goals to be a world-class industrial power with its own empire were growing.[40]

This yearning partly reflected a driving urge to match the other great powers and to achieve industrialization in the process. These ambitions were reflected in two slogans of the Meiji era noted by Marius Jansen: "civilization and enlightenment" and "be a success!" In the first decades of the Meiji period, Japanese "intellectuals shared a determination to remake their society with an idealism that would not reappear until the immediate post–World War II era in 1945."[41] "Enlightenment and self-improvement were efforts which Japanese embraced enthusiastically," Jansen writes.[42] He refers to "the restless ambition of Meiji youth determined to make a name for themselves in the new society."[43] The Meiji period saw an explosion in commercial sensibility, a rising emphasis on economic success, and a broader "enterprise fever."[44]

The Japanese case, of course, highlights the tremendous risk that can emerge when this characteristic runs out of control or generates angry reactions. In this case, national ambitions translated into an urge to industrialize and Westernize in ways that horrified traditionalists who worried that the aggressive, modern, cash-oriented new mentalities would undermine Japanese values. This tension produced an increasingly powerful "agrarian myth" and contributed to the rise of a romantic, antimodern sensibility in parts of Japanese society.[45] This in turn would nurture the grievances and nationalism that propelled the country into militaristic adventurism and, eventually, self-destruction.

***

Echoes of the same national self-confidence exist in China, where an undercurrent of social and cultural superiority comes to the fore and becomes especially influential during periods of competitive advance. Successive Chinese dynasties and regimes have felt a right and obligation to undertake a civilizing mission, in the sense of Confucian values, both for their own people and for their region. This form of "Confucian universalism" has fired the self-conception and foreign policies of China as a whole and specific dynasties during peri-

[40] Mark Ravina, *To Stand with the Nations of the World: Japan's Meiji Restoration in World History*, New York: Oxford University Press, 2017, p. 20.

[41] Jansen, 2000, loc. 6928.

[42] Jansen, 2000, loc. 6955.

[43] Jansen, 2000, loc. 6965.

[44] Gluck, 1985, pp. 161–162.

[45] Gluck, 1985, pp. 267–275.

ods of competitive advance.[46] Song China provides a good example of this relationship.[47] It did not yet span the complete territory of later Chinese dynasties, but it was an economic powerhouse, with the largest population of any political entity in the world, and a powerful commercial ethic. Production and trade boomed in areas such as tea, sugar, coal, copper, iron textiles, paper, and porcelains. Inland waterways boasted record amounts of water-borne trade.[48]

An ambition to understand, exchange with, and in some ways master the world has emerged at critical junctures of Chinese history. Niall Ferguson, for example, explains that Chinese inventors developed many critical technologies—such as movable-type printing, paper, matches, the magnetic compass money, and toilet paper. And he describes the case of Zheng He's famous early 15th-century exploration fleet of more than 28,000 people and ships, some of them many times the size of common European long-distance sailing vessels.[49]

Yet similar to some other societies that have experienced dramatic waxing and waning of dynamism and competitiveness, China has also seen many reactionary outbursts against this urge to engage with the world. Subsequent Chinese leaders prohibited long-distance exploration and in fact made ownership of a ship with more than two masts a crime punishable by death.[50] It is a wide generalization but holds significant truth to say that periods when Chinese rulers cracked down on ambition—international, to explore and trade, or domestic, to learn and understand—the country paid a competitive price.

This issue, in fact, helps clarify the argument we are making in this study. As with domestic ambition and motivation, the argument is *not* that given countries can be coded as "yes" or "no" on these qualities. It is far too simple to say that China reflected, or did not reflect, societal drive and ambition as a general rule. Our argument is instead that each case offers specific *examples* of the causal links between the societal characteristics and the competitive outcomes. Thus, in the case of China, it is possible to identify times, places, and context in which specific elements of national ambition and will influenced its national fate.

✳✳✳

Third and finally, our case studies reinforce the idea that, beyond international ambitions and a sense of national destiny, a more generalized sense of national adventurousness and ambition is associated with periods of peak national power and, as Jack Goldstone describes them, moments of national efflorescence. This pattern emerges, for example, in Renaissance

---

[46] We are grateful to Kenneth Pomeranz for stressing this point in communications with project staff and for offering this term.

[47] Dwight Perkins, "Government as an Obstacle to Industrialization: The Case of Nineteenth-Century China," *Journal of Economic History*, Vol. 27, No. 4, December 1967.

[48] We are grateful to Nicolas Tackett for highlighting the range of economic activity in the Song period.

[49] Ferguson, 2011, pp. 27–32.

[50] Ferguson, 2011.

Italy. These city-states held a vibrant sense of their exceptionalism:[51] Leaders of the Renaissance efflorescence "clearly felt themselves, and it was fully recognized by their time that they formed, a wholly new element in society."[52] Some of the Renaissance city-states were driven in part by a competitive ambition, by the goal of fame and glory and flaunting prestige. Jacob Burkhardt refers to the "boundless ambition and thirst after greatness, regardless of all means and consequences" that characterized the time.[53]

Renaissance societies were driven in part by an ambition to understand the world and an urge to explore and to share knowledge among explorers and businessmen.[54] Humanist values

> also gave a renewed thrust to old notions, such as man's right to rule over the rest of creation, the usefulness and beauty of the things at man's disposal, and "the capacities of the human mind, soul and body, for the work of ruling the sub-human universe." Here, then, we already have a domineering note. In discussion of "the dignity of man from Petrarch to Pico della Mirandola, there was a rising emphasis on sovereign man—on man the maker, inventor, ruler, sage, and beautiful being.[55]

Similarly, during its period of dramatic rise, from the 14th through the 16th centuries, the Ottoman state was founded on an essential doctrine of ambition. This was the "ideal of continuous Holy War and continuous expansion of" the realm of Islam, an ambition that translated into a "religious duty, inspiring every kind of enterprise and sacrifice."[56] Such a potent sense of national mission fueled the expansion of the Ottoman state. It inspired, for example, what Marc David Baer has termed the "Ottoman Age of Discovery," which involved more regional and global exploration than is sometimes appreciated.[57]

France offers another leading example of the connection between an outsized sense of national self and peak periods of competitive standing. Since the 17th century, French elites have believed that they had a rightful claim to regional prominence, even hegemony, and some degree of global influence and power as well.[58] This energizing myth or sense of

---

[51] Kenneth Bartlett, *The Renaissance in Italy: A History*, Kindle ed., Indianapolis, Ind.: Hackett Publishing Company, 2019, loc. 2246.

[52] Jacob Burkhardt, *The Civilization of the Renaissance in Italy*, New York: Start Publishing, 2013, p. 116.

[53] Burkhardt, 2013, p. 89.

[54] Burkhardt, 2013, pp. 171–173.

[55] Martines, 2013, loc. 4695–4699.

[56] Inalcik, 2001, loc. 210.

[57] Baer, 2021, pp. 165–187.

[58] Alice L. Conklin, *A Mission to Civilize: The Republican Idea of Empire in France and West Africa, 1895–1930*, Stanford, Calif.: Stanford University Press, 1997; Jennifer Pitts, "Introduction," in Alexis de Tocqueville, *Writings on Empire and Slavery*, Jennifer Pitts, ed. and trans., Baltimore, Md.: Johns Hopkins University Press, 2001; Douglas Porch, *The Conquest of the Sahara*, New York: Farrar, Straus and Giroux,

national élan vital, stemmed from various beliefs and impulses, from trade and economic ambitions, to French liberal ideologies, to pure power calculations.[59] The sense of French identity provided the fuel for regional and global ambitions, including an empire beginning in the 17th century. That empire, in turn, became an accepted and valorized reality that justified the country's sense of mission.[60]

Spain reflects a society with a sense of national mission during a very specific period. Its sense of exceptionalism and national mission became a potent fuel for conquest on the Iberian Peninsula and then for colonial adventures in the 15th and 16th centuries. Spain's own self-identity and national will were tied to religion, both the advancement of Catholic faith and the expulsion of Muslim power from the region. Spain's wider regional ambitions and religious sense of mission propelled it into distant wars—notably its quixotic effort to conquer the Netherlands—that had ruinous costs. It fought persistent wars for control of parts of Portugal, Italy, and France, and at one point famously sought to invade Britain. Habsburg Spain's national ambitions were mainly geopolitical in nature, but they were strongly associated with its period of national rise—and its subsequent overextension and collapse.

***

Some of our case studies reveal the other end of this spectrum—namely, countries with a weak sense of ambition and will and whose competitive position suffered for it. In the case of Austria-Hungary, it is true that there was significant economic activity within the empire and even urban areas with significant commercial classes. John Deak and other historians have written recent accounts cataloging the intense desire of several reformist leaders of the empire to modernize, industrialize, and try to match the social advances of their European competitors.[61] But our reading of the evidence suggests that it is fair to say that Austria-Hungary was simply not in the class of a France or Germany—and very far behind Britain—in terms of a coherent societal ambition and will fired by a widely embraced energizing myth and expressing itself in a drive for mastery, either internationally or, as a consistent social pattern, domestically.

Nor, over time, was the Soviet Union in this class—oddly so for a state whose very foundations rested on a claim of global ideological ambition. As the Cold War went on, the regime experienced a gradual corrosion of faith in communist ideology. People no longer believed in

---

2005; Alyssa Goldstein Sepinwall, *The Abbé Grégoire and the French Revolution: The Making of Modern Universalism*, Berkeley: University of California Press, 2005.

[59] Conklin, 1997; Pitts, 2001; Porch, 2005; Sepinwall, 2005; Michael Shurkin, "French Liberal Governance and the Emancipation of Algeria's Jews," *French Historical Studies*, Vol. 33, No. 2, 2010.

[60] Black, 1999.

[61] Deak, 2015.

the unifying myth of the state, and this drained energy and commitment from the society.[62] The dynamic sense of national ambition that had been present at the beginning and was so integral to the legitimacy of the system gave way to a growing despair and conviction that the system was bankrupt. We do not have truly accurate, measurable evidence for this—there were no reliable polls in that system, and polling data can vary significantly over relatively short periods. Nonetheless, there is elaborate qualitative and anecdotal evidence, both contemporaneous and later, that the Soviet Union underwent a sort of spiritual and ontological crisis starting in the 1970s, and for some people much earlier.

The Soviet case illustrates an important theme that crops up in several of the cases: National will begins to ebb when standards of living decline and a country is perceived to be failing to deliver on the promises of material advance. By the 1970s in the Soviet Union, gone was any widespread enthusiasm for communist ideology. Instead "frustrated consumerism, cynicism, and pleasure-seeking took its place," and any major efforts at improving conditions "quickly degenerated into . . . farce."[63] This case illustrates the ways in which ambition, will, and material progress exist in a mutually dependent relationship; positive or negative feedback loops can emerge among these factors. In the positive dynamic, ambition can help produce commercial vitality, innovation, and a work ethic that then generate growth and improved standards of living, which reinforce the rationale for the ambition. On the other side of a growth curve, long-term stagnation, especially if punctuated by repeated recessions and crises, can undermine the sense of national faith and energy, which in turn further impairs economic performance. Something like the latter dynamic was clearly evident in the Soviet case.

As much as any specific economic failure, this generalized loss of energy and faith, and the associated decline in support for truly ambitious domestic and global endeavors, therefore helps to explain the ultimate collapse of the Soviet Union. Whatever the material realities of the Soviet system, the associated spiritual crisis constituted the truly fatal blow to the society's collective will. That crisis, in the Soviet case as in many others, was accelerated by specific disasters and errors that lay bare the lies inherent in the system. In the Soviet case, the Chernobyl nuclear accident in 1986 was such an event.[64]

---

[62] Richard Sakwa, "The Soviet Collapse: Contradictions and Neo-Modernisation," *Journal of Eurasian Studies*, Vol. 4, No. 1, 2013, p. 67.

[63] Zubok, 2007, p. 277.

[64] Melvyn P. Leffler, *For the Soul of Mankind: The United States, the Soviet Union, and the Cold War*, New York: Hill and Wang, 2008, p. 390.

Tying National Ambition and Will to Competitive Outcomes: Other Evidence

It is challenging to identify anything like quantifiable evidence for this characteristic. We can find anecdotal descriptions of national ambition and will in many case studies, but the causal relationship between national will and competitiveness is necessarily imprecise. Just how much national ambition, domestic or foreign, is required for competitive success? Can other characteristics substitute for it? Must it take the same form in every case? Our research uncovered at least two empirical, causal connections where hints of this factor may be at work.

First, as suggested in the work of Joel Mokyr, David Landes, and others, an inherent societal drive to master the natural environment appears to be consistently tied to technological output, which in turn is a critical underpinning for competitive success.[65] The role of technology—a country's position in advanced industries (measured, for example, by proportion of global exports in those fields), its technological sophistication, its commitment to innovation and research and development—is central to competitive standing. One clear message of our survey of great power rivalries and rise and fall of civilizations is that mastering leading technologies, both civilian and military, is essential for competitive success.

Second, there is the empirical evidence, from the work of scholars focused on cultural values and national success, tying the associated characteristics of work ethic and a forward-looking time orientation to economic success. This evidence has been marshaled in part in the work of Lawrence Harrison and others who have done correlations between these social values and economic growth and development.[66]

Edmund Phelps has similarly tried to locate specific values associated with highly innovative economies. He emphasizes the critical role, in dynamic societies, of human agency, a drive for self-expression and mastery, and other forms of realizing human potential that are not unique to any one culture or nation but have become more characteristic of the modern era. Phelps counterposes these values with what he calls "traditional" values, such as unthinking respect for authority, which he believes retards innovation and progress: "In my account, attitudes and beliefs were the wellspring of the dynamism of the modern economies. It is mainly a culture protecting and inspiring individuality, imagination, understanding, and self-expression that drives a nation's indigenous innovation."[67] This sort of individualistic thirst for self-expression is part of the larger pattern of drive to influence and mastery characteristic of competitive societies.

---

[65] See, e.g., Mokyr, 2017; Landes, 1998.

[66] Harrison and Huntington, 2001. See also Lawrence Harrison, *Underdevelopment Is a State of Mind: The Latin American Case*, Lanham, Md.: Madison Books, 2000.

[67] Edmund S. Phelps, *Mass Flourishing: How Grassroots Innovation Created Jobs, Challenge, and Change*, Princeton, N.J.: Princeton University Press, 2013, p. x.

The Balance: Avoiding Overreach

This characteristic has one of the most obvious downside risks of any in our set: Excessive national will can easily produce overweening ambition and national overreach, which is one of the most common routes to national decline. Excessive ambition can also produce ecological devastation, as well as financial ruin, and it can destroy national values, such as sensible investment approaches and the need to conserve. National ambition and a desire for mastery must therefore be *balanced* against a pragmatic sense of limits and a constant capacity for self-reflection. This balance—between an urge to achieve and affect the world and a sense of limits, constraints, and prudence—is one of the most challenging for great powers to achieve. A sensible approach to this balance may be the single most important requirement for national competitive success, at least for great powers.

Overreach can also occur in areas other than military or geopolitical spheres. Japan's drive for industrial dominance—as with China's today—produced a backlash in the form of trade restrictions, competitive industrial policies, and other forms of reaction to perceived industrial imperialism.[68] In whatever form overreach takes, the general rule is clear: Excessive mastery seeking inevitably becomes competitively disadvantageous.

***

The dangers of military overreach formed the basis of Paul Kennedy's analysis of great power dynamics. If "too large a proportion of the state's resources is diverted from wealth creation and allocated instead to military purpose, then that is likely to lead to a weakening of national power over the longer term."[69] Overreach creates specific military and geopolitical vulnerabilities: Far-flung territories or interests can be harassed or attacked to distract or spread a state's resources thin. Overreach can also provoke negative alignment of major actors against a state. An example is how Austria-Hungary's participation in the Crimean War generated more-dangerous alignments of countries, including Russia.[70]

---

[68] One scholar discussing the concept of vitality in the Japanese case asked of Japan's hypercompetitive industrial policies, "are they provoking the very ends they seek to avoid? That is, is their expansion of market share so rapid that it triggers hostility and protectionist reactions to Japanese industry in other countries? Would it not be a greater sign of vitality to have a higher level of political consciousness on the part of major Japanese corporations which flood foreign markets with products, thereby inducing anti-Japanese political reactions?" (T. Murphy quoted in Clesse et al., 1997, p. 339).

[69] Kennedy, 1987, p. xvi.

[70] Mitchell, 2018, p. 273. Arnold Toynbee also stresses the risks of overextension. Few would quarrel, he asserts, with the idea that "geographical expansion, or 'painting the map red,' is no criterion whatever of the real growth of a civilization." Sometimes expansion is associated with a period of "qualitative progress," but even more often it "is a concomitant of real decline and coincides with a 'time of troubles' or a universal state—both of them stages of decline and disintegration." The reason, he argues, is that "times of trouble produce militarism, which is a perversion of the human spirit into channels of mutual destruction. . . . Geographical expansion is a by-product of this militarism." And militarism "has been by far the common-

History provides dozens of tragic examples of nations whose out-of-control ambition led them to overextend their power and produce backlash, war, destruction, and decline. Rome, for example, had "dreams of universal empire," but even Roman leaders were suspicious of these dreams and their implications. Eventually, the spread of the Roman Empire meant that "the demands on [leaders'] attention appeared limitless. Wars flared up everywhere." This drained finances but also demanded more-absolute forms of rule to govern the far-flung empire.[71]

A similar phenomenon cropped up in the Italian Renaissance city-states. Venice gradually sought to acquire large territories on the mainland of Italy in addition to its seafaring power. "It had also grown overly confident, indeed arrogant, in its dealings with other Italian and European states," writes Kenneth Bartlett. Eventually, the "aggressive, expansionist policies of the Venetians on the Italian mainland alienated their neighbors as well as committed the republic to constant and not always successful warfare. The cost was enormous and, as Doge [Giovanni] Mocenigo had prophesied, the wealth of both the state and its leading citizens decreased."[72]

Both the Spanish and Austrian Habsburg dynasties ultimately "simply had too much to do, too many enemies to fight, too many fronts to defend," in part because of the ambitions that had created such far-flung empires.[73] In Austria's case, this was partly a result of events beyond its choice—facing many surrounding enemies—but the Spanish Habsburgs certainly had ideological foundations for "one of the greatest examples of strategic over-stretch in history."[74] Austria-Hungary specifically went too far when it became seriously embroiled in Italy, which demanded "an ever-larger share of Habsburg attention while creating a stand-

---

est cause of the breakdowns of civilizations during the last four or five millennia" (Toynbee, 1947, p. 190). Later, he refers to the "suicidalness of militarism," related to three phases of overreach (which he defines in terms of three Greek words): the "psychological condition of being spoilt by success," the "consequent loss of mental and moral balance," and the eventual "blind headstrong ungovernable impulse which sweeps an unbalanced soul into attempting the impossible." He describes this combination as an "active psychological catastrophe in three acts," which was a common theme in classic Greek tragedy (Toynbee, 1947, pp. 336–337). One example was Sparta, which secured its neighborhood through "obstinate and repeated wars with neighboring peoples," which caused the city-state "to militarize Spartan life from top to bottom" (Toynbee, 1947, p. 4).

[71] Holland, 2005, pp. 370, 34, 154. Some Roman leaders would deeply regret such excesses, but it was at times as if Rome could not help itself—its essential national identity propelled it to such extremes. Yet it always convinced itself that it was under attack: "The Republic was never so dangerous as when it believed that its security was at stake. The Romans rarely went to war, not even against the most negligible foe, without somehow first convincing themselves that their preemptive strikes were defensive in nature" (Holland, 2005, p. 156).

[72] Bartlett, 2019, loc. 4538–4542, 4620.

[73] Kennedy, 1987, p. 48.

[74] Kennedy, 1987, p. 48.

ing source of crisis, virtually guaranteeing that a conflict facing Austria in any other theater would, unless effectively managed, quickly spread to a second front."[75]

The case of Japan in the 20th century shows how a generalized will to achieve and drive for honor can produce "a certain kind of animal vitality" that is destructive. There is no question of the potent sense of national will, ambition, and destiny that existed in Japan as of the Meiji era and ultimately expressed itself in both military and economic power seeking. These sentiments were held especially strongly in certain areas of Japanese society, notably the military. The resulting burst of imperialism in the 1930s, the distorted result of a gradual rise in nationalism and ambition that had begun before the turn of the century and took flight after the Russo-Japanese War and World War I, proved financially ruinous and provoked a decisive coalition to gather against it. In the 1930s, "Japan may have been characterized by vitality in the wrong direction, in terms of its domestic totalitarianism and aggression abroad." During this period, "Japan was a very vital country in terms of war-making."[76]

In the modern era, the Soviet Union stands as another paradigmatic case of a quasi-imperial power extending itself to the breaking point, in more than one way. Overly large military budgets and significant foreign adventures sapped the resource base of the society.[77] These were not solely responsible for the Soviet decline—the system was corrupt and moribund for structural reasons independent of its overextension. But that process put very specific burdens on the Soviet system that contributed to its failure. Moscow had creaking allies in Eastern Europe with substantial debt burdens and need for assistance, and its recurring political instability required expensive interventions. It was tempted into a rash of proxy wars and covert operations in the developing world, which added additional expense. The result was a crushing financial and policy-making burden by the 1980s.[78]

As the Soviet case implies, overreach is not merely a question of excessive spending, of a nation bankrupting itself on distant adventures. Long-term, large-scale efforts to protect power, whether in formal empires or other forms, also tend to reshape the societies of the adventurous nations.[79] Societies that become harnessed to endless global ambitions become distorted in ways that end up undermining their stability and dynamism. In the Ottoman

---

[75] Mitchell, 2018, p. 264.

[76] Ivan Hall quoted in Clesse et al., 1997, p. 313; A. Iriye quoted in Clesse et al., 1997, pp. 328–329. These quotes are from a 1992 conference about the "vitality of nations" organized by the Luxembourg Institute for European and International Studies in Tokyo and printed in the annex to Clesse et al., 1997. At a later conference on vitality, Christopher Coker noted that, in the 1930s, some in the West firmly believed that "[f]ascism produced a more vital society. After all, it traded in the vernacular of vitality, the will-to-power, the heroic in life, the need for sacrifice, including self-sacrifice." He described this as a form of "pathological vitality." Coker quoted in Clesse and Lounev, 2004, pp. 260, 305.

[77] Stephen Kotkin, *Armageddon Averted: The Soviet Collapse, 1970–2000*, Oxford, UK: Oxford University Press, 2008.

[78] Service, 2015, p. 6.

[79] Zubok, 2007, p. 228.

Empire, for example, as in many other cases, expansion empowered a military and elite class whose interests became associated with foreign adventures.

One factor that helps to determine a country's ability to balance ambition and overreach is the degree of adaptability, flexibility, and willingness to strategically retrench that characterizes national decisionmaking as it surmounts its peak power. The first essential component of such flexibility is to recognize that the country will not sustain the same degree of hegemony forever and begin to shed commitments and take other steps to sustain a kind of strategic solvency. This characterized elements of British diplomacy in the 19th and 20th centuries: Even amid the Suez Crisis and similar errors, British leaders managed to step back from some elements of their global role, including transferring some regional power to the emerging United States, in a way that sustained more relative power than it destroyed. Although it is not a societal characteristic per se, this sort of clever, self-aware strategic action obviously provides significant competitive advantage when it can be achieved.

***

Overreach abroad is a well-known problem. The role of such excessive ambition at home can be equally dangerous and is intimately connected to the same overblown view of national rights and potentials. A major issue is the focus of ambition in a society: Is it focused on productive ends (such as fame through magnificent cultural expression or scientific breakthroughs), or does it become nothing more than a grab for money or power?

The latter can occur in various ways. One is through the corruption of a country's elite class and its descent into rent seeking and manipulation of the state administration for personal gain. The general ambitions and competitive zeal of the elite can curdle into a blatant grab for power and wealth.

A second form of excessive domestic ambition can be a more wide-ranging obsession with wealth and conspicuous consumption on the part of a population. Social ambition can become directed toward showing off one's wealth rather than meaningful achievement that drives society forward. This was the pattern in the later Italian Renaissance, as Lauro Martines observes:

> The gradual change in the outlook and economic underpinnings of the Venetian nobility was accompanied by the growth of conspicuous spending. Thrift came to appear mean and dishonorable, unworthy of gentlemen—which is why, in the sixteenth century's mythology of class, to inherit wealth became one of the fundamental marks of nobility. Patricians made their houses larger and showier, the rooms spacious and more ornate. Families took on larger teams of servants. There was a pullulation of magnificent country villas: eighty-five at least built in the fifteenth century and more than 250 in the century following. And in the generation preceding, noblemen had developed a craze for portraits of self, family, and forebears.[80]

---

[80] Martines, 2013, loc. 3726–3732.

Ambition within a state can also go off the rails by ignoring externalities to the pursuit of wealth or power. A leading example, both modern and ancient—as Jared Diamond, Ian Morris, and others argue—is environmental degradation. Ambition to build, acquire, and control can produce environmental blowback every bit as dangerous as geopolitical reactions. This has been true in some historical cases and may be occurring again today.

***

Great societies in their most powerful and competitively effective moments have been driven in part by a potent will to exercise power and influence—a determination to comprehend and shape the natural world and associated societal values, such as a strong work ethic. The dynamism of highly competitive nations flows almost universally from some degree of this characteristic, stemming from an energizing myth that wraps national ambitions in a justifying narrative. This characteristic provides competitive advantage in several ways, most notably by underwriting national efforts and investments essential to competitive success.

This finding emerges consistently from our cases and broader research—even in the face of the unavoidable fact that this characteristic is abstract and difficult to define and will take different forms in different countries at different times. It has both international and domestic aspects. It cannot be measured in any overarching way.

Despite these uncertainties, our historical case studies speak in a unified voice about the importance of national ambition and will. Countries that compete effectively almost always do so under the influence of some combination of both internal and external societal ambitions, ones that energize scientific and economic progress and international activism. National dynamism in our broad sense is almost always correlated with such ambition.

But equally important is our parallel finding: Major powers lose competitive standing, and sometimes immolate themselves in strategic terms, when they allow this characteristic to run out of control, in either its international or its domestic forms. Overreach and overextension, excessive national hubris, and extreme ambition among specific actors in society are all strongly correlated with national decline and defeat. Exercising national will with the proper constraints, and keeping ambitions adequately in check, is the requirement for competitive success.

CHAPTER FOUR

Unified National Identity

Nations gain competitive advantage when their collective identity—the sense of a shared history, societal unity, and pride in a set of national values—is coherent and vibrant. National strength is sabotaged when identity is weak or fragmented. The precise degree of required unity varied from case to case in our research; there is no single threshold above which a nation has enough or below which it is vulnerable. Nonetheless, our research strongly suggests that countries have clearly benefited from high levels of coherent identity and suffered from its absence.

One of our historical cases nicely illustrates this point. Modern Japan has undergone two major leaps in competitive position, one broadly geopolitical and one broadly economic. The first was its rapid modernization and industrialization spurred by the Meiji Restoration; Japan's advancing industrial strength and military prowess, among other things, underwrote its success in the Russo-Japanese War of 1904–1905. The second competitive advance was Japan's rise as a global economic superpower in the aftermath and recovery from World War II. From 1950 to 2019, Japan's real GDP ballooned from $272 billion to over $5 trillion;[1] for a time, many expected Japan to surpass the United States in economic standing.

In each of those competitive surges, the unity and coherence of the Japanese nation appears to have been an important contributing factor in its rise. Japan's centralized and common sense of national identity took some time to cohere,[2] but when it did, a strong ethnic, linguistic, and historical set of linkages generated a strong basis for collective action. Partly this was an instrumental project, for competitive purposes: Japan's elites perceived a need to knit together a more unified nation out of the hundreds of semiautonomous local authorities. Mark Ravina notes that the result was that "a core principle of the new nation-state" must necessarily be "the unity of the Japanese people."[3] The resulting ability of Japanese governments and regimes to appeal to a resulting sense of community, and the willingness of Japanese citizens to sacrifice, work, and invest in actions designed to advance their nation, has

---

[1] Federal Reserve Bank of St. Louis, "Real GDP at Constant National Prices for Japan," updated November 8, 2021.

[2] Marius Jansen, for example, concludes that, in Tokugawa Japan, a "new civic religion bound society together in patterns of values and belief; a nation was emerging from the groupings of earlier days" (Jansen, 2000, loc. 2853).

[3] Ravina, 2017, p. 183.

been a significant competitive advantage. The sense of a collective identity enhanced domestic peace and stability and fostered patriotic commitment.

The role of national identity in this case was hardly simple or linear. Some scholars note that Japan has at times struggled to define a shared and coherent national project.[4] Indeed, the search for identity, the struggle to define a specific Japanese version, has been a major theme of modern Japan. Others have described the complexities of the modern Japanese encounter with nationalism. Kenneth Pyle notes that the country's sense of itself in the postwar era has been paradoxical and conflicted—at once self-confident and strictly self-effacing, economically aggressive, and diplomatically quiescent.[5] Kevin Doak stresses the tensions between commitment to an ethnically defined nation and a rationally organized state and shows how these twin forms of national identification generate tensions in Japanese self-conception.[6] The debate about Japan as a "normal nation," and the conflicted forms of national identity attached to that debate, indicates that the character of Japan's national identity remains far from settled.[7] Some modern surveys suggest that measures of modern patriotism are relatively low in Japan.[8]

Still, some of Japan's periods of national competitive advance, including the Meiji rush to modernize, were unmistakably grounded in a sense of national will and pride tied to an emerging identity.[9] In the modern world, sources of economic growth in Japan grew out of "the strong desire on the part of the Japanese people to catch up with the West and not be swallowed by the West," one Korean scholar concludes, a "drive to recover from defeat and

---

[4] Dharitri Chakravartty Narzary, "The Myths of Japanese 'Homogeneity,'" *China Report*, Vol. 40, No. 3, 2014. The management theorist Peter Drucker, who knew the country well and whose ideas influenced its business sector, explained in 1981 that the Japanese saw Western visions of a unified Japanese monolith as "a joke, and not a very funny one. They see only cracks and not, as the foreigner does, a monolith. What they experience in their daily lives are tensions, pressures, conflicts, and not unity. They see intense, if not cutthroat, competition both among the major banks and among the major industrial groups," as well as the "bitter factional infighting that characterizes their institutions: the unremitting guerilla warfare that each ministry wages against all other ministries and the factional bickering that animates the political parties, the Cabinet, the universities, and individual businesses" (Peter F. Drucker, "Behind Japan's Success," *Harvard Business Review*, January 1981).

[5] Pyle, 1982.

[6] Kevin M. Doak, "What Is a Nation and Who Belongs? National Narratives and the Ethnic Imagination in Twentieth-Century Japan," *American Historical Review*, Vol. 102, No. 2, April 1997. The Meiji Restoration did not inaugurate a new era of "national solidarity," he contends, but rather generated a "destabilizing disjuncture" grounded in a "tension between the state and the people" (p. 287).

[7] Zack Beauchamp, "Japan Is Weakening Its Constitutional Commitment to Pacifism," *Vox*, July 1, 2014.

[8] Brad Glosserman and Scott A. Snyder, *The Japan–South Korea Identity Clash: East Asian Security and the United States*, New York: Columbia University Press, 2017, p. 31.

[9] Tadashi Anno, "National Identity and Democracy: Lessons from the Case of Japan," *Asan Forum*, December 20, 2018. See also Eiko Ikegami, "Citizenship and National Identity in Early Meiji Japan, 1868–1889: A Comparative Assessment," *International Review of Social History*, Vol. 40, 1995; Gilbert Rozman, *East Asian National Identities: Common Roots and Chinese Exceptionalism*, Palo Alto, Calif.: Stanford University Press, 2012, Ch. 1.

restore their respectability in the eyes of the world."[10] The hardworking "salaryman" in Japanese industry saw himself toiling for the advancement of the nation. In recent years, survey evidence confirms the presence of a significant degree of national identity and pride. Japan's emergent sense of collective identity became enmeshed with its democratic principles, ultimately strengthening both.[11]

Carol Gluck's study of ideology in the late Meiji era lays out a fascinating and complex portrait of a more unified national identity under construction. Gluck makes clear that the 1930s and 1940s version of national identity, the quasi-religious faith in a superior race—a "society mobilized by its mythology in service to the national cause"—was unique to a particular time and not characteristic of the nation's recent history.[12] It had taken time to advance to that level of white-hot identity politics and had been much more qualified and contested during earlier periods. She carefully lays out the various interest groups in Japanese society that promulgated somewhat different versions of identity and contended with one another to define the national myth.

And yet Gluck's account still paints a portrait of a case in which a unifying identity, rooted in ethnic, historical, and linguistic foundations and strongly promoted by Meiji-era regimes, helped create what she refers to as "a sense of nation" and in the process made a difference in national development and, it would seem, competitive power.[13] After the Meiji Restoration of 1868, she writes, "Japanese leaders expressed their sense that institutions alone were insufficient to secure the nation." Japan's leaders feared that, on the verge of modernity, "in some profound and threatening way Japan was not yet prepared for the task that was upon it." To be a successful nation-state in the competitive swirl of a modern international system demanded a degree of unified effort. Generating a national identity with the capacity to unify and motivate the people therefore became a major project of successive governments. The result was a focus on "[n]ational spirit, national thought, national doctrine, national essence, nationality" and a legacy in which a "sense of nation of being Japanese," was imbued into the whole country.[14]

The Japanese case shows the importance of distinguishing among different forms of national identity. Especially in the postwar period, it may be misleading to look for evidence of garden variety "patriotism" in a country where excessive nationalistic affiliation had become almost a social taboo. But significant evidence suggests that the modern Japanese nation has clearly reflected a sense of collective membership, community, and national

---

[10] K. Kim quoted in Clesse et al., 1997, p. 333.

[11] Anno, 2018.

[12] Gluck, 1985, pp. 4–6.

[13] Gluck, 1985, pp. 21, 262–264.

[14] Gluck, 1985, pp. 3, 23, 286.

allegiance.[15] Other survey and research evidence suggests that many Japanese people have a strongly held sense of specific national traditions and values that set them apart from other nations and deserve protection, so much so that a generalized veneration of tradition can at times obstruct needed reform. As two scholars have put it, in the postwar era, "Japanese are proud of their country and their culture, but that pride does not equate with nationalism or chauvinism. Rather, it is a sense of belonging to a distinct group."[16] That sense of belonging, though, is very real and has inspired fierce efforts on behalf of the nation.

The Japanese case study thus hints at the claim embodied in this characteristic: Nations with a stronger sense of identity and societal coherence have a competitive advantage over nations with a more fragmented sense of self or without much allegiance to any sort of unified nationhood. Our case studies are brimming with examples that suggest as much. As with all our characteristics, we must accept the limitations of working with abstract and qualitative concepts: There is no way to put a precise value on the degree of national identity present in any nation at a given time. But there are indicators that hint at its level, and objective measures of national unity, as well as other ways to at least make broad and qualitative conclusions.

Like other nominated characteristics, this one comes with a clear downside risk: When unified identity hardens into a crushing and constraining orthodoxy, one that can become the basis for dictatorship, exclusion, and ideological restrictions, it flips from being a competitive advantage to being among the most profound drags on competitive dynamism we discovered. This emerges in the Japanese case as in many others: It shows the dangers of ways in which a formal campaign, or even an organic process, to develop national identity can congeal and become stifling, a classic conformist nationalism of loyalty and collective identity.[17]

In a sense, our proposed characteristic of completive diversity and pluralism (discussed in Chapter Nine) stands in tension with the characteristic of unified national identity. The two can be productively balanced, as the United States, for example, has shown. But when a rigid and tradition-bound form of national identification quashes pluralism of ideas and initiatives, it can become a strategic handicap rather than benefit.

---

[15] A recent study of national identity in five countries finds moderate levels of coherent national identity in Japan and posits that Japanese national identity showed "the importance of national heritage and cultural homogeneity, and the rather weak influence of belief system and consumer ethnocentrism" (Bruce D. Keillor and G. Tomas M. Hult, "A Five-Country Study of National Identity," *International Marketing Review*, Vol. 16, No. 1, 1999, p. 77). Another survey study of national pride in achievement in various areas—sports, arts and culture, economic development—finds that Japanese people have strong levels of national pride, equal, or nearly so, to levels in the United States and other advanced industrial democracies, in these areas (M. D. R. Evans and Jonathan Kelly, "National Pride in the Developed World: Survey Data from 24 Nations," *International Journal of Public Opinion Research*, Vol. 14, No. 3, 2002).

[16] Glosserman and Snyder, 2017, p. 52; see also pp. 35–36.

[17] Gluck, 1985, pp. 275–278.

Defining the Characteristic

Our research suggests at least two ways of conceptualizing and measuring unified national identity. One embodies a mixture of demographic, political, and sociological aspects. Is a nation relatively homogenous in terms of membership groups—national, ethnic, religious, linguistic, and otherwise? Or is it split among many contending populations with significantly divergent self-identities and interests? The second way of conceptualizing unity is ideational: Do the people of a nation share the same basic values? Are there well-established narratives of the nation, and do its citizens generally appreciate and endorse them? Do they feel themselves to be members of a community of shared values and identity?

The true essence of this characteristic cannot be measured in purely demographic terms. A coherent national identity can be based partly on a homogenous population, but much more important is what Peter Turchin, following the 14th-century Arab philosopher and scholar Ibn Khaldun, has referred to as *asabiya*—the sense of solidarity or fellow feeling, an intrinsic sense of unity, the social bonds that exist within a society (including nations but not limited to that level of governance). Turchin argues that rationalistic theories cannot adequately explain large-scale social cooperation. A more essential kind of solidarity, he believes, is necessary for nations to cohere and achieve.[18] Following Khaldun, he defines *asabiya* as a form of "group feeling" or solidarity, willingness and urge to collaborate with one's fellow group members. It exists in different ways and to different degrees in various groups within a society, but political communities, such as nations, also have overall degrees of the quality. It reinforces competitive dynamism, enhancing (here Turchin is quoting Khaldun) "the ability to defend oneself, to offer opposition, to protect oneself, and to press one's claims." As Turchin summarizes, "preponderance and *asabiya* renders one group superior to others."[19]

In some ways this concept has much in common with the degree of nationalism in a country—the level of commitment of a people to their nation, the sense that they owe duties and obligations to the national community and judge their own identity and satisfaction by

---

[18] Turchin, 2003, pp. 30–32.

[19] Turchin, 2003, p. 38. One interesting aspect of *asabiya* in Khaldun's theory is its relationship to the elite of a society. He argues that the rulers of any community "must be vested in a family or lineage that has the strongest and most natural claim to the control of the available *asabiyas*" (Turchin, 2003, p. 38). In a modern sense, in which power comes not from feudal lineages, one might say that leaders need to reflect the qualities or symbols associated with a nation's *asabiya*: In the United States, these could include status as a self-made person, middle-class roots, service in the military, or other qualities closely tied to national self-image. But Khaldun also notes that an elite group can have a degree of *asabiya* sufficient to power a people forward, even if it is not widely shared through the whole population. Khaldun also believes that wealth tends to degrade *asabiya* over time (Turchin, 2003, p. 39). Partly this is because of battles among elites for control of wealth, but one also gets the sense that—because it is struggle and hardship that provides the forge of *asabiya*—as societies gain excess wealth and leisure and begin to focus on luxury, the impulse for a competitive solidarity could be expected to fade. This is certainly a pattern which that emerges in many of the cases—a degree of self-satisfaction and focus on luxury and leisure that enfeebles the competitive drive of a people.

its standing.[20] The existence of a degree of *conceptual nationalism*, however, is not the same thing as *national unity*. A society could value many kinds of identity beyond the national one and still boast a strong and coherent national identification that contributes to competitive success.

Given these nuances, even using the twin measuring sticks proposed above and the literature on nationalism as a foundation, the existence of a firm national identity is not always a straightforward thing to assess.[21] In the mid-1990s, a Russian academic study of national identity discovered more than 400 themes and subthemes related to Russian identity—yet Russian governments have appealed to a singular national identity as a source of national strength, and the allegiance of Russians to a national identity appears in many ways to be immensely strong.[22] Russian national commitment was in abundant evidence during World War II, when millions of Russians—even many opponents of the Stalinist regime then in power—leaped at the chance to sacrifice everything for "Mother Russia." As we saw earlier, Japanese identity remains a highly debated and problematic subject despite the existence of seemingly very high degrees of homogeneity and a certain set of shared values and ideas.

A related factor that will almost always be closely associated with a strong and coherent national identity, its political cousin, is a degree of robust and strongly felt citizenship. In the histories of highly competitive nations, there are repeated references to this theme: People think of themselves as citizens of a valued collective body rather than as mere occupants of a territorial area or subjects of an abstract authority.

The strength of national identity is also related to a nation's experience in war, especially wars that pose existential threats to a people.[23] When a nation wins a conflict in which its very survival appears to be at stake, the legend and eventually myth of that conflict can become a potent fuel for national identity. America's self-conception is rooted in its success in the Revolutionary War; the Soviet Union used its victory in what it called the Great Patriotic War as a source of legitimacy for decades. A people can be bound together by a shared experience of

---

[20] See Anthony D. Smith, *Nationalism: Theory, Ideology, History*, 2nd ed., London: Polity, 2010. A typical baseline definition contends that nationalist programs are those that hold that the nation and the state are equivalent. More generally, a common understanding of nationalism, for example, involves "the attitude that the members of a nation have when they care about their national identity, and the actions that the members of a nation take when seeking to achieve (or sustain) self-determination" (Stanford Encyclopedia of Philosophy, "Nationalism," revised September 2, 2020). As another scholar puts it, "All nationalisms, therefore, share two features: (1) they define, at least roughly, the territorial boundaries that the nation has a right to control and (2) they define the membership boundaries of the population that makes up the nation—the group that deserves this territorial control and that is entitled to the supreme loyalty of other members of the collective." Part of this definition then does refer to an "emphasis on a unified national identity" (Lowell W. Barrington, "'Nation' and 'Nationalism': The Misuse of Key Concepts in Political Science," *PS: Political Science and Politics*, Vol. 30, No. 4, 1997, p. 713).

[21] René Grotenhuis, "Nation-Building: Identity and Identification, Process and Content," in *Nation-Building as Necessary Effort in Fragile States*, Amsterdam: Amsterdam University Press, 2016.

[22] A. Kara-Murza quoted in Clesse and Lounev, 2004, p. 214.

[23] We are grateful to William Anthony Hay for this suggestion.

common vulnerability and risk; cleverly employed, such an experience can resonate for generations. That bonding effect can be threatened in a number of ways: when the memory of the existential conflict fades, when its legacy is clouded by revisionist histories that undermine its mythology, or when the nation is drawn into new, much less critical and unifying wars that introduce fissures into the role of self-defense in national identity.

Defining *unified national identity*, then, is both straightforward and complex. In one basic and intuitive sense, it is a simple concept: To what degree does a nation represent a demographically, sociologically, and ideationally unified group; to what extent do the people of the nation see themselves as part of a coherent community guided by shared beliefs and values; and to what degree are they willing to sacrifice and labor on its behalf? What this means in practice, though, can vary, from one period or country to another.

The Theoretical Case for the Competitive Value of National Identity

Unified national identity could theoretically improve a nation's competitive vitality in several ways. It could inspire citizens to work and sacrifice in the name of the country—a pattern that many of our cases appear to reflect. It could reduce the potential for large-scale domestic instability. And it could provide a nation with a more well-defined cultural and societal model that others might respect and emulate. As the writer Tom McTague put it in 2022, describing the risks to Britain's coherent identity, a nation's "the imaginative sense of who we are" as a people is a critical foundation for competitive advantage. "States that have forgotten who they are tend not to last long," he adds, and continues:

> It seems to me that if Britain is to survive, It has to believe that there is such a thing as Britain and act as though that is the case. Joseph Roth wrote that the old Austro-Hungarian monarchy died "not through the empty verbiage of its revolutionaries, but through the ironical disbelief of those who should have believed in, and supported, it." In time, we might well say the same of Britain.[24]

It would be natural to assume that vibrant, dynamic nations will reflect a sense of self-worth and value that generally requires some degree of shared identity—and that this in turn can translate into optimism and a future orientation.[25] Unified national identity might also engender competitively valuable social norms, such as discipline, industriousness, and hard work. It is this theoretical expectation that has led political leaders and writers to celebrate the role of national identity. Fyodor Dostoevsky, to take one example, made the case that Russia

---

[24] Tom McTague, "How Britain Falls Apart," *The Atlantic*, January 5, 2022.

[25] See the comments of Christopher Coker in Clesse and Lounev, 2004, p. 261.

required a uniquely Russian sense of spirituality to be "a vital society as France and Britain were," a sense of spirituality connected to uniquely "Russian concepts and Russian history."[26]

Much of the literature on nationalism, especially in its modern varieties (and some see those as the only true forms of nationalism as a concept), assumes or suggests that constructing powerful national identities was critical to national strength. Scholars have suggested various reasons why potent nationalism ought to enhance state effectiveness—for example, by providing legitimacy and underwriting state authority, especially at significant distances from the central government.[27] Many major powers have "deliberately and actively homogenized their populations in order to obtain populations with a common national identity and culture"[28]—presumably out of a belief that it would enhance their power.

Countries with a stronger coherent national identity may also find it easier to enforce laws and thus produce stronger rule of law and adherence to norms, even at the level of such mundane but critical social transactions as contract enforcement. Higher levels of trust in societies ought to be associated with better economic performance. A strong national identity and sense of shared national community and fate, in turn, ought to create the conditions for high levels of trust. Institutions work better in such contexts: Transaction costs are reduced, and fears of domestic instability and lawlessness decline.

Finally, powerful national identity may provide countries with the willpower and commitment to better translate their resources and potential into actual national power. People who consider themselves citizens of an entity to which they owe allegiance and devotion will much more readily offer labor and loyalty to a nation. This translation capacity—as Ashley Tellis puts it, the issue of "national performance . . . accounts for variance in converting raw materials into physical and social products"—has major influence on levels of national power.[29]

Collective Identity and Competitive Outcomes: Evidence from Cases

Evidence for the competitive value of unified national identity emerges in a wide range of historical examples. Two leading cases—which illustrate two different ends of the spectrum— are Rome and Austria-Hungary.

---

[26] Clesse and Lounev, 2004, pp. 223–224.

[27] Jeffrey Herbst, *States and Power in Africa*, Princeton, N.J.: Princeton University Press, 2000, p. 126.

[28] Pelle Ahlerup and Gustav Hansson, "Nationalism and Government Effectiveness," *Journal of Comparative Economics*, Vol. 39, No. 3, 2011, p. 434.

[29] Ashley J. Tellis, "Assessing National Power in Asia," in Ashley J. Tellis, ed., *Foundations of National Power in the Asia-Pacific*, Washington, D.C.: National Bureau of Asian Research, 2015.

Rome and National Identity

Many historical sources suggest that Rome's strength—at least in our focus period of the late republic to the early empire—was grounded to some degree on a vibrant sense of shared identity and active citizenship, as well as a commitment to hard work that these values inspired. The idea of Rome, and the spiritual but also very practical implications of holding a Roman identity, had potent collective value during republican and early imperial times. It was arguably when such shared commitments gave way to looser civic allegiance—being bought off by bread and circuses—that the long, slow decline of Roman power began.

The Roman case highlights the importance of the role of deeply felt citizenship as part of the larger characteristic of national identity. Aspects of citizenship, such as voting rights, were not equally shared in all periods of Roman history, and the aristocratic society created barriers based on wealth and landholdings. However, in broad terms Romans—more so than most ancient societies—counted themselves as *citizens*, a membership title with almost religious overtones. Citizens were bound to a clear identity group and owed allegiance to each other and their city.

This identity group expanded over time as Rome granted citizenship to increasing numbers of incorporated and conquered peoples. It was not, eventually, a powerfully ethnic identity.[30] But the idea of Rome as an actor, and being Roman as an identity, continued to have a clear meaning. They called it "Romanitas," an idea of "Romanness" that implied a set of values and beliefs that distinguished Romans from others. Roman identity was expressed in formal citizenship and such associated ideas as blood (the basic way in which citizenship was passed down was through parentage), language,[31] clothing,[32] and other markers of membership.[33] The idea of a strong identity was obvious to Romans: Although they proved remarkably willing to absorb peoples of many ethnic, religious, and even racial identities, Romans drew a sharp line between themselves and others—the "barbarians" of the outside world.

Roman identity illustrates the competitive value of this characteristic not just internally, creating stronger bonds and a sense of commitment among a people, but also externally. Roman identity was one of the greatest sources of soft power influence in history: The clear identification it implied with a dominant power, the specific values and beliefs, the offer of shared citizenship, and the extension of an economic order of common currencies, weights,

---

[30] Erich S. Gruen, "Did Romans Have an Ethnic Identity?" *Antichthon*, Vol. 47, 2013; Erich S. Gruen, *Culture and National Identity in Republican Rome*, Ithaca, N.Y.: Cornell University Press, 1995.

[31] J. Adams, "Romanitas and the Latin Language," *Classical Quarterly*, Vol. 53, No. 1, May 2003.

[32] Ursula Rothe, *The Toga and Roman Identity*, New York: Bloomsbury, 2019.

[33] Ralph W. Mathisen, "'Roman' Identity in Late Antiquity, with Special Attention to Gaul," in Walter Pohl, Clemens Gantner, Cinzia Grifoni, and Marianne Pollheimer-Mohaupt, eds., *Transformations of Romanness: Early Medieval Regions and Identities*, Berlin, Boston: De Gruyter, 2018, pp. 255–274; Emma Dench, "Roman Identity," in Alessandro Barchiesi and Walter Scheidel, eds., *The Oxford Handbook of Roman Studies*, online ed., New York: Oxford University Press, 2012.

measures, and law.[34] National distinctiveness was expressed in the construction of thousands of cities according to strict Roman design principles and the building of awe-inspiring works of infrastructure. All of this attached to Roman identity. Tom Holland argues that part of Caesar Augustus's genius was to rekindle the sense of commitment and citizenship that had made Rome great. "The new era could be cast," Holland suggests, "as a moral challenge of the kind that the Romans had so often faced—and risen to triumphantly—in the past."[35] Augustus "summoned his countrymen to share with him the heroic task of revitalizing the Republic. He encouraged them, in short, to feel like citizens again." He sought

> to renew the rugged virtues of the ancient peasantry, to bring the Republic back to basics. It struck a deep chord, for this was the raw stuff of Roman myth: nostalgia for a venerated past, yes, but simultaneously a spirit harsh and unsentimental, the same that had forged generations of steel-hard citizens and carried the Republic's standards to the limits of the world.[36]

Rome thus illustrates one positive effect of strong and coherent national identity—it can encourage a sort of self-sacrificing, committed citizenship, a belief that the nation is a community with a common fate. When that fragments, a nation can suffer significant competitive costs.

This is especially true when the sense of common fate and national commitment ebbs among a country's elite classes. One subsidiary theme that emerges from many of our case studies, to which we will return later in the chapter, is the critical role of a public-spirited elite, a theme abundantly apparent throughout the Roman case but also many others. Many nations at their peak of competitive power benefit from elites who manifest a strong commitment to the common good, restraint in self-enrichment, and careful and thoughtful judgment on behalf of the nation. From the Renaissance exemplar of Cosimo de' Medici to the best examples of British aristocracy, with a sense of obligation to the common good, to the mid-20th-century American business elites, who viewed themselves as integral members of shared communities, the role of a public-spirited elite emerges again and again as a critical support system for a unified national identity. And a trend that was just as common in our case studies was the decay of altruistic habits among these elites into hoarding of wealth power and rent seeking.

---

[34] Janet Huskinson, ed., *Experiencing Rome: Culture, Identity and Power in the Roman Empire*, New York: Routledge, 1999; Martin Pitts and Miguel John Versluys, eds., *Globalisation and the Roman World: World History, Connectivity and Material Culture*, Cambridge, UK: Cambridge University Press, 2014.

[35] Holland, 2005, pp. 381–382.

[36] Holland, 2005, pp. 381–382.

The Risks of a Fractured Identity: Austria-Hungary

On the other side of the scale, the fate of Austria-Hungary offers a stark lesson about the competitive handicap that can arise when a nation lacks a truly unified and coherent sense of group identity and motivating purpose.[37] Without a unified identity, a state needs to impose cultural hegemony over its citizens—at much greater cost and with risk of blowback. This case suggests that any state must be "capable of inspiring an emotional attachment among its peoples by encouraging them to link their individual or group interests" to state interests.[38] The absence of such a collective commitment is a major competitive drag.

Modern scholars such as John Deak and Pieter Judson have done critical work to challenge the long-held view of the Austro-Hungarian Empire as a brittle and incoherent entity destined to collapse. Austria-Hungary included important pockets of national identity, for example, as when military officers retained strong national affiliations while pledging fealty to the emperor.[39] Austria-Hungary inspired sufficient identity for generations of national leaders to struggle mightily to maintain the empire and for successive armies to march off to war in defense of the realm. It stayed viable during four years of a tremendously destructive war and eventually brought a total of 8 million soldiers to arms in defense of the realm.[40] Absent the immense shock of World War I, it is not inconceivable that this structure could have held together—at least for further decades, if not longer.

And yet the Austro-Hungarian case still contrasts significantly with the Roman one and illustrates the competitive handicap that can emerge with a qualified and ebbing sense of unified national identity. Some in Austria-Hungary made the comparison quite directly at the time. Judson quotes a late 18th-century Austrian jurist and novelist who described the importance of citizenship in classical city-states: "The Greek or Roman father did not merely bring up a son for the family; he brought up a citizen for the Republic. The young man was quickly made aware of the advantages it conferred, learning to perceive in it a perfection wanting in other states, and was naturally moved by such perfection."[41] The point, by implication, was that Austria-Hungary lacked this degree of shared identity.

Politically and socially, the Austro-Hungarian Empire was in many ways constructed on the foundation of a fragmented identity. As Joel Mokyr puts it,

> Culturally and religiously the central European nations had always regarded themselves as part of the West, but politically the Habsburgs had more in common with the Romanovs and the Hohenzollerns than with the emerging Western democracies. Until

---

[37] The Ottoman Empire offers similar lessons that we will investigate: "the Turks could never create an Ottoman identity that commanded the loyalty of their diverse subjects" (Landes, 1998, p. 399).

[38] Pieter M. Judson, *The Habsburg Empire: A New History*, Cambridge, Mass.: Harvard University Press, 2016, p. 5.

[39] We are grateful to Pieter Judson for this insight.

[40] Deak, 2015, p. 273.

[41] Judson, 2016, p. 16.

the end the Habsburg Monarchy maneuvered awkwardly between Western notions of individual freedom and Eastern notions of autocracy.[42]

Coordination between Budapest and Vienna was not always good, and expressions of Hungarian nationalism, even if constrained within the larger empire, created a constant tension. Such disunions might not on their own have been enough to collapse the empire absent a war, though eventually nationalist fuses would probably have been lit by some combination of events.

Austro-Hungarian leaders were not ignorant of the risks associated with a lack of national unity. A series of reforms tried to bolster national identity by redefining "subjects as citizens—that is, as individual men and women with common legal rights and obligations anchored in their unmediated relationship to a central state."[43] Recent scholarship has stressed that it is wrong to characterize Austria-Hungary as an utterly incoherent mass; there was a sense of collective membership, as well as some degree of coordination, if imperfect, between the two major components of the system.

Yet these reform efforts were at best a partial success. Because of its many overlapping ethnic, national, religious, and political entities, the empire essentially forced on its citizens a constant burden of identity navigation.[44] Yes, there was room for a Habsburg self-conception at the top of the heap, but this still left the empire well short of several of its rivals in terms of a coherent and shared identity that could fuel competitive position. And those rivals could (and did) play on the complexities of Austro-Hungarian identity by fomenting attachment to competing identities, to create a centrifugal pressure within the empire. The collapse of the empire might not have come to fruition without the hammer blow of World War I, but it certainly did not help.

John Deak's superb account of Austro-Hungarian nation building nicely illustrates this fundamental tension.[45] He stresses the significance of rising state administrative capacities and the urgent efforts by successive regimes to improve unified governance and identity. But his history also shows that the repeated competitive challenges imposed on the society challenged its coherence. Ultimately, the competing identities in the empire could not be sufficiently reconciled to sustain it.

Other Cases: Identity and National Power

Many other historical cases also affirmed the connection between a coherent national identity and competitive advantage. Table 4.1 summarizes some of the essential evidence from

---

[42] Joel Mokyr, "And Thou, Happy Austria? A Review Essay," *Journal of Economic History*, Vol. 44, No. 4, December 1984, p. 1099.

[43] Judson, 2016, p. 51.

[44] We are grateful to John Deak for this insight.

[45] Deak, 2015.

TABLE 4.1

Unified National Identity and Competitive Advantage—Evidence from Cases

Case	Elements of the Role of Unified National Identity in Historical Cases
Rome	• Clear theme of citizenship and service to the state in Roman history • Demographically fairly unified in early phases and eventually quite diverse • Specific forms of Roman governance and civic life exported to areas absorbed into the empire; clear sense of what it meant to be a Roman town or region
China	• Coherent, unified national identity took time to emerge but became vibrant by modern era • Demographically and socially coherent and unified
Spain	• Evidence mixed; early periods of somewhat fragmented regional identity surmounted by some degree of national identity but unclear whether strong enough to provide competitive advantage
Austria-Hungary	• National and ethnic fragmentation generated competitive disadvantage • Evidence of lack of coordination of national policies • Incomplete commitment to the polity • Internal frictions and clashes that drained resources
Ottoman Empire	• Evidence mixed; despite diversity of empire, historical evidence for a widely shared sense of Ottoman-ness, yet the empire was still less coherent in identity and allegiance than some competitors
Renaissance Italy	• Strong sense of membership and identity within city-states • State identity used to rally public efforts and commitment • Commitment of public-spirited elite to city-state competitiveness
Britain	• Coherent, strong, loyalty-generating British identity emerged by 18th century • Specific evidence includes levels of national pride and patriotism, willingness to sacrifice for nation
Sweden	• Demographically and socially homogenous and relatively unified in periods before major national expression of power • Still, evidence somewhat mixed
France	• In modern era, strong sense of national identity provided basis for accumulating and projecting power, especially in postrevolutionary period
Japan	• Demographically homogenous and sense of strong group membership • Clear evidence of competitive advantage from appeals to national identity • Wartime evidence of the rallying effect of coherent national identity
Soviet Union	• Demographically and nationally diverse and increasingly fragmented over time • A created entity that never enjoyed the same degree of unified identity or citizen commitment as component republics
United States	• From fairly quickly in national history, strong sense of coherent identity and concept of meaningful citizenship • Demographically, ethnically, and racially increasingly diverse over time, but civic nationalism provided ideational links

each of the cases. As with all our characteristics, the relationship is not simple, linear, or consistent within each of the cases. The degree of coherent national identity waxed and waned in every nation. But most of them provide at least anecdotal evidence that high degrees of coherent identity are correlated with periods of competitive success and/or specific national strengths essential to competition.

In Renaissance Italy, collective membership in a political community appears to have been correlated to the dynamism and national competitive power of the major political units. While the notion of Italian-ness was still only in its embryonic stage during the Renaissance, the sense of identity and community allegiance within each of the city-states was in fact very profound.[46] Writers in Florence lionized the city's "special place . . . in Italy as the exemplar of republican liberty and freedom."[47] The embrace of a coherent identity was grounded in part in a revival of Roman values and culture that was a central component of Renaissance humanism: "Armed afresh with its culture, the Italian soon felt himself in truth citizen of the most advanced nation in the world."[48] According to Lauro Martines, the growth in political feeling in 13th-century Italy

> sprang from an ardent attachment to place, to city, and to commune, and it was turned into an unbridled local patriotism. Florence and Genoa, Milan and Bologna, Siena and Padua all seethed with local pride and bluster. The world in which the good life was possible seemed to stretch not much further than immediate political horizons.[49]

The Renaissance city-states also highlight the risks of an absence of collective identity, which can produce domestic instability that undermines competitiveness. During the intra-Italian wars among the city-states, governments at times had difficulty generating commitment or loyalty from populations in their surrounding areas. Political divisions and polarization within city-states also imposed significant competitive disadvantages, especially as elite groups became more self-interested and selfish over time, waging bitter contests to control the resources and power of the states.

Dynastic China makes for an interesting comparative case. Of the multiethnic empires that existed from the 17th century onward—the Ottoman, Habsburg or Austro-Hungarian, Russian, and Chinese—only China survives as a unified entity today.[50] This surely must have a great deal to do with the fact that successive Chinese dynasties eventually managed to generate a sense of shared national identity, joined with the force of shared national civic values, that others could not. Present-day events in Hong Kong, Taiwan, Tibet, and Xinjiang

---

[46] Bartlett, 2005; Burkhardt, 2013, p. 77; Guido Ruggiero, *The Renaissance in Italy: A Social and Cultural History of the Rinascimento*, New York: Cambridge University Press, 2014, p. 326.

[47] Bartlett, 2019, loc. 936.

[48] Burkhardt, 2013, p. 103.

[49] Martines, 2013, p. 125.

[50] We are grateful to Kenneth Pomeranz for this insight.

make quite clear that this unifying drive is not complete and may never be so. Still, there is a vast area that now counts as China, in terms of national identity: Even as late as 1800, the Qing dynasty acquired and ruled lands that previous dynasties had not, and the idea that everything that is now China would have fit into a single identity sphere would have seemed unlikely.

The challenge of sustaining a coherent and unified national identity was always an issue in the Ottoman Empire. Although the empire proved relatively adept at promoting a general sense of belonging to a single Ottoman entity, even in the disparate regions of the empire, it was, like Austria-Hungary, composed of many different nationalities, ethnicities, and religious faiths. Although, as with Austria-Hungary, it is easy to underestimate how much collective identity was generated even by this diverse, multiethnic polity. Still, it was never going to have the same degree of coherent identity as a more homogeneous national unit.[51] The strains affecting its identity became especially intense when, for example, movements of religious orthodoxy sprang up in places such as the Arabian Peninsula, which, as one scholar put it, "categorically rejected the legitimacy of Ottoman rule." Over time the empire also confronted internal challengers, such as disaffected military units and groups, guilds, and elites in provinces.[52]

A final modern case is Britain. Historically, Britain was not always a single nation: It comprises England, Scotland, Wales, and Northern Ireland. It was not until 1707 that the Act of Union formally created what we know as Great Britain. Even to the present day, overlapping identities contend for allegiance in Britain: a core English identity with very strong associations (of being an "Englishman") combined with Scottish, Welsh, and Irish nationalities and all housed under a "British" political unit.[53]

---

[51] "The most salient characteristic of the Ottoman Empire at the end of the eighteenth century was its decentralization. . . . In practice, the reach of the Ottoman government in Istanbul rarely extended beyond the central provinces of Anatolia and Rumelia, and then only weakly" (Hanioğlu, 2008, p. 6). This decentralized pluralism, demanded in part by powerful local leaders, created a degree of fragmentation that sapped the empire's power base. Ottoman leaders of the 18th and 19th centuries recognized that "a loosely-bound association of disparate, semi-independent territories could not expect to survive long in the Napoleonic era," and that the effort to create more unified identity and state power "was thus an existential imperative." But it was an imperative that would be subverted by the rise of nationalism and growing demands for self-determination in various parts of the empire—a process that "began to pull the empire apart at its ethno-religious seams" (Hanioğlu, 2008, pp. 40, 51).

[52] Quataert, 2005, p. 50.

[53] Eva-Maria Asari, Daphne Halikiopoulou, and Steven Mock, "British National Identity and the Dilemmas of Multiculturalism," *Nationalism and Ethnic Politics*, Vol. 14, No. 1, 2008. The writer Tom McTague argues that this knitted nation is beginning to come apart: "The problem is that Britain is not a traditional country like France, Germany, or even the United States." It is a "collection of nations and territories, combining England, Scotland, Wales, and the disputed land of Northern Ireland—while also being a legitimate, sovereign, and unitary nation-state itself." As a result, "Some of its citizens believe themselves to be British, while others say they are not British at all; others say they are British and another nationality—Scottish or Welsh, say. In Northern Ireland it is even more complicated, with some describing themselves as only British while others say they are only Irish" (McTague, 2022).

Still, the basic core of an English/British identity has exercised a powerful hold on national sentiments since at least the Middle Ages. The historical and cultural identity of the English people, stretching back to Anglo-Saxon times, provided a firm foundation and magnet for what became Britain. The resulting mosaic that built up around England had a more diverse self-identity but one that gradually acquired sufficient coherence to serve as the basic for national success. British identity is characterized variously by cultural expressions—notably the English language, Protestant Christianity, and the "othering" of rivals, including the French, the Germans, and those of different races.[54]

Significant levels of nationalism and patriotism are evident in British political discourse dating back to the early 19th century.[55] There is little direct public opinion data, but the strength of British identity can be inferred from a range of evidence: the degree of consistent service in the British armed forces and the ability of the nation to call on large numbers of recruits and replacements; the role of national identity and patriotic appeals in motivating national will during conflict, ranging from the War of 1812,[56] to the Napoleonic Wars,[57] to World War II; and consistent and repeated reference to British identity and national patriotism by national political figures. The degree of unified national identity would then have been reasonably strong by the period of our primary focus, the era of British competitive standing from the early 19th century through the early 20th.

The Soviet Union also highlights the risks of an incoherent sense of identity. It was a system based on the binding force of an ideology (and, to a degree, a police state backing it up) rather than national or religious identity per se—and thus always had the potential weakness that, if the ideology faltered, so would the binding identity. Stalin and his successors labored hard to use communist ideology as the rallying point for a coherent national identity, in part by investing heavily in traditional sources of Russian culture. By the end of Stalin's period—even as many artists were hauled off to prison camps—hundreds of others became

---

[54] There is an immense literature on British and English national identity. See, for example, Stephanie L. Barczewski, *Myth and National Identity in Nineteenth Century Britain: The Legends of King Arthur and Robin Hood*, Oxford, UK: Oxford University Press, 2000; Linda Colley, *Britons: Forging the Nation 1707–1837*, New Haven, Conn.: Yale University Press, 1992; Krishan Kumar, *The Making of English National Identity*, Cambridge, UK: Cambridge University Press, 2001 (chapter 6 of this volume explicitly treats the parallel development of British identity); Gerald Newman, *The Rise of English Nationalism*, London: Palgrave Macmillan, 1997; David Powell, *Nationhood and Identity: The British State Since 1800*, London: I.B. Tauris, 2002.

[55] J. H. Shennan, "The Rise of Patriotism in 18th-Century Europe," *History of European Ideas*, Vol. 13, No. 6, 1991; Raphael Samuel, ed., *Patriotism: The Making and Unmaking of British National Identity*: Vol. 1, *History and Politics*, London: Routledge, 1989; Miles Taylor, "Patriotism, History and the Left in Twentieth-Century Britain," *Historical Journal*, Vol. 33, No. 4, 1990.

[56] Maria Fanis, "In Defense of the British Empire: Great Britain's National Identity of Loyal Patriotism and the War of 1812," in *Secular Morality and International Security: American and British Decisions About War*, Ann Arbor: University of Michigan Press, 2011.

[57] Gareth Atkins, "Christian Heroes, Providence, and Patriotism in Wartime Britain, 1793–1815," *Historical Journal*, Vol. 58, No. 2, 2015.

dedicated servants of the Soviet communist state. Even by the end of the 1950s, Vladislav Zubok explains, "Soviet society continued to maintain not only a strong Cold War consensus but also a huge store of Communist romantic illusions."[58]

But the result was to narrow the aperture of allowed culture and encourage "triumphant conformism, kitsch, and mediocrity."[59] More broadly, the effort to create a national identity lashed to communist ideology could never win over all the population and shed more and more legitimacy with every collision between rhetoric and reality—in the emerging economic stagnation, the repeated interventions in Eastern Europe, and the cruel domestic repression. The legitimacy of this identity was therefore quickly under assault, not only from alienating state actions but also from the influence of the reality of the outside world—what happened when Soviet citizens got to see the consumer paradise that was the developed world or were exposed to Western cultural influences inside the Soviet Union.

Eventually, this disaffection—combined with the parallel rise of national identity—fractured the system: "What mattered in the end was the decline of Communist ideology inside the Soviet empire and among elites and the growing appeal of Western models of democracy and modernization." Soviet industrial muscle and military power "did not and could not compensate for [the system's] profound flaws—the erosion of ideological faith and political will in the Kremlin and among influential segments of Soviet elites."[60] It was the comprehensiveness of the ideological crisis, "affecting all versions of the Soviet model for the same reasons," that "became a delegitimizing factor in its own right."[61]

Collective Identity and Competitive Outcomes: General Evidence

Apart from the evidence from our case studies, more-general historical and political evidence suggests that a unified national identity makes nations more powerful and resilient. Strong national identities are often connected to national values that assert the importance of things beyond self-interest, to a shared set of values with some spiritual character. We survey two categories of evidence: the results of qualitative surveys of history and a few specific areas of empirical findings that can serve as proxy results for our broader theme.

The relationship between national identity and competitive advantage is of course not linear. Nationalism, for example—one expression (though hardly the only one) of commitment to a shared identity—can have mixed effects on national fates, especially if it becomes

---

[58] Zubok, 2007, p. 177.

[59] Zubok, 2007, p. 165.

[60] Zubok, 2007, p. 344.

[61] Johann P. Arnason, *The Future That Failed: Origins and Destinies of the Soviet Model*, London: Routledge, 1993, p. 179.

excessive and militarized.[62] David Landes argues, "One cannot generalize about the consequences of nationalist ideology for economic growth. Admittedly it can inspire to labor, but its influence may or may not be well directed."[63]

Nonetheless, many historical surveys have highlighted the role of national unity and a strong sense of community in promoting national success. A key factor governing the success of major powers, as Wess Mitchell argues in connection with Austria-Hungary, is the "ability of a state's population to provide a sufficient degree of unity to support the state's political aims."[64] Insufficient national will or political consensus, by contrast, can lead to a failure to act "with sufficient strength or resolve" in strategic competitions.[65] Some studies of cultural values point to the inherent advantages of a communitarian ethic with a strong collective identity and argue that this can be associated with better economic outcomes.[66]

Other studies have connected a unified national identity to economic success and, on the basis of that success, national competitive strength. Landes maintains that, in the race to industrial prominence,

> Britain had the early advantage of being a nation. By that I mean not simply the realm of a ruler, not simply a state or political entity, but a self-conscious, self-aware unit characterized by common identity and loyalty and by equality of civil status. Nations can reconcile social purpose with individual aspirations and initiatives and enhance performance by their collective synergy. The whole is more than the sum of its parts. Citizens of a nation will respond better to state encouragement and initiatives; conversely, the state will know better what to do and how, in accord with active social forces. Nations can compete.[67]

Liah Greenfeld's work stresses the importance of the dignity offered by national identity and the role that identity plays in promoting national stability and strength. She argues, for example, that China's advance was a product in part of "economic nationalism" and a shared national identity that fostered strong competitive postures.[68] Nationalism, she contends, "encourages an orientation to growth" because nations are "sovereign communities of essentially equal members." She continues, "When the source of dignity lies in national membership, individual dignity becomes tightly associated with the dignity of the nation, measured by its international position or prestige. The national population in each case is strongly com-

---

[62] One article points to the lack of empirical evidence to establish a link between "nationalistic sentiments and the ability of governments to formulate and implement good policies" (Ahlerup and Hansson, 2011, p. 432).

[63] Landes, 2003, p. 550.

[64] Mitchell, 2018, p. 59.

[65] Lacey, 2016, p. 6.

[66] Lodge and Vogel, 1987.

[67] Landes, 1998, pp. 218–219.

[68] Liah Greenfeld, "Nationalism's Dividends," *American Affairs*, Vol. 3, No. 2, Summer 2019, p. 151.

mitted to maintaining the prestige of its nation; this makes nationalism an inherently competitive ideology."[69]

A powerful sense of communitarian identity can engender a willingness to pay severe costs, which can enhance national resilience and fighting spirit. Part of the U.S. error in the Vietnam War was a serious underestimation of the North Vietnamese willingness to absorb punishment.[70] This was in part a result of a powerful collective identity.

Besides these qualitative and historical assessments, empirical evidence from a handful of specific issue areas also supports the connection between a strong commitment to a unified identity and national competitive advantage. Individual studies show causal relationships in a wide range of areas connected to this theme:

- Although the relationship is complex, one study finds the degree of ethnic fractionalization in a country to be related to levels of economic growth.[71] (This issue is complex in part because social diversity is a good thing for growth.[72])
- Some studies show a positive relationship between certain measures of nationalism and national identity and economic development.
- One of the strongest empirical findings related to this theme supports the connection between trust and economic outcomes.[73]

Taken together, this historical and quantitative research joins with the lessons of the case studies to provide significant support for the contention that strong unified identity contributes to national competitive advantage.

A critical aspect of shared national identity is the degree to which it is inclusive. A coherent and vibrant national identity appears to provide competitive advantage when it encompasses a whole people, rather than being held only by a small ruling class or foisted on a population by an autocratic regime. Identity provides advantage when it is felt and believed across the population—in other words, not when it is merely broadcast by a narrow elite. There is

---

[69] Greenfeld, 2019, pp. 154–155. For a more comprehensive argument in this score, about the role of national identity in promoting development and competitiveness, see Liah Greenfeld, *The Spirit of Capitalism: Nationalism and Economic Growth*, Cambridge, Mass.: Harvard University Press, 2001.

[70] John E. Mueller, "The Search for the 'Breaking Point' in Vietnam: The Statistics of a Deadly Quarrel," *International Studies Quarterly*, Vol. 24, No. 4, 1980.

[71] Alberto Alesina, Arnaud Devleeschauwer, William Easterly, Sergio Kurlat, and Romain Wacziarg, "Fractionalization," *Journal of Economic Growth*, Vol. 8, 2003.

[72] For a survey of the literature on ethnic diversity and economic performance, see Alberto Alesina and Eliana La Ferrara, "Ethnic Diversity and Economic Performance," *Journal of Economic Literature*, Vol. 43, No. 3, 2005.

[73] Knack and Keefer, 1996.

clear evidence, for example, that "people identify with their country when they see their own ethnic group represented in the national government."[74]

Such inclusiveness is a product, in part, of the contract a nation makes with its people, the benefits of citizenship. Powerful national identity and collective membership entails duty and responsibility, but, typically, especially in the modern world, it also implies powerful rights, benefits, and privileges—the obligations the nation undertakes to fulfill. When a nation fails to deliver on these obligations, its legitimacy declines and its competitive capacity presumably weakens.

This is one of several places among the characteristics where we find advantages of inclusion and representation. Achieving these outcomes does not require the existence of a formal democracy. Some Renaissance city-states were republics, though not in the fully representative sense that we would understand today; some were not; and some republics gradually fell into more autocratic and oligarchic patterns. Yet many of the city-states generated a sense of shared identity and pride, which fueled their competitive strength. The same was true of Japan in the Meiji and pre–World War II periods, Victorian Britain, and even Russia during World War II.

Nonetheless, this characteristic is closely related to the notion of citizenship. Whether the conceptual and practical version of citizenship is deep or shallow, in whatever type of political system a nation has, will help determine national coherence, strength, and dynamism.

The Basis for Unified Identity: A Public-Spirited Elite

Finally, a theme that emerged from our case studies is the importance of a public-spirited elite class that values, and is perceived to value, national interests. The full effect of shared identity can emerge only when a nation benefits from an elite class that sees itself as part of the community and that invests in and promotes the common good rather than pursuing selfish interests, rent seeking, and building separate enclaves to insulate itself from social challenges.

Several leading global histories have stressed the critical role that elites play in shaping national destiny, especially when they view themselves as full members of the larger society— citizens first and foremost—with a responsibility to ensure general harmony and development. Peter Turchin has amassed significant historical evidence for how elites respond to population and resource pressures, and he has cataloged ways in which elite abandonment of the common good contributes to decline.[75] The historian Walter Scheidel has described the ways in which inequality increases over time in part because elites become better at gaming

---

[74] Andreas Wimmer, "National Identity and Political Power," *Foreign Affairs*, April 16, 2018. A more extended version of the argument is Andreas Wimmer, "Power and Pride: National Identity and Ethnopolitical Inequality Around the World," *World Politics*, Vol. 69, No. 4, 2017.

[75] Turchin, 2003.

the system—inequality that then impairs national strength and competitiveness.[76] Daron Acemoglu and James Robinson catalog many ways in which noninclusive, elite-dominated institutions weaken societies.[77]

Nations gain tremendous competitive advantage through a combination of a strong, effective, coherent, and—most important—public-spirited (rather than rent-seeking or self-interested) elite and opportunity that reaches throughout the whole society. During periods of competitive flourishing, the societies we have studied—from ancient Greece and Rome, to the Italian Renaissance city-states, to modern Britain and the United States—have married these two qualities.[78] Our case histories produced a consistent lesson in this regard: A coherent, honest, law-abiding, self-aware, and public-spirited elite class may be a precondition for competitive success. When a nation's elite or a significant or dominant component of it becomes corrupt, self-interested, or rent seeking or favors tribal or family or other discrete groups, the competitive choices of the nation and its societal vibrancy and resilience will erode. The cases do not provide anything like a clear threshold for when this criterion is met, but it emerges again and again in the waxing and waning of national fates over time.

This pattern emerged in case after case. Especially in the later phases of competitive dominance, great powers tended to be enfeebled by the selfish demands of elites who used the state apparatus for self-enrichment and preserving their power rather than the common good or the long-term dynamism of the nation. This occurred in the Renaissance city-states, for example, as more strictly hierarchical social patterns returned, and elites became focused on hoarding wealth and limited political participation to select families. It occurred in the Soviet Union over time. It was characteristic of Rome, to some degree throughout its history but especially in the later periods of empire. Josiah Ober argues that one of the major lessons of the ancient Greek experience is that elite preferences and behavior are a critical supporting element of "superior state performance."[79]

The result of this pattern is not merely a direct drain on state effectiveness in terms of wealth or income. Nations dominated by a self-protective elite also tend to lose the ambition and future orientation so essential to dynamism and become obsessed with preserving the status quo. They become more traditional and orthodox in their values and habits and less concerned with the experimental, the creative, and the new. They become tired and stagnant.

---

[76] Walter Scheidel, *The Great Leveler: Violence and the History of Inequality from the Stone Age to the Twenty-First Century*, Princeton, N.J.: Princeton University Press, 2018.

[77] Acemoglu and Robinson, 2012.

[78] Dominant majorities in rising civilizations, Arnold Toynbee contends, do have the capacity to "produce an admirable governing class" (Toynbee, 1947, p. 373). One could say that the ideal combination—which we see in the best of ancient Greece and Rome, Victorian and post-Victorian England, colonial and postwar America—of an effective, relatively unified, temperate ruling class with the best interests of all the people at heart, and a substantial degree of equality and social mobility to ensure that the ranks that elite are constantly refreshed with diverse perspectives and that the general population perceives an opportunity to join its ranks. It is an elite class that it both relatively altruistic and open that underwrites dynamism.

[79] Ober, 2015, p. 170.

We see these patterns in the city-states of the Italian Renaissance. This was not equally true in all the city-states, of course, and not true in a fully modern sense anywhere. But in some places the elite cultivated a reputation as being more closely affiliated with the population at large and acting in the common good.[80] As Jacob Burkhardt describes it,

> great as were individual ambitions, and the vanities of nobles and knights, it remains a fact that the Italian nobility took its place in the centre of social life, and not at the extremity. We find it habitually mixing with other classes on a footing of perfect equality, and seeking its natural allies in culture and intelligence.[81]

This was reflected in specific leaders—Cosimo de' Medici being a leading example.

The Renaissance city-states also underscore the importance of one indicator of elites' public sensibility: where and how they lived. "The fact was of vital importance that, from certainly the 12th century onward, the nobles and the burghers dwelt together within the walls of the cities," Burkhardt writes.[82] This changed over time, however, and Italian elites began to behave and make decisions in the spirit of a self-interested oligarchy. By the 15th century, Lauro Martines explains, hard-edged divisions and the return of classic ideas of a persistent nobility undermined this sense of a public-spirited elite. The wealthy and powerful increasingly

> constituted a more cleanly delineated oligarchy; they were especially subject to the seductions of politics; they were the very ones—in an age of commercial risk—to court public office, to glorify the name of politics, and to give, accordingly, less and less time to the vocation of their ancestors, commercial enterprise.[83]

The elite in Britain have, at least at times, both acted and been perceived to act for the common good. This was of course the ideal—how often reflected in actual practice we cannot know—of Britain's system of aristocratic privilege. The fictional Robert Crawley, the Earl of Grantham in *Downton Abbey*, represents a somewhat airbrushed version of the ideal: a reflective and generous lord of the manor, holding a powerful sense of obligation to his servants, his tenants, his land, and his community.[84]

States and ruling groups without legitimacy have a much harder time competing, for obvious reasons. Populaces will be less willing to sacrifice for them, and the need to shore up their domestic position may make them feel less able to undertake bold new initiatives, whether

---

[80] Ruggiero, 2014, pp. 532–533.

[81] Burkhardt, 2013, p. 217.

[82] Burkhardt, 2013, p. 213.

[83] Martines, 2013, loc. 3769–3771.

[84] One real-life example sometimes offered to illustrate this type is Henry Charles Keith Petty-Fitzmaurice, the fifth Marquess of Lansdowne (1845–1927). See Simon Kerry, *Lansdowne: The Last Great Whig*, London: Unicorn, 2017.

domestic or foreign. Legitimacy relies on a belief, among the masses, that the elites have the best interests of the community at heart. Even nondemocratic states with strong levels of legitimacy—or societies reflecting highly unequal distributions of wealth and power—may inspire their people to consent to limits on popular voice and opportunity if they believe that the governing or elite classes ultimately are on their side.

Such a competitive drag can occur when elites have their own enrichment and power, rather than national betterment, in mind. The story of the Soviet Union is partly one of the degeneration of its ruling elite from an allegedly public-spirited, revolutionary cadre working on behalf of the common interest to an utterly corrupt, self-interested cabal. The lack of any willingness to fight to sustain the system at the end, one scholar explains,

> emerged from what has often been described as the total corruption of the elite, accompanied by their total incompetence. The system, from this perspective, was so corroded from within that it lacked the capacity to resist. The *nomenklatura* system had become a corrupt, piratical, privileged and corrupt elite, incapable of evolving into an active middle class, let alone an entrepreneurial bourgeoisie.[85]

This pattern—the descent of an elite into a self-interested, rent seeking, and exclusionary club—emerges repeatedly in our cases.[86] Jack Goldstone and Peter Turchin describe the pattern, and it is worth quoting their description at length:

> First, faced with a surge of labor that dampens growth in wages and productivity, elites seek to take a larger portion of economic gains for themselves, driving up inequality. Second, facing greater competition for elite wealth and status, they tighten up the path to mobility to favor themselves and their progeny. For example, in an increasingly meritocratic society, elites could keep places at top universities limited and raise the entry requirements and costs in ways that favor the children of those who had already succeeded. Third, anxious to hold on to their rising fortunes, they do all they can to resist taxation of their wealth and profits, even if that means starving the government of needed revenues, leading to decaying infrastructure, declining public services and fast-rising government debts. Such selfish elites lead the way to revolutions. They create simmering conditions of greater inequality and declining effectiveness of, and respect for, government.[87]

We see elements of this process in a Roman elite that gradually came to hold more tightly to social control and pour their money into land rather than more-productive investments.

---

[85] Sakwa, 2013, p. 70 (the *nomenklatura* refers to those people who were approved by the Communist Party to hold influential government jobs). The classic early treatment of the emerging self-protective Soviet elite is Milovan Djilas, *The New Class: An Analysis of the Communist System*, New York: Praeger, 1957.

[86] For one source that applies a version of this argument to modern Japan, see R. Taggart Murphy, *Japan and the Shackles of the Past*, New York: Oxford University Press, 2014.

[87] Jack A. Goldstone and Peter Turchin, "Welcome to the 'Turbulent Twenties,'" *Noema*, September 10, 2020.

We see it in the elite classes of several Renaissance Italian city-states that similarly devolved back into control by aristocratic families. We see it in the Ottoman Empire, with the gradually worsening corruption of the ulama and Janissary elite and subsequent groups of elites who strove to preserve their position in society and obstruct societal reform. And we see it in the modern Soviet Union, where a state apparatus became the servant of a self-protective and autocratic elite.[88]

The competitive disadvantage of self-interested elites comes through in elements of the Latin American experience. These patterns have well-examined historical roots stemming in part from Spain's extractive approach to its regional colonies and the different patterns of authority and governance that came into being as compared with those in British North America. Generalizations are dangerous; select countries in the region have enjoyed transparent and honest government and strong records of growth, and reforms have changed the situation over time. Nonetheless, self-interested oligarchies have been associated with economic stagnation and inequality and political repression for decades.[89]

In short, some nations with the raw societal material for a sustained strong competitive position—such as Spain or the Soviet Union—were handicapped in part by self-interested and corrupt elite and governing classes. Others, having reached world-leading heights of competitive advantage, saw that position erode as their elites lost a central allegiance to the community and became obsessed with selfish gains.

The Balance: The Risks of Excessive National Identification

Like national ambition, an intense commitment to national identity—and the resulting willpower—runs the risk of overreach. Indeed, excessive versions of our first two societal characteristics, national ambition and national identity, can work together to fuel overextension.

But national unity and a shared identity, when taken to extremes, can also have other negative effects on competitive standing. An exclusive and xenophobic version of identity can undermine the potential for diversity and cause a nation to exclude potential talents, whether at home or abroad.[90] Ethnic identity easily shades into various forms of bias, including racial

---

[88] Ironically, the Soviet Union saw one group of elites arise with a degree of public spiritedness and commitment to the common good. The reformist elites furnished opportunities to break out of old ways of thinking in the more open environment of the 1960s, many of whom, including Mikhail Gorbachev, would provide the core of the managers of glasnost and perestroika two decades later. They were "determined to reform and liberalize their country" (Zubok, 2007, pp. 164, 179–180).

[89] See, for example, Dennis Gilbert, *The Oligarchy and the Old Regime in Latin America, 1880–1970*, Lanham, Md.: Rowman and Littlefield, 2017; OxFam International, "Influence of Elites on Governments in Latin America Contributes to Increasing Poverty and Inequality," press release, November 16, 2018; James E. Sanders, "Histories of Elites, Redux: Oligarchs, Families, and Power," *Latin American Research Review*, Vol. 54, No. 3, 2019.

[90] Moses Abramovitz, "The Elements of Social Capability," in Bon Ho Koo and Dwight H. Perkins, eds., *Social Capability and Long-Term Economic Growth*, New York: St. Martin's Press, 1995, p. 30.

and ethnic hatred; as the characteristic on diversity and pluralism suggests, countries that deprive themselves of the full range of human talents in such ways—totally apart from the moral fault of such bias—saddle themselves with a profound competitive disadvantage.[91]

Anthony Marx explains the ways in which national solidarity can mutate into exclusionary, ethnocentric versions—and indeed, Marx catalogs how its deeper origins were just that, when early modern European leaders employed hostility directed at outsiders to help early state builders rally national unity. "State-building began before the emergence of matching popular allegiance," Marx argues, making it essential for elites to find ways to generate support for the new national entities. Nationalism demanded a situation "in which mass allegiance and institutional power coincide," and one way to do that was to pair the inclusive domestic aspects of nationalism with an aggressive, exclusivist attitude toward outsiders.[92] His research looks at the early period of state formation in Europe, but the same perilous connection, between nationalism and xenophobic aggression, has cropped up repeatedly throughout history.

An overly restrictive sense of national identity can also undermine other characteristics essential for competitiveness. A society in which identity factors tightly circumscribe the public debate—where a soft or hard form of autocracy prevails in the name of one ethnic, racial, or national identity—will undermine its openness to new ideas, its ability to learn, and its capacity to adapt. Such identity-fueled willpower can easily become a sort of imprisoning nostalgia.[93] The same dynamics can destroy effective strategizing by putting considerations of national pride and tradition over pragmatic judgments. The British case, as the historian Joyce Appleby explains, shows the central role of unfettered and sometimes hostile debate about fundamental issues. "The English were getting used to public discord," she says of the 16th and 17th centuries. Elsewhere in Europe, for the most part, governments clamped down on free thinking and scientific progress in part from a "fear of disorder." As she concludes, "Questioning authority proved critical to getting novelty accepted."[94] If a strict form of orthodoxy accompanying national identity were to undermine that openness to the new and radical, it would strike at the heart of the Renaissance spirit that represents the most dynamic and competitiveness-inducing combination of societal characteristics.

---

[91] In economic terms, Richard Rosecrance has pointed out that nationalist spurs to economic growth must be balanced by a significant degree of internationalism, for a country to operate in global networks of trade. Richard Rosecrance, "Money and Power," *National Interest*, Summer 2002.

[92] Anthony W. Marx, *Faith in Nation: Exclusionary Origins of Nationalism*, New York: Oxford University Press, 2003, pp. 5, 7, 192–193.

[93] Ian Morris describes some uncompetitive situations, such as 18th-century China, when "preserving the glories of the past seemed more important in China than addressing the kind of questions that global expansion was forcing onto Westerners' attention" (Morris, 2010, p. 481). Nostalgia had replaced a forward-directed national will to achievement.

[94] Appleby, 2010, loc. 1561, 1579, 1985.

The risk emerges, too, in the fear of outsiders and a strong social convention distinguishing members of the community from others.[95] An exclusionary identity can cause nations—as has occurred several times in Chinese and Japanese history—to isolate themselves from the kinds of productive networks and exchanges so essential to national power. It can make nations resistant to the value of immigrants. It can close off tolerance at the domestic level, generating discrimination. All of this works to constrain national competitive vitality.

Excessive national identification can have other risks. Jared Diamond describes how identity can have destructive effects on collective judgment. How Viking communities "viewed themselves," he maintains, affected their behavior. A powerful shared identity was a critical competitive advantage in some ways—but it also "prevented them from learning from the Inuit, and from modifying their identity in ways that might have permitted them to survive beyond four centuries."[96] David Landes makes a similar argument about France: The French nation of the early 17th and 18th centuries "dominated Europe, awed the rest of the world by her pomp and circumstance, scintillated by her artistic and intellectual achievements." In the process, important elements of French national identity became shared, coherent, and empowering. The country, Landes continues, developed, "especially at the upper levels of society, a highly integrated set of values, suffused with a sense of satisfaction and superiority." Yet a smug confidence in French superiority and its connection to national self-esteem made the country somewhat resistant to outside influences and less able to learn.[97] Potent national pride in a shared identity can become a barrier to openness and adaptation as much as a support system for national power. The United States has surely not been immune to this danger in its modern history.

One fascinating study looks specifically at the risks of excessive national identification. The authors hypothesize that "more nationalistic individuals should be more skeptical to new ideas or techniques if these in some way are not in line with national traditions." They find that, empirically, "the level of nationalism, measured by the level of national pride among the population, has an inverted U-shaped relationship with government effectiveness." The evidence suggests that "[m]ore nationalism is associated with better government effectiveness at low levels of nationalism, while the effect is the opposite at high levels of nationalism."[98] Such a changing causal relationship makes sense: Newly forming states need high degrees of national identity to solidify their standing. But well-established nations may suffer competitive disadvantages from the constraints imposed by a conformity-inducing national identity.

The Soviet Union provides a classic example of these dangers—a state in which adherence to the state ideology was necessary merely to stay out of prison. State emphasis on ideology was exacerbated by the pressures of the Cold War, which intensified the premium on

---

[95] Appleby, 2010, loc. 1662.

[96] Diamond, 2005, p. 193.

[97] Landes, 2003, p. 551.

[98] Ahlerup and Hansson, 2011, pp. 435, 446.

loyalty and thus made departure from the prevailing orthodoxy even more dangerous. The spirit of much state policy and propaganda became, "Those who are not completely with us are against us."[99] That constraining and repressive orthodoxy severely undercut national competitiveness.

Our research thus strongly suggests that a productive degree of unified national identity and critical associated values—a robust and rewarding sense of citizenship, a willingness to work on behalf of the community, and a public-spirited and community-focused elite—are important to national competitive advantage. They can be embraced to excess in ways that obstruct national learning and adaptation, but a foundation of national identity is essential for competitive dynamism. And that identity becomes even more effective when combined with the societal characteristic to which we now turn: Shared opportunity among a society allows a nation to build on the advantages of powerful identity by drawing the talents and commitments of the widest possible share of its population into the resulting national project.

---

[99] Zubok, 2007, p. 171.

CHAPTER FIVE

Shared Opportunity

The Italian Renaissance, that self-proclaimed period of rebirth that began in the late 14th century and ran through parts of the 17th, reflected a flowering of many remarkable social and political innovations. It saw the rise of a cluster of city-states—Florence, Venice, Genoa, Milan, Naples, and Rome—some of whose form of governance created a model for republican states to come. These states forged expansive trade networks in the Mediterranean and beyond. New industries, some based on technologies borrowed (or stolen) from the East, cropped up, underwriting the financing of an astonishing cornucopia of art, literature, and science.

This remarkable social efflorescence came about for many reasons. One of them—an important foundation for the dynamism of these societies—is our third societal characteristic associated with national competitive advantage: the degree to which a nation ensures shared opportunity that maximizes the human potential of its citizens. Select Italian city-states enhanced their power by tapping into the talents of a large number of people—at least by the standards of the time and in comparison to many rivals. Some of these city-states reflected a period of competitive vibrancy in which scholars, artisans, entrepreneurs, and officials competed to prove themselves as the best in their chosen fields.

This was still a premodern era. These were feudal or aristocratic societies, and social opportunity remained limited for many parts of the population. Structural discrimination against women was universal. Nonetheless, relative to societies before them, and to some of their major competitors, the leading city-states of the Italian Renaissance achieved greatness in part by unleashing, to a constrained but significant degree, the human potential to which they had access. Despite the profound inequities of these societies, they gained identifiable advantages by opening the aperture of opportunity to some degree, signaling to future societies the potential national gains from such a strategy.

In one sense this should not be a surprise, since the Italian Renaissance is in some ways defined by the ways in which it embodied a philosophy of humanism—the "discovery of the individual," or the truly autonomous person, in the 19th-century Swiss historian Jacob Burkhardt's famous conception. This emphasis on unleashing human potential through an expression of individual self-creation helped produce a context in which opportunity was inherently more shared. Burkhardt writes of this period, "Social intercourse in its highest and most perfect form now ignored all distinctions of caste, and was based simply on the existence of an educated class as we now understand the word." This fact was qualified, to be sure:

"[M]edieval distinctions still sometimes made themselves felt to a greater or less degree, if only as a means of maintaining equality with the aristocratic pretensions of the less advanced countries of Europe. But the main current of the time went steadily towards the fusion of classes in the modern sense of the phrase."[1]

The novelty of this concept can be exaggerated—even in ancient Greece, a form of humanism had begun to emerge, and the expression of individual identity had become a kind of civic practice and a source of Greek pride. But at a minimum, even with its limitations, the Renaissance pattern reinforced the basic lesson that societies more likely to tap a fuller degree of the talents and energies of their people, or at least an important component of them, could gain competitive advantage.[2]

The widening of opportunity also reflected the needs of city-states with a primary interest in trade and the accompanying impulse to gather commercial advantage from wherever they could find it. Artisans, such as glassmakers, gained new opportunity for social mobility because their skills were essential to the commercial success of the community. The involvement of the "richer part of the middle classes," the historian Lauro Martines argues, in "shipping and maritime trade in the thirteenth century," and the resulting weakening of rigid class divisions and the involvement of mercantile families into government, created a new "accessibility to the ruling class." This gave a "dynamic promise" to the life of artisans involved in commerce even at lower levels: "An exceptional man, born to a modest family around 1450, could end his life as a 'gentleman.'"[3]

Other scholars, such as the economist Dierdre McCloskey and the historian Joyce Appleby, see this link between opportunity and commerce as central to the story of national development and advantage.[4] A competitive, vibrant, ambitious commercial ethic was indispensable, they believe, in creating incentives for personal empowerment and realization of potential. The pursuit of wealth and commerce in the Italian city-states had the critical result of breaking down, to an imperfect but still profound degree, the social strictures holding class in place and opportunity in check.[5] Kenneth Bartlett, one of the leading experts on the Renaissance, puts it this way:

> The traditions of the Middle Ages had long proscribed social mobility—the rapid movement from one social class into another. Equally vilified was usury—the taking of interest on loans, no matter how minimal. But these proscriptions were unattractive to republican Florentines as they did not reflect the reality of their lives. In a republic run by merchants, social mobility was now possible.[6]

---

[1] Burkhardt, 2013, p. 213.

[2] Bartlett, 2019, loc. 607–611.

[3] Martines, 2013, loc. 2855–2857, 5382.

[4] McCloskey, 2016; Appleby, 2010.

[5] Ruggiero, 2014, p. 67.

[6] Bartlett, 2019, loc. 777.

Again, we should not exaggerate the extent to which opportunity and social mobility were shared by all in the Italian Renaissance city-states on anything like a modern scale.[7] These societies had vast working populations whose focus was to earn enough money or produce enough food to get through the day. Only a few percentage points of the adult population of most city-states were fully enfranchised. Humanistic values of self-discovery and fulfillment of opportunity were primarily manifest in the wealthy classes. Although it was true that these classes were more open to ambitious people from almost any background than before,[8] divisions in wealth remained stark, and poverty was rife among the laboring classes.[9] And the scholarship we reviewed for this analysis stresses that the later phases of the Renaissance also reflected new constraints on shared opportunity in the form of a reassertion of traditional patterns of hereditary nobility.[10]

Yet even with all these caveats, the Renaissance Italian city-states embraced social mobility and the discovery and fulfillment of individual potential to a degree remarkable by the standards of the time. And this embrace conveyed a competitive advantage, in anecdotal but clearly identifiable ways. It allowed talented entrepreneurs and financiers to rise to prominence, economically empowering the city-states as they did so. It allowed brilliant scientists and inventors to dream up and promote their ideas. It encouraged business enterprises and state institutions to choose people (to a somewhat greater degree) based on talent rather than name or connections or bribes (at least some of the time). And it fostered an environment of domestic competition in which the Italian Renaissance city-states were propelled to recruit or steal all the talent they could find—especially from one another—as they came to appreciate the growing relevance of human capital to state power.

This basic causal connection between shared opportunity to express talents and national strength would become a major theme over the subsequent centuries. The historian Eric Hobsbawm discusses the modern importance of a growing practice that "opened careers to

---

[7] Indeed, McCloskey makes the opposite case—that the Renaissance did not reflect a profound degree of shared opportunity. She refers to it as the "aristocracy-admiring Renaissance" and describes how it descended into a formalized hereditary aristocracy over time (McCloskey, 2016, pp. 522, 535). These things are true, but there is also strong evidence that, compared with many prior and contemporaneous societies, the Italian city-states valued the economic and cultural contributions of people from many backgrounds.

[8] "Their ideals of education, humanity, and political order could be realized only in a society with privileged elites—a society rather like their own" (Martines, 2013, loc. 4132). Kenneth Bartlett agrees that "[t]hose who commissioned the works of art, often those who produced them, and many of those who appreciated them were privileged, educated, influential members of the Renaissance 'one percent'" (Bartlett, 2019, loc. 281).

[9] Martines, 2013, loc. 3214–3217, 4042–4119.

[10] Ruggiero, 2014, 540; Barlett, 2019, loc. 4476–4480; Martines, 2013, loc. 2984. Over time, "true aristocratic status on a European level" became "increasingly difficult to gain unless one was from an established major family" (Ruggiero, 2014, p. 546; Martines, 2013, loc. 3022–3024). This tends to support the general trajectory suggested by Walter Scheidel, who describes how, as societies become firmly established and then develop economically, elites become more expert at various forms of rent seeking and institutional domination, and inequality increases (Scheidel, 2019).

talent, or at any rate to energy, shrewdness, hard work and greed."[11] Partly the expansion of opportunity reflected a drawn-out break from feudal or rigidly aristocratic patterns on the way to a more pluralistic society—and as David Landes observes, the societies that made this break earliest have the strongest economies to this day, having allowed the application of talent to competitive outcomes to run for the longest time.[12]

Yet shared opportunity for advancement and expression of talent and ideas can take a society only so far on their own. If the society's institutions are a shambles and its social map a fragmented array of mutually suspicious enclaves, it will not gain much from even radically inclusive avenues of opportunity. If the society has no habits of learning or adaptation, if it is homogenous and closed and imprisoned by a repressive orthodoxy rather than pluralistic and open and thirsty for bold new ideas, if it has no commercial ethic or vibrant marketplace to reward innovation, its dynamism will suffer even if many people can express their talents. This linkage of factors reemphasizes our key finding: It is the ways in which social characteristics *interact* with one another that determines the extent to which they will lead to decisive and lasting competitive advantage. In the case of the Italian city-states, a societal embrace of opportunity meshed with a strong sense of ambition and will, effective institutions (at least for the time), and other characteristics to make some of these polities the commercial and maritime leaders of their day, at least in the West.

Defining the Characteristic

The concept of shared opportunity to express talents and ideas refers to habits, practices, or beliefs that ensure that the wealth and investments of a society can benefit from the available talent, to fully maximize the potential of the society and provide real opportunity to the broadest number of people to express their capabilities. Competitive advantage stems from a society's ability to draw in contributions from all its members. A society's degree of social mobility is part of this equation: When classes or castes become locked into place, opportunity is necessarily constrained, and potential talent is wasted.

The role of shared opportunity emphasizes the importance of what we might today call *human capital*, but this notion involves more than is captured by the venerable economics concept of the intangible value of the skills and capacities of employees. The specific elements of the characteristic will be discussed below; for now, it is enough to define *shared opportunity* as *the degree to which all the people of a nation can work, advance in career and achievements, express and develop ideas, create, network, and in other ways contribute their full human potential to the life, prosperity, and power of the nation.* This characteristic would require that people's opportunities to express their ability—in their careers, in their ideas and creativity, in their general ambitions—would not be limited by their membership in any

---

[11] Hobsbawm, 1962, p. 189.

[12] Landes, 1998, pp. 238–242.

group. Opportunities in such societies are not blocked by gender, class, race, or ethnicity. People do not have to belong to a ruling, autocratic party, or to a specific family or tribe, to get good jobs or have full citizenship rights. And although the primary focus of this characteristic is the opportunities enjoyed by a nation's own citizens, the most successful societies have also extended the principle beyond their national boundaries: Recruiting talented people from abroad, either permanently or on loan, is a contributing factor to success in this area.

Shared opportunity is not easily measurable. We cannot, on the basis of the available data, plot its value on a precise curve, with a clear threshold defining how much of this quality is necessary for competitive success. Each of the premodern cases we examined reflect stark inequalities of wealth and strict barriers to opportunity for significant parts of the population. The question of how much is enough must be understood relative to competitors and thus will change over time. Our cases do not reflect a single degree of shared opportunity but rather shifting measures; any broad generalizations about single countries risk oversimplifying complex histories. And because competitive advantage is the combined result of many factors, nations have succeeded with imperfect degrees of shared opportunity and failed with substantial amounts of it. Yet a relatively widely shared degree of social opportunity, at least in specific ways or relative to others at the time, emerges again and again as a theme in our general research and case studies. The three most dynamic and sustained major powers— Rome, Britain, and the United States—each reflect clear examples (though in very different ways) of the benefits of widely shared opportunity for the expression of human talent.

***

We can understand shared opportunity as the sum of five factors. The first of these is *socioeconomic equality*. Shared opportunity is not synonymous with such equality: A society can embody powerful hierarchies and still allow a significant part of the population to express creative and productive talents. Britain of the 19th century was a profoundly class-bound society with stark degrees of inequality, and yet it managed to create enough avenues of opportunity to draw productive and innovative talents and ideas from a wide range of the population. Yet the tension between inequality and opportunity is unavoidable: Rigid social inequalities are likely to generate barriers to opportunity and mobility. And empirical evidence does suggest that, although the two factors do not move in lockstep, they are correlated.

A second and related component of shared opportunity is *social mobility*. Whether measured within generations or between them, by looking at income or wealth or education levels, social mobility is an excellent proxy for the degree to which a society is creating chances for people from all walks of life to contribute to national strength.[13]

---

[13] The ideal productive society, David Landes argues, "would be marked by geographical and social mobility. People would move about as they sought opportunity, and would rise and fall as they made something or nothing of themselves." The result would "tend to a more even distribution of income than is found with privilege and favor" (Landes, 1998, p. 218).

A third component of shared opportunity is *the potential for all subgroups in a nation—whether defined by gender, race, ethnicity, career field, sexual preference, or other aspects—to fully participate in that society's opportunities.* This speaks to the degree of inclusiveness of a society. To the degree that whole groups face discrimination or are otherwise held back by prejudice or formal barriers, a society's competitive engine is thwarted. An especially potent example is gender equality. Societies that do not grant fully equal opportunity to women suffer from a massive competitive weakness, missing out on a significant proportion of the talents, skills, innovations, and other contributions of half of their populations.[14] As Landes concludes, "The best clue to a nation's growth and development potential is the status and role of women."[15]

A fourth component of shared opportunity is *merit-based systems of social selection and advancement*, whether in civil service, business, scholarship, or the military. Societies with strongly shared opportunity are often marked by the availability of training, testing, and promotion systems based on objective standards. It is worth nothing that, over time, highly formalized and bureaucratized systems of assessment and merit can narrow and calcify routes to opportunity rather than expand them. Schooling, tests, and connections to established elites become necessary routes to advancement. This was the pattern in the Ottoman Empire over time,[16] and it can be seen in the Renaissance Italian city-states and the Soviet Union—as well as in the United States today, with the increasingly formalized credentials required in everything from jobs that needlessly demand a college degree to the certificates and training programs required to gain access to some career fields whose members once trained largely by apprenticeship.

Fifth, and finally, maximizing the talent opportunities of a society has also meant, for many competitively successful nations, *drawing talent from abroad* and then ensuring the freedom to express abilities and creativity. The Renaissance is one of the leading examples of this. Modern immigration policies—such as Canada's skills-based point system and the U.S. H-1B high-tech worker visa program—derive from the same basic impulse.

Shared opportunity, then, comprises a range of specific components that together highlight one basic finding: Societies that become transmission belts for the potential talents, ideas, and abilities of their people—and those they might attract—enjoy a significant competitive advantage.

The remainder of this chapter will first review the *theoretical* case for a connection between shared opportunity and competitive advantage—the basis for such a hypothesis in the first place. Next, it will describe the *historical* evidence for this connection—the lessons

---

[14] Landes, 1998, pp. 410–413.

[15] For his analysis of the Japanese example—why it remains imperfect but reflects some progress in women's roles—see Landes, 1998, pp. 417–421.

[16] Linda T. Darling, "The Sultan's Advisors and Their Opinions on the Identity of the Ottoman Elite, 1580–1653," in Christine Isom-Verhaaren and Kent F. Schull, eds., *Living in the Ottoman Realm: Empire and Identity, 13th to 20th Centuries*, Indianapolis: Indiana University Press, 2016.

of the historical cases examined for this study. Finally, it will take up more-recent *empirical research evidence* for the importance of opportunity to national competitive standing.

The Theoretical Case Linking Shared Opportunity and Competitive Advantage

The theoretical case for the strategic value of shared opportunity and talent development is straightforward, indeed almost tautological. It is based on the common-sensical assertion that societies that find ways to allow a higher proportion of their people to express their ambitions, talents, skills, and creativity become more dynamic and thus more competitive. This connection ought to be true in both direct and indirect ways.

In direct terms, granting opportunity adds fuel to a nation's economic, military, and cultural engines. The process will generate more inventions, more new businesses, more scientific breakthroughs, more cultural expressions that attract foreign notice, more military power and strategic judgment, and other benefits. In one sense this is simply an argument that more-energized human capital will make a nation more powerful and dynamic—but it should also be true in ways well beyond those measured by economics: opening the pathways for talented individuals to become military leaders or government officials, generating breakthroughs in basic science, and encouraging cultural expressions that broadcast the nation's dynamism.

In indirect terms, societies that maximize opportunity and provide avenues for talent development are likely to enjoy more social coherence and stability. Large-scale obstruction of ambitions, when a significant proportion of the people in a society feel blocked, marginalized, and dismissed, is a recipe for frustration and various forms of rebellion. We would expect weak social opportunity to be correlated with high inequality, low mobility, constraints on the advancement of specific groups, and other factors that are historically associated with social instability. A lack of social opportunity is likely to create resentment and loss of faith in the larger society in ways that drain the commitment of citizens to the common good.

Another indirect value of shared opportunity is its role as an especially critical support system for the synergy of factors mentioned in Chapter One. Shared opportunity lies at the hub of the most effective recipe for national success, the Renaissance spirit. It is all about creating an engine of dynamism through national unity and will, a learning and adapting mindset, an innovative drive and willingness to challenge established ways of thinking, and productive investment, all supported by effective institutions and an appropriately and efficiently energetic state apparatus. Shared opportunity connects to every piece of that recipe, opening critical pathways for achieving that delicate but hugely advantageous pattern of networked social entrepreneurialism. Societal combinations with even imperfect degrees of shared opportunity at the core have proved remarkably advantageous, as the British case amply demonstrates. As one scholar concludes:

In England . . . industrialization took off because events leading up to and including the Civil War of 1642–51, and the Glorious Revolution of 1688, had led to the abolition of monopolies and the establishment of more inclusive institutions. It was these institutions which enabled the great entrepreneurs of the Industrial Revolution, such as James Watt, Josiah Wedgwood, Richard Arkwright and Isambard Kingdom Brunel, to turn their ideas into commercial products, knowing that their property rights would be respected and that they would have access to markets where their innovations could be profitably sold. On the other hand, in the Austro-Hungarian and Russian empires, the absolute monarchs and aristocrats were more firmly entrenched, and were, therefore, able to block industrialization. As a result, their economies fell behind other European nations where economic growth took off during the nineteenth century.[17]

In most of our cases and historical research, providing fully shared opportunity does appear to have required at least a baseline level of open market economy, which provides transmission belts between that opportunity and economic, technological, and national-power outcomes.[18] Jack Goldstone brings out this theme in his analysis of the ways in which innovation fueled the Industrial Revolution. It was the connection of average inventors, artisans, and workers to elites, scientists, officials, entrepreneurs, and investors that helped bring about an innovative society. The "culture of innovation had to spread beyond any one social group or class," he writes, and do so in a context that made the best use of their innovations.[19] It was the mixture and collision of these individuals and groups that proved especially productive, a mixing that relied on and reflected a breaking down of boundaries between groups. "In fact," Goldstone writes, "what is striking is the way that the longstanding traditional barriers between upper-class philosophers, market-driven entrepreneurs, large-scale industrialists, and skilled craftspeople and technicians dissolved, so that all of these groups came together to initiate a culture of innovation that produced continuous, accelerating change." He concludes:

> For experiment and discovery to become the pursuit of a large number of individuals— across different occupations and social groups, all interested in linking scientific discovery to practical economic benefits—was truly exceptional. When this happened in eighteenth-century Britain, it set off a trajectory of scientific progress and economic growth that spread throughout the world and continues to this day.[20]

---

[17] David Sainsbury, *Windows of Opportunity: How Nations Create Wealth*, London: Profile, 2020, p. 44.

[18] Sainsbury, 2020, p. 144. Open, free-market societies did not suddenly create truly shared opportunity. "Capitalism didn't eliminate oppressive upper classes," Appleby argues. "It just changed the basis upon which they stood. The ladders for social mobility were spread about the landscape more generously, but those without capital suffered as had those without inherited status earlier" (Appleby, 2010, loc. 1967–1969).

[19] Goldstone, 2009, p. 134.

[20] Goldstone, 2009, pp. 163–164.

That same basic connection—among talent, opportunity, an open society, energetic commerce, innovation, and entrepreneurialism—inspires McCloskey's notion of a bourgeois ethic. Her main argument is about the "new dignity for trading and innovating in ordinary life" that emerged in Britain and other places in Europe and the effect of this development on national trajectories. "Give people liberty to work and to invent and to invest, and treat them with dignity," she argues, and economic development is the result.[21] And empowering a large proportion of the population to participate in this process is integral to the mechanism.[22] The dynamism of modern Europe was "released for the first time by a new liberty and dignity for commoners."[23]

In this process, McCloskey contends, the role of the petite bourgeoisie—small business-people and shopkeepers—was especially critical. It was when "the owner of the corner grocery store, the lower-middle manager, in former times the small but not subsistence farmer" and others like them received expanded opportunities that societies took off. "Most Americans, as Europeans did not, put the upper-working class in the bourgeoisie, and invited them into the bourgeois fraternal societies: the head clerk in the office, the electrician, the freight conductor, the chief sawyer," she concludes.[24] A vibrant small-business sector, then, and evidence that modest and obscure entrepreneurs are playing a significant role in the development of new products and technologies, will be important signals of shared economic opportunity.

Finally, growing wealth for a larger part of the population can be a spur to learning, creativity, and entrepreneurship in another way. It allows people to focus on issues other than daily concerns, giving them both the time and the money to support intellectual circles, scientific societies, and the like.[25]

The theoretical case is therefore powerful: Societies of widely shared opportunity ought to gain competitive advantage. They do so, however, in combination with other societal characteristics—as well as more material and structural factors.[26] This again harks back to our most central finding: It is dynamic combinations of factors producing competitive wholes greater than the sum of their parts that confer advantage. Like all the characteristics

---

[21] McCloskey, 2011, loc. 487, 1726–1728.

[22] McCloskey argues, for example, that European societies by the beginning of the 19th century were moving "away from, say, old South Asian or Korean levels of deference, and starting toward new American or Israeli levels. For their part the northwest European townspeople lost their grip on cozy medieval monopolies. They got in exchange a new dignity as innovators, tors, and a smaller social distance from the revered elite" (McCloskey, 2011, loc. 471–483).

[23] McCloskey, 2016, p. 12.

[24] McCloskey, 2010, p. 73.

[25] Jacob, 1988, p. 153.

[26] One example, brought to our attention by William Anthony Hay, is land availability in countries founded by settler communities. Although the true story of land provision and ownership in the American colonies is fraught with complexity, the idea that immigrants could acquire a significant piece of land, become self-supporting farmers, and build from that point was arguably a material factor aligned with shared opportunity.

that follow, shared opportunity should be seen not as a unique and severable tool of competitive advantage but as one critical piece of a mosaic.

Tying Shared Opportunity to Competitive Outcomes: Evidence from Cases

Given the paucity of data for many periods and the multiplicity of causal variables, it is impossible to produce a regression analysis or other quantitative assessment for this causal relationship. Indeed, the full participation of a population in a nation's competitive output is imperfectly related to competitive position. Sweden, to take just one example, was a highly aristocratic society that provided only limited opportunities to many of its people in the early 17th century even as it achieved geopolitical power. Even in the heart of the Industrial Revolution, Britain retained some sharp class distinctions.

And yet, as Table 5.1 suggests, the historical cases are bursting with anecdotal evidence of at least two things. First, societies that experience a competitive rise and a wider social and economic efflorescence do often reflect a degree of shared social opportunity notable for their time. Second, we can identify specific ways in which this characteristic contributed to competitive success in individual cases. This evidence, again, is not definitive. But it is strongly suggestive of important competitive advantages to be gained from shared opportunity and the resulting empowerment of human potential.

Several of the cases provide examples of discrete or limited pathways to opportunity that had some competitive effect, even when the larger society remained significantly hierarchical. Although the efflorescence of ancient Greece, in particular Athens, is not one of our primary cases, it offers very helpful insights into this characteristic. To be sure, like all the cases, the portrait is hardly one of generalized equality—but rather of a relative degree of societal egalitarianism and shared opportunity even alongside very sharp hierarchies (especially involving women, foreigners, and slaves). Greek equality was impressive only "when compared with the norms typical of premodern states."[27]

But with those qualifications, Athenian society, the historian Josiah Ober explains, was one in which "the normatively valued political conditions of democracy for an extensive body of citizens . . . were conjoined with economic growth whose benefits were widely shared." Its economic rise was a product in part of "the ability of an extensive middle class to consume goods and services at a level well above mere existence." Compared with other ancient societies, "wealth and income were quite equitably distributed. Many Greeks lived between the extremes of affluence and poverty and well above the level of bare subsistence." The result was the emergence of a "substantial middle class," at least by premodern standards, with significant potential for upward mobility. "It is uncontroversial," Ober adds, "to say that classical Greek society was characterized by historically exceptional levels of equality in terms of

[27] Ober, 2015, p. 103.

TABLE 5.1

Shared Opportunity and Competitive Advantage—Evidence from Cases

Case	Elements of the Role of Shared Opportunity in Historical Cases
Rome	• Role of freed slaves in economic life of Rome; potential for entrepreneurship • Military advancement for citizens other than aristocracy • Gradual and partial emergence of a middle class with expanding commercial ambitions • Inclusion of peoples beyond the city itself—in Italy and beyond—as citizens, even eventually emperors
China	• Some evidence of expanded opportunity in periods of premodern efflorescence, within constraints of social and political realities of the period and significant social conflict resulting from meritocratic competition • Modern China, although an autocratic system, eventually created (and invested in) pathways for economic, military, and political achievement for a broad swath of the population
Spain	• Mixed evidence; in early modern empire, opportunity more constrained to aristocratic classes; evidence of competitive disadvantage relative, for example, to Britain
Austria-Hungary	• Large parts of population stuck in peasantry, aristocratic society • Opportunity growing in 19th century, especially in Austria and among more urban and educated groups
Ottoman Empire	• System of recruiting talented young men as civil servants, especially in various reform periods beginning in the 18th century • Relative, qualified inclusion of all major social groups in social life • Potential for intellectual and military advancement for people from many backgrounds
Renaissance Italy	• General social value of self-development and expression • Conscious willingness to reward innovation and genius from all citizens
Britain	• Potential for commercial advancement for all citizens; many examples of entrepreneurs from limited means • Late-starting but eventually wide-reaching mass education to provide opportunity • Even within general aristocratic system, open channels of opportunity to wider proportion of population because of democratic and commercial values
Sweden	• Highly egalitarian modern society, but uncertain connection to competitive advantage in early modern period of peak power
France	• Postrevolution ethic of equality and shared opportunity, qualified by continuing role of exclusive elite (for example, a handful of leading universities training civil servants) • Mass education and commercial opportunities provide increasing basis for opportunity
Japan	• Meiji and postwar periods of growth emphasized education for all; general social commitment to egalitarianism and equal opportunity • Homogenous population reduces potential for exclusion; many entrepreneurs and businesspeople come from humble backgrounds
Soviet Union	• Theoretically drew talents from whole society but in practice excluded major groups, especially those at margins of Communist Party
United States	• Strong national ethic of shared opportunity; endless examples of economic, technological, scientific, and military value generated by average citizens • Mass education provides generally shared opportunity

access of native males to key public institutions." The result was a form of "rule egalitarianism" and equal treatment before the law, "which can have substantial effects on economic growth by building human capital." Such equality "encourages investments by individuals in learning new skills and increases net social returns to employment of diverse skills."[28]

The case that may speak most powerfully to this characteristic is the United States itself. From its founding, even with the echo of a class-based society that came from its British origins, American society reflected shared opportunity in ways that went beyond any major European power of the era. Basic measures of social mobility (which will be referenced in Chapter Ten) in the modern era reflect a strongly opportunity-based society. There are innumerable examples of ties between the effects of shared opportunity and national dynamism, including scientists and entrepreneurs who contributed directly to U.S. competitive advantage. In the following section, on empirical evidence, we cite many studies performed in the United States that demonstrate ways in which elements of shared social opportunity produce such advantage.

The American case also emphasizes the external component of shared opportunity. American national dynamism has been and continues to be fueled by immigrants, who have brought skills, ambition, and scientific and technical knowledge to American society. Abundant empirical evidence highlights the ways in which immigrants have made disproportionate contributions to economic outcomes, such as innovation and entrepreneurialism; contributed key skills and knowledge to basic science; and played critical leadership roles in society.[29] America's immigrant tradition has been and remains a significant competitive advantage in terms of drawing on the widest potential reservoir of talent.

Apart from those examples, five of our historical case studies stand out as providing especially interesting evidence on the connection between shared opportunity and competitive advantage. One is Renaissance Italy, described at the beginning of the chapter. The others are Rome, the Ottoman Empire, Britain, and Japan.

Ancient Rome: Unprecedented Opportunity . . . Within Strict Constraints

Ancient Rome provides an excellent example of the qualifications and limits that must be applied to claims about shared opportunity, while still offering clear evidence of the competitive advantages of this characteristic. Focusing especially on our core period of peak dyna-

---

[28] Ober, 2015, pp. xv, 4, 101, 111, 215, 243.

[29] Summaries of this evidence include Tom Jawetz, "Building a More Dynamic Economy: The Benefits of Immigration," testimony before the U.S. House Committee on the Budget, Washington, D.C.: Center for American Progress, June 26, 2019; Arloc Sherman, Danilo Trisi, Chad Stone, Shelby Gonzales, and Sharon Parrott, "Immigrants Contribute Greatly to the U.S. Economy," Center on Budget and Policy Priorities, August 15, 2019; Gordon Hansen and Matthew Slaughter, *Talent, Immigration, and U.S. Economic Competitiveness*, Long Beach, Calif.: Compete America Coalition, May 2013; Mohamad Ali, "Immigration Is at the Heart of U.S. Competitiveness," *Harvard Business Review*, May 15, 2017.

mism, from the late republic through the early empire, broadly defined, in many ways Roman society was hierarchical and strictly conservative.[30] It retained powerful class divisions and aristocratic prejudice, and it would be incorrect to think of Rome as reflecting shared opportunity on anything like a modern scale.[31] Roman elite mocked and despised social climbers, whether freedmen (former slaves promoted into a wide range of administrative and business positions) or the nouveau riche. Although routes to advancement did exist, Roman society did not valorize commercial achievement as later modern societies did, and we would be misguided to think of Rome as having a broad-based entrepreneurial mindset.[32]

Roman society was also strikingly unequal in economic terms. The historian Walter Scheidel has conducted some of the most-elaborate studies of inequality in the ancient world.[33] He concludes that the biggest Roman fortunes equaled about 1.5 million times the annual Roman income, similar to the massive ratio achieved by today's billionaires. "The net result," he concludes, "was an intensely stratified society in which the richest 1 percent or 2 percent absorbed much of the available surplus beyond bare subsistence."[34]

Yet Roman society did offer multiple avenues to advancement for talented individuals from many backgrounds, in ways that began to hint at more-modern approaches to shared opportunity. Increasingly over time, this included citizens born outside Rome itself and even outside Italy, as the empire granted citizenship to growing numbers of people in conquered lands and came to rely on military leaders, scientists, specialists, and even eventually emperors from places all across the wide swath of imperial rule. Rome clearly magnified its power to some degree by drawing on the talents of a reasonably wide range of its population—at least by the standards of an ancient civilization, and at least for a time. One historian, Kyle Harper, describes Rome as a "quasi-egalitarian polity."[35]

---

[30] As two scholars have concluded, "Roman society was obsessed with status and rank; a Roman's place in the social hierarchy was advertised in the clothes he wore, the seat he occupied at public entertainments, the number and social position of his clients and followers, and his private expenditures on slaves, housing and banquets" (Peter Garnsey and Richard Saller, *The Roman Empire: Economy, Society and Culture*, 2nd ed., Oakland: University of California Press, 2014, p. 232). An immense qualification to any catalog of shared opportunity in Rome is the prevalence of slavery, which constituted a major element of Roman economy and society. Romans actively worried about the threat of ambitious interlopers, the risk "that newcomers will displace them in society" (Temin, 2013, p. 3). Another was the lack of public involvement in the development of opportunity: "Rome's rulers showed virtually no interest in human capital or popular education" (Harris, 2007, p. 539).

[31] An outstanding general discussion of inequality in Rome at least in the early imperial period can be found in Garnsey and Saller, 2014, pp. 131–144.

[32] Garnsey and Saller, 2014, p. 71.

[33] Scheidel, 2018, p. 19.

[34] Scheidel, 2018, p. 91. Scheidel concludes that Roman inequality was close to the theoretical maximum—the highest degree of inequality possible to achieve in a premodern society: "At most a tenth of the population beyond the wealth elite would have been able to enjoy incomes well above bare subsistence levels" (Scheidel, 2018, p. 92).

[35] Harper, 2017, p. 6.

Some data support the image of a Roman society becoming more open and inclusive. Other scholars looking at the same data as Scheidel suggest that Roman society might have had a less intense concentration of wealth in the top 1 percent than some later societies (such as the Byzantine Empire), and a longer "tail" of wealthy citizens in the top 5 or 10 percent of the population—a distribution not totally unlike that of Britain at the end of the 18th century. These other studies suggest that Rome fell roughly in the middle of the measured historical societies in terms of distribution of wealth, even including many 19th-century societies.[36] Other evidence for an embryonic middle class comes from the fact that the spread of wealth beyond the uppermost classes would have produced demands for all manner of consumer goods—and archaeologists have found growing evidence for just such a pattern, including the remains of large numbers of an exceptional variety of consumer goods throughout society.[37]

Some scholars have also concluded that the generally strict division between upper classes and commoners became, through the late republic and early empire, "ever more permeable."[38] Common citizens could advance in the military, in business, even in politics to some degree—and the rich could fall and be left paupers. Although the concession is minimal and inhumane, Rome offered its enslaved population the possibility of purchasing or earning their freedom and becoming significant figures in society.[39] The position of women in Roman society (as, again, in almost all premodern societies) was starkly unequal, yet women's status in marriages did improve—for example, women did not, as in earlier Roman times,

---

[36] Branko Milanovic, Peter H. Lindert, and Jeffrey G. Williamson, "Ancient Inequality," unpublished manuscript, Harvard University, June 2008, pp. 30, 41–42. Scheidel himself, writing with another scholar, agrees that despite massive disparities, there might have been something like a Roman middle class that earned between 16 and 27 percent of income; Walter Scheidel and Steven J. Friesen, "The Size of the Economy and the Distribution of Income in the Roman Empire," *Journal of Roman Studies*, Vol. 99, 2009, p. 89.

[37] "For me, what is most striking about the Roman economy is precisely the fact that it was not solely an elite phenomenon, but one that made basic good-quality items available right down the social scale" (Ward-Perkins, 2006, p. 146; also see p. 88). Evidence for a sort of ancient version of a middle class comes in part from pottery and remnants of other textiles (Temin, 2013, p. 217), and other evidence of material wealth. The growing wealth in society "was not just the wealth of a small elite (although the elite did indeed grow significantly richer), but reached an increasingly prosperous subelite, and significant sections of the working population" (W. Jongman, "Gibbon Was Right: The Decline and Fall of the Roman Economy," in O. Hekster, G. de Kleijn, and Daniëlle Slootjes, eds., *Crises and the Roman Empire*, Leiden, Netherlands: Brill, 2007, p. 187).

[38] Holland, 2005, p. 22; also see M. K. Hopkins, "Social Mobility in the Later Roman Empire: The Evidence of Ausonius," *Classical Quarterly*, Vol. 11, No. 2, 1961.

[39] The scholar Robert Garland refers to this policy as "the boldest experiment in what sociologists call upward mobility that the world had ever seen" and concludes that, in terms of their enslaved population, the "Romans, unlike the Greeks, understood that their slave population included many highly talented and enterprising individuals, and that these people could greatly benefit Roman society once they had earned their freedom" (Robert Garland, "The Other Side of History: Daily Life in the Ancient World," Great Courses, course no. 3810, 2012, lecture 23).

transfer all their wealth to their husbands upon marriage.[40] As the classicist Emily Wilson explains, "In contrast to many slave-owning societies, both ancient and modern, the Romans allowed large numbers of their slaves to become free, and to acquire at least limited forms of citizenship." And in terms of gender relations, "The flexible vision of Romanitas [Roman self-identity] also meant that Roman women, at least in the elite classes, had access to far greater freedom and more legal rights than women in many other ancient societies."[41]

It is critical not to exaggerate the degree of shared opportunity in any ancient society, including Rome. Vast numbers of average citizens could aspire to little more than basic subsistence. Nonetheless, the potential for advancement for handfuls of lower-class individuals and more of the small but energetic middling classes did exist, and Rome did benefit from the talents of thousands of men who rose through some degree of social climbing. Some estimates suggest a 75 percent turnover in the composition of Roman elite families for each generation, [42] which implies that there was a constant process of churn that would provide new chances for advancement and no locked-in oligarchy. Men who had been slaves could rise to positions of significant authority in the Roman bureaucracy, although the line between those individuals and the true, "equestrian" elite remained very firm.[43]

Rome's partial and constrained embrace of shared opportunity appears to have bestowed several competitive advantages on the empire. Shared opportunity was part and parcel of Rome's key global strategy: offering citizenship to small numbers, but eventually many, of the peoples it conquered. This widely shared citizenship granted key legal and social benefits to eventually 60 million or more people. As the historian Douglas Boin describes it,

> If you lived at the empire's frontier, citizenship guaranteed your ability to hear a case before a Roman judge. If you grew up at the border, it ensured that you and your family could not suffer arbitrarily at the hands of slave traders, who stole boys and girls like hungry wolves. Citizenship also promoted a widespread public trust in investment and fostered economic growth.[44]

---

[40] "In sum, Roman women enjoyed a legal independence in marriage that is quite remarkable by comparison with the position of women in many other traditional agrarian societies" (Garnsey and Saller, 2014, p. 155).

[41] Emily Wilson, "The Secret of Rome's Success," *The Atlantic*, December 2015.

[42] See Garnsey and Saller, 2014, pp. 144–147.

[43] P. R. C. Weaver, "Social Mobility in the Early Roman Empire: The Evidence of the Imperial Freedman and Slaves," *Past and Present*, Vol. 37, No. 1, July 1967; Pedro López Barja De Quiroga, "Freedmen Social Mobility in Roman Italy," *Historia: Zeitschrift Für Alte Geschichte*, Vol. 44, No. 3, 1995.

[44] Douglas Boin, "Ancient Rome Thrived When the Empire Welcomed Immigrants: We Should Remember What Happened When That Changed," *Time*, June 9, 2020.

The result was a significant geostrategic advantage, in terms of the empire's ability to control, gather resources from, and avoid instability throughout its provinces.[45]

This expanding grant of citizenship had the direct and critical advantage of boosting the empire's manpower base, which turned out to be one of its essential competitive advantages. One historian argues that we cannot "overstress the importance of the practice of absorbing some conquered territory" and "extending forms of Roman citizenship to various Italian communities, and in all cases obliging subordinate states to contribute troops to the Roman army. This threefold policy allowed for the citizen population of Rome to grow so as to dwarf any single potential peninsular competitor, even the largest."[46] Rome's vast reservoirs of fighters proved to be a decisive response to repeated setbacks on the battlefield, beginning in the Punic Wars and continuing into the repeated recoveries of the Western Roman empire before its collapse in 476 CE.

Shared opportunity benefited the empire in economic ways as well. The commercial activities of some number of people drawn from the wider population, whether abroad or through advancement from lower classes or slave status, fueled the empire's economic vitality. Rome drew on ideas and scientific knowledge from many places, especially Greece, which Romans looked on as a source of great culture, employing many Greeks as teachers and administrators.

In sum, Rome's approach to relatively inclusive opportunity, ranging from opening avenues to entrepreneurship and riches (even for former slaves) to the enfranchisement of tens of millions of people in distant provinces, provided important competitive advantage. As the historian Michael P. Fronda writes:

> This constellation of political concepts and policies gave the Roman state a huge potential for growth because it detached citizenship from ethnic or linguistic origins: Roman citizenship became a bundle of rights and obligations that could be extended in whole or in part to whomever the Romans wished. This masterstroke also encouraged cooperation on the part of incorporated peoples and created bonds between the conquerors and conquered.[47]

The Ottoman Experience

The Ottoman state at its peak reflected a striking case of a multiethnic empire that drew on a highly diverse talent base and, in some ways like Rome, incorporated subject peoples—and

---

[45] Mary Beard, *SPQR*, New York: Liveright, 2015. As Wilson puts it, "the Romans pioneered a revolutionary understanding of citizenship. . . . The idea that one could be a citizen, even a partial citizen, of a place where one did not live, and had perhaps never been, was virtually unprecedented. So was the idea that one could have a dual identity, as both Roman and Mantuan, Roman and Sicilian, or Roman and Oscan (when the Romans conquered the peninsula), or—later—Roman and Greek, Hispanic, Gallic, or British" (Wilson, 2015).

[46] Fronda, 2010, p. 29.

[47] Fronda, 2010, p. 303.

in some cases assimilated their elites, through state policies that provided competitive advantage. Ultimately, however, it is possible to read especially the later history of the empire as a series of failed efforts to match Europe's gradually expanding degree of shared opportunity and widespread unleashing of talents. From the standpoint of this characteristic, the Ottomans could arguably never escape the simple fact that theirs was an empire, an identity, and a cause founded on a basic discrimination between Muslims and those of other faiths and, until very late in its tenure, embodied a strict and autocratic social and political hierarchy with the sultan at the top.

During its rise and the peak of its power, the Ottoman Empire represented a cosmopolitan civilization that embraced many nationalities, ethnicities, creeds, and religions even if not all enjoyed precisely the same rights.[48] There was significant toleration of many religions and ethnic groups and ways in which non-Muslims could pursue commercial and social achievements. The Ottomans were open to ideas and technical and scientific advances from many other peoples. The historian of the Ottoman world Marc David Baer describes it as a "conversion-based meritocracy" whose ideology sought a system that "balanced and properly utilized the diverse human resources at the empire's disposal."[49] Some European visitors, Baer reports, were impressed with the degree to which bureaucratic positions were filled based on skill and ability.

One way in which the Ottoman state took advantage of the talents of its full population was the practice of recruiting non-Muslim boys for administrative positions (the *devşirme*, or collection, a child levy system), and then educating them in the rigorous palace school systems, tapped widely into the talent available in the society.[50] The very best of these recruits became some of the highest officials in the land, and this system "offered extreme social mobility for males, allowing peasant boys to rise to the highest military and administrative positions in the empire" and allowed the empire "to tap into the manpower resources of its numerous Christian subject populations."[51]

Yet notwithstanding how powerful some of these bureaucrats could become, the practice amounted to a version of slavery or indentured servitude based on the state-sponsored kidnapping of children and forced conversion. Its goal might not have been so much freeing the talents of a wider segment of the population as much as replacing "the local Muslim aristocracy with a new and completely loyal class of servants devoted to their patron, the sultan."[52] If the *devşirme* was an avenue to social mobility, in other words, it was a rough and often cruel mechanism.

---

[48] Inalcik, 2001, loc. 230, 343, 3323.

[49] Baer, 2021, pp. 189–190.

[50] Finkel, 2005, pp. 74–75.

[51] Quataert, 2005, pp. 30–31.

[52] Baer, 2021, p. 44.

More broadly, the Ottoman case—in shared opportunity as in other characteristics, such as the quality of institutions and the role of learning and adaptation—illustrates the dangers of an incomplete and constrained embrace of key values. Even Baer, an eloquent defender of the qualities of Ottoman society, admits that its tolerant approach to some social groups existed within a fundamentally hierarchical society with male Muslims at the top, rather than anything like truly shared and equal opportunity. Conversion to Islam, even if sometimes voluntary, was an essential precondition for complete social mobility. Key social distinctions were "rigidly policed."[53]

Over time, these tensions expressed themselves in a series of counterreform movements in which the Muslim, male elite of the empire repeatedly sought to hold back the tide of spreading social status. Baer brilliantly outlines the contradictions that emerged—these elites saw themselves as "bearers and articulators of the meritocratic Ottoman Way," but the process of opening channels of social mobility quickly collided with reality. "Commoners," foreigners, women, and non-Muslims had to be excluded from social and political power and from the "privileged, ruling elite." Even the cosmopolitan reformer Selim III "was keen to maintain the gendered religious hierarchy of Ottoman society." As late as the mid-19th century, Baer writes, "elite Muslims" would not "relinquish the idea of the superiority of Islam or the primacy of Islamic law." Half a century later, at the dawn of the 20th century, Ottoman Muslims still "did not intend to relinquish their position as the empire's ruling element."[54]

Over the course of many centuries, from its rise through the 15th and 16th centuries, to perhaps the peak of power in the 17th, to the long, slow decline through the 18th century, the Ottoman Empire reflected complex patterns of social opportunity that cannot be boiled down to simple claims. But the research surveyed for this study does suggest that one major lesson is the competitive handicap imposed by significant limits on shared opportunity. Ultimately, the story of the empire's inability to keep pace with Europe may partly be about the unwillingness of a gendered, faith-based, hierarchical elite to open the aperture of social opportunity and mobility in dramatic ways.

Britain

Britain provides a modern case of the national competitive advantages that stem from shared opportunity, even if imperfect and qualified. If we focus on the period of peak British power—looking at British social patterns between perhaps 1820 and 1910, but also being mindful of groundwork that had been laid in the 18th century—the society that powered this competitive rise was, to be sure, highly stratified. British society right through the Victorian era and the heart of the Industrial Revolution was rigidly divided by class, on the basis of a landed

[53] Baer, 2021, pp. 11, 41, 252.

[54] Baer, 2021, pp. 256, 329–330, 423.

aristocracy that was slow to share power and privileges.[55] Nor did those patterns entirely disappear: Dierdre McCloskey refers to the "undertow" of aristocratic privilege that persisted, and to some degree persists to this day, in Britain.[56] Renewed debate broke out around 2018 over the degree to which advancement in the British civil service was constrained for those who did not attend elite schools or come from well-to-do or prominent backgrounds.[57]

And yet, in Britain as elsewhere, the Industrial Revolution was powered in part by an undeniably growing degree of inclusiveness.[58] Speaking of the Britain of the mid to late 19th century, David Landes argues that

> the Industrial Revolution created a society of greater richness and complexity. Instead of polarizing it into bourgeois minority and an almost all-embracing proletariat, it produced a heterogeneous bourgeoisie whose multitudinous shadings of income, origin, education, and way of life are overridden by a common resistance to inclusion in, or confusion with, the working classes, and by an unquenchable social ambition. For the essence of the bourgeois is that he is what the sociologists call upwardly mobile; and nothing has ever furnished so many opportunities to rise in the social scale as the Industrial Revolution.[59]

The result, Landes explains, was an "impulse given thereby to innovation," an impulse critically grounded in the "multiplication of points of creativity." That phrase is a wonderful shorthand summary of the essential character of highly competitive societies—it speaks both to expressions of talent and ideas and their synergistic connection in webs of productive exchange. Such a societal process, Landes argues, is to some degree "self-reinforcing: those economies that were freest seem to have been most creative; creativity promoted growth; and growth provided opportunities for further innovation, intended or accidental."[60]

---

[55] The most comprehensive study of British economic fortunes in these centuries concludes that income distribution "was profoundly unequal due to entrenched inequalities in access to the land, capital, education and political power upon which personal wealth depended. Gender, rank and servility and their differential legal rights were determined at birth. Privilege, patronage and position ensured that rent-seeking was rife" (Broadberry et al., 2014, p. 307).

[56] McCloskey, 2010, p. 73.

[57] Emma Sheppard, "Civil Servants on Being Working Class: 'It Feels the Odds Are Stacked Against You,'" *The Guardian*, March 26, 2018; "Britain's Civil Service Remains Upper-Middle Class," *The Economist*, May 22, 2021.

[58] Alan Macfarlane argues that English society had started to transition away from the rigidly hierarchical, patriarchal, isolated village life of peasant life and begun to shift toward a "fluid, individualistically oriented set of attitudes" (Alan Macfarlane, *The Origins of English Individualism: The Family, Property, and Social Transition*, Oxford, UK: Basil Blackwell, 1978; also see North, 1990, p. 115).

[59] Landes, 2003, p. 9.

[60] Landes, 2003, p. 19.

British society, though hierarchical, also became increasingly open during the 19th century as it reached its competitive peak, and the nobility did not operate as a "closed caste."[61] It is significant that only first sons of the elite inherited titles—other male heirs had to enter the military or business to at least partly make their own way. The system allowed for both upward and downward mobility, as wealthy merchants could earn themselves into the elite class and some nobles could fail so spectacularly that they were dropped from its rolls.[62] By the 18th century, "the idea of the 'self-made man' and the open society through which his industry, effort, thrift, and ability would propel him" had become "potent conceptions of society at the time."[63] This theme emerged prominently in literature and was a major narrative in British politics.[64] Despite many restrictions, "Englishmen and -women mingled more freely across lines of class and status than their peers elsewhere."[65]

There is abundant anecdotal evidence of leaders in business, science, the arts, and other spheres rising from middle and even lower classes to significant wealth and position in British society. We can point to the hundreds of inventors and entrepreneurs from the middle and lower classes whose ideas had immense economic value.[66] These range from James Hargreaves, the 18th-century inventor of the "spinning jenny"; to Richard Trevithick, inventor of the high-pressure steam locomotive; to the scientist of electromagnetism Michael Faraday, son of a blacksmith; to the blacksmith apprentice Michael Swan, who would go on to co-invent the incandescent light bulb. A society open to the ideas and inventions of a significant proportion of its whole population (though, in these earlier times, only its whole *male* population) ended up benefiting from the resulting imagination of people outside the elite classes.

In this context, the burgeoning scientific associations and intellectual networks helped break down boundaries by proclaiming themselves open to people from various religious groups and backgrounds.[67] British innovation was "indigenous and bottom-up—not, as was the case in" so many feudal, monarchical, autocratic, and dynastic societies—"the work of rulers and their courtiers."[68]

***

---

[61] We are grateful to William Anthony Hay for this insight.

[62] Paul Langford, *A Polite and Commercial People: England, 1728–1783*, Oxford, UK: Oxford University Press, 1989.

[63] Jason Long, "The Surprising Social Mobility of Victorian Britain," *European Review of Economic History*, Vol. 17, No. 1, February 2013, p. 2.

[64] Kathryn Hughes, "The Middle Classes: Etiquette and Upward Mobility," British Library, May 15, 2014.

[65] Appleby, 2010, loc. 2000.

[66] François Crouzet, *The First Industrialists: The Problems of Origins*, Cambridge, UK: Cambridge University Press, 1985.

[67] Ferguson, 2011, p. 69.

[68] Jacob, 2014, p. 10.

The historian Roy Porter's study of Britain in the 18th century stresses that it remained a hierarchical society whose "political institutions and . . . distributions of wealth and power were unashamedly inegalitarian, hierarchical, hereditary and privileged," a structure that remained in place at the beginning of the 19th century and indeed whose social hierarchy was intensifying in this period. Existing social authorities held tightly to their power and privilege, grounded in "landed estates, patronage, office and political and legal authority within the state" and other sources. Wealth was strikingly unequal throughout society, justified by a social ethic that asserted the natural condition of social stations. Women were denied most rights and forced into "constrictive roles."[69] When industrialization did begin to kick off, it drew masses of people into mines, factories, and eventually offices, many doing robotic jobs with high degrees of danger. British society remained resistant to change, with major social institutions locking in privilege rather than opening gates of mobility.

Yet even Porter recognizes the emerging industrialization, and the rise of "a self-confident manufacturing bourgeoise," that was beginning to force cracks into this edifice. Handfuls of entrepreneurs from limited backgrounds could get fabulously rich, and public institutions, though at first dominated by the wealthy, eventually became engines for advancement for a broader range of groups. The social hierarchy was "neither rigid nor brittle," and "[t]here was continual adaptiveness to challenge and individual mobility, up, down, and sideways. More than in other countries, money was a passport through social frontiers." Information flowed widely throughout society and that physical mobility was extensive, with people from rural areas visiting London. Above all, Porter describes the explosive commercial energy of the society that created ferment and generated opportunities that could not be kept restricted to a narrow few.[70]

Porter's rich account demonstrates again that we must be open-minded and flexible in what we mean by shared opportunity. It need not be perfect to achieve competitive advantage; strong social inequalities can be present, but with enough apertures for advancement, with enough chance for ambitious people and entrepreneurial energy to express themselves, the mechanism can work. Critical to this, however, is the absence of truly formalized, hard and fast class or other boundaries on the feudal model, the sort of blood-based aristocracy characteristic of much of the Continent during the period Porter is assessing. And his account highlights the critical role of commerce and economic ambition as a forcing function: "The dynamo of the market," he concludes, "was the secret of this transformation."[71] Sometimes, in other words, a significant, open-enough elite can be sufficient as the basis for national competitive advantage.

David Cannadine picks up the story of Britain in the 19th century and tells a similarly mixed tale. Society remained highly unequal in many ways, and up to three-quarters of the

[69] R. Porter, 1990, pp. 2–3, 14–17, 22–28, 48, 340.

[70] R. Porter, 1990, pp. 4, 15, 39, 97, 142, 185–187, 341.

[71] R. Porter, 1990, p. 342.

people toiled in lower middle-class or lower-class occupations. "The late eighteenth-century United Kingdom was, then, a very unequal society in terms of the distribution of wealth, power and status. It was probably less so than the Russian Empire, but it was certainly more inequitable than the United States. . . . [L]ife chances significantly deteriorated the lower down the social scale a person was situated." There were strict barriers between those who could vote and participate in significant political activity and those who could not, between men and women. Equality before the law, Cannadine reports, remained mostly an aspiration rather than a reality.[72]

And yet even by 1800, various "middling" classes were emerging across society, including bankers, financiers, leaders of the emerging private industries, lawyers, doctors, insurance professionals, clergy, and many others. Increasingly, "the landed elite and middle classes melded into each other." Cannadine later argues that major theorists of a fracturing, deeply divided society in Britain badly exaggerated the degree of division: British society was maturing into a highly complex, varied, and multilevel organism with all manner of layers in between the super wealthy and the desperately poor. Women's status in society, in terms of legal and political status and educational and career opportunities, was slowly but gradually improving throughout the century. By the later part of the century, the dominance of Parliament by old-style aristocrats was giving way to more influence for newer industrialists and professionals.[73]

***

Scholars have traced the role of *dissenters*—members of minority religious faiths—in spurring British entrepreneurship, as another form of shared opportunity.[74] Rosters of the faiths of leading businesspeople produce the conclusion that, as Joel Mokyr puts it, "[t]he importance of dissenting religions in the Industrial Revolution in supplying a much larger than proportional number of captains of industry is beyond question."[75]

Empirical research on inequality and mobility also suggests that British society toward the peak of its competitive position was beginning to display more shared, modern patterns of wealth. Multiple scholars suggest that British society—while class-based and constricted

---

[72] Cannadine, 2017, pp. 38, 357–359.

[73] Cannadine, 2017, pp. 35–36, 207, 250, 360–361, 490–497, 506–509. Margaret Jacob urges us not to exaggerate the role of "people with little or no education" in prompting the Industrial Revolution. The intellectual ferment surrounding that trend was very much an elite phenomenon, she argues (Jacob, 1988, p. 179). And yet the numbers of people from limited backgrounds who contributed to Britain's economic takeoff is quite large. Cannadine (2017, pp. 37, 320), for example, lists various emerging entrepreneurs and industrialists who joined the British upper classes during the 19th century.

[74] Jacob, 2014, pp. 7, 50.

[75] Mokyr, 2012a. It is important not to focus narrowly on the role of dissenters; the scientific and intellectual ferment of the 18th century onward penetrated widely in the British elite, and not all 18th-century entrepreneurs were dissenters (Jacob, 1988, p. 150; R. Porter, 1990, pp. 320–321).

in important ways—enjoyed significant and increasing amounts of social mobility as far back as the 19th century.[76] A new analysis of the levels of inequality in Britain before and during the Industrial Revolution indicates that inequality grew significantly between 1688 and 1798, then declined by 1867.[77] Prior research had already shown that the 18th century was a period of relative income growth for the richer segments of society, whereas the period 1846–1867 saw a dramatic rise in the relative incomes of working and lower classes. From the standpoint of simple inequality measures, Britain therefore underwent some reduction in inequality in roughly the same period that it grew to its most significant power.[78]

Although historical data for gender opportunity are scarce, some are available. One fascinating study of a "patriarchy index" combined factors such as female-headed households, proportion of young brides, and preference for sons to score European societies from the 18th through the early 20th centuries.[79] In terms of country ratings, the researchers find sig-

---

[76] See, for example, Andrew Miles, *Social Mobility in Nineteenth and Early Twentieth Century Britain*, London: Palgrave Macmillan UK, 1999. He argues that formal mobility was limited but that accessibility to different professions made Britain a relatively "open" society. See also Dean Rapp, "Social Mobility in the Eighteenth Century: The Whitbreads of Bedfordshire, 1720–1815," *Economic History Review*, Vol. 27, No. 3, August 1974. See also Landes, 2003, for a general discussion of these issues.

One important recent study of intragenerational occupational mobility offers a mixed picture of social mobility in Britain from the Victorian era through the 1970s. Social mobility was surprisingly strong in the Victorian era, more so that had traditionally been understood. Comparing the figures with modern Britain, Jason Long finds that social mobility has indeed increased over the longer term: "Total mobility is nine percentage points higher in 1972 than 100 years earlier, with virtually the entire difference due to a higher rate of upward mobility: 35.5 versus 26.8 percent." On the other hand, using what he admits are crude statistical tools for estimating Victorian-era income, Long also concludes that long-term income elasticity, or the income benefits of social mobility, are far less if they are noticeable at all. "By one measure at least," he concludes, "intergenerational mobility of earnings barely changed at all over the decades from the mid-nineteenth century to the late twentieth" (Long, 2013, pp. 14, 18). For additional details, see Jason Long, "Rural-Urban Migration and Socioeconomic Mobility in Victorian Britain," *Journal of Economic History*, Vol. 65, 2005.

[77] This study estimates the Gini coefficient (with 1.0 being perfect inequality) as 0.54 in 1688 and 0.53 by 1759 but rising to 0.60 by 1798 and holding at 0.58 by 1846. In just the next two decades, though, it fell to 0.48 (Allen, 2019). Peter Lindert also describes a context of rising inequality in the earliest phases of preindustrial and early industrial economies—for example, from the 18th through mid-19th centuries in Britain, followed by a reduction of inequality during the core period of industrialization (Peter H. Lindert, "Three Centuries of Inequality in Britain and America," in Anthony B. Atkinson and François Bourguignon, eds., *Handbook of Income Distribution*, Vol. 1, Amsterdam: North-Holland, 2000).

[78] Another study finds that British Gini coefficients in parts of the 18th and 19th centuries compared unfavorably with many other parts of the world. The authors' added concept of an "inequality extraction ratio"—given the constraints of the period, what proportion of total income that the wealthiest could acquire did they actually get—demonstrates that Britain of 1759 comes off substantially better, however. Indeed, when Gini figures are plotted against gross domestic income per capita, Britain and the Netherlands stand out as progressing in the most positive direction of any studied countries, making them part of the "less-exploitative pre-industrial countries" (Branko Milanovic, Peter H. Lindert, and Jeffrey G. Williamson, "Pre-Industrial Inequality," *Economic Journal*, Vol. 121, No. 551, March 2011).

[79] Mikołaj Szołtysek, Sebastian Klüsener, Radosław Poniat, and Siegfried Gruber, "The Patriarchy Index: A New Measure of Gender and Generational Inequalities in the Past," *Cross-Cultural Research*, Vol. 51, No. 3, 2017.

nificant regional variation even within countries. But generally, Western Europe—including Britain—had relatively lower levels of patriarchy according to this index than did Central or Eastern Europe. And 19th-century Britain had scores that matched the Nordic countries of the time, which we now think of as global leaders in gender equality. Some scholars of 19th-century British gender relations, for example, see that period as a time when women—taking advantage of the pluralistic, democratic, and open society and the ongoing Industrial Revolution that opened new career opportunities—were gaining increasing traction in challenging inequities.[80]

An early version of this pattern was then exported to Britain's American colonies, which supercharged the idea of shared opportunity. The critical factor in impelling dynamism in the British New World, Niall Ferguson argues, "was social mobility—the fact that a man . . . could arrive in a wilderness with literally nothing and yet within just a few years become both a property-owner and a voter." Opportunity in the New World was particularly tied to mechanisms of land ownership, as Ferguson writes. Widespread land ownership produces a more empowered and dynamic society; keeping land under the control of the Crown leaves many citizens as glorified serfs and magnifies barriers between classes. "Under Spanish rule" in the New World, as an emergent aristocracy controlled the land, "there was none of the upward mobility that characterized British America."[81]

Shared social opportunity was not the sole explanation for Britain's astonishing economic rise. It had to be combined with other supporting conditions—strong institutions, an effective catalytic state—to get these results. As Mokyr puts it, "The environment that made British entrepreneurship so effective during the Industrial Revolution consisted of institutions that created the right incentives, and the complementarities created by human capital, natural resources, and a more effective polity." Only because entrepreneurs were confident that their actions would be rewarded, due to strong rule of law and social trust and other factors, did their ambition translate into a significant degree of economic advancement.[82] Once again we find the critical importance of a comprehensive recipe for national dynamism and competitive advantage, one that allows each of the societal characteristics to magnify the effects of the others.

Japan

Modern Japan seems also to endorse the competitive advantages of drawing a higher proportion of the nation's talents into national economic and military outputs. Pre-Meiji Tokugawa Japan was characterized by a strict social grading. Many early societies organized people into

---

[80] Jan Marsh, "Gender Ideology and Separate Spheres in the 19th Century," Victoria and Albert Museum, undated.

[81] Ferguson, 2011, pp. 112–113.

[82] Mokyr, 2012a, p. 40.

such hierarchies, Marius Jansen argues, "but few have calibrated that status with the nice precision that distinguishes Tokugawa Japan."[83] This was not, he explains, a system built on the essential characteristic of social mobility but rather a regulated hierarchy with a divine emperor at the top. The Confucian emphasis on merit-based advancement did not sweep this system away.

The Meiji reforms of the late 19th century furnished more opportunities—through more widespread education, for example, and a more standardized and rationalized bureaucratic system—for a wider range of people. The Meiji period was surely characterized by formal policies designed to level classes and create a greater sense of egalitarianism.[84] Smashing the samurai class helped open chances for advancement to more Japanese citizens. Although many strict constraints remained in place (women, for example, continued to face barriers to equal opportunity),[85] in general it is fair to say that Japanese society became more egalitarian, and opportunity oriented in the Meiji era. Japan was to some degree opening the spigots on its human capital in partial imitation of the European powers it was rushing to match.[86]

Mark Ravina's deeply researched study of Meiji Japan calls into question typical assumptions about that period and lays out much of the complexity of the time—the gradualism of some of the reforms, for example, and the debates between groups of Meiji leaders. He notes that the urge to match international advances was nothing new in Japan's history; the Meiji period was, to his view, at least the third such period of cultural borrowing, and Japan was less isolated from the world before the Meiji than often believed. That period built on halfway reforms under the Tokugawa shogunate, which previewed many of the Meiji initiatives, such as reducing the authority of regional elites and fashioning a stronger central government. He stresses, too, that even many Meiji reforms—such as pushing toward a more egalitarian society—were justified by and grounded in traditional Japanese cultural values.[87]

Nonetheless, his account does support the idea that Meiji rulers actively employed or pursued several of our nominated characteristics to catch up to industrializing Western powers and gain competitive advantage. One of those was shared opportunity: The challenge to strict hereditary privileges and social class divisions that began during the Tokugawa period accelerated. This took time to develop fully. Even by about 1871, Ravina explains, "daily life was still governed by conventional hierarchies. Samurai still lorded over commoners. . . . Pariah

---

[83] Jansen, 2000, loc. 1506.

[84] Gluck, 1985, p. 17.

[85] As Carol Gluck notes of Japan, "Politics in 1890 was a subject reserved for the very few. The electorate of 450,000 comprised only 1.1 percent of the population." Quirks in the electoral laws favored tax-paying property owners, who were "heavily overrepresented" in the enfranchised voters. Still, though, many such property holders were upper middle class; access to the power-wielding groups was by merit and acquisition, not blood. When the new parliament was formed (the Diet), most of its members were middle-class rural "gentlemen of moderate means" (Gluck, 1985, pp. 67–69).

[86] We are grateful to Robert Hellyer for this insight.

[87] Ravina, 2017.

castes . . . were still bound by long-standing restrictions on work and residence."[88] But this gradually changed, with steps to pull back more and more symbols of samurai preeminence and invest in the sinews of a more equal society, such as mass education.

The comprehensiveness of this process should therefore not be exaggerated. A significant literature on the Meiji era, for example, speaks to resentments that cropped up against what became perceived as a regime led by elites.[89] But the thirst for a degree of equality and shared opportunity seems clear. And the legacy remains very much alive: Two scholars argue that Japan in the modern era did become a state that "promoted the notion of an egalitarian society." This tradition became deeply embedded in Japanese self-identity: Most Japanese view themselves as middle class, polling suggests. Fully half of Japanese people say that the gap between rich and small ought to be kept modest regardless of personal achievement.[90]

Empirical Evidence: Research on Shared Opportunity and Competitive Standing

Turning to more-modern forms of empirical evidence on the effects of opportunity (or the lack of it), we find extensive reason to believe that opening avenues to advancement, expression, and success to a wide component of a society will have significant positive effects on growth, development, innovation, and competitiveness.

A broad swath of research supports the idea, for example, that inequality is correlated with slower growth and constrained innovation. It has this effect through such mechanisms as inefficient human resource use, social instability, and lack of capital accumulation across the population.[91] International Monetary Fund researchers Andrew Berg, Jonathan Ostry, and Charalambos Tsangarides find, for example, that inequality contributes to highly uneven periods of growth spurts followed by stagnation and hard landings.[92] A recent RAND Cor-

---

[88] Ravina, 2017, pp. 13, 136.

[89] Jason G. Karlin, *Gender and Nation in Meiji Japan*, Honolulu: University of Hawaii Press, 2014, pp. 7–10; Doak, 1997, pp. 286–287.

[90] Glosserman and Snyder, 2017, pp. 33–34.

[91] Raquel Fernandez and Richard Rogerson, "Human Capital Accumulation and Income Distribution," Cambridge, Mass.: National Bureau of Economic Research, Working Paper 3994, 1992; Kevin M. Murphy, Andrei Shleifer, and Robert W. Vishny, "Income Distribution, Market Size and Industrialization," *Quarterly Journal of Economics*, Vol. 104, No. 3, 1989; Roberto Perotti, "Income Distribution, Politics, and Growth," *American Economic Review*, Vol. 82, No. 2, 1992; Torsten Persson and Guido Tabellini, "Is Inequality Harmful for Growth?" *American Economic Review*, Vol. 84, No. 3, 1994.

[92] Jonathan D. Ostry, Andrew Berg, and Charalambos G. Tsangarides, "Redistribution, Inequality, and Growth," Washington, D.C.: International Monetary Fund, April 2014. Ruchir Sharma has described ways in which inequality can "threaten the economy," including by becoming so severe that "the population turns suspicious of the way wealth is being created" (Sharma, 2016, p. 10). It can create a "stagnant and dominant elite" headed by hundreds of billionaires (p. 114). As Sharma concludes, "It is hard to dispute the

poration report finds that inequality is correlated with lack of opportunity, specifically measured by intergenerational transfers of wealth.[93]

Some analyses have modified this picture somewhat, arguing that economic opportunity—as distinct from inequality—is associated with economic growth.[94] Yet, overall, shared opportunity appears to be positively related to creativity and innovation in a society and, through those factors, to economic growth and productivity. The economist Raj Chetty explains:

> Children from rich families are 10 times as likely to become inventors as those from lower-income families. Further examination of these data suggests that a large portion of this innovation gap can, once again, be attributed to differences in childhood environment and exposure between low- and high-income families. These results imply that improving opportunities for social mobility could ultimately increase the rate of innovation in the economy and thereby benefit everyone, not just disadvantaged children. Hence, increasing mobility is of interest not just from the perspective of justice but also from the perspective of economic growth.[95]

This causal link emerges in a wide range of empirical studies. Some of that research points to lack of capital, educational opportunity, or other causal links between forgone opportunity and lower growth.[96] One study finds "robust support for a negative relationship between inequality of opportunity and growth."[97] Econometric studies suggest that the presence of society-wide innovative opportunity and drive are associated with economic dynamism.[98]

---

growing view that low levels of inequality fuel long runs of strong economic growth, and that high or rapidly rising inequality can prematurely snuff out growth" (p. 138).

[93] Francisco Perez-Arce, Ernesto F. L. Amaral, Haijing Crystal Huang, and Carter C. Price, *Inequality and Opportunity: The Relationship Between Income Inequality and Intergenerational Transmission of Income*, Santa Monica, Calif.: RAND Corporation, RR-1509-RC, 2016.

[94] Katharine Bradbury and Robert Triest write, "Inequality of opportunity prevents some potential workers in the economy from developing their full capacity, generating wasted resources and hence lower-than-possible output." Their analysis finds "a statistically significant positive coefficient on absolute mobility in explaining economic growth in either period, indicating a strongly negative effect of inequality of opportunity on growth" (Katharine Bradbury and Robert K. Triest, "Inequality of Opportunity and Aggregate Economic Performance," *RSF: The Russell Sage Foundation Journal of the Social Sciences*, Vol. 2, No. 2, May 2016, pp. 185, 189).

[95] Raj Chetty, *Improving Opportunities for Economic Mobility: New Evidence and Policy Lessons*, St. Louis, Mo.: Federal Reserve Bank of St. Louis, December 2016.

[96] Sarah Voitchovsky, "Inequality and Economic Growth," in Wiemer Salverda, Brian Nolan, and Timothy Smeeding, eds., *The Oxford Handbook of Economic Inequality*, Oxford, UK: Oxford University Press, 2009.

[97] Gustavo A. Marrero and Juan G. Rodriguez., "Macroeconomic Determinants of Inequality of Opportunity and Effort in the US: 1970–2009," working paper, Verona, Italy: Society for the Study of Economic Inequality, 2012. See also Gustavo A. Marrero and Juan G. Rodriguez, "Inequality of Opportunity and Growth," *Journal of Development Economics*, Vol. 104, September 2013.

[98] Edmund S. Phelps, Raicho Bojilov, Hian Teck Hoon, and Gylfi Zoega, *Dynamism: The Values That Drive Innovation, Job Satisfaction, and Economic Growth*, Cambridge, Mass.: Harvard University Press, 2020, p. xi.

Studies of the economic opportunity afforded to women and minority populations suggest that removing constraints on access to leading professions accounted for a significant proportion of productivity gains in those areas.[99]

A study from 2018 surveyed the striking lost opportunities from inequality. A quarter of U.S. productivity growth between 1960 and 2008, it reports, could be explained by expanding opportunity for women and minority groups. If Black and Hispanic business ownership in the United States were proportional to the national average, this would theoretically create as many as 1.1 million new businesses, employing 9 million additional people. All told, closing the racial equality gap in opportunity in the United States would add more than $8 trillion to U.S. GDP growth between 2018 and 2050.[100]

Research on the competitive advantages of social mobility is somewhat mixed. Some studies have found a weak relationship between mobility and economic growth,[101] yet a significant and growing set of studies suggests that there is indeed a causal link. Low levels of mobility, as two leading researchers explain, mean that a nation is "missing out on a sizable talent pool, fishing in the same small pond generation after generation. That is not just unfair for individuals to realize their potential but damaging to the nation's overall economic productivity." Studies have suggested that boosting social mobility could increase national GDP growth by 2 to 4 percent a year.[102] A 2020 World Economic Forum study, which ranked countries on a social mobility index, found that social mobility is a critical support system for national growth and productivity.[103] The World Bank has also developed the Human Capital Index, which it finds to be correlated with various measures of national growth, development, and productivity.[104] Historical cases also point to the importance of human capital to development and growth.[105]

---

[99] Chang-Tai Hsieh, Eric Hurst, Charles I. Jones, and Peter J. Klenow, "The Allocation of Talent and U.S. Economic Growth," Cambridge, Mass.: National Bureau of Economic Research, Working Paper 18693, 2013.

[100] Ani Turner, *The Business Case for Racial Equity: A Strategy for Growth*, Ann Arbor and Battle Creek, Mich.: Altarum Health and W.K. Kellogg Foundation, 2018.

[101] Richard Breen, "Inequality, Economic Growth and Social Mobility," *British Journal of Sociology*, Vol. 48, No. 3, 1997; Bradbury and Triest, 2016.

[102] Social mobility also turns out to be positively related to a country's creative output, which in turn can contribute to national strength in the categories of soft power (Lee Elliot Major and Stephen Machin, *What Do We Know and What Should We Do About: Social Mobility*, Los Angeles: Sage, 2020, p. 15). Helen Jenkins and Katie-Lee English, "Hidden Talent: The Economic Benefits of Social Mobility," Oxera, July 27, 2017.

[103] Major and Machin, 2020, p. 2; Lee Elliot Major and Stephen Machin, *Social Mobility and Its Enemies*, London: Pelican Books, 2018; World Economic Forum, *The Global Social Mobility Report 2020: Equality, Opportunity and a New Economic Imperative*, Geneva, 2020, pp. 11–12.

[104] World Bank, *Human Capital Index: 2020 Update*, Washington, D.C., 2021a.

[105] Francesco Cinnirella and Jochen Streb, "The Role of Human Capital and Innovation in Economic Development: Evidence from Post-Malthusian Prussia," *Journal of Economic Growth*, Vol. 22, 2017.

There are therefore many practical and theoretical reasons to believe that societies with poor social mobility are sacrificing opportunities that could lead to greater economic growth, technological innovation, and other positive ends.[106] As a major Organisation for Economic Co-operation and Development (OECD) study concludes,

> First and foremost, lack of social mobility can hurt the foundations of economic growth. Lack of upward mobility at the bottom of the income distribution means that many potential talents are missed out on or remain under-developed. It also means that many investment opportunities and potential businesses will never see the light. Poor people may not take advantage of investment opportunities because of borrowing or liquidity constraints, a lack of information about investment opportunities, or insufficient availability of family resources to insure against possible downside risks of the investment. This undermines productivity and potential economic growth at the national level.[107]

In similar ways, the Nobel Prize–winning economist Edmund Phelps emphasizes the importance—and the potential competitive advantage—of creating economies that offer productive labor, and the opportunity for creative and innovative work, to as many citizens as possible. Phelps argues that grassroots creativity is in fact the main engine of innovation. If so, then drawing as wide a swath of the population as possible into this process is essential.[108] During Britain in the Industrial Revolution, wealth and title were not necessary to make an economic impact: "It was enough to be creative and smart." He concludes, "The Industrial Revolution . . . was the age, above all, in history of matchless opportunities for penniless men with powerful brains and imaginations, and it is astonishing how quickly they came to the fore."[109]

What Phelps is getting at is the intersection of grassroots entrepreneurialism with what he calls "flourishing"—the fact that people in possession of such opportunities can fashion careers and vocations for themselves that serve as empowering outlets for creativity: "In such an economy, conceiving a new thing or new method, imagining an unseen possibility, and exploring the unknown are apt to be the most deeply rewarding sort of work experience."[110] There is some synergy here between opportunity, empowerment, self-realization, and national power.

In much this same vein, one recent study finds compelling evidence of the value of inclusion for national strength. The authors look at the effect of discrimination on military enlist-

---

[106] Federico Cingano, "Trends in Income Inequality and Its Impact on Economic Growth," OECD Social, Employment and Migration Working Paper No. 163, Paris: Organisation for Economic Co-operation and Development, 2014; Maia Güell, Michele Pellizzari, Giovanni Pica, and Sevi Rodriguez Mora, "Correlating Social Mobility and Economic Outcomes," *VoxEU*, November 26, 2018.

[107] OECD, *A Broken Social Elevator? How to Promote Social Mobility*, Paris, 2018, p. 23.

[108] Phelps et al., 2020, pp. 3–4.

[109] Phelps, 2013, p. 12.

[110] Phelps et al., 2020, p. x.

ment rates in World War II and find—as one would expect—that discrimination suppressed rates of enlistment among Black Americans. They contend that this is a good example of the connection between inclusion and state capacity, concluding: "[D]iscrimination can undermine an important dimension of state capacity, and that the social costs of discrimination can be far reaching. . . . [A] state that requires equal contributions from its citizens should treat its citizens equally."[111]

This social paradigm of inclusive opportunity turns out to be a critical component of the engine of national vitality and dynamism described in Chapter One. The most successful and competitive nations have reflected some degree—incomplete, qualified, relative to their time—of this widespread, grassroots pattern of shared opportunity that not only generates competitive advantage but also, as Phelps puts it, brings "to ordinary people of varying talents a kind of flourishing—the experience of engagement, personal growth, and fulfillment."[112]

The Competitive Risks of an Absence of Opportunity

Part of the reason why shared opportunity is so important to national competitive standing is that its *absence* is as much of a risk as its presence is a boon. This is true in economic terms, as we have seen, but it is also true in other ways. The failure to grant wide-enough opportunity is dangerous because it undermines the legitimacy of the social structure and provokes backlash. This theme emerges powerfully from our historical cases.

Eric Hobsbawn argues, drawing on his review of European history, that a lack of opportunity lays the groundwork for social revolt. Striving middle-class people in the early industrial period hoped more than anything to "escape the fate of being a poor laboring man, or at best to accept or forget poverty and humiliation."[113] A society that does not, or cannot, offer a wide cross-section of its people reliable avenues to at least potential advancement risks creating a resentful group of people stuck without hope or opportunity.[114] Broken social contracts regarding opportunity can foster a tinderbox of resentment.[115] Such situations create the risk of a classic revolution of rising expectations, in which economic progress and political change create hopes for the future that can then be dashed by continued limits on shared opportunity.

---

[111] Nancy Qian and Marco Tabellini, "Discrimination and State Capacity: Evidence from WWII U.S. Army Enlistment," Cambridge, Mass.: National Bureau of Economic Research, Working Paper 29482, November 2021, p. 28.

[112] Phelps, 2013, p. 15.

[113] Hobsbawm, 1962, p. 204.

[114] Hämäläinen, 2003, p. 161.

[115] John W. G. Lowe, *The Dynamics of Apocalypse: A Systems Simulation of the Classic Maya Collapse*, Albuquerque: University of New Mexico Press, 1985; Joseph A. Tainter, "Archaeology of Overshoot and Collapse," *Annual Review of Anthropology*, Vol. 35, 2006.

One of the important themes that emerged from our work was the critical role of the elites in any society in creating the conditions for shared opportunity. A lack of such opportunity and development of talent will often be associated with a situation in which a privileged few acquire such an intense sense of entitlement that their demands end up disrupting the whole society. This speaks to the relationship of elites to the larger society and the fact that elites' unwillingness to limit their own ability to acquire wealth can be destructive. When members of the larger populace come to believe that their advancement is blocked by self-interested elites, violence and instability can be the result.

Recent evidence indeed suggests that perception of decline in social mobility in many developed nations has become very real. According to an OECD study, "falling down the ladder—downward mobility—is becoming a greater risk in almost all OECD countries":

> a "broken social elevator" can have serious societal and political consequences. For one thing, perceived equal opportunities can reduce the probability of social conflicts. Higher rates of class movement are thought to weaken economic discontent and class struggle, even among those who are not mobile themselves. In contrast, stagnant societies do not offer much hope for change, and tend to create feelings of exclusion among disadvantaged groups. This fosters strong group identities and a division against those who are better-off.[116]

Part of the case for the role of opportunity in fueling competitive advantage, then, comes from an argument about what will happen if the characteristic goes unmet. A perception of intense barriers to expression of opportunity will cause societal anger and mistrust and a loss of connection to the community. Citizens will be less likely to sacrifice for a state that they do not believe offers them a fair chance. A perception of blocked paths to advancement alongside bitterly high disparities of income and wealth are a recipe for competitive decline.

There is also significant evidence from political science about the risks—to the stability, coherence, and governing effectiveness—for societies that fall into this noxious combination of low opportunity and high inequality. Although the empirical evidence about the relationship of inequality to specific outcomes is somewhat mixed (some studies, for example, do not show a strong correlation between inequality and political violence), there is sufficient evidence across many countries, studies, and issues to suggest a significant societal risk of growing and persistent inequality.[117] Inequality is also associated with democratic reversion and acceptance of authoritarianism.[118]

---

[116] OECD, 2018, p. 23.

[117] The literature on this point is voluminous. See, for example, Terry Lynn Karl, "Economic Inequality and Democratic Instability," *Journal of Democracy*, Vol. 11, No. 1, 2000; Edward N. Muller, "Income Inequality, Regime Repressiveness, and Political Violence," *American Sociological Review*, Vol. 50, No. 1, 1985.

[118] Ethan B. Kapstein and Nathan Converse, "Poverty, Inequality, and Democracy: Why Democracies Fail," *Journal of Democracy*, Vol. 19, No. 4, October 2008; Adam Przeworski, "The Poor and the Viability of Democracy," in Anirudh Krishna, ed., *Poverty, Participation, and Democracy: A Global Perspective*, New York: Cambridge University Press, 2008.

The perils of broadly constrained opportunity emerged in several of our case studies. One is Spain, a hierarchical society, both in terms of the gap between native Spaniards and the citizens of the empire, who were treated often as little more than a slave population, and among Spaniards themselves, where an aristocratic society was not as conducive to general advancement as the more open transmission belts of Britain or, in a very different way, France. The Renaissance case also offers cautionary lessons in this regard. In Milan, Lauro Martines explains, vast resources devoted to "glittering courtly expenditure," and foreign wars "made for a profundity of discontent that weakened government in its vitals."[119] After 1500, Martines notes,

> The continuing concentration of wealth resulted in more luxury at the top and misery at the bottom. A widening gulf separated privilege from institutional disability, and this increased suspicion as well as dislike between social classes. There was a greater emphasis on status over achievement, and a bullying new importance was attached to the claims of noble blood and antiquity of lineage. These towered over the "natural" inferiority of common folk and particularly over the stigma of anything that smacked of manual work.[120]

When broad swaths of a population perceive that an elite class is pursuing its own selfish interests at the expense of the larger society, loyalty and commitment to the national project can fray. Combined with gridlocked opportunity, and in a context of worsening inequality, this toxic mix can fatally weaken a nation. In many of our case countries, not at all points in history but at critical junctures—in Rome, Spain, France, the Ottoman Empire, China, and other countries—some mixture of these ingredients helped impair the legitimacy of the government, generate outright opposition or instability, and weaken bonds of national unity that underpinned competitive strength.

In the modern world, another case that highlights the long-term competitive risks of significant constraints on shared opportunity is the Soviet Union. It was not always a dismal story: There were phases in the postwar Soviet Union when state-promoted shared opportunity did create moments of optimism about the dynamism of the society.[121] The Soviet state expanded access to education, and the number of college students in the Soviet Union grew by a factor of twelve between 1928 and 1960: "The post-Stalin rulers wanted to prove that the Soviet model could produce a happy society of creative and highly educated people."[122]

But an autocratic society appears to be incompatible, in the long run, with any truly valid offer of shared opportunity. A consistent trend in the Soviet system was for bursts of economic growth, state-supported opportunity, and partial social relaxation of controls to pro-

---

[119] Martines, 2013, loc. 6382–6395.

[120] Martines, 2013, loc. 6526–6531.

[121] Arnason, 1993, p. 186.

[122] Zubok, 2007, p. 163.

duce new thinking, questioning, and innovative ideas—and then for the system to step in to crush this direction once people started asking fundamental questions about the regime. One example came with the end of the Stalinist period and Nikita Khrushchev's "secret" speech denouncing the evils of that era; once it became public, it undermined the faith of many in the regime. Other examples are the 1956 invasion of Hungary, the 1968 intervention in Czechoslovakia, and the recurring periods of economic stagnation in the 1950s and 1970s.[123] Official anti-Semitism was another huge barrier to truly shared opportunity, denying the state the talents and loyalty of tens of thousands of talented citizens. The example it set also "had an enormously divisive and corroding influence on Soviet elites and the educated society."[124]

Stymied by these irresolvable dilemmas, ultimately, Soviet the state had no real alternative to stagnation. By the Brezhnev period, Vladislav Zubok argues, "the Soviet leadership abandoned reformist projects. It was content to live with the fossilized ideology and sought to repress cultural dissent and force its participants into exile and immigration."[125]

The Balance: Competitive Merit and Psychological Resilience

A major finding of our research has been that competitive advantage, when considered with each characteristic, involves not pushing the dial to the highest setting—the most shared opportunity possible, for example—but finding the right balance between the good represented by that characteristic and other, conflicting factors. Even a seemingly unqualified good—for example, equal opportunity—must be balanced against countervailing characteristics. Our historical cases highlight at least one crucial balance: preserving a merit-based degree of competitive drive alongside shared opportunity.

Successful societies must allow for skill and meritocratic outcomes to preserve a competitive environment; mandating equal outcomes can have its own negative competitive effects. Other characteristics, discussed in the following chapters, will suggest that competitively successful nations need a striving ethic: Some degree of competition within the society is always associated with competitive advantage and social efflorescence. Cultivating ambition, drive, resilience, grit, and competitive fire at the same time as offering guarantees of basic human security is the route to competitive advantage. What that looks like in practice will be the subject of constant political negotiation.

---

[123] Zubok, 2007, pp. 164, 168. Other examples centered on the publication of classic modern Russian pieces of literature—*Doctor Zhivago* and *One Day in the Life of Ivan Denisovich*. In each case, a short-lived sense of excitement about the boundary-breaking novel was quickly quashed by suppression and attacks on the authors. When Soviet citizens, especially young people, spoke out about these issues, they were rounded up and imprisoned. Eventually the intellectual clash "realized that the entire, crude, ruthless force of the state opposed them" (Zubok, 2007, p. 189).

[124] Zubok, 2007, p. 166.

[125] Zubok, 2007, p. 191; Arnason, 1993, p. 185.

Shared opportunity, then, cannot become mandated equal outcomes or a societal habit of refusing to reward competitive drive and dedication. The right balance here is incredibly complex and what it would look like in the modern United States is well beyond the scope of this analysis. One bumper-sticker solution speaks of an "opportunity society," in which everyone has an equal starting point, and outcomes are left to individual initiative. That is part of the answer (though substantial policy changes are needed to create truly equal starting points). But it is not the whole answer: History and research suggest that economic precarity can undermine opportunity by making innovative and entrepreneurial chances seem too risky.

But the essential characteristic outlined here provides a building block for competitive advantage: shared opportunity. Nations that engage more of their population in their social and economic life lay the groundwork for economic development, social dynamism and stability, and a motivated population. Countries seeking to build a vibrant domestic base for competition would do well to structure social policy to encourage this outcome.

Indeed, our research suggests that the most dynamic and competitively successful nations combine the inclusive and humane quality of shared opportunity for the expression of talents with more hard-edged assertiveness. The most competitive nations reflect powerful ambitions and a competitive fire to outdo others, and sometimes to control them. They embody an urge to understand the natural world through science—but also to master it through technology and extend the opportunities generated by that mastery to the widest proportion of their people. And the efforts and determination of that society are magnified by a sense of shared identity.

These first three characteristics have begun to put critical building blocks of national dynamism into place. To organize the efforts of the society for specific ends, however, and to make sound judgments and adopt effective policies, the most competitive nations need something else. They need a strong and efficient state apparatus that can take the necessary steps to catalyze competitive advantage. They need an active state—the characteristic to which we next turn.

CHAPTER SIX

An Active State

If national ambition and will, a unified national identity, and shared opportunity create many of the essential preconditions for an engine of national dynamism, the governance expression of that coherence and will—an active, energetic, and competent state—in many ways constitutes the engine itself, or at least its driving mechanism. The proper role of any individual state in promoting competitive goals, such as development, growth, and innovation, is subject to intense debates, and our nomination of this characteristic does not pretend to resolve them. It does suggest, though, that considered in a more strategic and instrumental manner and with the proper limitations, what some scholars have called an *active state* is a critical support system for national competitiveness.

One of the countries we reviewed for this report is a leading example of the essential role of state action in promoting long-term competitive advantage. When its industrial sector was first emerging, this country used all manner of state-led development policies—enacting tariffs, sponsoring entrepreneurs and inventors, encouraging intellectual property borrowing and outright theft from established economic powers—to jump-start its economy.[1] Later it invested in research and development and in some cases state resources to guarantee early markets for new inventions. It supported domestic businesses seeking to invest abroad and created an elaborate set of laws and regulations to promote competition, including antitrust policies. This nation's experience makes clear that the idea of a strict opposition between *market* and *state* is far too simple: Dynamic nations have tended to use state instruments to shape the market for competitive advantage while always trying to avoid disrupting the bottom-up experimentation so critical to economic vitality.

This exemplar of the role of an active state in national competitive advantage is, of course, the United States.

In its early years, the young American nation became one of the classic practitioners of what today would be called state-led development—but was then simply common practice among nations seeking economic self-interest. This was the vision of Alexander Hamilton, whose conception of economic nationalism was strongly influential in the early republic. As Michael Lind puts it, Hamilton believed that

---

[1] See, for example, Paul Wiseman, "In Trade Wars of 200 Years Ago, the Pirates Were Americans," Associated Press, March 28, 2019.

one of the duties of the federal government . . . is the active promotion of a dynamic, industrial capitalist economy—not by government ownership of industry (which Hamilton favored only for military contractors) but by establishment of sound public finance, public investment in infrastructure, and promotion of new industrial sectors unlikely to be profitable in their early stages.[2]

In his famous *Report on Manufactures* (1791), Hamilton laid out a case and an agenda for an active federal state to jump-start the economic development of the new nation.[3] Not all his recommendations were put into effect, but the concept had long legs, and many components of state-led development emerged and remain in place to this day.

Today's federal government, as the scholar Mariana Mazzucato points out, "has for decades been directing large public investment programs in technology and innovation that underlie its past and current economic success. From the Internet to biotech and even shale gas," the active American state "has been the key driver of innovation-led growth."[4] This role has been evident in dozens of federal programs, agencies, and pieces of legislation. The Small Business Innovation Research and Small Business Investment Company programs and the Commerce Department's Advanced Technology Program offered chancy, early-stage funding to such companies as Compaq, Intel, and Apple. Other scholars have found, that across many of the high-technology firms that exploded onto the scene between the 1980s and the 2000s, government funding was equally if not more important than private investors in getting them off the ground.[5]

Other scholarship shows that just about every major area of U.S. technology advance since World War II—information technology, nuclear power, aviation systems, and more— has benefited from significant government support in some way, and likely would not have flourished as they did without it.[6] A review of the innovations celebrated by *R&D Magazine*'s annual awards between 1971 and 2006 reveals that almost 90 percent of them depended decisively on some form of federal investment or support.[7] Put simply, "Nearly all the technologi-

---

[2] Michael Lind, "Hamilton's Legacy," *Wilson Quarterly*, Vol. 18, No. 3, 1994, p. 43.

[3] See, for example, Douglas A. Irwin, "The Aftermath of Hamilton's 'Report on Manufactures,'" *Journal of Economic History*, Vol. 64, No. 3, 2004.

[4] Mazzucato, 2015, p. 1.

[5] P. E. Auerswald and L. M. Branscomb, "Valleys of Death and Darwinian Seas: Financing the Invention to Innovation Transition in the United States," *Journal of Technology Transfer*, Vol. 28, Nos. 3–4, 2003; Mazzucato, 2015, p. 55.

[6] V. Ruttan, "Social Science Knowledge and Induced Institutional Innovation: An Institutional Design Perspective," *Journal of Institutional Economics*, Vol. 2, No. 3, 2006; William Lazonick, "The Theory of Innovative Enterprise: A Foundation of Economic Analysis," in Jamee K. Moudud, Cyrus Bina, and Patrick L. Mason, eds., *Alternative Theories of Competition: Challenges to the Orthodoxy*, New York: Routledge, 2013.

[7] Fred Block and Matthew R. Keller, eds., *State of Innovation: The U.S. Government's Role in Technology Development*, London: Taylor & Francis, 2011; see also Mazzucato, 2015, pp. 68–70.

cal revolutions in the past—from the Internet to today's green tech revolution—required a massive push by the State."[8]

Many other historical cases parallel the U.S. experience and illustrate how important a powerful, goal-directed, and effective state structure is to competitive success. This, again, does not imply any specific degree of state intervention, and it certainly does not endorse anything close to state domination of the economy. The idea of an active state is not even synonymous with the well-worn (though often ill-defined) notion of *industrial policy*. An active state can take different forms in different countries: The U.S. version diverges from the French version, which contrasts with the Japanese and Finnish and Danish versions, which differ from the South Korean and Singaporean versions. And the role of an active state has changed over time: The pattern in Renaissance Italy is radically different from the 20th century Asian developmental state.

But the historical evidence suggests that competitively successful nations have all benefited from *some* version of an effective state apparatus actively pushing *some* agenda of competitive advantage. These include nurturing the public and private institutions essential for economic success and social stability, underwriting some level of state-led development, actively creating environments for the private sector to thrive, guaranteeing national stability, promoting strong education systems, ensuring sufficient markets for revolutionary technologies, protecting infant industries, rallying national willpower at critical moments, and so on. And our research suggests that the absence of effective state prompting of key capabilities is a competitive handicap.

This characteristic is closely related to another on our list: effective institutions. The two overlap substantially. A well-functioning, active state requires strong institutions to do its work; issue-specific institutions must be nested in a larger context of effective governance and state initiative to have their full effect.

Defining the Characteristic

The concept of an active state is not equivalent to state-controlled economies or societies, which are universally counterproductive for either economic growth and innovation or societal health.[9] The default recipe of a highly competitive society we have sketched out depends

---

[8] Mazzucato, 2015, p. 6.

[9] One leading analysis of several major recent case studies that make this point is James C. Scott, *Seeing Like a State: How Certain Schemes to Improve the Human Condition Have Failed*, New Haven, Conn.: Yale University Press, 1998. In the short to medium term, however, several cases—such as the early period of the Soviet Union—do show how such comprehensive state control can temporarily force-feed a certain degree of national development and competitive advantage. We include such a model as one of the recipes for competitive success described in Chapter Eleven. Yet there is abundant evidence that such a model cannot compete with more open, bottom-up, commercial models over the long term.

centrally on various forms of grassroots, uncontrolled, creative, and often disruptive energy too organic and chaotic to be managed by any state apparatus.

This characteristic reflects a more general but still important finding: In every sustainably competitive society we examined, the state played an important role in shaping the socioeconomic, military, and geopolitical contexts for success. This was especially true regarding the economy. Active states have helped create and preserve stable environments in which commerce and innovation can thrive. It was true in more limited ways in social matters. Active states have also diagnosed emerging social ills and worked to mitigate them. Competitive advantage demands active management—foresight, strategy, and action on the part of a catalyst working to promote the interests of the nation and help shape and manage interactions with outside trends, markets, and forces. Nations without an effective and energetic state undertaking these roles suffered strategic handicaps.

An active state need not "pick winners" or dictate the character of private-sector plans. Protecting state-controlled or state-favored companies—subsidizing a domestic automaker over foreign ones, say—may be politically sensible but is not what we have in mind here. Rather, our concept of an active state reflects the description of Eric Beinhocker. The "economic role of the state," he explains, "is to create an institutional framework that supports the evolutionary workings of markets, strikes an effective balance between cooperation and competition, and shapes the economic fitness function to best serve the needs of society."[10] The active state constantly assesses the competitive landscape and takes actions designed to put its people, firms, and institutions in the best position to succeed. It identifies materials, capabilities, and skills essential to competitive advantage and nurtures them. It anticipates threats and problems to the dynamism and stability of the society and works to mitigate them.

Our findings on active states and national competitiveness invite us to blur, rather than choose between, traditional ideological debates over the role of the state. One aspect of this debate that needs revision is the very distinction between *state* and *market*.[11] Steven Vogel argues that what we term *markets* are complex webs of institutions that can produce effective or ineffective patterns of activity, liberating or imprisoning power relations and tendencies toward innovation or orthodoxy.[12] The practice of governance in such societies is a shared endeavor between public and private actors, with various social institutions generating laws, rules, norms, patterns of behavior, and practices that shape the society. In this sense, the state

---

[10] Beinhocker, 2007, pp. 562–564.

[11] This question goes back at least as far as Karl Polanyi's *The Great Transformation*, and it was taken up in a substantial literature on developmental states in the 1970s and 1980s. See Karl Polanyi, *The Great Transformation: The Political and Economic Origins of Our Time*, rev. ed., Boston, Mass.: Beacon Press, 2001; Alice H. Amsden, *Asia's Next Giant: South Korea and Late Industrialization*, New York: Oxford University Press, 1992; Peter Evans, *Embedded Autonomy: States and Industrial Transformation*, Princeton, N.J.: Princeton University Press, 1990; Robert Wade, *Governing the Market: Economic Theory and the Role of Government in East Asian Industrialization* Princeton, N.J.: Princeton University Press, 1990.

[12] Steven K. Vogel, *Marketcraft: How Governments Make Markets Work*, New York: Oxford University Press, 2018.

is best viewed not as an opposing force to a clearly defined market but rather as one of a range of social actors helping produce social outcomes. Societies in which the state plays that role well—encouraging and sometimes mandating competitively effective behavior and discouraging self-defeating patterns—gain a competitive advantage.[13]

Without a commercial ethic and a grassroots, independent, and pluralistic business climate to produce new innovations, government intervention will be highly inefficient. And without a dynamic market to point capital and profits at successful innovations, a fully state-directed system would be utterly unable to keep up with the feedback loops of a fully productive market economy. The most competitive nations embody a productive symbiosis between state and market. They have found a sweet spot in which their active state embraces major elements of the positive roles states can play, even in the context of an unquestionably market-led economy and society.

***

One challenge in assessing this characteristic was to define the elements of an effective active state—to distinguish states performing the role in competitively advantageous terms from those that were not. This goal is complicated by the fact that there is no single portrait of what such an effective state looks like. To help identify states that successfully develop and sustain competitive advantage, we outline five defining factors:[14]

- Effective active states attend to investments and policies necessary to *safeguard the sovereign security of the state—and beyond that to enhance its power and prestige on the world stage*. Diplomacy and grand strategy are related to this, but so are a wide range of investments (in military forces and defense industries) and policies (regulations governing the flow of secret information) that underpin national security. Active states take a forward-looking, creative, and innovation-fostering approach to these matters.
- Effective states tend to look first to their role in *encouraging and shaping economic development, through supportive (but not domineering) rules and regulations, trade policies, investments in infant industries, and other steps to safeguard the environment for commerce and, most of all, underwrite creativity and innovation*. These states apply reasonably strict criteria to such activities to act and invest wisely but err on the side of being willing to try new ideas and experiment in new fields.
- Effective states are *urgently concerned with one of the most important distinguishing factors of competitive advantage: The proportion of national investment going into productive, creative, and innovative pursuits as opposed to investment in less productive or rent-*

---

[13] Even ancient historical cases show that states and markets are not independent, opposing functions but rather inextricably intertwined (Frier and Kehoe, 2007, p. 126).

[14] For a discussion of the elements of good governance in various literatures, see Francis Fukuyama, "Governance: What Do We Know, and How Do We Know It?" *Annual Review of Political Science*, Vol. 19, No. 1, 2016.

seeking activities. Effective active states work hard to shape this balance in the direction of productive investment—without, again, trying to control or dictate all that investment themselves.

- Active states also *attend to social and cultural trends in their countries to mitigate threats to social coherence and stability,* though these interventions are less reliably associated with competitive success.
- Effective active states also *undertake these tasks while managing their finances responsibly,* avoiding crippling levels of long-term debt.

These essential definitional points add up to the theoretical case for the value of an active state. States operating in these ways ought to generate competitive advantage almost by definition: playing these roles well will enhance states' military power and sustainable defense capabilities, strengthen their growth and innovation, and create a sense of national dynamism and efficacy that can have multiple spillover effects. The active state characteristic is much like the closely related characteristic of effective institutions: Both are essential support systems for all the other societal characteristics we have identified. Our case studies provide many examples of ways in which this theory plays out in reality.

Some might question whether an active state is truly a "societal" characteristic. It is, after all, a single institution, one consciously created and shaped by human choice. The degree of state intervention can shift significantly over time; it is not an embedded or inherent aspect of the society. Although admitting that this characteristic does sit on the boundary of our broad focus, some nations—because of inherent features of their social, cultural, and political heritage and nature—are more likely than others to make room for an effective active state. In effect, the *idea* of an active state shaping the fate of a nation, and the emergence of effective and legitimate institutions of national governance that can put the state's vision into practice, is itself a societal characteristic. Many of our characteristics involve some degree of public choice—for example, the level of investment in learning and education, the degree of adaptiveness in the corporate culture of leading firms, or national approaches to social opportunity.

Finally, active states are also shaped by a factor stressed in the last chapter's discussion of coherent national identity: a public-spirited elite. Having an elite class that views its primary obligation as fostering a strong community and powerful nation—as opposed to self-enrichment or narrower private-sector goals, such as profit or improved share price—is a critical component of competitive success. Without such a community-minded elite, an active state cannot achieve its full potential. In many cases, it was when elites turned the institutions of an active state to their own advantage that the nation began a competitive decline.

The Active State and Competitive Advantage: Evidence from Cases

The role of an active state (or lack of one) in generating (or hindering) competitive advantage is apparent in all our case studies. Table 6.1 very briefly summarizes some of the historical evidence from each case; we describe the evidence in more detail below.

In several of our case studies, a state apparatus, combined with a national will and urge for global power and influence, allowed a nation to rule over a very large area with a relatively streamlined administration. The typical pattern was one of allowing significant degrees of local autonomy while capturing varying levels of resources (through taxes and outright theft), co-opting local elites, militarily crushing those who directly challenged state power, and building an efficient if small bureaucracy. This pattern demonstrates how an active state can punch above its seeming weight. In more modern cases, the connection to national outcomes is more direct. As one scholar observes, "Industrialization entirely without state assistance, which some liberal economists considered both possible and desirable, was historically a great exception."[15]

Ancient and Premodern Cases

In cases before the modern era, the role of the state apparatus will necessarily be more constrained than modern examples. States had fewer resources and competencies and took charge of a much narrower range of social tasks. And yet we do find evidence for ways in which a prominent active state role provided competitive advantage.

Despite its limitations, the Roman state in the late republic and early empire actively shared the context for competitive advantage in multiple ways. In ancient Rome, the leading role of the state in promoting competitive advantage was probably in building and maintaining a dominant military. The state supported the emergence of a remarkably sophisticated financial sector, which will be discussed in the chapter on effective institutions. Through its efforts to bring stability and peace to the Mediterranean, the Roman state supercharged trade flows. It helped establish and manage ports and other supportive systems of trade and consistent coinage, weights and measures, and other practical underpinnings of commerce.

The Roman state intervened in markets to promote stability and to ensure enough food, especially in lean times. It standardized the money supply around a complex, multitiered set of coinage and even created legal penalties for traders who refused to accept the coins. In this role the state was "facilitating safe and smooth exchanges of goods at local, regional, and interregional level."[16] The early imperial state produced uniform standards for assessing taxes on agricultural land and engaged in certain embryonic forms of managed trade, espe-

---

[15] Osterhammel, 2014, p. 667.

[16] Elio Lo Casio, "Growth and Decline: The Roman Economy in Historical Perspective," *Rivista di storia economica*, No. 3, December 2007b.

TABLE 6.1

An Active State and Competitive Advantage—Evidence from Cases

Case	Elements of the Role of an Active State in Historical Cases
Rome	• Support for infrastructure; roads, water supplies, ports that support Rome's imperial control, trade networks, and legitimacy and power • Role of state in supporting economic foundations of success—e.g., coinage, trade
China	• In premodern times, role of the state in promoting industry, trade, culture, and stable finance • In modern times, role of developmental state in post-1950s China in generating levels of industrialization and growth; current state-directed competition plans • Excessive role of state in 1950s–1970; significant drag on development, especially in specific large-scale catastrophic episodes
Spain	• Mixed or limited • In 16th–17th centuries, role of monarchy in running the empire and organizing seizure of precious metals from New World • In more modern era, limits to role of state in promoting industry
Austria-Hungary	• Limited and constrained • Some efforts to use state to promote industry but bifurcated between two parts of empire; limited resources and finances; strategic handicap
Ottoman Empire	• During period of rise (14th–16th centuries), active state role for the period; cultivation of effective bureaucracy and investment in science and military technology • Decay of effective state role in promoting learning, technology, and industry in more modern period; significant competitive drag
Renaissance Italy	• Strong state role in promoting trade, specific industries, and culture; clear concept of an active state and its role in promoting the excellence and strength of a community • Over time declined into a pattern of elite capture of state institutions and self-enrichment
Britain	• Multiple examples of industrial-policy-style behavior in the rise of British industry • State role in promoting domestic requirements for competitiveness, including education, research, health, and welfare
Sweden	• Strong active state role in modern, social democratic era—at apex of power, Swedish leaders used state apparatus to build military and economic instruments of power
France	• Long history of active state role—early paradigmatic case is Napoleonic era, development of legal code and use of state power to enhance national strength • Many modern examples of industrial policy and related active state techniques, not all of which have proven effective
Modern Japan	• Associated with major era of Japanese national competitive rise—the classic case is the Meiji period and state role in attracting foreign expertise, supporting growth of new industries, making intentional leap to modernization • A postwar leading case of the role of the developmental state • Modern tradition of activist state promoting egalitarian society
Soviet Union	• Illustrates risks of active state overshoot; went beyond helpful role to state control of society in ways that ultimately proved competitively disastrous
United States	• More market reliant than some European and Asian cases, but still multiple examples of active state involvement to enhance competitiveness

cially in food but also, through the imperial seizure of control of mines, in critical metals. It enforced maritime security in the Mediterranean by fighting piracy and thus reduced the costs of trade.[17] "The imperial state could define and enforce the fundamental 'rules of the game' . . . not only in the Italian core but also in the provinces," according to one scholar.[18]

An especially significant—and lasting—use of state resources was in infrastructure. Rome saw the need for a strong institutional and infrastructural base to support its empire and to that end devoted significant resources to roads, ports, aqueducts, and large public buildings and shared spaces. Rome invested in its road systems, for example, from the fourth century BCE (with the famous Appian Way) up through the fifth and sixth centuries CE. Altogether, Roman engineers are estimated to have built between 50,000 and 200,000 miles of hard-surface roads throughout the empire. (Rome typically used private contractors to build the roads, but the financing was public.[19]) The result was not only the intended support for Rome's military power but also a profound investment in economic activity. Roads reduced transport costs, but they also gave rise to towns and guard stations along the way to safeguard and profit from commercial traffic. This network of roads required both the initial investment for construction and significant annual investment for ongoing maintenance.[20]

There were strict limitations to the active state's role in promoting advantage. Much of Rome's financial activity, for example, appears to have supported consumption "rather than land improvement and increased productivity."[21] As a society built on a landed aristocracy, possession of land and homes was the foundational investment, one that does not reflect an especially productive use of social capital. Successful commercial entrepreneurship in Rome was often viewed as something of a threat, not a benefit, to social stability because it challenged the existing bases of social status. Two scholars conclude that Rome's economy was characterized by a "failure to pursue the goal of higher productivity in industry or agriculture through heavy capital investment and economies of scale."[22] Despite these limits, the Roman state contributed to dynamism and competitiveness in many ways.

***

---

[17] Temin, 2013, pp. 2, 218.

[18] Lo Casio, 2007b, p. 626.

[19] Sarah Bond, "Investing in Infrastructure: Funding Roads in Ancient Rome and Today," *Forbes*, June 30, 2017.

[20] Confirmation of the long-term value of Roman investments in infrastructure comes from recent work associating the Roman road network with modern economic activity. One study concludes that "the density of ancient Roman roads at a given point in Europe strongly correlates with present-day prosperity, as measured by modern-day road density, population density and even satellite imagery of nighttime lighting" (Christopher Ingraham, "How 2,000-Year-Old Roads Predict Modern Prosperity," *Washington Post*, August 7, 2018).

[21] Garnsey and Saller, 2014, pp. 72–73.

[22] Garnsey and Saller, 2014, p. 79.

A similar pattern is seen in the Italian Renaissance city-states, where we find many examples of the ways in which effective state action, including steps to boost economic activity and to invest directly in key goals, made a competitive difference. The form was different, corresponding to the distinct governing structure of these smaller, more-personalized city-states. We see this in the rise of key powers on the peninsula, such as Florence, Milan, and Venice, where (at times) ruling families took an active interest in promoting the vibrancy of the state. They supported scientists, inventors, and artists; sponsored missions of trade and exploration, and built fleets to take advantage of (and dominate) what they found; erected impressive public works, including some of the great architecture in the world at the time; encouraged education; and more. The result was a degree of active promotion of state power that provided measurable economic and cultural advantages.

The decline of an effective and active competitive role for the state is part of the story of the decline of some of these same Italian city-states. The shift in the focus of investment from exploration and productive trade to controlling territory toward the interior of the peninsula is a major part of the story of Venice's loss of influence. As it increasingly sought to control nearby Italian cities, more Venetian noblemen bought land, including areas for large estates in the surrounding territories. "As the nobility diverted more and more capital into land," Lauro Martines explains,

> less went into trade and venturous enterprise. Alarming crises in public finance during the middle decades of the fifteenth century and again early in the next century dealt serious blows to public confidence in government bonds. Major banks were shaken or went under. Well into the sixteenth century, Venetians continued to stress the importance of the patriciate's devotion to trade, but historians are coming to detect a note of nostalgia and exaggeration in such emphasis. . . . By the late sixteenth century, notes one historian, 'the Venetian nobility's renunciation of trade had become almost general.' For about a century, moreover, it had been the custom of many noblemen, possibly a majority, to depend in part or in whole upon the income from public office—judgeships, advocacies, certain governorships, and a myriad of lesser offices.[23]

In the Spanish case, there are hints and harbingers of a productive active state that was hijacked by rent-seeking nobles and eventually autocrats who put the state in the service of personal and ideological rather than practical interests. And then there were efforts to build a unified, centralized state with more-rational management, stronger infrastructure, and other hallmarks of a modern nation-state that tipped too far in the other direction, pursuing a centralizing agenda with a zeal that generated a degree of authoritarianism and intolerance that undermined the competitive goals of the enterprise.[24] Despite this centralization, the state also remained fragmented. Richard Herr argues that "for all the centuries of expanding royal

---

[23] Martines, 2013, loc. 3707–3724 (Martines does not name the historian).

[24] Kenneth Andrien and Allan Kuethe, *The Spanish Atlantic World in the Eighteenth Century: War and the Bourbon Reforms, 1713–1796*, New York: Cambridge University Press, 2013.

authority, Spain remained in many ways a federation of self-governing municipalities."[25] It was also handicapped by such factors as byzantine land ownership laws, some related to the role of the Catholic Church, as well as an anachronistic, feudal-style system that imprisoned land in the hands of families that did not make full productive use of it.

China tells a somewhat different story, but one that still emphasizes the value of an active state. Even in premodern times, Song China reflected a state apparatus that some scholarship suggests was determined to promote commerce.[26] To this end, the state underwrote fiscal stability and sound currencies, built ports and harbors, and sought to promote trade. Centuries later, post-1960s China became one of the leading examples of state-led development, taking an even more directive and at times constricting role than that of late industrializers, such as Japan and South Korea. In other periods, however, the Chinese state has not had the resources to effectively promote modernization, was hostile to the notion, or did so ineffectually. In some premodern periods, investments relied on wealthy investors rather than public or state support.[27] This turned out to be a significant difference with Japan in the late 19th century and other periods, in which a potent, national, state-directed program of development, growth, and expanding military power set the stage for industrialization.[28]

The Chinese case also demonstrates the practical challenge of designing an agenda for an active state that generates deep, long-term competitive advantage. In the mid-19th century, for example, "the state took the levers of command." Provincial governors "embarked on a series of large-scale projects that all drew upon foreign technology and advisors," in areas such as arms production, shipbuilding, coal mining, and textile manufacturing. These state institutions were primarily motivated by a desire for military capability; some "70 percent of the capital was allocated to enterprises of military relevance."[29] Although these projects demonstrated China's inclination to incorporate foreign technology, they did not result in a generalized industrial takeoff. State activism—in the absence of social peace, stability, and similar characteristics; a diverse and entrepreneurial commercial sector; or an educated populace—cannot produce widespread competitive vibrancy.

***

The Ottoman case offers similarly complex and qualified lessons about the dangers of an incomplete active state. One story of the gradual enfeebling of the Ottoman Empire during

---

[25] Richard Herr, *Rural Change and Royal Finances at the End of the Old Regime*, Oakland: University of California Press, 1989, p. 44.

[26] See, for example, William Guanglin Liu, *The Chinese Market Economy, 1000–1500*, Albany: State University of New York Press, 2015; Richard Von Glahn, "Revisiting the Song Monetary Revolution: A Review Essay," *International Journal of Asian Studies*, Vol. 1, No. 1, 2004.

[27] Perkins, 1967, pp. 486–487.

[28] Osterhammel, 2014, p. 665.

[29] Osterhammel, 2014, p. 661.

its later period was the inability of the central state to promote a truly modern economy—and more broadly, the fact that the Ottoman state, though it displayed many impressive aspects, was not able to make the leap to a truly modern form.[30] There were elements of strength: As Niall Ferguson argues, Ottoman governments after the late 17th century were not "slower than many parts of Europe to embrace global commerce and, later, industrialization." And there was "no shortage of economic competition and autonomous corporate entitles like guilds in Ottoman lands."[31] Marc David Baer highlights the many qualities of Ottoman states at their apex, from a reasonably functioning bureaucracy to some effort to balance Islamic and secular law to at least a limited cultivation of the scientific and technological foundations of national power.[32] In both core areas and imperial possessions like the Balkans, the Ottomans developed a true centralized state which brought degrees of standard rules and norms to many elements of its domains based in part on a common Islamic law.[33]

And yet this scholarship also points out severe limitations to successive Ottoman state apparatuses. The Ottoman economy remained mostly premodern in character, and even use of money in transactions "was mostly limited to large towns." The state intervened to support favored interests and short-term goals, such as meeting the basic needs of the people by promoting imports of needed goods. One result was that the state ended up fostering massive trade deficits, borrowing, and debt. The state role in the Ottoman empire thus diverged sharply from an emerging, more forward-looking approach in Europe.[34] The Ottoman state was "an empire in the traditions of the ancient near-eastern states" and proved "ill-suited to the near era" of nation-states. As much as an idea of just governance was built into this tradition, it was still an essentially hierarchical and authoritarian understanding of relations between rulers and ruled.[35]

Ottoman leaders recognized the gap and strove to close it starting in earnest in the 19th century, with multiple bouts of reform in areas such as taxation, fiscal policy, population records, and the strength of the military, culminating in more than 30 years of bureaucratic-technocratic administration in the Tanzimat era, beginning in 1839. The result was a far more elaborate central administrative apparatus.[36] But our reading of the historical litera-

---

[30] Inalcik, 2001, loc. 336, 1365.

[31] Ferguson 2011, p. 59.

[32] Baer, 2021.

[33] Ottoman governments at various levels, for example, invested in infrastructure and created an elaborate network of travelers' rest stops and local security forces that facilitated movement throughout the empire. This system began as a more informal, grassroots, nonstate network and matured into a more state-directed system (Inalcik, 2001, loc. 3221–3265, 3307–3311). On the role of Islamic legal standards, extending even to issues such as weights and measures enforcement in business transactions, see Inalcik, 2001, loc. 3391–3425.

[34] Hanioğlu, 2008, pp. 19–20.

[35] Inalcik, 2001, loc. 160–163, 1402, 1417–1437.

[36] Hanioğlu, 2008, neatly summarizes these positive changes on pp. 208–209. See also Baer, 2021, pp. 194–196, 255–256, 328, 363.

ture indicates that these still left the Ottoman state relatively weak compared with European powers. And the reforms, magnifying as they did the dilemmas engendered by forcing a secular, liberal, rapidly evolving social model down onto a fundamentally conservative, hierarchical society, provoked sometimes violent reactions.[37] The challenges of developing an effective active state were also inextricably bound up with the Ottoman Empire's fragmentation and variety. The distribution of power throughout the empire heavily constrained the central government's ability to play its needed role.

As with shared opportunity and, as we will see, learning and adapting, much scholarship suggests that the Ottomans could simply not resolve the strong tensions between the demands of what we are calling the Renaissance spirit model and the nature of their society and government. Indeed, a major part of the Ottoman story is the consistently strong counterreform movements that arose to contest and often snuff out significant elements of the efforts to build elements of a more modern state.

Once the state fell into a vulnerable position, it had to grant numerous "capitulations" to outside powers in areas such as imports, which drastically reduced its power to shape its society and economy.[38] And a weak state sat at the center of a range of factors that constrained the emergence of a modern industrial economy. The state could not promote or invest in domestic manufacturing or protect it from international demands or competition. It did not significantly promote supportive social institutions, including infrastructure and education. As a result, "the overall picture from the mid-eighteenth century onward was one of stagnation and decline relative to Europe."[39] The absence of an effective active state was not the only explanation for this outcome, but it was certainly part of the reason.[40]

Two Defining Modern Case Studies: Britain and Japan

Two modern cases display especially strong evidence for the competitive value of a potent, effective state apparatus: Britain and Japan.

European states from the 17th to 19th centuries faced recurring problems of financial management. To enhance its fiscal muscle, Britain developed a "strong fiscal state."[41] These financial institutions were part of a larger drive that reflected a "political consensus among England's wealthy elites for an altogether stronger and more centralized state," which depended on more robust and effective institutions, especially those dealing with revenues

---

[37] Hanioğlu, 2008, pp. 70–71, 109–110.

[38] Inalcik, 2001, loc. 3059–3062.

[39] Hanioğlu, 2008, p. 23.

[40] Inalcik, 2001, loc. 1133–1140.

[41] Patrick K. O'Brien, "The Nature and Historical Evolution of an Exceptional Fiscal State and Its Possible Significance for the Precocious Commercialization and Industrialization of the British Economy from Cromwell to Nelson," *Economic History Review*, Vol. 64, No. 2, May 2011, p. 420.

and finance.[42] One of the advantages of a robust fiscal system is that it empowers a country to issue debt at reasonable rates, and Britain took advantage of this by borrowing heavily—with debt servicing ratios about 50 percent of total revenues—to fund "a far more aggressive stance in European power politics." No other European state in this period—not France, Spain, Austria, Denmark, Russia, or the Ottoman Empire—deepened its tax base or acquired the ability to issue debt at these rates.[43]

The quality of the resulting financial institutions and strength of the national financial base gave Britain a clear competitive advantage during the period of its rise to power and global heyday.[44] Early on, Britain and Holland seized the mantle of global financial leaders. In the 17th century, for example, Dutch capital helped the British economy grow and provided some of the foundation for a dominant navy. Later, Dutch and British money helped underwrite Austrian efforts against the French.[45] More broadly, Britain's financial centers and sources of income gave it a specific military advantage: Britain was able to sponsor allies and proxies to do most of the land fighting in Europe, freeing it to focus on building a dominant navy.[46]

Beyond finance, the British state took an active role in the economy and society—funding infrastructure and other foundations of economic development and national competitive strength and undertaking various forms of proto-industrial policy, including supporting entrepreneurs who acquired technology from abroad and investing in key technologies.[47] It fostered the rise of domestic industries by way of support for infrastructure, protective tariffs, and direct support for research.[48] Government sponsorship of science, engineering, and technical education played a notable role in the British Industrial Revolution, and the absence of this sponsorship—as can be seen in the Netherlands after its peak of power—left the nation at a disadvantage in the embrace of practical scientific learning.[49]

Yet the British case also makes clear how many conditions and qualifications apply to the argument for the competitive value of an active state. Margaret Jacob notes, "No understand-

---

[42] O'Brien, 2011, p. 426.

[43] O'Brien, 2011, p. 430.

[44] O'Brien, 2011, pp. 437–438.

[45] Schumann, 2016, pp. 316–317, 322, 325, 329, 335.

[46] Leggiere, 2016, pp. 339–340, 343.

[47] The 19th century, David Cannadine argues (2017, p. 85), "not only witnessed a revolution in the performance of the government of the United Kingdom as a war-making machine, with a new generation of young men committed to hard work and disinterested public service rather than apathy, self-interest and corruption. It also witnessed an unprecedented collaboration between state sponsorship and business, as many of the essential materials of war were provided and manufactured by private enterprise."

[48] As Jack Goldstone suggests, the image of Britain growing because of laissez-faire approach is a myth: The British economy grew rapidly "despite facing the highest tax rates, the highest tariffs, and one of the stiffest regulatory regimes on shipping in Europe, if not the entire world!" (Goldstone, 2009, p. 113).

[49] Jacob, 1988, pp. 189–191.

ing of British industrial development that downplays the importance of the state and state policies can begin to address what happened in the late eighteenth century."[50] But the ways in which they have done so are complex and sometimes widely divergent, and there is no simple way to draw a straight line from a single theory of state activism to competitive advantage. As she notes, 18th-century Britain was more laissez-faire than France, where the state was involved in a sort of proto-industrial policy and undertook more infrastructure projects.[51] In Britain, Matthew Boulton, James Watt, and other inventors and entrepreneurs were not directly supported by the state and often resented the interventions it did make. And yet "France lagged behind Britain in industrial development well into the nineteenth century."[52] The state offered legal guarantees for private investments in things like canals but did not take over their construction itself; such a system helped promote entrepreneurship with state support but not control.[53]

Indeed, the example of Britain's major Continental rival, France, offers useful cautions. French governments beginning even before the revolution, and certainly in the revolutionary period, became convinced that British schools were doing a better job of inculcating basic scientific and technical knowledge and set out—in a determined and centralized way—to close the gap. From the 1790s onward, revolutionary governments poured resources into education to generate industrial progress. At the same time, they invested in critical industries, sought to develop scientific knowledge, undertook projects to improve ports and highways, created contests and prizes to spur technical advances, and dispatched agents to steal British industrial secrets. And yet, in the main, they failed: France remained a laggard in industrial development for decades afterward.[54]

Clearly, a powerful and determined choice by a state to promote competitive advantage can only get so far on its own. An active state, like all our factors, is not itself a sufficient condition for dynamism or competitive position. In the French case, the revolutionary governments might have been running uphill against centuries of feudal traditions that had limited most scientific and technical training to the aristocracy and left the society with less grassroots entrepreneurial energy than Britain. Some of France's monarchs imposed religious constraints on learning and science, and this left France generations behind in exposure to the emerging sciences—and the Catholic Church's battle against many forms of scientific learning would persist.[55] The revolution's own fanaticism led to the slaughter or exile of large num-

---

[50] Jacob, 2014, pp. 14, 23.

[51] The British state was still relative underdeveloped through the first half of the 19th century, with limited national role in many areas of public life and sometimes weak city governance (Cannadine, 2017, p. 260).

[52] Jacob, 2014, p. 14.

[53] We are grateful to William Anthony Hay for pointing to this specific form of state role in the economy.

[54] Jacob, 2014, pp. 133–142.

[55] Even here Jacob makes clear that the reality is complex. Some monarchical regimes had seen the necessary instrumental value of science, and there were pockets of world-class scientific and engineering knowl-

bers of scientists and the abolition of scientific academies. The new Ècoles Centrales Group schools that were established throughout the country often lacked basic books and equipment. And then, in the years after 1815, the restoration shifted the balance of power back to traditionalists and the clergy, imposing another decades-long penalty on France's ability to keep up with Britain in intellectual and industrial applications.[56]

The French case also shows the risks of state control of a society's intellectual development. State sponsorship of science and engineering, Jacob explains, left French engineers with a mindset focused on military applications and, more broadly, "service to state and society" rather than a more generalized urge to explore whatever struck their fancy or offered the potential for profit. The "symbols of birth and authority" in French society (as distinct from the British) and the "political culture and value system of the *ancient règime*" played major roles in shaping intellectual energies.[57] When the winds blow against openness and toleration in governance and the state has control of the wheel, the result can be a long hiatus in learning and experimentation. In France, the pendulum swung back again after 1830—but, Jacob concludes, "the damage had been done. The change in direction came after nearly twenty years—a generation of young people—when the educational ideals of the French Revolution were systematically undermined."[58]

An active state has played a critical role in many of our case studies in underwriting national dynamism and competitiveness. But those cases also speak loudly to the essential superiority of a bottom-up, grassroots, trial-and-error, inclusive model of dynamism over a centrally directed and state-controlled model.

***

In the case of Japan, the nation's modern state arose from a diffuse, pluralistic set of regional or local authorities, not unlike the patterns in Italy and Germany before single states coalesced.[59] This began to be more centralized under the Tokugawa shogunate, beginning in 1603, which demanded a handful of the perquisites of centralized rule—notably allegiance and some taxes. Already, various levels of government in Japan were beginning to organize infrastructure and other investments and to create well-ordered urban areas. When Commodore Matthew Perry's fleet arrived in 1853, then, it was coming on a Japan that had already

---

edge throughout French society by the late 18th century—for example, among military engineers (Jacob, 2014, p. 148).

[56] Jacob, 2014, pp. 142–147, 152–159, 162–170.

[57] Another scholar notes that excessive state meddling with standards and procedures "stifled the innovative drive on the Continent," while state patronage of science and engineering "lured scientists and engineers away from manufacturing industry towards teaching, administration and military service" (R. Porter, 1990, p. 314).

[58] Jacob, 2014, pp. 150, 171.

[59] We are grateful to Robert Hellyer for this insight.

begun to make the first tentative investments in the demands of national competitive advantage: emerging commercial ventures, nationwide education, and rationalized administration. That Japan still lagged well behind European powers in these regards quickly became evident in the clash with American naval power, however. The resulting humiliation—combined with burgeoning social pressures in what remained a highly feudal society under the samurai— gave rise to a sense on the part of some Japanese that a coherent, effective active state was required to set it on a path to competing effectively.

The period of Japanese history that would come to be known as the Meiji era reflected this theme. Some Meiji leaders sought to build on the roots laid before to fast-track the construction of a competitive economy and government. They used state mandates and resources to forcibly advance Japanese society into the modern industrial era, ending the samurai system and replacing feudal domains with prefectures that reported to a central government. One scholar argues that Meiji rulers "did not aim to construct a permanent state economy." They provoked growth, supported technological imports, and took other actions, "then gradually withdrew from most industrial projects, not least to ease the strain on the budget."[60] They sought balance in the role of their active state.

Although sweeping generalizations about the Meiji period can therefore be dangerous, there is no question that, by building on tentative steps of the Tokugawa period, Meiji leaders "undertook a massive centralization of the Japanese state." This took place in fits and starts, with some reformers overstepping and generating backlash and the whole process involving a long period of negotiation with local elites. But eventually it picked up speed—in part driven by visits of Japanese elites to Western powers and partly by the recognition of many local notables that their larger political community, if it was to be safe from and competitive with the ravenous industrial powers, needed to become a full-fledged nation-state. Japanese leaders developed a "burning determination to join the company of the 'Great Powers' that had encircled it and restricted its sovereignty."[61] This lesson was driven home by Britain's defeat of China in the Opium War: To avoid China's fate, Japan needed to become more centralized, coherent, and industrialized. Even several years into this process the Japanese central state had significant limitations, but the direction was clear.[62] Japan began the Meiji era "as one of the modern world's most fractured polities" but "emerged within a generation as one of its most centralized states."[63]

This state then went about actively promoting the kinds of knowledge, infrastructure, and industry required to compete. This agenda included large infrastructure projects, such as railroad and telegraph lines; "direct government support for private enterprises"; efforts to "protect, promote, and nurture key industries until its people were more economically

---

[60] Osterhammel, 2014, p. 666.

[61] Jansen, 2000, loc. 5007–5059.

[62] Ravina, 2017, pp. 19, 67–68, 83, 121–128, 137–138, 167.

[63] Jansen, 2000, loc. 5050.

mature"; regulatory institutions stretching throughout the country; and a shared national system of rule of law.[64]

The resulting active state apparatus still preserved important aspects of decentralized initiative even within the general trend of central state authority.[65] Many of the new initiatives were taken by local and city governments—to sponsor the development of the growing tea industry, for example, and find jobs for newly unemployed samurai.[66] The scholar Sheldon Garon has referred to the "Japanese model" of national competitiveness in the late 19th and early 20th centuries as including, in part, "mass education, an interventionist bureaucratic state, [and] top-down organization of local associations."[67]

Over time, though, the state strongly promoted the idea of a single Japanese people and a unified nation, encouraging a growing sense of unified Japanese-ness that would become the basis for a more powerful and energetic active central state. The Meiji period did involve a significant centralization of state power, partly fueled by a desire to catch up with European levels of industrialization. It was this urge to compete, Carol Gluck explains, and a fear of socioeconomic weakness, that "helps to explain why, in Japan's case, the centralization of the state took precedence among the wholesale reforms after the Restoration," a process in which "hundreds of feudal lords agreed to surrender their ancestral lands, held in familial hands for generations, to the central government in 1869."[68]

It is perhaps in the postwar period of Japanese history, though, that we see the most significant connection between an active state and competitive advantage. The state underwrote postwar reconstruction in many ways, from basic national recovery to supporting extensive infrastructure projects to direct support of emerging business conglomerates. This did not involve "picking winners" or moving in the direction of anything like nationalized business enterprises, but it did represent many forms of activism to promote national competitiveness. A Japanese "activist state," two scholars argue, also worked to promote social equality. A 2008 poll found more than 84 percent of Japanese people agreeing that "the government should actively engage in closing the economic gap between citizens."[69]

---

[64] Ravina, 2017, pp. 179–180.

[65] See, for example, Kevin M. Doak, *A History of Nationalism in Modern Japan: Placing the People*, Netherlands: Brill, 2007.

[66] The scholar Carol Gluck has referred to the Meiji period as the "not-so-strong state," a period in which the "main protagonist of modernity in Meiji Japan . . . was not the state, but society. . . . For if one looks to the motors of change—not its enunciators but its engines—one finds them more often in society than in the government. The state often made grand claims, leaving the implementation—and the financing—of those claims to social rather than state actors, much as it did in the initial establishment of the national school system" (Carol Gluck, "Modernity in Common: Japan and World History," presented at the University of Washington Mitsubishi Lecture Series, Seattle, April 21, 2014, p. 30).

[67] Garon, 2017, p. 69.

[68] Gluck, 2014, p. 28.

[69] Glosserman and Snyder, 2017, pp. 33–34.

One problem with this narrative in the Japanese case is that this active state-led developmental engine slammed into multiple decades of economic stagnation beginning in the 1990s. This long-term social inertia led huge majorities of the Japanese people to conclude that the country was headed in the wrong direction and lose faith in major institutions. What this suggests, perhaps, is simply that an active state alone is not enough to guarantee dynamism or competitive advance. Japan's "lost decades" may have something to do with certain effects of overly ambitious active state roles, but they can also be traced to causes that hint at the role of other societal characteristics. Gluck, for example, argues for one explanation of Japan's travails: a social emphasis on "a stable social order" that limits major reforms to painfully slow incremental processes.[70] It is perhaps an incomplete social quality of learning and adapting—too much emphasis on stability and tradition and too little ambition and openness to change—that has contributed to Japan's stagnation. But this does not deny the competitive value Japan gained from having a state that actively sponsored earlier eras of development.

***

The case of Austria-Hungary complements the British and Japanese cases, showing, to some extent, the limits of halfway approaches to an active state. From the mid-19th through the early 20th century, the central government—or the twin set of governments—tried to make reasonable investments in transportation, railroads, electricity. It sought to spur industrialization at least in some sectors. It is not clear that levels of productive investment were dramatically lower than in other major European powers, although Austria-Hungary's significant financial constraints did put it at a competitive disadvantage to some degree. After 1850, Austria-Hungary invested in infrastructure and industrial development. As stressed in the last chapter, had it not been for the eventual shock, fiscal pressure, and ethno-political centrifugal forces of World War I, these efforts could have been more successful.

Nonetheless the empire's development lagged that of other European nations, and the reality of this lag feeds "the continuing suspicion that when all is said and done, the economic performance of the Empire left something to be desired."[71] Joel Mokyr notes that one scholar produced

> ample statistical illustration of the continuing relative backwardness of the Habsburg Empire. It is arguable that its failure to close the gap is the ultimate test of the Habsburg Monarchy, and that its inability to do so eventually sealed its military fate. . . . [E]ven the most advanced parts of Austria-Hungary were not keeping up with the leading regions in the West.[72]

---

[70] Gluck, 2014, pp. 36–37.

[71] Mokyr, 1984, p. 1096.

[72] Mokyr, 1984, p. 1096.

Mokyr concludes:

> [T]he Empire possessed much economic vitality. . . . [But] the acid tests of such economies remain how large the modern sector was relative to the traditional, and to what extent the modern sector created positive externalities for the rest of the economy. In this respect the Habsburg Empire remains a case in which deliberate efforts to modernize ran into physical and man-made constraints, producing a somewhat odd mixture of modernity and leftovers from feudalism.[73]

Financial constraints prevented the empire from making the investments necessary to get the sudden surge of growth and industrialization that would have allowed it to keep up with European leaders. Both national and local governments needed far more resources for modernization projects than their tax base would produce, and the result was debt, financial crisis, and ultimately limits on what could be accomplished.

Other Evidence: General Support for the Importance of an Active State

The most relevant general empirical confirmation for the role of an active state in promoting competitiveness comes from the literature on economic development—and in particular post–World War II development. Scholars have assessed the proposition that a "developmental state" has contributed to national success.[74] This refers to an effective state apparatus in a developing nation taking a rage of actions, from trade policy to sponsoring the rise of specific industries, to jump-start growth. As one review of the literature concludes,

> Key to rapid industrialization is a strong and autonomous state, providing directional thrust to the operation of the market mechanism. The market is guided by a conception of long-term national rationality of investment formulated by government officials. It is the "synergy" between the state and the market which provides the basis for outstanding development experience.[75]

Some of the empirical evidence for this proposition relates to the U.S. postwar experience. There is impressive research on the specific economic value of many U.S. postwar state investments, as well as rosters of the specific technologies created (directly and indirectly) through state support. Scholars have identified a range of civilian technologies, from personal computers to the internet, that emerged from the government's role in promoting key industries.

---

[73] Mokyr, 1984, p. 1099.

[74] Gordon White, ed., *Developmental States in East Asia*, London: Palgrave Macmillan UK, 1988.

[75] Ziya Öniş, "Review of *The Logic of the Developmental State*, by Alice H. Amsden, Frederic C. Deyo, Chalmers Johnson, and Robert Wade," *Comparative Politics*, Vol. 24, No. 1, 1991, p. 110.

Whereas some argue that the state mostly needs to get out of the way to promote dynamism, Joel Mokyr notes that the better reading of history is that "what seems to have worked best in the astonishing technological flourishing of the twentieth century is a cooperative effort," in which government and the private sector mutually support one another.[76]

This literature offers several findings that support the causal relationship of an active state and competitive success. One is evidence for the role of the state in promoting national success in specific industries. An active state role was critical to helping both Japan and South Korea gain market share, technological parity (and then advantage), and profits in high-tech and auto industries, among others.[77] In both cases, the state did not control the firms but rather encouraged active competition, allowing inefficient and badly run companies to fail.[78] The state did, however, play several specific roles—ensuring financing, shaping import policies, encouraging productive investment in the part of firms, and funding basic research—that underwrote industrial success.[79]

A second empirical finding tied an active state's role in development to growth rates, citing impressive economic growth in the East Asian "tigers" (Singapore, Hong Kong, Taiwan, and South Korea), at least during the 1970s and 1980s.[80] Additionally, this research suggests an important connection with another of our societal characteristics—effective institutions. The case for an active state depends on fair, effective national bureaucracies to manage the various components of governance. This has been true in paradigmatic cases, such as Japan, South Korea, and Taiwan, as well as other examples of developmental states, including Singapore. Although the developmental state model eventually became associated with a degree of overly cozy, even corrupt, state-corporate relations, these systems tended at first to be characterized by the generation of large and competent administrative systems that helped promote economic growth and social stability. These states placed a powerful emphasis on recruiting the most-talented people into their institutions, emphasizing quality of staff and leadership.[81]

---

[76] Joel Mokyr, "A Flourishing Economist: A Review Essay on Edmund Phelps's 'Mass Flourishing: How Grassroots Innovation Created Jobs, Challenge, and Change,'" *Journal of Economic Literature*, Vol. 52, No. 1, March, 2014, p. 192.

[77] Chalmers Johnson, *MITI and the Japanese Miracle: The Growth of Industrial Policy, 1925–1975*, Stanford, Calif.: Stanford University Press, 1982; Amsden, 1989.

[78] Two scholars write, "The state does not pick winners; it ensures that there is always a set of competitive companies, and then allows market competition to weed out losers. . . . Markets are merely a means to an end rather than an end in themselves" (Dan Breznitz and David Adler, "Reshoring Production and Restoring American Prosperity: A Practical Policy Agenda," *American Affairs*, Vol. 4, No. 4, Winter 2020).

[79] John Minns, "Of Miracles and Models: The Rise and Decline of the Developmental State in South Korea," *Third World Quarterly*, Vol. 22, No. 6, 2001.

[80] Cal Clark and Changhoon Jung, "Implications of the Asian Flu for Developmental State Theory: The Cases of South Korea and Taiwan," *Asian Affairs*, Vol. 29, No. 1, 2002, p. 17.

[81] Tom Ginsburg, "Dismantling the 'Developmental State'? Administrative Procedure Reform in Japan and Korea," *American Journal of Comparative Law*, Vol. 49, No. 4, 2001, pp. 585–586.

The concept and practice of the developmental state are not without controversy. Recent scholarship has pointed to the potential drawbacks of the model, in particular the ways in which state-led development can ossify into a bureaucratic corporatism that eventually stalls rather than promotes development. Growth rates in many of the Asian tigers slowed dramatically in the 1990s, most notably in Japan, which has since been stuck in an extended period of stagnation. Close government-business ties generated a degree of corruption that many of these countries have spent decades wringing out of their systems.[82] China is now running into headwinds that are in part demonstrating the limits and downsides of such a powerful state role in shaping economic choices. And in some cases, such as Taiwan, the success of small and medium-size businesses in the country's export model might have had less to do with the developmental state than the natural operation of the market.[83]

Scholars have also pointed to the complex societal implications of such a model, noting that a developmental state may impede the true sharing of political-economic power throughout a society.[84] It was precisely the unwinding of this imbalanced power structure—the growth of influence by a range of economic and social actors able to challenge the priorities of developmental states—that forced change in some of these systems over time.[85] And some experts argue that the 1997 Asian financial crisis was prompted by excessive government involvement in these economies and associated financial challenges, although others suggest that the connection is not so direct.[86]

A general pattern in these developmental states has been the need for a gradual ebbing of the role of the state and the search for a more lasting equilibrium between state and market forces. Different states have pursued this balance in distinct ways. Some have undertaken centrally directed liberalization programs, while others have worked more closely with labor and business to produce negotiated outcomes.[87] In Japan and South Korea, the independent power of the bureaucracies, while still substantial, has been shaved back in favor of greater checks and balances.[88] Taiwan pursued an interesting process of liberalization to seek an optimum balance between state and market.[89]

---

[82] David C. Kang, "Bad Loans to Good Friends: Money Politics and the Developmental State in South Korea," *International Organization*, Vol. 56, No. 1, 2002.

[83] Yongping Wu, "Rethinking the Taiwanese Developmental State," *China Quarterly*, No. 177, 2004.

[84] Alexius A. Pereira, "Whither the Developmental State? Explaining Singapore's Continued Developmentalism," *Third World Quarterly*, Vol. 29, No. 6, 2008.

[85] Minns, 2001.

[86] Clark and Jung, 2002.

[87] Darius Ornston and Mark I. Vail, "The Developmental State in Developed Societies: Power, Partnership, and Divergent Patterns of Intervention in France and Finland," *Comparative Politics*, Vol. 49, No. 1, 2016.

[88] Ginsburg, 2001.

[89] Christopher M. Dent, "Taiwan's Foreign Economic Policy: The 'Liberalisation Plus' Approach of an Evolving Developmental State," *Modern Asian Studies*, Vol. 37, No. 2, 2003.

Taken together, these assessments of the developmental state model offer important insights into the competitive advantages conferred by active states. Many 20th-century examples highlight the specific benefits, in terms of national competitive standing, of policies, investments, and guiding values that active states can provide. But, considering the modern experience since 1945, it is difficult to exaggerate the importance of balance in the active state's role.

The Balance: Avoiding Overbearing Interference

As much as an active state is essential to competitive advantage, when it is too intrusive, costly, or bureaucratic, an active state will obstruct rather than promote national dynamism. This is the essential goal for this characteristic: an active state that is energetic and powerful enough to create the conditions for success, but not so strong or constrained by orthodoxy or bureaucratically catatonic that it strangles the energy of the country. A good deal of evidence suggests that the state can easily go too far—that the vibrant energy of the most competitive societies is grounded first and foremost on grassroots initiatives, on the ability of vast numbers of average people to innovate, invent, express their ambitions for knowledge or commerce, and participate in many other forms of bottom-up energy.[90]

Many of our cases have reflected just such a balance. Alexander Hamilton's early vision for the United States, for example, while not fully implemented by the young republic, argued for clear limits to what the very powerful federal government would actually do. Britain during its period of rise benefited from a whole succession of competitiveness-supporting policies undertaken by a series of active states, which nonetheless cultivated the growth and health of a vigorous private sector and civil society outside the state's control.

It is when nations get this balance wrong that we can see trouble for their competitive position. The Soviet Union is a classic modern case in which the state quite consciously intervened in every aspect of social life—and in the process disastrously handicapped the energy, innovative potential, and adaptability of the Soviet society. The state sought to support modernization and the promotion of science and technology, but this had limited and mixed effects. In certain narrowly military areas, the effort produced impressive outputs and lavished state preferences on scientists and engineers. This characteristic reflects once again the same basic dilemma that confronted the Soviet system: It is exceptionally difficult to promote such intellectual energy in an autocracy, a dilemma magnified by the role of state intervention.[91]

The case of Japan highlights a different risk—the ways in which bold state intervention can ignite social tensions that ultimately destabilize the society. The Japanese state in the Meiji period was "determined to activate the nation" and was "adventurous in its encour-

---

[90] Appleby, 2010, loc. 1956–1961.

[91] Zubok, 2007, pp. 163, 166, 181.

agement of rapid change." But this provoked fears throughout the society about the loss of Japan's soul, its traditions, and its unique identity in the rush to match Western models.[92] The result was a toxic form of xenophobic nationalism.

This characteristic, therefore, comes with more qualifications and risks than most. An active state can turbocharge national competitive advantage—but only if its efforts are carefully targeted and tailored to achieve very specific results, and only if its role aligns with the socioeconomic realities of the age. The employment of state power for competitive advantage can easily go wrong and become excessive. On the far end of that spectrum, the evidence is very clear than total central control—a state-*run* economy and society, as opposed to a state-*empowered* economy and society—constitutes a serious and perhaps fatal competitive disadvantage. The periods of national competitive advance and efflorescence tend to reflect those in which states have somehow hit a decent balance, discovering the most effective and efficient ways for states to enhance national power.

Moreover, for this characteristic to work effectively, societies need a strongly associated quality working in their favor—effective institutions. An active state will not achieve meaningful results if public institutions are weak or corrupt. And it will not be able to make up for the competitive handicap of a society hamstrung with poor private and community institutions. It is to this critical societal characteristic of effective institutions that we now turn.

---

[92] Jansen, 2000, loc. 7116–7117.

CHAPTER SEVEN

Effective Institutions

Many factors contributed to the decline and eventual collapse of the Soviet Union, but one of the most important was surely the ineffectiveness, corruption, and oppressive weight of its social and government institutions. The Soviet governing structure was built on the idea that it could hardwire the operation of society and manage almost every aspect of economic and social life, right down to the amount of wheat needed to make a loaf of bread or the number of rivets needed to build a car. That these institutions and their associated processes ultimately proved sclerotic and fraudulent was perhaps the dominant factor associated with Soviet decline.

This was a tragically ironic result from the perspective of the architects of the Soviet system, which was built in part to shape social and economic outcomes more effectively than capitalist countries. As one scholar notes, Moscow generated an "elaborate network of state institutions that insinuated themselves into almost every aspect of society, from trade unions to chess clubs. . . . The institutional density of communist states was meant to serve as a mobilizing instrument."[1] The maintenance of its institutions of control was a high priority and ate up an immense amount of state resources. Officials were held accountable to production quotas and organizational metrics. Massively detailed data were accumulated on all manner of issues. And yet the formal network created to maintain the system ended up poisoning it.

Perhaps the core element of this institutional failure was a basic and structural level of inefficiency, resulting from a permanent mismatch between planned expectations and reality. Human societies are too vast and organic and unpredictable to be efficiently operated by such centralized mechanisms. A combination of grassroots market decisions with some state supervision and support—in the basic liberal model—was always destined to outcompete a central planning system whose choices would always be significantly misaligned with needs, desires, and risks. Soviet planners, Niall Ferguson concludes, could not anticipate "the desires of millions of individual consumers, whose tastes are in any case in a state of constant flux."[2]

Steven Solnick makes a persuasive case that the Soviet collapse was a product not merely of leadership mistakes or loss of faith in the masses but also the pervasive degeneration of the

---

[1] Charles King, "Review Article: *Post-Postcommunism: Transition, Comparison, and the End of 'Eastern Europe'* by Valerie Bunce, Karen Dawisha, Bruce Parrott, Richard Sakwa, and Daniel S. Treisman," *World Politics*, Vol. 53, No. 1, 2000, p. 158.

[2] Ferguson, 2011, p. 237.

working-level management of Soviet institutions. Midlevel authorities became infected with corruption and rent seeking and also found it impossible to control the ideas and activities of members. When some managers glimpsed the opportunity to use their position to enrich themselves and grab state resources, many others followed.[3] Control loosened, and senior managers had more and more difficulty managing or even staying aware of the activities of their subordinates.[4] Over time, institutions spent as much time waging bureaucratic warfare against one another as they did interacting with their supposed constituents, including obstructing any reforms that might threaten their position.

The Soviet system thus represents a case of an arrangement set up to generate competitive advantage but becoming instead a pivotal weakness because it fell catastrophically out of balance: A potentially dynamism-generating active state transformed into an imprisoning totalitarian structure. As Vladislav Zubok concludes, the "rigid bureaucratic apparatus . . . held the country in steel bands and blocked innovation and change."[5]

The institutional crisis of the Soviet system became acute after 1988, when the reforms begun by Mikhail Gorbachev effectively pulled the rug out from under popular faith and official reliance on key institutions of Soviet governance and legitimacy.[6] Once the system began change, its very institutional density became a source of instability.[7] A long, slow erosion metastasized into an urgent institutional crisis. And, combined with other blows—notably, the surge of nationalism in several Soviet republics straining to escape the Union—it proved fatal. From a political standpoint, when the Soviet system tried to replace socialist objectives with democratic principles, it was left suspended between two claims without a real support system. In fact, Soviet citizens learned to disdain products made in their own country and favor Western ones, simply on principle. The institutional superstructure governing their lives had become thoroughly discredited.

This characteristic emerges as our next major variable governing competitive success. A consistent theme across all the literatures surveyed for this research is the critical importance of effective institutions. Institutional quality *alone* does not explain national fates. Many scholars working on comparative history, including Niall Ferguson, Dierdre McCloskey, and Joel Mokyr, stress that institutions are critical, but typically they must be paired with broader values and habits in a society to produce necessary outcomes. Those values and habits, in turn, depend on an active state for full national competitiveness. Effective institutions, then, constitute a necessary though not sufficient building block of national dynamism: They pro-

---

[3] Steven Solnick, *Stealing the State: Control and Collapse in Soviet Institutions*, Cambridge, Mass.: Harvard University Press, 1998.

[4] Michael McFaul, "State Power, Institutional Change, and the Politics of Privatization in Russia," *World Politics*, Vol. 47, No. 2, 1995, pp. 221–222.

[5] Zubok, 2007, p. 179.

[6] Sakwa, 2013, p. 67.

[7] Valerie Bunce, *Subversive Institutions: The Design and the Destruction of Socialism and the State*, Cambridge, UK: Cambridge University Press, 1999.

vide key structures and capacities for the engine to operate. But they still rely on other components of that synergistic whole.

Defining the Characteristic

It turns out to be surprisingly complex to define the concept of *institutions* and even trickier to determine what constitutes *effectiveness* in institutions, as well as what role they play in the larger mosaic of variables affecting national competitive outcomes.

***

The term *institutions* would seem to imply solid, tangible structures—almost synonymous with organizations—but scholars use the term to encompass a wide variety of tangible and intangible things. In social science terms, institutions are part of the wider social structure of a nation, systems of rules, norms, habits, and organizations that shape behavior in the society. One analysis describes them this way:

> Institutions are the kinds of structures that matter most in the social realm: they make up the stuff of social life. The increasing acknowledgement of the role of institutions in social life involves the recognition that much of human interaction and activity is structured in terms of overt or implicit rules. Without doing much violence to the relevant literature, we may define institutions as systems of established and prevalent social rules that structure social interactions. Language, money, law, systems of weights and measures, table manners, and firms (and other organizations) are thus all institutions.[8]

Institutions thus include broad societal organizing patterns, such as markets and hierarchies, specific organizations or clusters of them, values and customs, and laws, regulations, and other formal rules. Douglass North defines institutions as "the rules of the game in a society or, more formally . . . the humanly devised constraints that shape human interaction. In consequence they structure incentives in human exchange, whether political, social, or economic."[9] They are far more than organizations; they constitute "the framework within which human interaction takes place. They are perfectly analogous to the rules of the game in a competitive team sport. That is, they consist of formal written rules as well as typically unwritten codes of conduct that underlie and supplement formal rules."[10]

---

[8] Geoffrey M. Hodgson, "What Are Institutions?" *Journal of Economic Issues*, Vol. 40, No. 1, 2006. See also B. Guy Peters, "Political Institutions, Old and New," in Robert E. Goodin and Hans-Dieter Klingemann, eds., *A New Handbook of Political Science*, Oxford, UK: Oxford University Press, 1996.

[9] North, 1990, p. 3.

[10] North, 1990, p. 4. In one sense, North's focus is narrower than ours: He is considering "the cooperation that permits economies to capture the gains from trade," not the institutional arrangements that make countries competitive full stop (North, 1990, loc. 72–77). But many of the factors would appear to overlap—

Institutions can be either formal (an organization or law) or informal (more-diffuse habits of a culture). Informal institutions in particular "evolve gradually with the national culture" and thus "provide the continuity and path-dependence that connects a society's present to its history and to the future." Such informal institutions "tend to be more durable than formal institutions which may be replaced overnight by new legislation and regulation, wars, revolution and so forth."[11] It is worth noting that these basic features—lasting, durable, habitual patterns of activity that can nonetheless evolve—also apply to our concept of societal characteristics. The category of informal institutions is one of the closest parallels in the scholarly literature to what we mean by societal characteristics.

Institutions are thus socially constituted rather than physical properties of a society. They emerge through social interactions and can change over time. Nations with poor or ineffective institutions can develop better ones; well-functioning institutions can decay into inertia and venality. Institutions are effective only when they generate shared habits among the population—in other words, the rules, or norms they aim to establish must be accepted.[12]

***

Turning then to what constitutes an *effective* institution, there is no similar agreed baseline in the scholarly literature.[13] Our research suggests several basic criteria with which we can assess institutional effectiveness:

- *Effectual in achieving economic and political purposes.* In the simplest sense, institutions are effective when they achieve, to a significant degree, the purposes for which they are established. Bureaucracies for taxation are effective if they collect the intended amount and nature of taxes. Regimes to protect intellectual property are effective to the degree they establish and enforce clear standards.
- *Respected and followed.* To have consistent effects, institutions must shape behavior in meaningful ways. The people of a society must come to accept their rules and norms as taken-for-granted aspects of social life and act accordingly. Institutions can exist in

---

the things that make countries better able to profit from trade also make them more competitive in other areas. Indeed, as he noted he is really considering the role of "institutions that create an hospitable environment fort cooperative solutions to complex exchange" (loc. 77).

[11] Hämäläinen, 2003, pp. 153–154.

[12] Geoffrey M. Hodgson, "On Defining Institutions: Rules Versus Equilibria," *Journal of Institutional Economics*, Vol. 11, No. 3, 2015.

[13] As one recent study put it, "While there is little disagreement that effective public administration is central to economic development, debates continue to rage about what are the building blocks of an effective and competent bureaucracy." Timothy J. Besley, Robin Burgess, Adnan Khan, and Guo Xu, "Bureaucracy and Development," Cambridge, Mass.: National Bureau of Economic Research, Working Paper 29163, August 2021, p. 2. This study offers a very helpful step toward defining an *organizational economics of the state*, ways of measuring more formally the institutional foundations for success.

some rhetorical or even organizational sense but be ignored or flouted, in which case they cannot be described as effective.

- *Professional.* Effective institutions will typically be at least partly professionalized—that is, run by a group of people trained in useful techniques and who uphold standards and norms that contribute to effectiveness. An accounting system, for example, depends on the basic shared practices of the field and the norms that guide the practice of specific accountants.
- *Objective and rule based.* Effective institutions must perform their duties and make their judgments largely on objective rules, standards, or norms, rather than being subject to corrupt influence, favoritism, or elite bias.
- *Perceived as legitimate.* Finally, to serve their broader role of enhancing social coherence by competently addressing social and economic challenges, institutions must be *perceived* as effective. This adds a significant wrinkle to the analysis because a major problem in many Western countries today is a loss of faith in institutions, whose objectively measured achievement of goals might not have shifted all that much.

Taken together, these criteria informed our assessment of whether institutions helped or hurt competitive standing. But they are only general and qualitative guidelines. Depending on the period of history, the country, and the ways in which institutions aid competitive advantage, the specific indicators of effective versus ineffective institutions will vary. But as we look across the case studies and through the empirical evidence for the effect of strong institutions, these criteria at least offer a useful road map.

The Theoretical Case for the Competitive Advantage of Strong and Effective Institutions

The theoretical argument for the importance of institutions to competitive advantage is foundational and stretches across all the other characteristics. Effective institutions are the route to the shared opportunity. They are essential for a workable active state and are tightly interwoven with the qualities of national ambition and will and unified national identity: Credible, effective, and legitimate institutions instantiate the somewhat abstract realities captured by those characteristics. Strong and effective institutions also help nations mobilize popular consent and effort, through such means as parliaments and public bureaucracies.

The defining modern case for the role of institutions is made by Douglass North. "The central puzzle of human history is to account for the widely divergent paths of historical change," he explains. Divergent outcomes are "perplexing," he points out, at least from the standpoint of economic theory, because that theory predicts convergence, not divergence.[14] The answer, he and others suggest, is closely related to the quality of national institutions,

---

[14] North, 1990, p. 6.

which are "the underlying determinant of the long-run performance of economies."[15] North contends that effective institutions are the basic factory of societal habits, rules, and norms that can be associated with competitive success. They achieve this effect in large measure through their role in promoting efficient transactions in a society, providing a foundational architecture for all manner of exchanges to take place.

Other scholars agree with the importance of institutions, but stress that they cannot achieve large-scale societal outcomes on their own. They must combine with other factors—notably, the prevailing norms and values in a society—to achieve lasting effectiveness.[16] It is the combination of institutions and values that is part of the secret sauce of national dynamism. Joel Mokyr, for example, argues,

> An economy that grows as a result of favorable institutions requires a world of well-delineated and respected property rights, enforceable contracts, law and order, a low level of opportunism and rent-seeking, a high degree of inclusion in political decision making and the benefits of growth, and a political organization in which power and wealth are as separate as is humanly possible.[17]

Mokyr notes that institutions like this do not account for the "growth of technological creativity and innovation in Europe and especially the surge following the middle of the eighteenth century. The Industrial Revolution . . . at first blush does not seem to have been a response to any obvious institutional stimulus." To explain such a broad social process as the Industrial Revolution we need another factor, which Mokyr describes as "useful knowledge," or the widespread pursuit of learning and knowledge and its application to practical scientific and technological advances and applications.[18] Yet the mutual dependence of these factors runs both ways. Without effective institutions, a society-wide commitment to useful knowledge will not have as much effect; without intellectual property protections and rule of law, for example, there is much less incentive to invent and innovate.[19]

---

[15] North, 1990, p. 107. He writes, "That institutions affect the performance of economies is hardly controversial. That the differential performance of economies over time is fundamentally influences by the way institutions evolve is also not controversial" (North, 1990, p. 3). North comes at the issue from the standpoint of a fundamentally neoclassical economic theory, but the role of institutions is stressed in many competing schools of economic thought.

[16] "If 'bad institutions' can too easily kill prosperity, there is no guarantee that 'good institutions' by themselves can foster a great enrichment. In fact, for millennia societies have enforced property rights and even adopted pro-market institutions without experiencing major economic progress" (Spolaore, 2020, p. 784).

[17] Mokyr, 2017, 5, pp. 9–12.

[18] Mokyr, 2017, pp. 5, 7.

[19] Deirdre McCloskey agrees that institutions hardly work if they are not supported by broader social habits and values. They must, she suggests, be supported by social ethics. "An institution works, if it does, mainly because of the good ethics of its participants, intrinsic motivations powerfully reinforced by the ethical opinion people have about each other," she writes (McCloskey, 2016, p. 23). A good example is Rome, where societal values such as reciprocity "made the fulfillment of contractual obligations a matter of per-

The economist Edmund Phelps has spoken to these same interrelationships, specifically in economic terms. Economic dynamism, he contends, relies on

> institutions and an economic culture that potentiate conceivers of new commercial ideas, facilitate entrepreneurs to develop these new ideas, allow employees to contract to work long and hard, and protect against fraud financiers willing to invest in or lend to enterprises and consumers (or other end-users) willing to try products found in the market.

The basic infrastructure of a modern capitalist economy, in other words, is nothing more than a set of effective institutions stretching across a range of economic functions, which Phelps describes as "a virtual infrastructure of legal rights and procedures."[20] These must be connected to a working commercial system and supportive social values to succeed, but the institutions themselves are the essential foundation for all these other endeavors.[21]

Other scholars similarly argue that it is the unique, case-specific interrelationship of institutions and cultural values that best explains national outcomes.[22] Still others trace specific mechanisms by which culture underpins institutional effectiveness.[23] These more-qualified views of the role of institutions hardly rule them out as an important contributing factor. Institutions clearly require the supporting context of social ethics to make their structures work. But even skeptics of the extreme case for institutions as the single or dominant explanation for national development agree that they are somewhat or even very significant as determinants of national power and growth. Effective institutions are necessary, if not sufficient on their own, to achieve national competitive advantage.[24]

---

sonal honor. The effects of laws therefore were amplified by the actions of individuals." These connections make clear that "the informal networks that underlie" institutions are critical to their success (Temin, 2013, pp. 12–13). Margaret Jacob (2014) also stresses the importance of values and norms underpinning institutional quality and effectiveness.

[20] Phelps, 2013, p. 203.

[21] North agrees, in fact. He highlights the close relationship between institutions and wider societal values and habits: "The cultural transmission of values, from the extension and application of formal rules to solve specific exchange problems," such as "[e]ffective traditions of hard work, honesty, and integrity[,] simply lower the cost of transacting and make possible complex, productive exchange. Such traditions are always reinforced by ideologies that undergird those attitudes" (North, 1990, p. 138).

[22] Alberto Bisin and Thierry Vierdier, "On the Joint Evolution of Culture and Institutions," Cambridge, Mass.: National Bureau of Economic Research, Working Paper 23375, April 2017.

[23] Alesina and Giuliano, 2013.

[24] Ferguson, 2011, pp. 11, 13–14.

Institutions and Competitive Outcomes: General Evidence

In the broad historical literature on national rise and fall, global economic history, and comparative history, there is ample evidence for the idea that strong, effective social institutions are a critical building block of national competitive advantage. As noted above, there is a bit of a debate, or at least need for qualification, on this point. Skeptics of North's view of institutions contend that some nations have grown quickly *before* they have good institutions and slowly *after* they have them.[25] Some research has come up with only modest results for the effect of institutions on economic growth or development.[26]

Yet our argument does not require proving the unique and distinct effect of institutions. It only demands proof that institutions are critical to competitive position—that, working in tandem with other characteristics, they are a necessary if not sufficient condition for competing well. The evidence for this more limited proposition is overwhelming. Most studies of national rise and decline emphasize the central role of effective institutions in underwriting national strength and competitiveness.[27] Dwight Perkins and Bon Ho Koo summarize the results of a range of empirical studies of "social capability" by arguing that "having well-trained people . . . is not enough. Institutions designed to mobilize this human capital capability are essential."[28] Cultivating strong and effective institutions is therefore a critical building block of competitive success.

General National Effectiveness

Perhaps the most general role of institutions across the breadth of a society is to smooth interactions, build trust, and otherwise boost societal capacity for cooperative action. Institutions, for example, play the critical if technical role of moderating transaction costs and allowing cooperation on complex problems of coordination and in many other ways greasing the wheels of a dynamic economic and social engine.[29] Beyond that basic conceptual role, many studies have discussed the manifold ways in which effective institutions have been critical for state development and competitive standing, from effective taxation to providing legitimacy

---

[25] Joel Mokyr, review of *Bourgeois Dignity: Why Economics Can't Explain the Modern World*, by Deirdre N. McCloskey, *Journal of Modern History*, Vol. 84, No. 2, June 2012b, p. 454.

[26] Edward J. Glaeser, Rafael La Porta, Florencio Lopez-De-Silanes, and Andrei Shleifer, "Do Institutions Cause Growth?" *Journal of Economic Growth*, Vol. 9, 2004.

[27] Georg Sørenson, *Changes in Statehood: The Transformation of International Relations*, Houndmills, UK: Palgrave, 2001; Jennifer Milliken and Keith Krause, "State Failure, State Collapse, and State Reconstruction: Concepts, Lessons and Strategies," *Development and Change*, Vol. 33, No. 5, 2002; Timothy Raeymaekers, "Collapse or Order? Questioning State Collapse in Africa," Berlin: Households in Conflict Network, Working Paper 01/01, 2005.

[28] Dwight H. Perkins and Bon Ho Koo, "Introduction," in Bon Ho Koo and Dwight H. Perkins, eds., *Social Capability and Long-Term Economic Growth*, New York: St. Martin's Press, 1995, p. 7.

[29] North, 1990, p. 133; Hämäläinen, 2003, pp. 153–154.

to the state to underpinning military power. One survey of this body of work outlines some basic findings, including the fact that bureaucratic or institutional quality is positively correlated with national development and economic growth.[30]

In an even more fundamental sense, the rule of law and basic standards of interaction provide the essential foundation for economic and social exchange.[31] Private property, an early institutional innovation, provided a foundational institution on which national development rests. Without the prospect of keeping the benefits of one's inventions—if they could merely be seized by a potentate or corporation—the incentive to invent was dimmed.[32] One example is the legal framework surrounding the modern company, including such aspects as bankruptcy law, "protection of companies from self-dealing by managers, protection of companies from employees who do not perform, limits on what companies may ask employees to do, and so forth."[33] Without the institution of the corporation, social norms and economic efficiency would be more difficult to protect.[34]

Institutions and Economic Vibrancy

Other research suggests that effective institutions provide the basis for productive activity, create competitive conditions not monopolies, and expand opportunities.[35] Competitive advantage comes from being able to make effective use of resources—but this in turn is a product of the "ability of a state's central government to dominate its constituent parts and efficiently organize their capacity"—that is, the quality of its institutions.[36] Additionally, "There is extensive evidence that societies with extractive and anti-market institutions have worse economic outcomes than similar societies with relatively better institutions."[37]

---

[30] Besley et al., 2021, pp. 5–10.

[31] "Medieval society had been held together by loosely defined, open-ended personal bonds between lord and vassal, seigneur and serf; but business could not operate in this realm of indeterminacy and needed a measure for all things. The new law provided the measure, and the new nation-state enforced it," Landes writes (Landes, 2003, p. 18).

[32] Landes, 2003, p. 16.

[33] Phelps, 2013, p. 205.

[34] Abramovitz, 1995, p. 37.

[35] North, 1990, p. 9; Acemoglu and Robinson, 2012. Indeed, there is a close connection between institutions and the related societal characteristic of shared opportunity: "Institutions, together with the standard constraints of economic theory, determine the opportunities in a society. Organizations are created to take advantage of those opportunities, and, as the organizations evolve, they alter the institutions. The resultant path of institutional change is shaped by (1) the lock-in that comes from the symbiotic relationship between institutions and the organizations that have evolved as a consequence of the incentive structure provided by those institutions and (2) the feedback process by which human beings perceive and react to changes in the opportunity set" (North, 1990, p. 7).

[36] Mitchell, 2018, p. 59.

[37] Spolaore, 2020, p. 784.

Dani Rodrik, Arvind Subramanian, and Francesco Trebbi marshal significant historical support for the importance of institutions in economic development. Their statistical
analysis of country growth rates finds "sharp and striking results. Most importantly, . . . the
quality of institutions trumps everything else. Once institutions are controlled for, integration has no direct effect on incomes, while geography has at best weak direct effects." They do
admit that the distinction between institutions and policies can be "murky" and that effective
macroeconomic policies have been shown by other research to have a critical role once institutions are controlled for.[38] But the importance of effective institutions nonetheless emerges
clearly from the data.[39]

More-recent studies of economic growth and national development also highlight the critical role of institutions. Paul Collier focuses on the ways in which the quality of governance
can affect national development. He especially focuses on "terrible governance and policies,"
which can "destroy an economy with alarming speed."[40] More generally, David Landes identifies the role of institutions—broadly defined and overlapping with cultural values—as the
true foundation of the Industrial Revolution in Britain. Especially critical were private property rights, personal liberty, rights of contract, and a "stable government" that is responsive,
honest, "moderate, efficient, ungreedy."[41]

The economic role of institutions emerges in historical comparisons as well. One scholar
argues that the modern Russian example of Wild West capitalism does not echo the robber
baron era in the United States precisely because the United States of that period had strong
political and economic institutions, ranging from independent political actors to powerful
national financial institutions and the rule of law. Those institutions could eventually get
control of the robber barons in ways we cannot necessarily expect in Russia today.[42] Indeed,
the capacity of government institutions is arguably the single most important distinguishing
factor between countries that have achieved rapid economic growth and converged with the
leading economies and those that have stagnated.[43]

Reviewing this range of evidence, Niall Ferguson concludes, "The critical point is that
the differential between the West and the Rest was institutional."[44] This emerged clearly,

---

[38] Rodrik, Subramanian, and Trebbi, 2002, pp. 4, 20.

[39] Robert E. Hall and Charles I. Jones, "Why Do Some Countries Produce So Much More Output per
Worker Than Others?" *Quarterly Journal of Economics*, Vol. 114, No. 1, February 1999.

[40] Collier, 2007, p. 64.

[41] Landes, 1998, pp. 215, 217–218.

[42] William Pfaff quoted in Clesse and Lounev, 2004, p. 253.

[43] Lawrence B. Krause, "Social Capability and Long-Term Economic Growth," in Bon Ho Koo and
Dwight H. Perkins, eds., *Social Capability and Long-Term Economic Growth*, New York: St. Martin's Press,
1995, p. 310.

[44] Ferguson, 2011, p. 13. Ferguson does admit that institutions on their own are not enough to explain why,
for example, the Industrial Revolution started in Britain rather than Holland or Germany; he adds the factors of more-expensive labor (which prompted labor-saving innovations) and access to coal (pp. 202–203).

he contends, in the differential degrees of success between British colonies, with their more grassroots-friendly system of property rights and open governance, and Spanish and Portuguese colonies in South America.

Political Stability

Empirical evidence shows that the credibility and legitimacy of public institutions are critical for the strength of democratic rule. One quantitative analysis of surveys on cultural values suggests that "the recent decline in institutional confidence around the globe may lead to political instability that threatens democratic institutions. Autocratic nations with high institutional confidence remain stable, further suggesting that no teleology exists that makes democracy inevitable and that disaffected populations will just as likely transition to autocracy as to democracy."[45]

The failure of institutions, or their dramatic ineffectiveness, can lead to social instability. This was true, for example, in Qing China, as its "innovative administrative infrastructure . . . became gradually outmatched and then overwhelmed by the increase of population density and size within fixed administrative units."[46] It was also true in imperial Spain and in the modern Soviet Union. Nations with institutions that cannot keep up with the managerial and strategic demands of their time stand at a tremendous critical disadvantage.

Social Capital, Institutions, and Economic and Political Success

Another way to understand the role of institutions is through the concept of *social capital*, which has been defined as "networks together with shared norms, values and understandings that facilitate co-operation within or among groups."[47] The importance of this underlying web of connections, many of which can also be considered as institutions, has been historically documented,[48] and it is connected to social stability, economic growth, and other beneficial outcomes. An example is the "gentlemanly ideals" of industrial-era Britain, which helped create a set of norms of conduct to underwrite economic exchanges and cooperation.[49] These norms were disseminated by a wide range of civil society organizations, from scientific to trade groups, that promoted norm-governed behavior and established implicit punishments for violations.

---

[45] Damian J. Ruck, Luke J. Matthews, Thanos Kyritsis, Quentin D. Atkinson, and R. Alexander Bentley, "The Cultural Foundations of Modern Democracies," *Nature: Human Behavior*, Vol. 4, 2020, p. 267.

[46] Goldstone, 2002, p. 352.

[47] OECD, *OECD Insights: Human Capital*, Paris, 2007, p. 103.

[48] David Sunderland, *Social Capital, Trust and the Industrial Revolution, 1780–1880*, London: Routledge, 2007.

[49] Mokyr, 2012a, pp. 188–191. For a comprehensive study of the concept of gentlemanly capitalism, see Peter Cain and Anthony G. Hopkins, *British Imperialism: Innovation and Expansion*, Essex, UK: Longman, 1993.

The importance of institutions is also reflected in the literature on the role of a vibrant and healthy civil society.[50] Recent arguments, including by Robert Putnam, about the importance of civil society basically amount to a subset of the argument for institutions. Social support structures such as guilds and associations and worker training organizations, when arrayed in a powerful network, strengthen social cohesion and competitiveness.[51] Other researchers have argued that associational activities themselves might not be strongly related to levels of growth and development, but two related factors—trust and civic cooperation—are. They may go together as a package, although some research suggests that the causal ties between the strength of civic associational life and trust or cooperation might not be linear.[52]

Beyond Simple Effectiveness: The Importance of Inclusive Institutions

Daron Acemoglu and James Robinson have recently added an important addendum to the case for institutions: Those that underwrite national success must not be merely strong and effective but inclusive.[53] "As institutions influence behavior and incentives in real life, they forge the success or failure of nations," they write.[54] Inclusive economic institutions,

> are those that allow and encourage participation by the great mass of people in economic activities that make best use of their talents and skills and that enable individuals to make the choices they wish. To be inclusive, economic institutions must feature secure private property, an unbiased system of law, and a provision of public services that provides a

---

[50] Indeed, even within the institutional realm there is a synergistic or combinatorial effect that must be understood. Competitively strong nations are characterized by the emergence of *many mutually support-ing institutions*, whose combined effect is the real advantage. The key factor is the "adaptively efficient characteristics of the institutional matrix (both the formal rules and the informal constraints embodied in attitudes and values) that produced an economic and political environment that rewarded productive activity of organizations and their development of skills and knowledge." But "exactly what was essential to that matrix, what was deliberately created to encourage productivity growth and flexible responses, and what was an accidental by-product of other objectives constitutes an important agenda for a much deeper understanding of economic growth" (North, 1990, p. 136).

[51] Morris, 2010, p. 510.

[52] Knack and Keefer, 1997.

[53] Acemoglu and Robinson, 2012, p. 43. "Egypt is poor," they argue, "precisely because it has been ruled by a narrow elite that have organized society for their own benefit at the expense of the vast mass of people." In the meantime, "Countries such as Great Britain and the United States became rich because their citizens overthrew the elites who controlled power and created a society where political rights were much more broadly distributed, where the government was accountable and responsive to citizens, and where the great mass of people could take advantage of economic opportunities" (Acemoglu and Robinson, 2012, pp. 3–4).

[54] Acemoglu and Robinson, 2012, p. 43.

level playing field in which people can exchange and contract; it also must permit the entry of new businesses and allow people to choose their careers.[55]

Such institutions are central to the characteristic of society-wide opportunity because they "create inclusive markets, which not only give people freedom to pursue the vocations in life that best suit their talents but also provide a level playing field that gives them the opportunity to do so." Inclusive institutions are more likely, Acemoglu and Robinson maintain, to generate productive societal investment in such collective goods as infrastructure and regulation "to prevent fraud and malfeasance"; they also "pave the way for two other engines of prosperity: technology and education."[56]

What Acemoglu and Robinson term *extractive* institutions, by contrast, retard opportunity, talent acquisition, and growth because they "concentrate power in the hands of a narrow elite and placed few constraints on the exercise of this power. Economic institutions are then often structured by this elite to extract resources from the rest of the society. Extractive economic institutions thus naturally accompany extractive political institutions."[57] In the case of the Spanish Habsburgs, massive silver discoveries in the Americas brought resources to the monarchy, but they were tightly held between the crown and a small number of merchants, did not spread throughout a middle class as in England and did not prevent successive regimes from defaulting on loans. Instead, they promoted monopolies on trade to enrich specific individuals.[58]

Acemoglu and Robinson do not argue that extractive institutions cannot generate growth, or that inclusive ones always do so. There are other variables involved, and sometimes an extractive regime (such as the Soviet Union in its early decades) can shove enough resources into the system to produce growth and some technological wonders.[59] But extractive institutions produce growth by applying current technologies and found resources rather than generating change. This approach is not sustainable over long periods, although it can go on for decades. The key missing factor is true technological change and innovation.[60]

---

[55] Acemoglu and Robinson, 2012, p. 74. One limitation of this analysis is that, beyond some general statements, the Acemoglu and Robinson never define precisely what counts as an inclusive political institution beyond these somewhat vague phrases. China's system has some elements of voice and inclusivity; the question is whether they are sufficient to overcome the extractive system trap.

[56] Acemoglu and Robinson, 2012, pp. 75–77. See also Sainsbury, 2020, p. 43.

[57] Part of the reason is that, in an extractive state, there will always be fights for control of the sources of extraction—control of the state. Acemoglu and Robinson argue that the later Roman Empire and the Mayan experience both provide examples of catastrophic civil warfare to control the real sources of wealth—the extractive state institutions (Acemoglu and Robinson, 2012, pp. 95, 150).

[58] Acemoglu and Robinson, 2012, pp. 81, 215, 219, 225.

[59] Acemoglu and Robinson, 2012, pp. 91, 124–127.

[60] Acemoglu and Robinson claim that China will eventually be seen as in this category: It is "similarly unlikely to generate sustained growth unless it undergoes a fundamental political transformation toward inclusive political institutions" (Acemoglu and Robinson, 2012, p. 151). The government still controls too

Effective Institutions and Competitive Outcomes: Evidence from Cases

As summarized in Table 7.1, the cases we reviewed provide many examples of the ways in which effective institutions underwrite national strength and dynamism—and how weak institutions can undermine those objectives. Good institutions alone are not the whole story. They must blend with other factors, including shared opportunity and habits associated with national ambition and will, to have their desired effects. But few countries have reached an apex of competitive vibrancy without institutions that are world-class for their time and context.

Much of the evidence that exists for these cases deals with what we would today call public or state institutions, as well as broader informal institutions, such as norms and conventions. There are some data on private associations, charities, private schools, and other nonstate institutions, but the discussions below focus in many cases on what our research suggested for state or state-supported institutions. Still, the evidence does highlight the basic connection between institutional quality and national competitive advantage.

Rome

Rome is a mixed and complex case, and one that changed substantially over time; Roman institutions of the early republic look nothing like those of the later empire. Rome's administrative institutions—the bureaucracy of empire—were, on the one hand, spectacularly effective; they were able to organize tax collection from provinces and empires, and they eventually maintained data on many Roman citizens. On the other hand, they were very limited in reach, function, and overall size compared with modern states. Some historians have suggested that Rome did not develop a managerial state as extensive or far-reaching as those of Chinese empires of the same era or the later Ottoman Empire.[61] Indeed, until well into its run, Rome had a central bureaucracy of remarkably modest scale: the Roman state simply did not seek to regulate the lives of its citizens in most essential ways.[62]

---

much of the economy, and China is likely to hit a wall. China mostly applies existing technology, entrepreneurs have to work through party cadres, property rights are not totally secure, and the government crashes down on firms without warning. This research says that growth under extractive institutions has been impressive, but "it will not be sustained" (pp. 437–443; quote from p. 441).

[61] Rome "did not, however, develop an imperial administration that matched the dimensions of the empire. A rudimentary apparatus of officialdom sufficed a government whose concerns were limited to essentials. The basic goals of the government were twofold: the maintenance of law and order, and the collection of taxes" (Garnsey and Saller, 2014, p. 35). Garnsey and Saller continue: "No emperor, in sum, was interested in introducing a substantially larger and more highly organized bureaucracy at any level, or in reorganizing local government systematically. Nor was there any need to do so. Despite more or less endemic corruption in the localities, tax revenues forwarded by the cities were adequate for the limited goals of the central government" (p. 52).

[62] Garnsey and Saller, 2014, pp. 36–40.

TABLE 7.1

Effective Institutions and Competitive Advantage—Evidence from Cases

Case	Elements of the Role of Effective Institutions in Historical Cases
Rome	• Modest but effective bureaucracy of empire; decentralized structure of local rule by incorporating elites complements central institutions • Emerging institutions of property rights, rule of law, judicial system • Military as core institution of competitive strength • Private institutions of trade, finance, engineering, and other disciplines
China	• Premodern China with world-class institutions of state administration (for the time) and finance • 20th-century growth fueled by effective state institutions
Spain	• Early modern Spain with mixed institutional quality; emphasis on effectiveness often secondary to other goals; at a significant institutional disadvantage in key areas—quality of military training and leadership, state finances • Seemingly less well-developed private institutional networks than Britain
Austria-Hungary	• Mixed quality • Some very strong strategy-making institutions and over time better state support for investment and industry • More fragmented and less coherent and generally high quality than some competitors
Ottoman Empire	• During period of competitive rise, strong institutions for the period: attention to high-quality state administration, military organizations • More corruption, ossification over time and less effective qualities
Renaissance Italy	• For the time, strong institutions of governance, finance, trade • Early form of private institutions in the form of scholarly associations, philanthropy by leading families, networks of learning and science • Decay over time as rigid hierarchical divisions and rent seeking recurred
Britain	• Industrial Revolution founded on key institutions stronger in Britain than elsewhere, from rule of law to state finances to stable parliamentary rule • At peak of empire, military and financial institutions lead the world • Extensive private institutions that underwrite learning, commerce, science
Sweden	• Mixed case; even at peak of European power the state had only incomplete effective institutions; arguably more personalized than institutionalized
France	• Early modern France develops core institutions of modern state—rule of law, state finances (though more uneven than Britain) • Napoleonic revolution in state capacity strengthens many key institutions, notably civil code, logistical basis for military power • Private institutions, such as associations, arguably less comprehensive and advanced than Britain
Japan	• Effective institutional management of two key periods of development and competitive rise—Meiji and post–World War II eras • Public-private linkages in institutional terms; at best synergistic, in excessive cases can become corrupt
Soviet Union	• Early institutional success story with management of massive injection of resources into industrialization • Eventual overshoot into sclerotic, corrupt bureaucratic stagnation
United States	• Reasonably strong institutions from the beginning, evolved to meet needs of time • In 20th century among the most effective institutional foundations of any case • Extensive private institutions complement public ones: associations, networks, philanthropy

The basic institutions of economics and commerce remained a work in progress during the period of peak influence we have defined, from the later republic through the early empire. Roman law, to take one example, did not allow for multigenerational business partnerships.[63] Public records of land and goods were incomplete, which limited the effectiveness of property rights to some degree. There was nothing like a generalized protection for intellectual property.[64] For much of Rome's history, it did not have a significant police force even for the capital, and Roman judicial institutions were limited to small numbers of cases. Nor was the bureaucracy professionalized in many cases—many positions were filled with political cronies, and there was often no requirement for training or experience.

Yet there are clear ways in which Rome—especially if we think in terms of the late republic and early empire under Augustus and his successors—appears to have benefited from institutional advantages over its competitors, specifically from its organizational and manufacturing capabilities. Rome was an immense, overpowering war machine with tremendous capacity for recovery from losses and setbacks, whose power was a function of several interconnected capacities:

> The Romans had always enjoyed a number of important advantages: they had well-built and imposing fortifications; factory-made weapons that were both standardized and of a high quality; an impressive infrastructure of roads and harbors; the logistical organization necessary to supply their army, whether at base or on campaign; and a tradition of training that ensured disciplined and coordinated action in battle, even in the face of adversity. Furthermore, Roman mastery of the sea, at least in the Mediterranean, was unchallenged and a vital aspect of supply. It was these sophistications, rather than weight of numbers, that created and defended the empire.[65]

These advantages can be traced in part to the quality of the institutions that supported them, which dealt with functions ranging from economic organization and commerce to the military itself to the logistical tools of state.

Within several areas crucial to Roman success, and relative to all other actors in ancient and even broadly premodern times, the Roman state produced numerous advanced, effective institutions. This included issuing coinage—an underappreciated but critical institution in premodern economies—and Roman law, especially regarding property rights, to govern both economic and social exchanges.[66] It included a centralized fiscal system that has

---

[63] Roman law "does not seem to have provided an institutional setting to accommodate ongoing, complex business enterprises that would continue to function regardless of who the owners or employees were" (Frier and Kehoe, 2007, p. 128).

[64] Frier and Kehoe, 2007, pp. 135–136.

[65] Ward-Perkins, 2006, p. 34.

[66] B. G. Abatino, G. Dari-Mattiacci, and E. C. Perotti, "Depersonalization of Business in Ancient Rome," *Oxford Journal of Legal Studies*, Vol. 31, No. 1, 2011; Craig Anderson, *Roman Law Essentials*, Edinburgh: Edinburgh University Press, 2009; Frier and Kehoe, 2007; Dennis P. Kehoe, "Agency, Roman Law, and

been described as the "metabolism of empire."[67] It included elaborate trade and commercial institutions—not all (or very many) state directed but nonetheless well established.[68] And it included, in a political sense, the Senate itself, for at least as long as it exercised real power (which was longer than the United States has existed as a nation, just to offer one comparison). Rome was institutionalized partly in what we would now call privatized or nongovernmental ways—with aristocrats taking responsibility for the provision of various public goods.

Among the most well-developed set of institutions in the republican and early imperial period of Rome was its legal structure, which was striking in the ancient world for its complexity and sophistication.[69] Among other Roman legal-institutional components were formal consensual contracts and partnerships, if only for the life of those involved in them. In the most basic sense, Roman law provided for common weights and measures. As early as the third or second century BCE, Roman law was already specifying multiple different legal remedies for broken contracts. Law and custom allowed Romans to employ slaves or freedmen as business managers, thus opening the way to commercial activity while avoiding "the opprobrium associated with too close and direct an involvement in sordid business affairs."[70]

Rome by the late republic had also developed a complex and sophisticated array of financial institutions. These included multiple ways of issuing, accounting for, and repaying debt, as well as multiple mechanisms for gathering capital to finance voyages of trade. Roman lending structures could adjust interest rates based on risk.[71] The historian Peter Temin has gone as far as to argue that "the surprising result is that financial institutions in the early Roman Empire were better than those of eighteenth-century France and Holland. They were similar to those in eighteenth-century London and probably better than those available elsewhere in England."[72]

That being said, these Roman institutions existed side by side with a political system that would not pass many modern tests for transparent or honest rule of law. Corruption of various forms remained endemic to the Roman system—indeed, taking advantage of the rent-seeking opportunities of the state was essentially celebrated as a public virtue, a problem that

---

Roman Social Values," in Dennis P. Kehoe and Thomas McGinn, eds., *Ancient Law, Ancient Society*, Ann Arbor: University of Michigan Press, 2017; Dennis P. Kehoe, *Law and the Rural Economy in the Roman Empire*, Ann Arbor: University of Michigan Press, 2007; Keith Roberts, *The Origins of Business, Money, and Markets*, New York: Columbia University Press, 2011, pp. 198–216. See also Harper, 2017, p. 37.

[67] Harper, 2017, p. 28.

[68] Temin, 2013; Bruce W. Frier, *Landlords and Tenants in Imperial Rome*, Princeton, N.J.: Princeton University Press, 1980, pp. 21–47.

[69] David Johnston, *Roman Law in Context*, New York: Cambridge University Press, 1999.

[70] Frier and Kehoe, 2007, p. 128, 130; Harris, 2007, p. 519; Neville Morley, "The Early Roman Empire: Distribution," in Walter Scheidel, Ian Morris, and Richard Saller, eds., *The Cambridge History of the Greco-Roman World*, Cambridge, UK: Cambridge University Press, 2007, p. 588; Temin, 2013, p. 3.

[71] Harris, 2007, pp. 521–523; Morley, 2007, p. 587.

[72] Temin, 2013, pp. 188–190.

worsened over time and corroded the legitimacy of the Roman state. Importantly, too, the competitive advantage was societal more than it was limited to government. Rome's wider commercial institutions helped support a system of regional and global trade that would not be equaled until perhaps the 19th century. Much of this was private and emergent rather than governmental and planned, but the result was still a series of institutions that provided Roman society with various competitive advantages. Taken as a whole, however, the Roman case does strongly suggest that some minimum level of institutional quality does seem to be necessary, if not sufficient, for sustained national competitiveness.

The Ottoman Empire

The Ottoman case offers similar lessons about the connection between effective institutions and national power. No single conclusion can be drawn about the complex, often highly local or regional, and shifting institutions of a multiethnic empire as wide-ranging as the Ottoman. Things changed over the more than six centuries of Ottoman history; Ottoman governments of various eras from the early 18th through the late 19th centuries made recurring efforts to improve the quality of state administration, with some degree of success. A gradual centralization of power produced the need for stronger core institutions of governance. The bureaucracy became more self-perpetuating, running its own schools and limiting positions to its own trainees. It sent many candidates to the West for education. For a time, the permanent bureaucracy essentially seized control of the state.[73]

Nonetheless, in the sense of the relative standing of Ottoman governments on this factor, there is substantial evidence that, despite periodic successes, Ottoman state and society labored under institutional handicaps relative to their emerging modern European competitors, especially in the later imperial period.

Some Ottoman central institutions were effective, and the administration of some provinces worked well. Ottoman society was also characterized by a proliferation of nonstate institutions, such as charitable societies that funded public works and offered aid and comfort to the poor.[74] But the pluralism of the empire made for a patchwork of institutional approaches even in the later empire (in the 18th century and afterward) that showed pockets of weakness.[75] And some foundations of effective state administration, such as population data, were "hopelessly out of date." Efforts at building a potent central administrative entity were hamstrung by "the enormous challenges posed by the fragmentation of the empire."[76] A

---

[73] Baer, 2021, p. 269.

[74] Inalcik, 2001, loc. 3072–3076; Baer, 2021, p. 97.

[75] One scholar explains, "Institutions that looked the same on paper worked quite differently in practice." The bureaucratic structure in Egypt, for example, was being transformed by the local leader into "a modern, effective machine of government," whereas the ruler of another region pursued a "despotic administration" that was "rigid and inefficient by comparison" (Hanioğlu, 2008, p. 7).

[76] Hanioğlu, 2008, pp. 7, 13, 50.

major reform drive in the early 19th century made some progress but always lagged behind European rivals.[77] One leading historian describes the period after the mid-17th century as "a record of the decayed forms of ancient imperial institutions."[78]

Law was another area in which successive Ottoman regimes, even in the later empire after the 18th century, fell behind their European rivals. Marc David Baer stresses the overall quality of Ottoman law and the strong efforts to rationalize Islamic with secular legal regimes.[79] But other scholars contend that, although in theory a central legal regime built partly on sharia law was applied "in a uniform manner throughout the empire," in practice "the dualistic character of the legal system, the different administrative regulations for the various provinces, and their somewhat arbitrary implementation resulted in uneven application of the law." The fragmented character of political rule "severely disrupted" the application of legal standards.[80]

The true quality and efficiency of these institutions remains subject to debate. Some scholars view the state role in managing trade, for example, as controlling and self-destructive; others see it as sensible and effective.[81] In certain core domains—running the state, organizing the army, and supporting scientific and intellectual advances that generated state power—the Ottomans could likely claim a reasonably effective set of institutions during their rise and apex of power. Fairly quickly, though, and certainly by about the 18th century, it became clear, to Ottoman rulers first and foremost, that their structures for managing governance and social life were lagging those of the most competitive nations. Issues of consistency, conflicts between Islamic and rational-legal standards, corruption, and the difficulty of creating a modern administrative state under a sultanic regime—and more broadly, this constant tension between the demands of an open, objective, rule-based, adaptive institutional structure and the societal traditions of the Ottoman Empire—worked to degrade the ways in which institutions could support competitive advantage.[82]

One risk—a danger that crops up across many cases—was that an increasingly strong and complex bureaucracy would harden into a barrier to competitiveness. This appears to have taken place in the Ottoman Empire to some degree. The Ottoman civil service, limited to about 2,000 people in about 1800, had grown to between 35,000 and 50,000 by 1918. "As the bureaucracy expanded in size, it embraced spheres of activity previously considered outside the purview of the state," such as running religious schools and charities.[83] This bureaucratic

---

[77] See Hanioğlu, 2008, pp. 60–63.

[78] Inalcik, 2001, loc. 163.

[79] Baer, 2021, pp. 10, 190, 194–196.

[80] Hanioğlu, 2008, p. 18.

[81] Quataert, 2005, pp. 32–33, 41–42.

[82] Baer, 2021, pp. 255–256.

[83] Quataert, 2005, pp. 62–63.

power would eventually be placed in the service of a neo-orthodoxy, an effort to reimpose traditional values and clamp down on free-wheeling intellectual and economic exchange.

Other Cases—Ancient, Premodern, and Modern

Other cases highlight the role of institutions in underwriting national dynamism. Although ancient Greece is not one of the core cases in the study, it still offers fascinating insight into this connection. The institutions and associated cultural values of the time, the classicist Josiah Ober argues, "encouraged individuals to take more rational risks and to develop more distinctive skills. They did so by protecting individuals against the theft by the powerful of the fruits of risk-taking and self-investment." The critical innovation was a set of "civic rights" that protected individuals against arbitrary assault and humiliation.[84] Relatively egalitarian institutions that guaranteed such shared rights, "by creating a fair playing field and limiting expropriation by the powerful, fostered competition and innovation."[85] All of this provided an essential foundation for the economic and social efflorescence of the period, Ober maintains.

At the same time, Ober's account of the ancient Greek example supports the qualification that institutions need accompanying variables—support systems of social values and habits, for example—to achieve their full result. He argues that the Greek efflorescence depended crucially on the combination of institutions, "understood as action-guiding rules, conjoined with civic culture, action-guiding social norms."[86] This is precisely the mutual dependency between institutions and values that emerges in all the cases.

Another interesting case is the Renaissance Italian city-states, which developed innovative institutional forms and practices, including highly effective new agencies of state finance.[87] "By the middle of the thirteenth century," the scholar Lauro Martines explains, "credit and its mechanisms governed the fiscal proceedings of the larger communes; auditing and tax collection were centralized in the course of the fourteenth and fifteenth centuries; and the public finance of the modern state was born."[88] In the public funding of art, culture, and science; the management of a trading system; and the financial systems of the time, the city-states gained notable competitive advantage from effective institutions.

Japan and China offer immensely complex stories about the role of institutions, although both support the basic causal relationship between good institutions and national success. Japan in the 19th century, for example, partly in its drive to emulate the effective governance structures of the West, developed a range of modern and effective institutions, from a com-

---

[84] Ober, 2015, pp. 15–16; see also pp. 5, 12, 102–103.

[85] Ober, 2015, p. 103, 114–117.

[86] Ober, 2015, pp. 101–102.

[87] Bartlett, 2019, loc. 770–773.

[88] Martines, 2013, loc. 3783–3784.

petent financial and banking sector to patent law. "Nothing distinguishes the Meiji period more," Marius Jansen argues, "than its disciplined search for models that would be applicable to Japan in the process of building its institutions."[89]

The result was a structure within which economic activity was encouraged and protected.[90] Meiji rulers were building on a reasonably strong foundation of effective and stable governance and in the process sought to develop organized, accountable, Western-style bureaucracies. To this end, they put in place key institutions that would guide Japan through the 20th century. This included regional and national agencies of governance, a centralized army, and the conscription and logistical architecture to support it, and nationally standardized aspects of rule of law and public administration.[91] Japan's postwar history offers another testament to the role of effective institutions in powering competitive dynamism. Japan's post–World War II governing institutions (especially those governing industrialization and trade), its massive business conglomerates, its networks of private social organizations, and many other institutional clusters contributed mightily to its rise.

China's story also highlights the competitive advantage of effective institutions, notably in trade, the rule of law, and finance, but in other areas as well. Premodern, dynastic China was institutionally weak in many ways. These states took only 2 to 3 percent of national income in taxes,[92] they employed a very small bureaucracy, and they had little control of details of governance outside their capitals. Although these limitations were common to many premodern nations, there were also important periods of institutional advance. The Song period, for example, appears to show advancing institutional quality in areas of governance and finance. Centrally kept administrative histories helped inform future bureaucrats, while contracts became the well-established basis for thriving commerce. And China's professionalized bureaucracy, even if tiny as a proportion of the population, became the envy of and model for similar state administrative institutions for surrounding countries, such as Korea and Japan.

In the case of France, relatively strong institutions, linked together in a competent, active state, also helped provide competitive advantage. These efforts built on established foundations, such as the initial early 17th-century state building of Henry IV and Cardinal Richelieu and the reforms of Jean-Baptiste Colbert in the late 17th century. They accelerated with Napoleon's modernizing and bureaucratizing spree in the early 19th century. Some institutional strengths—specifically, the national system of public, primary-school education mandated in 1833 that became the foundation for a high-quality, reasonably standardized system of national education and a transmission belt to influence and bureaucratic position—got fully underway only after France's peak of competitive power. Nonetheless, in many ways France

---

[89] Jansen, 2000, loc. 5356.

[90] Osterhammel, 2014, pp. 665–666.

[91] Jansen, 2000, loc. 6824–6826. See also Sydney Crawcour, "The Tokugawa Period and Japan's Preparation for Modern Economic Growth," *Journal of Japanese Studies*, Vol. 1, No. 1, Autumn 1974; Elise K. Tipton, *Modern Japan: A Social and Political History*, New York: Routledge, 2016, pp. 45–50.

[92] Perkins, 1967.

during its rise led the world in the centralizing and institution-building efforts designed to produce a competent and strong state.[93] These advances were correlated with France's rise in competitive position.

Yet in other ways French institutions suffered from handicaps relative to its competitors. France was always somewhat tradition bound and constrained in its institutional approaches. (We will see the same theme in the characteristic on learning and adapting.) When John Law, a Scottish financial entrepreneur who was advising the French court in the early 18th century, urged a more formalized system of a paper currency and public credit, France toyed with but abandoned the advice—and then watched Britain become the world's powerhouse financial institution, with a central bank, paper money, and public credit. Had France powered into a stronger set of financial institutions more quickly, its competitive trajectory would almost certainly have improved.[94]

Spain is sometimes presented as a sort of caricature of a state with weak and corrupt institutions, heavily dependent on empire. In truth the Spanish monarchy built reasonably competent institutions for a time, inspired in part by 18th-century reformers who saw the need for more effective and institutionalized administration. The monarchy's surprising decentralization created the context for a complex, overlapping mosaic of institutions that exercised effective governance and social order.[95] Yet the diversity and fragmentation of the monarchy's institutional makeup created competitive disadvantages; in fact, some senior Spanish officials at the time urged greater centralization and uniformity. And Spain's fiscal chaos, a result of its recurrent debt crises but also traceable to the absence of a Dutch- or British-quality fiscal state, was a massive competitive disadvantage.[96]

A somewhat countervailing example is Austria-Hungary, where the institutional record is mixed. Especially by the later 19th century, public and private institutions in the empire appear to have been of reasonable quality. Austria-Hungary's elite and cosmopolitan class saw a role for an active state to energize industrialization, education, and urbanization to help link the country with improved infrastructure and governance institutions.[97] It is wrong therefore to think of the empire as a fatally hamstrung polity. There were definitely problems and challenges because of the divided regime—policies in Budapest were not always mirrored

---

[93] Isser Woloch, *The New Regime: Transformations of the French Civic Order, 1789–1820s*, New York: W. W. Norton, 1994.

[94] John Shovlin, *Trading with the Enemy: Britain, France, and the 18th-Century Quest for a Peaceful World Order*, New Haven, Conn.: Yale University Press, 2021.

[95] We are grateful to Gabriel Paquette for this insight.

[96] Mauricio Drelichman and Hans-Joachim Voth, *Lending to the Borrower from Hell: Debt, Taxes, and Default in the Age of Philip II*, Princeton, N.J.: Princeton University Press, 2014.

[97] David F. Good, *The Economic Rise of the Habsburg Empire, 1750–1914*, Berkeley: University of California Press, 1984; Richard L. Rudolph, *Banking and Industrialization in Austria-Hungary: The Role of Banks in the Industrialization of the Czech Crownlands, 1873–1914*, Cambridge, UK: Cambridge University Press, 1976; J. Komlos, *The Habsburg Monarchy as a Customs Union: Economic Development in Austria-Hungary in the Nineteenth Century*, Princeton, N.J.: Princeton University Press, 1983.

in Vienna—but the various state apparatuses took an active role in building roads and stringing electrical wire, supporting industries, constructing hundreds of schools and other public buildings (including post offices), restoring earthquake-devastated towns, making national trade policy, and much more.[98] Yet one lesson of Austria-Hungary is that weakness in a few strategically critical institutions can be highly damaging to competitive position. In Austria-Hungary's case, this might have included the military and the foreign ministry, which some historians have characterized as being less adaptable and more hidebound than comparable institutions in other countries.[99] In other cases, weak financial institutions proved a critical competitive disadvantage, even when other institutions of governance worked well.

A Leading Modern Case: Britain

Broadly speaking, Britain surely counts as one of the first nations of the modern world to have developed a set of effective social institutions to manage and regulate its development. The British story, Douglass North argues, is one of "organizations that arose to take advantage of the resultant opportunities" created by good institutions—organizations such as "plantations, merchants, shipping firms, family farms," as well as parallel political institutions, including "town meetings and self-government, colonial assemblies, and the intellectual traditions from Hobbes and Locke."[100]

Some have denied the decisive and unique role of institutions in the British Industrial Revolution, favoring instead explanations that include access to coal or empire. As of the beginning of 19th century, Britain's institutional foundations were still very limited and incomplete, with no real police forces and few local governments of any meaning. There was limited understanding of the society, including basic demographic data. The country was one in which "the national and local ruling elites held a not wholly confident, certain or competent sway at the beginning of the nineteenth century."[101] If Britain had the basis of a competitive advantage in 1800, then, it was mostly embryonic and theoretical. Even as the century progressed, Britain's overall package of public institutions was not necessarily seen as clearly superior to those of France or the emerging state of Germany.

But the argument here is not so much whether British institutions were responsible for a specific economic surge in a narrow window, but whether British society was characterized by effective institutions over its long rise to power and whether institutions served as a com-

[98] We are grateful to John Deak for comments that helped inform this section. See also Jana Osterkamp, "Cooperative Empires: Provincial Initiatives in Imperial Austria," *Austrian History Yearbook*, Vol. 47, April 2016, pp. 128–146.

[99] We are grateful to Pieter Judson for emphasizing this theme.

[100] North, 1990, p. 135. A classic piece on institutions is Douglass C. North and Barry R. Weingast, "Constitutions and Commitment: The Evolution of Institutions Governing Public Choice in Seventeenth-Century England," *Journal of Economic History*, Vol. 49, December 1989.

[101] Cannadine, 2017, pp. 33, 43.

petitive advantage. This seems difficult to deny when we consider everything from the establishment of a credible and lasting parliamentary system (which endured as many European powers fell recurrently into bouts of autocracy); to strong financial institutions and British common law, which provided equal property protection; to a world-class navy built on efficiency and skill. In just one example of the resulting advantages, Britain's competent fiscal state allowed it to borrow at lower rates than many of its competitors.[102]

More specifically, capital markets and financial institutions were better and more quickly developed in England than in other places, providing the nation with a competitive advantage in the efficiency of allocating capital, interest rates, long-term management of finances, and other areas.[103] Voluntary associations, clubs, and other civil society organizations constituted a dense network of nongovernmental institutions critical to British growth.[104] British political institutions became stable with the establishment of a parliament and have remained coherent for centuries. The British military acquired a strong tradition of professionalism, and its institutional advantages in such areas as training, skills, and culture provided decisive on many occasions. In sum, Britain represents one of the leading cases of effective institutions contributing to national competitiveness.[105]

The British case is also the one in which, at least before the modern American example, private sector and community institutions became most advanced and influential of any major power. Leading examples, from a national competitive standpoint, were the networks of intellectual exchange and the thickening web of business clubs and associations which spurred synergies of knowledge and commercial alliance. Beyond them, private charities—spurred in part by occasional state prompting, such as Queen Victoria's emphasis on institutions of the public good—and a range of other institutions strengthened the sinews of social resilience and innovative energy.

Britain is also an excellent example of how our nominated societal characteristics are interdependent. British institutions worked in concert with its culture of learning and open debate, the national ambition and will of its commercial class, and its relatively open, mobile society to generate competitive advantage.[106] It was the combined, symbiotic effects of these

---

[102] We are indebted to William Anthony Hay for emphasizing this point. See John Brewer, *The Sinews of Power: War, Money, and the English State*, New York: Knopf, 1989.

[103] Wolfgang Keller, Carol H. Shiue, and Xin Wang, "Capital Markets in China and Britain, 18th and 19th Century: Evidence from Grain Prices," Cambridge, Mass.: National Bureau of Economic Research, Research Paper No. 21349, July 2015.

[104] Peter Clark, *British Clubs and Societies, 1580–1800: The Origins of an Associational World*, Oxford, UK: Clarendon Press, 2000.

[105] R. Porter, 1990, pp. 187–188. An excellent summary of this argument is Mokyr, 2012a. He concludes, "Thus the institutional developments in Britain in the eighteenth century were, on the whole, more conducive to entrepreneurship than elsewhere. This is not to say that British institutions were, by some standard, optimal or even very good. However, by the standards of the time Britain was clearly ahead of the competition" (p. 185).

[106] We are grateful to William Anthony Hay for the connection of institutions with other areas of advantage.

characteristics, not any one or two operating alone, that brought Britain to a level of unparalleled global hegemony.

Taken together, these various cases—Japan, China, France, Spain, Austria-Hungary, and Britain—demonstrate a host of specific ways in which strong and effective institutions can deliver competitive advantage—and weak ones can destroy it. None suggests that strong institutions alone are sufficient for national dynamism or competitive position. The story of institutions in the competitive trajectory of nations is of one piece in a larger mosaic, one factor that aligns with others to produce the sort of dynamic synergies characteristic of competitive nations.

The Balance: The Risk of Constraining Bureaucracy

As crucial as effective institutions are to national strength, even this powerful advantage cannot be developed without constraint. A societal trend of strong institutions must be *balanced* against overinstitutionalization—a managerial bureaucratization that stifles growth. The inverse of effective institutions, especially in the modern era and among highly developed nations, is not usually weak institutions. It is *excessive* institutionalization, the parallel risk to an intrusive active state.

Overinstitutionalization can ultimately become a competitive disadvantage through bureaucratic sclerosis and the potential for elite capture of institutions.[107] At its extreme, this trend becomes a form of kleptocratic rule, large-scale corruption and rent seeking, and state capture. A common competitive disadvantage for highly advanced nations is bureaucratic sclerosis—a loss of characteristics such as creativity, innovation, learning, adaptability, and shared opportunity due to the crippling constraint of a mass of rules, laws, procedures, requirements, forms, and other hallmarks of a hyperbureaucratized context.

Perhaps the most classic theory in this regard is Mancur Olson's argument about national competitive advantage. He begins with a logic of collective action—essentially, that smaller, more cohesive, and more homogenous groups have higher incentives to generate collective action than larger, more inclusive ones. A logical implication is that society should tend in the direction of policies, regulations, and behaviors that favor such distinct interests rather than general efficiency. And, over time, "stable societies with unchanged boundaries tend to accumulate more collusions and organizations for collective action over time." Such organizations seek their own interests, not general ones, and thus "special-interest organizations and collusions reduce efficiency and aggregate income in the societies in which they operate and make political life more divisive." Larger groupings of such organizations, or "distributional coalitions," tend to "slow down a society's capacity to adopt new technologies and to

---

[107] This concept of "institutional sclerosis" has attracted a good deal of criticism, but the empirical research does offer significant support (Jac C. Heckelman, "Explaining the Rain: *The Rise and Decline of Nations* After 25 Years," *Southern Economic Journal*, Vol. 74, No. 1, 2007).

reallocate resources in response to changing conditions, and thereby reduce the rate of economic growth."[108]

This pattern crops up in many of our case studies. Nations whose dynamic engines brought them to a place of competitive advantage or even dominance then saw those engines grind into neutral or even reverse as their social institutions imposed too much control, devolved into their own orthodoxies, became overly complex and impossible to navigate, or eventually became captured to a significant degree by self-interested elites. In earlier times, this trend was often accompanied by a reassertion of nearly feudal patterns of social relations in which the masses became structurally subservient to elites.[109]

The Renaissance Italian city-states represent a leading case of this phenomenon. As exemplars of competition, openness, and dynamism for a time, many of these polities eventually descended into corruption and rent seeking and were increasingly controlled by bands of aristocrats who sought to close off routes to advancement into their ranks.[110]

Britain provides another example if we consider the period of relative decline of British industrial prominence in the 20th century. There is a robust scholarly debate about the true causes of British industrial decline, characterized by a phenomenon some have dubbed "the British disease."[111] One review of multiple studies of British institutions argues that growing institutional rigidities, including collusion between industries and government in certain areas, proved a significant barrier to British growth and entrepreneurialism: "The last hundred years provide ample evidence of the timidity and vacillations of successive governments in responding to the need for new institutional arrangements conducive to economic

---

[108] Mancur Olson, *The Rise and Decline of Nations: Economic Growth, Stagflation, and Social Rigidities*, Kindle ed., New Haven, Conn.: Yale University Press, 1982, loc. 994–999. Japan offers a potential example of a balance gone wrong between strong and effective institutions and bureaucratized stagnation. In the Japanese case, "There is a trade-off between this organizational discipline and regimentation and the strengths and dynamism of each individual. . . . Certainly, this organizational strength has been the source of Japanese economic development. But, on the other hand, it is a difficulty in the process of Japan becoming more internationalized and acquiring the art of getting along with the rest of the world. . . . The tendency of the Japanese becoming totally mindless in the name of the organization is perhaps there is a conventional wisdom in Japanese society that to follow the majority opinion would be the safest way of dealing with the world" (Itaro Umezu quoted in Clesse et al., 1997, pp. 353–354).

[109] Two economists offer a general theory of economic growth that focuses largely on the constraining role of excessive institutional limits on investment and entrepreneurialism. These barriers include "regulatory and legal constraints, bribes that must be paid, violence or threat of violence, outright sabotage, and worker strikes" (Stephen L. Parente and Edward C. Prescott, "Barriers to Technology Adoption and Development," *Journal of Political Economy*, Vol. 102, No. 2, 1994, p. 299). Not all of these factors are bureaucratic, but this basic theory leaves large room for the growth-constraining effects of institutions that have outstripped their value.

[110] Martines, 2013, loc. 3969–3971.

[111] A very small sample is Bruce Collins and Keith Robbins, eds., *British Culture and Economic Decline*, New York: St. Martin's Press, 1990; M. W. Kirby, *The Decline of British Economic Power Since 1870*, London: Allen and Unwin, 1981; W. D. Rubinstein, *Capitalism, Culture and Decline in Britain, 1750–1990*, London: Routledge, 1993; Wiener, 1981.

progress." The author writes, "It seems legitimate to suggest that part of the explanation for relative industrial decline can indeed be ascribed to the sclerotic tendencies inherent within the country's institutional arrangements."[112]

As we discussed in the introductory chapter, our research points to two critical-feedback loops that affect competitive standing, one empowering and one constraining. Strong institutions and a learning and adapting society are cardinal elements of the positive synergies that are characteristic of competitively successful nations. Overbearing, highly bureaucratic, and constraining institutions combined with various forms of intellectually and economically limiting orthodoxies are among the most salient elements of the negative synergy that can undermine competitive standing. In this sense, nations that decline often do so because they get multiple balances wrong and thus create a powerful negative-feedback loop.

Strong and effective institutions, therefore, emerge as an indispensable complement to other societal characteristics—from national ambition and will to cohesive identity to shared opportunity—that underwrite national competitive standing. But our default recipe for success, that broad and abstract concept we have termed the Renaissance spirit, has at its core a habit of mind and approach to social life that goes beyond these spurs to dynamism. It demands a creative, inquisitive approach to the world—an openness to experimentation and change, a thirst for new knowledge, a willingness to question and debate and update the shared picture of the world. It demands, in other words, our next characteristic: A learning and adapting society.

---

[112] M. W. Kirby, "Institutional Rigidities and Economic Decline: Reflections on the British Experience," *Economic History Review*, Vol. 45, No. 4, November 1992, p. 656. One example is the financial system: "The new and potentially innovative British firms" in the late 19th and early 20th centuries "were often hamstrung by an overly cautious, ossified banking system" (Hudson, 2021, p. 120). Correlli Barnett has cataloged the decline of Britain from the world's leading industrial power to a much diminished economic and technological power with a growing trade deficit, decrepit industrial facilities, and poor marks on innovation. He focuses a good deal on institutional sclerosis but also describes a broader decay in societal characteristics underwriting success: "Industrial institutions and military institutions alike are, in general, expressions of their parent national society and its culture. And therefore . . . the explanation of the 'British disease' has to be sought beyond the confines of industry, in the nature of British society itself, its attitudes and values" (Barnett, 1986, p. 183).

CHAPTER EIGHT

A Learning and Adapting Society

Our next characteristic—a learning and adapting society—highlights the critical importance of the intellectual and policy climate within a country, as well as its openness to new ideas and ways of doing business. Nations gain significant advantage from a vigorous embrace of knowledge, learning, innovation, and experimentation. Highly dynamic and competitive nations are typically thirsty for new ideas and are excited, rather than intimidated, by fresh policies and approaches. They cultivate networks of scientific and intellectual discussion and debate and both allow and support the widespread public sharing of new knowledge. They apply learning in practical ways and continually reassess their ways of doing business.

This characteristic is manifest in the climate of discussion, debate, and intellectual ferment that had emerged in Britain by the 18th century. This climate was embodied in the coffee houses and clubs where issues of the day were discussed, the increasingly widespread public media where issues of state were reported and debated, and the vibrant scientific communities where new discoveries were shared. The historian David Cannadine writes of this sort of generalized enthusiasm for and pursuit of knowledge in 19th-century Britain:

> Such wide-ranging cultural activities, often combining politeness and sociability with the eager pursuit of knowledge and learning, indicated just how far the European Enlightenment had reached, both socially and geographically, in late eighteenth-century Britain. It was especially, but not exclusively, associated with the rise of a stable and prosperous middle class, which was increasingly attracted by the ideas and ideals of toleration and rationality, improvement and progress.[1]

Rapidly growing newspapers sold tens of millions of copies a day, and specialty magazines proliferated. "The United Kingdom at mid-century," Cannadine explains, "boasted a substantial reading public, with a broad appetite for a print culture that at its best was probably the most sophisticated in the world."[2]

A leading example of this process was the Royal Society, which emerged as early as the 17th century. "What made the Royal Society so important," Niall Ferguson argues, "was not so much royal patronage as the fact that it was part of a new kind of scientific community,

---

[1] Cannadine, 2017, p. 39.

[2] Cannadine, 2017, p. 257; see also p. 321.

which allowed ideas to be shared and problems to be addressed collectively through a process of open competition." The publication of results and debates that those journals produced offered a vital energy to the process. It meant that "scientific knowledge could grow cumulatively—albeit sometimes acrimoniously."[3] Similar groups, such as the Literary and Philosophical Society and the Mechanics' Institute, played a similar role in the following century, offering ready-made networks into which scientists, investors, entrepreneurs, and autodidacts could plug and gain access to the latest ideas—without much regard for class or faith.[4] Such innovations then set a pattern of intellectual ferment and experimentation that would grow and expand and help spur Britain's competitive rise.

This dynamic exchange of ideas was dependent, in part, on the rise of a scientific and technical sphere guided by some version of the scientific method—conducting experiments to see what is true of the natural world rather than operating on superstition or orthodoxy. It was intimately related to the societal characteristic of national ambition and will—notably, the drive to comprehend the natural world. It was strengthened by the related quality of shared opportunity: Some of these public dialogues drew in people from a range of backgrounds and classes, at least to a greater degree than most other countries at the time.[5] And Britain's spirit of learning, adapting, and experimenting was both spurred and rewarded by the country's vibrant commercial life and consumer economy. Scientific advances and technology networks centered on emerging industrial applications, and markets provided incentives for innovations.

The British case illustrates, too, that to have the full competitive effect, the emphasis on knowledge and learning cannot be merely theoretical. It must spread throughout society and be applied in practical ways to economic pursuits. Britain gained some degree of advantage, Jack Goldstone argues, because its scientific pursuits became "more experimental and commercially pragmatic, while continental science became more abstract, deductive, and formal." This drive to experiment, innovate, and learn was applied especially to "engine-centered science," which was a critical centerpiece of the Industrial Revolution.[6] Late in the 18th century, by contrast, some European universities were still refusing to teach Isaac Newton.

Margaret Jacob emphasizes the need for a powerful connection between theory and practice, arguing that British industrial advances of the 19th century were grounded in a particular form of learning and adapting—the "organized body of mechanical knowledge" that emerged in the 18th century and beyond. This connection between basic science, applied technical knowledge, and business and manufacturing skill produced a sort of Renaissance spirit in miniature. The same spirit encouraged a generalized practice of experimentation—applying new ideas, trying them out, discarding what did not work, and pushing forward with

---

[3] Ferguson, 2011, p. 70.

[4] Jacob, 2014, pp. 98–109.

[5] We are grateful to William Anthony Hay for this insight.

[6] Goldstone, 2002, pp. 370–371.

the successes. It was a culture in which "theory and practice were inextricably intertwined"; inventors, tinkerers, and hobbyists joined with scientists in developing new approaches. But at the foundation was knowledge, a grassroots sort of learning fed by an increasingly good education system but also powered by apprenticeship, self-study, and scientific and entrepreneurial societies.[7]

***

In Britain in the critical 19th century, this habit of reflecting, debating, experimenting, learning, and adapting spread throughout the whole society and created webs of interconnected debate and progress. Jack Goldstone argues that

> the scientific culture of England, steeped in engine culture, gained enthusiastic adherents broadly among English craftsmen, artisans, and entrepreneurs. The result was that England became the site where modern engineers—craftsmen who specialized in turning the principles of natural philosophy into mechanisms useful to entrepreneurs for production, relying on precise measurements with scopes, graphs, and instruments—originated and flourished. It was this engineering culture and the engineers it spawned who not only developed the steam engine, but its improvement and wide applications, as well as the improvement and application of a host of other inventions and borrowed ideas.[8]

As with all the nominated characteristics, learning and adapting depend on other factors. British political and social culture beginning in the 18th century   strong institutions, such as rule of law and commercial associations, stable parliamentary rule, and a pluralistic society not suppressed by religious orthodoxy—allowed for the full flowering of a curious, innovative, and adaptive society. As Goldstone concludes, some European countries had some of these factors, but "only in England did they all combine in a particular way with an engineering culture to take unique advantage of opportunities to transform production and trade."[9]

Indeed, elements of almost all our characteristics overlap to a significant degree with the quality of dynamic learning and adapting. In one sense, this characteristic might be the hub or centerpiece of the engine of national dynamism mentioned in Chapter One. It may be the master characteristic, the most foundational national quality underwriting competitiveness.

Yet Britain also came to reflect some shortcomings in the commitment to a learning society and thereby sowed at least some of the seeds of the eventual British industrial and innovative decline. David Landes contends that Britain made fewer investments in centralized higher education than, for example, the United States, partly because Britain was heir to a

---

[7] Jacob, 2014, pp. 1, 113–114, 125.

[8] Goldstone, 2002, p. 371.

[9] Goldstone, 2002, p. 374.

tradition of "learning by doing" and practical entrepreneurs and inventors.[10] This approach suited an early industrial era of decentralized production but proved inadequate to a period of much greater industrialization.[11] Toward the end of the 19th century, many key industries begin migrating out of Britain to Germany, France, and other places in part due to the availability of mass, highly educated workforces.

Major powers gain dynamism and competitive advantage that manage to cultivate open-minded inquiry and knowledge sharing, continual learning across many societal institutions and groups, willingness to change, and adaptability. This characteristic implies an absence of orthodoxy that limits intellectual exploration, as well as significant societal investments in learning. It requires a degree of willingness to act on that ongoing process of societal self-reflection—an adaptability and elasticity in strategy and policy.

Learning and *adapting* are therefore related but distinct qualities. Some version of each is required for both to work properly, but either alone is insufficient. "There is a difference between learning and adapting," the economist Eric Beinhocker writes. "Learning is the acquisition of knowledge in pursuit of a goal, while adapting is changing in response to selection pressures from one's environment."[12] We joined them into one characteristic because they are so integrally related. Learning is the essential foundation for adaptation, and adaptation is the practical application of learning, without which it is sterile. This makes for a less precise and simple characteristic to assess—but one that more accurately captures the essential competitive advantage of nations.

Defining the Characteristic

The essential building blocks of this characteristic include a habit of intellectual curiosity and investigation; the capacity for open debate and dialogue, even if constrained in some ways;

---

[10] British schooling took decades to become more broad-based in the 19th century. Even by about 1850, average length of schooling for most of the population was only a few years, and some social commentators and business leaders noted that British workers were starkly uneducated relative to their competitors in Europe and the United States. By the end of the century, however, this was improving, with school attendance mandatory until the age of 12 and often stretching well past that. In the meantime, British higher education grew in quality and reach (Cannadine, 2017, pp. 251, 502–504).

[11] There are contrasting views of this point. Margaret Jacob stresses that it is difficult to know much about British education—its quality or subject matter—because in the early 19th century it remained so highly decentralized. Yet she marshals extensive evidence that technical subjects began to infiltrate many schools as early as the mid-18th century and that the overall quality of British education should probably be seen as higher than often assumed (Jacob, 2014, pp. 6, 130–133). Correlli Barnett finds fault with the British education system and its bifurcated habit of turning out large numbers of poorly educated laborers and a tiny number of Oxbridge aristocrats—but men focused on the humanities rather than applied fields. Britain was simply not as dedicated to the practical application of scientific knowledge, whereas the "Europeans and above all the Germans looked from the very start . . . to organized science and technology, to thorough training at every level, as the necessary instrument of future industrial success" (Barnett, 1986, p. 98).

[12] Beinhocker, 2007, p. 469.

the existence of formal mechanisms of analysis, investigation, and debate in social institutions; national tradition and historical experience of adaptation in the face of learning; and a societal habit, and structures, oriented to the implementation of the fruits of learning. Some elements of these qualities can be identified in measurable ways, such as education levels and spending in a society, freedom-of-speech rankings and some criteria for adaptation and innovation in policy.[13]

This characteristic embodies a society-wide mindset of critical thought and includes social patterns of interaction, debate, investigation, and adaptation, alongside a strong commitment to innovation in the private sector. This idea—a network of thinking, research, experimentation, and dialogue—captures the basic portrait of many societies undergoing an efflorescence. Eric Beinhocker refers to the dynamic as a "Society of Minds," and some version of this intellectual and productive energy has characterized all highly competitive societies.[14]

***

This characteristic requires, in the most general sense, a quality of openness, to ideas and people and influences. Nations that score highly will reflect, both in their major institutions (state and otherwise) and throughout the population, an intellectual curiosity, a tolerance for new ideas, and an urgency to understand.

Such a dynamic can flourish much more easily in liberal societies. A truly open press was an important support system to this British competitive advantage, promoting the sharing of ideas.[15] This sharing of information, an open and unfettered public debate leading to shared conclusions that drive knowledge forward, is critical to these dynamic societies—one reason why, as we will see in Chapter Ten, the corruption of the information environment in an era of truth decay and disinformation is so perilous.

A capacity to absorb ideas and technologies—sometimes, to steal them—was central to the Great Divergence in which Europe lunged ahead of the rest of the world in economic development. European and Asian civilizations have, variously, been both open and closed to foreign influences and ideas from diverse parts of their societies. However, David Landes argues that during a critical early modern period, Europe imported everything from the stirrup to gunpowder, the compass, and printing, whereas China's sense of superiority caused it—at least for a specific period—to react harshly to foreign ideas.[16] A habit of "pervasive

---

[13] There is a significant literature on *learning organizations* in the business context, which we will examine to help add precision to this characteristic.

[14] Beinhocker, 2007, p. 462.

[15] Appleby, 2010, loc. 1511–1515.

[16] Landes writes, "The Chinese, for example, were wont to look at the rest of the world as a barbarian wasteland," and as a result their "contacts with Europeans in the eighteenth and early nineteenth centuries only confirmed their belief in their own superiority and enhanced the xenophobic component." Although the Japanese responded with alacrity and success to the technological and political challenge of the West," he

curiosity" drove the Industrial Revolution, Landes argues, a "readiness and even eagerness to learn from others."[17]

In addition to such a spirit of openness, this characteristic relies on a general habit of rational investigation and learning—an embrace of objective, fact-based assessment of evidence and means-ends relationships rather than superstition. It depends on the spread of scientific knowledge—the creation of networks of research and analysis that share results and insights. This sort of scientific community came to characterize Europe in the 17th and 18th centuries in part through the emergence of what became known as the "Republic of Letters," an ongoing correspondence among scientists and inventors across the continent.[18] Today, it is reflected in dense global networks of research and basic science.

In a different but parallel way, Song China reflects something of this practice, at least within the expansive boundaries of Chinese territory: Woodblock printing and other means of producing and sharing knowledge, as well as a burst of intellectual creativity, brought together thoughtful elites and scholars across China into networks of idea exchange.[19] Renaissance Italy saw the rise of exactly such networks of inquiry; some connections were spurred by competition—Florence stealing a scientist from Milan, or vice versa—but others linked scholars, scientists, and inventors in webs of knowledge and debate.

These networks, in turn, relied on a critical quality of societies and transnational scientific collaboration: trust. Trust among philosophers and scientists and inventors was a critical foundation for the diffusion of knowledge.[20] They came to view one another as members of a society or community, mutually devoted to the same goals of advancing knowledge and technological achievement. These webs of knowledge provide a leading example of one of the factors described in Chapter Two: Nations that become prominent hubs in networks of exchange—of trade, capital, or in this case knowledge—gain a competitive advantage.

---

argues, "the Chinese vacillated between disdainful rejection and reluctant, constrained imitation and fell between the two stools" (Landes, 2003, p. 28).

[17] Landes, 2003, p. 27.

[18] The scholar Karel Davids writes of the "circuits of knowledge" that emerged among Britain, the American colonies, and the Netherlands in the 18th century (Karel Davids, "The Scholarly Atlantic: Circuits of Knowledge Between Britain, the Dutch Republic and the Americas in the Eighteenth Century," in Gert Oostindie and Jessica V. Roitman, eds., *Dutch Atlantic Connections, 1680–1800: Linking Empires, Bridging Borders*, Leiden: Brill, 2014). These included personal travel, written exchanges, shared scientific and political texts, and other forms of knowledge exchange. These networks were centered on scholars and academics but also included entrepreneurs and settlers anxious to participate in European debates and apply emerging technologies and techniques. Exchanges were promoted in part by students traveling abroad for university. Topics of the knowledge exchange included electricity, fish and fishing, plants, and water.

[19] Nicolas Tackett, *The Origins of the Chinese Nation: Song China and the Forging of an East Asian World Order*, Cambridge, UK: Cambridge University Press, 2017.

[20] "In science, as in commercial transactions, trust is an information-cost saving device and as such was essential if useful knowledge was not only to be diffused but also verified and accepted" (Joel Mokyr, "The Intellectual Origins of Modern Economic Growth," *Journal of Economic History*, Vol. 65, No. 2, June 2005, p. 303).

In a more measurable and objective sense, a society's commitment to learning will turn up in the quality and reach of its education system. The numbers of children in school, the quality of education, the egalitarianism of that system reaching across classes and minority groups in the country, access to and quality of higher education—statistics on all these factors will tell part of the story about a nation's standing in this characteristic. The significance of such measures of educational attainment changes over time; premodern societies could be highly competitive with meaningful education reaching only a tiny part of the population. And there may be a threshold of educational attainment above which further progress might not confer extra competitive advantage. But quality and extent of educational attainment remain useful indicators of this characteristic.

***

Beyond learning and the basic application of the scientific method, this characteristic also includes the practical application of that learning and experimentation into technological and institutional advances—actual adaptation and innovation, with new tools and fresh ways of doing business. Dierdre McCloskey refers to the quality of "relentless experimentation" that characterized the European societies of the 18th and 19th centuries and that played a critical role in fueling the rapid economic takeoff of its leading powers.[21] Some objective measures can tell part of this story: Total R&D funding in the public and private sectors, numbers and quality of research institutes, numbers of high-quality patents, and scores on various indexes of innovativeness can all give clues to the degree of adaptive and experimental dynamism in a society.

This characteristic also relies heavily on a social quality mentioned in the characteristic on national ambition and will: a spirit of competition within the society. Competition drives learning and adapting in many ways. Many people involved in pushing the frontiers of science and technology in the 17th and 18th centuries, for example, sought fame and recognition, and this drive for personal achievement fueled their intellectual advances.[22] Economic competition spurred innovation, experimentation, and adaptation, as nations, companies, and individuals sought to create the basis for profits and dominance in markets. Learning and adapting do not arise on their own—they require the impulse of a competitive drive, whether intellectual or financial.

Nations that reflect these habits and qualities will also typically display a related quality, something often mentioned in the literature on cultural habits supportive of development: a future orientation.[23] A commitment to learning, innovation, and experimentation presup-

---

[21] McCloskey, 2011, loc. 1508.

[22] Mokyr, 2005, p. 310.

[23] Nations either "become a modern open state oriented toward the future" or "ossify in its identity and become a historical dinosaur—a specimen very interesting to look at but by no means a comfortable neighbor to live with" (V. Suprun quoted in Clesse and Lounev, 2004, pp. 221–222).

poses an embrace of the future. Our case studies suggest that the most-dynamic and most-competitive societies, especially in the modern era—Britain and the United States at their height, Japan in its periods of competitive acceleration, China over the last half century—look forward rather than backward, and their actions are based on the belief that they can influence and to some degree master the future. By contrast, a thorough presentism, a focus on ever-finer splitting of existing wealth and ideas and preserving what is rather than building something new, tends to be characteristic of nations on the competitive downslope.[24]

Edmund Phelps combines many of these elements of a learning and adapting society in his description of the qualities that led to the Industrial Revolution and subsequent growth in Europe. These societies emphasized innovation, creativity, and willingness, as well as a "drive to change things, the talent for it, and the receptivity to new things, as well as the enabling institutions. Thus dynamism, as it is used here, is the willingness and capacity to innovate, leaving aside current conditions and obstacles."[25] The basic "invention" was not specific technologies, he contends, but a set of interlocking social habits and patterns: "It was the fashioning of economies that drew on the creativity and intuition that lay inside them to attempt innovation. These were the world's first modern economies. Their economic dynamism made them the marvel of the modern era."[26]

***

Another, more abstract expression of this characteristic relates to a society's view of its relationship to the larger and natural world. One of the most persuasive accounts is the argument by Joel Mokyr that "modern economic growth or 'the Great Enrichment' depended on a set of radical changes in beliefs, values, and preferences," specifically focused on the human attitude toward the natural world. The critical shift, he believes, was the adoption of the "fundamental belief that the human lot can be continuously improved by bettering our understanding of natural phenomena and regularities and the application of this understanding to production has been the cultural breakthrough" that produced the Industrial Revolution. He calls this a focus on "useful knowledge."[27] This is, of course, a close cousin, perhaps even an identical twin, of the component of national ambition and will focused on mastering the natural world. And the quality is again closely related to a nation's basic orientation to time.[28]

---

[24] The issue of future orientation crops up repeatedly in the literature associating broad cultural values with economic success. Lawrence Harrison argues, "Progressive cultures emphasize the future; static cultures emphasize the present or past. Future orientation implies a progressive worldview-influence over one's destiny, rewards in this life to virtue, positive sum economics" (Harrison and Huntington, 2000, p. 299).

[25] Phelps, 2013, p. 20.

[26] Phelps, 2013, p. 14.

[27] Mokyr, 2017, pp. xiii, 4.

[28] One scholar argued in 1995 that "the West has been peering into the future for the last 200 years, whereas Russia has had a nostalgia for the past. Today the newly developing countries of East Asia are passionate

The same basic characteristic was an essential component of the emerging early European mindset and contributed to global exploration, pragmatic embrace of technology, a desire for improvement, and the spread of awareness that catalyzed advances. Paul Kennedy writes, "The cumulative effect of this explosion of knowledge was to buttress Europe's technological—and therefore military—superiority still further."[29] He goes on to define this as a "lack of cultural and ideological orthodoxy—that is, a freedom to inquire, to dispute, to experiment, a belief in the possibilities of improvement, a concern for the practical rather than the abstract, a rationalism which defied mandarin codes, religious dogma, and traditional folklore."[30]

The Theoretical Case for Competitive Advantage: A Learning and Adapting Society

The theoretical case for the competitive value of habits of learning and adapting is straightforward. Nations with powerful engines of learning and ideas, tied firmly to processes, institutions, and habits that drive those new ideas into practical adaptation and innovation, obviously stand to have a competitive advantage over those that lack such an intellectual and innovative engine. But the historical and theoretical literature we reviewed identifies a few specific reasons why we should expect this to be the case.

First, at the most general level, knowledge is the basic fuel for the engine of societal and competitive progress. Mokyr argues for the importance of what he has termed "practical knowledge." Kenneth Boulding has emphasized the competitive value of "'know-how," the idea that knowledge is the basic engine of history.[31] Eric Beinhocker suggests, "The origin of wealth is knowledge."[32] Goldstone writes that "changes in social attitudes to the creation and acquisition of particular kinds of knowledge" were essential for "the sudden onset of self-sustaining and accelerating growth in the nineteenth century."[33]

On the other end of the spectrum, a hostility to learning, science, and knowledge and an exclusionary attitude toward the outside world have been associated with uncompetitive

---

to get into the future very quickly" (Christopher Coker, quoted in Clesse and Lounev, 1997, p. 306). Jacob Burkhardt argues that "the pseudo-science which dealt with the stars proves nothing against the inductive spirit of the Italians of that day. That spirit was but crossed, and at times overcome, by the passionate desire to penetrate the future" (Burkhardt, 2013, p. 174).

[29] Kennedy, 1987, p. 29.

[30] Kennedy, 1987, p. 30.

[31] Kenneth Boulding, *Ecodynamics: A New Theory of Societal Evolution*, Beverly Hills, Calif.: Sage, 1978.

[32] Beinhocker, 2007, p. 423.

[33] Goldstone, 2002, p. 357.

societies. A skepticism about creativity and change is also harmful to competition.[34] David Landes compares Europe's success in the Industrial Revolution with the experience of China during the centuries-long period in which the country "lost its interest in technological innovation" and shut down many contacts with Europeans who could have brought new ideas—"a monumental error that cost some four hundred years of potential development."[35]

In a more institutional sense, Geoffrey Parker describes the role of learning, and state investments in learning, in helping major powers recover from the General Crisis of the 17th century.[36] Part of this was an emergent network of knowledge that promoted greater learning, creativity, and innovation among some nations. Although available data does not allow a precise estimate of its impact, the theory is strong: Investments in education by competitive great powers can be traced to the emergence of key discoveries and economic sectors.

Part of the explanation for the Industrial Revolution happening in Europe, David Landes argues, was the "accumulation of knowledge and know-how" across different fields, sciences, and industries.[37] This was in many ways a product of its learning culture—the "growing autonomy of intellectual inquiry"; the development of a common scientific method of proof "recognized, used, and understood across national and cultural boundaries"; and the "routinization of research and its diffusion."[38] Landes points to the French École Polytechnique and competing imitators in Austria, Switzerland, Russia, and elsewhere that nurtured a "pool of talent combined with enterprise and a research-oriented culture."[39]

A Learning and Adapting Society and Competitive Outcomes: Evidence from Cases

The historical cases we reviewed provide overwhelming evidence for the idea that the most competitive societies, in particular great powers at the apex of their influence, embody this characteristic (see Table 8.1). Goldstone argues that, across the last millennium, "If there was one ingredient to creating a new level of productivity growth and new kinds of economic activity that broke from the cycles of agrarian societies that had dominated the last 10 centuries, that ingredient was new ideas." Dynamic societies did not view new ideas as dangerous threats to social stability and existing political orders but instead embraced the risk of an adventurously experimental mindset.[40]

---

[34] Perkins and Koo, 1985, p. 6.

[35] Landes, 2003, loc. 131.

[36] Parker, 2013, pp. 642–660.

[37] Landes, 1998, p. 200.

[38] Landes, 1998, pp. 200–201.

[39] Landes, 1998, pp. 281–282, 290.

[40] Goldstone, 2009, p. 116.

TABLE 8.1

A Learning and Adapting Society and Competitive Advantage—Evidence from Cases

Case	Elements of the Role of a Learning and Adapting Society in Historical Cases
Rome	• Willingness to adopt technologies from abroad and apply them to state purposes • Continuing tradition of scientific and philosophical investigation, especially in peak era
China	• Strong emphasis on education in both premodern and modern China • Historically mixed commitment to learning and adapting—but their presence is associated with periods of efflorescence or competitive success, and absence (isolation, orthodoxy) with competitive failure • Habit of experimentation and adaptation central to modern Chinese strategy
Spain	• Mixed evidence • Early modern Spanish empire characterized by limits on this characteristic and presence of orthodoxy • Clear evidence that lack of embrace of this factor impaired competitive standing
Austria-Hungary	• Mixed evidence • Present in some parts of empire but not generally characteristic of society
Ottoman Empire	• Clear evidence of advantage of learning and adapting mindset in period of Ottoman rise: commitment to science, integration of new technologies, willingness to learn, and investment in learning from abroad • Evidence of the role of an end to open-minded inquiry in the empire's decline
Renaissance Italy	• Significant intellectual ferment and learning, experimentation, and adaptation in cultural and philosophical realms • Advances in knowledge in specific disciplines (mathematics, architecture) but not all • Competition for leading thinkers in selected disciplines
Britain	• One of the origin points of the modern scientific method and place of first flowing of its application to technological and industrial advances • Strong scientific communities, emphasis on basic research and shared knowledge • High-quality universities for some time; slower development of mass education
Sweden	• Limited evidence on direct connection to competitive standing
France	• Mixed evidence • Strong scientific, philosophical traditions; very high-quality education for top elite • More restraints on learning and innovation than, for example, in Britain or the United States: class/elite distinctions, narrow pipeline to intellectual positions, bureaucratic constraints on experimentation and innovation
Modern Japan	• Strong sense of desire to gather best ideas from abroad in both Meiji and modern postwar periods; clear evidence of connection to economic strength • Strong measures in modern era on educational reach and R&D investments • Periods of competitive decline associated with closing off from knowledge
Soviet Union	• In early years, strong investment in education, R&D, other state-led elements; potent scientific and technological sector • Over time, clear evidence of the constraining effect of autocratic system; fear of some new ideas, lack of incentives for deployment of others
United States	• Many indicators of importance of characteristic to early rise and peak power: levels of education, R&D investments, spirit of experimentation

The connection between learning and competitive standing is bound to be more apparent in the modern period, when the nexus between knowledge, technology, and power is perhaps more immediate and urgent than in previous eras. But we find this quality strongly reflected in the more competitive periods of ancient societies. Rome was an intensely conservative society in which a reverence for tradition and the past was a form of public religion. Yet it also reflects an appreciation for the value of knowledge alongside a willingness to employ cutting-edge scientific and engineering techniques. Although it was not a great advancer of technology, it was willing to borrow from others.[41] Roman leaders, businessmen, and inventors stole many technologies and techniques and put them to use for Roman purposes. This was part of Rome's openness to foreign ideas and breakthroughs—the absence of a constraining orthodoxy which prevented it taking advantage of others' ideas.[42]

These cases highlight the critical role of a strong tie between the theoretical and applied sides of this characteristic. Gathering knowledge is helpful; applying it to technological breakthroughs, social techniques, and other spurs to state power helps to translate theoretical knowledge into measurable competitive advantage. The Romans, for example, had a habit of making things work by gathering empirical knowledge from around the world to solve problems, partly guided by an ambitious orientation toward the future.[43] This trait—a faith in the ability to progress and a commitment to practical knowledge—underpinned some of their specific competitive characteristics, such as their engineering abilities.

***

Renaissance Italy reflects a powerful form of this characteristic, though one that was not unqualified or comprehensive, given the nature of the era's approach to science. Learning was often tied to sponsorship from wealthy patrons, but as a general commitment to knowledge took root, independent academies began to spring up. State-sponsored academics, one scholar explains, had the luxury of not worrying about earning an income and "could focus more easily on scholarship and the intellectual play that would provide the basis for intellectual innovation, especially in areas like the natural and mechanical sciences."[44] The peak eras of Renaissance learning and experimentation produced tremendous amounts of intellectual

---

[41] Harper, 2017, p. 6.

[42] As a useful benchmark, the historian Peter Temin compares Rome in the early imperial period with the Netherlands of around 1600. "Rome did not have a bond market, but it had a more sophisticated financial system than the Netherlands," he argues. Rome had "education, a functioning legal system, and an ethos of responsibility. Both places developed art and literature than still affects us today." Across many measures of national achievement in knowledge, institutions, and other elements of a competitive society, "Roman Italy was comparable to the Netherlands in 1600" (Temin, 2013, p. 259).

[43] Barry S. Strauss, "The War for Empire: Rome Versus Carthage," in James Lacey, ed., *Great Strategic Rivalries: From the Classical World to the Cold War*, New York: Oxford University Press, 2016, p. 107.

[44] Ruggiero, 2014, p. 540.

achievement advances.[45] Kenneth Bartlett describes the Florentine republic as a "laboratory for new ideas."[46]

There is some debate about the proper way to view the learning tradition of the Renaissance in the critical areas of science and technology. The period involved more emphasis on rediscovering the wisdom of ancient scientists rather than on observational, experimental natural science in areas such as physics, biology, and chemistry (though investigation and some degree of experimentation was underway in all of these areas). The Renaissance was characterized by a renewed emphasis on Neoplatonism and imposing somewhat mystical notions of essences and forms onto the natural world rather than trying to determine, through experiment and observation and testing of hypotheses, how it worked. Some historians have gone as far as to depict the Renaissance as a significant regression in scientific method and practice. The role of formal training and learning in building the basis for scientific insight was still mixed and incomplete, with a strong tradition of self-taught autodidacts using practical trial and error methods to generate usable inventions.

However, the Renaissance did serve as a critical bridge, in terms of learning and intellectual adaptation and experimentation, between the Middle Ages and the true Scientific Revolution, involving a firm focus on empirical science and symbolized by such figures as Copernicus, Kepler, Galileo, and Newton. Renaissance humanism's focus on individual perception and learning, and the goal of mastering the operation of the natural world, laid the groundwork for the mindset that could produce a scientific method—and a Scientific Revolution. Advances in mathematics were profound and supported related progress in such disciplines as navigation. Advances in anatomy and medicine were based on an increasingly experimental approach. New translations of ancient scientific works spurred debate and thinking about the natural world.[47] By the later Renaissance, moreover—the second half of the 16th century—the first stirrings of the Scientific Revolution were well underway, influenced by Copernican ideas.

Nor is there any doubt that in applied innovative technology and technique, the Renaissance represented a period of significant learning and adapting. The obvious example is the invention of movable-type printing, which led to the production of more than 6 million books by 1500 and played an absolutely central role in most further expressions of learning and intellectual advance in Europe. That innovation alone had profound effects on learning and adapting, but the Renaissance saw other inventions and advances in domains ranging from artillery and fortification to metalworking systems (e.g., blast furnaces) to nautical compasses and eyeglasses. It was a period of feverish invention.

---

[45] Martines, 2013, loc. 7302.

[46] Bartlett, 2005, lecture 7.

[47] We are grateful to Kenneth Bartlett for critical guidance in assessing these aspects of the Renaissance.

These city-states also promoted some increase in the reach of education, including both great universities and also schools in many towns.[48] Even though education primarily served the children of the elite—which was, again, open to ambitious people from varying backgrounds—it nonetheless helped to promote an ethic of learning and building a baseline of shared knowledge. Florence, like other city-states, came to host and be part of intellectual networks and societies extending throughout Europe.

The energy of these societies was fueled by the essential principle of competition, which as we have noted is closely related to the spirit of learning and adapting. When the city-states competed for talent, it was more typically poets, painters, architects, and applied inventors rather than true scientists, but the principle of rivalry for the best intellectual expression was well established. Philosophers and artists competed for official support and fame. Inventors vied to outdo one another, and entrepreneurs contended in business. One result of this intellectual ferment was that the Italian city-states innovated in a host of techniques and technologies that provided them with national competitive advantage. These included, according to the historian Lauro Martines, "the 'putting out' system, technology in textiles, the bill of exchange, deposit banking, double-entry bookkeeping, and the different types of business partnerships."[49]

The learning, adventuristic, and experimental spirit of the Renaissance city-states did not last forever. Eventually, as of about the middle of the 16th century, this spirit declined and curdled into the Counter-Reformation, giving way to bans on books and persecutions of provocative thinkers.[50] Eventually, some of these societies turned on groups that had once been a source of ideas and innovations—for example, in the later 16th century, the slaughtering of Jews and Protestants. But these city-states encouraged, for a time, advances in learning in specific areas (such as mathematics and anatomy) and a generalized humanistic urge to understand the natural world that laid critical foundations for continuing scientific and technological progress.

✳✳✳

Another historical case—the Ottoman Empire—reflects a mixed and evolving attitude toward free and open learning and bold adaptation. The early Abbasid Caliphate based in Baghdad, for example, a predecessor of the Ottomans, "led the world in scientific advances" through about the 12th century, and the Ottomans arguably took the lead for another two centuries. At various moments in Ottoman history, there was a profound "interest in science, medicine, and geography among the learned elite of the empire."[51] And for brief peri-

---

[48] Burkhardt, 2013, pp. 120–122.

[49] Martines, 2013, loc. 3623.

[50] Bartlett, 2019, loc. 7471–7617.

[51] Hanioğlu, 2008, pp. 37–40, 63.

ods, notably the 15th and early 16th centuries, in part with the support of the ruler Mehmet II, Ottoman scholars could produce world-leading insights in mathematics, astronomy, and other fields.[52]

Yet the primary lesson we took from the historical literature was that such efflorescences were more episodic in the Ottoman Empire than in Europe (or, later, even in places like Japan), more constrained, more subject to setback and counterreform. A change in policy in 1727 that allowed the printing of books in Turkish, for example, still left the Ottomans centuries behind Europe in the spreading of knowledge in printed form.[53] Its 15th- and 16th-century dynamism gave way to stagnation when religious elites, worried about instability, imposed "a traditional Islamic orthodoxy and halt[ed] all philosophical innovation. . . . Innovation became a particular object of the religious reformer's wrath, which condemned new ideas as leading only to error and decay."[54] Later, during the bold push for reform in the first half of the 19th century, these contradictions were again on display as the Ottoman government dispatched young people to Europe to be educated—but only in small numbers, and with instructions not to learn French or absorb European cultural influences.[55] Repeatedly, even the strong interest of a sultan in modern science eventually ran aground because of threatened interest groups or religious orthodoxy.

As a leading historian of the Ottoman state, Halil Inalcik, concludes, the Ottomans did borrow some technologies and scientific knowledge from Europe, but only that which narrowly enhanced military capabilities, and only that which could be reconciled with elements of Islamic teachings. Bouts of religious fundamentalism intermittently suppressed the societal capacity for bold, transformational, and dangerous forms of learning. Investments in scholarship usually meant more-elaborate programs to train religious authorities; a reference to learning in "science" often referred to highly expert knowledge of the Koran. "Ottoman scholarship was bounded by traditional Islamic concept[s]," Inalcik explains, "which saw religious learning as the only true science."[56] He concludes that

---

[52] Marc David Baer chronicles some of these bursts of learning, which involved the recruitment of Greek and Persian scholars, support for artists (both Ottoman and European) and impressive cultural outpourings, and active intellectual dialogues (Baer, 2021, pp. 96–100, 111–112). As late as the beginning of the 18th century, under Sultan Ahmed III, a new interest in European intellectual currents and cosmopolitan spirit gripped Istanbul: "Western European guests, Greek-speaking Muslims, and Ottoman Turkish-speaking Greeks gathered at Ahmed III's court to discuss the natural sciences, including astronomy, the utility of knowledge, natural philosophy, and virtue" (Baer, 2021, pp. 313–317).

[53] Even after that change, Ottoman printers managed to generate only 142 books between 1727 and 1838, and those in tiny numbers of copies. And in the centuries before that time, most books in the hands of even the elite had religious rather than scientific or social topics. Books printed in Arabic had been allowed as early as 1590; see also Inalcik, 2001, loc. 3788.

[54] Goldstone, 2009, pp. 48, 117.

[55] Hanioğlu, 2008, pp. 37–40, 63; Inalcik, 2001, loc. 3818–3826.

[56] Inalcik, 2001, loc. 3753.

> While a rapidly developing and humanistic Europe was ridding itself of all forms of medi-aevalism, the Ottoman Empire clung ever more zealously to the traditional forms of near-eastern civilization, becoming by the time of Süleymân I, when these reached their full perfection, self-satisfied, inward-looking and closed to outside influences. . . . [T]he Ottomans, convinced of their own religious and political superiority, closed their eyes to the outside world.[57]

"Tradition fettered Islamic thought," he adds, "and it became almost impossible for later Muslim thinkers to make any innovations. By the Ottoman period, precedent was the guiding principle not only in the religious law but in every aspect of Muslim scholarship."[58] Bold experimentation, radical new ideas, transformative breakthroughs in thinking—these were often viewed as threats to social order (and indeed sometimes offenses against God) rather than the raw material of national dynamism.

As the Ottomans began to suffer reverses, debates broke out about its seeming shortcomings relative to the West. Should it copy Western ways to generate better technology, or should it emphasize moral renewal and a return to rigid Islamic values?[59] The empire's leaders never quite resolved this question. Even by the 18th century, the historian Caroline Finkel explains, "there was no uncritical emulation of the West in Ottoman ruling circles at this time; there are limits to the adaptability and flexibility of every society, and it was never likely that ever closer Ottoman contact with Europe would result in deep cultural transformation."[60] The Ottomans did not really commit to broad-based education or literacy until the 19th century and even then only brought literacy rates up to perhaps 15 percent by the end of the century.[61] In sum, the impression of the Ottoman Empire is one of a society built on world-leading intellectual foundations but unable, as a consistent or long-term practical matter, to embrace the chaotic experimentalism, new thinking, impious scientific ideas, and nonhierarchical spirit required of a true habit of unfettered and ongoing learning.

***

Sources we reviewed for this study suggest that China has a fascinating, conflicted relationship with open, experimental, and pluralistic learning and adapting. Many Chinese dynasties have viewed themselves as superior to others, but not necessarily with an accom-

---

[57] Inalcik, 2001, loc. 1140–1147.

[58] Inalcik, 2001, loc. 3756. Inalcik gives the example (loc. 3891–3902) of the Ottoman observatory at Galata: Founded in 1577 by the sultan's chief astronomer, it rivaled Tycho Brahe's famed observatory, Uraniborg, for its technical sophistication. But religious extremists condemned it as sacrilegious, and just three years after it had been built, it was torn down. For more details of the general 17th- and 18th-century wars against intellectual novelty, see loc. 3902–3940.

[59] Quataert, 2005, pp. 50–51.

[60] Finkel, 2005, pp. 369–370.

[61] Quataert, 2005, p. 169.

panying drive to remake the world, as much as simply preside over it, content in their superiority. Such "cultural triumphalism combined with petty downward tyranny," David Landes writes, "made China a reluctant improver and a bad learner. Improvement would have challenged comfortable orthodoxies and entailed insubordination; the same for imported knowledge and ideas. In effect, what was there to learn? This rejection of the foreign was the more anxious for the very arrogance that justified it."[62] The result was a rejection of Western science and technology that severely impaired China's strategic position. Landes describes this as a form of "intellectual xenophobia."[63] Chinese history strongly suggests a causal association between hostility to open-minded learning—especially in terms of outside influences—and competitive stagnation or decline.

But not all periods of Chinese history reflected such hostility. Song China represents something close to the inverse, an efflorescence of economic vibrancy, culture, and social energy fueled in part by widespread learning and intellectual ferment. The period produced world-class poetry, painting, and textile arts. A large proportion of the population, as much as 10 percent, might have belonged to what could be called an educated elite.[64] Modern China has certainly embraced outside sources of knowledge and technology, and its experience since the 1970s demonstrates the inverse of the earlier lesson: Throwing open the gates of learning and experimentation produces national power, at least to a degree. An intellectual xenophobia is not inherent to Chinese culture, only to certain periods of its history—periods that readily demonstrate the competitive handicap such a mindset imposes.

The Soviet Union offers another example of how a society with constrained learning hampers competitiveness. As a closed, totalitarian system, the Soviet Union was generally hostile to uncontrolled information, especially anything coming from outside. Contacts between Soviet scientists and engineers and the outside world were strictly controlled. Even within the military and industrial sector, the system was biased in favor of applications and production, for example, and downplayed the importance of basic innovation.[65] Odd Arne Westad writes, "Soviet scientists and engineers had no problem understanding the progress that was made in the West. They could probably have delivered the same results for the Soviet Union, if there had been a system in place flexible enough to put such technology into production."[66] More broadly, the spirit of experimentation, of valuing crazy ideas, was simply not possible in such a system.

---

[62] Landes, 1998, pp. 335–336.

[63] Landes, 1998, p. 341.

[64] Robert Hymes, "Sung Society and Social Change," in John W. Chaffee and Denis Twitchett, eds., *Cambridge History of China:* Vol. 5, Pt. 2, *Sung China, 960–1279*, Cambridge, UK: Cambridge University Press, 2015.

[65] Odd Arne Westad, *The Cold War: A World History*, New York: Basic Books, 2017, p. 524.

[66] Westad, 2017, p. 524.

Moscow responded to signals of economic and technological decay by sinking further into orthodoxy. It exhibited the opposite of flexible adaptation. "Instead, the Soviet leadership under Leonid Brezhnev appeared to do everything possible to undermine the internal sources of renewal," one scholar concludes. The result was an "unremitting war against theoretical innovation and . . . dogmatic interpretation of ideology," a process in which efforts to build habits of innovation and creativity "gradually succumbed to the stifling of initiative and relative pluralism."[67]

National Adaptation and Creativity

This characteristic also includes adaptation and experimentation. Openness to ideas and an adaptive sensibility are supported by, and are critical fuel for, a commitment to innovation that goes well beyond individual technologies or policies to broad-based innovations in public policy, business models, military concepts and doctrines, art and culture, and many other aspects of social life. This characteristic provides an essential support system for a technologically advanced and innovative society, which is a critical competitive advantage.[68]

Eric Beinhocker has studied social patterns of growth and innovation and concludes that certain norms are associated with national flourishing. He refers to a basic quality of "deductive-tinkering" based on rational experimentation and some version of the scientific method. Dynamic cultures must be "tolerant of heresy and experimentation, as strict orthodoxy stifles innovation."[69] This kind of self-reflection and the ability to correct course and adapt turns out to be especially important during times of socioeconomic transformation.[70] Without such learning, curiosity, and a willingness to revise accepted thinking, however, adaptation becomes impossible, and societies become brittle. This is not always easy to measure—totaling up national R&D accounts and rankings on innovation indexes does not quite get us there—but its importance is undeniable.

The emphasis on adaptation recognizes that competitive advantage does not stem from knowledge alone. Some of our case study nations have, at some times in their history, failed to cultivate or preserve a societal habit of generalized invention and adaptation. As a result, many promising inventions were simply left to rot and never fully developed. Pure knowledge must be married to a grassroots enthusiasm for invention and for associated learning in the broadest sense—learning through trial and error, through apprenticeship in skilled crafts, through copying and improving on the inventions of others, and through a constant, self-

---

[67] Sakwa, 2013, p. 68.

[68] Part of learning is openness to ideas from other cultures, borrowing and sometimes stealing from them (Clesse et al., 1997, p. 314). Thus, a societal instinct toward learning is deeply related to another characteristic on our list—a welcoming attitude toward diversity and pluralism, including of foreign ideas and experts.

[69] Beinhocker, 2007, p. 568.

[70] Hämäläinen, 2003, pp. 58–59.

reinforcing process of adapting. And this must unfold, for maximum dynamic and competitive effect, adjacent to a vibrant commercial market.

Such a commitment to experimentation and adaptation—a drive to improve and make practical use of improvements—relies on many of the other societal characteristics on our list. It demands a degree of national ambition and will, it thrives in environments with better social institutions, and it is more likely in a society with diverse, pluralistic sources of creativity and indeed investment. A spirit of inquiry and willingness to question established truths is integrally related to a desire to master the world, the ambition to impose one's will on events. When such a mindset is lacking, empires and nations filled with brilliant scientists and productive inventors have fallen behind their competitors.

***

Meiji Japan is a striking example of a society that is committed to adaptation and experimentation—though also the limits and risks of an agenda of adaptation grounded mainly in the importation of foreign ideas. The fragmentation of Tokugawa rule created a fertile environment for trying new things and absorbing foreign ideas and technologies, and the Meiji leaders pursued these goals with determination.[71] Carol Gluck describes the resulting period as an "expansion of the intellectual horizons of the elite, an elite that had come over the course of the Tokugawa period to include not only samurai but also commoners, many of them with enhanced economic status and rising social, political, and especially, educational expectations."[72] During the Meiji period, Marius Jansen adds, "At every point the historian is impressed by the vigor of debate and the readiness of men to speak their minds."[73]

This emphasis on learning, adaptation, and gathering best practices and technologies from abroad were competitively driven, spurred by the shock at seeing how far ahead European industrial powers, such as Britain, had traveled.[74] The motivation of Meiji leaders was to place Japan on a par with European great powers. To do this, Meiji leaders recognized, they had to learn from the European powers, to understand the foundations of their industrial and military might, and to adapt society to catch up.

In a remarkable step, the Meiji government dispatched half its senior officials on a nearly two-year worldwide tour to learn and bring back best practices for Japanese power and imported experts from all over.[75] It drew at least two fundamental lessons, ones that point

---

[71] See, for example, D. Eleanor Westney, *Imitation and Innovation: The Transfer of Western Organizational Patterns to Meiji Japan*, Cambridge, Mass.: Harvard University Press, 1987; Hoi-Eun Kim, *Doctors of Empire: Medical and Cultural Encounters Between Imperial Germany and Meiji Japan*, Toronto: University of Toronto Press, 2014.

[72] Gluck, 2014, p. 27.

[73] Jansen, 2000, loc. 6228.

[74] Ravina, 2017, pp. 9, 57.

[75] Jansen, 2000, loc. 5358–5398, 6930–6934.

directly to a pair of our nominated societal characteristics: "Japan had entered a highly competitive world in which victory went to the educated and united."[76] Post–World War II Japan emphasized education even more, in particular as a route to shared opportunity.[77]

The social emphasis on learning was reflected in the growth of compulsory education, rising literacy, and a steadily growing market for newspapers, magazines, and books. The total numbers of publications in circulation remained relatively low, and readership was limited but still "reaching a wider social audience than ever before" and having related social effects.[78] This again built on progress begun in the Tokugawa period, in which literacy was expanding, the quality and number of schools was gradually but steadily growing, and specific leaders sought to promote widespread learning.[79] By the beginning of the 19th century, Japan had high rates of literacy among countries in a similar developmental stage, and the commitment to expanded education was never in doubt. Marius Jansen writes, "The underlying intent was clear: Popular education was to be a major goal of state policy."[80] As Jansen puts it, despite seeming stagnation in Japanese society in the 18th century, "in fact it had been transformed. The fruits of an intellectual renaissance had penetrated downward through society."[81]

Alongside such information-gathering tours, Japanese officials paid Western scientists, engineers, and educators to travel to Japan and advise their emerging economic strategy.[82] "One of the traditional strong points of Japan has been a timely ability to learn from other cultures," Endymion Wilkinson explains.[83] This was especially true during the Meiji period when

> it became the overriding objective of patriotic Japanese from the mid-19th century onwards to learn the strong points of the West, to catch up with it and surpass it, and thereby defend their country, saving it from further encroachments and possible subjugation. . . . Japan in the 1870s and 1880s entered into a feverish effort to adopt Western ways. This was the period of Europe's biggest influence. . . . European and U.S. institutions, laws, even ideas, were widely adopted.[84]

---

[76] Jansen, 2000, loc. 5425–5426.

[77] Jansen, 2000, loc. 11226–11229.

[78] Gluck, 1985, pp. 12, 68, 172–173.

[79] Jansen, 2000, loc. 2486–2491, 2854–2859.

[80] Jansen, 2000, loc. 6087; see also loc. 2886–2891.

[81] Jansen, 2000, loc. 2852.

[82] Graeme J. N. Gooday and Morris F. Low, "Technology Transfer and Cultural Exchange: Western Scientists and Engineers Encounter Late Tokugawa and Meiji Japan," *Osiris*, Vol. 13, 1998; Kenneth B. Pyle, "The Technology of Japanese Nationalism: The Local Improvement Movement, 1900–1918," *Journal of Asian Studies*, Vol. 13, No. 1, November 1973.

[83] Endymion Wilkinson, *Japan Versus the West: Image and Reality*, New York: Penguin, 1990, p. 40.

[84] Wilkinson, 1990, p. 43. See also Garon, 2017, p. 73.

During the Meiji period and afterward, Tokyo sent representatives to international meetings to compile detailed reports on the substantive issues at stake. Between 1868 and 1900, the Japanese government invited about 2,400 foreign experts to visit and train government ministries and schools in Western ways.[85] "The Japanese systematically studied Western countries," but not only the largest ones—Japanese scholars and officials gathered information on helpful policies from places such as Denmark and New Zealand.[86] Japan became known for world-class scientific knowledge in areas especially relevant to the country, such as seismology. Tokyo sent hundreds of medical students to learn at European medical schools and sent civil servants to study governance and military mobilization programs throughout Europe. The drive to learn, take good ideas, and then tinker, experiment, and adapt is associated particularly with Japan's periods of competitive efflorescence, both in the 19th century and post-1945.

This process was hardly linear or without backsliding. Compulsory education spread slowly, with much 18th-century schooling still private.[87] Even in the Meiji period there were limits on free speech and assembly and a shift back to emphasis on "loyalty and filial piety" rather than "the acquisition of knowledge and skills."[88] Like all of our characteristics, the trend toward a habit of learning and adapting in Meiji Japan reflects a complex trajectory. But the role in generating national dynamism and competitive power is undeniable.

***

Classic assessments of the fates of civilizations have stressed a related and bracing point: Adaptation often requires forcing functions—that is, events or trends that demand change and experimentation, partly by posing a threat to established ways of doing things. Arnold Toynbee famously argues that it is the recurring confrontation and overcoming of challenges that marks rising or successful civilizations. But nations cannot adapt successfully to new situations, or surmount challenges, without some degree of an instinct for learning, appreciation for intellectual engagement, and openness to adaptation. Only when societies are tested do they realize their full ability to pursue new techniques, business models, policy concepts, and other new ways of doing business—but only when their responses are grounded in a learning and adapting mindset can they respond effectively to such tests. Growth in civilizations is the product of "creative personalities and creative minorities" and the process of *mimesis*—copying—that they inspire in the civilization in reaction to threats or opportunities, such as a traditional rival racing ahead in scientific skill or industrial muscle.[89]

---

[85] Wilkinson, 1990, p. 57.

[86] Garon, 2017, pp. 68–69.

[87] Jansen, 2000, loc. 2423.

[88] Ravina, 2017, p. 178.

[89] Toynbee, 1947, pp. 276–277.

Not all societies react well to these challenges. Toynbee stresses "the part played in the breakdown of civilizations by the intractability of old institutions to the touch of new social forces." He describes the risk of the "idolization of an ephemeral technique" and warns that societies can become "arrested" through their obsession with an anachronistic societal model or technique. He quotes a scholar who makes an analogy to the natural world—specifically, a species of fish that did not adapt to changing climactic conditions: "They were committed, could not readjust, and so they vanished."[90] This danger—the risk that societies become stuck in ways of thinking, gripped by tradition and orthodoxy—is the flip side of the characteristic of learning, experimentation, and adaptation. It is a common route to societal decline.

Orthodoxy: The Enemy of Learning and Adapting

Our research strongly suggests that societies that embrace intellectual curiosity, venerate and invest in the creation of knowledge, and reflect a spirit of openness to change, possess a willingness to consider radical ideas, tolerate dissent, support experimentation and research by a wide range of people, and have other hallmarks of openness and an adventurous mind will have a tremendous competitive advantage. Societies, on the other hand, that reject and repress learning, that become stuck in traditional ways of thinking and organizing themselves, that become unable to adapt or innovate, suffer crippling competitive weaknesses. Nations gripped by constraining orthodoxies cannot keep up with those that are more tolerant, open-minded, and adventurous. Of course, openness to new and outside ideas is not itself enough—it must be supported by a domestic capacity to innovate on those ideas, to produce the resulting products, and more. But the willingness to think broadly is the beating heart of the enduring recipe for national competitive advantage.

Edmund Phelps emphasizes the risk to societal dynamism inherent in what he terms "traditional" values—by which he means a closed and restricted mindset. The "genius" of the dynamic eras of modern history, according to Phelps, was

> a restless spirit of conceiving, experimenting, and exploring throughout the economy from the bottom up—leading, with insight and luck, to innovation. This grassroots spirit was driven by the new attitudes and beliefs that defined the modern era, and a full return to high dynamism will require that those modern values prevail again over traditional ones: Nations will have to push back against the resurgence of traditional values that have been so suffocating in recent decades and revive the modern values that stirred people to go boldly forth toward lives of richness.[91]

---

[90] Toynbee, 1947, pp. 307, 326–327; quoting Gerald Heard, *The Source of Civilization*, London: Cape, 1935, pp. 66–67.

[91] Phelps, 2013, p. 324.

The tension here is between a spirit of wanting to learn and experiment with few constraints, accepting the changed knowledge and social practices that come with that spirit, and a desire to control, clamp down, limit intellectual investigation, and impose a state- or elite-directed set of values and understandings onto society. Nations that reflect the former set of habits have tended to gain tremendous competitive advantage over those that did not.[92] The historical cases demonstrate the ways in which fundamentalism and orthodoxy can ruin the learning and experimental basis of social dynamism.[93]

Walter Scheidel points to the risks that emerged when "new insights and ways of doing things clashed with hallowed tradition or religious doctrine." For dynamism to flourish, he contends, surveying the sweep of history, "[i]nnovators had to be able to follow the evidence wherever it led, regardless of how many toes they stepped on in the process." Such a spirit faced barriers everywhere, from religious leaders in Europe to politically sensitive managers of China's imperial court. It was where these barriers thinned and broke down that competitive advantage could arise. He writes, "Over time, the creation of safe spaces for critical enquiry and experimentation allowed scientists to establish strict standards that cut through the usual thicket of political influence, theological vision and aesthetic preference: the principle that only empirical evidence counts."[94]

We find some version of this pattern—with significant differences based on the period or cultural context—in ancient Greece, Rome, Renaissance Italy, Song China, the Netherlands at its height of global power, Britain before and during the Industrial Revolution, and the modern United States. These were societies with a tolerance for new and sometimes dangerous ideas, for the oddball iconoclast with a different way of looking at things, for the troubling implications of new scientific understandings.

Of course, all these societies retained areas of tradition and orthodoxy. Rome was an intensely traditional society in many ways. Britain retains to this day many legacies of what was once a powerfully constricting aristocratic society. As with many of our characteristics, there is no way around the fact that it can be difficult to draw a precise line in terms of how much openness is enough or how much orthodoxy will ruin a nation's competitive prospects. But the contrast is real, as are the cases that show the risks of constrained intellectual dynamism.[95] David Landes argues that orthodoxy kept Muslim nations from benefiting as much from foreign ideas as European countries did, in part by generating suspicion of radical new

---

[92] A similar notion is reflected in the theory of economic development offered by Stephen Parente and Edward Prescott. Their emphasis is on barriers to the entrepreneurial and creative energies of firms and individuals, and some of this can emerge from normative or bureaucratic objections to new products, grounded in part in a societal orthodoxy. Their evidence suggests that, in places where "the adoption of technology was met with fierce resistance," development has tended to lag (Parente and Prescott, 1994, p. 299).

[93] Inalcik, 2001, pp. 3950–3975.

[94] Scheidel, 2021.

[95] McCloskey, 2016, p. 204.

ideas. Among Muslim nations, "the effect of this suspicion and hostility was to isolate the scientific community, place its representatives in an apologetically defensive posture, and render difficult, if not impossible, the kind of triumphant cumulative advance that was to occur in the West some hundreds of years later."[96]

Spain offers an example of a society that, at certain points and to a significant but not total degree, chose absolutism over learning and adapting and suffered for it. After fostering impressive intellectual achievement and seeing the growth of world-class universities, Spain and Portugal suffered the rise of the Inquisition and related oppression, which of course obstructed science and learning and adapting. Spain even went to war to try to impose its religious orthodoxy elsewhere in Europe. Books were banned, travel prohibited, skilled outsiders thrown out. This is the behavior of a nation seemingly trying to handicap itself in competition. One source suggests that only 12 Spanish students went abroad to study between 1560 and 1599. As a result, "Iberia and indeed Mediterranean Europe as a whole missed the train of the so-called scientific revolution."[97]

Orthodoxy can come in many flavors. The term tends to evoke connection to religious belief or perhaps autocratic societies. In fact, there are many orthodoxies in U.S. public discourse today that establish taken-for-granted assumptions about many issues. Even a free-wheeling democratic society that would appear to score very highly on any index of learning and adapting can have its competitive dynamism constrained by more-discrete issue- or domain-specific traditions and orthodoxies. A sense of smugness, of believing one's own culture to be the highest and not needing to learn or advance or draw in ideas from others, has always been a sign of impending competitive decline.[98]

Learning and Adapting: General Evidence

In addition to the anecdotal evidence from the case studies—both positive and negative, the advantages of learning and adapting, as well as the risks of a rigid orthodoxy—we found four sources of empirical or historical support for the claim that societies strong in measures of learning and adapting will have competitive advantages.

The first comes from the powerful set of world historical survey analyses that highlight the competitive advantage gained by societies that emphasize open, creative, and bold habits of learning and adapting. The work of such scholars as Joel Mokyr, David Landes, Margaret Jacob, Edmund Phelps, and Dierdre McCloskey—as much as they disagree on some issues—showcases the competitive advantages generated by a dynamic synergy of intellectual energy and productive societal experimentation and innovation. These sources go beyond the individual cases noted in this chapter to identify more-general historical trends and associations.

---

[96] Landes, 2003, pp. 28–29.

[97] Landes, 1998, p. 180.

[98] For the example of 18th-century China, see Ferguson, 2011, p. 47.

A second collection of supporting studies ties excellence in societal practices of learning, such as educational attainment, with competitive success, at least in the modern era. The relationship is not linear and universal. The role of education is very different in the modern world, for example, compared with ancient and premodern contexts. Skill and knowledge are at a much greater premium now than in the past. Yet even granting these differences,[99] there is a substantial literature affirming the connection between education and economic growth and development.[100]

A third source of supporting empirical research highlights the competitive value of high societal levels of innovation and associated practices. Extensive research has connected barriers to innovation with impediments to economic growth.[101]

Fourth and finally, more-recent case studies support the connection between a society of active, forward-leaning learning and experimentation and competitive success—in part by demonstrating the costs imposed by the inverse of those qualities. One of the most powerful recent assessments of the importance of a mindset of learning, adapting, and experimenting is Kenneth Pollack's study of the military effectiveness of Arab armies. He aims to explain significant underperformance of Arab armies, and specifically a pattern in which

> Arab tactical commanders regularly failed to demonstrate initiative, flexibility, creativity, independence of thought, an understanding of combined arms integration, or an appreciation for the benefits of maneuver in battle. These failings resulted in a dearth of aggressiveness, responsiveness, speed, movement, intelligence gathering, and adaptability in Arab tactical formations that proved crippling in every war they fought.[102]

Pollack finds in these armies a tendency to hoard and compartmentalize information, an inability to adapt to changing circumstances, and an unwillingness to challenge directives from higher authorities. He documents a consistent presence of conformity and a hesitation to endorse new ideas. "One result of this constant pressure to conform is a corresponding stifling of originality," he explains. Innovation is not as much rewarded as punished for seeming

---

[99] Amatul R. Chaudury, Asim Iqbal, and Syed Yasir Mahmood Gillani, "The Nexus Between Higher Education and Economic Growth: An Empirical Investigation for Pakistan," *Pakistan Journal of Commerce and Social Sciences*, Vol. 3, 2009; Yousif Khalifa Al-Yousif, "Education Expenditure and Economic Growth: Some Empirical Evidence from the GCC Countries," *Journal of Developing Areas*, Vol. 42, No. 1, Fall 2008.

[100] P. B. Eregha, R. I. Irughe, and J. Edafe, "Education and Economic Growth: Empirical Evidence from Nigeria," *Managing Global Transitions*, Vol. 16, No. 1, 2018; L. I. Hongyi and Liang Huang, "Health, Education, and Economic Growth in China: Empirical Findings and Implications," *China Economic Review*, Vol. 20, No. 3, 2009; L. Marquez-Ramos and E. Mourelle, "Education and Economic Growth: An Empirical Analysis of Nonlinearities," *Applied Economic Analysis*, Vol. 27, No. 79, 2019.

[101] Xavier Cirera and William F. Maloney, *The Innovation Paradox: Developing-Country Capabilities and the Unrealized Promise of Technological Catch-Up*, Washington, D.C.: World Bank Group, 2017; Klaus Desmet and Stephen Parente, "Unleashing Growth: The Decline of Innovation-Blocking Institutions," *VoxEU*, May 18, 2013.

[102] Pollack, 2019, pp. 29–30.

to deviate from shared practices. This encourages a passivity and tendency to wait for guidance from above rather than taking initiative.[103]

The elements of a "shame and honor culture" present in some of these countries served to exacerbate this imperative: "In Arab society, to do something wrong generally is much worse than to do nothing at all. In this way, the dominant Arab culture creates a disincentive for taking initiative or action." These effects are not universal among Arab societies, and there is always a risk of cultural essentialism in broad-brush assessments of countries and regions. But Pollack's analysis does offer evidence for the narrower claim being made here: Societies suffer competitive disadvantage when their major institutions do not reflect a spirit of learning, intellectual inquiry, innovation, and adaptation. That is true in European, Asian, Arab, and other societies alike.[104]

The Balance: The Need for a Grounding Tradition

All our characteristics involve some degree of balance, as stressed in Chapter One. In no case is the requirement simply to push the settings to maximum. Every one of these qualities must be balanced against competing considerations—sometimes in the form of other characteristics.

In the case of a learning and adaptive mindset, from the standpoint of competitive advantage, a society's openness to change must be balanced against the need for strong traditions and norms that provide a stable sense of national identity and ballast against a changing world. The lack of any unifying tradition can destabilize a society and create weakness in other traits. In this sense the characteristic of learning and adapting trades off with another one of our nominated sources of competitive advantage—a unified national identity. That characteristic inevitably demands some degree of orthodoxy—certainly some traditions—that will end up constraining the full play of intellectual freedom in some ways.

As noted above, there is no way to demonstrate precisely where this balance should be struck for maximum advantage. That choice will differ depending on the country, the era, the nature of the competitors, the character of the society, and many other variables. Moreover, sometimes a society's general setting can be very positive, but policies or habits in specific areas or sectors can be subverted by unquestioned orthodoxies in thinking.

Our cases also underscore the importance of moderation. An unrestrained commitment to innovation can leave a major power unmoored to any consistent policies; a society without a unifying *energizing myth*, as was described in the chapter on national identity, and the shared traditions and values and beliefs that go with it, will be weaker as a result. The importance of this partly opposed pair of characteristics points again to the need for an ongoing, strategically minded balancing act.

---

[103] Pollack, 2019, pp. 437, 441.

[104] Pollack, 2019, pp. 447–448, 463–466.

A learning, adapting mindset therefore interacts with many of our other nominated societal characteristics. It is closely related to national ambition and will. It requires a degree of shared opportunity to achieve its full effect. It depends on effective institutions to protect and spur creative invention and to shepherd the practical application of knowledge and experimentation into the marketplace. And social habits of learning, experimentation, and open-minded engagement with the future will be much stronger in societies that embody one additional quality: a high degree of diversity and pluralism. This is our final characteristic, to which we now turn.

CHAPTER NINE

Competitive Diversity and Pluralism

Many scholarly assessments that catalog the rise of Europe to global predominance in the period after the 16th century, and in particular in the 19th, stress the competitive value of its pluralistic mosaic of states and peoples and the dynamics of productive rivalry this unleashed. Paul Kennedy emphasizes the "political fragmentation" of early modern Europe as a factor behind the continent's development—the multiplicity and decentralization of political units in competition with one another, a diversity grounded in a divided geography, full of rivers and forests and mountains breaking up the landscape and reducing the potential for territorial conquest. This political and geographic partition meant that many centers of innovation and economic activity were at work and could not be suppressed or controlled from one place. It also made for a competitive dynamism, as the different units (and eventually states) sought to better one another—essentially, it was an engine of progress. And it created a general requirement for all peoples to look constantly abroad—for threats, for trade and barter, for technological innovations—rather than the "turning in upon themselves" that characterized China and Japan in later eras.[1]

Other scholars highlight the same factor as critical to Europe's development. Walter Scheidel notes that the decay of the Roman Empire ultimately proved a blessing by ushering in a far more dispersed power structure—one with short-term costs of instability but long-term advantages, a competitive "patchwork quilt" of actors pushing innovation and technology ahead:

> So many different power structures intersected and overlapped, and fragmentation was so pervasive that no one side could ever claim the upper hand; locked into unceasing competition, all these groups had to bargain and compromise to get anything done. Power became constitutionalised, openly negotiable and formally partible; bargaining took

---

[1] Kennedy, 1987, pp. 17–21, 23. Ian Morris similarly stresses that "Europe's peninsula made it easy for small kingdoms to hold out against would-be conquerors." And it provided multiple potential sources of investment in innovative ideas: Unified Chinese governments could decide to shut down foreign exploration, but "[i]n fragmented Europe, by contrast, monarch after monarch could reject Columbus's crazy proposal, but he could always find someone else to ask" (Morris, 2010, p. 17). This contrasted with China, which, "dominated by a single great empire," did not have the same incentive for constant competitive improvement (Morris, 2010, p. 484). But competition is not the whole answer; it does not explain why some parts of this competitive European landscape (e.g., Portugal and Spain) "stagnated for centuries" while England and the Netherlands moved ahead, to be joined by others (North, 1990, p. 130).

place out in the open and followed established rules. However much kings liked to claim divine favour, their hands were often tied—and if they pushed too hard, neighbouring countries were ready to support disgruntled defectors.[2]

The result, Scheidel argues, was a "deeply entrenched pluralism" that became embedded in these societies and continued to influence their evolution for centuries, even during periods when monarchs and autocrats tried to rein it in. Explanations for the Great Divergence that pushed Europe ahead all rely in part on this factor: "Pluralism is the common denominator." Progress, Scheidel concludes, "was born in the crucible of competitive fragmentation." China, by contrast, was shaped by an embedded sense of imperially justified unity, which restrained innovation and generated far less motive for ambition and adaptation. Niall Ferguson agrees that European pluralistic fragmentation was an engine of competitive advances.[3]

This fragmentation had drawbacks. In the wars, rivalries, constraints on free trade, and other inefficiencies introduced by multiple partitions, European political division weakened national competitiveness in various ways. Dierdre McCloskey concludes that "Europe's fragmentation led to a beneficent intergovernmental competition for business, in the way American cities and states are forced to compete for business. It continued after 1800. Yet from an economic point of view the quarrel-provoking fragmentation of Europe was as much bad news as good."[4] Wars took an immense toll, even as they prompted advances in technology.

On balance, though, Europe's pluralistic struggle appears to have spurred progress in its member countries, in part by encouraging a competitive copying of new technologies and techniques among nations. One example is the way in which the fragmented competition encouraged European leaders to pursue exploration and, at times, imperialism, thus feeding the ambitions of these societies. Pluralism "propelled Europeans to seek opportunities—economic, geopolitical and religious—in distant lands."[5] European powers envied and raced one another, copied one another's innovations, stole each other's intellectual property, and recruited each other's leading generals and scholars and inventors. Centralization of economic and intellectual judgment had severe costs in places such as China and the Ottoman Empire, where a combination of orthodoxy and centralized control clamped down on dynamism. Pluralism is an enemy of coercive bureaucracy, one of the main threats to innovation.

Although the European example speaks to the value of a pluralistic *external* context (that is, a competitive mosaic of states), the value of *internal* pluralism and diversity, found within states, is the primary focus of this chapter. The basic principle is the same: A competition among groups and interests in a society, and an embrace of the resulting diversity, creates a broader range of ideas and talents that a society can draw on. A pluralistic context also creates more-competitive fire to strengthen domestic actors, whether firms or military services, by

---

[2] Scheidel, 2021.

[3] Ferguson, 2011, pp. 37–39, 42.

[4] McCloskey, 2016 p. 133; see also McCloskey, 2011, loc. 1514–1523, 1532–1534, 1561–1569.

[5] Ferguson, 2011, p. 39; also see pp. 36–45.

subjecting their claims and plans to contrary arguments and by providing alternatives. As we will see, pluralism can take many forms: Our cases show that ethnically and racially homogenous nations, such as Japan or Victorian-era Britain, can still produce significant degrees of political and commercial pluralism, which provides their own competitive advantage.

Diversity as defined in our modern sense also carries potential competitive advantage. Nations—and organizations—that draw on a diverse set of experiences and perspectives are likely to benefit from a wider range of ideas. They have a built-in mechanism for avoiding an orthodoxy that suppresses competitive dynamism and a social structure that makes it easier to attract talent from abroad—talent that sees a ready home for itself in the varied mosaic of the nation's culture.

From a competitive standpoint, it is fair to say—on the basis of historical cases and persuasive research evidence—that diversity and pluralism beat uniformity and regimentation. This basic truth emerged again and again in the trajectories of great powers. But like national ambition and will, this characteristic carries an obvious risk of excess: Too much pluralism becomes social fragmentation, political polarization, and even societal strife and instability. Competitive nations keep this characteristic in balance, finding ways to nurture diverse, pluralistic contexts, without spiraling into division. Partly, then, the challenge for nations is to strike a balance between two of our nominated characteristics: building a strong, unified national identity while allowing substantial degrees of diversity and pluralism within that unified whole.

Defining the Characteristic

This characteristic includes two closely related but somewhat distinct elements. One is *diversity*, defined as the level of overall variation in a society—not only in terms of gender, race, ethnicity, sexual orientation, and so on but also in every other way that diversity can be defined. This can include a wide range of education, training, career paths, and skill sets; people from geographically distinct parts of the nation with different cultural traditions and even languages; and people with divergent major experiences (military service versus creative arts, for example). The inverse of diversity would be a largely homogenous society.

The second element of this characteristic is *pluralism*. This concept is defined in many ways. We use it to highlight two aspects of a society: the degree to which it has overlapping sources of authority, rulemaking, and governance and the degree to which its people value, and tolerate, multiplicity. In the first, structural, sense, pluralism is embodied in such related factors as the degree and health of civil society, strong and multifarious public and private institutions, and the level of decentralization and federalism in a political system. In the second, normative sense, pluralism creates an environment in which people tolerate differences in allegiance or membership, rather than viewing other social groups with suspicion and disdain.

These two qualities are tightly interlinked. Most pluralistic societies are inherently diverse, to the degree that their multiple authorities or groups or components represent diversity. And a diverse society will generate a significant degree of pluralism. Diversity and pluralism are, in crucial ways, two sides of the same coin, though the degree of overlap does vary in the historical cases.[6]

Diversity and especially pluralism produce competitive advantage in one central way—by fueling domestic rivalries. Geopolitically successful societies are themselves internally competitive: They reflect contending approaches to technologies, markets, solutions to social problems, artistic expression, and much else. It is hard to exaggerate the link between a generalized atmosphere of competitive drive and ambition and the dynamism that drives—and sustains—competitive success. A diverse range of empowered actors helps fuel borrowing from other cultures. And the more these actors compete, the more likely they are to become entrepreneurs of imported innovation.[7]

The Theoretical Case for Competitive Diversity and Pluralism

There are many reasons to expect that diversity and pluralism will underwrite competitive advantage. A more diverse and pluralistic society is likely to generate a wide range of ideas and concepts, contributing to economic, military, and intellectual development. These societies could also be more resilient, with a broader range of social actors on whom they can call to respond to different challenges.

This theoretical expectation is based on a general appreciation for the role of pluralistic experimentation within the U.S. government. In the defense realm, although there are always a handful of massive core procurement programs, U.S. efforts also include a partly decentralized, semirandom, constant stream of small bets. These take place in part through the work of specific offices and agencies that exist to foment just such a pluralistic set of experiments, including the Defense Advanced Research Projects Agency, Intelligence Advanced Research Projects Activity, and In-Q-Tel.

Part of the theoretical foundation for this characteristic is the value of diversity for any organization or community—diversity of ideas, approaches, policies, and solutions. It is a basic principle of evolution that variety is a source of strength; difference is the lifeblood of evolutionary advance. This is as true for countries as it is for organisms. Eric Beinhocker writes eloquently on this, noting that a superabundant supply of ideas and strategies makes businesses more competitive. He recommends something that reflects the essential insight of

---

[6] As we will note, there are some cases of a largely homogenous society that reflected some degree of political pluralism. Japan in different periods represents such an example. Typically, though, diversity and pluralism will go together to some degree, and the most-powerful examples of societies benefiting from this characteristic involve nations that pursued both together.

[7] See Clesse and Lounev, 2004, p. 265.

this characteristic—a "portfolio of experiments"—to generate as much fact-based discussion and debate as possible.[8] More ideas of different kinds from different places, in a competitively diverse and pluralistic society, is a recipe for competitive advantage. It was precisely in reflecting these concepts that Europe's pluralism provided much-needed space for disruptive innovation.[9]

The case for diversity and pluralism also emerges in many of our other characteristics. A nation could provide shared opportunity, for example, only to a very constricted, nondiverse group, but that would forfeit many of the presumed advantages of that characteristic. A learning and adapting society will pair best with one that is also diverse and pluralistic, at least to some degree, to create the most dynamic cocktail of ideas. In these and other ways, diversity and pluralism achieve their positive effects only when meshing with other societal characteristics—notably, shared opportunity and a learning and adapting society.[10] Diverse and pluralistic societies create an opening for dynamism and competitive advantage—but the other characteristics are necessary for a nation to take advantage of that opportunity.

This characteristic, too, can run to excess and must be pursued in balance with other societal qualities. Our historical cases underscore the risk that an extreme degree of pluralism can lead to incoherence and fragmentation, and thus act as a competitive handicap. But others, especially those in which diversity and pluralism are balanced against a unified national identity, make clear that a competitively lively pluralism is an essential foundation for long-term national dynamism.

The classicist Josiah Ober explains how this characteristic helped fuel national efflorescence in ancient Greece. That degree of dynamism was spurred in part by interactions among a "startlingly large number of surprisingly small states" and the laboratories of social, scientific, and technological advance that they represented. Ober refers to these using the political science category of "dispersed-authority cultures," as distinguished from large imperial "centralized authority" cultures. The dispersed cultures "can be compared to a natural ecology, characterized by a rich variety of plant and animal species, none of which is dominant." Conflict "remains endemic" in such systems, but they can also be powerful engines of competitively generated growth and innovation. Federalism, Ober argues, was ultimately a competitive advantage for Greek city-states for many of the reasons described here—competitive drive, resilience, and diverse sources of ideas.[11]

---

[8] Beinhocker, 2007, pp. 448–450.

[9] Koyama, 2021, p. 641.

[10] McCloskey, 2016, p. 598.

[11] Ober, 2015, pp. 6–12, 170.

Diversity and Pluralism: Evidence from Cases

Some of our cases, such as the modern United States, offer clear if anecdotal evidence of specific ways in which these qualities can improve national dynamism and stability. Others, such as the later Ottoman Empire and the Cold War Soviet Union, demonstrate the risks of quashing pluralistic competition and thought. Still others, such as the Austro-Hungarian Empire, demonstrate the perils of excessive diversity and pluralism. Table 9.1 summarizes the basic historical patterns that emerged in our research.

Edmund Phelps, in his studies of the sources of national dynamism, also points to the importance of a diverse, pluralistic set of entrepreneurs, sources of finance, and other components of the socioeconomic system: "The modern system thrives on diversity within the society. How willing and able to innovate a society is—its propensity to innovate or, for short, its economic dynamism—obviously depends not only on the variety of situations, backgrounds, and personalities among potential conceivers of new ideas." Phelps adds that "a country's dynamism also depends on the pluralism of views among financiers." One implication of this, Phelps argues, is the importance of a vibrant private sector. This diverse "system of creativity and vision . . . exploded in the private sector, not the public sector."[12]

Jack Goldstone's analysis of the sources of the Industrial Revolution stresses the value of productive interactions, guided by a driving ambition to innovate and experiment, among a wide range of social actors. It was the interaction of scientists, inventors, entrepreneurs, established businesspeople, scholars, and others that powered Britain into a period of explosive growth. Goldstone suggests a related principle, namely that economic growth is fastest in periods "when different cultural and philosophical traditions are allowed to mix."[13]

The importance of diversity extends to sources of investment. The Italian Renaissance, and indeed the wider European phenomenon, was distinguished in part by the competition among states and private investors. An inventor (or indeed an artist) who found limited support from one patron could turn to others. When there is only one source of funds, however, or a small number of them, or if the available funders have rigidly uniform criteria for their investments, the space for creativity shrinks. There is some risk, as we will see, that this is precisely what is going on in the United States today.

Some of the cases highlight the value of social diversity in addition to political pluralism. These societies have more nodes of different ideas and creativity, more sources of distinct innovation, more ways of approaching problems. Other cases highlight the risks of a single dominant belief system, whether religious or political. Looking at societies that experienced an efflorescence—early modern Islamic civilization, Song China, Medieval Spain, Renaissance Italy, Holland, Britain—Goldstone notes that they tolerated the existence of many religions under a general spirit of pluralism rather than trying to impose a single faith or view-

---

[12] Phelps, 2013, p. 38.

[13] Goldstone, 2009, p. 141.

TABLE 9.1

Competitive Diversity and Pluralism and Competitive Advantage—Evidence from Cases

Case	Elements of the Role of Competitive Diversity and Pluralism in Historical Cases
Rome	• Incorporation of peoples beyond Rome itself as full citizens; eventually highly diverse • Some degree of political and social pluralism in the early republic and even in competing factions in imperial period
China	• More-limited role of this characteristic; significant limits on diversity in society or political pluralism • Some degree of pluralism in premodern and early modern periods; competition among dynasties and groups • In periods of growth and efflorescence, arguably a greater degree of or respect for diversity in backgrounds, as well as moderately greater pluralism
Spain	• Some degree of pluralism within political components of the Iberian Peninsula, but unclear connection to competitive advantage • Some evidence from key historical periods of the opposite—constraints on diversity and pluralism and imposition of orthodoxy as competitive disadvantage
Austria-Hungary	• Some limited anecdotal gains from pluralism—notably, varying contributions to national strength from parts of bifurcated empire • Major case of competitive disadvantage of excessive pluralism/fragmentation; lack of coherent national policies; internal disputes and instability
Ottoman Empire	• During period of rise, pluralism and diversity within empire produced benefits from mixture of multiple influences; evidence seen in scientific, economic, military fields • Clear competitive disadvantage of excessive fragmentation and incoherence of larger imperial entity over time
Renaissance Italy	• Pluralism among city-states created microcosm of productive competition characteristics of Europe as a whole • Some degree of diversity in citizenries of city-states; skilled immigrants often welcomed and recruited • Republican systems provided basis for pluralistic political systems
Britain	• Signal case of growth of pluralism over time in political and economic terms • Part of pluralistic European system whose competitions generated dynamism • Modern Britain benefited from expanding diversity
Sweden	• Limited case applicability • Largely homogenous nation, though made use of mercenaries and other outsiders • No clear tie between diversity and pluralism and competitive strength
France	• Not a clear case on this characteristic; elements of it exist in early modern and modern France, but direct tie to competitive advantage not clearly identifiable
Japan	• Pluralism exists within industrial sector, with the state encouraging competing conglomerates to generate a range of ideas • Diverse not so much demographically but in terms of ideas and concepts, such as during the Meiji period about ways to benefit from outside ideas
Soviet Union	• Clear competitive disadvantage of centrifugal pressures in fragmenting empire • Lack of diversity and pluralism inherent to system
United States	• Political and economic pluralism from early days of nation has competitive costs (including in domestic conflict) but also advantages • Diversity is a strength, both native- and foreign-born talents

point. The end of such golden ages was "almost always marked by the return or imposition of a crushing official religious orthodoxy," he concludes.[14]

***

The Ottoman Empire embodied tremendous, perhaps historically unique, degrees of diversity and pluralism. As one scholar concludes, "the Ottoman Empire succeeded because it incorporated the energies of the vastly varied peoples it encountered, quickly transcending its roots in the Turkish nomadic migrations from Central Asia into the Middle East." The empire is best viewed as a "highly effective blend of influences," combining Byzantine, Turkish, Balkan, and Islamic ideas and practices. Tapping into this diversity produced an "exceptional flexibility, a readiness and ability to pragmatically adapt to changing conditions."[15] Such variety appears to have helped fuel the rise of the Ottoman Empire during its period of competitive advance. The strength of the empire, during its rise and centuries of peak power, was the incorporation of diversity into a multiethnic empire.[16]

Taking advantage of the multifarious character of the multiethnic empire demanded a significant degree of tolerance across many populations. Although the Ottoman state was not uniformly tolerant in a modern sense, scholars nonetheless refer on balance to "the tolerant model of administration that it offered during most of its existence." This included legal protections for minority religious groups to practice their faiths. These were not always observed, and persecutions did occur. But for "most of its history . . . the Ottoman Empire offered an effective model of a multi-religious political system to the rest of the world."[17]

The Ottoman Empire, however, was a dynastic state, with intense court politics and a limited talent pool for the most senior rulers. The fact that ultimate absolute authority rested in those rulers' hands meant that it cannot be compared with truly pluralistic modern societies. And the risks of excessive diversity and pluralism were certainly present in the Ottoman system, which engaged in an ongoing struggle to balance its essentially hierarchical and Muslim identity and tolerance.[18] Exchanges, reforms, and change were "counterbalanced by an impulse to protect what was unique to Ottoman political and cultural life, particularly the religious substructure on which it rested, for this, like the temporal power of the dynasty, was in danger of being undermined by the empire's ever closer involvement with Europe."[19]

***

---

[14] Goldstone, 2009, p. 48.

[15] Quataert, 2005, pp. 2, 4, 18.

[16] Baer, 2021, pp. 13, 82.

[17] Quataert, 2005, pp. 5–6.

[18] Baer, 2021, pp. 45, 190.

[19] Finkel, 2005, p. 371.

Perhaps the paradigmatic premodern case that speaks to the competitive value of pluralism is the Italian Renaissance. Pluralistic dynamism existed both within city-states and between them, creating overlapping networks of intellectual drive, technical experimentation, and sources of new ideas.[20] "That mosaic of states, that fragmentation of authority that constituted Italy during the period of the Renaissance," Kenneth Bartlett explains, "resulted in constant and almost obsessive competition." In "every field, competition and genius were the means to success." The Italian city-states "wanted to not just perfect the internal operation of each individual place, but they wanted to outdo their neighbors. They wanted to succeed in all ways, not just economically and militarily but also culturally and intellectually. That experimentation that allowed for a thousand flowers not just to bloom, but in fact to be carefully cultivated." Later, as the Italian city-states were subsumed under outside control, this dynamic pluralism was crushed. "With a single model imposed, with a single Habsburg hegemony over the continent and over the Italian peninsula, there was nothing that was left of this experimentation," Bartlett notes. "It simply no longer worked; nor could it work. All that mattered was that you met the needs of the emperor."[21]

Again, qualifications must be acknowledged, and exceptions too. Guido Ruggiero explains that as the aristocratic elite in some of the Italian city-states imposed more control, trying to keep the free-wheeling inclusive energy of an opportunity society in check, a by-product was a crackdown on diversity. Foreigners, Jews, the urban poor—these and other groups were increasingly shoved aside or hemmed in.[22] But for their time, at least, and in many places, the Italian city-states tolerated a significant degree of diversity of background and opinion. Partly this was a mindset encouraged by the prominence of trade and commerce in the city-states: Trade is naturally supportive of openness and toleration, and membership in trading networks cannot be easily reconciled with orthodoxy or uniformity.

Other cases demonstrate a positive relationship between dynamic pluralism and competitive advantage. Although Japan is thought of as highly homogenous, during times of especially great vitality—such as the Tokugawa period—it also reflected diversity in the form of local governance, the somewhat independent regions that generated a sort of decentralized innovation.[23] Meiji Japan inaugurated a more institutionalized and national level of pluralistic competition that did not demand ethnic or other forms of diversity but still found ways to encourage productive competition. A rotating cast of senior Japanese officials and prominent individuals exercised significant influence over policy, which helped promote an energetic competition of ideas.

---

[20] One scholar argues, "There would seem to be a case for talking about the pluralism of worldviews in Renaissance Italy, a pluralism which may well have been a stimulus to intellectual innovation" (Peter Burke, *The Italian Renaissance: Culture and Society in Italy*, 3rd ed., Princeton, N.J.: Princeton University Press, 2014, p. 214).

[21] Bartlett, 2005, lecture 35.

[22] Ruggiero, 2014, p. 550.

[23] Clesse et al., 1997, p. 348.

The same form of pluralistic competition emerged in the economic realm and would eventually extend to postwar economic development. Contrary to common misperception, postwar Japanese governments did not pick single national champions in various areas as much as sponsor various competing firms, helping to provide capital, acquire technology, and create markets. The winner was then decided by the market. Peter Drucker argued in 1981 that Japanese postwar success is "not the result of some uniformity of thought and action. It is the result of something far more interesting—habits of political behavior that use the diversity in Japanese national life to produce effective economic action."[24] Partly this comes from the clash of interest groups—the Ministry of International Trade and Industry versus various industries, some companies versus others, and the active role of economic and industry associations, professional societies, and labor groups.

There are also strict limits to diversity and pluralism in Japan. The country handicaps itself by not admitting more ethnic and racial diversity, it scores low on gender equality in the workplace, and it has a tightly constrained policy on immigration. Arguments about Japanese homogeneity being an advantage in the 1980s "cover up, at times, a certain inertia and therefore a non-vital sort of insularism . . . that tends to prevent Japan from making perhaps its greatest possible vital contribution to the global system today, a contribution commensurate with its economic and financial power."[25]

Of the modern cases, it is the United States that may offer the paradigmatic case for the advantages of pluralism. In the U.S. case, this characteristic points to the potential value of federalism: The existence of 50 states as laboratories of policy experimentation and competitive engines seeking best practices for economic development offers a potentially significant competitive advantage.[26] States and localities provide a range of solutions to public policy challenges, offer regulatory and policy contexts suitable for various industries, bid for talent and industry, and in other ways energize national dynamism through their competition, sharing of best practices, and other interactions.

The American experience makes clear that—in an echo of the early modern European example—a pluralism of competing political entities has costs as well as benefits.[27] Federalism or decentralization on the American model has costs as well as advantages. It can institutionalize inequalities between regions, if for example one state chooses to spend more on

---

[24] Drucker, 1981.

[25] Ivan P. Hall quoted in Clesse et al., 1997, p. 313.

[26] Richard R. Nelson, ed., *National Innovation Systems: A Comparative Analysis*, New York: Oxford University Press, 1993, p. 30. Some have suggested that these advantages have come to the fore during the COVID-19 pandemic, when states experimented with various policy responses and in some cases "performed admirably" (Caroline Chang, Scott Moore, and Ali Wyne, "Federalism in the Time of Coronavirus: A Comparative U.S. Advantage," *The Diplomat*, May 29, 2020).

[27] Albert Breton, "Federalism and Decentralization: Ownership Rights and the Superiority of Federalism," *Publius*, Vol. 30, No. 2, 2000.

health care than another.[28] It can cause inefficiencies when multiple political units do duplicative work to develop programs or capabilities.

Diversity and Pluralism: General Evidence

This characteristic boasts some of the most extensive empirical support of any of our seven: Multiple studies demonstrate the competitive advantage to be gained by diverse and pluralistic nations and organizations.

There is broad and persuasive experimental evidence for the competitive value of diversity in organizations. This is true both in overall composition and in leadership teams. Research by McKinsey, for example, shows performance boosts of between 15 and 35 percent for firms with higher diversity in their leadership.[29] That study establishes that gender, ethnic, and cultural diversity all have significant advantages. Deloitte has surveyed research that demonstrates even greater advantages in areas like innovation, with more-diverse, tolerant firms generating as much as 80 percent more innovation-based revenue.[30] More-diverse organizations draw from a wider range of potential ideas, for example, and they incorporate the skills and talents of a wider range of potential employees. Other studies show that democracies gain long-term strategic advantages from their more open version of pluralism for similar reasons.[31]

In systemic terms, a pluralistic environment is more naturally conducive to generating the kind of portfolio of experiments that Eric Beinhocker associates with innovation. Beinhocker explains how Microsoft, when facing early challenges, did not make one big bet but instead created multiple partly competing lines of approach to the next generation of operating systems:

> What Gates created was not a focused big bet, but a portfolio of strategic options. One way of interpreting what Gates did was that he set a high-level aspiration—to be the leading PC software company—and then he created a portfolio of strategic experiments that had the possibility of evolving toward that aspiration. Rather than try to predict the future,

[28] Robert A. Schapiro, "States of Inequality: Fiscal Federalism, Unequal States, and Unequal People," *California Law Review*, Vol. 108, No. 5, October 2020.

[29] Vivian Hunt, Lareina Yee, Sara Prince, and Sundiatu Dixon-Fyle, *Delivering Through Diversity*, Los Angeles, Calif.: McKinsey & Company, January 18, 2018.

[30] Deloitte, "Diversity and Inclusion as a Competitive Advantage," webpage, undated.

[31] According to Landes, "European science and technology derived considerable advantage from the fact that the continent was divided into nation-states, rather than united under the rule of an ecumenical empire. Fragmentation, as we have seen, entailed competition, specifically competition among equals" (Landes, 2003, p. 31).

Gates created a population of competing Business Plans within Microsoft that mirrored the evolutionary competition going on outside in the marketplace.[32]

From the perspective of strategy, a pluralism and diversity of concepts and ideas is a major source of competitive advantage, especially when organized into a formalized structure like Beinhocker's "portfolio of experiments." As he explains, "the objective is to be able to make lots of small bets and only make big bets as a part of amplifying successful experiments when uncertainties are much lower. Being forced to make all-or-nothing bets under uncertainty means that a company is boxed in."[33] More-uniform, homogenous nations and organizations are more likely to find themselves in that predicament.

Research also suggests that a pluralistic and diverse societal structure offers a richer basis of ideas and innovations from a wider range of people, both individually and in rich and creative mixtures.[34] It has the potential to draw on the skills and talents of a more comprehensive part of the population and to draw talented individuals from abroad. Pluralism also helps mitigate potential risks of state capture of society and extractive institutions (which is one reason Daron Acemoglu and James Robinson speak of the connection between inclusive political institutions and economic ones).[35] Promoting competition among firms keeps the society from becoming dominated by a few state-connected entities.[36]

For all these reasons, a pluralistic society is likely to be inherently more open to experimentation and change than a more uniform one. Scott Page argues, in response to Jared Diamond's theory, that a critical difference between the singular cultures Diamond examined and the current world—in terms of risks of overshoot—lies precisely in the diversity of actors on the stage today, creating room for experimentation: "Cultural and institutional diversity also provides insurance against widespread collapse. Regardless of what the future holds, some culture is likely to have the required skills to thrive in it."[37]

The Balance: Avoiding Societal Instability

Like all the characteristics we examine, diversity and pluralism can be taken to excess. If excessive pluralism undermines a coherent national identity, it can lead to social instability,

---

[32] Beinhocker, 2007, pp. 445–446.

[33] Beinhocker, 2007, p. 449.

[34] Scott E. Page and Lu Hong, "Groups of Diverse Problem Solvers Can Outperform Groups of High-Ability Problem Solvers," *Proceedings of the National Academy of Science*, Vol. 101, No. 46, November 2004.

[35] Acemoglu and Robinson, 2012.

[36] Toynbee refers to the dangers of "a tendency towards standardization and uniformity," which is the opposite of the "tendency towards differentiation and diversity which we have found to be the mark of the growth stage of civilizations" (Toynbee, 1947, p. 555).

[37] Page, 2005, p. 1066; see Diamond, 2005.

which becomes a competitive handicap. Social instability, in turn, can lead to political fragmentation and stagnation, making it harder for a nation to govern effectively or pursue major projects. The pattern can also express itself in violence. Civil war is obviously the extreme form of social instability, but it can take many other forms, from insurgency to violent crime.

The required balance here is straightforward: a sufficient appreciation for diversity and pluralism on the one hand (to gather talents and ideas from as wide a range as possible) and a sufficiently unified national identity on the other (to create a sense of membership in a clear group and a commitment to the success of that group against others). Needless to say, this balance is very difficult to strike in practice. One source of the competitive success of Europe and the United States during the 19th and 20th centuries may be that they were in the process of striking that balance better than others. Clearly, the appreciation for diversity, for example, in late 19th- and early 20th-century America or France was highly imperfect. But it was improving, gradually becoming better than in societies that were much more xenophobic and nationalistically exclusive.[38]

In short, to achieve competitive advantage countries, must have sufficient diversity and pluralism to generate creative, innovative, and competitive dynamics, but the countries must also retain a sufficient degree of national coherence and identity. One survey of the literature has shown that diversity can have tremendous value for economic development—but excessive fragmentation can be a competitive drag.[39] Too much incoherent, fragmented pluralism becomes a handicap.[40]

Nineteenth-century China offers a tragic example of the competitive price of massive societal instability, even after a period of great efflorescence. A typical explanation for China's competitive decline relative to Europe during the period of the Great Divergence focuses on an allergy to foreign influences, and this is certainly the case. But the country suffered through a series of major dynastic and civil wars right up through the end of World War II, and the constant instability and conflict were a critical factor in holding back its competitive capabilities.

The Soviet Union also had competitive difficulties in balancing the demands and varying goals of a complex mosaic of nationalities. It represented more than 90 distinct nationalities,

---

[38] A related thesis may be that civic nationalism—which embraces diversity in many forms under a set of unifying ideas—is in the long run more competitively advantageous than forms of ethnic nationalism, which by definition cannot cast the net of opportunity and intellectual embrace as wide.

[39] Alesina and La Ferrara, 2005. Another intriguing study of the connection between cultural values and business performance makes the same point: Diversity within cultures is an important competitive advantage—"provided that there is also sufficient commonality of culture to prevent factionalism of the society" (Mark Casson, "Cultural Determinants of Economic Performance," *Journal of Comparative Economics*, Vol. 17, No. 2, June 1993).

[40] On this see Goldstone, 2009, pp. 141–143, 169. As one scholar writes of the German case, for example, "It is crystal clear that the separate German states suffered economically from being a crazy quilt of states rather than a group under a national blanket" (Appleby, 2010, loc. 2878).

and at one point fully a sixth of its population was Muslim.[41] National identity was baked into the Soviet Union's constitution, which represented subordinate nations as semiautonomous areas with their own languages.[42] The growing nationalism of these areas played a significant role in the Soviet Union's dissolution.[43] This was especially true because of the gap between rhetoric and reality embodied in a system in which nearly all leadership positions went to Slavic Russians, and ethnic minorities faced significant barriers to equal opportunity: "In conditions of democratisation where a number of republics were as wealthy or even wealthier than Russia, and with a rich arsenal of potent symbolic and actual grievances, the shift from coercion to consent in the management of federal relations proved too wide a chasm to be bridged by the methods of perestroika." In the end, the final "crisis of the Soviet Union was above all a crisis of federalism."[44]

Spain also provides an example of the competitive effect of profound degrees of pluralism. Often depicted as a centralized, autocratic monarchy devoted to brutal religious orthodoxy, the Spanish Empire did accommodate both local autonomy and forms of pluralism, whether in possessions in Italy and the New World or in provinces within Spain itself, such as Catalonia. As the scholar Gabriel Paquette suggests, Spain was a "composite monarchy" that reflected a "legal mosaic."[45] The result, as another scholar sees it, were "centripetal impulses toward centralization and centrifugal tendencies toward localism."[46] Still another scholar describes Spanish governing institutions as a "dynamic balance between the principles of authority and flexibility."[47] Partly the issue was one of overlapping authorities: As in many premodern or early modern societies, central rulers had to constantly negotiate outcomes with potent local or regional leaders.[48] This created a constant dialogue rather than a simple process of central direction. Over time, Spanish rulers came to view this reality as a competitive handicap. As much as overlapping realms of governance might offer some pluralistic

[41] Barbara Anderson and Brian Silver, "Growth and Diversity of Population in the Soviet Union," *Annals of the American Academy of Political and Social Science*, Vol. 510, June 1990.

[42] Mark Beissinger, *Nationalist Mobilization and the Collapse of the Soviet State*, Cambridge, UK: Cambridge University Press, 2010. See also Mark Beissinger, "Nationalism and the Collapse of Soviet Communism," *Contemporary European History*, Vol. 18, No. 3, 2009.

[43] Ben Fowkes, *The Disintegration of the Soviet Union: A Study in the Rise and Triumph of Nationalism*, London: Palgrave-Macmillan, 1997.

[44] Sakwa, 2013, pp. 68–69.

[45] We are grateful to Gabriel Paquette for this insight.

[46] Jack P. Greene, "State Formation, Resistance, and the Creation of Revolutionary Traditions in the Early Modern Era," in Michael A. Mornson and Melinda S. Zook, eds., *Revolutionary Currents: Nation-Building in the Transatlantic World*, Lanham, Md.: Rowman and Littlefield, 2004, p. 4.

[47] John Leddy Phelan, "Authority and Flexibility in Spanish Imperial Bureaucracy," *Administrative Science Quarterly*, Vol. 5, No. 1, 1960.

[48] J. H. Elliott, "A Provincial Aristocracy: The Catalan Ruling Class in the Sixteenth and Seventeenth Century," in *Spain and Its World*, New Haven, Conn.: Yale University Press, 1990, p. 90.

variety and energy, the inability to govern the state with a firm hand left Spain lagging more rapidly centralizing powers, such as Britain and France.

But probably the defining case, from those we examined in depth, of excessive pluralism and diversity becoming an inherent competitive advantage is Austria-Hungary. As long ago as 1981 the historian John Boyer cast a light on "those features of the Imperial political system which contributed to its stability and functionality," arguing that the "important fact about the monarchy before 1918 was not that it fell apart, but that it proved capable of surviving for so long."[49] Austria-Hungary was in some ways a dynamic and potentially sustainable state whose collapse was not foreordained had it not been for the immense pressures of finding itself at the epicenter of the most destructive conflict in world history to that point.[50]

The empire was divided into multiple national and ethnic groups and suffered from a lack of coherence relative to many key competitors. As noted in previous chapters, recent scholarship has modified the view of the empire as a fragmented and unstable house of cards ready to collapse.[51] It had many strengths and was even managing its odd, split-governance structure somewhat effectively before the war. Especially on the Austrian side, a significant degree of decentralization allowed local towns and communities to govern aspects of their own affairs and encouraged more allegiance to the system.

Nonetheless, the Austro-Hungarian case certainly illustrates the limits to the competitive advantage of pluralistic societies. Austria-Hungary had to deal with a constant concern for domestic stability and the risk of flaring tensions among ethnic groups, especially the role of the Slavs in Hungary, and contend with an ongoing battle for ethnic supremacy between various components of the empire, with different pieces trying to undermine others.[52] As Wess Mitchell catalogs, the ethnic and national fragmentation of the empire—and the multiple decisionmaking units within it—severely handicapped Austria-Hungary as a strategic actor.[53] The empire's fragmentation affected its administrative efficiency, which in turn "stunted its development as a geopolitical actor at a critical moment when continental powers like France and Prussia were achieving greater efficiency in matters of state and war."[54] The ethnic complexity of the empire created "equivocal loyalties" that weakened the empire as a strategic actor.[55]

---

[49] John W. Boyer, *Political Radicalism in Late Imperial Vienna: Origins of the Christian Social Movement, 1848–1897*, Chicago: University of Chicago Press, 1981, p. xiv.

[50] We are grateful to both John Deak and Pieter Judson for contributing to our understanding on this point.

[51] We are grateful to the advice and counsel of John Deak and Pieter Judson, who offered extremely thoughtful inputs to the study on this case. The conclusions represented here, of course, are ours.

[52] Samuel R. Williamson, "Austria-Hungary and the International System: Great Power or Doomed Anachronism?" in *Austria-Hungary and the Origins of the First World War*, London: Macmillan Education UK, 1991.

[53] Mitchell, 2018, pp. 52–81.

[54] Mitchell, 2018, p. 61.

[55] Mitchell, 2018, p. 61.

More generally, our historical cases highlight a different and paradoxical insight: Sometimes, societal instability and crisis laid the foundations for later strength. Some economists and historians have suggested that the Black Death cleared the way for later social progress by putting labor at a premium and forcing more social mobility and investments in technology. In both Britain and China, civil wars and violent social turbulence (in the 17th and 19th centuries, respectively) forced changes to governance and created new patterns of social relations that turned out to underpin later competitive strengths. Walter Scheidel argues that major progress against social inequality occurs only in the aftermath of major social upheavals.[56]

None of this is to endorse a societal crisis or collapse as a useful tool to enhance national competitiveness. The final message of this characteristic—as with all of them—is the critical importance of balance. Diversity and pluralism, as measured in distinct and sometimes surprising ways, is a clear competitive advantage for nations. But they must be achieved in ways that allow for unified national identity, stability, and the activities of an effective, coherent active state.

---

[56] Scheidel, 2018.

CHAPTER TEN

Assessing U.S. Standing in the Characteristics

The final step in our analysis was to assess the United States' current and prospective competitive situation using the characteristics identified in this study. If these seven characteristics and the associated insights—such as the importance of balance, the role of synergies of factors producing dynamism, and the importance of a public-spirited elite—provide important clues to a nation's competitive potential, where does the United States stand today? Is it in good or bad shape, and why?

To evaluate these questions, we identified specific measurable variables that could be associated with each characteristic, gathered data on those variables, and reviewed recent literature on the U.S. standing in various societal measures of competitive strength. The findings are partial and preliminary. We did not conduct a comprehensive assessment of outcome variables, such as levels of economic growth, standard of living, or indexes of well-being in societies.[1] Nor was this, yet, a comparative assessment, ranking the United States relative to its main competitors. The purpose was narrower: We offer some initial findings on the characteristics likely to govern U.S. standing on the global stage, informed by our assessment of the societal characteristics essential to competitive advantage. The result is an interpretive assessment rather than a mere report of data, but it is grounded in an extensive assessment of available literature. The research that produced these findings included the following:

- *Gathering data on our seven societal characteristics.* We sought trends and data on social opportunity, measures of national ambition and will, the condition of U.S. public and private institutions, and other aspects of the seven characteristics. Because the basic theme of each characteristic is broader than any one category of data, we often had to seek proxy variables or compile results from multiple indicators.
- *Reviewing general literature on the condition of U.S. society.* There is a rich and growing literature on challenges facing U.S. society, and we reviewed this literature for key evidence and insights.
- *Evaluating the possible role of prior routes to competitive decline.* In the process of assessing the current U.S. situation, we applied the lessons of the project's historical case

---

[1] Examples are the Social Progress Imperative, World Population Review, and World Bank.

studies used to generate the seven positive societal characteristics. That research also pointed to ways in which shortcomings in those areas could cause national decline, and this helped us identify the societal dangers listed below.

One of the challenges was to objectively assess abstract social trends and realities—such as national morale and will, a society's level of "entitlement," the much-discussed issue of "decadence"—which might not be measurable by simple variables. These can be analytically perilous concepts, but an analysis that ignores such inchoate trends would offer an incomplete portrait. In each of the categories below, although we focus mainly on discrete, often measurable variables, we also consider more-abstract factors that help define the competitive standing of American society.

The overall message of this application is somewhat daunting. The United States of the second half of the 20th century might have represented the most complete package of competitive advantages—the most ideal representation of the Renaissance spirit—of any great power in history. The nation retains many structural and societal legacies of that period: a relatively high degree of social mobility, political pluralism, and an important degree of domestic social ambition, to take three examples. But trends in many of these characteristics appear to be running in a disempowering direction, and this analysis raised stark questions of how well the U.S. competitive engine is functioning today. Beyond the specific characteristics, the evaluation points to a wider sense of national sluggishness and rigidity with worrying parallels to other great powers on the far side of their dynamic peak.

Characteristic 1: National Ambition and Will

The initial characteristic immediately confronts us with this problem of evaluating abstract qualities: When applied to any current case, it is challenging to assess in any measurable way. Polling on, for example, faith in institutions and expectations for the future can be an unreliable guide because opinions rise and fall and because the results are strongly affected by momentary events. But data reviewed for this analysis provide at least five sources of evidence that suggest a risk of declining national ambition and will—a loss of commitment to the "energizing myth" of the nation and a broader determination to master its environment.

The first of these is the most qualitative: The theme of waning national will emerges again and again in public discussions and debates, with numerous commentaries and books using anecdotal conversations and general insight to suggest that this is a major trend.[2] Writers and scholars alike, some referring to polling evidence, have argued that the spirit of adventurous-

---

[2] See, for example, David Brooks, "America Is Having a Moral Convulsion," *The Atlantic*, October 4, 2020; Yuval Levin, "How Did Americans Lose Faith in Everything?" *New York Times*, January 18, 2020; Douthat, 2020.

ness, experimentation, and determination to remake the future have all ebbed in the American character. This coincidence of subjective assessment may tell us something.

Second, survey evidence consistently suggests that younger Americans do not view the nation, its inherent values, and its ambitions in the same way as previous generations. A 2019 Eurasia Group Foundation study reported on polling data that showed a significant generational shift in the proportion of Americans who believe that the country represents something exceptional.[3] Some 75 percent of Americans age 60 and older believe that the country is exceptional, compared with just 45 percent of Americans 18 to 29. Over half of people in that age group agreed with the statement that "America is not an exceptional nation," but rather, like all others, acts in accordance with its interests. Many other surveys have produced similar results.[4]

Third, other polling data indicate that many Americans have little faith in the trajectory of their nation. These views are not unique in the developed world; the analysis here is not a relative assessment but rather indicates where the United States stands relative to its recent history. Some three-quarters of Americans in 2019 were dissatisfied with the way things were going in the country.[5] These numbers fluctuate, and a poll in one year can be contradicted the next. One 2018 Harvard Kennedy School poll found that more than 60 percent of younger Americans had "more fear than hope" about the future of the country.[6] By 2021, Harvard reported on a new survey that showed that 56 percent of those younger Americans were now hopeful about the future of the country.[7] The trend is not simple and linear over the last half century,[8] but the country has settled into a long-term situation in which two-thirds to three-quarters of the people believe the country is on the wrong track.

---

[3] Mark Hannah and Caroline Grey, "Indispensable No More? How the American Public Sees U.S. Foreign Policy," white paper, New York: Eurasia Foundation, November 2019.

[4] Pew polling in 2019, for example, found most Americans to be strikingly cynical or pessimistic about the country's ability to surmount key challenges. Fully 60 percent said that the United States would likely be less important in world affairs in 30 years. Seventy-three percent said that they expected the divide between rich and poor to grow even more over that time frame. Sixty-five percent thought that political divides would be worse. And 87 percent of Americans were fairly or very worried about the ability of the political system to solve any of its chief problems. See Kim Parker, Rich Morin, and Juliana Menasce Horowitz, "Looking to the Future, Public Sees an America in Decline on Many Fronts," Pew Research Center, March 21, 2019.

[5] Pew Research Center, *Trump Begins Third Year with Low Job Approval and Doubts About His Honesty*, Washington, D.C., January 18, 2019. See also Carol Graham, "Premature Mortality and the Long Decline of Hope in America," Brookings Institution, May 10, 2018; Mark Penn, "Americans Are Losing Confidence in the Nation but Still Believe in Themselves," *The Atlantic*, June 27, 2012.

[6] See results at Institute of Politics, Harvard Kennedy School, "Nearly Two-Thirds of Young Americans Fearful About the Future of Democracy in America, Harvard Youth Poll Finds," April 2018.

[7] Michael P. Nietzel, "New Harvard Poll Finds Rising Hopes for the Nation's Future Among Young Americans," *Forbes*, April 23, 2021.

[8] One long-term set of Gallup polls, for example, shows public confidence with "the way things are going" in the mid-30th percentile for the past decade or so, which is below general averages for the previous decades

Fourth, the degree of skepticism and cynicism about major social institutions, especially the federal government, has been disturbingly high for some time.[9] This derives in part from a perception of loss of accountability, that major institutions have simply gotten beyond our control. And the result is a striking degree of conspiratorial thinking and a growing proportion of Americans (again, especially younger people) who have significant skepticism about the openness, honesty, or legitimacy of social institutions.

Like attitudes about expectations for the future, Americans' views of social institutions have not unfolded in a straight line. Trust in government fell through the late 1960s and into the 1970s, hit modern lows of around 20 percent in the mid-1990s, recovered significantly after September 11 to over 40 percent, but then collapsed back down into the 20th percentile and has largely stayed there.[10] The United States won the Cold War, in other words, and spent three decades at the pinnacle of world power, while still laboring under some trust-in-government metrics as low as the ones we have today. Alone, clearly, this indicator does not foretell competitive disaster. But many trends of loss of faith in institutions may be accumulating to create a more generalized loss of energy and dynamism in the country.

A closely related data point is levels of trust: Various polls suggest that trust among Americans and trust in institutions have declined significantly since the postwar peak of the 1950s and early 1960s.[11] Part of the reason for this trend is a deeply entrenched view that many public (as well as private) institutions are deeply unfair and corrupt.[12] Seventy percent of Americans believe that campaign donations are corrupt and that "offices are for sale to the highest bidder."[13] Although trust is not equivalent to national ambition, will, and faith in the national project, a falling level of intersubjective trust in a society is very likely to have negative ramifications for the degree of national ambition and willpower, both internationally and domestically.

---

but was matched in the 1970s and 1990s. See Gallup, "Satisfaction with the United States," last updated March 2022.

[9] Megan Brenan, "Americans' Confidence in Major U.S. Institutions Dips," Gallup, July 14, 2021.

[10] See Gallup, "Public Trust in Government, 1958–2021," May 17, 2021.

[11] Lee Rainie, Scott Keeter, and Andrew Perrin, "Trust and Distrust in America," Pew Research Center, July 22, 2019. See also Baker Center for Leadership and Governance, "2018 American Institutional Confidence Poll: The Health of American Democracy in an Era of Hyper Polarization," undated.

[12] The role of money in politics has become endemic: The 2020 U.S. election cost candidates over $14 billion, making this election the most expensive on record; OpenSecrets.org, "2020 Election to Cost $14 Billion, Blowing Away Spending Records," October 28, 2020. Lobbyists spent $3.5 billion in 2016 alone, and polling and anecdotal evidence suggest that "the vast sums spent on political campaigns in the United States are amplifying the sense among ordinary Americans that they're being marginalized, politically and economically" (Celestine Bohlen, "American Democracy Is Drowning in Money," New York Times, September 20, 2017).

[13] Sandra Knipsel, "Corporate Money in Politics Threatens US Democracy—or Does It?" University of Rochester, July 6, 2020.

Fifth and finally, recent surveys find growing disquiet with the basic values on which the country was founded, especially democracy. One 2018 survey finds that only 10 percent of Americans are "very satisfied" with how democracy is working, as opposed to 25 percent who are neutral and 36 percent who are somewhat or very dissatisfied. In the same poll, only about 55 percent of Americans ages 18–40 affirm that "democracy is always preferable" to other forms of government; a third of those same cohorts agree that "non-democracies can be preferable." Only half of Americans 18–40 believe that "democracy serves the people," half agree that "democracy serves the elite," and two-thirds or more of all age groups agree with the statement that "public officials don't care what I think."[14]

Another recent poll found that almost a third of Americans approve of the idea of a "strong incumbent leader who does not have to bother with Congress and elections." This matches the findings of the World Values Survey, which in 2017 found that 38 percent of Americans— up from 24 percent in the mid-1990s—approved of an "unchecked leader."[15] Two leading scholars on the issue have concluded that in the United States and much of the developed democratic world, "citizens of mature democracies have become markedly less satisfied with their form of government and surprisingly open to nondemocratic alternatives. A serious democratic disconnect has emerged. If it widens even further, it may begin to challenge the stability of seemingly consolidated democracies."[16]

In broader and more abstract terms, Ross Douthat raises the question of whether the United States is becoming, in terms related to these, a "decadent" nation. By this he means something very specific—not moral or sexual excess but rather an absence of energy and drive, the predominance of "boredom and fatigue," a society trying to become "comfortably numb," accepting "futility and the absurd as normal." Decadence, according to Douthat, denotes

> economic stagnation, institutional decay, and cultural and intellectual exhaustion at a
> high level of material prosperity and technological development. It describes a situation
> in which repetition is more the norm than innovation; in which sclerosis afflicts public
> institutions and private enterprises alike; in which intellectual life seems to go in circles;
> in which new developments in science, new exploratory projects, underdeliver compared

---

[14] Sean Kates, Jonathan M. Ladd, and Joshua A. Tucker, "New Poll Shows Dissatisfaction with American Democracy, Especially Among the Young," *Vox*, October 31, 2018.

[15] Michael Albertus and Guy Grossman, "Americans Are Officially Giving Up on Democracy," *Foreign Policy*, October 16, 2020.

[16] These scholars cite World Values Survey findings from 2011 showing that almost a quarter of Americans ages 16 to 24 say that a democratic system is a "bad" or "very bad" way to run the country. Political apathy, they report, is growing among younger generations as well. Roberto Stefan Foa and Yascha Mounk, "The Danger of Deconsolidation: The Democratic Disconnect," *Journal of Democracy*, Vol. 27, No. 3, July 2016. There is some conflicting evidence on this point. Some polls show support for democracy if the question is asked differently. Others show no clear trend or a more recent rebound in support for democratic systems; see Christopher Classen, "Support for Democracy Is Declining—but Not in the U.S. or Other Western Democracies," *Washington Post*, July 5, 2018.

with what people recently expected. And, crucially, the stagnation and decay are often a direct consequence of previous development. The decadent society is, by definition, a victim of its own significant success.[17]

A profound question facing the United States today is whether it, indeed, has become a version of a "satisfied society," one that has turned its back on any urgency in its drive to achieve and explore and master. The risk is of a society-wide inertia, a reaching of plateaus on many goals and efforts to solve problems, a generalized habit of coasting on established positions rather than building new ones. This pattern can also reveal itself in a habit of rent seeking, market capture, elite-privilege protection, and other forms of preserving established advantage rather than exploration or creation.

Characteristic 2: Unified National Identity

There are reasons to believe that the degree of national unity and political coherence in the United States has declined in recent years. Yet where this leaves the United States in broader historical terms, and specifically in relation to the actions necessary for competition, is less clear.

One can easily exaggerate the degree to which the United States has been unified in the past. Often, the celebrated eras of national community and cooperation emerged only in response to an external threat, including in various wars and the rivalry with the Soviet Union. There is no objective way to measure whether degrees of national disconnection are greater now than during the Red Scare of the 1950s or the Vietnam-era period of instability in the late 1960s. It is not enough to say that the present moment feels different in terms of the intensity of divergent and polarized views among the American people and their political leaders.

But several signs do suggest that current trends may harbor significant risk to unified national identity. One has to do with the degree to which *a population sees itself as part of a coherent whole*.[18] On one level, general polling data suggest a relatively stable degree of commitment to national identity. Yet a countervailing trend is clearly underway—there is a growing belief on the part of a significant number of Americans that the country is divided into mutually incompatible ideological groups.[19]

---

[17] Douthat, 2020, pp. 8–9.

[18] George Packer, "How America Fractured into Four Parts," *The Atlantic*, July–August 2021.

[19] Bill Bishop and Robert Cushing, *The Big Sort: Why the Clustering of Like-Minded America Is Tearing Us Apart*, New York: Mariner Books, 2009. The book includes data on perceptions of ideological affinity; the general thesis has been criticized. See Samuel J. Abrams and Morris P. Fiorina, "The Myth of the 'Big Sort,'" Hoover Institution, August 13, 2012. Some subsequent research supported the idea of spatial sorting; see Richard Florida, "America's 'Big Sort' Is Only Getting Bigger," Bloomberg, October 25, 2016.

A second engine of fragmenting national identity and coherence consists of *structural factors that obstruct collective action and shared identity*. Two such structural factors are gerrymandering and the democratization of U.S. presidential nomination processes. The former has intensified partisanship in the U.S. House of Representatives by creating districts locked in for one or another party, where the only real fight is in the primary. Candidates have little incentive to tack to the center to capture middle-ground voters.

Although not formally structural, the political affiliation of individual American states is also becoming informally locked into partisan place. From 1979 to 1980, 27 states had split Senate delegations—one senator from each party—suggesting a mixed and somewhat bipartisan state-level political affiliation. By 2021, the number of states with split delegations had fallen to six, the lowest in the period of direct election of senators.[20] This is a symptom of a larger secular trend, again not formally structural but increasingly locked in: a national phenomenon of "ideological sorting" in which people with certain political views tend to congregate in specific geographical areas.[21] Recent evidence suggests that increasing numbers of Americans do not want to live in communities with, or have their children marry, people who belong to the other political party.[22]

A third source of danger to national identity is demographic. *A country with a rapidly diversifying population—though it gains competitive advantages from this diversity—will also face greater hurdles to sustaining a sense of coherent national identity*. As the pollster Bruce Stokes notes, "The percentage of non-white people in the United States has tripled in the last half-century. The portion of foreign-born persons has also tripled. The share of births to unmarried women has quadrupled." Those trends offer competitive advantage, as our characteristic dealing with diversity and pluralism makes clear. But they also pose challenges. Stokes adds, "it is the unprecedented pace of change that is currently straining the fabric of American society because some of the fundamental pillars of human psychological identity—the sense of family, ethnic cohesiveness, the workplace, religion, the relations between the sexes—have been rapidly eroding. All of these changes are happening at the same time, interacting with each other, often in negative ways."[23]

Finally, the trajectory of national disunion has been *measurably accelerated by a fragmenting, silo-based information environment in which misinformation and conspiracy theories—some of them generated and popularized specifically to undermine norms of shared identity—can easily spread*. We examine this trend in the following section. Through both intentional

---

[20] Drew Desilver, "U.S. Senate Has Fewest Split Delegations Since Direct Elections Began," Pew Research Center, February 11, 2021.

[21] Morris P. Fiorina, *Unstable Majorities: Polarization, Party Sorting and Political Stalemate*, Stanford, Calif.: Hoover Institution Press, 2017.

[22] Nate Cohn, "Polarization Is Dividing American Society, Not Just Politics," *New York Times*, June 12, 2014.

[23] Bruce Stokes, "America's Identity Crisis," German Marshall Fund of the United States, December 17, 2021.

and unintentional processes, involving the accidental but uninformed spread of misinformation and the active use of inaccuracies and fabricated reports to intensify polarization, this phenomenon significantly exacerbates divisions.[24]

The result is not merely political polarization but a deeper emerging degree of tribalism across many identity categories. Pew Research Center has conducted a decade or more of surveys designed to measure this variable, and the trend has been consistently negative. The numbers are clear and striking:

- A 2014 Pew analysis remains one of the defining assessments of growing polarization.[25] This study introduced the famous graphic of diverging political values over time (see Figure 10.1).
- On many core public policy issues, such as race, gender, and immigration, the differences between the parties are immense and, in some cases, unprecedented in modern polling.[26]
- Each political side increasingly sees the other as not merely holding views they disagree with but as actively dangerous to the country.[27] Before the 2020 election, 80 percent of Americans said that their disagreements with political opponents dealt with "core American values, and roughly 9 in 10—again in both camps—worried that a victory by the other would lead to 'lasting harm' to the United States."[28] As another Pew survey of research concluded in 2020, "The elected officials who take the oath of office in January will be representing two broad coalitions of voters who are deeply distrustful of one another and who fundamentally disagree over policies, plans and even the very problems that face the country today."[29]

---

[24] Three of these six dangers could indeed be viewed as a highly integrated joint trend. A society that becomes more unequal and believes that it is losing a culture of opportunity—*and* that is characterized by growing tribalism and polarization, *and* that suffers from a corrupted information environment—is a society in serious danger of descent into instability or undemocratic forms of rule.

[25] Pew Research Center, "Political Polarization in the American Public," June 12, 2014.

[26] When asked in late 2020 whether it was "a lot more difficult" to be a Black person than a White person in the United States, 74 percent of those who voted for Joe Biden agreed, as opposed to only 9 percent of those who voted for Donald Trump. Eighty-four percent of Biden voters agreed that a growing number of immigrants strengthens U.S. society versus only 32 percent of Trump voters. Seventy-nine percent of Biden voters agreed with the statement that women face greater obstacles to getting ahead than men, as opposed to just 26 percent of Trump voters. See Pew Research Center, "Voters' Attitudes About Race and Gender Are Even More Divided Than in 2016," September 20, 2020.

[27] Philip Bump, "Most Republicans See Democrats Not as Political Opponents but as Enemies," *Washington Post*, February 10, 2021.

[28] Michael Dimock, "America Is Exceptional in Its Political Divide," *Trust Magazine* (Pew Research Center), Winter 2021.

[29] Claudia Deane and John Gramlich, "2020 Election Reveals Two Broad Voting Coalitions Fundamentally at Odds," Pew Research Center, November 6, 2020.

FIGURE 10.1

Distribution of Democrats and Republicans on a Ten-Item Political Value Scale

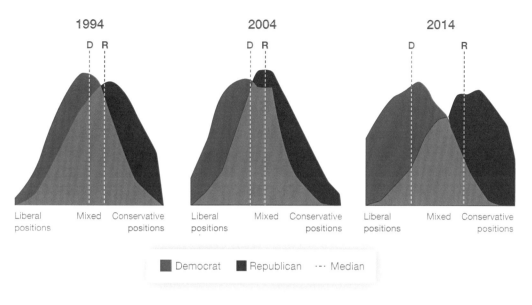

SOURCE: Pew Research Center, "The Partisan Divide on Political Values Grows Even Wider," October 5, 2017.

- The ideological polarization of members of Congress has measurably grown in recent years, reaching a post–Civil War high by 2016.[30]
- In comparative terms, global Pew research suggests that the United States is more politically divided, at least on issues related to current public policy crises, than 19 other democracies, including France, Spain, Japan, Italy, and Germany.[31] Another major study finds similar results looking at 12 OECD members.[32] Among that set, six countries saw a decrease in polarization and five others saw an increase—but none experienced a rise in polarization close to the U.S. rate.

This stark and growing polarization weakens U.S. international competitiveness in direct ways.[33] It is making the United States less able to form and sustain international agreements or conduct foreign policy with bipartisan support. Under a context of severe partisanship, the party out of power becomes more likely to undercut and embarrass the party with the White

---

[30] Laura Paisley, "Political Polarization at Its Worst Since the Civil War," *USC News*, November 8, 2016.

[31] Dimock, 2021.

[32] Levi Boxell, Matthew Gentzkow, and Jesse M. Shapiro, "Cross-Country Trends in Affective Polarization," Cambridge, Mass.: National Bureau of Economic Research, Working Paper 26669, August 2021.

[33] Frank Newport, "The Impact of Increased Political Polarization," Gallup, December 5, 2019.

House, even if this tends to undermine U.S. credibility.[34] One result is to reduce the durability of U.S. policy—which in general ought to be higher in a democratic context that can make more-credible long-term commitments.[35]

Some scholars reject the idea that the United States is ideologically polarized. They point to evidence that, on many major values, most Americans are not especially politically involved, do not hold strong political views, and overlap in their beliefs on many significant issues. It is the extreme activists in both parties who make the landscape appear more polarized than it is.[36] This especially shows up when Americans are asked to rate themselves on an ideological spectrum: "[T]he way that Americans self-categorize their ideological positions has changed little in four decades. The General Social Survey (GSS) series is flat, showing nothing beyond sampling variability."[37] Table 10.1 represents a mixed picture consistent with this view: Members of the two parties differ widely on their faith in certain institutions—but agree strongly on others.

Some argue that what really is going on is party sorting along ideological lines, not intensifying polarization to the extremes. The center still exists in American politics—centrists have become independents, whose numbers have grown, whereas each party has moved somewhat away from the center.[38] Data from the American National Election Studies surveys paint a somewhat mixed picture about such trends. On one scale, intensity of ideological affiliation, the proportion of Americans describing themselves as "extremely" liberal or conservative has risen—but only from about 1 or 2 percent of the population in the 1990s to 5 or 6 percent today. Still, the number of those describing themselves as "moderate" has declined by about 10 percent, so the general picture is of more intense polarization. Another question shows that the number of Americans describing themselves as nonpartisan declined, while the number of those describing themselves as "strongly partisan" is up 20 percentage points since about 1980, to a striking 44 percent of the total.[39]

---

[34] This can reach extreme heights. As one scholar suggests, "It is becoming possible to imagine a world in which the Democratic and Republican parties not only have orthogonal foreign policy priorities but also maintain different relationships with key foreign allies and adversaries" (Rachel Myrick, "America Is Back—but for How Long?" *Foreign Affairs*, June 14, 2021).

[35] Lisa L. Martin, *Democratic Commitments: Legislatures and International Cooperation*, Princeton, N.J.: Princeton University Press, 2000; Kenneth A. Schultz, *Democracy and Coercive Diplomacy*, Cambridge, UK: Cambridge University Press, 2001).

[36] Morris P. Fiorina, Samuel J. Abrams, and Jeremy C. Pope, *Culture War? The Myth of a Polarized America*, 3rd ed., New York: Longman, 2010.

[37] Morris P. Fiorina, "The Myth of Growing Polarization," *Defining Ideas* (Hoover Institution), September 14, 2016.

[38] Matthew Dickinson, "Sorted, Not Polarized: Why the Distinction Matters," *Presidential Power* (Middlebury College), July 11, 2014.

[39] The data for these two specific points can be found in American National Election Studies, "Liberal-Conservative Self-Identification 1972–2020," August 16, 2021a; American National Election Studies, "Strength of Partisanship 1952–2020," August 16, 2021b.

TABLE 10.1

Confidence Levels in Major U.S. Institutions: Partisan Divides

Institution	Republicans (%)	Democrats (%)
There are significant divides on confidence in a few institutions . . .		
Police	76	31
Organized religion	51	26
Newspapers	8	35
Television news	6	25
Public schools	20	43
. . . but also striking agreement on many others		
Military	78	62
Small business	76	64
Big business	19	17
Supreme Court	39	35
Banks	35	33
Criminal justice	20	19

SOURCE: Gallup; see Brenan, 2021.

Other polling suggests that most Americans still do adhere to a core set of beliefs about the nature of the country. More than 90 percent in one wide-ranging 2021 poll agreed that being "truly American" involves commitment to essential freedoms. Less than 20 percent thought being of Western European heritage was a critical defining aspect of Americanness—a signal of widespread appreciation for diversity as a core national trait. When asked directly whether they preferred the country to be diverse, strong majorities agreed or at least moderately supported that goal. Some 75 percent affirmed that the national goal of "from many, one" (*e pluribus unum*) remained possible. But the same poll uncovered ideological divides: More than 60 percent of Republicans defined being Christian as an important aspect of being American—as opposed to 35 percent of Democrats. Almost 80 percent of Republicans, as opposed to half of Democrats, said that capitalism was essential to being truly American. And the poll found fears of identity loss: Four in ten Americans said that change was so rapid that they "sometimes feel like a stranger" in their country, and over half agreed that America was "in danger of losing its culture and identity."[40]

---

[40] The survey tested support for these values by asking for reactions to specific statements of principles, such as, "All people are equal, regardless of race, ethnicity, gender, physical appearance, or any other personal characteristics." See Public Religion Research Institute, "Competing Visions of America: An Evolving Identity or a Culture Under Attack? Findings from the 2021 American Values Survey," November 1, 2021.

Another 2021 survey found that more than 80 percent of Americans aligned with generally agreed-on national values, such as equality, liberty, and progress. Strikingly, it found a gap of only a few percentage points between 2020 Trump and Biden voters on these most basic values.[41] Even that survey found evidence of rising ideological cleavages, though. And other surveys and focus groups have identified significant gaps in how Americans define some basic terms: The pollster Frank Luntz reports that more than 80 percent of Americans agree with the statement that the country "is more divided today than at any other time in my lifetime."[42]

The *potential* to draw Americans together around a persistent set of shared beliefs and values therefore appears to exist. Despite that, however, there is abundant evidence of a significant and growing ideological divide and significant concerns about the fragmenting identity of the country.[43] Moreover, there is evidence of an emerging structural fragmentation of the country that, while driven in part by ideological cleavages, goes well beyond them.[44]

Other reasons for concern in this and related characteristics relate to what some have characterized as the rise of an insular, self-interested, and wealthy American elite, a theme that has become a major topic of recent assessments of American society.[45] The precise degree of public spiritedness among America's elites is beyond the scope of this work, though, as the previous section noted, there are some reasons for concern. Broad generalizations are bound to be misleading, concealing tremendous variation. Whatever the qualities of America's elite classes today, our study supports the proposition that a self-interested, acquisitive, wealth-flaunting elite class is associated with loss of social dynamism. As noted in earlier chapters, that connection emerged in Rome at its peak, in the later Renaissance and Ottoman Empire, and in the Soviet Union and other cases. Such a trend can generate significant competitive risk for nations, leading to a situation in which the selfish elite undermines many of the essential societal characteristics necessary to compete. If such a trend is indeed underway in the United States, it holds unsettling implications for the future of national power, cohesion, and stability.

---

[41] Siena College Research Institute, "Americans, Deeply Divided, yet Share Core Values of Equality, Liberty and Progress," October 25, 2021.

[42] Frank Luntz, "No Wonder America Is Divided: We Can't Even Agree on What Our Values Mean," *Time*, October 26, 2018.

[43] Alan I. Abramowitz and Kyle L. Saunders, "Is Polarization a Myth?" *Journal of Politics*, Vol. 70, No. 2, 2008; Shanto Iyengar, Yphtach Lelkes, Matthew Levendusky, Neil Malhotra, and Sean J. Westwood, "The Origins and Consequences of Affective Polarization in the United States," *Annual Review of Political Science*, Vol. 22, No. 1, 2019; Christopher Hare and Keith T. Poole, "The Polarization of Contemporary American Politics," *Polity*, Vol. 46, No. 3, 2014; Marc J. Hetherington, Meri T. Long, and Thomas J. Rudolph, "Revisiting the Myth: New Evidence of a Polarized Electorate," *Public Opinion Quarterly*, Vol. 80, No. S1, 2016.

[44] Packer, 2021.

[45] Edward Luce and Rana Foroohar, "That Creeping Sense of Western Dread," *Financial Times*, October 29, 2021.

Characteristic 3: Shared Opportunity

The United States continues to manifest many aspects of a society with opportunities and many effective institutions of social advancement. Recent decades have seen significant improvement in the degree of shared opportunity enjoyed by some groups in society. But our research pointed to two concerning realities: The United States is losing significant potential competitive advantage because opportunity for a significant part of the population continues to be limited, and trends are running in the wrong direction in areas of general national equality.

Historically, nations have gained competitive advantage by empowering greater and greater proportions of their people. Despite progress, there are still very significant gaps in the potential opportunity of many groups in the United States.

The best-known challenge has been offering full opportunity to the country's African American and Native American populations.[46] Several numbers indicate the degree of shortfall:

- A U.S. Chamber of Commerce report from 2020 catalogs evidence of the opportunity gap affecting African Americans and other Americans of color, especially men.[47]
- According to that same study, African Americans constitute over 12 percent of the population but only about 9 percent of business owners. A major reason for this is lack of access to business capital: African American entrepreneurs are less than half as likely to get outside funding as their White counterparts, and over 70 percent of African American entrepreneurs must rely on personal or family capital. This study suggested that if Americans of color were supported to an equal degree, this would add 1.1 million businesses, 9 million jobs, and $300 billion in economic activity to the economy.[48]
- Millions of Americans across many economic classes are facing an opportunity crisis, according to a major 2009 report that surveys several categories of opportunity, including social mobility, economic equality, political voice, and economic security.[49]

---

[46] The situation for Hispanic Americans is somewhat different, with greater intergenerational mobility (within a few percentage points of White mobility), but barriers remain to full opportunity. See Raj Chetty, Nathaniel Hendren, Maggie R. Jones, and Sonya R. Porter, "Race and Economic Opportunity in the United States: An Intergenerational Perspective," *Quarterly Journal of Economics*, Vol. 135, No. 2, May 2020.

[47] The evidence ranges from significant educational gaps, particularly in early grades, to vast differences in economic standing (Black children live in poverty at a rate double that of White children); only 15 percent of Black students go on to complete a bachelor's degree, compared with 23 percent of White students. Some 23 percent of Black workers were in occupations in the lowest-earning groups, compared with 13 percent of White workers. On the other end of the spectrum, over 50 percent of White workers are in the highest earning groups (management, technical, professional), compared with 25 percent of Black workers. U.S. Chamber of Commerce, "America's Opportunity Gaps: By the Numbers," June 24, 2020.

[48] U.S. Chamber of Commerce, 2020.

[49] Meredith King Langford, *The State of Opportunity in America*, New York: Opportunity Agenda, 2009.

- Female, African American, and Latino researchers are underrepresented in scientific and technological fields and in teaching positions associated with them.[50]
- Some 40 percent of African American students and 37 percent of Latino students transfer out of science, technology, engineering, and mathematics majors before earning a degree, and research suggests some of the reasons relate to lack of preparatory resources and support systems in these fields.[51]
- One driver of unequal opportunity has been the disproportionate incarceration rates for African American males, strongly affecting the economic potential of that community.[52]

Shared opportunity is not strictly an issue of race, ethnicity, or gender; it is also affected by geography. Another group that faces significant barriers to full realization of talents is the population of rural areas and Rust Belt cities that have been left hollowed out by the departure of the manufacturing industry. Many rural areas suffer from significant barriers to economic opportunity: weak job creation, a relative absence of new business starts, lack of high-speed digital connections, and in some cases higher rates of child poverty.[53] Measures of unemployment and drug addiction are higher in former manufacturing cities, and indicators of social opportunity—such as quality of local schools and college attendance rates—have shown significant declines.

Constraints on shared opportunity also show up in the skewed distribution of venture capital and investment. Broad access to capital and investment was a major contributing factor to prior competitive surges.[54] Yet the evidence has been clear for decades that access to capital in the United States is highly unequal. To take just one example, minority-owned firms are less likely to receive loans, less likely to apply for them for fear of rejection, and more likely to pay higher interest rates than nonminority-owned firms. The amount of equity

[50] Diyi Li and Cory Koedel, "Representation and Salary Gaps by Race-Ethnicity and Gender at Selective Public Universities," *Educational Researcher*, Vol. 46, No. 7, 2017.

[51] Emily Arnim, "A Third of Minority Students Leave STEM Majors: Here's Why," EAB, October 8, 2019.

[52] Noah Smith, "America, Land of Equal Opportunity? Still Not There," Bloomberg, April 3, 2018.

[53] Jared Bernstein, "Improving Economic Opportunity in the United States," testimony before the U.S. Congressional Joint Economic Committee, April 5, 2017; Institute for Research on Poverty, "Many Rural Americans Are Still 'Left Behind,'" January 2020.

[54] Jack Goldstone (2009, p. 159) argues that part of the genius of the British system in the Industrial Revolution was that the "adoption of the experimental method and the availability of the latest scientific findings turned craftspeople and instrument makers into modern engineers." The idea is that average people could be investors, working engineers were conversant with the latest scientific breakthroughs, and everyone was endeavoring to push knowledge and innovation forward. It was a highly inclusive, grassroots-powered economic engine.

investment they receive is smaller.[55] Although the evidence is mixed, rural areas also appear to suffer from unequal access to capital, especially in the venture and "angel" categories.[56]

A second category of data also suggests reasons for concern: the growth of income and wealth inequality in the United States. As Chapter Five explained, inequality is not perfectly correlated with opportunity. Historically, some societies (from the rising period of the Ottoman Empire to Victorian England) have combined dramatic gaps in wealth and privilege with significant avenues for advancement for people from many parts of society. Indeed, some of our competitively successful nations have existed with, or lived through periods of, striking inequality. The United States only recently returned to levels of inequality last seen in the 1920s, for example. In world-leading Britain just before World War I, the top 10 percent of households by wealth "held a staggering 92 percent of all private wealth, crowding out pretty much everybody else."[57]

Nonetheless, a society becoming more unequal will surely be erecting some new barriers to shared opportunity in some overarching ways. Research has linked inequality to both limits on opportunity and anticompetitive economic outcomes, such as slowed economic growth. The very perception of inequality can become a barrier to citizens feeling empowered to claim shared opportunity.

The numbers on trends in U.S. levels of inequality are clear and daunting. Between 2001 and 2016, the median net worth of America's middle class fell by 20 percent and the working class by 45 percent: "Even after multiple economic expansions, the total net worth of the bottom 50 percent of Americans is 20 percent less than it was in 1990. The top 1 percent of families has $41 trillion in assets."[58] As Walter Scheidel—in his magisterial history of inequality across the centuries—puts it:

> The wealthiest twenty Americans currently own as much as the bottom half of their country's households taken together, and the top 1 percent of incomes account for about a fifth of the national total. And to the one who has, more will be given: in the United States, the best-earning 1 percent of the top 1 percent (those in the highest 0.01 percent income

---

[55] Robert W. Fairlie and Alicia M. Robb, *Disparities in Capital Access Between Minority and Non-Minority-Owned Businesses*, Washington, D.C.: U.S. Department of Commerce, Minority Business Development Agency, January 2010. See also Robert W. Fairlie, Alicia Robb, and David T. Robinson, "Black and White: Access to Capital Among Minority-Owned Startups," Cambridge, Mass.: National Bureau of Economic Research, Working Paper 28154, November 2020.

[56] Alicia Robb, "Rural Entrepreneurship and the Challenges Accessing Financial Capital: An Overview of Funding in Rural America," presentation to the Small Business Capital Formation Advisory Committee, November 16, 2021.

[57] Scheidel, 2018, p. 18.

[58] Ron Ivey and Tim Shirk, "Ending America's Antisocial Contract," *American Affairs*, Vol. 5, No. 3, Fall 2021.

bracket) raised their share to almost six times what it had been in the 1970s even as the top tenth of that group (the top 0.1 percent) quadrupled it.[59]

Scheidel adds that 60 percent of all income growth between 1979 and 2007 went to the top 1 percent of the income bracket; the bottom 90 percent of Americans as measured by income received only 9 percent of that income growth.[60]

Such inequality translates directly into unequal opportunity. One study finds that *noncollege* graduates who are the children of wealthy parents are two and a half times more likely to have high incomes as adults than poor college graduates.[61] Other research suggests that inequality is directly tied to declining intergenerational mobility. As shown in Figure 10.2,

FIGURE 10.2

Percentage of Children Earning More Than Their Parents, by Year of Birth

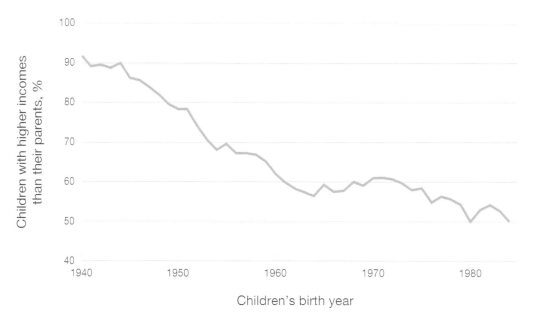

SOURCE: Chetty et al., 2016.

---

[59] Scheidel, 2018, p. 17.

[60] Scheidel, 2018, p. 431.

[61] Bernstein, 2017. Two analysts refer to "the decline of economic mobility," in part because the "hoarding of wealth and opportunity became geographically entrenched," and children in poor neighborhoods "were becoming less and less likely to exit poverty and succeed in life." Meantime tax policy has become even more focused on aiding the wealthy, with the richest 5 percent of Americans getting 43 percent of the 2017 tax cuts the year after they were passed—a number that will rise to 99 percent by 2027. One result is that 99 percent of Americans pay over double the tax rate as the wealthiest 1 percent (Ivey and Shirk, 2021).

Raj Chetty and coauthors note the negative trend: Each successive postwar generation has been less likely to make more than their parents.[62]

This entrenched and growing inequality may correlate with a related trend—the intensification of barriers between the rich and the rest of society. A significant vein of recent social criticism has been that class divides in the United States are hardening while opportunity is narrowing. Ross Douthat argues that

> from New York to London, Paris to San Francisco, our upper class is not only richer and bigger but also more self-segregated and well defended than fifty years ago—flocking to the same unchanging list of grade-inflated elite schools, planting themselves in the same small group of "global" cities, concentrating their privileged families in exclusive neighborhoods protected by stringent zoning rules, defending their turf by pricing out everyone except the necessary service class, which is largely composed of immigrants welcomed because they'll work harder for less money than the upper class's fellow countrymen. Small wonder that mobility and entrepreneurship are declining: if you're an outsider to, say, Silicon Valley, you can't "go West" to pursue the opportunities it offers if you can't afford to live and work there.[63]

Those are broad and qualitative claims, but they are backed up by a range of statistics that highlight continuing and even intensifying divisions between the wealthy and others in society. Elite U.S. universities, for example, give significant admissions preferences to "legacy" students, locking in a generational bias.[64] The number of Americans, especially from the wealthy or upper middle class, living in gated communities has grown in recent years.[65] Wealthy Americans are seeking out private schools for their children, and the decline of Catholic and other less expensive private alternatives means that private education has become more limited to the elite. In turn, a vastly disproportionate number of students at elite Ivy League colleges have attended private secondary school: roughly a quarter as of

[62] Raj Chetty, David Grusky, Maximilian Hell, Nathaniel Hendren, Robert Manduca, and Jimmy Narang, "The Fading American Dream: Trends in Absolute Income Mobility Since 1940," *Science*, Vol. 356, No. 6336, December 2016.

[63] Douthat, 2020, pp. 31–32. The Nobel Prize–winning economist Edmund Phelps and coauthors similarly argue, "It must be said that it is not only the decline in relative wages that has aroused anger among middle-income workers. It is also the corruption, barriers to competition, cronyism, and other obstacles that have blocked these people's sense of having a 'fair shot.' They lack the connections, or 'strings,' that they—for the most part—would need to get ahead" (Phelps et al., 2020, p. 203).

[64] Daniel A. Gross, "How Elite U.S. Schools Give Preference to Wealthy and White 'Legacy' Applicants," *The Guardian*, January 23, 2019. As of 2021, as one report concludes, "over a quarter of Harvard freshmen come from families that are wealthier than 94 percent of Americans. Nearly half have parents that make double the U.S. average"; see Amy Y. Li, "Freshmen Skew Wealthy, as Always: Harvard Isn't Helping," *Harvard Crimson*, September 15, 2021.

[65] Andrew Stark, *Drawing the Line: Public and Private in America*, Washington, D.C.: Brookings Institution Press, 2009, Ch. 1; Keith C. Veal, "The Gating of America: The Political and Social Consequences of Gated Communities on the Body Politic," dissertation, University of Michigan, 2013.

2021.[66] Inflated real estate and rental prices in major urban areas constrain opportunity for Americans who cannot afford sky-high housing costs.[67]

The scholars Anne Case and Angus Deaton catalog disturbing evidence of one outcome related to rising inequality and constrained opportunity: the rise of "deaths of despair" in the United States, such as opioid overdose and suicide. Gaps between rich and poor, symbolized by such distinctions as college degrees, are not merely economic issues; they also have implications for human identity and dignity. Case and Deaton's most recent research found that for White Americans, "the age-adjusted alcohol-related mortality rate increased by 41 percent between 2013 and 2019 for those aged 25–74 without a BA, the suicide rate climbed by 17 percent, and the drug-related mortality rate increased by a stunning 73 percent." Drug-related mortality among Black and Hispanic Americans without a college degree doubled in the same period. "We see the increasing mortality and declining adult life expectancy of less-educated Americans," they conclude, "not only as a catastrophe in its own right but as a powerful indicator that American society is not working for the majority of its population."[68]

These trends can undermine other societal sources of competitive advantage. A strict distinction between haves and have-nots poisons the essential tolerance at the core of a pluralistic society.[69] Over the long term, such trends can also spark social conflict. Using extensive historical comparative examples, Peter Turchin claims that political instability is associated with a toxic mix of inequality, stagnating wages, and rising debt. "Historically," he argues, "such developments have served as leading indicators of looming political instability."[70]

Finally, we considered evidence about social mobility, both inter- and intragenerational. The balance sheet for U.S. performance in this domain, according to the best available evidence, shows signals of concern alongside evidence of stability. In a major recent OECD study, the mobility of the United States, while not as strong when measured by earnings and health indicators, still compared well with other OECD countries when assessed by intergenerational education and occupation mobility.[71] The World Economic Forum's global social

---

[66] Alia Wong, "Private Schools Are Becoming More Elite," *The Atlantic*, July 26, 2018. See also Caitlin Flanagan, "Private Schools Have Become Truly Obscene," *The Atlantic*, April 2021.

[67] Edward J. Glaeser and David Cutler, "The American Housing Market Is Stifling Mobility," *Wall Street Journal*, September 2, 2021.

[68] Anne Case and Angus Deaton, "The Death Divide: Education, Despair, and Death," Cambridge, Mass.: National Bureau of Economic Research, Working Paper 29241, September 2021, p. 2.

[69] "Political systems have effectively come to represent two kinds of elites—the well-educated and the rich," and in the process "they have left little space for the expression of the interests of the most disadvantaged citizens." Amory Gethin, Clara Martínez-Toledano, and Thomas Piketty, "How Politics Became a Contest Dominated by Two Kinds of Elite," *The Guardian*, August 5, 2021a.

[70] Peter Turchin, "Correspondence: Political Instability May Be a Contributor in the Coming Decade," *Nature*, Vol. 463, February 2010. See also Amory Gethin, Clara Martínez-Toledano, and Thomas Piketty, *Political Cleavages and Social Inequalities: A Study of Fifty Democracies, 1948–2020*, Cambridge, Mass.: Harvard University Press, 2021b.

[71] OECD, 2018, p. 38.

mobility report ranks the United States 27th, mostly behind small, more homogenous countries in Europe but also behind France, Germany, Britain, and South Korea. But the differences are mostly slight: The U.S. score is 70.4, with Denmark in first at 85.2 and bigger countries (e.g., France, Japan, Australia, and Canada) scoring in the mid-70s.[72]

When we look at social mobility and opportunity for specific segments of the population, we find significant degrees of improvement over the last half century. This is not at all to imply that opportunity is now equal or that forms of discrimination have been fully surmounted. The claim here is very narrow and specific: Relative to the situation in 1900 or even 1950, the opportunities enjoyed by women and minorities in the United States have measurably improved. The gender gap in schooling, for example, not only closed but in fact female students now achieve higher average rates of schooling than male students.[73]

Yet there are also worrisome trends here. One recent study looks at U.S. intergenerational mobility during the whole 20th century. It finds various sources of improved mobility in the early and middle parts of the century but suggests that the midcentury leap was not sustained.[74] Perception of shared opportunity can be as important as the objective reality. And in this regard, the trend is unambiguously negative: Americans increasingly believe that their society constrains opportunity to those with wealth, power, and position.

Characteristic 4: An Active State

A challenge in assessing the U.S. standing on this characteristic is to identify the minimum or desirable level of state action to support competition. More is not necessarily better, and any comprehensive judgment about the sufficiency of the U.S. active state today would have to try to estimate the potential value of more state activity in specific issue areas—e.g., education, industrial protection, trade promotion, and R&D spending. That is beyond the scope of our analysis. More research would be required to identify objective shortcomings in the potential contributions of an active state, including a ground-up evaluation of the policies undertaken by the federal and state governments to support national competitiveness.

The evidence that does exist does, however, lend itself to several conclusions. Taken together, the data suggest that the United States is leaving significant competitive advantage on the shelf by undershooting the possible gains to be achieved by a slightly more active state.

---

[72] World Economic Forum, 2020.

[73] Wittgenstein Centre for Demography and Global Human Capital, "Wittgenstein Centre Data Explorer," version 2.0, undated.

[74] Elisa Jácome, Ilyana Kuziemko, and Suresh Naidu, "Mobility for All: Representative Intergenerational Mobility Estimates over the 20th Century," Cambridge, Mass.: National Bureau of Economic Research, Working Paper 29289, September 2021.

One specific measure of an active state is support for innovation, and this is lagging in the United States, at least in the public sphere.[75] Figure 10.3 shows the overall national picture. At the federal level, the trend is more decidedly negative. One estimate suggests that federal R&D spending will lose $95 billion between 2013 and 2021 because of cuts from sequestration.[76] Federal funding of research in physical sciences declined 45 percent between 1976 and 2004.[77]

Some experts argue that a public role in this area is unnecessary because private R&D has grown to make up the gap. Yet recent years have seen a decline in research designed to generate breakthrough technologies and products in favor of shorter-term efforts to generate additional profit from existing capacities. Private R&D is also increasingly offshored: One study finds that in recent years U.S. foreign affiliates grew their R&D spending 50 percent

FIGURE 10.3

R&D Spending, United States and China, 2000–2018, as Percentage of GDP

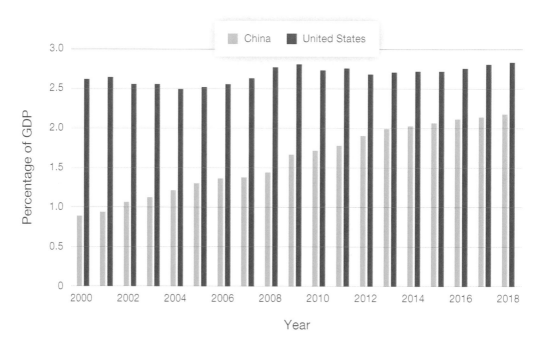

SOURCE: World Bank, "Research and Development Expenditure (% of GDP)," September 2021b.

---

[75] Robert D. Atkinson, "How the U.S. Government Falters on Support for Innovation," Information Technology and Innovation Foundation, August 28, 2019.

[76] Mazzucato, 2015, p. 14.

[77] Vijg, 2011, p. 218.

faster than the U.S.-based parent company.[78] And research by MIT and others suggests that the decline of corporate labs, such as PARC and Bell Labs, has helped to dampen the energy of R&D and innovation; within a highly bureaucratic firm structure, these labs provided islands of less constrained innovative thinking and experimentation.[79]

Moreover, private-sector R&D cannot fully take the place of an active state in promoting innovation. The technologies or capabilities essential for national competitive advantage are often different from those that firms see as advantageous for improved market performance. A good example emerged in the COVID-19 pandemic: Pharmaceutical firms might have lacked sufficient business incentive to pursue a consistent program of anticipatory research before the crisis, either for vaccines or for therapeutic treatments, that might have left the United States better protected earlier in the crisis.

A second measure of an active state might assess policies in specific issue areas, identifying socioeconomic and security challenges and evaluating the degree to which the American state is energetically responding. In at least several such issue areas—many of which center on information competitions—the U.S. government is not taking full advantage of the opportunity of boosting competitive standing; see Table 10.2. Partly this is a result of an across-the-board stagnation in major national legislation that will be discussed in the next section. Simply put, the U.S. government is not actively and productively engaging with many of the major barriers to competitive position.

There are signs, prompted by considerations around the China threat and concerns about disinformation, that the U.S. government is beginning to embrace a more active role. There is much more urgency around information security, with new offices being formed to deal with it, new coordination mechanisms being developed, and a consideration of new national policies to improve research and innovation. In the area of economic competition, the formation of the International Development Finance Corporation from several existing agencies and the creation of a pool of $60 billion in investment funds in various categories, along with the creation of the Blue Dot Network to promote transparent, high-quality infrastructure investments, constituted important moves in the direction of a more active international economic policy.[80] These totals remain relatively small compared with China's Belt and Road Initiative,

---

[78] Sainsbury, 2020, p. 188.

[79] Mazzucato, 2015, p. 31.

[80] See U.S. Department of State, "Blue Dot Network," webpage, undated. One recent example of the potential for a more active state role in promoting U.S. competitive position was the June 2021 Senate passage of a $250 billion technology package, known as the U.S. Innovation and Competition Act (S.1260), advertised to counter China but including investments in many areas of technology. As of this writing, the bill has not passed the House, which has somewhat different and complementary legislation pending. Partly as reflected by this legislation, the debate over "industrial policy" has also been shifting, seeming to clear the way for some additional active state measures to promote competition. Jared Cohon, Mary Sue Coleman, and Robert Conn, "US Innovation and Competition Act Will Ensure Continued US Leadership," *The Hill*, September 7, 2021.

TABLE 10.2

Competitive Issue Areas and Current Responses

Policy Area	Current U.S. Government Response
Cybersecurity	Intensifying, but by general agreement still not decisive or coordinated enough; no clear strategy combining norms and diplomacy with resilience
Disinformation and corrupted information environment	Still weak; only beginning to confront problem; no definition of standards of digital citizenship or consensus on legal framework to address problems
Global information competition	No core U.S. government institution on the model of the U.S. Information Agency; no clear strategy for contesting global narratives; weak tools for doing so
Global economic competition	Some initial actions with the formation of the Blue Dot Network and the International Development Finance Corporation
Productive investment	No national consensus on moving from short-term share value model or limiting such profit-sweeping tools as stock buybacks
Climate security	Federal and state roles in laws and investments growing, but investments modest relative to potential threat; opportunity to gain competitive advantage through climate technologies

however, and the U.S. economic responses to Chinese influence and belligerence remain slow and halting.

One signal of the continuing potential of the U.S. government to catalyze action emerged in some institutional elements of the U.S. government in dealing with the COVID-19 pandemic. That role, while imperfect and at times controversial, at least in several of its elements reflected an active use of state power for national benefit. The author David Adler catalogs the many achievements of some components of Operation Warp Speed in the U.S. response to the COVID-19 pandemic—developing and distributing huge numbers of vaccines in record time. The experience "demonstrates the strength of the U.S. developmental state," he argues, "despite forty years of ideological assault."[81] Another writer argues that, to deal with the economic fallout of the pandemic, the

> American fiscal state was rumbling to life. American fiscal policy has largely been dormant since the Reagan revolution, largely restricted to tax policy and military spending. . . . The first CARES [Coronavirus Aid, Relief, and Economic Security] Act and ensuing stimuli were a radical departure from the previous policy regime. Just as importantly, the Federal Reserve changed its stance to prioritize employment over a strict inflation target of 2%. These policies worked. Instead of a feared repeat of the Great Depression,

---

[81] David Adler, "Inside Operation Warp Speed: A New Model for Industrial Policy," *American Affairs*, Vol. 5, No. 2, Summer 2021.

the American economy has remained largely stable and prosperous, considering the circumstances.

This author concludes that "the United States has more state capacity than we imagined at the start of the pandemic—it is simply that some of the muscles of the state have not been exercised, while others have not been put to use."[82]

In sum, although there is no objective measure of the right size and shape of an effective active state, the U.S. government appears to be well short of that threshold in relation to several critical issues of competitive standing. But the nation retains tremendous latent power and capability and, in some areas, has begun to act more energetically to promote its competitive position.

Characteristic 5: Effective Institutions

Data related to effective institutions demonstrate a similar pattern—an enduring foundation of well-established institutions held to be generally transparent, effective, and legitimate on global rankings, alongside concerning recent trends.

Although perceptions of institutional quality have declined, for example, the studies that attempt to measure and assess U.S. institutional quality and effectiveness have remained unchanged for some time. Several indexes provide such a portrait of the quality of U.S. governance institutions. Transparency International's Corruption Perception Index, for example, reviews 13 sources of data on perceived corruption levels and offers results on a scale of 0–100, where 0 equals the highest level of perceived corruption and 100 equals the lowest level of perceived corruption. The U.S. score has hovered around 70–75, a strong showing, especially for a large and diverse nation. It did dip to 69 in 2019, a five-point decline from two years earlier and a concerning trend that bears watching.[83] But the basic message of this index is that the United States is a nation whose institutions retain some key aspects of effectiveness—transparency and relative honesty.

A similar theme emerges in the World Bank's Governance Effectiveness Indicators.[84] This index plots results on a scale of –2.5 to +2.5: "perceptions of the quality of public services, the quality of the civil service and the degree of its independence from political pressures, the quality of policy formulation and implementation, and the credibility of the government's commitment to such policies." The index (Figure 10.4) shows the United States remaining roughly stable since 2000, with a very slight decline that bears watching.[85]

---

[82] Yakov Feygin, "The American Fiscal State Rumbles to Life," *Noema*, April 27, 2021.

[83] Transparency International, "Corruption Perception Index, 2020," undated.

[84] World Bank, "Worldwide Governance Indicators," undated-a.

[85] The World Bank also compiles the Governance Effectiveness Indicators, a data set that "reflects perceptions of the extent to which agents have confidence in and abide by the rules of society, and in particular

FIGURE 10.4

U.S. Governance Effectiveness Index

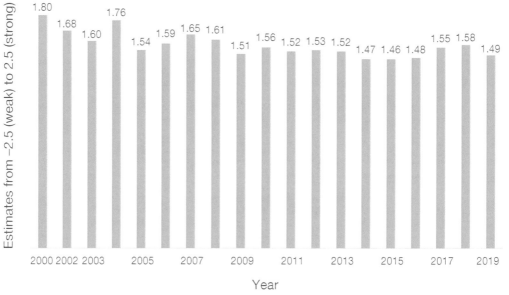

SOURCE: World Bank, undated-a.

The same pattern shows up in the oft-discussed metric of trust in major social institutions. As Figure 10.5 indicates, there has been some drop-off since the 1990s, but the broader pattern can best be characterized as stagnation trending slightly in the wrong direction.

Somewhat in tension with these global rankings, some scholars argue that large U.S. bureaucratic institutions have over the past several decades proved repeatedly incoherent or incompetent at managing major national crises or issues. Paul Light, one of the country's leading experts on governance, argues in a 2014 assessment that failures in government policy and crisis response have become more common over time. He writes that the rate of "major failures" was accelerating, from about one to one and a half per year under the Ronald Reagan and George H. W. Bush administrations to around three per year under George W. Bush and Barack Obama. Failures included the September 11 attack, Hurricane Katrina, and the 2008 financial crisis.[86]

---

the quality of contract enforcement, property rights, the police, and the courts, as well as the likelihood of crime and violence." On the same scale (–2.5 to +2.5), the U.S. rating has hovered right about 1.5 for some 20 years. This index again shows a slight dip in 2018–2019, though this may recover, given recent political trends.

[86] Paul C. Light, *A Cascade of Failures: Why Government Fails, and How to Stop It*, Washington, D.C.: Brookings Institution, Center for Effective Public Management, July 2014.

FIGURE 10.5

Average Confidence Ratings for Major U.S. Institutions

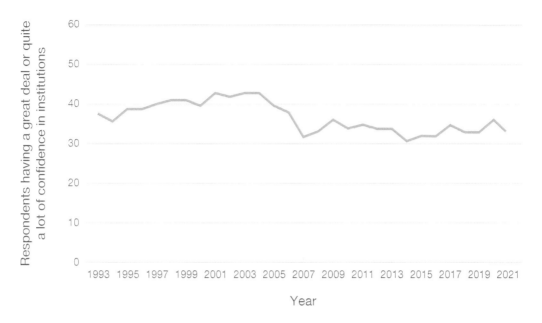

SOURCE: Gallup; see Brenan, 2021.
NOTE: Gallup computed the average from 14 institutions that it has polled yearly from 1993 to 2021.

Other examples of institutional ineffectiveness seem increasingly commonplace. U.S. federal investment projects, whether defense or nondefense, are typically characterized by massive cost overruns and administrative complexity.[87] Effective, coherent responses increasingly tend only to emerge in crises, and not always even then.[88] To some degree, institutional effectiveness may be constrained by an ever-constricting web of regulations, laws, and rules that govern public policy, a deepening bureaucratic quicksand that imposes inefficiencies and suppresses innovation and growth. This trend is not limited to government: A parallel superstructure of rules, regulations, processes, forms, and other constraints has sprouted up in the private sector. This, too, can be difficult to quantify in objective terms, but it is a trend

---

[87] Alon Levy, "What Is the Cost of Building a Subway?" presentation, *Pedestrian Observations*, November 19, 2019. The result, to take just one example, is that the per-mile cost of railroads is significantly higher in the United States: It costs an astonishing $550 million per kilometer to build a rail network in the United States, compared with $300 million in Germany or Taiwan, about $250 million in France, and well under $200 million in Italy, Israel, and Japan. See Jerusalem Demsas, "Why Does It Cost So Much to Build Things in America?" *Vox*, June 28, 2021. See also Urban C. Lehner, "Can Slow-Building Democracies Compete with China?" *Asia Times*, August 23, 2021.

[88] Daniel Immerwahr, "The Strange, Sad Death of America's Political Imagination," *New York Times*, July 2, 2021.

that crops up in analyses from a host of disciplines. We summarize this evidence in the following pages.

In many ways this danger represents an updated and modified version of Mancur Olson's classic thesis about the deepening bureaucratization and "social rigidities" that emerge over the long term, which was cited in Chapter Seven. "Stable societies with unchanged boundaries," he argues, "tend to accumulate more collusions and organizations for collective action over time."[89] Single-issue organizations tend to reduce the efficiency and standard of living in countries, to create more political divisions, and to constrain innovation.[90] Olson's analysis would lead us to expect such a trend in a mature industrial society like the United States and thus raise concerns about the country's future dynamism.

There has been a good deal of critical commentary about Olson's prediction. He holds these rigidities to blame for slowing growth in major economies,[91] but research since the publication of his book does not consistently uphold the idea that growth slows over time as institutions accumulate—the relationship is simply not that linear.[92] Yet a growing body of evidence does suggest that very large public and private social institutions have become so regulated and rationalized as to constrain individual initiative and innovation. In more abstract terms, this speaks to a society in which rule-following under the shadow of immense organizations and risk suppression becomes the dominant value. This is an argument not about "big government" but rather about bureaucratic sclerosis running through public, private, and charitable institutions of the whole society.[93]

The management scholar Gary Hamel studies the growth and effect of bureaucracy in the private sector. He and coauthor Michele Zanini argue that excess management and red-tape cost $3 trillion *per year* in lost output in the United States. They provide telling figures: The proportion of Americans working for large organizations (more than 500 people) grew from 47 percent to almost 52 percent between 1993 and 2013. During the same period, whereas general employment grew 40 percent, the number of managerial positions grew almost 200 percent. By 2014, almost 14 percent of the U.S. workforce held positions classified as managerial or supervisory. More than 5 million held administrative positions: "That's a bureaucratic class of 23.8 million people, with one manager/administrator for every 4.7 work-

---

[89] Olson, 1982, p. 41.

[90] Olson, 1982, p. 47.

[91] Olson writes, "Of two societies that were in other respects equal, the one with the longer history of stability, security, and freedom of association would have more institutions that limit entry and innovation." One result is that "there has been a strong and systematic relationship between the length of time a state has been settled and its rate of growth of both per capita and total income. . . . [T]he longer a state has been settled and the longer the time it has had to accumulate special-interest groups, the slower its rate of growth" (Olson, 1982, pp. 87, 97).

[92] Theresa Hager, "Special Interest Groups and Growth: A Meta-Analysis of Mancur Olson's Theory," working paper, Linz, Austria: Institute for Comprehensive Analysis of the Economy, September 2020.

[93] For a related argument, see Michael J. Mazarr, "Abstract Systems and Social Trust," *American Affairs*, Vol. 6, No. 1, Spring 2022.

ers." Their research on internal corporate activity leads them to conclude that "roughly half of all bureaucratic work adds little or no value."[94] Hamel argues that the costs of these management layers include delay, inefficiency, a "hefty tax" in the form of overhead costs, and an autocratic constraint on employee activities.[95]

Hamel and Zanini conducted a survey of more than 7,000 U.S. business executives. One question was about the degree of bureaucratic bloat: On their 1–100 Bureaucratic Mass Index (BMI), where scores over 60 indicate excess bureaucracy, 64 percent of respondents tallied a BMI of over 70, and less than *1 percent* scored under 40. The average score for large organizations was 75. Two-thirds of respondents reported that their organizations had become more bureaucratic over the past year; only 13 percent said that the organizations had become less bureaucratic. In terms of the negative effects of these trends,

> BMI survey-takers reported spending an average of 28% of their time—more than one day a week—on bureaucratic chores such as preparing reports, attending meetings, complying with internal requests, securing sign offs and interacting with staff functions. Moreover, a significant portion of that work seems to be creating little or no value. Less than 40% of respondents found typical bureaucratic processes (e.g. budgeting, goal-setting, performance reviews) to be "very helpful."[96]

This crushing weight of bureaucracy also constrains innovation: "Only 20% of respondents said that unconventional ideas were greeted with interest or enthusiasm in their organization. Eighty percent said new ideas were likely to encounter indifference, skepticism, or outright resistance."[97]

Beyond these general estimates of administrative functions, recent analyses and surveys provide abundant evidence of the pervasiveness of excess bureaucracy and its costs:

- The Boston Consulting Group's index of "complicatedness" shows that "companies have increased the level of bureaucracy by approximately 7 percent annually—compounded for the last five decades."[98] Analysts at the firm have argued that the "underlying" cause of declining U.S. productivity has been "the ongoing, long-term rise of complicatedness," which they define as "the increase in organizational structures, processes, pro-

---

[94] Gary Hamel and Michele Zanini, "Bureaucracy: Where to Liberate $3 Trillion," *London Business School Review*, September 4, 2017b. See also Gary Hamel and Michele Zanini, "Excess Management Is Costing the U.S. $3 Trillion per Year," *Harvard Business Review*, September 5, 2016.

[95] Gary Hamel, "First, Let's Fire All the Managers," *Harvard Business Review*, December 2011.

[96] Gary Hamel and Michele Zanini, "What We Learned About Bureaucracy from 7,000 HBR Readers," *Harvard Business Review*, August 10, 2017a.

[97] Hamel and Zanini, 2017a.

[98] Fredrik Erixon and Björn Weigel, "Capitalism Without Capitalists," *American Affairs*, Vol. 1, No. 3, Fall 2017, p. 12; see Reinhard Messenböck, Yves Morieux, Jaap Backx, and Donat Wunderlich, "How Complicated Is Your Company," Boston Consulting Group, January 16, 2018.

cedures, decision rights, metrics, scorecards, and committees that companies impose to manage the escalating complexity of their external business environment." Their research suggests that such increases in administrative complexity "hampers growth by slowing innovation and the deployment of new products and services. And it cuts margins by injecting inefficiency and cost into operations"; their research finds that companies with lower complicatedness perform measurably better on these metrics.[99]

- A Deloitte study from Australia finds that employees spend almost a fifth of their time on "internal compliance" tasks, between 12 and 24 percent of which were unnecessary. If this were applied to the U.S. economy, it would amount to a waste of 3.2 million person-years.[100]

- Doctors, who were once "not hesitant to take initiative in developing new treatments," are today too busy with paperwork, and too restricted by regulatory demands and the threat of lawsuits, to experiment very much.[101]

- The "institutional sclerosis and bureaucratic ossification" in the U.S. intelligence and national security communities prevented the sharing of information and agile response to warning before September 11, 2001.[102]

- Obscure and incredibly dense bureaucratic processes surrounding U.S. arms transfers, defense coproduction, and other military cooperation processes make it very difficult for allies to work with the United States.[103]

- In U.S. universities, the growth of managerial and administrative positions has out-paced the rise of teaching and advising jobs. In 1981, U.S. universities spent 26 percent of their budgets on administrative and overhead expenses and 41 percent on instruction. By 2011, the categories were about even: 24 percent administrative and 29 percent instructional.[104] In the quarter century leading up to 2014, administrative positions at U.S. universities doubled, "vastly outpacing the growth in the number of students and faculty."[105] Even during the recession after 2008, the number of administrative jobs rose 15 percent amid college spending cuts.[106]

---

[99] Messenböck et al., 2018. This essay defines eight elements of a complicatedness index, including such issues as layers of management, clear versus obscure definition of roles, and the nature of staff development programs.

[100] Cited in Hamel and Zanini, 2017b.

[101] Vijgl, 2011, pp. 70–72.

[102] Ariel Cohen, "Intelligence Disaster, Bureaucratic Sclerosis," Heritage Foundation, September 16, 2001.

[103] Stephen Rodriguez, "The Fox in the Henhouse: How Bureaucratic Processes Handicap US Military Supremacy and What to Do About It," Atlantic Council, February 26, 2020.

[104] Caroline Smith, "Bureaucrats and Buildings: The Case for Why College Is So Expensive," *Forbes*, September 5, 2017.

[105] New England Center for Investigative Journalism, "New Analysis Shows Problematic Boom in Higher Ed Administrators," *Huffington Post*, February 6, 2014.

[106] Jon Marcus, "The Reason Behind Colleges' Ballooning Bureaucracies," *The Atlantic*, October 6, 2016.

- In 2017, U.S. health care providers spent more than $800 billion on administration, and administrative costs represented more than a third of total U.S. health care spending.[107]
- Bureaucracy slows and complicates medical research. One study from the United Kingdom finds that navigating various government health requirements delayed results by a year and increased costs between 30 and 40 percent.[108] A U.S. analysis of cancer research finds that the "proliferating complexity and unnecessary formalities involved in developing and testing cancer therapies have stifled innovation, driven up costs, and delayed development of new treatments." The impact of this process emerges in a stark statistic: The average cost of research exploded from $3,000–$5,000 per subject around 1990 to $75,000–$125,000 by 2013. Stifling bureaucracy also suppressed innovation, because studies aimed at incremental improvements on existing treatments may have easier routes to approval than bold and dramatic new approaches.[109]

That list is only the tip of the iceberg. There are thousands of similar examples of both the growth of bureaucratic control in the United States and its pernicious effects. Extended to a national level, these figures and themes clearly illustrate the ways in which the relative growth of bureaucracy becomes a drag on competitive advantage, and the competitive engine of the country becomes deeply enfeebled. This pattern emerges in many of our historical case studies. It attacks the lifeblood of any truly competitive society: the combination of openness to new ideas, learning orientation, tolerance for pluralism of ideas and perspectives and ambition for bold change. Gary Hamel explains that bureaucracies, in contrast, are "built to ensure conformity and predictability."[110]

Characteristic 6: A Learning and Adapting Society

To assess the current standing of this characteristic in the United States, we looked at data in a few major areas. The first was education: A learning society will tend to be one that values education at all levels and in all forms. As with prior civilizations, data on the role of education in American society can provide one indication of a learning mindset. In *The Economist*'s Worldwide Educating for the Future Index,[111] the U.S. score improved between 2018

---

[107] Linda Carroll, "More Than a Third of U.S. Healthcare Costs Go to Bureaucracy," Reuters, January 6, 2020.

[108] Helen Snooks, Hayley Hutchings, Anne Seagrove, Sarah Stewart-Brown, John Williams, and Ian Russell, "Bureaucracy Stifles Medical Research in Britain: A Tale of Three Trials," *BMC Medical Research Methodology*, Vol. 12, No. 1, 2012.

[109] David P. Steensma and Hagop M. Kantarjian, "Impact of Cancer Research Bureaucracy on Innovation, Costs, and Patient Care," *Journal of Clinical Oncology*, Vol. 32, No. 5, 2014.

[110] Hamel, 2011.

[111] Economist Intelligence Unit, *The Worldwide Educating for the Future Index 2019: A Benchmark for the Skills of Tomorrow*, London, 2019.

and 2019 and rated well, with an overall score of 58.9 in 2018 and 61.4 the following year. This is significantly below the very top performers, mostly northern European and Nordic countries, but consistent.

Yet here too we see evidence of stagnation. The mean for years of schooling in the United States has idled at about 13 and is not projected to change through 2040.[112] This will also contribute to continued stagnation in productivity levels.[113] The National Center for Education Statistics issues an annual report on the condition of American education, and many indicators in the 2021 report show basically flat lines over the last decade,[114] such as the percentage of three- to five-year-olds enrolled in school, overall school enrollment, school finances, and college enrollment rates. (There was one area that showed improvement: the precollege dropout level, which declined from 8.3 percent of children in 2010 to 5.1 percent in 2019.)

The National Assessment of Educational Progress's study, the largest national study of high school achievement, shows concerning results: The 2020 survey found that only 37 percent of American high school graduates could perform in both reading and math at levels that would be demanded in freshman-year college courses.[115] Data on science, technology, engineering, and mathematics outcomes in U.S. K–12 education are particularly mediocre, reflecting stagnation on testing results, while many U.S. economic competitors have improved their position.[116]

A second and potentially even greater long-term threat to the context for effective learning and adaptation is the corrosion of the information environment in U.S. society. Competitive societies are in many ways information-processing mechanisms, whose various components take insights about the world and turn them into behavior. The sort of dynamic interplay of ideas described in the introduction and Chapter Eight—a context in which competitive societies, both within their boundaries and in the bigger global environment, benefit from

---

[112] Wittgenstein Centre for Demography and Global Human Capital, undated.

[113] As one study concludes, "it will become increasingly difficult to increase the educational attainment of a labor force when the great majority of workers already have at least a high-school degree and a large portion have attended college" (Robert Shackleton, "Total Factor Productivity Growth in Historical Perspective," Washington, D.C.: Congressional Budget Office, Working Paper 2013–01, March 2013).

[114] Véronique Irwin, Jijun Zhang, Xiaolei Wang, Sarah Hein, Ke Wang, Ashley Roberts, Christina York, Amy Barmer, Farrah Bullock Mann, Ritsa Dilig, and Stephanie Parker, *Report on the Condition of Education 2021*, Washington, D.C.: National Center for Education Statistics, May 2021.

[115] Lauren Camera, "Reading Scores Fall Among U.S. High School Seniors," *U.S. News and World Report*, October 28, 2020.

[116] In one example, the United States ranked 25th out of 27 OECD nations in math proficiency among 15-year-olds; see Allison Gillespie, "What Do the Data Say About the Current State of K–12 STEM Education in the US?" National Science Foundation, September 9, 2021. See also Drew Desilver, "U.S. Students' Academic Achievement Still Lags That of Their Peers in Many Other Countries," Pew Research Center, February 15, 2017; Bart Gordon, "U.S. Competitiveness: The Education Imperative," *Issues in Science and Technology*, Vol. 23, No. 3, Spring 2007.

being at the center of a rich and creative dialogue about science, technology, ethics, and other topics—requires a healthy information environment.

There is little question that the U.S. information marketplace is being corrupted in various ways.[117] Threats to the information environment include a growing virality and sensationalism of the media landscape, in which false information spreads very quickly and sensationalism spreads more quickly than truth; the fragmentation of information sources (a decline in trusted, mediating institutions of accurate information and the existence of multiple competing takes on reality); the related and growing role of echo chambers, silos of self-reinforcing knowledge sharing that can reinforce various biases and collective misapprehensions, as well as exacerbate social divisions; and the emergence of a "trolling ethic" that allows and encourages a level of hostility and mean-spiritedness as a consistent element of public discourse. "The result," one RAND report that outlines these trends concludes, "could be an infosphere that is increasingly disaggregated in ways that undermine social coherence, interconnected in ways that create networked vulnerabilities, and extreme and sensational in ways that persistently skew public perceptions and depress ontological security, trust in the future, and social institutions."[118]

By many measures, the proportion of misinformation and "fake news" in the public sphere has been growing. Websites promoting misinformation doubled as a share of social media engagements from 2019 to 2020, from 8 percent to 17 percent, while the total number of those engagements also doubled (from 8.6 billion to 16.3 billion).[119] Significant numbers of Americans adhere to conspiracy theories: more than 20 percent endorse various forms of coronavirus conspiracies,[120] 50 percent believe one major conspiracy theory,[121] and astonishingly, in 2021, 15 percent of Americans concurred with the basic claim of the fringe conspiracy theory QAnon—that U.S. society is run by "a group of Satan-worshipping pedophiles who run a global child sex trafficking operation."[122]

Some research is more reassuring, finding that the scale of misinformation remains more limited than these figures would indicate.[123] One large-scale study found that Americans still rely on television for news five times as much as social media, and that identifiably "fake"

---

[117] Alesina et al., 2020.

[118] Michael J. Mazarr, Ryan Bauer, Abigail Casey, Sarah Heintz, and Luke J. Matthews, *The Emerging Risk of Virtual Societal Warfare: Social Manipulation in a Changing Information Environment*, Santa Monica, Calif.: RAND Corporation, RR-2714-OSD, 2019, p. 40.

[119] Emily Stewart, "America's Growing Fake News Problem, in One Chart," *Vox*, December 22, 2020.

[120] Rainer Zitelman, "How Many Americans Believe in Conspiracy Theories?" *Forbes*, June 29, 2020.

[121] J. Eric Oliver and Thomas J. Wood, "Conspiracy Theories and the Paranoid Style(s) of Mass Opinion," *American Journal of Political Science*, Vol. 58, No. 4, 2014.

[122] Chuck Todd, Mark Murray, and Carrie Dann, "Study Finds Nearly One-in-Five Americans Believe QAnon Conspiracy Theories," NBC News, May 27, 2021.

[123] Even in 2020, with 2.8 billion social media engagements with websites judged not credible, there were 13.5 billion engagements with credible sites (Stewart, 2020).

stories accounted for just 0.15 percent of Americans' total media diet.[124] The trend, though, seems clear. More Americans are reaching for sources of information that—intentionally or not—spread large-scale misinformation, and more Americans have become prey to conspiracy theories. The prevalence of misinformation across many platforms exposes more Americans to such claims.[125] The danger is also rising in part because powerful social actors are working to advance rather than combat them, believing, apparently, that they benefit from a world in which the concept of truth has been fatally weakened.[126] Private firms and individual entrepreneurs have now gotten into the business of "disinformation for hire," intensifying the collapse of the public knowledge sphere[127] and practicing a sort of "weaponized misinformation."[128] "Disinformation has become an industry," argues Joan Donovan of the Harvard Shorenstein Center on Media, creating an environment of engineered fake news.[129]

A RAND report on Truth Decay focuses on a different angle of the fraying infosphere: not the presence of misinformation per se but the degree of disagreement and lack of commitment to shared reality in environments where objective facts are available.[130] The American public is not simply misinformed about some key policy issues; it is increasingly mistrustful of experts and intermediaries who provide mediating sources of factual data.[131]

These trends are sapping the health of several societal characteristics essential for competitive success. The trends undermine a sense of unified national identity, for example, by

---

[124] Jennifer Allen, Baird Howland, Markus Mobius, David Rothschild, and Duncan J. Watts, "Evaluating the Fake News Problem at the Scale of the Information Ecosystem," *Science Advances*, Vol. 6, No. 14, April 2020.

[125] Melissa Chan, "Conspiracy Theories Might Sound Crazy, but Here's Why Experts Say We Can No Longer Ignore Them," *Time*, August 15, 2019.

[126] This political strategy has roots in the behavior of the tobacco industry in the 1970s and 1980s, which sought to undermine public awareness of and confidence in the growing scientific consensus that smoking was destructive to health. The political concept that a given political party may benefit from a destabilization of objective public discourse can be traced in part to the theories of the political consultant Frank Luntz. Infamously, Luntz sought to undermine the early scientific consensus on global warming by rebranding it as "climate change" and calling into question the science behind the trend. See Oliver Burkeman, "Memo Exposes Bush's New Green Strategy," *The Guardian*, March 3, 2003.

[127] Max Fisher, "Disinformation for Hire, a Shadow Industry, Is Quietly Booming," *New York Times*, July 25, 2021.

[128] Ari Rabin-Havt and Media Matters, *Lies, Incorporated: The World of Post-Truth Politics*, New York: Anchor Books, 2016.

[129] Quoted in Miles Parks, "Trump Is No Longer Tweeting, but Online Disinformation Isn't Going Away," NPR, March 5, 2021.

[130] Jennifer Kavanagh and Michael D. Rich, *Truth Decay: An Initial Exploration of the Diminishing Role of Facts and Analysis in American Public Life*, Santa Monica, Calif.: RAND Corporation, RR-2314-RC, 2018.

[131] Research has also shown how poor average citizens are at distinguishing fact from opinion and substantive information from advertisements. See, for example, Sam Wineburg, Sarah McGrew, Joel Breakstone, and Teresa Ortega, *Evaluating Information: The Cornerstone of Civic Online Reasoning*, Stanford, Calif.: Stanford History Education Group, 2016.

ruining shared narratives that help produce an equilibrium in national attitudes. There is substantial evidence that social media divisiveness spills over into political attitudes and the views of Americans toward one another.

A corrosion of a democracy's information environment also tends to weaken social institutions, especially but not solely those related to the sharing of information. The effect on media institutions is straightforward: The current fragmentation of the information landscape tends to undermine support for traditional media organizations. But the result of the current era of sensational disinformation has been to accelerate a decline in citizens' faith in social institutions of all kinds.

A corrupted information environment also has the effect of blocking full opportunity on the part of some Americans victimized or traumatized by the resulting extreme opinions. Misinformation has particularly targeted minority and less privileged groups, both in direct attacks (such as racist screeds) and in their effect on behavior.

Finally, the decay of the U.S. information environment disrupts the key elements of a learning culture. Intense echo chambers allow people to deny reality and fail to learn and adapt.[132] Forms of extremism and fundamentalism are the enemies of a learning mindset and social adaptation, and the spread of misinformation undermines Americans' accurate knowledge about their own society.[133]

From a competitive standpoint, a degraded information environment is far more than a mere inconvenience. It poses a potentially decisive threat to aspects of social functioning— that is, the networking of knowledge—that are historically essential to building and sustaining an economically, technologically, and strategically dynamic nation. If the ongoing dialogue, debate, and shared research and thinking endeavors of a dynamic society are fundamentally disrupted by a combination of misinformation, disinformation, biased echo chambers, and hostile attacks, the capacity of that society to generate competitive advantage may be critically impaired. The result, like today, was to undermine the dynamism of the society's engine of knowledge, its technical and economic creativity, and its competitive standing. For a democracy and pluralistic society that requires objective but also mutually respectful debate to thrive, no trend could be more dangerous.

Characteristic 7: Competitive Diversity and Pluralism

Ample data are available on the status of diversity and pluralism in the United States, but the challenge is relating them to competitive advantage and determining whether current levels

---

[132] Hämäläinen, 2003, pp. 61, 65.

[133] Jack Goldstone and Peter Turchin write, "Americans no longer have an accurate sense of their own society. For example, a poll showed that Americans, on average, think Muslims are seventeen times as large a portion of the U.S. population as they actually are. Another poll showed that most Americans think a majority of immigrants are in the country illegally (in fact, 77% of all immigrants have fully legal status)" (Goldstone and Turchin, 2020).

are sufficient for U.S. competitive goals. The United States is gradually becoming a more diverse country—one of the most thoroughly diverse nations on Earth. Given that the United States rose to global prominence with significantly less diversity than it now possesses, and that its essential forms of political pluralism remain largely the same, our baseline conclusion is that the United States rates sufficiently high on this characteristic for competition. If it won the Cold War as a much less diverse country, for example, it should be able to excel today.

Where shortcomings exist, they may relate more to an absence of shared opportunity rather than insufficient diversity. The competitive challenge for the United States is not becoming more diverse but in providing full opportunity for its various ethnic, racial, regional, class, gender, and other groups to realize their full potential.

The same can be said, for the most part, about pluralism. The United States gains competitive advantage because it is a collection of 50 state laboratories of governance (and, in fact, hundreds of metropolitan ones as well) that experiment with different solutions to public policy challenges and learn from each other's successes and failures. The innovative and adaptive energy in states and cities is a major source of the resilience of the U.S. system. This system remains as it has been in the postwar era and therefore ought to provide sufficient pluralistic energy for competitive purposes.

Other Competitive Influences: Factors Other Than Societal Characteristics

To assess the U.S. competitive position, we also briefly reviewed evidence relating to the factors laid out in Chapter Two—the factors *other than* societal characteristics that contribute to competitive success and failure. Some of these, such as natural disasters and geography, are outside the control of the United States. Others, such as America's role in networks of trade or intellectual exchange (especially relative to its competitors), continue to display some degree of strength. We present our overall assessment of these factors in Table 10.3; next, we focus on two issues that emerged from our research as significant potential competitive challenges: a decline in productive investment and unsustainable financial habits.

The Rise of Rent-Seeking Investment Behaviors

From an economic standpoint, one leading competitive risk to the United States is the decline of more-productive uses of capital in favor of various forms of rent seeking and profit grabbing. This is a core symptom of the larger society-wide phenomenon of coasting on accumulated success. Simply put, many private actors are devoting a significant proportion of their available capital to stock buybacks, gobbling up and then shutting down or absorbing potential competitors, dividend payments, and other actions designed to achieve two goals: protecting market position and maximizing share price.

TABLE 10.3

Nonsocietal Sources of National Competitive Advantage: Assessment

Factor	Components and Examples	Verdict
Demographic indicators	• Population growth rate • Dependency ratio	**Competitive advantage** relative to major rivals, partly due to immigration but still bad enough to generate fiscal challenges
Resilience indicators	• Ecological sustainability • Climate resilience • Disease preparedness • Natural disaster response and recovery	**Mixed and unclear status** because the United States remains very vulnerable, but so are major rivals; the United States is missing out on a major potential source of competitive advantage
National policies and characteristics underwriting economic strength	• National investment as a proportion of GDP • Degree of productive investment • Sustainable fiscal position in both public and private sectors	**Clear competitive challenges** and risks to U.S. ability to maintain competitive position; rivals have challenges as well
Role in international webs and networks	• Formal alliances • Informal coalitions, groupings • International institutions • Networks of economic exchange • Scientific and intellectual networks	**Mixed and unclear pattern** because the United States retains strong competitive advantage in most alliances and networks relative to major rivals, but China is gaining traction in many key networks: scientific research, 5G, trade, and finance
Sustainable energy sources	• Resilient, secure, reliable energy network • Competitive advantage in accessibility and sustainability of energy sources	**Mixed and unclear pattern** because China is ahead of the United States in some renewable technologies; security of U.S. energy network is in serious question

At first glance, data on levels of investment in the U.S. economy suggest a consistent and relatively strong trend. Overall levels of investment relative to other developed economies are reasonably good. As Figure 10.6 indicates, overall U.S. investment, apart from a collapse during the financial crisis, has generally run more than 20 percent of GDP.

Yet there is a bigger trend at work: Private firms are allocating a growing proportion of capital away from long-term product development and R&D and into stock buybacks and other forms of share-boosting activities. The resulting focus on quarterly returns drives companies to reduce investment in favor of acquisitions and stock buybacks.[134] American corporate behavior has shifted to "value extraction," finding ways to generate cash rather than investing in productive assets[135] in what one scholar has termed the "financialization of the

---

[134] Smithers, 2020.

[135] William Lazonick and Jang-sup Shin, *Predatory Value Extraction: How the Looting of the Business Corporation Became the U.S. Norm and How Sustainable Prosperity Can Be Restored*, New York: Oxford University Press, 2019. The philosopher Nancy Fraser argues, "Financialized capitalism . . . is a deeply predatory and unstable form of social organization, which liberates capital accumulation from the very constraints

FIGURE 10.6

Total U.S. Investment as Percentage of GDP

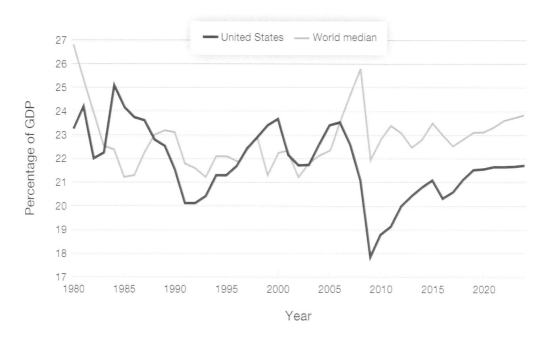

SOURCE: World Bank, "TCdata360: Total Investment (% of GDP)," undated-b.

American elite."[136] In the decade up to 2014, the Fortune 500 spent $4 trillion on stock buy-backs.[137] The pattern is evident even in industries heavily reliant on research, such as the pharmaceutical industry:

> In 2011, along with $6.2 billion paid in dividends, Pfizer repurchased $9 billion in stock, equivalent to 90 per cent of its net income and 99 per cent of its R&D expenditures. Indeed, from 2003 to 2012, Pfizer spent amounts equivalent to 71 per cent and 75 per cent of its profits, respectively, on share buybacks and dividends. Since 2002, the cost of Amgen's stock repurchases has surpassed the company's R&D expenditures in every year

---

(political, ecological, social, moral) needed to sustain it over time. . . . As social life as such is increasingly economized, the unfettered pursuit of profit destabilizes the very forms of social reproduction, ecological sustainability, and public power on which it depends. Seen this way, financialized capitalism is an inherently crisis-prone social formation. The crisis complex we encounter today is the increasingly acute expression of its built-in tendency toward self-destabilization" (Nancy Fraser, "From Progressive Neoliberalism to Trump—and Beyond," *American Affairs*, Vol. 1, No. 4, Winter 2017, p. 63; see also Matt Stoller, "The War Within Corporate America," *American Affairs*, Vol. 4, No. 1, Spring 2020).

[136] Sam Long, "The Financialization of the American Elite," *American Affairs*, Vol. 3, No. 3, Fall 2019.

[137] William Lazonick, "Profits Without Prosperity," *Harvard Business Review*, September 2014.

except 2004, and for the period 1992–2011 was equal to fully 115 per cent of R&D outlays and 113 per cent of net income.[138]

The incentives are now such that even corporate tax cuts often do not produce much new investment, only more buybacks. As the Bank of England governor Andrew Bailey put it in a 2020 speech, "We live in a time where there appears to be no shortage of aggregate saving, but investment is weak."[139]

A related issue is that so much of the private investment in the United States is now directed by a small number of institutional investors—hedge and pension funds, venture capitalists, major investment banks—who relentlessly seek short-term gains.[140] Such investors now own a majority of U.S. corporate stock and impose managerial rules for investment.[141] Their goals, while perfectly appropriate for their own institutional incentives, are not necessarily supportive of effective long-term competition as much as quarterly and annual stock price value. It may be that, even in a capitalist economy, outside investor control in some cases has an effect not unlike central control of state-owned enterprises in a closed system—imposing rules that restrict creative activity.

---

[138] Mazzucato, 2015, p. 32.

[139] Quoted in Robin Harding, "Pension Funds Need a Radical Rethink," *Financial Times*, January 5, 2020. One disturbing result is that a good deal of the rise of the U.S. stock market since the 1980s has in fact been a Potemkin economic phenomenon. Three economists assess the sources of stock price growth since the 1950s. They find that, between 1952 and about 1988, economic growth explained basically all the rise in equity prices. But since that time, though $34 trillion in share price value has been created, "44% of this increase was attributable to a reallocation of rewards to shareholders in a decelerating economy, primarily at the expense of labor compensation. Economic growth accounted for just 25%" (Daniel L. Greenwald, Martin Lettau, and Sydney C. Ludvigson, "How the Wealth Was Won: Factors Shares as Market Fundamentals," Cambridge, Mass.: National Bureau of Economic Research, Working Paper 25769, April 2021).

[140] Even pension funds, which ought to be well positioned "to model 'patient capital' behavior," "don't demonstrate patience: In fact, they have led the pack in the search for high short-term returns" (Clayton M. Christensen and Derek van Bever, "The Capitalist's Dilemma," *Harvard Business Review*, June 2014, p. 65).

[141] In the 1960s, U.S. individuals owned 84 percent of public stock; by 2013 that rate was down to 40 percent. One outcome is a centralization of equities: An OECD study contended that leading financial institutions—investment funds, insurance companies, and pension funds—owned $93 trillion of the world's assets in 2013 (cited in Erixon and Weigel, 2017, p. 8). Not only do institutional investors own most equities but the holdings within the institutional investor domain are also becoming more concentrated. Historically, U.S. companies had "a dispersed and fragmented shareholder base." But from 1998 to 2017, the "big three" institutional investors—Vanguard, State Street, BlackRock—went from holding 5.2 percent of stocks in S&P 500 companies to over 20 percent. Given current trends, their stake will be well over 30 percent by 2038 (Moarefy, 2020, pp. 12, 3; see also Bebchuk and Hirst, 2019). These investing institutions have become the dominant voting shareholders in many firms, casting more than 25 percent of the votes for directors at S&P 500 companies. If current ownership trends continue, these three megainvestors will hold over 40 percent of voting shares by 2038 (Sahand Moarefy, "The New Power Brokers: Index Funds and the Public Interest," *American Affairs*, Vol. 4, No. 4, 2020).

Clayton Christensen points to complex ways in which this trend has dissuaded firms from investing in market-transforming innovations. In a survey of Harvard Business School graduates, he reports,

> Our alumni expressed deep frustration over the way that the resource allocation process is biased against profitable, high-growth opportunities in new markets and favors predictable investments focused on current customers. This leads to a paradox: Competing for a point of share in an established market appears to be easy, even in the face of fierce competition. Investing to create a new market appears to be hard, even in the absence of headwinds and with the prospect of a much more sizable, and profitable, opportunity.[142]

"This, then, is the capitalist's dilemma," he concludes. "Doing the right thing for long-term prosperity is the wrong thing for most investors, according to the tools used to guide investments. In our attempts to maximize returns to capital, we reduce returns to capital. Capitalists seem uninterested in capitalism—in supporting the development of market-creating innovations."[143] The trends of share price ownership are related to another development that also tends to depress productive investment: the financialization of the U.S. economy—the dominance of the financial sector in profit making and the victory of the mindset of short-term-profit-oriented investors over longer-term value creation.[144]

***

These constraints on the productive value of investment impair American competitiveness in several ways. One is to depress corporate investment. The economist Dietrich Voll-

---

[142] Christensen and van Bever, 2014, p. 66.

[143] Christensen and van Bever, 2014, p. 66. Another scholar concludes, "In a 2004 survey of more than four hundred US executives, 80 per cent said that they would decrease discretionary spending on areas such as R&D, advertising, maintenance and hiring, in order to meet short-term earnings targets; while more than 50 per cent said they would delay new projects even if it meant sacrificing value creation. . . . As a result of the pressures from financial markets for immediate returns, profits have gone disproportionately into dividend payments and share buy-backs, rather than investment. This has happened in the case of US manufacturers, with the ratio of dividends paid to the amount invested in capital equipment increasing from 20 per cent in the late 1970s and early 1980s, to around 40–50 per cent in the early 1990s, to above 60 per cent in the 2000s" (Sainsbury, 2020, p. 190).

[144] The economist Edmund Phelps and coauthors argue that, in the United States today, "There has also been a visible change in the business culture. Short-termism that aims at maximizing bonuses and seeking rent within companies reduces the incentive to innovate." The prevailing mindset becomes one of profit-taking and minimal risk: "What is valued is a steady rise in consumption and leisure brought about by gradual gains in efficiency" (Phelps et al., 2020, p. 108; see also Phelps, 2013, pp. 243–244). The private-equity sector is becoming skewed as well, with hedge-fund-style investors seeking out quick equity hits by buying even small firms and flipping them—partly based on the mythology that "outside investor/managers" can improve their performance. But repeated studies show that this rarely is the case and mostly what investors add is debt. Private-equity deals are now heavily debt financed (Daniel Rasmussen, "Private Equity: Overvalued and Overrated?" *American Affairs*, Vol. 2, No. 1, Spring 2018).

rath explains that the private U.S. net investment rate declined significantly after 2000. Corporate net investment

> hovered around 30%–40% for the period 1950–2000, with a dip in the early 1990s. That run-up of corporate investment in the later 1990s was largely due to massive investments in computers. But following 2000, the average rate of net investment by corporations fell to around 20%–25%, even ignoring the sharp drop in investment occasioned by the financial crisis in 2008 and 2009.[145]

The result is that true productive investment is lower than the overall figures would suggest. This pattern affects competitive standing because it drains the economy of productive investment, innovation, and capital for entrepreneurship: "Was Cisco outflanked by Huawei, China's state-sponsored competitor, because it shifted into value extraction mode via buybacks, on which it spent $118.7 billion between 2002 and 2018? That's a tough one, but it certainly didn't help. Huawei . . . doesn't do buybacks."[146] A related outcome is to starve small and medium-size businesses of capital needed for expansion and innovation.[147] "Finance does not support real investment the way its advocates claim," economist Steve Brent writes. "On the contrary, the financial sector's high profits have coincided with low investment in the real economy." He explains one natural outcome: "If investment is low, productivity advances will be limited."[148]

A second and related outcome is that profit taking and rent seeking tend to depress a specific form of investment—research and development funding.[149] A third competitive result is the shift to outsourcing and cost-cutting in manufacturing industries, which has often reduced their ability to control quality. Boeing's embrace of outsourcing created quality problems with its initial 787 Dreamliner aircraft, for example: "Outsourcing removed assets from Boeing's balance sheet but also made the 787's supply chain so complex that the company couldn't maintain the high quality an airliner requires. Just as the engineers had predicted, the result was huge delays and runaway costs."[150]

---

[145] Vollrath, 2020, p. 118.

[146] Duff McDonald, "Managing Decline: The Economy of Value Extraction," *American Affairs*, Vol. 4, No. 2, Summer 2020, p. 57.

[147] Craig Zabala and Daniel Luria, "New Gilded Age or Old Normal?" *American Affairs*, Vol. 3, No. 3, Fall 2019, p. 27.

[148] R. Stephen Brent, "Misunderstanding Investment in the United States and China," *American Affairs*, Vol. 4, No. 4, Winter 2020, pp. 96–97.

[149] Mariana Mazzucato explains, "While causality may be hard to prove, it cannot be denied that at the same time that private pharma companies have been reducing the R of R&D, they have been increasing the amount of funds used to repurchase their own shares—a strategy used to boost their stock price, which affects the price of stock options and executive pay linked to such options" (Mazzucato, 2015, p. 32).

[150] Gautam Mukunda, "The Price of Wall Street's Power," *Harvard Business Review*, June 2014. The article continues, "Research by the economists John Asker, Joan Farre-Mensa, and Alexander Ljungqvist shows

This process may gradually give rise to a private sector that is managerial rather than innovative, risk averse rather than adventurous and experimental. Two scholars refer to the resulting mindset as "managerial capitalism," which "limits the space for eccentric ideas, let alone eccentric people. It is a control-and-monitor culture. . . . And under its regime, companies take machinelike approaches to every new opportunity and to their development."[151]

These trends have profound national security implications, undermining as they do domestic production of critical goods. Webs of interdependent technologies, techniques, and capabilities are essential in specific industries, and the United States has been steadily losing such networks and thus a competitive position in key industries. These include machine tools, rare-earth-element processing, rechargeable batteries, telecommunications equipment, LED manufacturing, and semiconductor fabrication. The story of U.S. industrial loss has moved from general outsourcing and reliance on foreign suppliers to outsourcing even of the R&D behind the products. "Once lost," one assessment concludes, "capabilities tend not to return," in part because they are based on ecosystems of knowledge that become fractured.[152] The United States has allowed industries to decline and be offshored not based on their strategic significance but by their asset returns.[153]

The end point of this process is what one writer has called the "Nikefication" of the U.S. economy, in which firms become mostly a brand and a headquarters and contract with other firms for nearly all their activities.[154] Some major hotel chains, for example, now lease their actual properties from real estate investment firms and contract out staffing to other companies. The companies themselves are only a brand. In theory this could happen to a country as well: It becomes a brand name contracting out major economic activities and profiting off the financial engineering that goes on with asset values.

Finally, the current patterns of investment exacerbate trends in inequality. Ron Ivey and Tim Shirk refer to the present situation as a "hoarding economy, in which both elected officials and central bankers have turned the policy dials to encourage the wealthiest to hoard power and prosperity at the expense of middle-class Americans." They contrast this pat-

---

that a desire to maximize short-term share price leads publicly held companies to invest only about half as much in assets as their privately held counterparts do. Pressure to reduce assets made Sara Lee, for example, shift from manufacturing clothing and food to brand management. Sara Lee's CEO explained, 'Wall Street can wipe you out. They are the rule-setters . . . and they have decided to give premiums to companies that harbor the most profits for the least assets.' In the pursuit of higher stock returns, many electronics companies have, like Boeing and Sara Lee, outsourced their manufacturing, even though tightly integrating R&D and manufacturing is crucial to innovation."

[151] Erixon and Weigel, 2017, p. 11.

[152] Keith B. Belton, "The Emerging American Industrial Policy," *American Affairs*, Vol. 5, No. 3, Fall 2021.

[153] Julius Krein, "The Value of Nothing: Capital Versus Growth," *American Affairs*, Vol. 5, No. 3, Fall 2021.

[154] Gerald F. Davis, "What Might Replace the Modern Corporation? Uberization and the Web Page Enterprise," *Seattle University Law Review*, Vol. 39, 2016.

tern with "[b]uilding wealth through entrepreneurship, wise risk-taking, and investment."[155] They worry that this pattern could generate social conflict.

A Long-Delayed Fiscal Reckoning

Another challenge to the U.S. engine of competitiveness is the risk to sustainable finances. A collapse of state revenues, exploding debt, and associated inability to invest in critical capabilities is one of the most common routes to competitive decline in our case studies. The question is whether the United States is now headed down the road of Spain, the Austro-Hungarian Empire, the Ottoman Empire (in some periods), and other great powers that ultimately lost their competitive position because they ran out of money.

The United States continues to have the potential to have a strong, sustainable financial basis for its competitive position. The potential scale of its tax and revenue base and the needed investments in various competitive areas could in theory be well aligned. However, in practice the United States does face several major areas of concern in the societal approach to finances.

The first and most obvious is an unwillingness to live within its means, which has characterized the United States for decades. Total U.S. public debt exceeded $17 trillion in 2020 and is on pace to add *more than $100 trillion in new debt* over the next three decades.[156] Figure 10.7 traces the history and projections for U.S. annual budget deficits. The trend tells a clear story: Like many great powers before it, the United States has become perpetually unable to live within its fiscal means. Figure 10.8 shows the growth of the federal debt as a percentage of GDP.

Low interest rates have provided a temporary relief from the consequences of this trend.[157] But this situation is set to worsen in coming decades, as the health care and pension costs of an aging population intensify. By the period 2027–2031, the U.S. Congressional Budget Office projects that net interest on the federal debt will total 2.3 percent of GDP per year. Net interest payments are projected to reach $712 billion in 2029, $808 billion in 2030, and $910 billion in 2031—placing interest on the debt as almost equal to projected defense spending in that year.

Looking further ahead—where projections become admittedly more uncertain—is even more concerning. The Congressional Budget Office estimates that by 2051, on current trends,

---

[155] Ivey and Shirk, 2021, pp. 44, 49.

[156] Brian Riedl, "Behind CBO's $100 Trillion in Projected Deficits over 30 Years," Manhattan Institute, November 19, 2020.

[157] At this writing in 2022, moreover, rates of inflation have risen significantly, which will have the effect of depressing the relative scale of accumulated debt. But inflation comes with its own challenges, some of which affect fiscal sustainability and in any case will not provide enduring relief from debt. This is especially true because inflation is likely to drive up interest rates, which will raise the cost of borrowing. Tom Fairless, "As Inflation Eases Public Debt Load, Economists Sound Cautionary Note," *Wall Street Journal*, May 1, 2022; Chris Giles, "Fiscal Relief from Inflation Is Transitory, IMF Says," *Financial Times*, April 20, 2022.

FIGURE 10.7

U.S. Federal Deficits and Percentage of GDP, 1971–2031

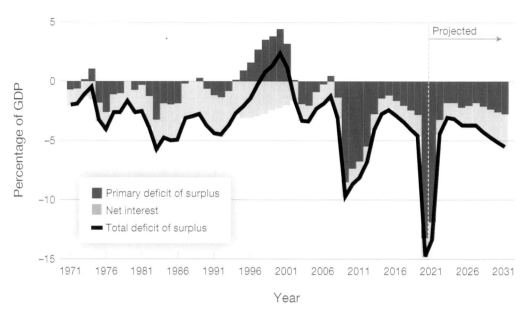

SOURCE: U.S. Congressional Budget Office, "Additional Information About the Updated Budget and Economic Outlook: 2021 to 2031," July 2021.

FIGURE 10.8

U.S. Federal Debt as Percentage of GDP, 1941–2031

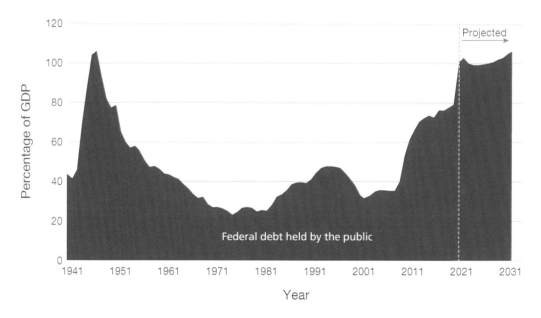

SOURCE: U.S. Congressional Budget Office, 2021.

U.S. debt will reach more than 200 percent of GDP. Interest payments on that debt will consume *almost half* of federal revenues (even assuming a significant rise in those revenues, to more than 30 percent of GDP by 2050). And this assumes very low and slowly rising interest rates: In one scenario, if those rates rose more quickly, into the range of 4.5 percent, the debt would hit 125 percent of GDP by 2031 and 244 percent by 2015. By 2031, interest payments would consume almost a third of current federal revenue levels—and almost 60 percent by 2051.[158] One economist suggests that every 1 percent rise in rates would add, over the following three decades, some *$3 trillion* in added interest obligations.[159]

U.S. fiscal prospects are worsened by the country's unwillingness to tax itself at rates equal to recent U.S. history, which would close the spending gap significantly. The United States has developed a yawning gap between what Americans want their government spending to produce and how much they are willing to tax themselves to generate those desired programs. This is partly a product of years of powerful rhetoric directed at federal programs, spending, and the role of the government in society. This analysis supports no specific position on that debate, except to say that this rhetoric has made it effectively impossible for the country to increase taxes in any meaningful way, seemingly locking in a perpetual annual deficit. As Figure 10.9 shows, since the late 1980s, the United States has pursued a series of major tax cuts—while increasing spending on both domestic and foreign priorities. As a result, relative to other OECD nations, the United States takes a relatively small proportion of its national income in taxes.[160] The U.S. Government Accountability Office estimates that closing the current fiscal gap would require either a 27 percent cut in noninterest federal expenditure or a 36 percent increase in revenue.[161]

***

This report has noted that major powers very typically get into competitive trouble when their fiscal situations become desperate. The United States has not reached the level of debt relative to resources as some of the classic fiscal weaklings of history did, but current trends pose serious dangers to the nation's competitive position in at least three ways.

First, the general fiscal tightness constrains new investments in areas that could provide competitive advantage. Second, the United States may be losing the fiscal flexibility to respond to the next crisis. After September 11 and during the 2008 financial crisis and the COVID-19 pandemic, the federal government stepped in with trillions in spending, loans, and bailout packages to keep the economy from an even worse catastrophe. In a future crisis,

---

[158] The Concord Coalition, "Why the National Debt Still Matters," July 28, 2021.

[159] Brian Riedl, "Rising Federal Debt Still Matters," *National Review*, September 30, 2021.

[160] Andrea Louise Campbell, "America the Undertaxed: U.S. Fiscal Policy in Perspective," *Foreign Affairs*, September–October 2012.

[161] U.S. Government Accountability Office, "America's Fiscal Future," webpage, undated.

FIGURE 10.9

Federal Revenues and Outlays, 1980–2016

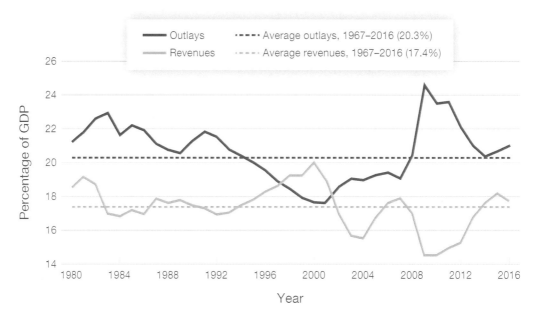

SOURCE: U.S. Congressional Budget Office, 2021.

if interest rates are higher and debt-servicing costs are already huge, it may be far more difficult to respond in decisive fiscal ways.

Third, emerging levels of debt could themselves spark a classic debt crisis, with major implications for U.S. credibility and economic power. The economist John Cochrane describes how one might emerge:

> Imagine that five or even 10 years from now we have another crisis, which we surely will. It might be another, worse, pandemic, or a war involving China, Russia, or the Middle East.... At this point, the US has, say, 150 percent debt to GDP. It needs to borrow another $5 trillion–$10 trillion, or get people to hold that much more newly printed money, to bail out once again and pay everyone's bills for a while. It will need another $10 trillion or so to roll over short-maturity debt. At some point, bond investors see the end coming, as they did for Greece, and refuse. Not only must the US then inflate or default, but the normal crisis-mitigation policies—the firehouse of debt relief, bailout, and stimulus that everyone expects—are absent, together with our capacity for military or public-health spending to meet the shock that sparks the crisis.[162]

---

[162] John H. Cochrane, "Debt Still Matters," *Chicago Booth Review*, November 12, 2020.

This trend of fiscal decline interacts with many other threats to competitiveness—as fiscal decline *has* done with every previous major power that has suffered this fate. It interacts with the degree of opportunity in society by draining resources from investments designed to widen that opportunity. It can negatively affect national will by generating a sense of exhaustion and, in practical terms, leaving no resources available for new projects. It directly affects levels of productive investment in both public and private sectors. In sum, an unsustainable fiscal profile serves as a major drag on competitive advantage for any major power—and it is in the process of doing so for the United States.

Findings and Conclusions

As part of this study, we conducted an initial, exploratory analysis of risks to the U.S. competitive position from major societal trends. We did not conduct a comprehensive assessment of American society but rather identified specific perils to the sources of societal competitive advantage proposed by this study. As reflected in Table 10.4, our analysis highlights multiple risks to the U.S. competitive position.

These tentative findings about the specific position of the United States in these seven areas are both hopeful and concerning, each in very specific ways. On the hopeful side of the ledger, as it has done for much of its modern history, the United States reflects a reasonably strong position and clear inherent strengths in each of the major characteristics contributing to competitive advantage. Part of the reason for its disproportionate share of global power over the last half century has been exactly this: It has excelled in many characteristics across this broad range. Even given some negative trends in certain areas, the United States has very powerful strengths to build on, and our analysis suggests that it possesses the raw material and residual strength across the board in these characteristics to maintain a broadly superior competitive position versus China.

To take one example in relation to our first characteristic, the United States has reflected, and continues to reflect, an opportunity society.[163] Social mobility and opportunity for specific segments of the population has improved over the last half century. Opportunity remains unequal and many forms of discrimination remain, but relative to the situation in

---

[163] In a major recent OECD study, relative to OECD countries, U.S. social mobility ranked highly for intergenerational education and occupation mobility, but medium or low to medium for mobility as measured by earnings and health indicators (OECD, 2018, p. 38). One of the leading scholars in the field and coauthors find generally stable rates of social mobility relatively stable for several decades, if measured by intergenerational earnings elasticity (Raj Chetty, Nathaniel Hendren, Patrick Kline, and Emmanuel Saez, "Where Is the Land of Opportunity? The Geography of Intergenerational Mobility in the United States," *Quarterly Journal of Economics*, Vol. 129, No. 4, 2014).

TABLE 10.4

U.S. Standing in Societal Characteristics

Characteristic	Current U.S. Situation
National ambition and will	Strong foundation of national "energizing myth" but significant evidence for waning of ambitions and willpower for national public endeavors
Unified national identity	Major negative trends in polarization, partisanship, and sense of national fracturing pose a real danger to degree of unity
Shared opportunity	Major aspects of an opportunity society remain in place, though with much untapped potential talent and serious negative trends in inequality
An active state	Strong accumulated state power and potential, but unevenly deployed to enhance national competitive standing
Effective institutions	Public and private institutions objectively effective in many cases; perception of institutional quality very poor, with gaps in some areas
A learning and adapting society	Strong environment for research, intellectual exchange, and institutional adaptation, but now threatened by corrosion of information environment
Competitive diversity and pluralism	Remains a highly diverse and pluralistic nation

1900 or even 1950, the life opportunities enjoyed by women and minorities in the United States have improved.[164]

In other areas, too, accumulated U.S. strengths remain potent. In terms of national will, public opinion data on the U.S. role in the world and America's global interests mainly indicate stability and continued commitment to a global leadership role. In terms of openness and effective institutions, the World Bank's ranking on ease of doing business may serve as an interesting proxy for one component of national ambition.[165] It includes elements designed to show the status of the legal, financial, regulatory, and entrepreneurial context in a nation. By this index, the United States improved in its ranking, from a score of 60 in 2014 to almost 80 by 2020. The parallel index for ease of starting a business also rose by about 20 rating points during that period.[166]

Moreover, the United States has clearly represented, since 1945 and perhaps earlier, the most potent example of the ideal recipe of interactions among those factors—the Renaissance spirit described in Chapter One and emphasized throughout the study. The United States' strong sense of national mission has been one justification for the helpful interventions of its

---

[164] The gender gap in schooling, for example, not only closed but female students now achieve higher average rates of school than male. See Wittgenstein Centre for Demography and Global Human Capital, undated.

[165] World Bank, "Doing Business," March 7, 2022.

[166] World Bank, 2022.

catalytic state. Its openness and learning culture have increasingly been tied to an opportunity society. Such a strong interactive engine, grounded in long-term cultural and political characteristics, will retain a certain degree of dynamism.

Yet the balance of the evidence offers clear cause for concern. The United States increasingly displays characteristics of once-dominant powers on the far side of their peak of competitiveness: complacent, highly bureaucratized, in search of short-term gains and rents rather than long-term productive breakthroughs, socially and politically fragmented and divided, and cognizant of needed reforms yet unwilling or unable to tackle them.

***

Indeed, a worrisome pattern throughout these assessments is that most U.S. strengths that emerge across the characteristics derive from momentum and path dependence, not new energy, ideas, or initiatives. This initial, tentative assessment suggests that the United States may be living off its accumulated social strengths rather than actively nurturing and advancing them. That is a very broad generalization. It does not apply to every social issue, government agency, or private-sector firm. Yet evidence across many characteristics associated with national dynamism and competitive position does raise this worrisome possibility.

This is reflected, in part, in the generalized pattern of stagnation in many of the indexes we examined. There is quantitative, polling, and qualitative evidence for the conclusion that the American competitive advantage is weakening, that the U.S. societal condition betrays an overarching sluggishness, lack of dynamism, and inertia. This pattern shows up across many indicators. It has been evident in slowing economic growth and stalled productivity, an economic picture some have described as "secular stagnation."[167] It shows up in a decline in productive investment, especially in new technologies.[168] It appears to be evident in the level of business entrepreneurialism and new business energy: As one economist notes, "over the past few decades there has been a distinct decline in the volume of turnover in the number of firms and jobs in the economy, with fewer new firms entering the economy, fewer old firms exiting, and fewer movements of people from one job to another."[169]

---

[167] Barry Eichengreen, "Secular Stagnation: The Long View," *American Economic Review*, Vol. 105, No. 5, 2015; Patrizio Pagano and Massimo Sbracia, "The Secular Stagnation Hypothesis: A Review of the Debate and Some Insights," occasional paper, San Francisco, Calif.: Bank of Italy, 2014; Antonin Bergeaud, Gilbert Cette, and Rémy Lecat, "Long-Term Growth and Productivity Trends: Secular Stagnation or Temporary Slowdown?" *Revue de l'OFCE*, Vol. 157, No. 3, 2018.

[168] Henrique Basso and Juan F. Jimeno, "Demographics and Technology Explain Secular Stagnation and More," *VoxEU*, November 29, 2019.

[169] Vollrath, 2020, p. 7. Ross Douthat adds, "American entrepreneurship has been declining fairly steadily since the 1970s: during the Carter presidency, hardly an ideal time for the American economy, 15 percent of all US businesses had been founded in the previous year; today that rate is about 8 percent. It's become harder to survive as a nonincumbent, with the share of start-ups failing in the first year having risen from around 20 percent in the mid-1980s to closer to 30 percent today. In 1990, 65 percent of US companies were less than ten years old; today it's about 52 percent" (Douthat, 2020, pp. 25–26).

The evidence we reviewed adds up to a reality that most Americans sense: Their country may be stuck in neutral, idling; the powerful forward momentum of an earlier era—even a few decades ago—has been somehow lost. Other countries appear to see the United States in this way, which will have its own competitive risks. China has already begun a forceful campaign to depict the United States as a power on the decline in part because of this widely shared view that the dynamism has gone out of the American project, that its forward momentum has been interrupted—or permanently halted.

***

The slow seizing up of a nation's engine of dynamism and competitive advantage can take various specific forms. In Chapter One, we laid out an engine of dynamism, a construct for the way in which our seven nominated characteristics of social competitiveness can spur each other and interact synergistically in ways that produce the most decisive energy and power, the most impressive societal efflorescences in history. We termed it the Renaissance spirit. There is a similar negative feedback mechanism among the danger signs in these seven characteristics. Together these signals help define the condition of many competitively declining nations in history: Negative trends in each area feed on each other, each exacerbating the others, generating dramatic social and geopolitical decline.

Figures 10.10 and 10.11 offer two distinct cycles of negative feedback as possibilities: one deals primarily with economic and national power, the other with national political and social coherence. Both of those negative cycles, or some combination of them, could easily emerge. These are not individual dangers: If not addressed, individually and as a group, they could feed on and intensify one another.

As noted in the introduction to this chapter, we do not seek to make a general, overarching judgment about the condition of U.S. society. In addition to the dangers cited here, as well as the wider theme of stagnation, there remain many reasons for hope and optimism. American society continues to reflect the spirit of many of our seven characteristics of competitiveness better than many other countries—certainly more so than its leading rivals, Russia and China.

But taking account of all the evidence surveyed for this concluding assessment, we must conclude that the balance sheet looks daunting. The issue is not just that the United States has social challenges—it has always had them. The primary reasons for concern are twofold: the significant number of intersecting dangers to U.S. competitiveness and the fact that the United States seems, more than any other time in its modern history, to be obstructed from taking decisive action to deal with them.

It is easy to imagine a potent national agenda that would attend to many of these risks; it is much more difficult to imagine the current U.S. political system and wider social context rallying itself to overcome present divisions and misinformation to implement such an agenda. Some of the current disquiet on the part of Americans—their expressed concerns about their future and the effectiveness of their institutions and even the sustainability of their demo-

FIGURE 10.10

Cycle of Decline 1: Waning National Energy

FIGURE 10.11

Cycle of Decline 2: Fragmenting National Identity and Coherence

cratic model—surely reflects an awareness of this fact. (As to what that the agenda should be, this analysis has not assessed possible solutions. Each could be addressed in different ways, and a set of public policies to deal with them must await a deep analysis of the likely effects, feasibility, and risk of various alternatives.)

Professor Kenneth Bartlett is a scholar of the Italian Renaissance. In the concluding lecture of his Great Courses series on that period, he speaks of the reasons for the collapse of the values of pluralism, tolerance, genius, and competition that were at the heart of the competitive advantage of the Italian city-states.[170] In the place of energy, dynamism, and genius, what many Italians then came to accept, Bartlett argues, was mediocrity. "The thing about mediocrity," he explains, "whether it's in government or politics or economics or art, it that it's safe. If something is mediocre it doesn't challenge the weak and the unable. It doesn't set a standard that others feel they can never reach. It doesn't [maintain] a set of principles that make those who are in positions of power and authority feel insecure." This appealed to Italian city-states that had suffered through numerous wars and crises and political collapses in part because they had learned that "freedom and genius were just too expensively bought. Ultimately freedom just wasn't worth the effort." Genius was appealing if it could be contained and controlled, but "genius uncontrolled and unconfined can lead you in areas that you could not control or even foresee. . . . In many ways the late Italian Renaissance is a celebration of mediocrity—and therein lies its failure."

Many elements of that portrait ought to sound familiar. A nation facing serious challenges yet having lost the will to truly confront them. A period of energy, risk taking, and celebration of competition that has given way to managing risk and seeking stability above all. Willingness to trade parts of a society's freedom and dynamism for control. A failure, in the end, of societal will, based in part on the fact that the "energizing myth" of that society had run its course.

This is the portrait of a self-reinforcing negative-feedback cycle of many social trends that lead to a position of lack of competitiveness, lack of dynamism and energy, and a loss of faith in the conceptual project that the nation had represented. The question is whether the United States is headed for the same fate—not disaster, necessarily, or permanent calamity, or war, or instability, but a sort of societal stagnation and mediocrity that blocks the potential for a new competitive advance, a new Renaissance spirit.

---

[170] Bartlett, 2005, lecture 35.

CHAPTER ELEVEN

Findings and Implications

As the Soviet Union began its long, slow decline—as its institutions seized up, corruption grew, output and growth slacked off, consumer goods became increasingly scarce, and frustration and resentment escalated—many of its leaders understood that they were in deep trouble. They knew that the Soviet Union's problems went well beyond a handful of specific policies to the essential character of the system. They needed to act, but the scale of the required change staggered them. Not to mention that many of the elites in a position to effect change continued to live comfortably under the existing system and benefit from its gross inequities, rent seeking, and corruption.

And so the decline persisted. Unproductive industries soaked up state investments. State-run production chains became ever more inefficient. Major civilian industries fell further and further behind their international rivals. Corruption escalated as midlevel officials turned many aspects of the Orwellian bureaucracy to their own protection and enrichment. Faith in the system ebbed, resentment deepened, the previous sense of national purpose disappeared. Eventually, national identities within the Soviet empire increasingly came to the fore and tore the state apart.

We see roughly similar signposts in many great powers or civilizations that begin to lose competitive standing. It is a negative-feedback loop, a poisonous synergy, the mirror image of the model of positive interaction we have termed the Renaissance spirit. Opportunity becomes less shared, and society slips into increasingly unequal patterns in which the well-off and powerful hoard wealth and power. National willpower recedes as a society becomes self-satisfied, focused on preservation rather than discovery, losing the adventurous spirit—both for international achievement and for domestic intellectual, social, and scientific advances—that had spurred its competitive advance. National unity fragments under centrifugal pressures and partisan or ideological quarrels. The social obsession with learning and openness to experimentation, creativity, and adaptation gives way to different forms of orthodoxy. Social institutions become weak and inept in some cases and overbearing and strangled with bureaucracy in others. The productive role of an active state seizes up, with state institutions unable to take bold action to solve problems or create new opportunities.

Nations that begin to suffer from some version of such a mixture of social ills are then sometimes confronted with other major challenges—the factors surveyed in Chapter Two. In a desperate bid to retain an exalted strategic position, great powers may overextend themselves geopolitically and financially. State and even private resources increasingly flow into investments with minimal productive value, such as lurid amounts of conspicuous consumption at home, especially among the wealthy, and needless wars abroad spurred by pride and a refusal to limit the nation's ambitions. The nation's position at the hub of global networks of exchange recedes—sometimes because the networks themselves decay, sometimes because the natural evolution of commerce shifts trade and investment away from them, sometimes because a competitor consciously and strategically infiltrates the networks and elbows them aside. Neighboring or competing powers that had been weak create new challenges by growing strong and bellicose. Many such weakening societies have then confronted a coup de grâce from some exogenous shock—a natural disaster, a disease, the grinding effects of climate change.

If this portrait produces unease, it should. The United States might have begun to take on the familiar and disturbing aspect of a great power whose engine of social dynamism is being encumbered by stagnation and social instability. This is not the same as claiming that the United States confronts decline, whether relative or absolute. The size of its economy and military, its position in major alliances, and the signal weaknesses of its leading rivals may keep the United States from sinking too far in the hierarchy of world politics. And its rivals, notably China, face their own litany of constraints and crises, which may be even more daunting and systemic than those of the United States. But a great power can give an impression of conserving its overall power levels while still being hollowed out from the inside as the gears and levers of its competitive engine grind to a halt. Often, nations that give every outward indication of remaining near their peak of objective power and influence have actually begun to rot inside. And at that point, if history is any guide, the nation or civilization loses resilience and becomes vulnerable to profound shocks, whether from rivals or some other source.

Our study suggests that the challenges to U.S. competitive standing from many of the seven societal characteristics are unmistakable. They may constitute a more comprehensive challenge to U.S. national dynamism than at any time in the country's modern history.

***

Chapter One summarized the five basic findings of this study. The first is simply that an identifiable set of societal characteristics, our seven nominated qualities of dynamic nations, do appear to be related to competitive success. This emerged from the methodology described in Chapter One and is demonstrated in the analysis reported in Chapters Three through Nine.

The second finding highlights the importance of a prudent balance in seeking sources of national advantage. All these societal characteristics can take on an excessive form that undermines rather than enhances competitive position. In terms of national ambition and desire to master the world, for example, that critical impulse has also produced competitive disadvantage—either temporary or permanent—in many countries (such as Greece, Rome, France, Spain, the Soviet Union) when their ambitions pushed them into strategic overreach.

The role of the state is another area in which balance is essential. Some cases (such as the Soviet Union) show the risks of an overly intrusive state control of economy and society; others (such as Austria-Hungary) demonstrate the core weakness that can emerge when private actors and local and city governments are free to conduct business largely outside the state's control and financial remit.

The third finding was that a set of distinct factors *other than* societal characteristics is associated with national competitive standing. Chapter Two described those factors. Fourth, the study found that positive-feedback synergies—combinations of mutually supporting societal characteristics—delivered the most-profound competitive advantage. And the fifth finding was that one specific synergistic recipe, which we have termed the Renaissance spirit, offers by far the most-significant advantages.

This chapter offers concluding analysis and builds on those essential findings with additional themes. It elaborates on the issue of recipes for success by describing several leading synergies that nations have employed to gain competitive advantage. It points toward the aspects of the most-effective such synergies by examining ways in which societal characteristics provide lasting and sustained, rather than fleeting and temporary, advantage. The chapter suggests broader implications of our work—ways of seeing major trends in world politics in the modern period that are highlighted by the study's findings. Finally, the chapter offers concluding thoughts about the implications of this analysis for efforts to enhance U.S. competitive standing.

In producing these findings, this study's aim was diagnostic, not prescriptive. We sought to identify societal characteristics that contribute to national competitive success. What should be done about those characteristics—what set of national policies would best enhance shared opportunity, or ways to encourage strong but not excessive unified national identity or empower any of the other characteristics—is a very different question, one we have not tried to address.

The Synergy of National Dynamism

The most important theme that emerges from this work was one of the findings outlined in Chapter One—the importance of *holistic packages of competitive advantage*.[1] Small asymmetries in power or capabilities rarely make a decisive difference in a competition. Real advantage derives from combined effects—the ways in which multiple characteristics interact with each other to produce dynamism.[2]

---

[1] Lacey, 2016, p. 61.

[2] David Landes explains that the advances of many parts of industry were made in the Industrial Revolution, "and all of these together, mutually reinforcing," drove the revolution (Landes, 1998, p. 186). A community of intellectuals was not enough—which was why "it could not have happened in Renaissance Florence. Even less in ancient Greece. The technological basis had not yet been laid; the streams of progress had to come together." And changes in individual technologies were not enough: "What was needed was techno-

Just about every global history we reviewed for this study suggests the same basic truth. In the Industrial Revolution, David Landes concludes, "change begat change. For one thing, many technical improvements were feasible only after advances in associated fields."[3] Joel Mokyr and Jack Goldstone point out that the mutually supporting, self-reinforcing aspects of many variables around a basic application of the scientific method are key to industrial takeoff.[4] Edmund Phelps argues that, in the development of modern European economies, "the success of this system depends also on the degree of interactivity within it."[5] Another source notes that a "conjunction of geographical, historical, institutional and fortuitous circumstances" promoted explosive growth in Britain and the wider northern European areas after 1500.[6] Jürgen Osterhammel suggests that a critical synergy of factors in Scotland and England—networks of scholars working on problems under the guidance of the scientific method, effective institutions, and a commercial market to encourage application of ideas—generated a combinatorial breakthrough, which he describes as the "normalization of technological innovation."[7] A nation's "dominant needs, cognitive frames, attitudes, beliefs and opinions, values, behavioral norms, social theories and ideologies and established behavioral patterns form a synergistic whole," he argues.[8]

The theme of synergy and packages of qualities that produce effects beyond the sum of their parts emerges in particular sectors of society and specific issue areas as well. One example is the constellations of corporate institutions, universities, research centers, educational systems and policies, immigration policies, availability of local resources, and other factors that contribute to an economy's ability to master advanced technology and large-scale manufacturing. The importance of such collections is one reason for the lagging of the British economy in certain sectors, such as chemicals, relative to Germany and the United States even after Britain staked such a commanding early lead in mastering the Industrial Revolution.[9]

---

logical change of mighty leverage, the kind that would resonate through the market and change the distribution of resources" (Landes, 1998, p. 206). Moreover, the story of why the Industrial Revolution happened in Britain first is to a significant degree the story of a predominant mosaic of factors, a decisive mixture: advances in energy and fuel supply; a maritime tradition that underwrote global trade, exploration, and (it must be admitted) exploitation; good investment in high-quality domestic infrastructure; strong cottage industries as the foundation of industrial growth; a powerful community of inventors and scientists; a rapidly advancing financial sector; and a strong agricultural foundation that freed up resources and attention for more-advanced pursuits (Landes, 1998, p. 213).

[3] Landes, 2003, p. 2.

[4] Goldstone, 2002, p. 356.

[5] Phelps, 2013, p. 38.

[6] Broadberry et al., 2014, p. 396.

[7] Osterhammel, 2014, p. 644.

[8] Hämäläinen, 2003, pp. 31, 59; Scott and Lodge, 1985, p. 70.

[9] Carl J. Dahlman and Richard Nelson, "Social Absorption Capability, National Innovation Systems and Economic Development," in Bon Ho Koo and Dwight H. Perkins, eds., *Social Capability and Long-Term Economic Growth*, New York: St. Martin's Press, 1995, p. 85. See also Barnett, 1972, 1986.

This finding suggests that the United States must think in terms more holistic and interactive than individual policies. Ross Douthat argues that "the economic, demographic, intellectual, and cultural elements of our predicament are all connected, so that you can't just pick out a single cause or driver of stagnation and repetition or solve the problem with a narrow focus on one area or issue." An American Renaissance, he suggests, could not be based on any one approach or small number of them. It would have to "look more like the birth of the modern world, when the Renaissance and the Reformation and Counter-Reformation and the scientific revolutions and the age of discovery were happening on top of one another, influencing each other and driving each other forward."[10] The question facing the United States, in terms of both its overall competitiveness as a society and its position in the emerging rivalry with China, is: What is the best way to reinvigorate this synergistic engine of national dynamism, this American version of a Renaissance spirit, that has been its most profound competitive advantage?

***

Different combinations of these factors can provide distinct models of competitive advantage and different routes to national dynamism.[11] Some countries might build their advantage largely on the characteristics that produce powerful economic growth and technological expression. Others might focus on sources of normative and ideological power. Some may rely heavily on strong central state institutions for state-led development, very effective strategic decisionmaking, potent national identity, and perhaps one or more other characteristics.[12]

Just as recipes differ among countries at the same moment, recipes for success can also evolve. Ancient societies could thrive with only two or three of these qualities; modern competitors require a much more comprehensive package of effective characteristics. The same country or civilization might assemble different combinations of factors at different times in its history. The story of industrialization is different, in important ways, in just about every case, even if some parts of the story are common.[13]

Yet not all engines of national dynamism, not all synergies of societal characteristics, are created equal—at least not in the modern world. There is a recurring pattern in the most-competitive modern societies built around a few key qualities: openness, an embrace of diversity and the benefits of pluralistic governance structures, opportunity fueled in part by a

---

[10] Douthat, 2020, pp. 229–230.

[11] Osterhammel, 2014, p. 645; see also pp. 650–651; Goldstone, 2002, pp. 330, 358.

[12] In his study of social capabilities, Moses Abramovitz concludes, "Quite different constellations of characteristics appear to have been compatible with successful development and growth" (Abramovitz, 1995, p. 29). "In a world in which cultures as varied as Japan's and Norway's are among the most economically successful," Eric Beinhocker writes, "such claims of one perfect formula are easily dismissed" (Beinhocker, 2007, p. 567).

[13] Osterhammel, 2014, pp. 646–648.

strong commercial ethic, and a learning and experimenting mindset, grounded in powerful national identity and ambition and supported by effective institutions and an active state. We termed this the Renaissance spirit. With some variations, this most potent source of national dynamism, built around the competitive advantages of a tolerant, open, opportunity-granting, effectively governed society, rises above the others.

This finding ought to be reassuring for the United States, at least in theory. It has immense accumulated power across these categories, although some are increasingly constrained by the challenges examined in Chapter Ten. In terms of the basic qualities of its society, the United States remains potentially more capable of reflecting a Renaissance spirit than China or any other potential rival. Whatever its current challenges, *in theory* the United States can maximize a higher number of these especially valued characteristics and the synergy among them and strike the necessary balances, better than any competitor. But as Chapter Ten warned, there are reasons for concern that the elements of the powerful American engine of national dynamism are weakening and that the United States may be increasingly incapable of realizing these advantages.

Transient Power Versus Sustainable Competitive Vibrancy

In the process of assessing recipes for competitive success, our research highlighted a related theme—the difference between transient and lasting competitive advantage. Lasting advantage in an uncertain global environment and a changing economic and technological context calls for emergent, bottom-up creativity, constant experimentation, and a spirit of adaptation. The most successful powers in the long run are not those that force-feed their engines of dynamism through immense centralized muscle. They are the nations that nurture competitive systems capable of organically breeding ideas, inventions, innovations, concepts, cultural brilliance, and other expressions of national imagination, power, and culture from a wide range of people and institutions.

The dominance of such an emergent, grassroots route to competitive advantage was not as true in the premodern or early modern eras. But it has been true for most of the modern era, and it is likely to provide an even better guide to competitive advantage in the 21st century.

Perhaps the classic modern example is the Soviet Union. From the 1950s through the 1970s, it appeared to be an economic, technological, and geopolitical juggernaut. The Soviet Union produced immense amounts of natural resources and industrial products, including steel, through the 1970s. But it achieved these results with an exhausting, focused application of societal resources to create a sort of Potemkin degree of competitiveness.

The pattern, the historian Marshal Goldman explained at a conference on Russian national vitality, was that "Russia jumps ahead and then falls back and then tries to jump ahead and then falls back." He gave the example of Peter the Great, whose lunge toward modernization demanded tremendous resources: "Peter had to find investment funds and investment basically came from exploiting the peasants—in effect enserfing them—taking away their ability to move, so that they could be taxed."[14] This was not a recipe for creating a truly vibrant, diverse, networked society that could create self-generating growth. A similar pattern—of drilling into economies and populations for surge levels of resources to force-feed development or state building—can be seen in other great powers whose competitive positions proved temporary (even if they lasted for some time).[15]

Table 11.1 outlines some of the elements of sustained advantage that emerged from our research. As it suggests, several indicators would appear to stand out in terms of identifying a transitory competitor. Is the country, for example, achieving progress largely through state- or leader-directed development of centrally chosen priorities? Is it devoting a large proportion of available capital to state-directed projects? Is it accumulating substantial debt, or robbing other parts of society of capital, to throw resources at competitive goals? Does it suffer from extreme and xenophobic bouts of nationalism, which then produce an excessive degree of foreign adventurism?

The most sustainably competitive nations become engines of investigation, innovation, and trial and error and in the process become resilient against many futures. Eric Beinhocker has a powerful phrase that captures the essential requirement: Strategic action on the part of successful organizations—and presumably nations—can be seen as a "portfolio of experiments." Such an approach involves making "lots of small bets, and only make big bets as a part of amplifying successful experiments when uncertainties are much lower. Being forced to make all-or-nothing bets under uncertainty means that a company is boxed in." Such an approach requires tolerance for radical ideas and most powerfully emerges from a foundation

TABLE 11.1

Transitory Versus Sustainable Competitiveness

Transitory	Sustainable
• State-led development often in the form of major projects run by the state; picking winners • High degree of centralization • Large proportion of available capital devoted to state-led projects • High quotient of xenophobic nationalism (though leaders may seek to steal or learn from foreign ideas) • Aggressive geopolitical goals • Weak rule of law and societal institutions	• Development led by commercial sector but catalyzed and supported by state action • State role strong but supportive, creating the conditions for emergent societal strength • Capital allocated based on bottom-up criteria of efficiency, productivity • Moderate nationalism; open to ideas and influences throughout society • Primarily commercial goals • Strong rule of law and societal institutions

---

[14] Marshal Goldman quoted in Clesse and Lounev, 2004, p. 230.

[15] This theme reflects a wider idea—that, as the economist Eric Beinhocker argues, "All competitive advantage is temporary." In the private sector, for example, companies do not tend to sustain a leading position for a long period. He reports on one finding that only 5 percent of companies sustained superior performance, leading their industry or in terms of profits or share price or other metrics, for more than ten years. Less than a half a percentage sustained such performance for two decades (Beinhocker, 2007, pp. 436–439). The percentages for countries might be similar: Of our cases studies, only three—Rome, Britain, and the United States—sustained true dominance for well over a century. All other stories involve far more waxing and waning.

of diversity: "[A]n evolutionary strategy requires tolerance of people going in different directions at once and experimenting with risky ideas."[16]

Another scholar, describing the sort of social creativity needed to rejuvenate 21st-century economies, puts the challenge in very similar terms. Citizens of dynamic societies should be provided with the essential skills and sense of safety to help generate "a storm of experiment and innovation. Such a storm does not happen spontaneously; it needs to be aroused."[17] This again emphasizes the essential role of the state in competitive nations: to create the conditions for such "a storm of experiment and innovation" to occur. Markets will not necessarily do so on their own—but a vibrant market is an indispensable context for vibrant social experimentation.

These themes question whether a closed, autocratic system can generate truly sustained competitive advantage. Historically, such regimes have been able to do so for sometimes extended periods—such as the Soviet Union's remarkable ability to force-feed economic growth and technological advances for several decades. Ultimately, though, the character of those systems, and the way they violated some of these rules for lasting advantage, ultimately caught up to them. One of the leading questions in world politics today is whether the same fate awaits the Chinese communist system.

A Framework for Understanding Trends in World Politics

Many efforts to understand the fundamental driving forces in world politics and national development have dealt with issues such as modernization, democratization, and globalization. Our findings suggest three additional ways of understanding such long-term trends.

First, our roster of dynamic societal characteristics, and the history of national efforts to cultivate them, offers a new lens on the process of global isomorphism in the pursuit of national power. Once a leading or dominant recipe for national competitive advantage became evident and produced results, others sought to copy it in part or in full, in places such as Japan, Russia, the Ottoman Empire, and, later, China. These were, in one sense, efforts to "modernize" and catch up to Western industrialization, but there was always more going on than that: The countries involved were striving to replicate a comprehensive model of national dynamism. For reasons partly related to accident and unplanned evolution, European societies stumbled into the leading recipe for success in ways that provided competitive advantage. In theory China or the Ottoman Empire or Japan or India could have done so, although each of them retained social patterns that kept them from embracing these characteristics as fully as Europe did. Once these nations did begin to fall behind, worried about their competitive standing, they saw what was working elsewhere and strove to mimic those factors. A clear pattern then emerged: the gradual spread of a default recipe for national com-

---

[16] Beinhocker, 2007, pp. 443, 449–450.

[17] Roberto Mangabeira Unger, "Britain's Project," *New Statesman*, March 17, 2021.

petitive success, the effort of others to adopt some version of it, and, in some cases, the resulting social instability and resistance to the imported models.

Carol Gluck describes this process in the Japanese case.[18] States are heavily influenced, Gluck adds, by what she terms the "available modern"—the patterns of modern life on display in the leading powers, or, to put it another way, the prevailing global paradigm. Several factors gradually emerged as representative of the essential modern recipe for national success, she explains: the "political form of the nation-state," industrialization, and integration into global networks of ideas and commerce. Advocates and entrepreneurs of modernity in Japan, from the Meiji period forward, sought to bring many of these elements to their nation. They were pursuing "aspirational modernity," impelled by the desire for national prestige, power, and prosperity, and pulled by the magnet of the dominant model of successful modernity.[19]

Yet not all societies could effectively embrace this recipe. A nation whose politics, socioeconomic patterns, and established history and culture are at odds with key elements of the model will be blocked from easily adopting its core components and benefiting from its competitive effects. Such a society then fall into a long, slow decline, sometimes punctuated by defeat at the hands of more-competitive nations and then anger and scapegoating. This appears to be, from our reading of the evidence, part of the story of the Ottoman Empire: Although at times it expressed degrees of institutional quality, learning and intellectual pursuits, and shared opportunity that rivaled some of its European competitors, over the long term the character of its political and social life could not be aligned with the demands of the Renaissance spirit or anything like it. The Soviet Union provides a similar, later example of a state trying to gain the persistent benefits of a combination of social characteristics its system could simply not embrace.

***

Our analysis highlights a second insight into long-term patterns in world politics—the recurring pattern of nations or societies that stagnate and lose competitive standing. Many lose competitive energy for similar reasons: They become increasingly bureaucratized, governed by constraining orthodoxies, and captured by an oligarchic elite whose essential values and habits curdle over time into self-interest rather than public interest; next, institutions decay and the role of the active state becomes less effective or ebbs away. And then something happens—reform efforts collapse, or a major outside shock occurs, or an attack comes from some outside power—that thrusts the nation into a steeper decline.

This pattern connects our findings to several fascinating theories about cyclical dynamics in world politics.[20] Our research supports the narrow claim that nations' ability to sustain peak competitive performance may have a time limit. What appears to happen—as reflected

---

[18] Gluck, 2014, pp. 26–30.

[19] Gluck, 2014, pp. 26–30.

[20] One fascinating recent example is the investor Ray Dalio's (2021) concept of civilizational cycles.

in the cases of Rome, Britain, the late Ottoman Empire, the Soviet Union, and others—is that the nations lose the ability to maintain a productive balance in several of the characteristics. They become too ambitious and aggressive, allow their state apparatus to become too encompassing, or see a productive pluralism descend into a crippling degree of social fragmentation. Striking the right balance in a critical mass of these characteristics is a challenging task, it appears, and—if the historical pattern of gradual descent into stagnation is any guide—nations have difficulty doing so indefinitely.[21] The phases of world politics that appear in some theories might be not the result of mysterious structural long cycles but a natural product of degeneration and imbalance that tend to emerge while a nation tries to maintain equilibrium in its pursuit of societal advantages.

***

The third and final implication of our analysis for larger trends in world politics has to do with the most effective manner of achieving global influence. Those nations that have come to embody the prevailing paradigm for dynamism, and whose social characteristics best align with it, sustain the most-lasting competitive advantage. In the cases of Rome, Britain, and the United States,[22] the dominant powers were countries whose package of societal advantages matched the demands of the era, whether they be demographic muscle and national will, industrial output and commercial connections, or grassroots initiative and technological advance. Partly as a product of these factors but also as the result of strategic choice, these nations then placed themselves at the hub of regional or international networks of economic, intellectual, and cultural exchange. The result was that they came to dominate critical components of the international orders of their day.

The realist scholar of international relations Hans Morgenthau, though emphasizing the predominant role of political-military power as the basic currency of world politics, nonetheless well understands the effect of more-ephemeral forms of influence:

> [C]ultural imperialism is the most subtle and, if it were ever to succeed by itself alone, the most successful of imperialistic policies. It aims not at the conquest of territory or at the control of economic life, but at the conquest and control of the minds of men as an instrument for changing the power relations between two nations. If one could imagine the culture and, more particularly, the political ideology . . . of State A conquering the minds of all the citizens determining the policies of State B, State A would have won a more

---

[21] One typical pattern is the gradual capture of state and societal institutions by elite oligarchies, which then skew the operation of those institutions to their advantage, with the effect of reducing support to broadly shared opportunity, intensifying the stifling effect of bureaucracies, and sparking resentment throughout society.

[22] One could also make an argument for the Ottoman Empire as a candidate for this list, at least in a regional context. During its peak of power, it spent more than two centuries as the acknowledged geopolitical leader and socioeconomic hub of its area of influence. The Netherlands and the trading states of the Italian Renaissance, notably Venice, could be said to represent more-conditional versions of the same pattern.

complete victory and would have founded its supremacy on more stable grounds than any military conqueror or economic master.[23]

This idea gives a sense of the kind of power that nations wield when they come to embody the prevailing paradigm—that is, nations whose societal characteristics best meet the demands of a specific moment, including commercial and military aspects. The model of one of these nations will have inherent appeal as a source of national strength as much as a preferred way of organizing society. The nation will gain influence via the leading international elites trying to become part of its networks of exchange or mimic its package of societal characteristics. The scientific and cultural energy of the society will produce followers around the world. Mastering the essential characteristics of societal advantage produces national competitive advantage not only by fueling the nation's domestic dynamism but by creating a magnet for international alignment and ideas.

A country's *soft power*—the inherent appeal of a society, its magnetic force in world politics—is very much a function of the quality of its societal characteristics. Such a tie is implicit in the concept of soft power itself, which is all about the ways in which a country's basic qualities reverberate outward and provide influence and power. This analysis helps illustrate the more specific national characteristics that produce such soft power advantage. Some of the characteristics on our list do so directly, by, for example, creating an opportunity society that others view as a model for their own countries. These characteristics can also do so indirectly: Strength in learning, science, and education, for example—combined with nonsocietal factors, such as position in trade networks—can help establish a nation's language as the dominant means of shared global communication in many fields. This has certainly happened with English, a product of both British and American societal strengths and competitive position.

In this sense, though, our research also highlights a very real danger. Acquiring and then holding on to this role at the center of the global order begins with, and depends on, the strength of social characteristics in the leading power. As they ebb, so will its ability to preserve its claim to being the hub or embodiment of the paradigm of the era. The risks to American societal competitiveness outlined in Chapter Ten threaten not only domestic dynamism but also America's hold on world politics.

The Potential for an American Competitive Renaissance

Roberto Mangabeira Unger, discussing the British conundrum post-Brexit, argues that the various challenges of British life and society all highlight the same conclusion: the requirement for a "national project." Britain, this author says,

---

[23] Hans Morgenthau, *Politics Among Nations: The Struggle for Power and Peace*, brief ed., New York: McGraw Hill, 1993, p. 72.

does not have one. What kind of project would respond to the opportunities implied by those circumstances—a project not beholden to the fantasies and interests of the cosmopolitan elite that does business and makes policy in and around London? The very idea of a national project may seem anachronistic to that elite, which can barely disguise its distaste for the national idea and its skepticism about transformative ambition in politics.[24]

The analysis in Chapter Ten suggests that much the same could be said about the United States: To rejuvenate national competitive dynamism, it needs some form of a new national project, an agenda for national renewal based on an assessment of the factors that underwrite an engine of dynamism. This study has sought to contribute to such a dialogue by offering an admittedly partial assessment of what those factors—and that agenda—might be. An agenda for competitive success would look for ways to enhance each of the core societal characteristics, without going to excessive lengths and throwing them out of balance, and would seek to manage the U.S. position in the four major nonsocietal sources of advantage that can be affected with strategy.

This is a very broad injunction, in part because this study was never designed to generate specific policy proposals. But our research does allow us to identify the main elements of such a project at the level of broad societal characteristics. An agenda to rejuvenate America's engine of societal dynamism would likely include

- a renewed commitment to shared opportunity and to unleashing the national creativity and power that resides in underserved and underachieving parts of the population
- an unapologetic celebration of an American national community and spirit—a restatement and recommitment to the "energizing myth" of American society
- a somewhat stronger and more consistently active role for the state, but one that is precisely targeted based on the best available evidence of what interventions bring the most return on investment
- policies to encourage more-productive use of capital and less emphasis on such objectives as short-term boosts in stock price, including avenues to making capital more broadly available to a wider number of people and smaller firms[25]

---

[24] Unger, 2021.

[25] Some scholars discuss the potential value of a "democratization of capital," with the goal to "disperse capital through more accountable institutions that are independent from one another. More broadly dispersed capital would reduce the chances of mistakes being distributed nationally or internationally and make it more likely that capital would be matched with talents—the necessary condition of prosperity" (Reuven Brenner, "How the Financial Crisis Did Not Change the World," *American Affairs*, Vol. 3, No. 1, Spring 2019). The British political theorist and parliamentarian Maurice Glasman offers a similar idea, which he has termed "deconcentrating capital"—making more capital available to more people in society, specifically "locally focused, regionally oriented" elements of a country's "financial ecosystem." He refers to the need for "a new civic ecology" and recommends specific institutions in the British context—such as the Industrial and Commercial Finance Corporation to promote regionally based small and medium-size businesses—to expand access to capital (Maurice Glasman, "Deconcentrating Capital," *American Affairs*, Vol. 4, No. 1, Spring 2020). Edmund Phelps similarly argues that a more grassroots approach to lending and

- improved investment in the core elements of a learning and experimenting society, from research and development to research institutes and new models of education[26]
- a new war against bureaucratic excess and administrative constraints on creativity in the private and public sectors
- a much more urgent program to combat mis- and disinformation in society, better equip citizens to be critical information consumers, and strengthen the sources of sound and accurate versus misleading data.

This last priority may be of special importance. The poisoning of the basic atmosphere of information undermines needed societal characteristics across the board. It fragments national unity and makes effective learning and adaptation far more difficult. Our research suggests, in fact, that Truth Decay and the related explosion of misinformation and fragmented beliefs about reality may be the single most deadly threat to American societal dynamism, coherence, and competitiveness of any major trend today.[27]

It should be obvious that these findings, and proposed agenda items, have a thoroughly nonpartisan character in the United States. Some of them—an emphasis on the essential role of a vibrant commercial market, the risks of stifling bureaucracy, the fuel provided by a strong sense of national community and identity—are typical conservative ideas. Others are more commonly associated with liberal policies, including the need for an active state to shape markets in the public good and the moral but also instrumental value of socioeconomic equality and shared opportunity. Some elements represent ideas often shared across the political spectrum: an emphasis on local and grassroots initiatives, the energy that comes from an idealistic and ambitious desire to make a better future, and a desire to have social investments work for the common good.

The current American predicament—and opportunity—has imperfect but still-telling parallels to many of our historical cases. One of the most interesting, and worrying, comes from the Italian Renaissance. In many ways, the peak of Renaissance economics, art, culture, and politics was a very close early modern analogue to the sort of grassroots synergistic dynamism the United States would later come to reflect. But in the same way, the decay of the Italian city-states into a new kind of restrictive set of social hierarchies, and ultimately the orthodoxy and autocratic rule imposed by outside occupiers, ended that brilliant efflorescence.

---

investment would boost national dynamism. Phelps advocates for the competitive advantage conferred by a "landscape of the economy dotted with local investors and lenders" and proposes the idea of a national bank specifically oriented to making loans to start-up ventures (Phelps, 2013, p. 322).

[26] One review of the literature points to state actions which appear most measurably to bolster innovation. They are tax incentives for private research and development; direct government support for research, especially when linked to supporting local ecosystems of universities and research institutes; and seeking to enhance the human capital available for innovation by investing in expanded university programs in key areas as well as increasing skilled immigration (Nicholas Bloom, John Van Reenen, and Heidi Williams, "A Toolkit of Policies to Promote Innovation," *Journal of Economic Perspectives*, Vol. 33, No. 3, Summer 2019).

[27] Kavanagh and Rich, 2018.

We have cited the historian of the Renaissance Kenneth Bartlett on several occasions throughout this report. We will conclude by quoting at length from his series of lectures on that period. He ends those lectures with a melancholy meditation on the sources of national stagnation and decline. "The Renaissance ended," he explains,

> because the sets of attitudes and beliefs and self-confidence, that energizing myth that [was] the motive power of the Renaissance mind, simply ceased to function. The Renaissance could not continue in the form that it had. It couldn't be sustained because ultimately the failure wasn't military or political or economic, although all of these provided the context of the truly great failure which was psychological: The failure of will, the failure to confront the crises that the Italians knew that they were in, the decision—the hard decision, and the decision that is so natural in human nature, to accept what is known and safe and stable.[28]

That decision killed off many of the intellectual energies that had fired the greatness of the period. In the process, the "self-reinforcing energizing myth" that had driven the Italians "to do such great things—to extend human experience so far in such a short period of time," simply "evaporated."[29]

Whether current American society has begun to reflect similar patterns is for the reader to judge. In Chapter Ten we offered some concerning evidence about the major trends in each of our seven societal characteristics and some of the other factors associated with national competitiveness. But Bartlett is hinting at something broader, a more generalized personality trait of a civilization, something about the overarching mindset that comes to characterize a nation. He is speaking to the essential dynamism and vitality of a society—or, on the other side of the coin, the lack of ambition or commitment to learning, fear of the experimental and innovative, and commitment to grab as much power and profit as possible.

Our research does not allow for a final judgment on where the United States stands on these very abstract measures. What we can suggest is that the country's competitive standing, generally and in particular in the rivalry with a powerful and in some ways aggressive China, will be determined in large measure by which side of this coin comes to reflect American societal realities. Setting the country up for competitive success is ultimately far more about attending to these factors than deploying impressive military systems or sustaining large numbers of bases. The real test of whether the United States is up for this competition, then, is not the size of its defense budget but the seriousness of its commitment to rejuvenate its engine of national dynamism. The real test is whether the United States can generate a new era of dynamism and national competitive advantage by rediscovering its Renaissance spirit.

---

[28] Bartlett, 2005, lecture 35.

[29] Bartlett, 2005, lecture 35.

Methodology

David Landes was a Harvard professor of economics and history who tackled some of the most-grueling analytical problems of his day. He examined the fates of nations, the sources of economic development and national advantage, and the values that underpinned both. Landes described the difficulties of his task—drawing clear lines from cause to effect amid a welter of factors—this way:

> A definitive answer is impossible. We are dealing here with the most complex kind of problem, one that involves numerous factors of variable weights working in changing combinations. This sort of thing is hard to deal with even if one has precise data that lend themselves to refined techniques of analysis. But we have almost no evidence of this kind for the pre-modern period (say, before the eighteenth century), so that any judgment must be based on an impressionistic examination of the record.[1]

Our challenge in this project was similar. For this study we aimed to identify the societal characteristics that helped countries improve their competitive advantage. But answering this question is complicated by the buzzing swarm of variables that contribute to that outcome. Distinguishing the precise effect of any specific factor is difficult and in many cases impossible.

The difficulty was compounded by the complexity, and frankly the ambiguity, of the outcome we set ourselves to assess—national dynamism or competitive position. It is not a single factor or variable, like the rate of economic growth or level of defense spending. We quickly concluded that the more analytically clean our definition, the less analytically satisfying it was. We could take a nation's proportion of world GDP as a proxy for competitive standing and measure other variables against that single number. But a nation's slice of world GDP is *not* a reliable indicator of its competitive strength, as shown by China's mixture of vast relative GDP and military weakness during parts of the 19th century. If we defined competitive standing as equivalent to territory and population, on the other hand, it slipped into an uninteresting surrogate for a nation's mass.

As Landes implies, too, when making historical assessments (or even current ones, given the unreliable data on Chinese or Russian economic performance), the information available

---

[1] Landes, 2003, p. 14.

will often be painfully limited. For some historical periods and on certain issues, it is simply absent. Even had we decided to choose very discrete, measurable variables to serve as our societal characteristics and competitive outcome, we would not have then been able to simply populate a vast model with the necessary figures and turn the crank. The data are too thin.[2]

Smaller countries also had to have a voice in our story. We needed to define competitive success or failure in such a way that it did not rule out a country scoring high on our scale merely because it was small or strictly because it chose not to throw its geopolitical weight around. There was some tension here, because at the end of the day we *are* interested in the leading great powers and the societal fuel for their competitive standing. But valuable societal characteristics can improve the position of small and medium-size countries as much as big ones. A small country can be as highly competitive as its economic and military size will allow, and long-term success can be understood in more ways than success in war, global power, or territorial expansion.

The economist Dierdre McCloskey argues that "the entire, popular business of thinking of ranks and league tables and races and football yardage in which nations are 'beaten' or 'decline' or 'lose' tells the story the wrong way." In historical competitions, she explains, the

> prize for merely second place, or tenth place, was not poverty, or even loss of political hegemony. "Beaten" Britain is still the eighth-largest economy in the world, the second-largest source of direct foreign investment, and a permanent member of the United Nations Security Council; and London is the second-largest financial center in the world. Before the British, the leading case of "failure" was the United Provinces of the Netherlands in the eighteenth and early nineteenth centuries. With what result? Disaster? Poverty? No. True, the Netherlands has ended small and militarily weak, a tiny linguistic island in a corner of Europe. Yet by any historical or international standard it has become fabulously wealthy and indeed it is still among the most influential investors in the world. Relative "decline" is no decline at all.[3]

This distinction highlights, in part, the difference between absolute and relative power. Britain and the Netherlands have remained prosperous and successful as societies in absolute terms even as their relative competitive position has sagged. But that is partly an unavoidable

---

[2] Broadberry et al., 2014, p. 188; Studer, 2015, p. 3.

[3] McCloskey, 2011, loc. 1676–1682. The writer Ross Douthat similarly argues, "Neither the trajectory of morals nor aesthetics yields to simple narratives of rise and fall, and their connection to political strength is likewise highly contingent. Empires can fall at the height of their political and cultural vigor if they face a potent-enough enemy, and cultures can give in to appetitive excesses without necessarily seeing their political stability undone. (It was more than four hundred years from Nero's reign to the actual fall of Rome)" (Douthat, 2020, pp. 7–8). Writing about the Ottoman Empire, Marc David Baer (2021, p. 258) notes similarly that claims of an Ottoman "decline" made by reformist officials in the 17th century, after the time of Suleiman I, were premature. "We should not call this 'decline,'" he argues. "If there was a political decline of the empire, it came much later." The empire "lasted 356 years beyond his death, representing a very long decline."

result of their size: Once China got its economic act together, neither Britain nor the Netherlands could possibly remain a peer competitor. Yet for our analysis, the trick is that both nations have many helpful and competitively advantageous social qualities. They cannot be included in our rosters as competitive failures merely because of relative decline.

Moreover, as noted in Chapter One, our initial focus, and in some ways the true obsession of this study, was something more than competitive success. We were interested in that more fundamental, abstract, and ultimately elusive quality of national vitality or dynamism. The right societal characteristics add up to dynamism, which produces competitive success. Smaller states that succeed in ways short of geopolitical power indexes can still reflect a dynamic society, and their experience can tell us important things.

To incorporate all these ideas—measuring relative position but in qualitative ways that avoided crude and misleading proxy variables, understanding success and failure in nuanced terms, keeping in mind the essential focus on national dynamism, dealing with the absence of key data, and identifying societal qualities independent of national size or mass—we had to open the aperture and think of competitive position in a broad and complex way. That approach ruled out the hunt for any singular value, or even an index of several of them, against which to assess our societal characteristics.

Finally, as noted in Chapter One, the *primary* finding of this research is not about individual societal characteristics at all. It is about the synergies among and between them that produce a dynamic engine of national competitiveness. The most critical thing is the way our various characteristics mix, combine, strengthen, and support one another to produce effects greater than the sum of the parts. That fact complicates our assessment yet further: We had to be on the lookout for such intersections as much as the presence of specific national capacities.

The upshot of these considerations is that we can make only a qualified claim. We believe that we have identified seven societal characteristics that contribute to the competitive success of nations. But that overall conclusion is qualified in at least three ways. First, societal qualities are not the only factors that influence competitive standing. In Chapter Two, we survey others—from geography to participation in trade networks to the quality of national strategy—that also shape a country's competitive standing. Societal characteristics play a role, but they are part of a larger picture. Second, we cannot assign a specific value to any of the characteristics for any given nation at any specific time. Our analysis does not prove that a 10 percent boost in some measurable component of any given characteristic, for example, will lead to a 2 or 3 or 15 percent rise in competitive position. Third, we cannot promise that these seven are the only characteristics of societies that affect competitive standing. There may be others.

Nonetheless, our research provides a solid foundation for making important but limited claims. Nations that have positive expressions of the seven societal characteristics outlined here—either all of them or some subset clustered into a specific recipe for national strength—will gain competitive advantage. The absence of these qualities will most often prove a competitive disadvantage. Steps designed to maximize them therefore ought to help the United States improve its relative position in the current strategic competitions.

The Methodological Challenge of Complex Historical Causality

Any effort to clarify the causal relationship between two complex and somewhat abstract factors—in this case, what we are calling societal characteristics and national competitive position—must contend with a complex mosaic of factors and variables at work in that causal link. Debates about such relationships stem in part from the fact that different scholars combine those variables into competing theories and frameworks that purport to explain the reasons for events. There is, for example, "a traffic jam of contending theories" that claim to offer the real causes of Rome's decline.[4] Too many variables whose causal interrelationships are only imperfectly understood jostle for analytical attention.[5] In methodological terms, the problem is sometimes referred to as "endogeneity," a situation in which "a whole array of variables are mutually influencing each other and changing simultaneously in the process."[6]

For our purposes, the difficulty of identifying causal connections is complicated by the fact that even seemingly critical variables do not track neatly with national competitive trajectories. For example, "Stalled technological progress does not coincide with decline."[7] Nor, we might agree, do variables such as strong institutions of property rights and governance, measures of human capital, or the degree of national unity.

This has not kept scholars from trying to identify the master cause or causes, the single or small number of variables that are responsible for major historical outcomes, including wars, degrees of national development, and relative power. Whether they emphasize "cultural values," climate change, Peter Turchin's notion of "cliodynamics," Deirdre McCloskey's focus on the competitive effects of free market economies, Ian Morris's case for energy capture or

---

[4] Harper, 2017, pp. 12, 20.

[5] Landes puts it with characteristic elegance: "Economic analysis cherishes the illusion that one good reason should be enough, but the determinants of complex processes are invariably plural and interrelated. Monocausal explanations will not work" (David S. Landes, "Culture Makes Almost All the Difference," in Lawrence E. Harrison and Samuel P. Huntington, eds., *Culture Matters: How Values Shape Human Progress*, New York: Basic Books, 2000, p. 3). Dierdre McCloskey also emphasizes Alexander Gerschenkron's point about "essential prerequisites for economic growth," where he argues that "one thing can 'substitute' for another" (McCloskey, 2011, loc. 2319–2320). Such substitution effects make it impossible to prove that any one factor is essential or has a consistent and generalizable effect on competition: If it can be substituted for with other things, its role is only case specific.

[6] Studer, 2015, p. 3.

[7] Vijg, 2011, p. 204.

other factors, these analyses apply various (often quantitative) methods to the horde of variables at work and hope to pick out the few that are most decisive.[8]

Moreover, as noted above, using such models to explain historical periods of national rivalry is confounded by the fact that the data simply are not there. Scholars attacking the analytically simpler challenge of discovering the causes for economic growth in Europe since about the 15th century have admitted as much. Going back much before the 18th century in any rigorous quantitative way is extremely difficult.

The inevitable conclusion is that complex outcomes, such as economic development or national competitive position, can be explained only with the help of many causal variables. One discussion of the sources of the Great Divergence puts it well:

> In terms of an overall explanation for such far-reaching change, this study confirms more traditional lines of argument that go against mono-causal explanations and stress a "seamless web of historical change." Several things seem to have happened simultaneously and probably interdependently, reinforcing each other. The various factors that seem to account for Europe's early rise include better institutions, favorable geographical features, increasing political stability, and increasingly rapid advances in science and technology. We thus depart from popular research strategies . . . in naming one decisive factor or even a clear place and point in time as the main origin of economic integration or economic development.[9]

Our research confirmed the need for such a multicausal assessment of the sources of societal competitive advantage. This basic decision, however, generated many subsidiary questions. Without assigning quantitative associations between variables, how could we make rigorous conclusions about the role of societal characteristics in producing outcomes? A major problem with multicausal assessment is the requirement, in research designed to preserve some echo of a scientific method, for falsifiability. It is well and good to suggest that national will provides competitive advantage. But is this a falsifiable claim? Can we, in theory, prove it wrong? Partly this would seem to demand finding cases in which an absence of national will ruined national competitive standing.

Then there is the problem of generalizability. Scientific theories pursue it doggedly, trying to identify causal relations that hold across nature. Yet in a multicausal analysis, if a swarm of causes work together to generate certain outcomes, and if the swarm can look different in dif-

---

[8] Turchin, 2003; McCloskey, 2010; Morris, 2013. In this they follow Landes's description of the methodological temptation when offering a complex explanation for complex issues: "How much more agreeable it would be to reduce everything to a handful of aspects and explain these by a handful of causes!" (Landes, 2003, p. 554).

[9] Studer, 2015, p. 181. The famed political scientist Kenneth Boulding built theories that were more mechanistic than the approach we have designed. But he still argues that his approach is "unfriendly to any monistic view of human history that seeks to explain it by a single factor. . . . [It] sees human history as a vast interacting network of species and relationships of many different kinds, and there is really no 'leading factor' always in the forefront" (Boulding, 1978, p. 19).

ferent cases—if a distinct set of variables can cause the same outcome—then it is simply infeasible to generate a comprehensive, generalizable theory, and falsification becomes impossible for any single variable. As noted in Chapter Eleven, recipes for success can—and do—take different shapes in different contexts. Any analysis must therefore ultimately determine what societal characteristics are important to success in a *specific* competition, rather than to competition in general. But if three or seven or fifteen combinations of social characteristics can produce success, how can we say anything definitive about them?

One implication of these difficulties was that a quantitative model that tried to produce something as pure and simple as a plot of variables could never work for our purpose. The variables involved are too numerous, too incommensurable, in many cases too abstract to measure properly. Any coding of variables in a model would inevitably involve heroic levels of subjective judgment—and with a very large error margin in many of the codings across dozens of variables, the resulting findings would be more noise than signal.

Nonsocietal Factors, Time, and Intervening Variables

The difficulty of multicausal analysis was not the only methodological hurdle we confronted. We also had to account for the competitive role of factors other than societal character. Various analyses of great power competition have stressed factors other than the character of a society, such as geography and demographic profile.[10] If these factors are decisive, then success or failure in strategic competitions might not have much to do with societal character at all. And because this analysis does not envisage a comprehensive survey of all factors bearing on competition, we would not be able to make claims about the relative importance of societal characteristics relative to other things. The analysis can only try to identify such characteristics that are strongly associated with competitive success; it will not be able to precisely measure their degree of importance.

Further, we had to decide how timeless and universal these characteristics might be. Historical analyses of the competitive role of societal characteristics might be of little use if each case is unique.[11] Because of limits on data, it would be difficult if not impossible to conduct adequate statistical analyses comparing variables from most historical periods.

In premodern times the basis for competitive advantage was surely different. Walter Scheidel examines the common authoritarian, highly unequal patterns of premodern societies and points out, "Centralized authoritarian states commonly outcompeted differently structured rivals. Defying this considerable diversity of context, the best-known among them

---

[10] Michael Beckley, "The Power of Nations: Measuring What Matters," *International Security*, Vol. 43, No. 2, Fall 2018a.

[11] "Each country, region, historical period, and indeed each human being is unique in many ways," Mancur Olson concludes. "Thus the fact that a country with an unusually high growth rate has this or that distinctive trait provides no justification for the inherence that there is a causal connection" (Olson, 1982, loc. 163).

developed into strikingly similar entities." At the same time, "the residue of ancestral egalitarianism was replaced by belief in the merits of inequality and acceptance of hierarchy as an integral element of the natural and cosmic order." He refers to the

> competitive advantage of a particular type of state: far-flung imperial structures held together by powerful extractive elites. This is where empire thrived: for thousands of years, most of humanity lived in the shadow of these behemoths, with a few coming to tower far above ordinary mortals. This was the environment that created what I call the "original 1 percent," made up of competing but often closely intertwined elite groups that did their utmost to capture the political rents and commercial gains mobilized by state-building and imperial integration.[12]

This approach to competitive advantage—centralized authoritarian empires relying on networks of extractive elites—is close to the inverse of the most-powerful modern recipes for competitive success. The contrast raises a potent question today, two decades into a century that many expect to see significant changes in human social and economic organization. If the 21st century is indeed the time of the "network society" and if networks, connections, and interdependencies provide decisive competitive advantage, then the most-advantageous societal characteristics might be things totally unknown in earlier eras.[13] We must identify the traits needed to do well in the *current* competition, partly through assessing the wider socioeconomic context and the demands it will make on nations.

Yet another methodological challenge was to identify possible intervening factors that could disrupt the causal relationships. Consider the simplified relationship depicted in Figure A.1.

In that relationship, it is the factors in the second box—the intervening products of democratic governance—that generate the actual competitive advantage. The question then is whether a state could produce *those* factors in the absence of democracy: Could a state sidestep the more typical route to openness and flexibility with innovative structures inside an autocratic system? And if so, are there in fact any societal qualities that are either necessary or sufficient for competitive advantage—or can the right set of national policies alone cir-

FIGURE A.1
Levels of Factors

[12] Scheidel, 2018, pp. 57–58.

[13] Manuel Castells, *The Rise of the Network Society*, Oxford: Blackwell Publishers, 1996.

cumvent the importance of such characteristics? Part of the challenge is to avoid an endless regression to more-essential causes that often cannot be reliably identified.[14]

A good example of this challenge emerges from a review of Michael Beckley's book comparing U.S. and Chinese power.[15] Many of the factors he highlights as competitive advantages (such as high levels of societal wealth, strong economic productivity, low levels of domestic crime and unrest, and accountable institutions) are best viewed as intervening factors. All flow from more-fundamental roots. But if the sources of those roots are highly contested—if there is no agreement, for example, on where productivity comes from—then we will be incapable of locating more-basic characteristics, habits, or behaviors that will reliably produce those outcomes. And if it turns out that there are many possible policy levers to generate each of the desired outcomes, then societal characteristics may be exogenous to competitive success.

Our research uncovered many variables that fit into this category—the critical *intervening factors*, the considerations between the baseline societal characteristics and the competitive outcomes. These are national advantages or qualities that successful competitors must achieve, but they are downstream from societal characteristics. These are domestic measurable outcomes that represent transmission belts of the effects of national characteristics into relative competitive advantage. Examples might include the following factors.

The Well-Being of a Nation's People

It could be that national well-being, understood in a very broad sense, is a precondition for effective long-term competition. This factor is not a societal characteristic, but nor is it a relative outcome. It is not in any way zero sum or even relative between countries; it is therefore not easily used as an outcome measure of a competition. And yet various versions of this factor figure prominently in just about all national security strategies, measures of national power, and indexes of national competitiveness; scoring highly on this metric is surely seen as a leading measure of a "successful" society. And there is some evidence that national well-being enhances such variables as national will, resources available for competition, political and social stability, and other factors that contribute to competitive success; whereas declining well-being is associated with instability and weakness.

---

[14] Olson makes a similar argument with regard to arguments about the "sources" of economic development and growth: Evidence of the "sources" of growth "do not tell us about the ultimate causes of growth. They do not tell us what incentives made the saving and investment occur, or what explained the innovations, or why there was more innovation and capital accumulation in one society or period than in another. They do not trace the sources of growth to their fundamental causes; they trade the water in the river to the streams and lakes from which it comes, but they do not explain the rain" (Olson, 1982, loc. 78–82).

[15] Michael Beckley, *Unrivaled: Why America Will Remain the World's Sole Superpower*, Ithaca, N.Y.: Cornell University Press, 2018b.

The Legitimacy and Allegiance Commanded by the National Governing System

A similarly important intervening factor could be the ability of the government of a nation—either a specific regime or the governance system over time—to command legitimacy in the eyes of its people. Many societal characteristics could have the effect of producing (or undermining) such legitimacy, which would then have many second-order effects in terms of the nation's ability to generate the national effort and will to compete.

Economic Growth, Both General and Per Capita

Growth of a country's GDP could be the critical intervening variable because it is the engine of just about everything else—domestic social stability, military power, and international influence. Advantageous societal characteristics could be beneficial *because* they boost a country's growth rate.

Productivity Levels

Virtually every major study of national competitive advantage in an economic or business context ultimately comes back to the central role of national levels of productivity. It could be that some important societal characteristics are associated with competitive advantage precisely *because* they generate higher productivity.

Innovation Measures and Proxies

Finally, Michael Porter's work also stresses the degree to which innovation, change and adaptation are central characteristics of competitive firms, and the societal characteristics that encourage that outcome are critical for nations.[16] Stagnation may be a central variable in determining competitive failure.

Such intervening metrics could point in the direction of relatively simple indicators to assess a country's competitive standing—metrics that can serve as second-order indicators or proxies for the societal characteristics we hope to identify. On the basis of this list, for example, a sample measure of broadly defined well-being, a rating of a government's perceived legitimacy and effectiveness, growth rates of GDP and total factor productivity (or a related productivity measure), and some overall measure of innovative progress could tell an important story. But it would be a story of symptoms rather than causes, of the suggestive indications of the more underlying and fundamental sources of national competitive advantage. If this analysis can identify the fundamental societal characteristics that produce these measures, understanding a society's competitive trend lines would still demand knowing the status of those characteristics.

---

[16] M. Porter, 2019.

The Core Causal Approach: Middle-Range Mechanisms

Because of the constraints on our analysis—the complexities of the factors involved, the limits of available data, the multiple potential alternate causalities—we cannot say that any one of our nominated characteristics will have a predictable degree of effect on competitive standing. Nor will the characteristics have the same value for different countries. The characteristics will have different effects at different periods in history or if assembled in different ways in divergent packages of social qualities. We cannot, therefore, claim to have discovered an invariant, lawlike causal relationship between these characteristics, individually or as a set, and competitive advantage.

Yet not all causal relationships in the real world are subject to that demanding level of proof. To take one example, hundreds of studies have shown the general value of physical exercise for enhancing health—but the way this plays out with any given individual is subject to great variation and uncertainty. To say that no lawlike relationship exists between a specific form or amount of exercise and a particular health outcome does not necessarily deny the truth of a broad causal association, one that justifies changes in behavior.

Much social scientific analysis of causal relations is designed to be *explanatory* and *exploratory* rather than designed to generate precise, universal relationships. Rather than claiming a definitive and predictive cause-and-effect relationship between two variables, such analysis can describe causal links "in more general terms."[17] In fact, some methodologies seeking to demonstrate such lawlike causal relationships, such as randomized controlled trials, often produce results that turn out to be highly localized and contingent.[18]

It is in this spirit of exploration and explanation that we approached the methodology of this study. Rather than trying to build models that assert a replicable and direct causal relationship between two precisely defined variables, we looked for an evidence-based causal association between them. We have discovered abundant evidence supporting the claim that each of these characteristics is associated with national competitive advantage—in different ways at different times but persistently. Such abstract and less quantifiable causal relationships clearly exist and are relevant for understanding outcomes in world politics.

The challenge is how to approach them in the most analytically demanding manner possible. At its worst, such argumentation can become hand-waving around ill-defined terms. This problem infects, for example, Edward Gibbon's argument about the decline and fall of Rome.[19] He attributes the decline in important part to moral weakness, in part brought on by the rise of Christianity. But he never defines that variable. He cannot come close to measuring it; indeed he has no idea whether and to what degree Roman leaders reflected such attitudes

---

[17] Connable et al., 2018, pp. 34–36.

[18] Nancy Cartwright, "Will This Policy Work for You? Predicting Effectiveness Better: How Philosophy Helps," *Philosophy of Science*, Vol. 79, No. 5, December 2012.

[19] Gibbon and Mueller, 2005.

at any given time. He cannot connect moral weakness to specific competitive outcomes—the decline of economic performance, for example, or the loss of a particular battle.

The risk of less precise connections, of course, is that we could confuse correlation with causation. One could say, for example, that a thousand Americans were fired last year within a week of riding a roller coaster. The fact of a correlation in these cases does not prove that the rides caused the dismissals—and only "causal laws" can be the foundation of good public policy.[20] We need large-scale studies that prove with statistical certainty that riding roller coasters leads to firing.

In the world of social and political events, such strict causal laws are difficult to demonstrate. But again, exact and definitive causal proof cannot be the sole standard against which we judge analysis. Other levels of analytical proof can still indicate causal confidence at a level somewhere between random correlation and strict causal laws. These would be relationships supported by strong narrative, qualitative, and related empirical evidence that all strongly suggest that factor A is related to outcome B. We are terming these relationships *demonstrated causal associations*.

These associations differ from causal laws in several ways. The associations are not universal—they will be true to different degrees in different contexts.[21] They are not linear or precise; the level of correlation will change in various places and across time. They are subject to multiple other intervening factors that can enhance or depress their effect. But they nonetheless highlight a causal relationship that is common enough and repeatable enough to allow a confident claim that it will often be true. They represent, in some ways, the equivalent of saying "exercise is generally good for you, and especially under the following conditions"—a causal claim supported by vast empirical and anecdotal evidence, but one whose measurable degree will vary from case to case.

In the same way that the general causal insight about exercise is good enough to recommend behavioral changes, such demonstrated causal associations in social science ought to be strong enough to influence public policy decisions, if they take seriously a certain margin of error and need for experimentation to see the best ways to make use of the relationship. Yet pointing to such associations still leaves us one step short of choosing the right specific policy interventions. That sort of research, to find the policy interventions with the highest return on investment, is well beyond the aspirations of this effort.

∗∗∗

In an interesting way, this insight—the need to remain constantly open to revised evidence about causal relationships and to experiment with causal associations rather than

---

[20] Nancy Cartwright, "How to Do Things with Causes," *Proceedings and Addresses of the American Philosophical Association*, Vol. 83, No. 2, November 2009.

[21] In technical terms, the associations relax the invariable requirement for causal claims. They are not scientific laws in this sense, arguing that under specified conditions, input A will always produce output B.

leaping to one grand policy solution—meant that our methodology ended up reflecting our research findings. Our analysis strongly suggests that the most dynamic and ultimately competitive nations have strong grassroots energy. These nations encourage, explicitly and implicitly, creativity and innovation and entrepreneurialism and experimentation across a wide range of the society. They create, as the economist Eric Beinhocker suggests, a "portfolio of experiments" in service of societal or economic goals and let experience and evidence and markets—regulated by a state enforcing standards of common good—sort out the best.[22] Each of those causal relationships can be highly qualified and case specific; a given policy intervention may only work in one type of community, for a limited period, or with the right secondary support policies.

Such an approach combines a limited top-down identification of key goals and a strong bottom-up set of experiments to determine the more precise causal relationships that support those broad goals. In *neither* of those cases is the public official seeking ironclad causal laws. The cases are operating first on rigorously identified causal associations that point generally in the right direction, and then nourishing thousands of experiments to generate more-discrete and sometimes definitive causal relationships. But neither case is held to be universal.

This is roughly the combination we have in mind with our approach to causality. We can identify certain strong associations, validated by analysis, but leave it to experience and issue-specific research to generate a collection of public policies that moves the ball forward gradually. This has much in common with the philosopher Nancy Cartwright's proposed criteria for good community-based experimentation to discover causal relationships. She argues for ongoing, interactive research agendas that are numerous, diverse, "mutually scrutinizing," connected to other disciplines and practices, and wide-ranging across available knowledge,[23] an approach that matches the essential nature of the engine of dynamism we described in Chapter One. Both involve a spirit of intellectual inquiry and evidence-based experimentation. Both recognize the value of grassroots involvement of many actors and diversity among them. Both embody an urge to understand and, to a degree through causal awareness, master the world around us.

***

The resulting methodological approach has much in common with an alternative strategy for assessing causation, which has been termed *middle-range theory* or sometimes *mechanisms* or *middle-range law mechanisms*.[24] Two scholars define *middle-range theory* as

> a clear, precise, and simple type of theory which can be used for partially explaining a range of different phenomena, but which makes no pretense of being able to explain all

---

[22] Beinhocker, 2007.

[23] Cartwright, 2020, pp. 306–307.

[24] Cartwright, 2020.

social phenomena. . . . It is a vision of sociological theory as a toolbox of semigeneral theories[,] each of which is adequate for explaining a limited range or type of phenomena.[25]

Cartwright offers the example of democratic peace theory as a classic modern case of such middle-range theorizing.[26] The claim that democracies tend not to go to war with one another is not an *invariant* lawlike proposition: It admits exceptions and will be true for different reasons in different cases. Nonetheless, it states a causal relationship, between the characteristics of democracies and choices for war, that is true across time and geography.

Jon Elster argues for a similar approach, the use of explanatory "mechanisms" in social science that make important claims of causal relationship short of invariant, lawlike causalities. He defines such mechanisms as "frequently occurring and easily recognizable causal patterns that are triggered under generally unknown conditions or with indeterminate consequences."[27] The idea is frequently used to describe more discrete and limited causal relationships than the ones we discuss in this work. But the basic comparison—between lawlike regularities and general causal relations that admit many qualifications and exceptions—informs our methodological approach.

In employing such rigorous but less lawlike causal arguments, Cartwright argues that precision in defining terms is important—democratic peace theorists spend exhaustive effort defining *democracy*. And yet not all of them do so in the same way, and she ends up concluding that useful middle-range theories can get away with "employing loosely characterized concepts." She argues that "the fact that a middle-range law mechanism is loose does not mean that its use is uncontrolled. . . . We can equally do it with knowledge-how, reflected in a thick tangle of critically evolved practices."[28] In other words, a "thick tangle" of multimethod approaches based on historical narrative and disciplinary understanding, focused on clear but still somewhat loosely defined concepts, can say meaningful causal things.

***

Middle-range mechanisms can be stated as bald assertions rather than carefully defined analytical arguments (such as, "nations with a stronger moral fiber are more competitive"). To bring methodological rigor to qualified causal associations, we established several conditions for such claims. They require the analyst to ask five questions, listed in Table A.1 (a reprint of Table 1.2), along with examples drawn from one of our seven societal characteristics—

---

[25] Hedström and Bearman, 2011, p. 31.

[26] Cartwright explains, "The claim 'democracies do not go to war with democracies' is an example of a middle-range theory par excellence. It is in the middle with respect to the abstractness of the concepts employed and the breadth of the claim's applicability, i.e. between high social theory and more specific social science claims that use more detailed concepts about more specifically identified issues" (Cartwright, 2020, p. 277).

[27] Elster, 1998, p. 45. See also Elster, 2015.

[28] Cartwright, 2020, pp. 314–315.

TABLE A.1

Elements of Demonstrated Causal Associations—Shared Opportunity

Question and Criterion	Example
Can we *define the factor we are trying to assess* with sufficient detail, rigor, and precision to test its effect in real settings?	Shared opportunity can be understood as the ability of all or a large part of a population—both in absolute terms and relative to its competitors—to express its talents in economic, political, and social contexts; partial elements include such measurable indicators as social mobility, numbers of entrepreneurs from middle and lower classes, availability of capital, and quality and reach of mass education.
Is there a strong *theoretical reason* to believe in this causal association that specifies the pathways by which the factor will achieve outcomes?	In theory it ought to be the case that a superior ability to tap into a nation's human resources ought to enhance national power and thus competitiveness.
Do historical cases or surveys provide *multiple concrete examples of various types of this association* that confirm some causal relationship and show how the factor generates outcomes?	Such causal ties show up in multiple case studies. The British case, for example, indicates how opening opportunity to a wide range of the population to become inventors and entrepreneurs can provide national access to critical new technologies.
Is there *issue-specific empirical evidence* validating the causal effect of one or more subsets of the association?	Economic research has shown a relationship between greater opportunity, including such proxy factors as social mobility, and aspects of national dynamism, including economic performance; other empirical evidence shows that the denial of opportunity has effects that degrade national stability and coherence.
Are there any cases or alternative causalities that *decisively contract the causal relationship*?	We found no major cases of nations that achieved sustained dynamism or competitive advantage while displaying significantly less shared opportunity than their direct rivals or competitors.

shared opportunity. In the process, this analysis seeks to specify the pathways for causal effect, exactly *how* a factor will achieve its effects.[29]

This approach begins to satisfy two of Cartwright's proposed criteria for assessing the rigor of middle-range theories or mechanisms. Her call for a deeply "tangled" or comprehensive mixed-methods approach with evidence from multiple sources and disciplines employed to assess the causal relationship is embodied here in the evidence from various disciplines and methods, including case analysis and issue-specific empirical tests, that are reflected in answering these five questions. Cartwright also suggests that such mechanisms can be assessed by the degree to which they confirm prior descriptive models applied to similar cases. We bring this test to bear through our reliance on existing global histories and previous efforts to identify characteristics associated with national dynamism.[30]

---

[29] On the importance of reasons why a factor causes an outcome as opposed to "black box" explanations, see Elster, 1998, pp. 47–48.

[30] Cartwright, 2020, p. 315.

In our assessment of disconfirming cases, we were partly trying to determine whether such alternate causality could explain the effects of our nominated characteristics. This is much more difficult in historically based social analysis because the data do not exist to simply pull one of the variables out of the picture. Still, we did interrogate our cases with this question partly in mind: Do any of them suggest that the outcome—for example, of strong economic dynamism—can be sustainably achieved by using techniques A and B instead of many of the characteristics we propose? A good example here is the contrast between state-dominated, force-fed economic development and technological progress versus dynamism based on opportunity, learning and adapting, diversity and pluralism, and other characteristics we highlight.

***

The chapters on the characteristics, Chapters Three through Nine, follow this approach and are organized roughly according to these five questions or categories. Each first seeks to define the societal characteristic being proposed, both as a general concept and in terms of specific recognizable expressions in the real world. Each chapter outlines the theoretical case for the association between that characteristic and competitive success. Each chapter then surveys the case studies and global histories for anecdotal evidence to support the association. In the process, we looked for clearly disconfirming cases; in some cases, chapters will mention possible candidates. And each offers empirical evidence that demonstrates the competitive effects of subcomponents of the characteristic.

There are still risks, even in such a humbler approach to causal analysis. Cartwright worries about a specific form of variance in causal relationships—what she terms *fragility*. "So many of the causal laws I know break, and so readily," she explains, "when we try to use them. Winding up the toy soldier causes him to march—if only you don't wind too tightly."[31] Once we relax rules of universality and invariance, causal relationships begin to become less predictable and more brittle. If a proposed relationship becomes too fragile, it ceases to have any analytical or policy value. We do believe that the evidence reviewed for this study strongly supports the tie between the seven nominated characteristics and national competitive success. But when turning to policy, that connection must be investigated gradually, through experiments, and with humility, knowing that the causal relationships we have identified are somewhat contingent and uncertain.

Identifying Cases for Comparative Analysis

The next step toward assessing causal connections was choosing the historical case studies we would lean on in developing the evidence. Discrete historical cases represent only one of several major components of the research basis for our findings. Ultimately, though, under-

---

[31] Cartwright, 2009, p. 12.

standing the trajectories of specific great powers is an essential starting point in identifying societal characteristics that influenced those trajectories. Building a baseline set of focus countries—and then developing a snapshot of the competitive position of each of them over time—was therefore a critical foundation for the analysis.

Building a Roster of Cases

In one sense, choosing historical cases to mine for evidence on characteristics of societal competitiveness was straightforward. We conducted research into leading examples of great powers, particularly those that had experienced significant competitive success or failure, over the history of international relations. But to assure that we were not missing any potential sources of evidence, we reviewed three categories of literature for candidate societies.

First, we reviewed the literature on international rivalry, particularly on both bilateral and multilateral great power rivalries in the modern era. This literature highlighted several well-known great power cases over roughly the past five centuries. These included

- Austro-Hungarian Empire
- China
- Britain
- France
- Italy (including maritime city-states, such as Venice and Genoa)
- Japan
- Netherlands
- Prussia and Germany
- Russia and the Soviet Union
- Ottoman Empire
- Sweden
- United Habsburgs
- United States.[32]

Second, we identified specific periods of bilateral rivalries over since the 19th century.[33] We did so to support potential analysis of success and failure. In identifying the winners and

[32] Jack Levy, "Historical Trends in Great Power War, 1495–1975," *International Studies Quarterly*, Vol. 26, No. 2, 1982.

[33] Empirical and historical sources that address this specific factor include Michael P. Colaresi, Karen Rasler, and William R. Thompson, *Strategic Rivalries in World Politics: Position, Space and Conflict Escalation*, Cambridge, UK: Cambridge University Press, 2008; Karen Rasler, William R. Thompson, and Sumit Ganguly, *How Rivalries End*, Philadelphia: University of Pennsylvania Press, 2013; Paul F. Diehl and Gary Goertz, *War and Peace in International Rivalry*, Ann Arbor: University of Michigan Press, 2000; D. Scott Bennett, "Security, Bargaining, and the End of Interstate Rivalry," *International Studies Quarterly*, Vol. 40, No. 2, 1996; Zeev Maoz and Ben D. Mor, *Bound by Struggle: The Strategic Evolution of Enduring International Rivalries*, Ann Arbor: University of Michigan Press, 2002.

losers of such rivalries, we could begin to create the general outcome judgments to support a causal analysis of societal characteristics. Table A.2 lists the rivalries that appear in major sources in this literature.

TABLE A.2
Major Rivalries Since 1816

Rivalry	Start Year	End Year
U.S.-Britain	1816	1904
U.S.-Spain	1816	1819
U.S.-France	1830	1871
U.S.-Germany	1889	1918
U.S.-Japan	1898	1945
U.S.-Germany	1933	1945
U.S.–Soviet Union	1945	1989
U.S.-China	1949	1972
U.S.-China	1996	Ongoing
U.S.-Russia	2007	Ongoing
Britain-France	1816	1904
Britain-Russia/Soviet Union	1816	1956
Britain-China	1839	1900
Britain-Germany	1896	1918
Britain-Japan	1932	1945
Britain-Germany	1934	1945
Britain-Italy	1934	1945
France-Austria-Hungary	1816	1918
France-Germany	1816	1955
France-Russia	1816	1894
France-China	1856	1900
France-Italy	1881	1940
Prussia-Austria-Hungary	1816	1870
Germany-Poland	1918	1939
Germany–Soviet Union/Russia	1890	1945
Germany-China	1897	1900

Table A.2—Continued

Rivalry	Start Year	End Year
Poland-Russia	1918	1939
Austria-Hungary-Russia	1816	1918
Austria-Hungary–Ottoman Empire	1816	1908
Austria-Hungary-Italy	1847	1918
Italy–Ottoman Empire/Turkey	1884	1943
Russia–Ottoman Empire	1816	1918
Russia/Soviet Union–China	1816	1949
Russia/Soviet Union–Japan	1894	1945
Soviet Union–China	1958	1989
China-Japan	1873	1945
China-India	1948	Ongoing
China-Taiwan	1949	Ongoing
China-Japan	1996	Ongoing

SOURCES: William R. Thompson, "Identifying Rivals and Rivalries in World Politics," *International Studies Quarterly*, Vol. 45, No. 4, December 2001; J. David Singer, "Reconstructing the Correlates of War Dataset on Material Capabilities of States, 1816–1985," *International Interactions*, Vol. 14, No. 2, 1987.

Third, we reviewed the literature on the rise and fall of societies to identify other major powers or city-states, largely from eras before the modern period of great power rivalries. The most prominent such premodern powers that appear in this literature include

- Ancient Egypt
- Ancient Greece (Athens, Sparta, others)
- Rome (republican and imperial periods)
- African empires beyond Egypt (such as the Mali and Songhai)
- Assyrian Empire
- Persian/Safavid Empire
- Maya Empire
- Inca Empire
- Anasazi civilization
- premodern Chinese empires and states
- Mongol Empire
- Nordic societies (Greenland, Norway, Viking)
- Italian Renaissance city-states (Florence, Venice, Genoa, Milan)
- Mughal Empire.[34]

---

[34] Acemoglu and Robinson 2012; Diamond, 2005; Morris, 2010.

Ultimately, we focused on 12 more-detailed historical cases, listed in Table A.3 (a reprint of Table 1.3). We addressed them with a combination of internal RAND assessments and commissioned papers from leading historians specializing in these cases. In addition to those 12, we conducted more in-depth research on several other important countries in relation to their competitive position over time. These included classical Greece (specifically Athens), Italy, Germany (and its Prussian predecessor), the Netherlands, and South Korea.

Identifying Periods of Competitive Advantage (and Failure)

Having developed a roster of nations, empires, and civilizations to examine for evidence, we sought to create an initial, rough periodization of their competitive positions. Ultimately, our assessment of the value of the societal characteristics was not solely dependent on alignment to trajectories of national competitive advantage. We also sought issue-specific historical and empirical evidence for the characteristics' value. If studies show that broad-based social opportunity empowers a nation's economy and military, for example, that demonstrates the value of the characteristic. But many of these cases represent centuries of gradual rise, peak power, and eventually decline (relative or absolute), and we could not trace the effect of the characteristics across such immense time spans. At a minimum we wanted to identify the periods of peak competitive standing to help our evaluation of the role of characteristics in producing it.

Appendix B discusses our definition of *competitive success and failure* at more length. Here we briefly summarize the general trends—periods when nations or societies were gener-

TABLE A.3
Historical Cases Assessed for the Study

Case	Analyses Conducted
Rome	RAND analysis
China (premodern and modern)	RAND and external analyses
Spain	RAND and external analyses
Austria-Hungary	RAND and external analyses
Ottoman Empire	RAND and external analyses
Renaissance Italy	RAND analysis
Britain	RAND and external analyses
Sweden	RAND analysis
France	RAND analysis
Japan	RAND and external analyses
Soviet Union	RAND analysis
United States	RAND analysis

ally successful or rising and periods when they were declining or failing. There is insufficient reliable historical data to allow very specific causal analysis across fine-grained periods of national history. This analysis is therefore ultimately qualitative and case specific. Table A.4 offers such an initial assessment.

TABLE A.4

Periodization of Competitive Advantage

Case Study	Competitive Advantage
Rome	Rome's long period of predominant power remains by far the most extended of any case study subject on our list. The full space of its dominant competitive position in the Western world might run from 146 BCE, when it defeated Carthage in the Third Punic War, through to the fall of the Western empire in 476 CE, although there were of course many peaks and valleys in Roman competitive position during that time.
China (ancient to modern)	The premodern and early modern trajectory of Chinese power is somewhat contested (relative to Europe) and determined in part by whether China is judged as a collection of states or the leading state. Two obvious peaks include the societal and cultural efflorescence of the Song Dynasty in 960–1279 CE and the premodern height of Chinese power in the Qing Dynasty, 1636–1912. An obvious fallow period was 1839 to 1949, when China fell substantially behind the West, running from the Opium Wars, through Japanese occupation and the postwar civil war, to the establishment of the People's Republic.
Spain	The Spanish monarchy persisted for three centuries, but its period of peak competitive position was shorter than some of the cases on our list. Its rise began in the late 15th century and accelerated early in the 16th century CE, with an apex of power in the first half of the 16th century, during the reign of Charles V (1500–1558), when Spain controlled Portugal and parts of the Netherlands and Germany and had massive New World colonies generating huge amounts of resources (35 million total pesos between 1591 and 1959). By the 1550s Habsburg armies significantly outnumbered those of France and England combined (150,000 versus 50,000 and 20,000, respectively), an advantage that persisted into the 1630s. But constant wars and a decline in New World revenues (down to 12 million pesos in 1646–1650, only 1.2 million of which went into crown coffers) undermined the empire's power. Its regional advantage had ended by the 1659 defeat in the Franco-Spanish War.
Austria-Hungary	Although the empire emerged from a broader European Habsburg power base, and the emergence of parliamentary systems and representation began in 1848 CE, the national project of Austria-Hungary had a relatively short period of peak power, just half a century, between 1867 and 1918.
Ottoman Empire	The overall trajectory of the empire runs from the end of the 13th century CE to a peak of power from the late 14th century to the late 17th century, with periods of discrete relative rise and fall alongside a gradual decline through the 19th century, which ended in a collapse just after World War I.
Renaissance Italy	There was an initial major phase of economic and political development in the 12th and 13th centuries CE, and then a second phase through the 16th century. Spanish and French invasions began in the early 16th century; thereafter, the Italian city-states were more beleaguered. Different cities reached their peak power at different times, but broadly speaking the peak of their competitive position was roughly between 1300 and 1500.
Britain	Britain's peak of competitive position can be marked as the height of its empire and the peak of its global economic dominance thanks in part to its early-mover advantages in the Industrial Revolution—a period beginning in about the 1820s CE and running through the beginning of the 20th century. Historians debate the point at which British societal advantages truly began working to create competitive advantage; some highlight trends underway before the 1820s–1830s.

Table A.4—Continued

Case Study	Competitive Advantage
Sweden	Sweden's globally relevant competitive position was brief—this case considers Gustav II and his successor's efforts to position the nation as a dominant military player at least in northern Europe in the period roughly from 1610 to 1670 CE.
France	France was a major European power rising through the 16th and 17th centuries CE. France's peak power was in the early 18th century, with predominant population, land armies that demanded multinational coalitions to balance, and leading cultural, intellectual, and political influence and example. Post-1815 brought relative decline: France fell behind Britain in the Industrial Revolution and had repeated military defeats to single opponents but remained a top-rank world power.
Japan	There was a long period of relative isolation and weakness after the invasion of Korea in the 1590s CE and subsequent defeats. The main period of competitive rise and advance was the 1860s to the present, when Japan industrialized, became a major world economic power, won wars against European powers (e.g., Russia) and Asian ones (e.g., China), and recovered from World War II to again become a dominant economic player.
Soviet Union	This case considers the whole history of the Soviet Union, from its postrevolutionary origins and turmoil, through World War II, to a primary focus on the Cold War and the end of the Soviet Union in 1989–1991. The peak of its competitive position probably lies in the early to mid Cold War, when at least in terms of military power and global geopolitical influence it rivaled and in some narrow fields surpassed the United States.
United States	The general trajectory of the United States' power involves its rise as a leading industrial power in the later parts of the 19th century, more significant arrival onto the world stage in 1898–1918, and then an obvious peak with the collapse of the Soviet Union in 1989. But the United States dominated some indexes of noncommunist economic and military power by about 1950.

We sought to examine not only the reasons for competitive success but also the sources of national inertia and infirmity. A few of our cases eventually became known as weak states, and in some cases their empires or national coherence simply collapsed—the Austro-Hungarian and Ottoman Empires, for example. The Soviet Union is a leading example of social decline: As one source explains, "The decade after 1975 became known in Soviet history as the time of stagnation (*zastoi*)[,] . . . a time of drift and inertia, bereft of ideological, economic, and social vitality."[35] Another source notes that the "revolutionary imagination was depleted" in the Soviet Union by the later 1970s.[36] Each of these competitive declines can be attributed to

---

[35] Vladislav Zubok, "Soviet Foreign Policy from Détente to Gorbachev, 1975–1985," in Melvyn P. Leffler and Odd Arne Westad, eds., *The Cambridge History of the Cold War*: Vol. 3, *Endings*, Cambridge, UK: Cambridge University Press, 2010.

[36] Jan-Werner Müller, "The Cold War and the Intellectual History of the Late Twentieth Century," in Melvyn P. Leffler and Odd Arne Westad, eds., *The Cambridge History of the Cold War*: Vol. 3, *Endings*, Cambridge, UK: Cambridge University Press, 2010, p. 1.

a multiplicity of factors, but we sought to identify specific societal characteristics associated with the trends.

Beyond those very broad and qualitative indicators of rise and decline, our research highlighted three sets of nations for analysis according to the trend of their competitive position (noted in Figure A.2). There are three cases of long-term competitive excellence—Rome, Britain, and the United States. They stand head and shoulders above the other cases in terms of the sustained degree of dominance they were able to attain and therefore bear special scrutiny for characteristics that might have empowered that success.

A second set of countries are those that achieved some peak of *geopolitical* power or competitive advantage which then faded, partly due to their smaller size, but which maintained world-class levels of *social indicators* more broadly. The Netherlands cannot be viewed as a nation with "weak" societal characteristics that have caused it to "fail." It is a highly successful advanced country that ranks very highly on our nominated characteristics. As we tied those characteristics to competitive outcomes, therefore, we had to bear in mind that outcomes critically dependent on the size of a country, such as relative geopolitical power or the share of the world economy, are not the only yardsticks for assessing the effect of social capacity.

The third set of nations or empires did sustain both geopolitical and social declines, either in basic political stability or coherence, economic development rates, or other measures. This set has the competitive failures, for want of a more nuanced term. Even here there is a range: Italy has sustained pockets of economic excellence, and parts of Italian economic and industrial life could easily be said to belong in the second group. Spain, after a long postimperial decline leading to a lagging standard of living among industrialized nations through the mid-20th century, has made significant progress of late. Broadly speaking, though, relative

FIGURE A.2

Categorizing Case Studies by Degree of Competitive Success

Dominant Long-Term Hegemons	Peak Power with Sustained Competitiveness	Peak Power with Impaired Competitiveness
Nations that achieved and sustained an unquestioned leading position in world politics	These nations might have only briefly achieved predominant geopolitical power, but their subsequent histories represented economic power, high standards of living, and high ranking on international competitiveness indexes	These nations achieved relatively brief geopolitical predominance, and their subsequent histories have at least long periods of lack of economic and societal competitiveness (even if they have recovered)
Rome, Britain, United States	France, Italy (from Renaissance city-states), Japan, Sweden, UK (after peak hegemony); the non-case-study nations of the Netherlands and Germany would also fit into this category	Austro-Hungarian Empire, Ottoman Empire, Spain, Soviet Union/Russia

to their peak power, these are nations that can be most profitably assessed for the factors that produced their relative decline or persistent lagging competitive position.

Basic Research Approach: Indicators of Causal Relationships

Given these challenges and constraints with identifying demonstrated causal associations through the method of middle-range causal mechanisms, we sought to relate societal characteristics to national competitive outcomes by reviewing five categories of evidence that together offered the best possible qualitative basis for such claims. They were (1) global histories that have sought causal explanations, (2) case studies, (3) general disciplinary assessments seeking explanatory variables for historical trends, (4) confirmation of empirical research evidence, and (5) existence of clearly disconfirming cases or alternate causalities.

For category 1, **global histories that have sought causal explanations**, we first examined the broad literature on national rise and fall, civilizational fates, the Great Divergence, and other treatments that have tried to isolate the causes of national rise and decline over the centuries. Examples of the sort of global histories we consulted include classical treatments, such as that of Arnold Toynbee, as well as more recent scholarship from Acemoglu and Robinson, Diamond, Ferguson, Goldstone, Jacob, Landes, McCloskey, Mokyr, Morris, Pomeranz, and more (see the bibliography for these publications).

From this research, we collected an initial list of hypothesized societal characteristics that may offer competitive advantage. From a crosscutting assessment of these various treatments, we discovered an initial set of findings that appear as consistent themes in these global histories. These factors included sound and effective institutions, stable finances, and the importance of a strong and coherent national identity.

For category 2, **case studies**, we conducted deeper case studies of a dozen nations and empires (see Table A.4) to examine possible connections between societal characteristics and competitive outcomes. These were necessarily qualitative assessments, trying to derive broad relationships that were nonetheless supported by specific evidence. Some of the relationships we sought were subsidiary or proxy relations. Each of the societal characteristics comprises a set of related activities or qualities, and some of those can be measured or assessed independently. For example, in modern cases we looked for any proven causal relations between (1) aspects of a learning and adapting society (such as investments in education) and (2) economic growth and technological sophistication. We often had to look beyond the measurable to the qualitative, finding telling examples or anecdotes that, combined with the expert judgment of an experienced historian, could support the case for a characteristic in promoting or undermining competitive standing. To take one example, the relationship between the British system's ability to empower entrepreneurs and inventors from many backgrounds and classes, even amid a highly class-bound aristocratic society, clearly helped to fuel its Industrial Revolution. This can be quantified only at the margins (though some historians have tried), but the general relationship is strong and supported by the evidence.

In some cases, these causal relations were very clear: Finances, for example, both fueled Spain's rise (through its access to New World precious metals) and then (as those supplies dwindled) played a major role in its relative decline. In other cases, the effects might be notable but not dominant. In the case of France, shared opportunity throughout society did exist to a degree greater than in some other major powers of the time (such as Russia), but there is no persuasive evidence that this factor alone made a decisive difference in the country's ultimate competitive position. In a few cases there was no reason to believe that a given characteristic had any meaningful effect on a specific country's competitive trajectory.

In nearly all cases, specific evidence emerged to support a clear competitive advantage or disadvantage associated with that issue. Significant uncertainties emerged in the *degree* of the association, however. In some cases, such as the role of shared opportunity in 19th-century Britain or a pluralistic competition in the United States, a "strong" coding was clearly warranted. In many cases, however, the precise influence of a given factor could not be determined. Partly this is a methodological issue of a classic causal relationship involving many variables whose individual causal effect cannot be precisely determined.

For category 3, **general disciplinary assessments seeking explanatory variables for historical trends**, in addition to the general global histories employed in category 1, we reviewed broad, long-term surveys (specific to a single discipline) that sought to identify critical variables influencing the dynamism and competitive standing of nations. Most of these were in the field of economics—studies nominating key variables that help explain growth rates, long-term economic development, and the birth of the Industrial Revolution. These qualitative and quantitative analyses provided rich sources of insight and evidence for our assessment of potential characteristics.

For category 4, **confirmation of empirical research evidence**, after identifying specific characteristics contributing to national success, broadly defined, we sought confirmatory evidence from other disciplines on issue areas related to those characteristics. There is independent, empirical work on many specific subcomponents of the societal characteristics and subelements of competitive success. For example, economists have assessed the relationship between inequality or social mobility and economic growth and innovation. There is strong evidence showing the value of diversity to firms, research that establishes principles that ought to work as well for nations.

For category 5, **existence of clearly disconfirming cases or alternate causalities**, we looked for clearly disconfirming cases for each proposed characteristic or cases that denied the validity of any of our characteristics by demonstrating alternative causes for their effects. A single country that succeeded without a given social quality would not be disconfirming, because these seven characteristics offer the raw materials for various recipes of success. As we reviewed the global histories and case studies, however, we identified cases in which a successful nation clearly flouted one of the proposed criteria (or a failed one boasted by many other nations).

The evidence from these five categories allows us to confidently able to say that our final list of societal characteristics is strongly associated with competitive success and failure.

Ruined finances are a route to competitive decline—in Spain, in France, and in China—just as a vibrant and well-managed financial foundation is a critical support system for competitive advantage (as in Britain). National incoherence, disunity and civil instability, and violence are a serious drag on competitiveness—in the Austro-Hungarian and Ottoman Empires and in various periods in Rome. Shared economic and societal opportunity is consistently present—to varying degrees, depending on the historical period—in the most-successful nations.

As this list makes clear, our causal analysis was *not* completely dependent on fitting characteristics to national trajectories. We did not seek to match high "measures" of these qualities with peak relative power—to say, for example, that social opportunity in Britain, or its habit of societal learning and intellectual energy, rose in tandem with its power in the 19th century. These causal relations will generally be too indirect and qualitative to see such alignments in measured trends. In most cases, too, we simply do not have the data to create such quantitative assessments. Instead, we sought evidence of demonstrated causal associations *across these five areas of evidence*: Does the nation generally reflect these societal qualities during its competitive rise? Are there anecdotal examples of the societal quality producing specific advantage, especially related to a nation's peak power? Are there specific research data proving an important component of an overall causal relationship? Our causal argument is therefore about the overall weight of evidence rather than a direct causal tie to rise and decline.

To be even more explicit about the basis for our findings, Table A.5 outlines the forms of evidence employed to sustain our claim that each of these characteristics contributes to competitive success.

Results of the Case Analyses

Table A.6 briefly summarizes the results of these case analyses designed to look for the effects of specific characteristics in particular countries. As it suggests, the cases did mostly confirm the lessons of the general historical research. The bulk of our list can be said to have been supported by these cases. In all these assessments—seven characteristics assessed in 12 cases, or a total of 84 judgments—only six were coded as not available, suggesting that we found little evidence linking the characteristic to competitive success or failure in the case. In all other cases, we found persuasive evidence linking the characteristic to competitive outcomes.

In the coding of the cases, there was little uncertainty about assigning a positive value of some sort to specific characteristics. Because of the limited availability of hard data for nearly all these countries and characteristics, there was no opportunity to establish measurable criteria for the application of codings. These are subjective judgments, drawing on extensive historical research and an ability to cite some specific numbers, cases, or other evidence in support. The distinction between strong and moderate effects could not be objectively established for all factors; again, it represents a research-informed judgment of the basic distinc-

TABLE A.5

Categories of Evidence

Societal Characteristic	Evidence for Causal Relationship to Competitive Outcomes
National ambition and will	• Consistent historical association across many cases; ability to identify the theme in national values and political principles • Presence of such ambition in key leaders and ruling elites who energized national competitiveness • In a more generalized sense, association of an ethic of ambition to master the natural world with nations that achieve efflorescence
Unified national identity	• Qualitative case evidence correlating the degree of coherent and shared national identity with competitive outcomes • Specific examples of the inverse relationship—times and places where weak or fragmented national identity was a competitive handicap (such as Austria-Hungary or the Soviet Union)
Shared opportunity	• Evidence from general global historical literature, specifically the general historical-economic assessments of such authors as McCloskey, Mokyr, and Phelps • Case study evidence for the role of opportunity in providing new technology, economic growth, good leaders • Modern empirical evidence for the economic and other advantages of equality, mobility, and group opportunity • Absence of modern counterexamples—nations that sustained long-term competitive advantage while denying opportunities to large segments of the population
An active state	• Historical assessment of state role in promoting economic development, military power, and other aspects of competitive standing across many cases • Relationship of active-state approach to outcomes in leading cases of the most-competitive nations • Specific examples of beneficial results of active-state policies (such as technological spin-offs) • Cases supporting competitive value of the two major subthemes—productive investment and stable finances • Empirical research on the requirement for productive investment to fuel growth
Effective institutions	• Evidence from general global historical literature, specifically Acemoglu and Robinson; presence of theme even when not offered as the leading variable (Landes, Mokyr) • Issue-specific analyses—for example, the role of institutions, linked with supporting norms and values, in creating military effectiveness • Case study evidence for the role of effective institutions in underwriting economic growth and other favorable outcomes • Modern empirical evidence for the economic and other advantages of effective institutions
A learning and adapting society	• Correlative evidence from social patterns of adaptation versus orthodoxy in major cases (for example, Britain versus the late Ottoman Empire or Soviet Union) • Identifiable competitive advantages from innovation, learning, and adaptation (specific technologies or techniques) • Empirical research showing measurable positive effects of education on economic growth and other beneficial outcomes • Empirical research showing measurable ties between aspects of innovation and adaptation and firm-level results
Competitively diversity and pluralism	• Global historical evidence for a competitive pluralism and its effect on innovation, technology, and military power (in cases such as the Italian Renaissance city-states and the fragmented European political map) • Qualitative evidence for the beneficial effects of competition within a pluralistic system • Empirical evidence for the value of diversity in organizations

TABLE A.6

Case Study Results: The Role of Hypothesized Societal Characteristics in Determining Competitive Position

	National Ambition and Will	Unified National Identity	Shared Opportunity	An Active State	Effective Institutions	A Learning and Adapting Society	Competitive Diversity and Pluralism
Rome	●	●	▸	●	▸	▸	▸
China	●	●	●	●	●	▸	▸
Spain	●	▸	●	▸	▸	●	
Austria-Hungary	▸	●	▸		▸		●
Ottoman Empire	●	●	●	▸	▸	●	●
Renaissance Italy	●	●	●	●	●	●	▸
Britain	●	●	●	●	●	●	●
Sweden	▸	▸	▸	●	▸		
France	●	●	●	●	●	▸	▸
Japan	●	●	●	●	●	●	
Soviet Union	●	●	▸	●	●	▸	
United States	●	●	●	●	●	●	●

NOTES: ● indicates clear historical evidence to support association—not that the association is necessarily positive, only that the case offers a strong causal link, whether positive or negative. ▸ indicates weaker evidence. Blank cells indicate that the case did not offer clear evidence for the causal effect of that characteristic.

tion between a factor that had some measurable effects not far from decisive ones and a factor whose effects were central to a nation's competitive position.

Some of these cases stretch over decades, centuries, or even—in the case of Rome—nearly a millennium. Many of these countries had periods of rise, fall, and stagnation. The association of specific characteristics with competitive position shifted over time. A good example is the Cold War Soviet Union: Some characteristics (such as effective institutions and an active state) were associated with the period of relative growth and competitive success it enjoyed during the 1950s and 1960s. But rising corruption and overinvestment in military instruments of statecraft became competitive drags in the later Cold War. Again, the question was whether the characteristics were associated with competitive outcomes. A strong rating on institutions for the Soviet Union does not indicate that its institutions were always strong but rather that the association between institutional effectiveness and competitive outcomes was generally sustained across time periods.

Many of the causal relationships we identified in these cases were therefore a product of the conditions at the time. The sources of competitive advantage for ancient societies, or for Habsburg Spain or Austria, were a product of various aspects of the historical context, from the nature of warfare to the character of ancient or early modern societies. The degree to which and way in which such characteristics as shared opportunity and effective institutions contributed to competitive standing have obviously changed over time, and these cannot be translated simply or automatically into a 21st-century context. The case studies discuss these issues. Our research continues to suggest, however, that these general categories are both historically supported and relevant today.

Summary

In sum, then, we believe that these approaches allow us to say, based on rigorous analysis, that certain societal characteristics appear to be associated with national efflorescence and competitive advantage. Merely because we cannot quantify the precise degree of their effect does not suggest that they are unimportant. Across many cases and many forms of evidence, the characteristics laid out in Chapters Three through Nine have emerged as consistently associated with nations that achieve and sustain strong competitive position.

The importance of these factors will vary by the case and the historical period. Not all of them are essential for national competitive success; nations can cobble together different packages of characteristics that represent distinct recipes for success. And other factors outside societal characteristics can emerge to boost (or crush) a nation's competitive standing.

Defining Concepts

If written as a crude equation, the research question of this study would propose a causal relationship between societal characteristics and competitive outcomes. But that begs the question of what we mean by the concepts on both sides of that causal relationship. What is a *societal characteristic*? What is success in competition, or *competitive position*? Chapter One offered a brief summary of this study's view of those concepts. This appendix describes them in more detail to provide further insight into the methodology and approach employed for this study.

Defining *competitive success* may be the easier task, although the result will still be a complex mosaic of factors. Countries that are succeeding in rivalries tend to be doing well economically (in terms of gross GDP, growth rates, productivity, and finances). They tend not to lose major, decisive wars (but can in fact lose smaller, peripheral wars at an astonishing rate and still ultimately prevail). They sustain their territorial integrity and may even grow. They create the context for rising safety, security, and prosperity on the part of their people. And they do all of this in ways at least parallel with, and often exceeding, the rates of major rivals.

Even here, there are significant debates. Michael Porter's emphasis on "the competitive advantage of nations," for example, produced strong rejoinders from economists and others who argued, in effect, that there was no such thing—that firms compete but nations do not.[1] Recent innovations, such as the World Economic Forum's "competitiveness index," have been criticized for including a misleading set of variables, and the World Bank suspended its "ease of doing business" competitiveness index after charges that the data were shifted to favor China.[2]

Deciding what we mean by a societal characteristic is an even more challenging task. As noted in Chapter One, there is a long and spotty history of scholars trying to prove that various "cultural" factors underwrote the success of one or another civilization, from Thucydides's assessment of Athens and Sparta to Confucian values as an explanation for the rise of Asian economic powers to claims that rock-ribbed American family ties and traditional values

---

[1] M. Porter, 2019.

[2] Tom Wilson, "World Bank Suspends Its Business Climate Index over Data 'Irregularities,'" *Financial Times*, August 28, 2020; World Economic Forum, 2020; World Bank, 2022.

powered its Cold War victory.[3] These sorts of essentialist explanations have not aged well, in part because of the mismatch in trend lines: Confucian values have been in place for centuries during which China's competitive position has fluctuated wildly. Our goal was to identify more-precise patterns of social life that might be characteristic of more-successful nations.

We began our search on more universal ground—the idea that some broad quality of *national dynamism* or *national vitality* was the essential fuel for competitive success. This, too, is a hoary conceit and one that has had some fascinating recent investigations. Ultimately, though, we decided that these concepts were hopelessly broad. They took meaning only when defined in more-specific ways—which led us to the basket of possible factors we are terming *societal characteristics*.

This appendix sets the foundation for the later analysis by first reviewing the broad concepts. It then defines the narrower idea of a societal characteristic and finally defines what we mean by *competitive success*.

Defining Societal Characteristics

To develop a list of societal characteristics, we had first to define the category. Just what *is* a societal characteristic in the way in which we mean it here? How can we distinguish social characteristics from other types of variables? What distinguishes a societal characteristic, for example, from one of the cultural habits or practices that some of the literature connects to national fates?[4]

***

Several existing approaches have much in common with the idea of societal characteristics. One was the scholar and diplomat Armand Clesse's effort to develop a notion of national "vitality."[5] That research program produced many specific insights that we rely on, but the

---

[3] Clesse and Lounev, 2004, p. 261.

[4] As implied here, the question of unit of analysis is an important one in any search for variables shaping social outcomes (Clesse et al., 1997, p. 316). Our unit is the *society*, by which we mean, in practical modern terms, the nation-state and, more generally, a single societal unit under shared governance. Some of the cases we have examined are city-states or empires, but the basic unit is the same. Societal characteristics blur that unit choice somewhat because they draw in the habits, values, and behaviors of individuals and groups within societies, but we are ultimately interested in how those factors shape the fates of nations.

[5] In fact, the notion, as many participants in the conferences organized by Clesse pointed out, was never actually defined and allowed to encompass a wide range of issues; see, for example, Clesse et al., 1997, pp. 314–315, 351, 354, 357. Clesse at one point argues, "It is quite evident that competitiveness is not necessarily vitality," though, like this analysis, his approach did presume that characteristics of vitality would provide a country with competitive advantage (Clesse et al., 1997, p. 308). Factors that came up in his projects include economic growth and productivity, social stability, resilience, education levels, artistic output, technological innovation, and military power, but they are not knitted together in any single framework.

focus on a single term shows the risk of trying to shoehorn all the desired qualities into one single overarching quality whose meaning will necessarily remain obscure.

A second related approach was the economist Walt Rostow's concept of "propensities." These factors offered ways of understanding how the basic qualities of a society expressed themselves in economic behavior and growth.[6] Partly his goal was to integrate political and social factors (or what he calls at one point "the social frame of a society") into economic analysis, to create a more holistic portrait of the sources of development—to take seriously intervening variables between neoclassical economic factors and true national outcomes. "The character, scale, and capacity for growth of an economy," he explains, "are closely related to the whole society of which it is a part."[7] We would say the same for a nation's competitive capabilities.

Rostow defines several propensities related to economic growth and development—the tendency to invest in basic science or degree of economic investment. He also suggests that these propensities "reflect the scheme of ideas and values relevant to economic action with which a community equips the individual and which are incorporated in the community's institutions." They are the "means by which an individual interprets what he sees around him; and they afford a degree of security and stability in confronting complex and otherwise chaotic circumstances."[8] These defining elements mirror much of that we have in mind with the concept of societal characteristics.

A third similar analytical concept is Moses Abramovitz's idea of "social capability." By this he means not a single factor but, as with this approach, a collection of factors that added up to overarching patterns of economic advantage.[9] Other scholars note that the concept

---

For other concerns about definitions, see Clesse and Lounev, 2004, pp. 223, 263. The "dependent variable is not yet defined," conference participant Robert Legvold complains, "and as a consequence I can't explain it because I don't know what I'm explaining" (p. 263).

[6] Rostow describes these as "variables which incorporate the human response to the challenges and material opportunities offered by the economic environment. These variables are designed to constitute a link between the domain of the conventional economist on the one hand, and the sociologist, anthropologist, psychologist, and historian on the other" (Rostow, 1962, p. 11). See also Guy Ortolano, "The Typicalities of the English? Walt Rostow, *The Stages of Economic Growth*, and Modern British History," *Modern Intellectual History*, Vol. 12, No. 3, 2015, p. 669. Rostow adds that the concept involved a "frank abandonment of the effort to make economic behavior solely a function of what are conventionally regarded as economic motives" (Rostow, 1962, p. 35). Indeed, he implies a similar mining of the societal characteristics of nations when he says that propensities "are their determinants"—even deeper aspects of the societies that generate the propensities themselves. The propensities "are themselves determined by a much wider range of forces," he suggests (p. 35).

[7] Rostow, 1962, pp. 21, 20.

[8] Rostow, 1962, pp. 22, 40–41.

[9] Moses Abramovitz, "Catching Up, Forging Ahead, and Falling Behind," *Journal of Economic History*, Vol. 46, No. 2, June 1986; Moses Abramovitz, "The Search for the Sources of Growth: Areas of Ignorance, Old and New," *Journal of Economic History*, Vol. 53, No. 2, June 1993. Like Clesse, however, Abramovitz

"includes a wide variety of institutions and human resources that make it possible for some nations to develop more rapidly than others."[10]

Abramovitz centers the concept on the idea of a combination of education levels and the quality and efficiency of large-scale organizations in society, especially those responsible for productive investment. But he also includes notions of adaptation and institutional sclerosis:

> Social capability, finally, depends on more than the content of education and the organization of firms. Other aspects of economic systems count as well—their openness to competition, to the establishment and operation of new firms, and to the sale and purchase of new goods and services. Viewed from the other side, it is a question of the obstacles to change raised by vested interests, established positions, and customary relations among firms and between employers and employees.[11]

A fourth and final broad concept or analytical category that overlaps with our notion of social characteristics is the idea of social capital.[12] This is the notion popularized by Robert Putnam and others, that the strength of social ties and connections is an essential foundation for the stability and health of a national community. Putnam defines it as "features of social life—networks, norms, and trust—that enable participants to act together more effectively to pursue shared objectives."[13] The French social scientist Pierre Bourdieu defines *social capital* as "the aggregate of the actual or potential resources which are linked to possession of a durable network of more or less institutionalized relationships of mutual acquaintance and recognition."[14] In many ways, these relationships amount to networks of trust.[15]

In the face of some critiques that argue that social capital is not adequately objective and measurable, three scholars propose instead an idea of "civic capital, i.e., those persistent and

---

admits that the trouble with his concept is that "no one knows just what it means or how to measure it" (Abramovitz, 1986, p. 388).

[10] Perkins and Koo, 1985, p. 3. Yet the definitional confusion persists: Even here the authors admit, "No single definition of social capability is attempted." They associate it with factors producing technological progress (grouped as "technological capability"), including "the development of human resources through education," but this is only part of the equation. They even say that "there is no consensus . . . as to just how education affects development" (p. 4).

[11] Abramovitz, 1986, p. 389.

[12] Guiso, Sapienza, and Zingales, 2008; Luigi Guiso, Paola Sapienza, and Luigi Zingales, "Civic Capital as the Missing Link," in Jess Benhabib, Alberto Bisin, and Matthew Jackson, eds., *Handbook of Social Economics*, Vol. 1A, Amsterdam: North-Holland, 2011.

[13] Robert D. Putnam, "Tuning In, Tuning Out: The Strange Disappearance of Social Capital in America," *PS: Political Science and Politics*, Vol. 28, No. 4, 1995.

[14] Quoted in Guiso, Sapienza, and Zingales, 2011, p. 419.

[15] Eric Beinhocker (2007, p. 464) offers the closely related idea of social architecture: "We will define a social architecture as having three components: The behaviors of the individual people in the organization. The structures and processes that align people and resources in pursuit of an organization's goals. The culture that emerges from the interactions of people in the organization with each other and their environment."

shared beliefs and values that help a group overcome the free rider problem in the pursuit of socially valuable activities." They suggest that this idea "makes it clear that social capital is not about networks or just about values, but about values and beliefs, which are shared by a community and persist over time, often passed on to its members through intergenerational transmissions, formal education, or socialization."[16]

∗∗∗

Even with these echoes in other scholarship, the concept of societal characteristics is not an established category in political science or economics. It is not the same as values, norms, institutions, classes, or even general social structures. Although these cultural traits can be real in some times and places, they furnish a crude instrument for understanding national competitive advantage. Our notion of societal characteristics refers to more-specific patterns of organization and activity than cultural values.

Another important distinction, as noted in Table B.1, is between such characteristics and national policies. In trying to identify societal characteristics that contribute to competitiveness, we are explicitly avoiding more-temporary, policy-based actions.

Robert Hall and Charles Jones suggest the importance of what they called "social infrastructure," by which they mean

> the institutions and government policies that determine the economic environment within which individuals accumulate skills, and firms accumulate capital and produce output. A social infrastructure favorable to high levels of output per worker provides an environment that supports productive activities and encourages capital accumulation,

TABLE B.1
Categories of Competitive Drivers

Category of Characteristic	Definition	Examples
Cultural values and norms	General qualities of social life in a given nation or culture; elements of basic worldview or belief system of a people	Trust, cooperation, hierarchy, frugality, work ethic
Lasting societal characteristics	Habitual patterns of social, cultural, economic, or political organization and behavior; can be shifted with large-scale policy effort but only over medium to long term	Degree of shared opportunity; level of national identity; national willpower and ambition; quality of institutions in society
Specific competitive policies	Legislative, regulatory, or executive actions that establish specific rules, laws, requirements, or levels of spending; can be readily changed	Level of spending on defense, policies toward immigration, legal and regulatory treatment of business investment, levels of taxation

---

[16] Guiso, Sapienza, and Zingales, 2011, pp. 419, 423.

> skill acquisition, invention, and technology transfer. Such a social infrastructure gets the prices right so that . . . individuals capture the social returns to their actions as private returns.[17]

This broad conception of an ecosystem of norms, habits, and institutions mirrors what we have in mind with societal characteristics. The proxies Hall and Jones use are a combination of good governance models, indexes of countries that prevent diversion, and openness to trade, which they see as an indication of the practices of good social infrastructure. Their research uncovers strong associations between their metrics of social infrastructure and such outcomes as output per worker and productivity.[18]

Michael Porter argues that the association of national success with singular, essentialist cultural variables—such as "frugality" or "cooperativeness"—elides too many complexities. But he still maintains that there are "supportive attitudes and values" that fuel national competitiveness, in ways that closely mirror our effort conceptualize societal characteristics:

> Innovation is good, competition is good, accountability is good, high regulatory standards are good, investment in capabilities and technology is a necessity, employees are assets, membership in a cluster is a competitive advantage, collaboration with suppliers and customers is beneficial, connectivity and networks are essential, education and skills are essential to support more productive work, and wages should not rise unless productivity rises, among others. These can be contrasted with unproductive attitudes and values: monopoly is good, power determines rewards, rigid hierarchy is needed to maintain control, and self-contained family relationships should determine partnership.[19]

These categories also speak to the category of variables we aim to emphasize: more general than specific policies (a societal habit of emphasizing and rewarding educational achievement, for example), yet less abstract, generic, and essentialist than singular "cultural values." What we have in mind is similar to the "patterned normative order through which the life of a population is collectively organized" that the sociologist Talcott Parsons discusses, composed of "norms and rules" but also institutions, processes, and habits.[20]

Drawing on these concepts and literatures and informed by the historical research conducted for the project, we then offer the following definition of *societal characteristics*: the essential and persistent social qualities of a nation, including norms, values, institutions, and practices, that shape measurable outputs of national competitive advantage and influence its patterns of behavior.

---

[17] Hall and Jones, 1999, p. 84.

[18] Hall and Jones, 1999, pp. 84, 103, 110.

[19] M. Porter, 2000, p. 22.

[20] Hämäläinen, 2003, p. 25, discussing Parsons.

More specifically, our research—and a review of the sorts of variables and factors used by other studies—suggests four main criteria for a factor to count as a societal characteristic. That factor must be

1. related to inherent qualities of the society—representing habits, idea, ideologies, cultural values, or other features of social life, aspects that go beyond individual policy decisions and that are widely internalized as taken-for-granted values or behaviors
2. equipped with sociopolitical or socioeconomic features rather than physical ones, reflecting the competitive advantages of a society rather than a location or some resource endowment
3. lasting and persistent over time, although not necessarily permanent (even habitual characteristics undergo change and evolution and can be subject to some intentional revision through intentional policy measures)
4. representative of multiple individual measures or variables and not reducible to a single proxy variable; this criterion speaks to the fact that societal characteristics are necessarily somewhat abstract and holistic factors.

We continued to refine these criteria as we evaluated and revised our list of characteristics and encountered additional sources.

Defining Competitive Success and Failure

To judge which societal characteristics make a nation competitive, we had to identify outcomes to assess them against. What does it mean to be more rather than less competitive in national terms? By what criteria can we identify national vibrancy in a competitive sense? The difficulty in answering these questions can be seen in our historical case of Rome.

Rome's immense and multifaceted trajectory does not lend itself to easy analysis of rise and fall or success and failure. Some sources put the transition from early monarchical regimes to the republic at about 509 BCE. Broadly speaking, the full span of the Roman Empire, past the decline of the Western Empire and through the span of the Eastern, lasted over a millennium, to about 600–650 CE. Rome was becoming the dominant Mediterranean power by the time of its wars against Carthage from 264 to 146 BCE. The republic gave way to the empire with (and through) the rule of Augustus (63 BCE to 14 CE), reached an arguable early peak during the rule of Marcus Aurelius (161–180 CE), and then underwent peaks and valleys of strength in the West through the fourth century CE, up to the sack of Rome by Goths in 410 CE and the later assaults in 455 and 476 CE. But the empire recovered to a degree even in the West and remained potent in the East for at least another two centuries. As late as the early to mid sixth century CE, Eastern Emperor Justinian brought new energy, reformist zeal, massive construction projects, and efforts to reconquer some lost territory so that Rome remained as significant and powerful in some ways as it had been during Marcus Aurelius's time.

During these centuries, Rome won and lost numerous battles, and even some wars, but the losses only temporarily slowed its march to dominance. A good example is Cannae in 216 BCE: The Roman force was annihilated by Hannibal, and perhaps 50,000 men were killed—yet within about 70 years, Scipio Aemilianus was standing over the ruins of a destroyed Carthage. The Roman army sustained one of its most catastrophic losses at Adrianople in 378 CE but again recovered and went on to win major battles. Then, over a millennium, the social, political, and economic entity that was "Rome" underwent profound changes, many bearing on the societal characteristics we have identified. To take just one example, the later empire integrated soldiers, scholars, scientists, and even Latin linguists from well beyond Italy in ways that did not happen in the republican period.

For all these reasons it is impossible to draw a straightforward linear trajectory of Rome's competitive position or to tell a simple story of the societal characteristics that help explain those outcomes. Rome rose and fell too many times, and underwent too many societal transformations, for any simple causal correlations with societal characteristics. We have therefore reviewed relevant treatments for general causal associations between such characteristics and Roman strength broadly defined.

Defining the power trajectory of the Ottoman Empire is just as challenging. The origins of the empire run to about 1300 in Asia Minor, when the Ottomans were still just "one of many Turcoman, or Turkish, tribal groups of Central Asian origin vying for control in Anatolia—the land between the Black Sea, the Mediterranean and the Aegean."[21] The Ottoman state rose to immense prominence by the later 17th century and came close to conquering Vienna in 1529 and 1683, a period that represents in some ways the apex of Ottoman power. Even by the late 17th century, the tide was beginning to shift against the empire; in some ways the siege of Vienna in 1683 represented the last high-water mark. But the empire remained firmly in place, a viable entity, though clearly in decline, until after 1918.

In comparative terms, too, at any one moment in history, it can be difficult to pick out the dominant or most competitive of the great powers. During the 16th century, for example, many great powers vied for dominance: the Ottoman Empire, England, Habsburg Spain, France, the Netherlands, and the Holy Roman Empire; in Italy, Venice and Genoa were significant seagoing powers. In Iran there was a Safavid dynasty and the Mughal Empire in India.[22] These rose and fell in absolute terms and against one another. It would be very difficult to identify precise measurable differences in competitive standing from one year to the next.

There are other complications. Countries such as Denmark, Norway, and Singapore are not driven to engage in geopolitical rivalry in the same way as, for example, China, but they have high levels of societal well-being and reflect many elements of what we would call the engine of dynamism. They are dynamic societies in many ways—in terms of technology, busi-

---

[21] Finkel, 2005, p. 3.

[22] Quataert, 2005, p. 3.

ness output, cultural creativity, and diplomatic savvy. They are competitively successful—they check all the seven boxes to a degree. Is it strictly the barrier of scale that denies them membership in the competitiveness top ranks? Or have they also lost a certain drive and energy—our characteristic of national ambition and will—and fallen into the ranks of satisfied, slow-growing, relatively unambitious states whose only goal is to maximize the short-term well-being of their people?

Or we could consider a bigger country such as Germany. On many of the same measures of competitive standing—the well-being of its people, a world-class economy, impressive artistic and cultural achievements—it must be counted as dynamic. Yet its geopolitical competitive profile relative to China or Russia remains limited. If a country chooses not to express its military and international power to the degree that theoretically it could, but it embodies the seven characteristics to impressive degrees, where should we categorize that nation?

As these examples suggest, our definition of competitive success embodied both a generalized dynamism and measures of relative power. A country can be small and dynamic but not powerful. It can be medium-sized and dynamic and simply choose not to compete globally with much energy. It can be very large and not dynamic at all but still force its way into certain indexes of national power by dint of its population or land mass or raw GDP. As we considered the historical cases, we were on the lookout for both outcomes: We sought out countries that reached high levels of dynamism, as indicated by such metrics as high growth rates, surges of scientific and technological discovery and innovation, brilliant and transformative military techniques, leading industrial sectors, and world-class cultural expressions. But we also assessed the competitive trajectory of countries, in terms of their position in the geopolitical hierarchy, to determine competitive standing.

Sometimes these two basic outcome indicators overlapped, as in Britain at the height of its power or the United States from perhaps the 1920s through the 1990s. Sometimes a country or political unit achieved a localized golden age without the same degree of geopolitical predominance. Song China might be an example of this, a society that reached a brilliant moment of efflorescence yet remained in some ways politically weak and geopolitically vulnerable. Nations could sometimes temporarily achieve very high global power ranking without rating very high on elements of dynamism, such as the Soviet Union in the Cold War. But these typically could not sustain their competitive position for very long.

The upshot is that it becomes impossible to make easy, uncomplicated causal connections between characteristics and outcomes on any discrete or short-term basis. It is not the specific swings in competitive prospects that we can seek to explain but the long-term trends. In doing so, we developed more-specific understandings of the way to track competitive standing.

Baseline Indicators of Success and Failure: War and Economic Predominance

We decided not to choose one outcome indicator of success that would have provided a single unitary metric: *victory or loss in war*.[23] Most existing theoretical treatments of national rivalries use this outcome as the dominant variable to assess desired outcomes.[24] That criterion was not going to be enough to judge the competitive effect of societal characteristics in the present context, in part because U.S. rivals appear committed to achieving every possible gain short of major conflict. The United States could lose this competition without ever losing a war. This analysis is meant to identify characteristics that provide advantage in long-term competitions and in all elements of national power, not merely in war-making.

But success in war is far from the only way to judge whether societies have successful competitive characteristics. Nations can go decades or even centuries without engaging in major wars, particularly in the nuclear age; to judge competitive success only by this metric would ignore trends and developments in the intervening periods. Countries also sometimes lose wars because vital national interests are not involved, and countries do not make a comprehensive national effort. The United States arguably lost in Vietnam and did not achieve unqualified victory in Iraq or Afghanistan—but in none of these cases did the United States bring to bear anything close to its comprehensive national resources, and the partial or complete failures do not really give a clear indication of the degree of national competitive strength. The United States simply decided not to apply the strength it had.

And in any case, nations can lose wars for many reasons other than a lack of effective societal characteristics, however defined. Germany before World War II had many societal characteristics that offered some degree of competitive advantage. It arguably lost not because of a lack of dynamism but because its ambitions eventually brought into being a dominant opposing coalition.

Most would agree that Athens stood head and shoulders above Sparta on any list of societal characteristics helpful to prevailing in a long-term conflict. And yet Athens lost—partly because it was ravaged by a plague but also because of some questionable strategic choices (in the management of allies and undertaking wasteful expeditions to Egypt and Sicily) and because its opponent excelled in one critical societal characteristic—war-making. On the other hand, if we open the aperture and consider national success in terms broader than one conflict (such as regional influence, cultural standing, longevity of a political culture, and historical impact), Athens was clearly the more successful society despite its loss in that single

---

[23] Another possible outcome metric, the collapse or disintegration of a society, also did not work for several reasons. It captures too few cases to be useful. States can become gradually less competitive without collapsing; collapse is not the only measure of noncompetitiveness. But states can also collapse for idiosyncratic reasons—a suddenly changing climate, for example—that do not reflect a true verdict on its societal strengths and weaknesses.

[24] This is true for example, of Paul Kennedy (1987): Although his analysis is about the "rise and fall" of the great powers, he focuses on the relationship between economic change and outcomes in military conflict.

war. In the "societal competition" between Athens and Sparta, it might be said, Sparta won the war—but Athens won the contest of historical influence, fame, and longevity.

Put into the present context, for example, China's centralized system can focus resources on critical technologies and systems that could, in an analogy to Sparta, produce excellence in warfighting. Whether China's autocratic, informationally closed, bureaucratic, belligerent, and hierarchical approach to domestic and global relationships can generate the creativity, attractiveness, and foreign partnerships necessary to acquire and sustain true systemic predominance is another matter.

A second broad criteria could have been merely *factors that promote economic growth and development*. A large and fast-growing economy may be the essence of competitive vibrancy. Societal characteristics that promote economic vibrancy could thus be equated to overall competitive characteristics. Some analyses of national competitive advantage, such as those of Michael Porter and Ruchir Sharma,[25] use this factor as the essential measure of success.

Yet we decided not to employ this singular criterion for several reasons. First, economists bitterly debate the real sources of economic growth; without a clear consensus on the matter, it would be impossible to identify broadly agreed characteristics that produce it. Second, and as would be expected given the lack of consensus, even a cursory glance at the cases we identified shows a wide variation in characteristics associated with either fast or slow growth: Some fast-growing economies are state-directed, others liberal; some represent societies with high degrees of individualism, others do not; and so forth. Third and finally, our review of the qualities of competitive powers made clear that there are factors other than economic strength that play into a society's overall strength and influence.

We therefore concluded that defining success in strategic competitions required indicators that are more varied and numerous than victory in war or a growing economy. We eventually turned to a range of literatures to nominate such factors—but first reviewed what was the most comprehensive modern debate on the issue of national competitiveness.

Jack Goldstone agrees that looking at history as periods of "growth" and "non-growth" is not helpful. He offers instead the idea of a succession of "efflorescences" in national histories, which he defines as "a sharp and fairly sudden burst of economic expansion and creative innovation,"[26] or more specifically as

> a relatively sharp, often unexpected upturn in significant demographic and economic indices, usually accompanied by political expansion and institution building and cultural synthesis and consolidation. Such "efflorescences" . . . are often seen by contemporaries or successors as "golden ages" of creativity and accomplishments. Moreover, they often set new patterns for thought, political organization, and economic life that last for many generations.[27]

---

[25] M. Porter, 2019; Sharma, 2016.

[26] Goldstone, 2002, p. 353.

[27] Goldstone, 2002, p. 333.

These golden ages may be propelled by economic dynamism, but they cannot be reduced to measurements of economic growth. They are characterized instead by interrelated progress in multiple areas of social development—political institutions, economic growth and development, technological innovation, rising productivity, and improving objective measures of national well-being and development. Yet he also argues that each efflorescence tends to sow the seeds of its own decline: The advances become a new "equilibrium or inertial state" in which "new technological innovations slowed or ceased, and economic and political elites sought to defend existing social patterns. Such inertial states were prone to decay . . . and the collapse of complexly interwoven economic and political structures."[28] The typical trajectory, he argues, is "for an efflorescence to create a number of interlocking practices that are initially fruitful, but then tend to stabilize and be actively defended. Only a major social or political upheaval is then likely to create new opportunities for major episodes of growth." The result is that such periods "tend to reach a ceiling—a new and higher ceiling to be sure— but then to suffer stagnation or decline. It is no coincidence that later generations tend to look back to these periods as 'golden ages.'"[29] This concept comes as close as any to describing what we had in mind with successfully dynamic nations—the sorts of results that competitively advantageous societal characteristics will help produce.

Two Relevant Debates: The Great Divergence and Great Enrichment

Two other helpful literatures discuss national competitive advantage through the lens of a pair of epochal global developments that occurred across roughly the past 500 years. Each has been the focus of immense literatures. One is typically called the Great Divergence—the period, largely centered on and after the Industrial Revolution of the early to mid 19th century, when European powers raced ahead of the rest of the world in economic, technological, and military terms.

The second global development is sometimes called the Great Enrichment, the hockey-stick-like explosion of economic growth and living standards starting at about the same time. As Dierdre McCloskey argues, "The Great Enrichment of the past two centuries has dwarfed any of the previous and temporary enrichments. Explaining it is the central scientific task of economics and economic history, and it matters for any other sort of social science or recent history."[30]

Taken together (and as a package), those two developments have conferred a significant proportion of national competitive advantage that has emerged since 1800. Taken together, these two historical trends helped to produce the incredible growth trajectory of, first, the Netherlands, then Britain, and then the United States and other parts of the world. This amazing path broke from all historical tradition, which largely involved centuries of relative

---

[28] Goldstone 2002, p. 378.

[29] Goldstone, 2002, pp. 354–355.

[30] McCloskey, 2016, p. 12.

stagnation in living standards: In 1800, workers in England and Hollard were earning about the same, adjusted for inflation, as their ancestors 300 years before.[31]

Debates continue to rage over the true causes of each of these interrelated developments. Some scholars, for example, raise questions about the true status of relative economic and technological progress between Europe and China over time. A good case can be made that many parts of Europe and Asia stood at similar levels of development in the early modern period; the precise point when Europe surged ahead—as it surely did—is contested, as are the domains in which that advance was most critical. Some suggest that the real European lead did not emerge until the Industrial Revolution. Even by about 1800, some contend, there was no European miracle, no sense that European culture furnished critical competitive advantages over others.

We could not seek to resolve these debates in this study. But the literatures surrounding these issues provided important insight into our conception of both societal characteristics and how to define competitive advantage.

Potential Indicators of Competitive Success and Failure

To go beyond these singular options and nominate specific indicators of competitive success, we reviewed several sources of candidate outcome factors. First, in an earlier project, we used the international relations literature to identify the kinds of goals that nations typically seek in the international system.[32] These would give us a clue as to the ends against which national competitiveness would be judged, and they include the following:

- relative power (economic and military)
- domestic security and stability, as well as continuation of rule of the current government
- status and prestige
- control over and access to resources
- acquisition of territorial claims
- promotion of the state's values and ideology
- capability to shape the prevailing global paradigm.

---

[31] Goldstone, 2009, p. 25.

[32] Lacey, 2016; Douglas Lemke and William Reed, "War and Rivalry Among Great Powers," *American Journal of Political Science*, Vol. 45, No. 2, 2001; Charles A. Kupchan, *How Enemies Become Friends: The Sources of Stable Peace*, Princeton, N.J.: Princeton University Press, 2010; Kennedy, 1987; Paul W. Schroeder, "The Nineteenth Century System: Balance of Power or Political Equilibrium?" *Review of International Studies*, Vol. 15, No. 2, 1989; Robert K. Massie, *Dreadnought: Britain, Germany, and the Coming of the Great War*, New York: Random House, 1991; Paul K. MacDonald and Joseph M. Parent, *Twilight of the Titans: Great Power Decline and Retrenchment*, Ithaca, N.Y.: Cornell University Press, 2018; Joshua R. Itzkowitz Shifrinson, *Rising Titans, Falling Giants: How Great Powers Exploit Power Shifts*, Ithaca, N.Y.: Cornell University Press, 2018; Stacie E. Goddard, *When Right Makes Might: Rising Powers and World Order*, Ithaca, N.Y.: Cornell University Press, 2018.

Second, we reviewed recent U.S. national security strategies for lists of national interests and objectives,[33] as well as secondary sources that summarized U.S. interests.[34] A list of interests common to multiple strategies provides some sense of the outcomes that would constitute success from the standpoint of U.S. national power:

- protect the homeland and survival of the nation, prevent catastrophic attack, and foster an international environment that promotes this objective
- promote global norms, institutions, rules and promote democratic values
- manage international alignments and power balances, prevent the emergence of hostile powers and great power dominance of regions, and preserve and strengthen alliances and partnerships
- preserve the security and stability of global economic system
- suppress terrorism and extremism
- maintain productive relations with rivals
- sustain lead in key technological areas and industries.

Third, we reviewed indexes of national power to identify characteristics commonly associated with national strength.[35] Table B.2 lists the factors included in four major power indexes.[36] Classic versions of such indexes typically relied on a handful of clear-cut measures of

---

[33] The strategies reviewed include William J. Clinton, *A National Security Strategy of Engagement and Enlargement: National Security Strategy 1994*, Washington, D.C.: White House, July 1994; William J. Clinton, *A National Security Strategy of Engagement and Enlargement: National Security Strategy 1996*, Washington, D.C.: White House, February 1996; George W. Bush, *The National Security Strategy*, Washington, D.C.: White House, September 2002; Barack Obama, *National Security Strategy*, Washington, D.C.: White House, May 2012; Donald J. Trump, *National Security Strategy of the United States of America*, Washington, D.C.: White House, December 2017.

[34] Graham T. Allison, Dimitri K. Simes, and James Thomson, *America's National Interests*, Cambridge, Mass.: Commission on America's National Interests, Belfer Center, Harvard University, July 2000; Terry L. Diebel, *Foreign Affairs Strategy: Logic for American Statecraft*, New York: Cambridge University Press, 2007.

[35] See the Composite Index of National Capability at Correlates of War, "National Material Capabilities," version 5.0, undated; J. David Singer, Stuart Bremer, and John Stuckey, "Capability Distribution, Uncertainty, and Major Power War, 1820–1965," in Bruce Russett, ed., *Peace, War, and Numbers*, Beverly Hills, Calif.: Sage, 1972; Jonathan D. Moyer, Tim Swijs, Mathew J. Burrows, and Hugo Van Manen, *Power and Influence in a Globalized World*, Washington, D.C.: Atlantic Council of the United States, 2018; Jacob L. Heim and Benjamin M. Miller, *Measuring Power, Power Cycles, and the Risk of Great-Power War in the 21st Century*, Santa Monica, Calif.: RAND Corporation, RR-2989-RC, 2020; Lowy Institute, "Asia Power Index 2020," webpage, undated. See also Richard L. Merritt and Dina A. Zinnes, "Validity of Power Indices," *International Interactions*, Vol. 14, No. 2, 1988; Richard L. Merritt and Dina A. Zinnes, "Alternative Indexes of National Power," in Richard J. Stoll and Michael D. Ward, eds., *Power in World Politics*, Boulder, Colo.: Lynne Rienner, 1989; Ray S. Cline, *World Power Assessment: A Calculus of Strategic Drift*, Boulder, Colo.: Westview Press, 1975; Hyung-min Kim, "Comparing Measures of National Power," *International Political Science Review*, Vol. 31, No. 4, 2010.

[36] One of these indexes is something of an outlier: The Foreign Bilateral Influence Index, compiled by the Hague Center for Strategic Studies and the Pardee Center at the University of Denver, aims to capture a

TABLE B.2

Factors in National Power Indexes

Correlates of War National Materiel Capabilities Index	Lowy Institute Asia Power Index	National Intelligence Council Global Power Index	Foreign Bilateral Influence Index
• Total population • Urban population • Iron and steel production • Energy consumption • Military personnel • Military expenditure	• Economic capability: Size; leverage (multinational corporations, role of currency); technology; connectivity • Resilience: Internal stability, resource security, geopolitical security, nuclear deterrence • Military capability: Defense spending, armed forces, weapons and platforms, signature capabilities, military posture • Cultural influence: Cultural, information and people flows • Diplomatic influence: Diplomatic network, multilateral power, achievement of foreign policy goals • Defense networks: Regional alliance network, regional defense diplomacy, global defense network • Economic relationships: Trade relations, investment ties, economic diplomacy • Future resources: Economic, military and general resources to 2030; demographic resources in 2050	• Military capacity: Nuclear weapons, military forces • Economic capacity: GDP, trade • Technological capacity: Innovation • Political capacity: Governance • Human capacity: Population	• Bandwidth • Total trade • Trade agreements • Percentage of total trade • Total arms transfers • Percentage of arms imports • Military alliances • Level of diplomatic representation • Intergovernmental membership • Dependence • Trade as percentage of GDP • Aid, as percentage of total aid and percentage of GDP • Arms imports as percentage of military spending

national weight, such as size of the economy, size of the population, and total defense spending. More-recent versions have expanded these baseline categories to a much more comprehensive set of factors and indicators.[37]

measure of dyadic influence between pairs of countries. Its measures therefore speak to the importance of one country's power and activities relative to one another—the proportion of trade dependent on that one partner and percentage of total foreign assistance or military imports received from that country. Nonetheless, many of the categories speak to the sorts of outcomes that a highly competitive power would seek. See Jonathan D. Moyer, Collin J. Meisel, Austin S. Matthews, David K. Bohl, and Mathew J. Burrows, *China-US Competition: Measuring Global Influence*, Denver, Colo.: Atlantic Council and Frederick S. Pardee Center for International Futures, University of Denver, Josef Korbel School of International Studies, May 2021.

[37] One especially interesting concept is the new measure of state economic strength offered in Gwang-Nam Rim, Sun-Nam Jang, Chol-Ju An, Sun-Hui Hwang, and Son-Hui Ri, "State Economic Strength and

Finally, we examined indexes of national competitiveness for sets of factors commonly used to identify success.[38] The World Economic Forum Competitiveness Index is the leading such measure; Table B.3 lists the factors from that source and one competing index. These indexes tend to have a strong economic, indeed specifically business-centric, flavor: They represent measures of the characteristics that allow nations to generate and sustain strong business and economic activity and to attract multinational firms, capital investment, and high-skill immigration.[39]

Despite that somewhat narrower purpose, these competitiveness indexes provide at first glance a close analogue to our goal—to develop a set of the qualities and outcomes that char-acteristics of societal competitiveness ought to produce. It would be theoretically possible to employ something like the World Economic Forum index as a comprehensive proxy for the outcome variables we are seeking. Nonetheless, because of the broader conception of national power and outcomes we had in mind—which emphasized both relative and geopolitical power to a degree not highlighted in the World Economic Forum index—we did not use it as a singular proxy. Modern competitiveness indexes tend to focus more on a country's ability to attract and provide a supportive context for business activity than a broader sense of the relative advantages it might have in a range of competitions with other countries.

Some Methodological Issues on Its Assessment," *Social Indicators Research*, Vol. 152, 2020. The authors' first criterion is state self-reliance, which they define as possessing the "versatile and synthetic economic strength to domestically satisfy the national demand for material means. Versatile economic foundation is what consists of production sectors which can meet all the material demands arising in economic construc-tion and people's livelihood improvement; synthetic economic foundation means what includes the whole course of social production ranging from raw materials exploitation to finished goods production and all the organically-connected links of reproduction cycle" (Rim et al., 2020, p. 613). They also include techno-logical sophistication and the ability of an economy to "satisfy the need of people for bountiful and cultured life," including broad-based measures of material well-being. They translate these categories into somewhat more-specific indicators, many of which center on human capital factors, human and knowledge resources, production totals, and capital availability.

[38] World Economic Forum, *Global Competitiveness Report 2019*, Geneva, 2019; IMD World Competitive-ness Center, *World Competitiveness Yearbook 2020*, Lausanne, Switzerland, 2020. See also IMD World Competitiveness Center, *Methodology and Principles of Analysis*, Lausanne, Switzerland, 2017; IMD World Competitiveness Center, "All Criteria List," 2021. These indexes have been the subject of some concern regarding methodology, most notably the risks of aggregating measures from different sources, the diffi-culty of defining key terms (such as *institutional quality*), the inability to capture interrelationships among the variables, and the fact that they may reflect an ideological bias.

[39] A related index is the World Bank's "government effectiveness" index. This tends to replicate many of the basic governance variables included in other indexes. There has been some controversy about possible manipulation of data for this index; see Josh Zumbrun, "World Bank Cancels Flagship 'Doing Business' Report After Investigation," *Wall Street Journal*, September 16, 2021.

TABLE B.3

Factors in Modern Competitiveness Indexes

World Economic Forum Global Competitiveness Index	IMD World Competitiveness Index
12 pillars with hundreds of indicators: • Institutions: Security, social capital, checks and balances, public-sector performance, transparency, property rights, corporate governance, future orientation of government • Infrastructure: Transport, utility • Information and communications technology adoption • Macroeconomic stability • Health • Skills: Education and skills of current and future workforce • Product market: domestic market competition, trade openness • Labor market: flexibility, meritocracy, and incentivization • Financial system: Depth, stability • Market size • Business dynamism: Administrative requirements, entrepreneurial culture • Innovation capability: Diversity and collaboration, research and development, commercialization	338 total indicators in four major categories: • Economic performance: Domestic economy, international trade, international investment, employment, prices • Government efficiency: Public finance, tax policy, institutional framework, business legislation, societal framework • Business efficiency: Productivity and efficiency, labor market, finance, management practices, attitudes and values • Infrastructure: Basic, technological, scientific, health and environment, education

Outcome Indicators: A Proposed Framework

On the basis of this analysis, we built a roster of factors more aligned with national security and relative global power and influence that could help us contrast competitive success and failure in at least somewhat objective terms. Table B.4 lists the resulting proposed variables. These factors do seek to assess where a given nation stands in comparison to others, but some are absolute rather than relative measures—they offer ways of identifying the success of each nation on its own terms, rather than a simple comparison of strength. Some, such as comparative military power assessments, speak to relative standing. Nor are most zero-sum measures. All the competitors in a strategic rivalry could rate very highly on the ability to protect their homelands. These factors are likely to display some interactions. They might conflict, with success in one making it harder to succeed in another. More commonly, there could be mutually supportive relationships: A strong trade position is likely associated with a strong paradigmatic position and military power.

One important qualification to this list is that states seek different combinations of these outcomes, based on their size, strength, governance model, ideology, history, and other factors. Simply put, success means different things to different countries. Countries perceive themselves as competing over different things, and both success and failure can take multiple forms. So can the recipe or formula for success: As Chapter Eleven suggests, countries

TABLE B.4

Outcome Indicators—Factors to Measure Competitive Success

Indicator of Competitive Success and Advantage	Historical and Current Examples and Metrics
Longevity in terms of long-term socioeconomic and geopolitical resilience that maintains national identity over an extended period and promotes extended cultural and social influence	• Trends in measures of national power • Collapse or surrender by rival • Long-term, indirect, and diffuse social, cultural, or political influence
Sovereign ability to protect the safety and prosperity of citizens against capabilities or threats of other states, nonstate actors, and systemic risks	• Power to prevent large-scale territorial aggression against homeland • Ability to prevent harassment or disruption of society short of war
Geopolitical freedom of action in terms of the ability to make free and unconstrained sovereign decisions and to take actions in the international system to the greatest degree that relative power will allow	• Absence of coercive control by regional or global hegemon • Self-sufficiency in materials and factors necessary for freedom of action
Military advantage or dominance, locally or globally, and the ability to project power	• Global military dominance, either generally (e.g., Rome, post–Cold War United States) or in specific domains (e.g., British maritime dominance) • Ability to project power from a distance
Leadership of or membership in predominant alignments of military and geopolitical power	• Modern treaty-based alliances, multilateral or bilateral • Less formal security relationships
Predominant economic strength—globally, within a region, or within one or more industries	• Total or per capita GDP • Share of global trade, investment, or research in critical industries
Strong to predominant position in global trade, investment, and capital markets (relative to size of GDP and other factors)	• Role in regional or global trade networks (Egypt, Rome, Britain, United States) • Dominance of national currency • Predominant power in economic institutions
Strong to predominant position in ideological and paradigmatic categories and global narratives and norms, attractive power, and international institutions and standards	• Cultural influence • Alignment with leading global norms and values • Leadership of international organizations and norm-setting processes
Strong or leading position in frontier technology; leading or dominant role in key emerging industrial sectors	• Domestic capabilities and industries in leading industries of the era • Measures of relative technological standing • Proportion of R&D spending in key industries

can display competitive advantage composed of many different combinations of the societal characteristics.

Taken together, these insights suggest a critical interim finding: For national competitive advantage, success or failure is a case-specific phenomenon, not a generalized one. Understanding whether a nation has the characteristics to succeed means first defining its specific goals in the competition (as distinct from those of other countries), and then understanding the formula for success that is allowed by its specific combination of societal characteristics. What this meant, in part, was that our analysis had to ultimately focus on individual cases and ask the qualitative and interpretive question of whether specific characteristics helped a specific country achieve success on its terms.

A related challenge involved how to handle countries that excel on an individual basis but do not have overall national power that compares to the leading states of the era. This was the challenge posed by societies such as the Nordic countries and Singapore: By purely internal measures and on a per capita basis, they display very high ratings on many competitiveness indexes. They have high standards of living and strong health and well-being measures, develop human capital, have world-class technology firms and research, and express values consistent with dominant global narratives.

Partly as a result, such countries often appear at the top of current indexes of national competitiveness. Among the top 15 most competitive nations in the 2020 World Economic Forum index, for example, are Singapore, Hong Kong, the Netherlands, Switzerland, Sweden, Denmark, Finland, and Canada.[40] Some current power indexes make clear that some smaller or medium powers punch above their weight in certain measures of global power and influence, in part because of such essential advantages. Yet their high rankings would not make them able to contest U.S. or Chinese global or regional power, and we must think about their degree of competitive strength differently.

Figure B.1 offers one way of doing so, organizing selected countries according to two vectors: domestic measures of competitiveness, regardless of size or power, and the degree to which they count as true great powers, with large populations, world-leading economies, and predominant military forces. The placements are broad and qualitative, but the figure begins to hint at how nations fall out according to these two basic variables.

Such a global competitiveness map could also provide some guidance to U.S. strategy in terms of targeting specific classes of nations. It would provide a way of measuring relative global alignment, for example, by looking at the "proportion of global competitive national strength" or some similar measure that is aligned with the United States.

Another way we sought to account for competitive advantages in smaller but still competitively successful powers—countries in the top-left portion of Figure B.1—was through a more indirect and emergent form of national competitive advantage: The ability of a nation or civilization to continue to exercise influence long after its period as a hegemon or even great power has faded. We included this in two variables in Table B.4: longevity and paradigmatic influence. In both cases, we have reserved an opportunity to highlight a civilization or a nation's ability, through key societal characteristics, to exercise a long-term influence on social, cultural, and political life, in each region or beyond, even apart from its direct national power measures.

To take one distant example, Athens exercised significant power over the Greek world for some time and helped defeat Persian efforts to subordinate the region—but it lost the major war it fought against another Greek city-state and eventually declined to a secondary position even within Greece. Yet the long-term effect of political, scientific, philosophical, cultural,

---

[40] World Economic Forum, 2020.

FIGURE B.1

Categorizing Competitive Nations

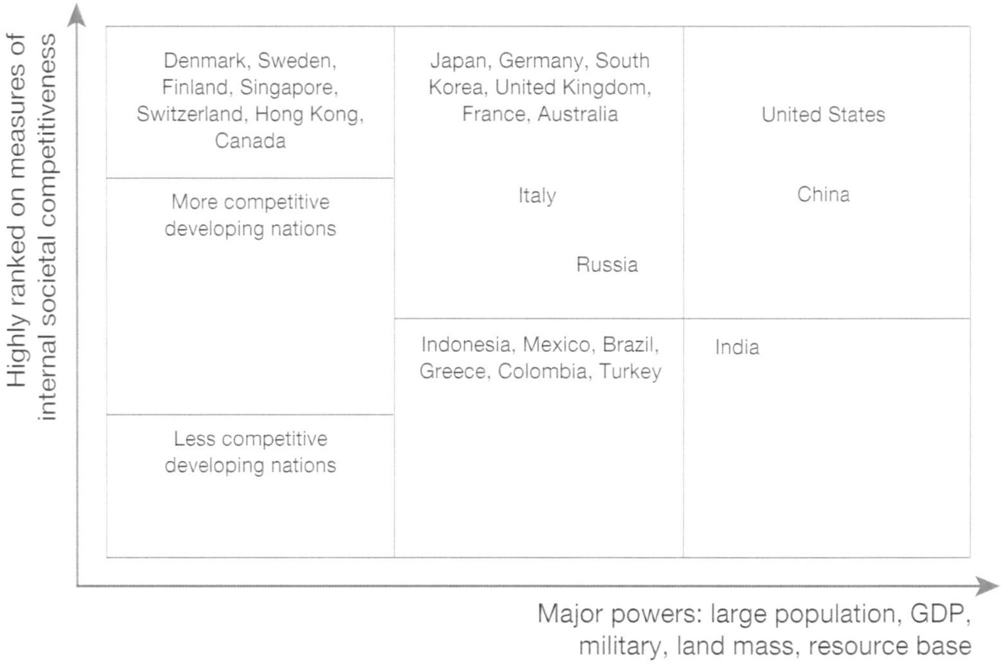

Denmark, Sweden, Finland, Singapore, Switzerland, Hong Kong, Canada	Japan, Germany, South Korea, United Kingdom, France, Australia	United States
More competitive developing nations	Italy	China
	Russia	
	Indonesia, Mexico, Brazil, Greece, Colombia, Turkey	India
Less competitive developing nations		

(Vertical axis: Highly ranked on measures of internal societal competitiveness)

(Horizontal axis: Major powers: large population, GDP, military, land mass, resource base)

and other ideas and innovations associated with Athens had a disproportionate impact on the course of Western history. The same has arguably been true of some of the great Italian city-states of the Renaissance period, northern European states of the late Renaissance and the Industrial Revolution, and the United States early in its history and again in the 20th century. Meanwhile, the city-state that defeated Athens in the Peloponnesian War—Sparta—lives on as myth and image but bequeathed no significant cultural or political legacy to history.

The ability to exercise such extended influence may be of less concern to policymakers focused on the immediate interests and ambitions of their country. And it will offer little reassurance to countries that lose wars or suffer major social collapses: In 404 BCE, as a starving and surrounded Athens surrendered to the Spartan army, few in the famed city would have been comforted by the idea that later civilizations would stand on the cultural, philosophical, artistic, political, and scientific foundations that they laid. Nonetheless, national competitive advantage can be expressed in both immediate and gradual ways.

In sum, we conceptualized competitive advantage in three broad ways. First, from the historical literature, our case studies, and modern indexes of competitiveness, we identified the nine defining factors of national competitive success listed in Table B.4. The aim of this list is to identify countries that are internally dynamic and competitive, *not* to assess their relative global standing. This set of factors allows us to start with a baseline of success that incorporated measures of how effective a society is in meeting its own domestic needs and goals, partly independent of its relative geopolitical standing. It helps us take seriously the fact that the Netherlands is a hugely successful and competitive society today even though it is no longer a world-spanning great power in classic historical terms. It also allowed us to assess that vague but suggestive idea of national dynamism in more-precise ways. A dynamic and vital society will be one that shows up well in these nine factors.

We then added a second lens focused on relative geopolitical standing: We defined the competitive peak or apex of global power of our case study countries and looked especially for the factors that drove their success. In the case of Britain, for example, we highlighted the period from the early 19th century through World War I as its moment of peak competitive standing. The Ottoman state rose to peak prominence in roughly the 15th through the 17th centuries, remaining powerful for an extended period after that but beginning a gradual relative decline—which prompted a series of reform efforts to catch up with European powers— beginning in the 18th century. For Rome's peak of power and influence, we chose the period from the late republic through the early empire.

For a third and final lens on competitive advantage, we turned to global histories tracking large-scale shifts in power and influence beyond the fates of individual nations, especially those that sought to identify causal factors explaining such shifts. The literature on the Great Divergence was especially useful, since it speaks directly to the factors responsible for Europe attaining a peak of competitive standing.

As we stressed in Chapter One, the resulting causal associations are a mix of objective data (such as figures on societal inequality, specific policies of an active state, or the numbers of students in school) and—much more commonly—subjective judgment about the role of specific factors, as suggested by the historical record. This approach does not allow us to estimate the precise effect of each societal characteristic on specific outcomes or even to quantify the overall effect of a characteristic across all of them. But the evidence is sufficient to hypothesize a meaningful competitive advantage effect from each of the seven nominated characteristics through a demonstrated causal association that has a strong theoretical basis for being valid, that stretches across multiple historical cases, and that is backed by other, more-discrete empirical evidence.

Abbreviations

BMI	Bureaucratic Mass Index
GDP	gross domestic product
OECD	Organisation for Economic Co-operation and Development
R&D	research and development

Bibliography

Abatino, B., G. G. Dari-Mattiacci, and E. C. Perotti, "Depersonalization of Business in Ancient Rome," *Oxford Journal of Legal Studies*, Vol. 31, No. 1, 2011, pp. 365–389.

Abramovitz, Moses, "Catching Up, Forging Ahead, and Falling Behind," *Journal of Economic History*, Vol. 46, No. 2, June 1986, pp. 385–406.

———, "The Search for the Sources of Growth: Areas of Ignorance, Old and New," *Journal of Economic History*, Vol. 53, No. 2, June 1993, pp. 217–243.

———, "The Elements of Social Capability," in Bon Ho Koo and Dwight H. Perkins, eds., *Social Capability and Long-Term Economic Growth*, New York: St. Martin's Press, 1995.

Abramowitz, Alan I., and Kyle L. Saunders, "Is Polarization a Myth?" *Journal of Politics*, Vol. 70, No. 2, 2008, pp. 542–555.

Abramowitz, Alan I., and S. W. Webster, "Negative Partisanship: Why Americans Dislike Parties but Behave Like Rabid Partisans," *Political Psychology*, Vol. 39, 2018, pp. 119–135.

Abrams, Samuel J., and Morris P. Fiorina, "The Myth of the 'Big Sort,'" Hoover Institution, August 13, 2012. As of February 14, 2022:
https://www.hoover.org/research/myth-big-sort

Acemoglu, Daron, and Pascual Restrepo, "Secular Stagnation? The Effect of Aging on Economic Growth in the Age of Automation," *American Economic Review*, Vol. 107, No. 5, 2017, pp. 174–179.

Acemoglu, Daron, and James A. Robinson, *Why Nations Fail: The Origins of Power, Prosperity, and Poverty*, New York: Currency, 2012.

Adams, J., "Romanitas and the Latin Language," *Classical Quarterly*, Vol. 53, No. 1, May 2003, pp. 184–205.

Adelman, Jeremy, *Sovereignty and Revolution in the Iberian Atlantic*, Princeton, N.J.: Princeton University Press, 2006.

———, "The Age of Imperial Revolutions," *American Historical Review*, Vol. 113, No. 2, 2008, pp. 319–340.

Adler, David, "Inside Operation Warp Speed: A New Model for Industrial Policy," *American Affairs*, Vol. 5, No. 2, Summer 2021.

Ahlerup, Pelle, and Gustav Hansson, "Nationalism and Government Effectiveness," *Journal of Comparative Economics*, Vol. 39, No. 3, 2011, pp. 431–451.

Albertus, Michael, and Guy Grossman, "Americans Are Officially Giving Up on Democracy," *Foreign Policy*, October 16, 2020.

Alden, Edward, *Failure to Adjust: How Americans Got Left Behind in the Global Economy*, New York: Council on Foreign Relations, 2016.

Alesina, Alberto, Arnaud Devleeschauwer, William Easterly, Sergio Kurlat, and Romain Wacziarg, "Fractionalization," *Journal of Economic Growth*, Vol. 8, 2003, pp. 155–194.

Alesina, Alberto, and Paola Giuliano, "Culture and Institutions," Cambridge, Mass.: National Bureau of Economic Research, Working Paper No. 19750, December 2013.

Alesina, Alberto, Armando Miano, and Stefanie Stantcheva, "The Polarization of Reality," *AEA Papers and Proceedings*, Vol. 110, 2020, pp. 324–328.

Alesina, Alberto, and Eliana La Ferrara, "Ethnic Diversity and Economic Performance," *Journal of Economic Literature*, Vol. 43, No. 3, 2005, pp. 762–800.

Ali, Mohamad, "Immigration Is at the Heart of U.S. Competitiveness," *Harvard Business Review*, May 15, 2017.

Allen, Jennifer, Baird Howland, Markus Mobius, David Rothschild, and Duncan J. Watts, "Evaluating the Fake News Problem at the Scale of the Information Ecosystem," *Science Advances*, Vol. 6, No. 14, April 2020.

Allen, Robert C., "The Rise and Decline of the Soviet Economy," *Canadian Journal of Economics/Revue Canadienne d'Economique*, Vol. 34, No. 4, 2001, pp. 859–881.

———, "Class Structure and Inequality During the Industrial Revolution: Lessons from England's Social Tables, 1688–1867," *Economic History Review*, Vol. 72, No. 1, February 2019, pp. 88–125.

Allison, Graham T., Dimitri K. Simes, and James Thomson, *America's National Interests*, Cambridge, Mass.: Commission on America's National Interests, Belfer Center, Harvard University, July 2000.

Al-Yousif, Yousif Khalifa, "Education Expenditure and Economic Growth: Some Empirical Evidence from the GCC Countries," *Journal of Developing Areas*, Vol. 42, No. 1, Fall 2008, pp. 69–80.

American National Election Studies, "Liberal-Conservative Self-Identification 1972–2020," August 16, 2021a. As of April 15, 2022:
https://electionstudies.org/resources/anes-guide/top-tables/?id=29

———, "Strength of Partisanship 1952–2020," August 16, 2021b. As of April 15, 2022:
https://electionstudies.org/resources/anes-guide/top-tables/?id=23

Amsden, Alice, *Asia's Next Giant: South Korea and Late Industrialization*, New York: Oxford University Press, 1989.

Anderson, Barbara, and Brian Silver, "Growth and Diversity of Population in the Soviet Union," *Annals of the American Academy of Political and Social Science*, Vol. 510, June 1990.

Anderson, Craig, *Roman Law Essentials*, Edinburgh: Edinburgh University Press, 2009.

Anderson, James H., "A New Global Paradigm: The United States Versus Russia," in James Lacey, ed., *Great Strategic Rivalries: From the Classical World to the Cold War*, New York: Oxford University Press, 2016.

Andrien, Kenneth, and Allan Kuethe, *The Spanish Atlantic World in the Eighteenth Century: War and the Bourbon Reforms, 1713–1796*, New York: Cambridge University Press, 2013.

Anno, Tadashi, "National Identity and Democracy: Lessons from the Case of Japan," *Asan Forum*, December 20, 2018.

Appleby, Joyce, *The Relentless Revolution: A History of Capitalism*, New York: W. W. Norton, 2010.

Arbesman, Samuel, "The Life-Spans of Empires," *Historical Methods: A Journal of Quantitative and Interdisciplinary History*, Vol. 44, No. 3, 2011, pp. 127–129.

Armitage, David, *The Ideological Origins of British Empire*, Cambridge, UK: Cambridge University Press, 2000.

Arnason, Johann P., *The Future That Failed: Origins and Destinies of the Soviet Model*, London: Routledge, 1993.

Arnim, Emily, "A Third of Minority Students Leave STEM Majors: Here's Why," EAB, October 8, 2019. As of February 23, 2022:
https://eab.com/insights/daily-briefing/
student-success/a-third-of-minority-students-leave-stem-majors-heres-why/

Asari, Eva-Maria, Daphne Halikiopoulou, and Steven Mock, "British National Identity and the Dilemmas of Multiculturalism," *Nationalism and Ethnic Politics*, Vol. 14, No. 1, 2008.

Atkins, Gareth, "Christian Heroes, Providence, and Patriotism in Wartime Britain, 1793–1815," *Historical Journal*, Vol. 58, No. 2, 2015, pp. 393–414.

Atkinson, Robert D., "How the U.S. Government Falters on Support for Innovation," Information Technology and Innovation Foundation, August 28, 2019. As of May 4, 2022:
https://itif.org/publications/2019/08/28/how-us-government-falters-support-innovation

Atkinson, Robert D., and Michael Lind, "National Developmentalism: From Forgotten Tradition to New Consensus," *American Affairs*, Vol. 3, No. 2, Summer 2019.

Auerswald, P. E., and L. M. Branscomb, "Valleys of Death and Darwinian Seas: Financing the Invention to Innovation Transition in the United States," *Journal of Technology Transfer*, Vol. 28, Nos. 3–4, 2003, pp. 227–239.

Baer, Marc David, *The Ottomans: Khans, Caesars, and Caliphs*, New York: Basic Books, 2021.

Baker Center for Leadership and Governance, "2018 American Institutional Confidence Poll: The Health of American Democracy in an Era of Hyper Polarization," undated. As of February 23, 2022:
http://bakercenter.wideeyeclient.com/aicpoll/

Banfield, Edward C., *Moral Basis of a Backward Society*, New York: Free Press, 1958.

Barnett, Correlli, *The Collapse of British Power*, New York: William Morrow & Company, 1972.

——, *The Pride and Fall: The Dream and Illusion of Britain as a Great Nation*, New York: Free Press, 1986.

Barczewski, Stephanie L., *Myth and National Identity in Nineteenth Century Britain: The Legends of King Arthur and Robin Hood*, Oxford, UK: Oxford University Press, 2000.

Barrington, Lowell W., "'Nation' and 'Nationalism': The Misuse of Key Concepts in Political Science," *PS: Political Science and Politics*, Vol. 30, No. 4, 1997, pp. 712–716.

Bartlett, Kenneth, "Italian Renaissance," Great Courses, course no. 3970, 2005. As of June 27, 2021:
https://www.thegreatcourses.com/courses/italian-renaissance

——, *Short History of the Italian Renaissance*, Toronto: University of Toronto Press, 2013.

——, *The Renaissance in Italy: A History*, Kindle ed., Indianapolis, Ind.: Hackett Publishing Company, 2019.

Bartsch-Zimmer, Shadi, "The Romans, Just Wars, and Exceptionalism," *Formations* (Stevanovich Institute on the Formation of Knowledge, University of Chicago), September 28, 2017. As of November 8, 2021:
https://sifk.uchicago.edu/news/the-romans-just-wars-and-exceptionalism/

Basso, Henrique, and Juan F. Jimeno, "Demographics and Technology Explain Secular Stagnation and More," *VoxEU*, November 29, 2019. As of February 25, 2022:
https://voxeu.org/article/demographics-and-technology-explain-secular-stagnation-and-more

Baszak, Gregor, "A New Cultural Cold War?" *American Affairs*, Vol. 4, No. 4, 2020.

Beard, Mary, *SPQR*, New York: Liveright, 2015.

Beauchamp, Zack, "Japan Is Weakening Its Constitutional Commitment to Pacifism," *Vox*, July 1, 2014. As of March 9, 2022:
https://www.vox.com/2014/7/1/5861768/abe-security-alliance

Bebchuk, Lucian, and Scott Hirst, "The Specter of the Giant Three," *Boston University Law Review*, Vol. 99, May 2019, pp. 721–741.

Beckley, Michael, "The Power of Nations: Measuring What Matters," *International Security*, Vol. 43, No. 2, Fall 2018a, pp. 7–44.

———, *Unrivaled: Why America Will Remain the World's Sole Superpower*, Ithaca, N.Y.: Cornell University Press, 2018b.

Beinhocker, Eric D., *The Origin of Wealth: The Radical Remaking of Economics and What It Means for Business and Society*, Boston, Mass.: Harvard Business Review Press, 2007.

Beissinger, Mark, "Nationalism and the Collapse of Soviet Communism," *Contemporary European History*, Vol. 18, No. 3, 2009, pp. 331–347.

———, *Nationalist Mobilization and the Collapse of the Soviet State*, Cambridge, UK: Cambridge University Press, 2010.

Bell, Alexander, Raj Chetty, Xavier Jaravel, Neviana Petkova, and John Van Reene, "Who Becomes an Inventor in America? The Importance of Exposure to Innovation," Cambridge, Mass.: National Bureau of Economic Research, Working Paper 24062, November 2017.

Belton, Keith B., "The Emerging American Industrial Policy," *American Affairs*, Vol. 5, No. 3, Fall 2021.

Bennett, D. Scott, "Security, Bargaining, and the End of Interstate Rivalry," *International Studies Quarterly*, Vol. 40, No. 2, 1996, pp. 157–183.

Bergeaud, Antonin, and Gilbert Cette, and Rémy Lecat, "Long-Term Growth and Productivity Trends: Secular Stagnation or Temporary Slowdown?" *Revue de l'OFCE*, Vol. 157, No. 3, 2018, pp. 37–54.

Berger, Mark T., "States of Nature and the Nature of States: The Fate of Nations, the Collapse of States and the Future of the World," *Third World Quarterly*, Vol. 28, No. 6, 2007, pp. 1203–1214.

Bernstein, Jared, "Improving Economic Opportunity in the United States," testimony before the U.S. Congressional Joint Economic Committee, April 5, 2017.

Berthold, Norbert, and Klaus Gründler, "On the Empirics of Social Mobility: A Macroeconomic Approach," Würzburg, Germany: Julius Maximilian University of Würzburg, 2014.

Besley, Timothy J., Robin Burgess, Adnan Khan, and Guo Xu, "Bureaucracy and Development," Cambridge, Mass.: National Bureau of Economic Research, Working Paper 29163, August 2021.

Biasi, Barbara, David J. Deming, and Petra Moser, "Education and Innovation," Cambridge, Mass.: National Bureau of Economic Research, Working Paper 28544, March 2021.

Bishop, Bill, and Robert Cushing, *The Big Sort: Why the Clustering of Like-Minded America Is Tearing Us Apart*, New York: Mariner Books, 2009.

Bisin, Alberto, and Thierry Vierdier, "On the Joint Evolution of Culture and Institutions," Cambridge, Mass.: National Bureau of Economic Research, Working Paper 23375, April 2017.

Bisley, Nick, *The End of the Cold War and the Causes of Soviet Collapse*, Basingstoke: Palgrave Macmillan, 2004.

Black, Jeremy, *From Louis XIV to Napoleon: The Fate of a Great Power*, London: University College London Press, 1999.

Blanchette, Jude, "Xi's Confidence Game," *Foreign Affairs*, November 23, 2021.

Block, Fred, and Matthew R. Keller, eds., *State of Innovation: The U.S. Government's Role in Technology Development*, London: Taylor & Francis, 2011.

Bloom, Nicholas, John Van Reenen, and Heidi Williams, "A Toolkit of Policies to Promote Innovation," *Journal of Economic Perspectives*, Vol. 33, No. 3, Summer 2019, pp. 163–184.

Bohlen, Celestine, "American Democracy Is Drowning in Money," *New York Times*, September 20, 2017.

Boin, Douglas, "Ancient Rome Thrived When the Empire Welcomed Immigrants: We Should Remember What Happened When That Changed," *Time*, June 9, 2020.

Bond, Sarah, "Investing in Infrastructure: Funding Roads in Ancient Rome and Today," *Forbes*, June 30, 2017.

Bonnueil, Noël, "History and Dynamics: Marriage or Mésalliance?" *History and Theory*, Vol. 44, No. 2, May 2005, pp. 265–270.

Boulding, Kenneth, *Ecodynamics: A New Theory of Societal Evolution*, Beverly Hills, Calif.: Sage, 1978.

———, *Evolutionary Economics*, Beverly Hills, Calif.: Sage, 1981.

Boyd, Brian, and Kirk Doran, "Governance for Good Jobs: The Need for Pro-Productivity Reforms," *American Affairs*, Vol. 5, No. 3, Fall 2021.

Boyer, John W., *Political Radicalism in Late Imperial Vienna: Origins of the Christian Social Movement, 1848–1897*, Chicago: University of Chicago Press, 1981.

Boxel, Levi, Matthew Gentzkow, and Jesse M. Shapiro, "Cross-Country Trends in Affective Polarization," Cambridge, Mass.: National Bureau of Economic Research, Working Paper 26669, August 2021.

Bradbury, Katharine, and Robert K. Triest, "Inequality of Opportunity and Aggregate Economic Performance," *RSF: The Russell Sage Foundation Journal of the Social Sciences*, Vol. 2, No. 2, May 2016, pp. 178–201.

Breen, Richard, "Inequality, Economic Growth and Social Mobility," *British Journal of Sociology*, Vol. 48, No. 3, 1997, pp. 429–449.

Brenan, Megan, "Americans' Confidence in Major U.S. Institutions Dips," Gallup, July 14, 2021. As of February 25, 2022:
https://news.gallup.com/poll/352316/americans-confidence-major-institutions-dips.aspx

Brenner, Reuven, "How the Financial Crisis Did Not Change the World," *American Affairs*, Vol. 3, No. 1, Spring 2019.

Brent, R. Stephen, "Misunderstanding Investment in the United States and China," *American Affairs*, Vol. 4, No. 4, Winter 2020.

Breton, Albert, "Federalism and Decentralization: Ownership Rights and the Superiority of Federalism," *Publius*, Vol. 30, No. 2, 2000, pp. 1–16.

Brewer, John, *The Sinews of Power: War, Money, and the English State*, New York: Knopf, 1989.

Breznitz, Dan, and David Adler, "Reshoring Production and Restoring American Prosperity: A Practical Policy Agenda," *American Affairs*, Vol. 4, No. 4, Winter 2020.

"Britain's Civil Service Remains Upper-Middle Class," *The Economist*, May 22, 2021.

Broadberry, Stephen, Bruce M. S. Campbell, Alexander Klein, Mark Overton, and Bas van Leeuwen, *British Economic Growth, 1270–1870*, New York: Cambridge University Press, 2014.

Brog, David, "Up from Laissez-Faire: Reclaiming Conservative Economics," *American Affairs*, Vol. 4, No. 4, Winter 2020.

Brooks, David, "America Is Having a Moral Convulsion," *The Atlantic*, October 4, 2020.

Brooks, Stephen G., and William C. Wohlforth, "The Rise and Fall of the Great Powers in the Twenty-First Century," *International Security*, Vol. 40, No. 3, 2015–2016, pp. 7–53.

Bump, Philip, "Most Republicans See Democrats Not as Political Opponents but as Enemies," *Washington Post*, February 10, 2021.

Bunce, Valerie, *Subversive Institutions: The Design and the Destruction of Socialism and the State*, Cambridge, UK: Cambridge University Press, 1999.

Burckhardt, Jacob, *The Civilization of the Renaissance in Italy*, New York: Start Publishing, 2013.

Burke, Marshall, Sol Hsiang, and Ted Miguel, "Economic Impact of Climate Change on the World," Stanford University, webpage, undated. As of March 25, 2022: https://web.stanford.edu/~mburke/climate/map.php

Burke, Peter, *The Italian Renaissance: Culture and Society in Italy*, 3rd ed., Princeton, N.J.: Princeton University Press, 2014.

Burkeman, Oliver, "Memo Exposes Bush's New Green Strategy," *The Guardian*, March 3, 2003.

Bush, George W., *The National Security Strategy*, Washington, D.C.: White House, September 2002.

Butzer, Karl W., and Georgina H. Endfield, "Critical Perspectives on Historical Collapse," *Proceedings of the National Academy of Sciences*, Vol. 109, No. 10, 2012, pp. 3628–3631.

Byman, Daniel L., and Kenneth M. Pollack, "Let Us Now Praise Great Men: Bringing the Statesman Back In," *International Security*, Vol. 25, No. 4, 2001, pp. 107–146.

Cain, Peter, and Anthony G. Hopkins, *British Imperialism: Innovation and Expansion*, Essex, UK: Longman, 1993.

Callahan, William, "Chinese Visions of a World Order: Post-Hegemonic or New Hegemony?" *International Studies Review*, Vol. 10, No. 4, 2008.

Camera, Lauren, "Reading Scores Fall Among U.S. High School Seniors," *U.S. News and World Report*, October 28, 2020.

Campbell, Andrea Louise, "America the Undertaxed: U.S. Fiscal Policy in Perspective," *Foreign Affairs*, September–October 2012.

Cannadine, David, *Victorious Century: The United Kingdom, 1800–1906*, New York: Penguin Books, 2017.

Carment, David, "Assessing State Failure: Implications for Theory and Policy," *Third World Quarterly*, Vol. 24, No. 3, 2003, pp. 407–427.

Carroll, Linda, "More Than a Third of U.S. Healthcare Costs Go to Bureaucracy," Reuters, January 6, 2020.

Cartwright, Nancy, "How to Do Things with Causes," *Proceedings and Addresses of the American Philosophical Association*, Vol. 83, No. 2, November 2009, pp. 5–22.

———, "Will This Policy Work for You? Predicting Effectiveness Better: How Philosophy Helps," *Philosophy of Science*, Vol. 79, No. 5, December 2012, pp. 973–989.

———, "Middle-Range Theory," *Theoria: An International Journal for Theory, History and Foundations of Science*, Vol. 35, No. 3, 2020, pp. 269–323.

Case, Anne, and Angus Deaton, "The Death Divide: Education, Despair, and Death," Cambridge, Mass.: National Bureau of Economic Research, Working Paper 29241, September 2021.

Casson, Mark, "Cultural Determinants of Economic Performance," *Journal of Comparative Economics*, Vol. 17, No. 2, June 1993, pp. 418–442.

Casson, Mark, and Andrew Godley, "Entrepreneurship in Britain, 1830–1900," in David S. Landes, Joel Mokyr, and William J. Baumol, eds., *The Invention of Enterprise: Entrepreneurship from Ancient Mesopotamia to Modern Times*, Princeton, N.J.: Princeton University Press, 2010, pp. 211–242.

Castells, Manuel, *The Rise of the Network Society*, Oxford: Blackwell Publishers, 1986.

Chan, Melissa, "Conspiracy Theories Might Sound Crazy, but Here's Why Experts Say We Can No Longer Ignore Them," *Time*, August 15, 2019.

Chang, Caroline, Scott Moore, and Ali Wyne, "Federalism in the Time of Coronavirus: A Comparative U.S. Advantage," *The Diplomat*, May 29, 2020.

Chaudhary, Amatul R., Asim Iqbal, and Syed Yasir Mahmood Gillani, "The Nexus Between Higher Education and Economic Growth: An Empirical Investigation for Pakistan," *Pakistan Journal of Commerce and Social Sciences*, Vol. 3, 2009, pp. 1–9.

Chetty, Raj, *Improving Opportunities for Economic Mobility: New Evidence and Policy Lessons*, St. Louis, Mo.: Federal Reserve Bank of St. Louis, December 2016.

Chetty, Raj, David Grusky, Maximilian Hell, Nathaniel Hendren, Robert Manduca, and Jimmy Narang, "The Fading American Dream: Trends in Absolute Income Mobility Since 1940," *Science*, Vol. 356, No. 6336, December 2016, pp. 398–406.

Chetty, Raj, Nathaniel Hendren, Maggie R. Jones, and Sonya R. Porter, "Race and Economic Opportunity in the United States: An Intergenerational Perspective," *Quarterly Journal of Economics*, Vol. 135, No. 2, May 2020, pp. 711–783.

Chetty, Raj, Nathaniel Hendren, Patrick Kline, and Emmanuel Saez, "Where Is the Land of Opportunity? The Geography of Intergenerational Mobility in the United States," *Quarterly Journal of Economics*, Vol. 129, No. 4, 2014, pp. 1553–1623.

Christensen, Clayton M., and Derek van Bever, "The Capitalist's Dilemma," *Harvard Business Review*, June 2014.

Cirera, Xavier, and William F. Maloney, *The Innovation Paradox: Developing-Country Capabilities and the Unrealized Promise of Technological Catch-Up*, Washington, D.C.: World Bank Group, 2017.

Cingano, Federico, "Trends in Income Inequality and Its Impact on Economic Growth," OECD Social, Employment and Migration Working Paper No. 163, Paris: Organisation for Economic Co-operation and Development, 2014.

Cinnirella, Francesco, and Jochen Streb, "The Role of Human Capital and Innovation in Economic Development: Evidence from Post-Malthusian Prussia," *Journal of Economic Growth*, Vol. 22, 2017, pp. 193–227.

Clark, Cal, and Changhoon Jung, "Implications of the Asian Flu for Developmental State Theory: The Cases of South Korea and Taiwan," *Asian Affairs*, Vol. 29, No. 1, 2002, pp. 16–42.

Clark, Peter, *British Clubs and Societies, 1580–1800: The Origins of an Associational World*, Oxford, UK: Clarendon Press, 2000.

Classen, Christopher, "Support for Democracy Is Declining—but Not in the U.S. or Other Western Democracies," *Washington Post*, July 5, 2018.

Clesse, Armand, Takashi Inoguchi, E. B. Keehn, and J. A. A. Stockwin, eds., *The Vitality of Japan: Sources of National Strength and Weakness*, Basingstoke, UK: Macmillan Press, 1997.

Clesse, Armand, and Sergei Lounev, eds., *The Vitality of Russia*, Luxembourg: Luxembourg Institute for European and International Studies, 2004.

Cline, Eric, *1177 B.C.: The Year Civilization Collapsed*, Princeton, N.J.: Princeton University Press, 2014.

Cline, Ray S., *World Power Assessment: A Calculus of Strategic Drift*, Boulder, Colo.: Westview Press, 1975.

Clinton, William J., *A National Security Strategy of Engagement and Enlargement: National Security Strategy 1994*, Washington, D.C.: White House, July 1994.

———, *A National Security Strategy of Engagement and Enlargement: National Security Strategy 1996*, Washington, D.C.: White House, February 1996.

Cochrane, John H., "Debt Still Matters," *Chicago Booth Review*, November 12, 2020. As of August 5, 2021:
https://review.chicagobooth.edu/economics/2020/article/debt-still-matters

Cohen, Ariel, "Intelligence Disaster, Bureaucratic Sclerosis," Heritage Foundation, September 16, 2001. As of February 25, 2022:
https://www.heritage.org/defense/commentary/intelligence-disaster-bureaucratic-sclerosis

Cohn, Nate, "Polarization Is Dividing American Society, Not Just Politics," *New York Times*, June 12, 2014.

Cohon, Jared, Mary Sue Coleman, and Robert Conn, "US Innovation and Competition Act Will Ensure Continued US Leadership," *The Hill*, September 7, 2021.

Colaresi, Michael P., Karen Rasler, and William R. Thompson, *Strategic Rivalries in World Politics: Position, Space and Conflict Escalation*, Cambridge, UK: Cambridge University Press, 2008.

Colley, Linda, *Britons: Forging the Nation 1707–1837*, New Haven, Conn.: Yale University Press, 1992.

Collier, Paul, *The Bottom Billion: Why the Poorest Countries Are Failing and What Can Be Done About It*, New York: Oxford University Press, 2007.

Collins, Bruce, and Keith Robbins, eds., *British Culture and Economic Decline*, New York: St. Martin's Press, 1990.

Comin, Diego, William Easterly, and Erick Gong, "Was the Wealth of Nations Determined in 1000 B.C.?" Boston, Mass.: Harvard Business School, Working Paper 09-052, 2008.

Concord Coalition, "Why the National Debt Still Matters," July 28, 2021. As of February 25, 2022:
https://www.concordcoalition.org/special-publication/why-national-debt-still-matters

Conklin, Alice L., *A Mission to Civilize: The Republican Idea of Empire in France and West Africa, 1895–1930*, Stanford, Calif.: Stanford University Press, 1997.

Connable, Ben, Michael J. McNerney, William Marcellino, Aaron B. Frank, Henry Hargrove, Marek N. Posard, S. Rebecca Zimmerman, Natasha Lander, Jasen J. Castillo, and James Sladden, *Will to Fight: Analyzing, Modeling, and Simulating the Will to Fight of Military Units*, Santa Monica, Calif.: RAND Corporation, RR-2341-A, 2018. As of March 15, 2022:
https://www.rand.org/pubs/research_reports/RR2341.html

Correlates of War, "National Material Capabilities," version 5.0, undated. As of April 27, 2022:
http://www.correlatesofwar.org/data-sets/national-material-capabilities

Crane, Gregory, "The Fear and Pursuit of Risk: Corinth on Athens, Sparta and the Peloponnesians," *Transactions of the American Philological Association*, Vol. 122, 1992, pp. 227–256.

Crawcour, Sydney, "The Tokugawa Period and Japan's Preparation for Modern Economic Growth," *Journal of Japanese Studies*, Vol. 1, No. 1, Autumn 1974, pp. 113–125.

Crouzet, François, *The First Industrialists: The Problems of Origins*, Cambridge, UK: Cambridge University Press, 1985.

Dahlman, Carl J., and Richard Nelson, "Social Absorption Capability, National Innovation Systems and Economic Development," in Bon Ho Koo and Dwight H. Perkins, eds., *Social Capability and Long-Term Economic Growth*, New York: St. Martin's Press, 1995, pp. 82–121.

Dalio, Ray, *Principles for Dealing with the Changing World Order: Why Nations Succeed and Fail*, New York: Avid Reader Press, 2021.

Darling, Linda T., "The Sultan's Advisors and Their Opinions on the Identity of the Ottoman Elite, 1580–1653," in Christine Isom-Verhaaren and Kent F. Schull, eds., *Living in the Ottoman Realm: Empire and Identity, 13th to 20th Centuries*, Indianapolis: Indiana University Press, 2016, pp. 171–181.

Davids, Karel, "The Scholarly Atlantic: Circuits of Knowledge Between Britain, the Dutch Republic and the Americas in the Eighteenth Century," in Gert Oostindie and Jessica V. Roitman, eds., *Dutch Atlantic Connections, 1680–1800: Linking Empires, Bridging Borders*, Leiden: Brill, 2014.

Davis, Gerald F., "What Might Replace the Modern Corporation? Uberization and the Web Page Enterprise," *Seattle University Law Review*, Vol. 39, 2016, pp. 508–511.

Deak, John, *Forging a Multinational State: State Making in Imperial Austria from the Enlightenment to the First World War*, Stanford, Calif.: Stanford University Press, 2015.

Deane, Claudia, and John Gramlich, "2020 Election Reveals Two Broad Voting Coalitions Fundamentally at Odds," Pew Research Center, November 6, 2020. As of August 17, 2021:
https://www.pewresearch.org/fact-tank/2020/11/06/2020-election-reveals-two-broad-voting-coalitions-fundamentally-at-odds/

Deloitte, "Diversity and Inclusion as a Competitive Advantage," webpage, undated (no longer available).

Demsas, Jerusalem, "Why Does It Cost So Much to Build Things in America?" *Vox*, June 28, 2021. As of July 13, 2021:
https://www.vox.com/22534714/rail-roads-infrastructure-costs-america

Dench, Emma, "Roman Identity," in Alessandro Barchiesi and Walter Scheidel, eds., *The Oxford Handbook of Roman Studies*, online ed., New York: Oxford University Press, 2012.

Denmark, Abraham, and Matthew Rojansky, "American Success Abroad Is Anchored to Problem-Solving at Home," *War on the Rocks*, June 25, 2020. As of June 26, 2020:
https://warontherocks.com/2020/06/american-success-abroad-is-anchored-to-problem-solving-at-home/

Dent, Christopher M., "Taiwan's Foreign Economic Policy: The 'Liberalisation Plus' Approach of an Evolving Developmental State," *Modern Asian Studies*, Vol. 37, No. 2, 2003, pp. 461–483.

Desilver, Drew, "U.S. Students' Academic Achievement Still Lags That of Their Peers in Many Other Countries," Pew Research Center, February 15, 2017. As of April 25, 2022:
https://www.pewresearch.org/fact-tank/2017/02/15/u-s-students-internationally-math-science/

———, "U.S. Senate Has Fewest Split Delegations Since Direct Elections Began," Pew Research Center, February 11, 2021. As of August 17, 2021:
https://www.pewresearch.org/fact-tank/2021/02/11/u-s-senate-has-fewest-split-delegations-since-direct-elections-began/

Desmet, Klaus, and Stephen Parente, "Unleashing Growth: The Decline of Innovation-Blocking Institutions," *VoxEU*, May 18, 2013.

De Vries, Jan, "The Industrial Revolution and the Industrious Revolution," *Journal of Economic History*, Vol. 54, No. 2, June 1994, pp. 249–270.

———, "Secular Cycles by Peter Turchin and Sergey A. Nefedov," *Population Studies*, Vol. 64, No. 2, July 2010, pp. 203–204.

DeVries, Kelly, "A Medieval Enterprise: England Versus France I," in James Lacey, ed., *Great Strategic Rivalries: From the Classical World to the Cold War*, New York: Oxford University Press, 2016.

Diamond, Jared, "Ecological Collapses of Ancient Civilizations: The Golden Age That Never Was," *Bulletin of the American Academy of Arts and Sciences*, Vol. 47, No. 5, 1994, pp. 37–59.

———, *Collapse: How Societies Choose to Fail or Succeed*, New York: Viking, 2005.

Dickinson, Matthew, "Sorted, Not Polarized: Why the Distinction Matters," *Presidential Power* (Middlebury College), July 11, 2014. As of August 17, 2021:
https://sites.middlebury.edu/presidentialpower/2014/07/11/sorted-not-polarized-why-the-distinction-matters/

Diebel, Terry L., *Foreign Affairs Strategy: Logic for American Statecraft*, New York: Cambridge University Press, 2007.

Diehl, Paul F., and Gary Goertz, *War and Peace in International Rivalry*, Ann Arbor: University of Michigan Press, 2000.

Dill, Joshua, "Nonliberal Capitalism: The Exception or the Rule?" *American Affairs*, Vol. 4, No. 4, 2020.

DiMaggio, Paul, "Culture and Economy," in Neil Smelser and Richard Swedberg, eds., *The Handbook of Economic Sociology*, Princeton, N.J.: Princeton University Press, 1994, pp. 27–57.

DiMaggio, Paul J., and Walter W. Powell, "The Iron Cage Revisited: Institutional Isomorphism and Collective Rationality in Organizational Fields," *American Sociological Review*, Vol. 48, No. 2, April 1983, pp. 147–160.

Dimock, Michael, "America Is Exceptional in Its Political Divide," *Trust Magazine* (Pew Research Center), Winter 2021. As of August 17, 2021:
https://www.pewtrusts.org/en/trust/archive/winter-2021/
america-is-exceptional-in-its-political-divide

Djilas, Milovan, *The New Class: An Analysis of the Communist System*, New York: Praeger, 1957.

Doak, Kevin M., "What Is a Nation and Who Belongs? National Narratives and the Ethnic Imagination in Twentieth-Century Japan," *American Historical Review*, Vol. 102, No. 2, April 1997, pp. 283–309.

———, *A History of Nationalism in Modern Japan: Placing the People*, Netherlands: Brill, 2007.

Doornbos, Martin, "State Collapse and Fresh Starts: Some Critical Reflections," *Development and Change*, Vol. 33, No. 5, 2002, pp. 797–815.

Douthat, Ross Gregory, *The Decadent Society: How We Became the Victims of Our Own Success*, New York: Avid Reader Press, 2020.

Drelichman, Mauricio, and Hans-Joachim Voth, *Lending to the Borrower from Hell: Debt, Taxes, and Default in the Age of Philip II*, Princeton, N.J.: Princeton University Press, 2014.

Drucker, Peter F., "Behind Japan's Success," *Harvard Business Review*, January 1981.

Easterbrook, Gregg, "Global Warming: Who Loses—and Who Wins?" *The Atlantic*, April 2007.

Economist Intelligence Unit, *The Worldwide Educating for the Future Index 2019: A Benchmark for the Skills of Tomorrow*, London, 2019.

Edgerton, David, *The Shock of the Old: Technology and Global History Since 1900*, New York: Oxford University Press, 2011.

Eichengreen, Barry, "Secular Stagnation: The Long View," *American Economic Review*, Vol. 105, No. 5, 2015, pp. 66–70.

Elliott, J. H., "A Provincial Aristocracy: The Catalan Ruling Class in the Sixteenth and Seventeenth Century," in Elliott, *Spain and Its World*, New Haven, Conn.: Yale University Press, 1990, pp. 71–91.

Elster, Jon, "A Plea for Mechanisms," in Peter Hedström and Richard Swedberg, eds., *Social Mechanisms: An Analytical Approach to Social Theory*, Cambridge, UK: Cambridge University Press, 1998, pp. 45–73.

———, *Explaining Social Behavior: More Nuts and Bolts for the Social Sciences*, Cambridge, UK: Cambridge University Press, 2015.

Eregha, P. B., R. I. Irughe, and J. Edafe, "Education and Economic Growth: Empirical Evidence from Nigeria," *Managing Global Transitions*, Vol. 16, No. 1, 2018, pp. 59–77.

Erixon, Fredrik, and Björn Weigel, "Capitalism Without Capitalists," *American Affairs*, Vol. 1, No. 3, Fall 2017, pp. 3–16.

Evans, M. D. R., and Jonathan Kelley, "National Pride in the Developed World: Survey Data from 24 Nations," *International Journal of Public Opinion Research*, Vol. 14, No. 3, 2002.

Evans, Peter, *Embedded Autonomy: States and Industrial Transformation*, Princeton, N.J.: Princeton University Press, 1990.

Fairless, Tom, "As Inflation Eases Public Debt Load, Economists Sound Cautionary Note," *Wall Street Journal*, May 1, 2022.

Fairlie, Robert W., and Alicia M. Robb, *Disparities in Capital Access Between Minority and Non-Minority-Owned Businesses*, Washington, D.C.: U.S. Department of Commerce, Minority Business Development Agency, January 2010.

Fairlie, Robert W., Alicia Robb, and David T. Robinson, "Black and White: Access to Capital Among Minority-Owned Startups," Cambridge, Mass.: National Bureau of Economic Research, Working Paper 28154, November 2020.

Fanis, Maria, "In Defense of the British Empire: Great Britain's National Identity of Loyal Patriotism and the War of 1812," in *Secular Morality and International Security: American and British Decisions About War*, Ann Arbor: University of Michigan Press, 2011, pp. 13–56.

Federal Reserve Bank of St. Louis, "Real GDP at Constant National Prices for Japan," updated November 8, 2021. As of April 8, 2022:
https://fred.stlouisfed.org/series/RGDPNAJPA666NRUG

Ferguson, Niall, *Empire: How Britain Made the Modern World*, London: Allen Lane, 2003.

———, *Civilization: The West and the Rest*, New York: Penguin, 2011.

Fernandez, Raquel, and Richard Rogerson, "Human Capital Accumulation and Income Distribution," Cambridge, Mass.: National Bureau of Economic Research, Working Paper 3994, 1992.

Feygin, Yakov, "The American Fiscal State Rumbles to Life," *Noema*, April 27, 2021.

Finkel, Caroline, *Osman's Dream: The History of the Ottoman Empire*, New York: Basic Books, 2005.

Fiorina, Morris P., "The Myth of Growing Polarization," *Defining Ideas* (Hoover Institution), September 14, 2016. As of February 27, 2022:
https://www.hoover.org/research/myth-growing-polarization

———, *Unstable Majorities: Polarization, Party Sorting and Political Stalemate*, Stanford, Calif.: Hoover Institution Press, 2017.

Fiorina, Morris P., Samuel J. Abrams, and Jeremy C. Pope, *Culture War? The Myth of a Polarized America*, 3rd ed., New York: Longman, 2010.

Fisher, Max, "Disinformation for Hire, a Shadow Industry, Is Quietly Booming," *New York Times*, July 25, 2021.

Flanagan, Caitlin, "Private Schools Have Become Truly Obscene," *The Atlantic*, April 2021.

Florida, Richard, "America's 'Big Sort' Is Only Getting Bigger," Bloomberg, October 25, 2016. As of February 27, 2022:
https://www.bloomberg.com/news/articles/2016-10-25/
how-the-big-sort-is-driving-political-polarization

Flynn, Dennis O., "Fiscal Crisis and the Decline of Spain (Castile)," *Journal of Economic History*, Vol. 42, No. 1, March 1982, pp. 139–147.

Foa, Roberto Stefan, and Yascha Mounk, "The Danger of Deconsolidation: The Democratic Disconnect," *Journal of Democracy*, Vol. 27, No. 3, July 2016.

Fowkes, Ben, *The Disintegration of the Soviet Union: A Study in the Rise and Triumph of Nationalism*, London: Palgrave-Macmillan, 1997.

Franke, Richard H., Geert Hofstede, and Michael H. Bond, "Cultural Roots of Economic Performance: A Research Note," *Strategic Management Journal*, Vol. 12, No. S1, 1991, pp. 165–173.

Fraser, Nancy, "From Progressive Neoliberalism to Trump—and Beyond," *American Affairs*, Vol. 1, No. 4, Winter 2017, pp. 46–64.

Frier, Bruce W., *Landlords and Tenants in Imperial Rome*, Princeton, N.J.: Princeton University Press, 1980.

Frier, Bruce W., and Dennis P. Kehoe, "Law and Economic Institutions," in Walter Scheidel, Ian Morris, and Richard Saller, eds., *The Cambridge History of the Greco-Roman World*, Cambridge, UK: Cambridge University Press, 2007.

Fronda, Michael P., *Between Rome and Carthage: Southern Italy During the Second Punic War*, New York: Cambridge University Press, 2010.

Fukuyama, Francis, "Governance: What Do We Know, and How Do We Know It?" *Annual Review of Political Science*, Vol. 19, No. 1, 2016, pp. 89–105.

Gallup, "Public Trust in Government, 1958–2021," May 17, 2021. As of April 15, 2022: https://www.pewresearch.org/politics/2021/05/17/public-trust-in-government-1958-2021/

———, "Satisfaction with the United States," last updated March 2022. As of April 15, 2022: https://news.gallup.com/poll/1669/general-mood-country.aspx

Ganesh, Janan, "How the Pandemic Exposed the Myth of the Anglosphere," *Financial Times*, January 18, 2022.

Garland, Robert, "The Other Side of History: Daily Life in the Ancient World," Great Courses, course no. 3810, 2012.

Garnsey, Peter, and Richard Saller, *The Roman Empire: Economy, Society and Culture*, 2nd ed., Oakland: University of California Press, 2015.

Garon, Sheldon, "Transnational History and Japan's 'Comparative Advantage,'" *Journal of Japanese Studies*, Vol. 43, No. 1, Winter 2017, pp. 65–92.

Gelfand, Michele, "The Threat Reflex: Why Some Societies Respond to Danger Better Than Others," *Foreign Affairs*, July–August 2021.

Gethin, Amory, Clara Martínez-Toledano, and Thomas Piketty, "How Politics Became a Contest Dominated by Two Kinds of Elite," *The Guardian*, August 5, 2021a.

———, *Political Cleavages and Social Inequalities: A Study of Fifty Democracies, 1948–2020*, Cambridge, Mass.: Harvard University Press, 2021b.

Gibbon, Edward, and Hans-Friedrich Mueller, *The Decline and Fall of the Roman Empire*, Vols. 1–3, New York: Modern Library, 2005.

Gilbert, Dennis, *The Oligarchy and the Old Regime in Latin America, 1880–1970*, Lanham, Md.: Rowman and Littlefield, 2017.

Giles, Chris, "Fiscal Relief from Inflation Is Transitory, IMF Says," *Financial Times*, April 20, 2022.

Gillespie, Allison, "What Do the Data Say About the Current State of K–12 STEM Education in the US?" National Science Foundation, September 9, 2021. As of April 25, 2022: https://beta.nsf.gov/science-matters/what-do-data-say-about-current-state-k-12-stem-education-us

Ginsburg, Tom, "Dismantling the 'Developmental State'? Administrative Procedure Reform in Japan and Korea," *American Journal of Comparative Law*, Vol. 49, No. 4, 2001, pp. 585–625.

Glaeser, Edward J., and David Cutler, "The American Housing Market Is Stifling Mobility," *Wall Street Journal*, September 2, 2021.

Glaeser, Edward J., Rafael La Porta, Florencio Lopez-De-Silanes, and Andrei Shleifer, "Do Institutions Cause Growth?" *Journal of Economic Growth*, Vol. 9, 2004, pp. 271–303.

Glasman, Maurice, "Deconcentrating Capital," *American Affairs*, Vol. 4, No. 1, Spring 2020.

Glosserman, Brad, and Scott A. Snyder, *The Japan–South Korea Identity Clash: East Asian Security and the United States*, New York: Columbia University Press, 2017.

Gluck, Carol, *Japan's Modern Myths: Ideology in the Late Meiji Period*, Princeton, N.J.: Princeton University Press, 1985.

———, "Modernity in Common: Japan and World History," presented at the University of Washington Mitsubishi Lecture Series, Seattle, April 21, 2014.

Goddard, Stacie E., *When Right Makes Might: Rising Powers and World Order*, Ithaca, N.Y.: Cornell University Press, 2018.

Goldstone, Jack, "Efflorescences and Economic Growth in World History: Rethinking the 'Rise of the West' and the Industrial Revolution," *Journal of World History*, Vol. 13, No. 2, Fall 2002, pp. 323–389.

———, *Why Europe? The Rise of the West in World History, 1500–1850*, New York: McGraw-Hill, 2009.

Goldstone, Jack A., and Peter Turchin, "Welcome to the 'Turbulent Twenties,'" *Noema*, September 10, 2020.

Gong, Yooshik, and Wonho Jang, "Culture and Development: Reassessing Cultural Explanations on Asian Economic Development," *Development and Society*, Vol. 27, No. 1, 1998, pp. 77–97.

Good, David F., *The Economic Rise of the Habsburg Empire, 1750–1914*, Berkeley: University of California Press, 1984.

Gooday, Graeme J. N., and Morris F. Low, "Technology Transfer and Cultural Exchange: Western Scientists and Engineers Encounter Late Tokugawa and Meiji Japan," *Osiris*, Vol. 13, 1998, pp. 99–128.

Gordon, Bart, "U.S. Competitiveness: The Education Imperative," *Issues in Science and Technology*, Vol. 23, No. 3, Spring 2007.

Graham, Carol, "Premature Mortality and the Long Decline of Hope in America," Brookings Institution, May 10, 2018. As of April 15, 2022: https://www.brookings.edu/blog/future-development/2018/05/10/premature-mortality-and-the-long-decline-of-hope-in-america

Granato, Jim, Ronald Inglehart, and David Leblang, "The Effect of Cultural Values on Economic Development: Theory, Hypotheses, and Some Empirical Tests," *American Journal of Political Science*, Vol. 40, No. 3, 1996, pp. 607–631.

Grant, Michael, *The Fall of the Roman Empire*, New York: Simon and Schuster, 1990.

Grant, Robert M., "Porter's *Competitive Advantage of Nations*: An Assessment," *Strategic Management Journal*, Vol. 12, 1992, pp. 535–548.

Greene, Jack P., "State Formation, Resistance, and the Creation of Revolutionary Traditions in the Early Modern Era," in Michael A. Mornson and Melinda S. Zook, eds., *Revolutionary Currents: Nation-Building in the Transatlantic World*, Lanham, Md.: Rowman and Littlefield, 2004, pp. 1–34.

Greenfeld, Liah, *The Spirit of Capitalism: Nationalism and Economic Growth*, Cambridge, Mass.: Harvard University Press, 2001.

———, "Nationalism's Dividends," *American Affairs*, Vol. 3, No. 2, Summer 2019.

Greenwald, Daniel L., Martin Lettau, and Sydney C. Ludvigson, "How the Wealth Was Won: Factors Shares as Market Fundamentals," Cambridge, Mass.: National Bureau of Economic Research, Working Paper 25769, April 2021.

Greer, John Michael, "How Civilizations Fall: A Theory of Catabolic Collapse," in *The Long Descent: A User's Guide to the End of the Industrial Age*, Gabriola Island, B.C.: New Society Publishers, 2008, pp. 225–240.

Greif, Avner, and Murat Iyigun, "What Did the Old Poor Law Really Accomplish? A Redux," Bonn, Germany: Institute of Labor Economics, Discussion Paper 7398, 2013.

Gross, Daniel A., "How Elite U.S. Schools Give Preference to Wealthy and White 'Legacy' Applicants," *The Guardian*, January 23, 2019.

Grotenhuis, René, "Nation-Building: Identity and Identification, Process and Content," in *Nation-Building as Necessary Effort in Fragile States*, Amsterdam: Amsterdam University Press, 2016, pp. 73–92.

Gruen, Erich S., *Culture and National Identity in Republican Rome*, Ithaca, N.Y.: Cornell University Press, 1995.

———, "Did Romans Have an Ethnic Identity?" *Antichthon*, Vol. 47, 2013, pp. 1–17.

Güell, Maia, Michele Pellizzari, Giovanni Pica, and Sevi Rodriguez Mora, "Correlating Social Mobility and Economic Outcomes," *VoxEU*, November 26, 2018. As of June 24, 2021: https://voxeu.org/article/correlating-social-mobility-and-economic-outcomes

Guiso, Luigi, Paola Sapienza, and Luigi Zingales, "Does Culture Affect Economic Outcomes?" *Journal of Economic Perspectives*, Vol, 20, No. 2, Spring 2006, pp. 23–48.

———, "Social Capital as Good Culture," *Journal of the European Economic Association*, Vol. 6, Nos. 2–3, April–May 2008, pp. 295–320.

———, "Civic Capital as the Missing Link," in Jess Benhabib, Alberto Bisin, and Matthew Jackson, eds., *Handbook of Social Economics*, Vol. 1A, Amsterdam: North-Holland, 2011.

Hager, Theresa, "Special Interest Groups and Growth: A Meta-Analysis of Mancur Olson's Theory," working paper, Linz, Austria: Institute for Comprehensive Analysis of the Economy, September 2020.

Hall, Robert E., and Charles I. Jones, "Why Do Some Countries Produce So Much More Output per Worker Than Others?" *Quarterly Journal of Economics*, Vol. 114, No. 1, February 1999, pp. 83–116.

Hämäläinen, Timo J., *National Competitiveness and Economic Growth: The Changing Determinants of Economic Performance in the World Economy*, Cheltenham, UK: Edward Elgar, 2003.

Hamel, Gary, "First, Let's Fire All the Managers," *Harvard Business Review*, December 2011.

Hamel, Gary, and Michele Zanini, "Excess Management Is Costing the U.S. $3 Trillion per Year," *Harvard Business Review*, September 5, 2016.

———, "What We Learned About Bureaucracy from 7,000 HBR Readers," *Harvard Business Review*, August 10, 2017a.

———, "Bureaucracy: Where to Liberate $3 Trillion," *London Business School Review*, September 4, 2017b.

Hanioğlu, M. Şükrü, *A Brief History of the Late Ottoman Empire*, Princeton, N.J.: Princeton University Press, 2008.

Hankins, James, "Regime Change with Chinese Characteristics," *American Affairs*, Vol. 4, No. 4, 2020.

Hannah, Mark, and Caroline Grey, "Indispensable No More? How the American Public Sees U.S. Foreign Policy," white paper, New York: Eurasia Foundation, November 2019.

Hansen, Gordon, and Matthew Slaughter, *Talent, Immigration, and U.S. Economic Competitiveness*, Long Beach, Calif.: Compete America Coalition, May 2013.

Harding, Robin, "Pension Funds Need a Radical Rethink," *Financial Times*, January 5, 2020.

Hare, Christopher, and Keith T. Poole, "The Polarization of Contemporary American Politics," *Polity*, Vol. 46, No. 3, 2014, pp. 411–429.

Harper, Kyle, *The Fate of Rome: Climate, Disease, and the End of an Empire*, Princeton, N.J.: Princeton University Press, 2017.

Harris, William V., "The Late Republic," in Walter Scheidel, Ian Morris, and Richard Saller, eds., *The Cambridge History of the Greco-Roman World*, Cambridge, UK: Cambridge University Press, 2007.

Harrison, Lawrence, *Underdevelopment Is a State of Mind: The Latin American Case*, Lanham, Md.: Madison Books, 2000.

Harrison, Lawrence, and Samuel P. Huntington, eds., *Culture Matters: How Values Shape Human Progress*, New York: Basic Books, 2000.

Heard, Gerald, *The Source of Civilization*, London: Cape, 1935.

Heckelman, Jac C., "Explaining the Rain: *The Rise and Decline of Nations* After 25 Years," *Southern Economic Journal*, Vol. 74, No. 1, 2007, pp. 18–33.

Hedström, Peter, and Peter Bearman, "Analytical Sociology and Theories of the Middle Range," in Peter Hedström and Peter Bearman, eds., *The Oxford Handbook of Analytical Sociology*, Oxford, UK: Oxford University Press, 2011, pp. 25–47.

Heim, Jacob L., and Benjamin M. Miller, *Measuring Power, Power Cycles, and the Risk of Great-Power War in the 21st Century*, Santa Monica, Calif.: RAND Corporation, RR-2989-RC, 2020. As of April 22, 2022:
https://www.rand.org/pubs/research_reports/RR2989.html

Herbst, Jeffrey, *States and Power in Africa*, Princeton, N.J.: Princeton University Press, 2000.

Herman, Arthur, "America Needs an Industrial Policy," *American Affairs*, Vol. 3, No. 4, Winter 2019.

Herr, Richard, *Rural Change and Royal Finances at the End of the Old Regime*, Oakland: University of California Press, 1989.

Hetherington, Marc J., Meri T. Long, and Thomas J. Rudolph, "Revisiting the Myth: New Evidence of a Polarized Electorate," *Public Opinion Quarterly*, Vol. 80, No. S1, 2016, pp. 321–350.

Hobsbawm, Eric J., *The Age of Revolution: 1789–1848*, New York: New American Library, 1962.

Hodgson, Geoffrey M., "What Are Institutions?" *Journal of Economic Issues*, Vol. 40, No. 1, 2006.

———, "On Defining Institutions: Rules Versus Equilibria," *Journal of Institutional Economics*, Vol. 11, No. 3, 2015, pp. 497–505.

Hofstede, Geert, *Culture's Consequences: Comparing Values, Behaviors, Institutions, and Organizations Across Nations*, Thousand Oaks, Calif.: Sage, 2001.

Holland, Tom, *Rubicon: The Last Years of the Roman Republic*, New York: Anchor Books, 2005.

Homer-Dixon, Thomas F., "On the Threshold: Environmental Changes as Causes of Acute Conflict," *International Security*, Vol. 16, No. 2, 1991, pp. 76–116.

———, "Environmental Scarcities and Violent Conflict: Evidence from Cases," *International Security*, Vol. 19, No. 1, 1994, pp. 5–40.

———, "The End of Ingenuity," *New York Times*, November 29, 2006.

Hongyi, L. I., and Liang Huang, "Health, Education, and Economic Growth in China: Empirical Findings and Implications," *China Economic Review*, Vol. 20, No. 3, 2009, pp. 374–387.

Hopkins, M. K., "Social Mobility in the Later Roman Empire: The Evidence of Ausonius," *Classical Quarterly*, Vol. 11, No. 2, 1961, pp. 239–249.

Hopkins, Terence K., and Immanuel Wallerstein, "Cyclical Rhythms and Secular Trends of the Capitalist World-Economy: Some Premises, Hypotheses, and Questions," *Review*, Vol. 2, No. 4, 1979, pp. 483–500.

Hsieh, Chang-Tai, Eric Hurst, Charles I. Jones, and Peter J. Klenow, "The Allocation of Talent and U.S. Economic Growth," Cambridge, Mass.: National Bureau of Economic Research, Working Paper 18693, 2013.

Hudson, Walter M., "Analogy and Strategy: U.S.-China Competition Through an Edwardian Lens," *American Affairs*, Vol. 5, No. 3, Fall 2021.

Hughes, Kathryn, "The Middle Classes: Etiquette and Upward Mobility," British Library, May 15, 2014. As of April 14, 2022:
https://www.bl.uk/romantics-and-victorians/articles/
the-middle-classes-etiquette-and-upward-mobility#

Hunt, Vivian, Lareina Yee, Sara Prince, and Sundiatu Dixon-Fyle, *Delivering Through Diversity*, Los Angeles, Calif.: McKinsey & Company, January 18, 2018.

Huskinson, Janet, ed., *Experiencing Rome: Culture, Identity and Power in the Roman Empire*, New York: Routledge, 1999.

Hyam, Ronald, *Britain's Imperial Century, 1815–1914: A Study of Empire and Expansion*, 2nd ed., Lanham, Md.: Barnes and Noble Books, 1993.

Hymes, Robert, "Sung Society and Social Change," in John W. Chaffee and Denis Twitchett, eds., *Cambridge History of China*: Vol. 5, Pt. 2, *Sung China, 960–1279*, Cambridge, UK: Cambridge University Press, 2015, pp. 526–664.

Ikegami, Eiko, "Citizenship and National Identity in Early Meiji Japan, 1868–1889: A Comparative Assessment," *International Review of Social History*, Vol. 40, 1995, pp. 185–221.

IMD World Competitiveness Center, *Methodology and Principles of Analysis*, Lausanne, Switzerland, 2017.

———, *World Competitiveness Yearbook 2020*, Lausanne, Switzerland, 2020.

———, "All Criteria List," 2021.

Immerwahr, Daniel, "The Strange, Sad Death of America's Political Imagination," *New York Times*, July 2, 2021.

Inalcik, Halil, *The Ottoman Empire: The Classical Age, 1300–1600*, Kindle ed., London: Phoenix Press, 2001.

Ingraham, Christopher, "How 2,000-Year-Old Roads Predict Modern Prosperity," *Washington Post*, August 7, 2018.

Institute of Politics, Harvard Kennedy School, "Nearly Two-Thirds of Young Americans Fearful About the Future of Democracy in America, Harvard Youth Poll Finds," April 2018. As of April 15, 2022:
https://iop.harvard.edu/about/newsletter-press-release/
nearly-two-thirds-young-americans-fearful-about-future-democracy

Institute for Research on Poverty, "Many Rural Americans Are Still 'Left Behind,'" January 2020. As of August 23, 2021:
https://www.irp.wisc.edu/resource/many-rural-americans-are-still-left-behind/

Irwin, Douglas A., "The Aftermath of Hamilton's 'Report on Manufactures,'" *Journal of Economic History*, Vol. 64, No. 3, 2004, pp. 800–821.

Irwin, Véronique, Jijun Zhang, Xiaolei Wang, Sarah Hein, Ke Wang, Ashley Roberts, Christina York, Amy Barmer, Farrah Bullock Mann, Ritsa Dilig, and Stephanie Parker, *Report on the Condition of Education 2021*, Washington, D.C.: National Center for Education Statistics, May 2021.

Ivey, Ron, and Tim Shirk, "Ending America's Antisocial Contract," *American Affairs*, Vol. 5, No. 3, Fall 2021.

Iyengar, Shanto, Yphtach Lelkes, Matthew Levendusky, Neil Malhotra, and Sean J. Westwood, "The Origins and Consequences of Affective Polarization in the United States," *Annual Review of Political Science*, Vol. 22, No. 1, 2019, pp. 129–146.

Jackson, Joshua Conrad, Michele Gelfand, and Carol R. Ember, "A Global Analysis of Cultural Tightness in Non-Industrial Societies," *Proceedings of the Royal Society B*, Vol. 287, No. 1930, July 2020.

Jacob, Margaret C., *The Cultural Meaning of the Scientific Revolution*, Philadelphia: Temple University Press, 1988.

———, *The First Knowledge Economy: Human Capital and the European Economy, 1750–1850*, New York: Cambridge University Press, 2014.

Jácome, Elisa, Ilyana Kuziemko, and Suresh Naidu, "Mobility for All: Representative Intergenerational Mobility Estimates over the 20th Century," Cambridge, Mass.: National Bureau of Economic Research, Working Paper 29289, September 2021.

Jansen, Marius B., *The Making of Modern Japan*, Kindle ed., Cambridge, Mass.: Harvard University Press, 2000.

Jawetz, Tom, "Building a More Dynamic Economy: The Benefits of Immigration," testimony before the U.S. House Committee on the Budget, Washington, D.C.: Center for American Progress, June 26, 2019.

Jenkins, Helen, and Katie-Lee English, "Hidden Talent: The Economic Benefits of Social Mobility," Oxera, July 27, 2017. As of June 24, 2021:
https://www.oxera.com/insights/agenda/articles/
hidden-talent-the-economic-benefits-of-social-mobility/

Johnson, Chalmers, *MITI and the Japanese Miracle: The Growth of Industrial Policy, 1925–1975*, Stanford, Calif.: Stanford University Press, 1982.

Johnston, David, *Roman Law in Context*, New York: Cambridge University Press, 1999.

Jongman, W., "Gibbon Was Right: The Decline and Fall of the Roman Economy," in O. Hekster, G. de Kleijn, and Daniëlle Slootjes, eds., *Crises and the Roman Empire*, Leiden, Netherlands: Brill, 2007, pp. 183–199.

Judson, Pieter M., *The Habsburg Empire: A New History*, Cambridge, Mass.: Harvard University Press, 2016.

Kagan, Donald, *A New History of the Peloponnesian War*, Ithaca, N.Y.: Cornell University Press, 1969.

———, *The Peloponnesian War*, New York: Penguin, 2004.

Kang, David C., "Bad Loans to Good Friends: Money Politics and the Developmental State in South Korea," *International Organization*, Vol. 56, No. 1, 2002, pp. 177–207.

Kaniewski David, Elise Van Campo, Joël Guiot, Sabine Le Burel, Thierry Otto, and Cecile Baeteman, "Environmental Roots of the Late Bronze Age Crisis," *PloS ONE*, Vol. 8, No. 8, 2013, e71004.

Kapstein, Ethan B., and Nathan Converse, "Poverty, Inequality, and Democracy: Why Democracies Fail," *Journal of Democracy*, Vol. 19, No. 4, October 2008, pp. 57–68.

Karl, Terry Lynn, "Economic Inequality and Democratic Instability," *Journal of Democracy*, Vol. 11, No. 1, 2000, pp. 149–156.

Karlin, Jason G., *Gender and Nation in Meiji Japan*, Honolulu: University of Hawaii Press, 2014.

Kates, Sean, Jonathan M. Ladd, and Joshua A. Tucker, "New Poll Shows Dissatisfaction with American Democracy, Especially Among the Young," *Vox*, October 31, 2018. As of February 28, 2022:
https://www.vox.com/mischiefs-of-faction/2018/10/31/18042060/
poll-dissatisfaction-american-democracy-young

Kaufmann, Eric, "Liberal Fundamentalism: A Sociology of Wokeness," *American Affairs*, Vol. 4, No. 4, 2020.

Kavanagh, Jennifer, and Michael D. Rich, *Truth Decay: An Initial Exploration of the Diminishing Role of Facts and Analysis in American Public Life*, Santa Monica, Calif.: RAND Corporation, RR-2314-RC, 2018. As of February 28, 2022:
https://www.rand.org/pubs/research_reports/RR2314.html

Kehoe, Dennis P., Kehoe, *Law and the Rural Economy in the Roman Empire*, Ann Arbor: University of Michigan Press, 2007.

———, "Agency, Roman Law, and Roman Social Values," in Dennis P. Kehoe and Thomas McGinn, eds., *Ancient Law, Ancient Society*, Ann Arbor: University of Michigan Press, 2017, pp. 105–132.

Keillor, Bruce D., and G. Tomas M. Hult, "A Five-Country Study of National Identity," *International Marketing Review*, Vol. 16, No. 1, 1999, pp. 65–82.

Keller, Wolfgang, Carol H. Shiue, and Xin Wang, "Capital Markets in China and Britain, 18th and 19th Century: Evidence from Grain Prices," Cambridge, Mass.: National Bureau of Economic Research, Research Paper No. 21349, July 2015.

Kennan, George, "George Kennan's 'Long Telegram,'" History and Public Policy Program Digital Archive, National Archives and Records Administration, Department of State Records, Record Group 59, February 22, 1946.

Kennedy, Paul, *The Rise and Fall of the Great Powers: Economic Change and Military Conflict from 1500 to 2000*, New York: Random House, 1987.

Kerry, Simon, *Lansdowne: The Last Great Whig*, London: Unicorn, 2017.

Kim, Hoi-Eun, *Doctors of Empire: Medical and Cultural Encounters Between Imperial Germany and Meiji Japan*, Toronto: University of Toronto Press, 2014.

Kim, Hyung-min, "Comparing Measures of National Power," *International Political Science Review*, Vol. 31, No. 4, 2010, pp. 405–427.

King, Charles, "Review Article: *Post-Postcommunism: Transition, Comparison, and the End of 'Eastern Europe'* by Valerie Bunce, Karen Dawisha, Bruce Parrott, Richard Sakwa, and Daniel S. Treisman," *World Politics*, Vol. 53, No. 1, 2000, pp. 143–172.

Kirby, M. W., *The Decline of British Economic Power Since 1870*, London: Allen and Unwin, 1981.

————, "Institutional Rigidities and Economic Decline: Reflections on the British Experience," *Economic History Review*, Vol. 45, No. 4, November 1992, pp. 637–660.

Kissinger, Henry, *World Order*, New York: Penguin, 2014.

Klingler-Vidra, Robyn, "Building the Venture Capital State," *American Affairs*, Vol. 2, No. 3, Fall 2018.

Knack, Stephen, and Philip Keefer, "Does Social Capital Have an Economic Payoff? A Cross-Country Investigation," *Quarterly Journal of Economics*, Vol. 112, No. 4, 1996.

Knack, Stephen, and Paul Zak, "Trust and Growth," *Economic Journal*, Vol. 111, No. 470, 2001, pp. 295–321.

Knipsel, Sandra, "Corporate Money in Politics Threatens US Democracy—or Does It?" University of Rochester, July 6, 2020. As of March 1, 2022: https://www.rochester.edu/newscenter/does-money-in-politics-threaten-us-democracy-442802/

Komlos, J., *The Habsburg Monarchy as a Customs Union: Economic Development in Austria-Hungary in the Nineteenth Century*, Princeton, N.J.: Princeton University Press, 1983.

Koo, Bon Ho, and Dwight H. Perkins, eds., *Social Capability and Long-Term Economic Growth*, New York: St. Martin's Press, 1995.

Kota, Sridhar, and Tom Mahoney, "Reinventing Competitiveness: The Case for a National Manufacturing Foundation," *American Affairs*, Vol. 3, No. 3, Fall 2019, pp. 3–17.

Kotkin, Stephen, *Armageddon Averted: The Soviet Collapse, 1970–2000*, Oxford, UK: Oxford University Press, 2008.

Koyama, Mark, "Counterfactuals, Empires, and Institutions: Reflections on Walter Scheidel's Escape from Rome," *Journal of Economic Literature*, Vol. 59, No. 2, 2021, pp. 634–650.

Krause, Lawrence B., "Social Capability and Long-Term Economic Growth," in Bon Ho Koo and Dwight H. Perkins, eds., *Social Capability and Long-Term Economic Growth*, New York: St. Martin's Press, 1995, pp. 310–327.

Krien, Julius, "The Value of Nothing: Capital Versus Growth," *American Affairs*, Vol. 5, No. 3, Fall 2021.

Krugman, Paul, "Competitiveness: A Dangerous Obsession," *Foreign Affairs*, Vol. 73, No. 2, March 1994, pp. 28–44.

Kumar, Krishan, *The Making of English National Identity*, Cambridge, UK: Cambridge University Press, 2001.

Kupchan, Charles A., *How Enemies Become Friends: The Sources of Stable Peace*, Princeton, N.J.: Princeton University Press, 2010.

Kwon, Roy, "Hegemonies in the World-System: An Empirical Assessment of Hegemonic Sequences from the 16th to 20th Century," *Sociological Perspectives*, Vol. 54, No. 4, 2011, pp. 593–617.

Lacey, James, "Introduction," in James Lacey, ed., *Great Strategic Rivalries: From the Classical World to the Cold War*, New York: Oxford University Press, 2016, pp. 1–52.

Lambert, Andrew, *Seapower States: Maritime Culture, Continental Empires and the Conflict That Made the Modern World*, New Haven, Conn.: Yale University Press, 2018.

Landes, David S., *The Wealth and Poverty of Nations: Why Some Are So Rich and Some So Poor*, New York: W. W. Norton and Co., 1998.

———, "Culture Makes Almost All the Difference," in Lawrence E. Harrison and Samuel P. Huntington, eds., *Culture Matters: How Values Shape Human Progress*, New York: Basic Books, 2000, pp. 2–13.

———, *The Unbound Prometheus: Technological Change and Industrial Development in Western Europe from 1750 to the Present*, Cambridge, UK: Cambridge University Press, 2003.

Langford, Meredith King, *The State of Opportunity in America*, New York: Opportunity Agenda, 2009.

Langford, Paul, *A Polite and Commercial People: England, 1728–1783*, Oxford, UK: Oxford University Press, 1989.

Lazonick, William, "The Theory of Innovative Enterprise: A Foundation of Economic Analysis," in Jamee K. Moudud, Cyrus Bina, and Patrick L. Mason, eds., *Alternative Theories of Competition: Challenges to the Orthodoxy*, New York: Routledge, 2013, pp. 127–159.

———, "Profits Without Prosperity," *Harvard Business Review*, September 2014.

Lazonick, William, and Jang-sup Shin, *Predatory Value Extraction: How the Looting of the Business Corporation Became the U.S. Norm and How Sustainable Prosperity Can Be Restored*, New York: Oxford University Press, 2019.

Leffler, Melvyn P., *For the Soul of Mankind: The United States, the Soviet Union, and the Cold War*, New York: Hill and Wang, 2008.

Leggiere, Michael V., "Napoleon's Quest: Great Britain Versus France III," in James Lacey, ed., *Great Strategic Rivalries: From the Classical World to the Cold War*, New York: Oxford University Press, 2016, pp. 289–320.

Lehner, Urban C., "Can Slow-Building Democracies Compete with China?" *Asia Times*, August 23, 2021. As of March 1, 2022:
https://asiatimes.com/2021/08/can-slow-building-democracies-compete-with-china/

Lemke, Douglas, and William Reed, "War and Rivalry Among Great Powers," *American Journal of Political Science*, Vol. 45, No. 2, 2001, pp. 457–469.

Lepore, Jill, "A New Americanism: Why a Nation Needs a National Story," *Foreign Affairs*, March–April 2019.

Levin, Yuval, "How Did Americans Lose Faith in Everything?" *New York Times*, January 18, 2020.

Levy, Alon, "What Is the Cost of Building a Subway?" presentation, *Pedestrian Observations*, November 19, 2019.

Levy, Jack, "Historical Trends in Great Power War, 1495–1975," *International Studies Quarterly*, Vol. 26, No. 2, 1982.

Li, Amy Y., "Freshmen Skew Wealthy, as Always: Harvard Isn't Helping," *Harvard Crimson*, September 15, 2021.

Li, Diyi, and Cory Koedel, "Representation and Salary Gaps by Race-Ethnicity and Gender at Selective Public Universities," *Educational Researcher*, Vol. 46, No. 7, 2017, pp. 343–354.

Light, Paul C., *A Cascade of Failures: Why Government Fails, and How to Stop It*, Washington, D.C.: Brookings Institution, Center for Effective Public Management, July 2014.

———, "Trade Wars Are Strategic Sector Wars," *American Affairs*, Vol. 4, No. 4, 2020.

Lind, Michael, "Hamilton's Legacy," *Wilson Quarterly*, Vol. 18, No. 3, 1994, pp. 40–52.

Lindert, Peter H., "Three Centuries of Inequality in Britain and America," in Anthony B. Atkinson and François Bourguignon, eds., *Handbook of Income Distribution*, Vol. 1, Amsterdam: North-Holland, 2000, pp. 167–216.

Liu, William Guanglin, *The Chinese Market Economy, 1000–1500*, Albany: State University of New York Press, 2015.

Lo Casio, Elio, "The Early Roman Empire: The State and the Economy," in Walter Scheidel, Ian Morris, and Richard Saller, eds., *The Cambridge History of the Greco-Roman World*, Cambridge, UK: Cambridge University Press, 2007a.

———, "Growth and Decline: The Roman Economy in Historical Perspective," *Rivista di storia economica*, No. 3, December 2007b, pp. 269–282.

Lodge, George C., and Ezra F. Vogel, eds., *Ideology and National Competitiveness: An Analysis of Nine Countries*, Cambridge, Mass.: Harvard Business School Press, 1987.

Long, Jason, "Rural-Urban Migration and Socioeconomic Mobility in Victorian Britain," *Journal of Economic History*, Vol. 65, 2005, pp. 1–35.

———, "The Surprising Social Mobility of Victorian Britain," *European Review of Economic History*, Vol. 17, No. 1, February 2013, pp. 1–23.

Long, Sam, "The Financialization of the American Elite," *American Affairs*, Vol. 3, No. 3, Fall 2019, pp. 169–190.

Lowe, John W. G., *The Dynamics of Apocalypse: A Systems Simulation of the Classic Maya Collapse*, Albuquerque: University of New Mexico Press, 1985.

Lowy Institute, "Asia Power Index 2020," webpage, undated. As of April 27, 2022: https://power.lowyinstitute.org/

Luce, Edward, and Rana Faroohar, "That Creeping Sense of Western Dread," *Financial Times*, October 29, 2021.

Lukianoff, Greg, and Jonathan Haidt, *The Coddling of the American Mind: How Good Intentions and Bad Ideas Are Setting Up a Generation for Failure*, New York: Penguin, 2018.

Luntz, Frank, "No Wonder America Is Divided: We Can't Even Agree on What Our Values Mean," *Time*, October 26, 2018.

Lustgarten, Abrahm, "How Russia Wins the Climate Crisis," *New York Times Magazine*, December 16, 2020.

MacBride, Elizabeth, "Why Venture Capital Doesn't Build the Things We Really Need," *Technology Review*, June 17, 2020.

MacDonald, Paul K., and Joseph M. Parent, *Twilight of the Titans: Great Power Decline and Retrenchment*, Ithaca, N.Y.: Cornell University Press, 2018.

Macfarlane, Alan, *The Origins of English Individualism: The Family, Property, and Social Transition*, Oxford, UK: Basil Blackwell, 1978.

MacLeod, W. Bentley, "On Economics: A Review of *Why Nations Fail* by D. Acemoglu and J. Robinson and Pillars of Prosperity by T. Besley and T. Persson," *Journal of Economic Literature*, Vol. 51, No. 1, 2013, pp. 116–143.

Maddison, Angus, *Contours of the World Economy, 1–2030 AD: Essays in Macro-Economic History*, Oxford, UK: Oxford University Press, 2007.

Major, Lee Elliot, and Stephen Machin, *Social Mobility and Its Enemies*, London: Pelican Books, 2018.

———, *What Do We Know and What Should We Do About: Social Mobility*, Los Angeles: Sage, 2020.

Mann, Michael, *The Sources of Social Power*, Vol. 1, Cambridge, UK: Cambridge University Press, 1986.

———, *The Sources of Social Power:* Vol. 3, *Global Empires and Revolution, 1890–1945*, Cambridge, UK: Cambridge University Press, 2012.

Maoz, Zeev, and Ben D. Mor, *Bound by Struggle: The Strategic Evolution of Enduring International Rivalries*, Ann Arbor: University of Michigan Press, 2002.

Marcus, Jon, "The Reason Behind Colleges' Ballooning Bureaucracies," *The Atlantic*, October 6, 2016.

Marquez-Ramos, L., and E. Mourelle, "Education and Economic Growth: An Empirical Analysis of Nonlinearities," *Applied Economic Analysis*, Vol. 27, No. 79, 2019, pp. 21–45.

Marrero, Gustavo A., and Juan G. Rodriguez., "Macroeconomic Determinants of Inequality of Opportunity and Effort in the US: 1970–2009," working paper, Verona, Italy: Society for the Study of Economic Inequality, 2012.

———, "Inequality of Opportunity and Growth," *Journal of Development Economics*, Vol. 104, September 2013, pp. 107–122.

Marsh, Jan, "Gender Ideology and Separate Spheres in the 19th Century," Victoria and Albert Museum, undated.

Martin, Lisa L., *Democratic Commitments: Legislatures and International Cooperation*, Princeton, N.J.: Princeton University Press, 2000.

Martines, Lauro, *Power and Imagination: City-States in Renaissance Italy*, New York: ACLS Humanities E-Book Project, 2013.

Marx, Anthony W., *Faith in Nation: Exclusionary Origins of Nationalism*, New York: Oxford University Press, 2003.

Massie, Robert K., *Dreadnought: Britain, Germany, and the Coming of the Great War*, New York: Random House, 1991.

Mathisen, Ralph W., "'Roman' Identity in Late Antiquity, with Special Attention to Gaul," in Walter Pohl, Clemens Gantner, Cinzia Grifoni, and Marianne Pollheimer-Mohaupt, eds., *Transformations of Romanness: Early Medieval Regions and Identities*, Berlin: De Gruyter, 2018, pp. 255–274.

Mayer, Jane, "The Big Money Behind the Big Lie," *New Yorker*, August 2, 2021.

Mazarr, Michael J., "Abstract Systems and Social Trust," *American Affairs*, Vol. 6, No. 1, Spring 2022.

Mazarr, Michael J., Ryan Bauer, Abigail Casey, Sarah Heintz, and Luke J. Matthews, *The Emerging Risk of Virtual Societal Warfare: Social Manipulation in a Changing Information Environment*, Santa Monica, Calif.: RAND Corporation, RR-2714-OSD, 2019. As of February 23, 2022:
https://www.rand.org/pubs/research_reports/RR2714.html

Mazzucato, Mariana, *The Entrepreneurial State: Debunking Public vs. Private Sector Myths*, New York: PublicAffairs, 2015.

McCloskey, Dierdre N., *The Bourgeois Virtues: Ethics for an Age of Commerce*, Kindle ed., Chicago: University of Chicago Press, 2010.

———, *Bourgeois Dignity: Why Economics Can't Explain the Modern World*, Chicago: University of Chicago Press, 2011.

———, *Bourgeois Equality: How Ideas, Not Capital or Institutions, Enriched the World*, Chicago: University of Chicago Press, 2016.

McDonald, Duff, "Managing Decline: The Economy of Value Extraction," *American Affairs*, Vol. 4, No. 2, Summer 2020, pp. 49–62.

McFaul, Michael, "State Power, Institutional Change, and the Politics of Privatization in Russia," *World Politics*, Vol. 47, No. 2, 1995, pp. 210–243.

McInnes, Neil, "The Great Doomsayer: Oswald Spengler Reconsidered," *National Interest*, No. 48, 1997, pp. 65–76.

McTague, Tom, "How Britain Falls Apart," *The Atlantic*, January 5, 2022.

Merriam-Webster.com Dictionary, "Dynamism," Merriam-Webster, undated-a. As of March 14, 2022:
https://www.merriam-webster.com/dictionary/dynamism

———, "Vitality," Merriam-Webster, undated-b. As of March 14, 2022:
https://www.merriam-webster.com/dictionary/vitality

Merritt, Richard L., and Dina A. Zinnes, "Validity of Power Indices," *International Interactions*, Vol. 14, No. 2, 1988, pp. 141–151.

———, "Alternative Indexes of National Power," in Richard J. Stoll and Michael D. Ward, eds., *Power in World Politics*, Boulder, Colo.: Lynne Rienner, 1989.

Messenböck, Reinhard, Yves Morieux, Jaap Backx, and Donat Wunderlich, "How Complicated Is Your Company," Boston Consulting Group, January 16, 2018. As of April 25, 2022:
https://www.bcg.com/publications/2018/complicated-company

Meyer, Timothy, and Ganesh Sitaraman, "It's Economic Strategy, Stupid: The Case for a Department of Economic Growth and Security," *American Affairs*, Vol. 3, No. 1, Spring 2019.

Milanovic, Branko, Peter H. Lindert, and Jeffrey G. Williamson, "Ancient Inequality," unpublished manuscript, Harvard University, June 2008.

———, "Pre-Industrial Inequality," *Economic Journal*, Vol. 121, No. 551, March 2011, pp. 263–265.

Miles, Andrew, *Social Mobility in Nineteenth and Early Twentieth Century Britain*, London: Palgrave Macmillan UK, 1999.

Milliken, Jennifer, and Keith Krause, "State Failure, State Collapse, and State Reconstruction: Concepts, Lessons and Strategies," *Development and Change*, Vol. 33, No. 5, 2002, pp. 753–774.

Minns, John, "Of Miracles and Models: The Rise and Decline of the Developmental State in South Korea," *Third World Quarterly*, Vol. 22, No. 6, 2001, pp. 1025–1043.

Mitchel, Fordyce, "Athens in the Age of Alexander," *Greece and Rome*, Vol. 12, No. 2, 1965, pp. 189–204.

Mitchell, A. Wess, *The Grand Strategy of the Habsburg Empire*, Princeton, N.J.: Princeton University Press, 2018.

Moarefy, Sahand, "The New Power Brokers: Index Funds and the Public Interest," *American Affairs*, Vol. 4, No. 4, 2020.

Modelski, George, "The Long Cycle of Global Politics and the Nation-State," *Comparative Studies in Society and History*, Vol. 20, No. 2, 1978, pp. 214–235.

———, *Long Cycles in World Politics*, Seattle: University of Washington Press, 1987.

Mokyr, Joel, "And Thou, Happy Austria? A Review Essay," *Journal of Economic History*, Vol. 44, No. 4, December 1984, pp. 1094–1099.

———, *The Lever of Riches: Technological Creativity and Economic Progress*, New York: Oxford University Press, 1990.

———, "The Intellectual Origins of Modern Economic Growth," *Journal of Economic History*, Vol. 65, No. 2, June 2005, pp. 285–351.

———, "Entrepreneurship and the Industrial Revolution in Britain," in David S. Landes, Joel Mokyr, and William J. Baumol, eds., *The Invention of Enterprise: Entrepreneurship from Ancient Mesopotamia to Modern Times*, Princeton, N.J.: Princeton University Press, 2012a, pp. 183–210.

———, review of *Bourgeois Dignity: Why Economics Can't Explain the Modern World*, by Deirdre N. McCloskey, *Journal of Modern History*, Vol. 84, No. 2, June 2012b, pp. 453–456.

———, "A Flourishing Economist: A Review Essay on Edmund Phelps's 'Mass Flourishing: How Grassroots Innovation Created Jobs, Challenge, and Change,'" *Journal of Economic Literature*, Vol. 52, No. 1, March 2014, pp. 189–196.

———, *A Culture of Growth: The Origins of the Modern Economy*, Princeton, N.J.: Princeton University Press, 2017.

Morgan, William M., "Pacific Dominance: The United States Versus Japan," in James Lacey, ed., *Great Strategic Rivalries: From the Classical World to the Cold War*, New York: Oxford University Press, 2016.

Morgenthau, Hans J., *Politics Among Nations: The Struggle for Power and Peace*, revised by Kenneth W. Thompson, 6th ed., New York: Alfred A. Knopf, 1985.

———, *Politics Among Nations: The Struggle for Power and Peace*, brief ed., New York: McGraw Hill, 1993.

Morley, Neville, "The Early Roman Empire: Distribution," in Walter Scheidel, Ian Morris, and Richard Saller, eds., *The Cambridge History of the Greco-Roman World*, Cambridge, UK: Cambridge University Press, 2007.

Morris, Ian, *Why the West Rules—for Now: The Patterns of History, and What They Reveal About the Future*, New York: Farrar, Straus and Giroux, 2010.

———, *The Measure of Civilization: How Social Development Decides the Fate of Nations*, Princeton, N.J.: Princeton University Press, 2013.

Morton, Frederic, *Thunder at Twilight: Vienna, 1913–1914*, Boston, Mass.: Da Capo Press, 2014.

Moyer, Jonathan D., Collin J. Meisel, Austin S. Matthews, David K. Bohl, and Mathew J. Burrows, *China-US Competition: Measuring Global Influence*, Denver, Colo.: Atlantic Council and Frederick S. Pardee Center for International Futures, University of Denver, Josef Korbel School of International Studies, May 2021.

Moyer, Jonathan D., Tim Swiejs, Mathew J. Burrows, and Hugo Van Manen, *Power and Influence in a Globalized World*, Washington, D.C.: Atlantic Council of the United States, 2018.

Mueller, John E., "The Search for the 'Breaking Point' in Vietnam: The Statistics of a Deadly Quarrel," *International Studies Quarterly*, Vol. 24, No. 4, 1980, pp. 497–519.

Mukunda, Gautam, "The Price of Wall Street's Power," *Harvard Business Review*, June 2014.

Muller, Edward N., "Income Inequality, Regime Repressiveness, and Political Violence," *American Sociological Review*, Vol. 50, No. 1, 1985, pp. 47–61.

Müller, Jan-Werner, "The Cold War and the Intellectual History of the Late Twentieth Century," in Melvyn P. Leffler and Odd Arne Westad, eds., *The Cambridge History of the Cold War*: Vol. 3, *Endings*, Cambridge, UK: Cambridge University Press, 2010, pp. 1–22.

Murphy, Kevin M., Andrei Shleifer, and Robert W. Vishny, "Income Distribution, Market Size and Industrialization," *Quarterly Journal of Economics*, Vol. 104, No. 3, 1989.

Murphy, R. Taggart, *Japan and the Shackles of the Past*, New York: Oxford University Press, 2014.

Murray, Williamson, "A Whale Against an Elephant: Britain and Germany," in James Lacey, ed., *Great Strategic Rivalries: From the Classical World to the Cold War*, New York: Oxford University Press, 2016.

Myrick, Rachel, "America Is Back—but for How Long?" *Foreign Affairs*, June 14, 2021.

Narzary, Dharitri Chakravartty, "The Myths of Japanese 'Homogeneity,'" *China Report*, Vol. 40, No. 3, 2014.

Nelson, Richard R., ed., *National Innovation Systems: A Comparative Analysis*, New York: Oxford University Press, 1993.

New England Center for Investigative Journalism, "New Analysis Shows Problematic Boom In Higher Ed Administrators," *Huffington Post*, February 6, 2014. As of March 1, 2022:
https://www.huffpost.com/entry/higher-ed-administrators-growth_n_4738584

Newman, Gerald, *The Rise of English Nationalism*, London: Palgrave Macmillan, 1997.

Newport, Frank, "The Impact of Increased Political Polarization," Gallup, December 5, 2019. As of March 1, 2022:
https://news.gallup.com/opinion/polling-matters/268982/impact-increased-political-polarization.aspx

Nietzel, Michael P., "New Harvard Poll Finds Rising Hopes for the Nation's Future Among Young Americans," *Forbes*, April 23, 2021. As of March 1, 2022:
https://www.forbes.com/sites/michaeltnietzel/2021/04/23/
new-harvard-poll-finds-rising-hopes-for-the-nations-future-among-young-americans/

North, Douglass C., *Institutions, Institutional Change and Economic Performance*, Kindle ed., Cambridge, UK: Cambridge University Press, 1990.

North, Douglass C., and Barry R. Weingast, "Constitutions and Commitment: The Evolution of Institutions Governing Public Choice in Seventeenth-Century England," *Journal of Economic History*, Vol. 49, December 1989, pp. 803–832.

Obama, Barack, *National Security Strategy*, Washington, D.C.: White House, May 2012.

Ober, Josiah, *The Rise and Fall of Classical Greece*, Princeton, N.J.: Princeton University Press, 2015.

O'Brien, Patrick K., "Fiscal Exceptionalism: Great Britain and Its European Rivals from Civil War to Triumph at Trafalgar and Waterloo," working paper, London: Department of Economic History, London School of Economics, October 2001.

———, "The Nature and Historical Evolution of an Exceptional Fiscal State and Its Possible Significance for the Precocious Commercialization and Industrialization of the British Economy from Cromwell to Nelson," *Economic History Review*, Vol. 64, No. 2, May 2011, pp. 408–446.

OECD—*See* Organisation for Economic Co-operation and Development.

Oliver, J. Eric, and Thomas J. Wood, "Conspiracy Theories and the Paranoid Style(s) of Mass Opinion," *American Journal of Political Science*, Vol. 58, No. 4, 2014, pp. 952–966.

Olson, Mancur, "Rapid Growth as a Destabilizing Force," *Journal of Economic History*, Vol. 23, No. 4, 1963, pp. 529–552.

———, *The Rise and Decline of Nations: Economic Growth, Stagflation, and Social Rigidities*, Kindle ed., New Haven, Conn.: Yale University Press, 1982.

———, "Why Nations Rise and Fall," *Challenge*, Vol. 27, No. 1, 1984, pp. 15–23.

Öniş, Ziya, "Review of *The Logic of the Developmental State*, by Alice H. Amsden, Frederic C. Deyo, Chalmers Johnson, and Robert Wade," *Comparative Politics*, Vol. 24, No. 1, 1991, pp. 109–126.

OpenSecrets.org, "2020 Election to Cost $14 Billion, Blowing Away Spending Records," October 28, 2020. As of March 1, 2022:
https://www.opensecrets.org/news/2020/10/cost-of-2020-election-14billion-update/

Organisation for Economic Co-operation and Development, *OECD Insights: Human Capital*, Paris, 2007.

———, *A Broken Social Elevator? How to Promote Social Mobility*, Paris, 2018.

Ornston, Darius, and Mark I. Vail, "The Developmental State in Developed Societies: Power, Partnership, and Divergent Patterns of Intervention in France and Finland," *Comparative Politics*, Vol. 49, No. 1, 2016, pp. 1–21.

Ortolano, Guy, "The Typicalities of the English? Walt Rostow, *The Stages of Economic Growth*, and Modern British History," *Modern Intellectual History*, Vol. 12, No. 3, 2015, pp. 657–684.

Osterhammel, Jürgen, *The Transformation of the World: A Global History of the Nineteenth Century*, Patrick Camiller, trans., Princeton, N.J.: Princeton University Press, 2014.

Osterkamp, Jana, "Cooperative Empires: Provincial Initiatives in Imperial Austria," *Austrian History Yearbook*, Vol. 47, April 2016, pp. 128–146.

Ostry, Jonathan D., Andrew Berg, and Charalambos G. Tsangarides, "Redistribution, Inequality, and Growth," Washington, D.C.: International Monetary Fund, April 2014.

OxFam International, "Influence of Elites on Governments in Latin America Contributes to Increasing Poverty and Inequality," press release, November 16, 2018. As of April 13, 2022: https://www.oxfam.org/en/press-releases/ influence-elites-governments-latin-america-contributes-increasing-poverty-and

Oxford English Dictionary, "Dynamism," undated-a.

———, "Vitality," undated-b.

Packer, George, "How America Fractured into Four Parts," *The Atlantic*, July–August 2021.

Pagano, Patrizio, and Massimo Sbracia, "The Secular Stagnation Hypothesis: A Review of the Debate and Some Insights," occasional paper, San Francisco, Calif.: Bank of Italy, 2014.

Page, Scott E., "Are We Collapsing? A Review of Jared Diamond's Collapse: How Societies Choose to Fail or Succeed," *Journal of Economic Literature*, Vol. 43, No. 4, December 2005, pp. 1049–1062.

———, *The Difference: How the Power of Diversity Creates Better Groups, Firms, Schools, and Societies*, Princeton, N.J.: Princeton University Press, 2007.

Page, Scott E., and Lu Hong, "Groups of Diverse Problem Solvers Can Outperform Groups of High-Ability Problem Solvers," *Proceedings of the National Academy of Science*, Vol. 101, No. 46, November 2004.

Paisley, Laura, "Political Polarization at Its Worst Since the Civil War," *USC News*, November 8, 2016. As of August 17, 2021: https://news.usc.edu/110124/political-polarization-at-its-worst-since-the-civil-war-2/

Parente, Stephen L., review of *Bourgeois Dignity: Why Economics Can't Explain the Modern World*, by Deirdre N. McCloskey, *Journal of Economic Literature*, Vol. 49, No. 4, December 2011, pp. 1234–1237.

Parente, Stephen L., and Edward C. Prescott, "Barriers to Technology Adoption and Development," *Journal of Political Economy*, Vol. 102, No. 2, 1994, pp. 298–321.

———, "A Unified Theory of the Evolution of International Income Levels," in Philippe Aghion and Steven N. Durlauf, eds., *Handbook of Economic Growth*, Vol. IB, Amsterdam: North-Holland, 2004, pp. 1371–1416.

Parker, Geoffrey, "Crisis and Catastrophe: The Global Crisis of the Seventeenth Century Reconsidered," *American Historical Review*, Vol. 113, No. 4, October 2008, pp. 1053–1079.

———, *Global Crisis: War, Climate Change and Catastrophe in the Seventeenth Century*, New Haven, Conn.: Yale University Press, 2013.

———, "Incest, Blind Faith, and Conquest: The Spanish Habsburgs and Their Enemies," in James Lacey, ed., *Great Strategic Rivalries: From the Classical World to the Cold War*, New York: Oxford University Press, 2016.

Parker, Kim, Rich Morin, and Juliana Menasce Horowitz, "Looking to the Future, Public Sees an America in Decline on Many Fronts," Pew Research Center, March 21, 2019. As of August 23, 2021: https://www.pewresearch.org/social-trends/2019/03/21/ public-sees-an-america-in-decline-on-many-fronts/

Parks, Miles, "Trump Is No Longer Tweeting, but Online Disinformation Isn't Going Away," NPR, March 5, 2021.

Penn, Mark, "Americans Are Losing Confidence in the Nation but Still Believe in Themselves," *The Atlantic*, June 27, 2012.

Pereira, Alexius A., "Whither the Developmental State? Explaining Singapore's Continued Developmentalism," *Third World Quarterly*, Vol. 29, No. 6, 2008, pp. 1189–1203.

Perez-Arce, Francisco, Ernesto F. L. Amaral, Haijing Crystal Huang, and Carter C. Price, *Inequality and Opportunity: The Relationship Between Income Inequality and Intergenerational Transmission of Income*, Santa Monica, Calif.: RAND Corporation, RR-1509-RC, 2016. As of February 23, 2022:
https://www.rand.org/pubs/research_reports/RR1509.html

Perkins, Dwight H., "Government as an Obstacle to Industrialization: The Case of Nineteenth-Century China," *Journal of Economic History*, Vol. 27, No. 4, December 1967, pp. 478–492.

Perkins, Dwight H., and Bon Ho Koo, "Introduction," in Bon Ho Koo and Dwight H. Perkins, eds., *Social Capability and Long-Term Economic Growth*, New York: St. Martin's Press, 1995, pp. 3–9.

Perotti, Roberto, "Income Distribution, Politics, and Growth," *American Economic Review*, Vol. 82, No. 2, 1992.

Persson, Torsten, and Guido Tabellini, "Is Inequality Harmful for Growth?" *American Economic Review*, Vol. 84, No. 3, 1994, pp. 600–621.

Peters, Guy, "Political Institutions, Old and New," in Robert E. Goodin and Hans-Dieter Klingemann, eds., *A New Handbook of Political Science*, Oxford, UK: Oxford University Press, 1996, pp. 205–220.

Pew Research Center, "Political Polarization in the American Public," June 12, 2014. As of August 17, 2021:
https://www.pewresearch.org/politics/2014/06/12/political-polarization-in-the-american-public/

———, "The Partisan Divide on Political Values Grows Even Wider," October 5, 2017. As of May 2, 2022:
https://www.pewresearch.org/politics/2017/10/05/1-partisan-divides-over-political-values-widen/

———, *Trump Begins Third Year with Low Job Approval and Doubts About His Honesty*, Washington, D.C., January 18, 2019.

———, "Voters' Attitudes About Race and Gender Are Even More Divided Than in 2016," September 20, 2020. As of August 17, 2021:
https://www.pewresearch.org/politics/2020/09/10/
voters-attitudes-about-race-and-gender-are-even-more-divided-than-in-2016/

Phelan, John Leddy, "Authority and Flexibility in Spanish Imperial Bureaucracy," *Administrative Science Quarterly*, Vol. 5, No. 1, 1960, pp. 47–65.

Phelps, Edmund S., *Mass Flourishing: How Grassroots Innovation Created Jobs, Challenge, and Change*, Princeton, N.J.: Princeton University Press, 2013.

Phelps, Edmund S., Raicho Bojilov, Hian Teck Hoon, and Gylfi Zoega, *Dynamism: The Values That Drive Innovation, Job Satisfaction, and Economic Growth*, Cambridge, Mass.: Harvard University Press, 2020.

Pierrakis, Yannis, *Venture Capital: Now and After the Dotcom Crash*, London: National Endowment for Science, Technology and the Arts, 2010.

Pitts, Martin, and Miguel John Versluys, eds., *Globalisation and the Roman World: World History, Connectivity and Material Culture*, Cambridge, UK: Cambridge University Press, 2014.

Pitts, Jennifer, "Introduction," in Alexis de Tocqueville, *Writings on Empire and Slavery*, Jennifer Pitts, ed. and trans., Baltimore, Md.: Johns Hopkins University Press, 2001, pp. ix–xxxviii.

Polanyi, Karl, *The Great Transformation: The Political and Economic Origins of Our Time*, rev. ed., Boston, Mass.: Beacon Press, 2001.

Pollack, Kenneth M., *Armies of Sand: The Past, Present, and Future of Arab Military Effectiveness*, New York: Oxford University Press, 2019.

Pomeranz, Kenneth, *The Great Divergence: China, Europe, and the Making of the Modern World Economy*, Princeton, N.J.: Princeton University Press, 2009.

Porch, Douglas, *The Conquest of the Sahara*, New York: Farrar, Straus and Giroux, 2005.

Porter, Michael E., "Attitudes, Values, Beliefs, and the Microeconomics of Prosperity," in Lawrence E. Harrison and Samuel P. Huntington, eds., *Culture Matters: How Values Shape Human Progress*, New York: Basic Books, 2000, pp. 14–28.

———, *The Competitive Advantage of Nations*, New York: Free Press, 2019.

Porter, Roy, *English Society in the Eighteenth Century*, rev. ed., London: Penguin Books, 1990.

Potter, Simon J., "Empire, Cultures and Identities in Nineteenth- and Twentieth-Century Britain," *History Compass*, Vol. 5, No. 1, January 2007.

Powell, David, *Nationhood and Identity: The British State Since 1800*, London: I.B. Tauris, 2002.

Pratt, Edward E., *Japan's Protoindustrial Elite: The Economic Foundations of the Gōnō*, Cambridge, Mass.: Harvard University Asia Center, 1999.

Przeworski, Adam, "The Poor and the Viability of Democracy," in Anirudh Krishna, ed., *Poverty, Participation, and Democracy: A Global Perspective*, New York: Cambridge University Press, 2008, pp. 125–146.

Public Religion Research Institute, "Competing Visions of America: An Evolving Identity or a Culture Under Attack? Findings from the 2021 American Values Survey," November 1, 2021. As of April 15, 2022:
https://www.prri.org/research/competing-visions-of-america-an-evolving-identity-or-a-culture-under-attack/

Putnam, Robert D., "Tuning In, Tuning Out: The Strange Disappearance of Social Capital in America," *PS: Political Science and Politics*, Vol. 28, No. 4, 1995, pp. 664–683.

Pyle, Kenneth B., "The Technology of Japanese Nationalism: The Local Improvement Movement, 1900–1918," *Journal of Asian Studies*, Vol. 13, No. 1, November 1973.

———, "The Future of Japanese Nationality: An Essay in Contemporary History," *Journal of Japanese Studies*, Vol. 8, No. 2, 1982, pp. 223–263.

Qian, Nancy, and Marco Tabellini, "Discrimination and State Capacity: Evidence from WWII U.S. Army Enlistment," Cambridge, Mass.: National Bureau of Economic Research, Working Paper 29482, November 2021.

Quataert, Donald, *The Ottoman Empire 1700–1922*, 2nd ed., Cambridge, UK: Cambridge University Press, 2005.

Quiroga, Pedro López Barja De, "Freedmen Social Mobility in Roman Italy," *Historia: Zeitschrift Für Alte Geschichte*, Vol. 44, No. 3, 1995, pp. 326–348.

Rabin-Havt, Ari, and Media Matters, *Lies, Incorporated: The World of Post-Truth Politics*, New York: Anchor Books, 2016.

Rachman, Gideon, "Lousy Demographics Will Not Stop China's Rise," *Financial Times*, May 4, 2021.

Raeymaekers, Timothy, "Collapse or Order? Questioning State Collapse in Africa," Berlin: Households in Conflict Network, Working Paper 01/01, 2005.

Rahe, Paul A., "The Primacy of Greece: Athens and Sparta," in James Lacey, ed., *Great Strategic Rivalries: From the Classical World to the Cold War*, New York: Oxford University Press, 2016.

Rainie, Lee, Scott Keeter, and Andrew Perrin, "Trust and Distrust in America," Pew Research Center, July 22, 2019. As of March 2, 2022:
https://www.pewresearch.org/politics/2019/07/22/trust-and-distrust-in-america/

Rapp, Dean, "Social Mobility in the Eighteenth Century: The Whitbreads of Bedfordshire, 1720–1815," *Economic History Review*, Vol. 27, No. 3, August 1974, pp. 380–394.

Rasler, Karen, William R. Thompson, and Sumit Ganguly, *How Rivalries End*, Philadelphia: University of Pennsylvania Press, 2013.

Rasmussen, Daniel, "Private Equity: Overvalued and Overrated?" *American Affairs*, Vol. 2, No. 1, Spring 2018, pp. 3–16.

Ravina, Mark, *To Stand with the Nations of the World: Japan's Meiji Restoration in World History*, New York: Oxford University Press, 2017.

Reeves, Richard V., "The Economic Case for Social Mobility," Brookings Institution, August 16, 2013. As of June 24, 2021:
https://www.brookings.edu/opinions/the-economic-case-for-social-mobility/

Reynolds, David, "Science, Technology and the Cold War," in Melvyn P. Leffler and Odd Arne Westad, eds., *The Cambridge History of The Cold War*: Vol. 3, *Endings*, Cambridge, UK: Cambridge University Press, 2010, pp. 378–399.

Riedl, Brian, "Behind CBO's $100 Trillion in Projected Deficits over 30 Years," Manhattan Institute, November 19, 2020. As of March 2, 2022:
https://www.manhattan-institute.org/behind-cbos-100-trillion-projected-us-deficits-over-30-years

———, "Rising Federal Debt Still Matters," *National Review*, September 30, 2021.

Rim, Gwang-Nam, Sun-Nam Jang, Chol-Ju An, Sun-Hui Hwang, and Son-Hui Ri, "State Economic Strength and Some Methodological Issues on Its Assessment," *Social Indicators Research*, Vol. 152, 2020, pp. 607–636.

Robb, Alicia, "Rural Entrepreneurship and the Challenges Accessing Financial Capital: An Overview of Funding in Rural America," presentation to the Small Business Capital Formation Advisory Committee, November 16, 2021.

Roberts, Keith, *The Origins of Business, Money, and Markets*, New York: Columbia University Press, 2011.

Roberts, Michael, *Sweden as a Great Power, 1611–1697: Government, Society, Foreign Policy*, New York: St. Martin's Press, 1968.

Rodriguez, Stephen, "The Fox in the Henhouse: How Bureaucratic Processes Handicap US Military Supremacy and What to Do About It," Atlantic Council, February 26, 2020. As of March 2, 2022:
https://www.atlanticcouncil.org/blogs/new-atlanticist/the-fox-in-the-henhouse-how-bureaucratic-processes-handicap-us-military-supremacy-and-what-to-do-about-it/

Rodrik, Dani, Arvind Subramanian, and Francesco Trebbi, "Institutions Rule: The Primacy of Institutions over Geography and Integration in Economic Development," Cambridge, Mass.: National Bureau of Economic Research, Working Paper 9305, October 2002.

Rosecrance, Richard, "Long Cycle Theory and International Relations," *International Organization*, Vol. 41, No. 2, Spring 1987, pp. 283–301.

———, "Money and Power," *National Interest*, Summer 2002.

Rostow, Walt W., *The Process of Economic Growth*, New York: W. W. Norton, 1962.

Rothe, Ursula, *The Toga and Roman Identity*, New York: Bloomsbury, 2019.

Rozman, Gilbert, *East Asian National Identities: Common Roots and Chinese Exceptionalism*, Palo Alto, Calif.: Stanford University Press, 2012.

Rubinstein, W. D., *Capitalism, Culture and Decline in Britain, 1750–1990*, London: Routledge, 1993.

Rubio, Marco, "Common Good Capitalism: An Interview with Marco Rubio," *American Affairs*, Vol. 4, No. 1, Spring 2020.

Ruck, Damian J., Luke J. Matthews, Thanos Kyritsis, Quentin D. Atkinson, and R. Alexander Bentley, "The Cultural Foundations of Modern Democracies," *Nature: Human Behavior*, Vol. 4, 2020, pp. 265–269.

Rudolph, Richard L., *Banking and Industrialization in Austria-Hungary: The Role of Banks in the Industrialization of the Czech Crownlands, 1873–1914*, Cambridge, UK: Cambridge University Press, 1976.

Ruggiero, Guido, *The Renaissance in Italy: A Social and Cultural History of the Rinascimento*, New York: Cambridge University Press, 2014.

Ruggie, John Gerard, "International Regimes, Transactions, and Change: Embedded Liberalism in the Postwar Economic Order," *International Organization*, Vol. 36, No. 2, 1982, pp. 379–415.

Ruttan, V., "Social Science Knowledge and Induced Institutional Innovation: An Institutional Design Perspective," *Journal of Institutional Economics*, Vol. 2, No. 3, 2006, pp. 249–272.

Sainsbury, David, *Windows of Opportunity: How Nations Create Wealth*, London: Profile, 2020.

Sakwa, Richard, "The Soviet Collapse: Contradictions and Neo-Modernisation," *Journal of Eurasian Studies*, Vol. 4, No. 1, 2013, pp. 65–77.

Samuel, Raphael, ed., *Patriotism: The Making and Unmaking of British National Identity*: Vol. 1, *History and Politics*, London: Routledge, 1989.

Sanders, James E., "Histories of Elites, Redux: Oligarchs, Families, and Power," *Latin American Research Review*, Vol. 54, No. 3, 2019, pp. 739–746.

Schama, Simon, *The Embarrassment of Riches: An Interpretation of Dutch Culture in the Golden Age*, New York: Vintage Books, 1987.

Schapiro, Robert A., "States of Inequality: Fiscal Federalism, Unequal States, and Unequal People," *California Law Review*, Vol. 108, No. 5, October 2020.

Scharf, W. Fred, and Seamus Mac Mathuna, "Cultural Values and Irish Economic Performance," in Susanne Niemeier, Charles P. Campbell, and René Dirven, eds., *The Cultural Context in Business Communication*, Amsterdam: John Benjamins, 1998, pp. 145–166.

Scheidel, Walter, *The Great Leveler: Violence and the History of Inequality from the Stone Age to the Twenty-First Century*, Princeton, N.J.: Princeton University Press, 2018.

———, *The Failure of Empire and the Road to Prosperity*, Princeton, N.J.: Princeton University Press, 2019.

———, "The Road from Rome," *Aeon*, April 15, 2021. As of March 2, 2022: https://aeon.co/essays/how-the-fall-of-the-roman-empire-paved-the-road-to-modernity

Scheidel, Walter, and Steven J. Friesen, "The Size of the Economy and the Distribution of Income in the Roman Empire," *Journal of Roman Studies*, Vol. 99, 2009, pp. 61–91.

Schroeder, Paul W., "The Nineteenth Century System: Balance of Power or Political Equilibrium?" *Review of International Studies*, Vol. 15, No. 2, 1989, pp. 135–153.

Schularick, Moritz, "Public and Private Debt: The Historical Record (1870–2010)," *German Economic Review*, Vol. 15, No. 1, 2013, pp. 197–207.

Schultz, Kenneth A., *Democracy and Coercive Diplomacy*, Cambridge, UK: Cambridge University Press, 2001.

Schumann, Matt J., "A Contest for Trade and Empire: England Versus France II," in James Lacey, ed., *Great Strategic Rivalries: From the Classical World to the Cold War*, New York: Oxford University Press, 2016.

Scott, Bruce R., and George C. Lodge, *U.S. Competitiveness in the World Economy*, Boston, Mass.: Harvard Business School Press, 1985.

Scott, James C., *Seeing Like a State: How Certain Schemes to Improve the Human Condition Have Failed*, New Haven, Conn.: Yale University Press, 1998.

Sepinwall, Alyssa Goldstein, *The Abbé Grégoire and the French Revolution: The Making of Modern Universalism*, Berkeley: University of California Press, 2005.

Service, Robert, *The End of the Cold War: 1985–1991*, New York: PublicAffairs, 2015.

Shackleton, Robert, "Total Factor Productivity Growth in Historical Perspective," Washington, D.C.: Congressional Budget Office, Working Paper 2013–01, March 2013.

Sharma, Ruchir, *The Rise and Fall of Nations: Forces of Change in the Post-Crisis World*, New York: W. W. Norton, 2016.

———, *The 10 Rules of Successful Nations*, New York: W. W. Norton, 2020.

Shennan, J. H., "The Rise of Patriotism in 18th-Century Europe," *History of European Ideas*, Vol. 13, No. 6, 1991, pp. 689–710.

Sheppard, Emma, "Civil Servants on Being Working Class: 'It Feels the Odds Are Stacked Against You,'" *The Guardian*, March 26, 2018.

Sherman, Arloc, Danilo Trisi, Chad Stone, Shelby Gonzales, and Sharon Parrott, "Immigrants Contribute Greatly to the U.S. Economy," Center on Budget and Policy Priorities, August 15, 2019. As of April 13, 2022: https://www.cbpp.org/research/poverty-and-inequality/immigrants-contribute-greatly-to-us-economy-despite-administrations

Shifrinson, Joshua R. Itzkowitz, *Rising Titans, Falling Giants: How Great Powers Exploit Power Shifts*, Ithaca, N.Y.: Cornell University Press, 2018.

Shovlin, John, *Trading with the Enemy: Britain, France, and the 18th-Century Quest for a Peaceful World Order*, New Haven, Conn.: Yale University Press, 2021.

Shurkin, Michael, "French Liberal Governance and the Emancipation of Algeria's Jews," *French Historical Studies*, Vol. 33, No. 2, 2010, pp. 259–280.

Siena College Research Institute, "Americans, Deeply Divided, yet Share Core Values of Equality, Liberty and Progress," October 25, 2021. As of April 15, 2022:
https://scri.siena.edu/2021/10/25/americans-deeply-divided-yet-share-core-values-of-equality-liberty-progress/

Singer, J. David, "Reconstructing the Correlates of War Dataset on Material Capabilities of States, 1816–1985," *International Interactions*, Vol. 14, No. 2, 1987.

Singer, J. David, Stuart Bremer, and John Stuckey, "Capability Distribution, Uncertainty, and Major Power War, 1820–1965," in Bruce Russett, ed., *Peace, War, and Numbers*, Beverly Hills, Calif.: Sage, 1972, pp. 19–48.

Smeltz, Dina, Ivo H. Daalder, Karl Friedhoff, Craig Kafura, and Brendan Helm, *2020 Chicago Council Survey*, Chicago: Chicago Council on Global Affairs, September 17, 2020. As of April 25, 2022:
https://www.thechicagocouncil.org/research/public-opinion-survey/2020-chicago-council-survey

Smith, Anthony D., *Nationalism: Theory, Ideology, History*, 2nd ed., London: Polity, 2010.

Smith, Caroline, "Bureaucrats and Buildings: The Case for Why College Is So Expensive," *Forbes*, September 5, 2017. As of March 2, 2022:
https://www.forbes.com/sites/carolinesimon/2017/09/05/bureaucrats-and-buildings-the-case-for-why-college-is-so-expensive/

Smith, Noah, "America, Land of Equal Opportunity? Still Not There," Bloomberg, April 3, 2018. As of August 23, 2021:
https://www.bloomberg.com/opinion/articles/2018-04-03/u-s-doesn-t-deliver-on-promise-of-equal-opportunity-for-all

Smithers, Andrew, "Investment, Productivity, and the Bonus Culture," *American Affairs*, Vol. 4, No. 2, Summer 2020, pp. 18–31.

Snooks, Helen, Hayley Hutchings, Anne Seagrove, Sarah Stewart-Brown, John Williams, and Ian Russell, "Bureaucracy Stifles Medical Research in Britain: A Tale of Three Trials," *BMC Medical Research Methodology*, Vol. 12, No. 1, 2012, pp. 1–9.

Solar, Peter M., "Poor Relief and English Economic Development Before the Industrial Revolution," *Economic History Review*, Vol. 48, No. 1, 1995, pp. 1–22.

Soll, Jacob, *The Reckoning: Financial Accountability and the Rise and Fall of Nations*, New York: Basic Books, 2014.

Solnick, Steven, *Stealing the State: Control and Collapse in Soviet Institutions*, Cambridge, Mass.: Harvard University Press, 1998.

Sørenson, Georg, *Changes in Statehood: The Transformation of International Relations*, Houndmills, UK: Palgrave, 2001.

Spawforth, Tony, *The Story of Greece and Rome*, New Haven, Conn.: Yale University Press, 2018.

Spolaore, Enrico, "Commanding Nature by Obeying Her: A Review Essay on Joel Mokyr's *A Culture of Growth*," *Journal of Economic Literature*, Vol. 58, No. 3, 2020, pp. 777–792.

Stanford Encyclopedia of Philosophy, "Nationalism," revised September 2, 2020. As of April 10, 2022:
https://plato.stanford.edu/entries/nationalism

Stark, Andrew, *Drawing the Line: Public and Private in America*, Washington, D.C.: Brookings Institution Press, 2009.

Steensma, David P., and Hagop M. Kantarjian, "Impact of Cancer Research Bureaucracy on Innovation, Costs, and Patient Care," *Journal of Clinical Oncology*, Vol. 32, No. 5, 2014, pp. 376–378.

Stewart, Emily, "America's Growing Fake News Problem, in One Chart," *Vox*, December 22, 2020. As of March 3, 2022:
https://www.vox.com/policy-and-politics/2020/12/22/22195488/fake-news-social-media-2020

Stokes, Bruce, "America's Identity Crisis," German Marshall Fund of the United States, December 17, 2021. As of April 13, 2022:
https://www.gmfus.org/news/americas-identity-crisis

Stoller, Matt, "The War Within Corporate America," *American Affairs*, Vol. 4, No. 1, Spring 2020.

Strauss, Barry S., "The War for Empire: Rome Versus Carthage," in James Lacey, ed., *Great Strategic Rivalries: From the Classical World to the Cold War*, New York: Oxford University Press, 2016.

Studer, Roman, *The Great Divergence Reconsidered: Europe, India, and the Rise to Global Economic Power*, Cambridge, UK: Cambridge University Press, 2015.

Stulz, Rene M., and Rohan Williamson, "Culture, Openness, and Finance," *Journal of Financial Economics*, Vol. 70, No. 3, 2003, pp. 313–349.

Sunderland, David, *Social Capital, Trust and the Industrial Revolution, 1780–1880*, London: Routledge, 2007.

Supple, Barry, review of *The Verdict of Peace: Britain Between Her Yesterday and the Future*, by Correlli Barnett, *English Historical Review*, Vol. 117, No. 472, June 2002, pp. 672–673.

Szołtysek, Mikołaj, Sebastian Klüsener, Radosław Poniat, and Siegfried Gruber, "The Patriarchy Index: A New Measure of Gender and Generational Inequalities in the Past," *Cross-Cultural Research*, Vol. 51, No. 3, 2017, pp. 228–262.

Tackett, Nicolas, *The Origins of the Chinese Nation: Song China and the Forging of an East Asian World Order*, Cambridge, UK: Cambridge University Press, 2017.

Tainter, Joseph A., "Plotting the Downfall of Society," *Nature*, Vol. 427, February 5, 2004.

———, "Archaeology of Overshoot and Collapse," *Annual Review of Anthropology*, Vol. 35, 2006, pp. 59–70.

Taylor, Miles, "Patriotism, History and the Left in Twentieth-Century Britain," *Historical Journal*, Vol. 33, No. 4, 1990, pp. 971–987.

Tellis, Ashley J., "Assessing National Power in Asia," in Ashley J. Tellis, ed., *Foundations of National Power in the Asia-Pacific*, Washington, D.C.: National Bureau of Asian Research, 2015.

Temin, Peter, *The Roman Market Economy*, Princeton, N.J.: Princeton University Press, 2013.

Thompson, William R., "Identifying Rivals and Rivalries in World Politics," *International Studies Quarterly*, Vol. 45, No. 4, December 2001.

Thompson, William R., and Leila Zakhirova, *Racing to the Top: How Energy Fuels System Leadership in World Politics*, New York: Oxford University Press, 2019.

Thucydides, *The Landmark Thucydides: A Comprehensive Guide to the Peloponnesian War*, Robert B. Strassler, ed., New York: Free Press, 1998.

Tipton, Elise K., *Modern Japan: A Social and Political History*, New York: Routledge, 2016.

Todd, Chuck, Mark Murray, and Carrie Dann, "Study Finds Nearly One-in-Five Americans Believe QAnon Conspiracy Theories," NBC News, May 27, 2021. As of March 3, 2022:
https://www.nbcnews.com/politics/meet-the-press/
study-finds-nearly-one-five-americans-believe-qanon-conspiracy-theories-n1268722

Toynbee, Arnold J., *A Study of History: Abridgement of Volumes I–VI by DC Somervell*, New York: Oxford University Press, 1947.

Transparency International, "Corruption Perception Index, 2020," undated. As of May 13, 2021:
https://www.transparency.org/en/cpi/2020/

Trump, Donald J., *National Security Strategy of the United States of America*, Washington, D.C.: White House, December 2017.

Turchin, Peter, *Historical Dynamics: Why States Rise and Fall*, Princeton, N.J.: Princeton University Press, 2003.

———, "Correspondence: Political Instability May Be a Contributor in the Coming Decade," *Nature*, Vol. 463, February 4, 2010.

Turchin, Peter, and Sergey A. Nefedov, *Secular Cycles*, Princeton, N.J.: Princeton University Press, 2009.

Turner, Ani, *The Business Case for Racial Equity: A Strategy for Growth*, Ann Arbor and Battle Creek, Mich.: Altarum Health and W.K. Kellogg Foundation, 2018.

Unger, Roberto Mangabeira, "Britain's Project," *New Statesman*, March 17, 2021.

U.S. Chamber of Commerce, "America's Opportunity Gaps: By the Numbers," June 24, 2020. As of March 3, 2022:
https://www.uschamber.com/diversity/america-s-opportunity-gaps-the-numbers

U.S. Congressional Budget Office, "Additional Information About the Updated Budget and Economic Outlook: 2021 to 2031," July 2021.

U.S. Department of State, "Blue Dot Network," webpage, undated. As of April 23, 2022:
https://www.state.gov/blue-dot-network/

U.S. Government Accountability Office, "America's Fiscal Future," webpage, undated. As of March 3, 2022:
https://www.gao.gov/americas-fiscal-future

Veal, Keith C., "The Gating of America: The Political and Social Consequences of Gated Communities on the Body Politic," dissertation, University of Michigan, 2013.

Vijg, Jan, *The American Technological Challenge: Stagnation and Decline in the 21st Century*, New York: Algora Publishing, 2011.

Vogel, Steven K., *Marketcraft: How Governments Make Markets Work*, New York: Oxford University Press, 2018.

Voitchovsky, Sarah, "Inequality and Economic Growth," in Wiemer Salverda, Brian Nolan, and Timothy Smeeding, eds., *The Oxford Handbook of Economic Inequality*, Oxford, UK: Oxford University Press, 2009.

Vollrath, Dietrich, *Fully Grown: Why a Stagnant Economy Is a Sign of Success*, Chicago: University of Chicago Press, 2020.

Von Glahn, Richard, "Revisiting the Song Monetary Revolution: A Review Essay," *International Journal of Asian Studies*, Vol. 1, No. 1, 2004, pp. 159–178.

Wade, Robert, *Governing the Market: Economic Theory and the Role of Government in East Asian Industrialization* Princeton, N.J.: Princeton University Press, 1990.

Ward-Perkins, Bryan, *The Fall of Rome: And the End of Civilization*, New York: Oxford University Press, 2006.

Wawro, Geoffrey, "A New Europe with New Rivalries: The Franco-German Rivalry," in James Lacey, ed., *Great Strategic Rivalries: From the Classical World to the Cold War*, New York: Oxford University Press, 2016.

Weaver, P. R. C., "Social Mobility in the Early Roman Empire: The Evidence of the Imperial Freedman and Slaves," *Past and Present*, Vol. 37, No. 1, July 1967, pp. 3–20.

Westad, Odd Arne, *The Cold War: A World History*, New York: Basic Books, 2017.

Westney, D. Eleanor, *Imitation and Innovation: The Transfer of Western Organizational Patterns to Meiji Japan*, Cambridge, Mass.: Harvard University Press, 1987.

White, Gordon, ed., *Developmental States in East Asia*, London: Palgrave Macmillan UK, 1988.

Wiener, Malcolm H., *The Collapse of Civilizations*, Cambridge, Mass.: Belfer Center for Science and International Affairs, Harvard Kennedy School, September 2018.

Wiener, Martin, *English Culture and the Decline of the Industrial Spirit, 1850–1980*, Cambridge, UK: Cambridge University Press, 1981.

Wilkinson, Endymion, *Japan Versus the West: Image and Reality*, New York: Penguin, 1990.

Williamson, Samuel R., "Austria-Hungary and the International System: Great Power or Doomed Anachronism?" in *Austria-Hungary and the Origins of the First World War*, London: Macmillan Education UK, 1991, pp. 4–12.

Wilson, Emily, "The Secret of Rome's Success," *The Atlantic*, December 2015.

Wilson, Tom, "World Bank Suspends Its Business Climate Index over Data 'Irregularities,'" *Financial Times*, August 28, 2020.

Wimmer, Andreas, "Power and Pride: National Identity and Ethnopolitical Inequality Around the World," *World Politics*, Vol. 69, No. 4, 2017, pp. 605–639.

———, "National Identity and Political Power," *Foreign Affairs*, April 16, 2018.

Wineburg, Sam, Sarah McGrew, Joel Breakstone, and Teresa Ortega, *Evaluating Information: The Cornerstone of Civic Online Reasoning*, Stanford, Calif.: Stanford History Education Group, 2016.

Wiseman, Paul, "In Trade Wars of 200 Years Ago, the Pirates Were Americans," Associated Press, March 28, 2019.

Wittgenstein Centre for Demography and Global Human Capital, "Wittgenstein Centre Data Explorer," version 2.0, undated. As of April 6, 2021: http://dataexplorer.wittgensteincentre.org/wcde-v2/

Wolf, Laurence G., "Carroll Quigley: The Evolution of Civilizations," *Comparative Civilizations Review*, Vol. 38, No. 38, 1998.

Woloch, Isser, *The New Regime: Transformations of the French Civic Order, 1789–1820s*, New York: W. W. Norton, 1994.

Wong, Alia, "Private Schools Are Becoming More Elite," *The Atlantic*, July 26, 2018.

Woodruff, Jerry, "Prophet of Decline: Spengler on World History and Politics Review," *Occidental Quarterly*, Vol. 2, No. 1, 2001.

Wootton, David, *The Invention of Science: A New History of the Scientific Revolution*, New York: Harper, 2015.

World Bank, "Worldwide Governance Indicators," undated-a. As of May 13, 2021: http://info.worldbank.org/governance/wgi/

———, "TCdata360: Total Investment (% of GDP)," undated-b. As of May 13, 2021: https://tcdata360.worldbank.org/indicators/inv.all.pct

———, *Human Capital Index: 2020 Update*, Washington, D.C., 2021a.

———, "Research and Development Expenditure (% of GDP)," September 2021b. As of May 2, 2022:
https://data.worldbank.org/indicator/GB.XPD.RSDV.GD.ZS

———, "Doing Business," March 7, 2022. As of April 25, 2022: https://datacatalog.worldbank.org/dataset/doing-business

World Economic Forum, *Global Competitiveness Report 2019*, Geneva, 2019.

———, *The Global Social Mobility Report 2020: Equality, Opportunity and a New Economic Imperative*, Geneva, 2020.

Wright, Gordon, *France in Modern Times*, New York: W. W. Norton, 1995.

Wu, Yongping, "Rethinking the Taiwanese Developmental State," *China Quarterly*, No. 177, 2004, pp. 91–114.

Zabala, Craig, and Daniel Luria, "New Gilded Age or Old Normal?" *American Affairs*, Vol. 3, No. 3, Fall 2019.

Zhao, Dingxin, "*Historical Dynamics: Why States Rise and Fall* by Peter Turchin," *American Journal of Sociology*, Vol. 112, No. 1, July 2006, pp. 308–310.

Zitelman, Rainer, "How Many Americans Believe in Conspiracy Theories?" *Forbes*, June 29, 2020. As of March 3, 2022:
https://www.forbes.com/sites/rainerzitelmann/2020/06/29/
how-many-americans-believe-in-conspiracy-theories/

Zubok, Vladislav M., *A Failed Empire: The Soviet Union in the Cold War from Stalin to Gorbachev*, Chapel Hill: University of North Carolina Press, 2007.

———, "Soviet Foreign Policy from Détente to Gorbachev, 1975–1985," in Melyvn P. Leffler and Odd Arne Westad, eds., *The Cambridge History of the Cold War*: Vol. 3, *Endings*, Cambridge, UK: Cambridge University Press, 2010, pp. 89–111.

Zumbrun, Josh, "World Bank Cancels Flagship 'Doing Business' Report After Investigation," *Wall Street Journal*, September 16, 2021.